The Age of
CUNARD
A Transatlantic History
1839–2003

Daniel Allen Butler

The Age of
CUNARD
A Transatlantic History
1839–2003

Daniel Allen Butler

Lighthouse Press Publication
a division of **ProStar** Publications, Inc.

© 2003 by Daniel Allen Butler. All rights reserved. Except for use in a review, no part of this book may be reproduced or utilized in any form or by any means, electronic or mechanical, including photocopying, recording, or by an information storage and retrieval system, without written permission from the publisher.

ISBN: 1-57785-348-2
Printed in the United States

Published by:

Lighthouse Press
a division of **ProStar** Publications, Inc.

3 Church Circle
Suite 109
Annapolis, MD 21401
(800) 481-6277
Email: editor@prostarpublications.com
Website: www.prostarpublications.com

Also by Daniel Allen Butler

Unsinkable—The Full Story of RMS Titanic
The Lusitania: The Life, Loss, and Legacy of an Ocean Legend
Warrior Queens—the Queen Mary and Queen Elizabeth in World War Two

Original Cover Design Concept:
Brian Jeffers

Cover Design and Production:
Ron Ligrano

Book Design and Production:
Carole Ann Thomas

The Cunard logo and the Cunard crest are used with the permission of Cunard Line Ltd. This use and permission does not indicate an endorsement of this book.

Library of Congress Cataloging-in-Publication Data

Butler, Daniel Allen.
The age of Cunard : a transatlantic history 1839-2003 / Daniel Allen Butler.-- 1st ed.
    p. cm.
Includes bibliographical references and index.
ISBN 1-57785-348-2 (hardcover : alk. paper)
1. Cunard Steamship Company, Ltd.--History. 2. Steam-navigation--Atlantic Ocean--History.
3. Ocean liners--History. I. Title.

HE945.C9B88 2004
387.5'42'0916309034--dc22   2004001172

To the memory of
Harold Butler
(1927-2002)

Sailor, soldier,
builder, and mentor,
but most important of all,
my father and my friend.

Dad, I'm really going to miss you.

CONTENTS

POEM 9
INTRODUCTION 11
PROLOGUE 17

Chapter 1   The North Atlantic 19
Chapter 2   Samuel Cunard 35
Chapter 3   Setting the Pace 51
Chapter 4   The Yankee Rival 71
Chapter 5   The Struggle for Supremacy 85
Chapter 6   White Star Rising 103
Chapter 7   The German Challenge 129
Chapter 8   Cunard Ascendant 147
Chapter 9   The Glory Years 179
Chapter 10 The Great War 203
Chapter 11 Collapse 233
Chapter 12 Return to Glory 259
Chapter 13 The Second World War 285
Chapter 14 The Warrior *Queens* 309
Chapter 15 Cunard Triumphant 331
Chapter 16 Decline and Fall 361
Chapter 17 Limbo 387
Chapter 18 Resurrection 409

Epilogue 433
Appendix 437
Author's Note 451
Bibliography 455
Index 458

Romance! Those first class passengers they like it very well,
Printed an' bound in little books; but why don't poets tell?
I'm sick of all their quirks an' turns—the loves an' doves they dream—
Lord, send a man like Robbie Burns to sing the Song o' Steam!
To match wi' Scotia's noblest speech yon orchestra sublime
Whaurto—uplifted like the Just—the tail-rods mark the time.
The crankshaft-throws give the double-bass, the feed pump sobs an' heaves,
An' now the main eccentrics start their quarrel in the sheaves:
Her time, her own appointed time, the rocking link-head bides,
Till—hear that note?—the rod's return whings glimmerin' through the guides.
They're all awa'! True beat, full power, the clangin' chorus goes
Clear to the tunnel where they sit, my purrin' dynamos.
Interdependence absolute, foreseen, ordained, decreed,
To work, Ye'll note, at ony tilt an' every rate o' speed.
Fra' skylight-lift to furnace bars, backed, bolted, braced an' stayed,
An' singin' like the Mornin' Stars for joy that they are made;
While, out o' touch o' vanity, the sweatin' thrust-block says:
"Not unto us the praise, or man—not unto us the praise!"
Now, a' together, hear them lift their lesson—theirs an' mine:
"Law, Order, Duty an' Restraint, Obedience, Discipline!"
Mill, forge an' try-pit taught them that when roarin' they arose,
An' whiles I wonder if a soul was gied them wi' the blows.
Oh for a man to weld it then, in one trip-hammer strain,
Till even first class passengers could tell the meanin' plain!
But no one cares except mysel' that serve and understand
My seven thousand horse-power here. Eh, Lord! They're grand—they're grand!

—from McAndrew's Hymn by Rudyard Kipling

INTRODUCTION

For a century and a half, the single most important sea lane in the world was the transatlantic route linking the Old World and the New. Governments formulated their foreign policies around it, nations' economies were dependent on it, navies were built to protect—or interdict—it, wars were fought over it, empires rose because they controlled it, and fell because they didn't. And during that span of time, one shipping line more than any other became inseparably associated with the North Atlantic run, its history, its triumphs, its tragedies, and ultimately, its demise: the Cunard Line.

At the beginning of the fourth decade of the 19th century, Great Britain stood pre-eminent among the nations of the earth, the world's greatest maritime power with the largest, most dynamic economy of any of the Great Powers, and an empire that girdled the globe. More than a third of all shipping tonnage was British-registered—a proportion which would steadily grow as the century progressed—as thousands of ships sailed to and fro between the far-flung marches of that empire. The jewel in that maritime crown, so to speak, was the collection of shipping lanes that spanned the Atlantic. What made them so valuable was simple: Great Britain's single most important trading partner was the United States. While Britain's economy was the largest in the world, that of the United States' was the fastest growing. But American industry, like the nation itself, was a fledgling giant and not yet capable of meeting the needs, let alone the wants, of the burgeoning American economy and population. That role fell to Great Britain, who supplied most of the demands of American heavy industry, as well as meeting the requirements for precision manufactures that were as yet beyond the Americans' ability to produce. In fact, for most of the century, the volume of British manufactured goods shipped to the United States exceeded the volume produced by the Americans themselves. Nor was the role of Britain's shipping confined to carrying British manufactures: Russian oak from the Baltic states, German-produced railroad rolling stock, Austrian crystal and optics, French wines and fabrics, all were carried to the United States in British ships. On their return crossings, those same ships would have cargo holds full of raw cotton from the American South, Canadian and American ores, pine and fir from the Pacific Northwest and Canada, and of course, countless tons of grain and beef, as Britain had long since ceased to be self-supporting in producing her own food supply.

For three hundred years, sailing ships had sufficed to carry cargoes and people back and forth between the Old World and the New, but there was an inherent vulnerability that all sailing vessels shared—their dependence on favorable weather. No matter how hard they were driven, or how much canvas their skippers crowded on in a gale, sailing ships were at the mercy of the wind, and an unexpected calm could suddenly transform a potential record-breaking crossing into an arduous trek of more than a month. While such a happenstance might be acceptable in the relatively relaxed tempo of mercantile-era trade, the demands of Steam Age business and commerce could make no such allowances. Just as the steam engine had allowed railroads to replace the unpredictability of stagecoaches and post-chaises on land with regularity and dependable schedules, steam engines, in the form of steamships, promised to bring similar reliability to crossing the Atlantic. This is where the story of the Cunard Line began.

That story spans more than 160 years, starting in 1839 when Samuel Cunard, a Halifax, Nova Scotia businessman, organized the rather clumsily named British and North American Royal Mail Steam Packet Company, which almost instantly became known to the general public as simply the Cunard Line. It ended in 1998, when Cunard was purchased by Carnival Corporation.

The fleet of ships that the Cunard Line would put to sea reads like an honor roll of the North Atlantic run, including names like the *Scotia, Persia, Carpathia, Mauretania, Aquitania, Berengaria, Caronia, Queen Mary, Queen Elizabeth*, and *Queen Elizabeth 2*. Passenger lists were replete with people as famous and diverse as Oscar Wilde, Alfred Vanderbilt, John Jacob Astor, Sir Winston Churchill, Bob Hope, Stan Laurel and Oliver Hardy, the Prince of Wales, Charlie Chaplin, Fred Astaire, and Clark Gable, to name just a few. The ships themselves were often the paragons of luxury at sea, while fourteen of the forty-two ships that would ever hold the Blue Ribband, the appellation given to the fastest ship on the North Atlantic run, were Cunard liners.

There is far more, though, to the story of the Cunard Line than just a recounting of the line's ships and their service: For more than a hundred-fifty years the North Atlantic run was the stage on which some of the most revolutionary products of science and industry made their debut, and where some of the greatest political, military, social, and economic dramas of the 19th and 20th Centuries were played out. By a quirk of fate, Cunard became the benchmark by which all other steamship lines measured their ambitions, and while the line was rarely an innovator—and never revolutionary—the imprimatur of Cunard acceptance meant that any new development in steamship design or service was here to stay, and destined to become an industry standard. As the 19th century progressed, Cunard was always at the center of the great rivalry among the various British and American shipping lines for the Blue Ribband, and when that commercial rivalry turned into a nationalistic competition between Great Britain and Germany for maritime supremacy on the North Atlantic, it was Cunard that would seal the British victory by introducing the magnificent *Lusitania* and *Mauretania*.

The greatest influence Cunard would have on world events would be the leading role the line would take in the last half of the 19th century, when the great migration from the Old World to the New would transform the populations of Europe, the United States, and Canada. What began as a trickle of immigrants in the middle of the century would rapidly become a torrent, then eventually a flood, as millions of Europeans flowed to the shores of the New World, hoping to find their fortunes in such exotic locales as New York, Pittsburgh, or Chicago. As the decades passed, increasing numbers of central and southern Europeans emigrated to America, though the majority of those leaving the Old World for the New were still Anglo-Saxon. Many were Germans, whose Fatherland was undergoing a bewilderingly rapid transformation from an agrarian society to an industrial juggernaut, with all the attendant social dislocations; many others were Britons, often skilled or semi-skilled workers, sometimes craftsmen, occasionally members of the professions, forced to seek employment in America as Britain began her slow decline industrially and economically. These people sought transportation to take them from Southampton (or Cherbourg or Queenstown) to New York or Halifax. In achieving this goal, Cunard would serve them admirably.

Along the way there would be great dramas, great triumphs and great tragedies. In the first years of the 20th century, the existence of the line was threatened when the American shipping conglomerate International Mercantile Marine (IMM) attempted to acquire a controlling interest in all of the major shipping lines on the North Atlantic, including Cunard. The near-epic struggle that followed was a microcosm of the economic struggle that was being waged between the established business world of the British Empire and the burgeoning American economy, as one strove to maintain its world dominance and the other to attain it. Acknowledging the public outcry opposing the sale of Cunard to IMM as well as recognizing political and military realities, Prime Minister Arthur Balfour chose to intervene and allow the Government to subsidize Cunard, preserving the line's independence. There would be the remarkable career of the first *Mauretania,* possibly the most beloved steamship in history, and the only liner to hold the Blue Ribband for more than twenty years; the long-lived *Aquitania,* veteran of two World Wars whose interior was widely regarded as the most handsome ever installed in a ship; the magnificence of the *Queen Mary* and *Queen Elizabeth*; the wartime tragedies of the destruction of the *Lusitania* in 1915 and the dreadful collision between the *Queen Mary* and HMS *Curacoa* in 1942. War's devastation would come to the Cunard Line not once but twice, as the power of the German submarine fleet—built with one purpose in mind, to sever the North Atlantic shipping lanes—threatened Great Britain's very existence, and in so doing decimated the ranks of the Cunard fleet. In both World Wars, Cunard's pre-eminence among the shipping lines was acknowledged by the fact that the line was given the responsibility for organizing and coordinating the efforts of all the British shipping firms.

The line's ultimate ambition was finally realized after the Second World War, when the *Queen Mary* and the *Queen Elizabeth* began an alternating, weekly trans-Atlantic schedule, fulfilling Sir Samuel's prescient vision that one day just two enormous ships would be needed to maintain a regular trans-Atlantic service, and do so with such regularity that would rival train schedules. Despite a resurgent French Line and a newly dynamic Italian Line, as well as a challenge thrown down by the Americans in the form of the S.S. *United States*, the line had twelve ships in service, including the two greatest ships ever to sail the route, and completely dominated the transatlantic trade. Incredibly profitable during these years, the *Queens* were booked solid on most voyages. With commercial air travel still in its infancy, the ocean liner was still, in John Maxtone-Graham's felicitous phrase, "the only way to cross." It was Cunard's finest hour.

Yet it would ultimately prove a hollow victory, for the ever-dynamic business of carrying travelers across the Atlantic took a turn that no one had imagined, let alone foreseen. All during those golden years, the numbers of people crossing the Atlantic by airplane were slowly but steadily growing. By 1963, more people were choosing to travel to Europe or America by airplane than by steamship, and Cunard found itself losing money for the first time since the end of the Second World War, the *Queens* alone running a combined deficit of over £3,000,000 that year. It was the beginning of the end. Sir Winston Churchill, watching the airplane supplant the steamship as the favored means of travel, not just on the Atlantic but around the world, and understanding the implications of that eclipse for Great Britain, was moved to observe, "You came into great things by an accident of sea power…. By an accident of air power, you will probably cease to exist." He was declaiming a eulogy of sorts for the British Empire, but he could have well been pronouncing an epitaph for the steamship service on the North Atlantic. During the mid-1960s, Cunard quietly disposed of many of its smaller ships, while several of its competitors abandoned the North Atlantic altogether, among them the Italians, the Dutch and the Americans. By 1967 Cunard had to face the inevitable, and announced that the *Queen Mary* would be withdrawn from service and sold the following year—the *Queen Elizabeth* would suffer the same fate a year later. It was the death knell of the North Atlantic run, and the beginning of the end for Cunard.

Once again Cunard's history was serving as a microcosm for the world economy, as it had in the first years of the 20th century. During the 1980s and 1990s, the company was bought and sold by a succession of British holding companies, eventually becoming ensnared in the world of corporate mergers. Cunard was awash in a sea of red ink, and this time there would be no knight in shining armor in the form of Her Majesty's Government, and the line was absorbed by the giant Carnival Corporation in 1998.

Cunard has been reduced to a shadow of its former self as ocean liners have become luxuries: no longer "the only way to cross," ocean liners have lost their reason for being, becoming charming anachronisms, nothing more. They gave embodiment to the Age of Sea Power, the Age of Steam, the Age of the Machine, but in the Electronic Age and the Age of Air Power, they are no longer necessary. The economies that produced them and were dependent on them, the societies that needed them and demanded them, the industries that built them and maintained them, have all passed away, supplanted by new economies, societies and industries just as they had supplanted those that came before. It had been a heroic age, one that shaped its own world and the world that would come after it. It had been the Age of Cunard.

PROLOGUE

All that really mattered was speed.

It was in early 1840 that an ambitious Canadian businessman named Samuel Cunard formed the British and North American Royal Mail Steam Packet Company, a risky venture that proposed to establish a regular steamship service between Great Britain and the United States for the purpose of delivering mail and passengers between the United Kingdom and the United States. Though not quite in their infancy anymore, steamships were still far from being a reliable mode of transportation, and compared to sailing ships, were costly to build and operate. Only if his proposed quartet of paddlewheel steamers could maintain the regular, scheduled service across the Atlantic that Cunard claimed for them, could he hope to ever make a profit. The best packet boats, as the transatlantic square-riggers of the day were called, could make an eastbound passage in as little as fifteen days—though contrary winds could triple that time when the ships were westbound. So the key for Cunard's ships lay in speed—not blinding, ferocious speed, but consistent, predictable speed, maintained day after day, hour after hour, which would permit regular departures and arrivals, something even the best packet boats could never hope to rival.

No one could have imagined that the story of the little steamship company Cunard was forming would eventually span more than a century and a half, or that the company itself would grow into the greatest passenger steamship line in history, and become a household word on four continents. In the spring of 1840, what the distant future held really didn't matter—all that really mattered was speed....

CHAPTER ONE

The North Atlantic

No one knows for sure who were the first men to cross the North Atlantic. Some say the Egyptians could have, in their surprisingly sturdy papyrus reed boats. Others argue that it was the Phoenicians, while there are fanciful tales of Roman ships sailing westward from Spain to reach the shores of lands that would one day be known as Mexico or Texas. Certainly the Vikings crossed the northern ocean, though their attempts to colonize the strange new territory they christened "Vinland" met with little success. But for centuries the vast northern sea was more of a barrier than a pathway: it was a forbidding expanse of water, chimerical and capricious. Swept periodically by violent gales, at times studded with ice floes, at others, shrouded with banks of near-impenetrable fog, even in the summer months the North Atlantic was a dangerous place to be.

The first man to cross these perilous waters and leave a record of his crossing was an English explorer, John Cabot, who discovered what would become the aptly named Newfoundland in 1497. It was the beginning of what would, over the next three centuries, become a predominantly Anglo-Saxon flood as the entire North American coast from the St. Johns River at the base of the Florida peninsula in the south to Baffin Island up astride the Arctic Circle was colonized by ever increasing numbers of Englishmen, Scots, and Irishmen, along with a leavening of French, Germans and Dutch.

Some came to settle and make new lives and new homes for themselves and their families. Others came to make their fortunes, for the resources of North America were vast and seemingly inexhaustible. Wood, ores, furs, tobacco, cotton all presented opportunities for entrepreneurs, who in turn were followed by businessmen who brought regularity and organization to the fruits of the explorers findings. Business meant the transport of cargoes between the New World and the Old, and, with increasing frequency, travel by men, sometimes alone, sometimes in the company of their wives and children, back and forth across the Atlantic in order to meet the demands of their businesses and make them prosper.

With business came government, and soon communications between the various colonies and their mother countries became a priority. A revolution took place in the Old World, an industrial revolution, and it was fed and fueled by the products of the New; the demand for cotton and timber and copper ore and corn, grew at an astonishing rate. Another revolution broke out, this one of politics, and suddenly a handful of colonies was a nation in their own right, but the flow of goods and people between the British Isles and North America continued virtually unabated. Some years later, still another revolution took place, this time in Europe, and a gentle, befuddled king lost his head, his place eventually taken by the most insidious tyrant the world had yet known: the demand for the raw materials of the New World became even greater as war intervened and sources in the Old World were cut off to Great Britain.

And just as the island nation took in ever more of that produce, the lands that had been colonies and those that still were, constantly demanded more of the manufactures that Great Britain disgorged. Machinery, tools, cannon, cloth, spirits, tableware, china, furniture, clocks, a thousand different items that were beyond the ability of the colonies to produce in kind or quality, all found places in the holds of ships sailing westward.

For more than three hundred years, a steady procession of sailing ships passed endlessly back and forth between Europe and America. First came the galleons, in the decades when the Spanish and Portuguese were plundering the cultures and empires of Central and South America. Full bellied, with steep-sided hulls and high forecastles and poop decks, they were slow, cumbersome, and at best only indifferent sailors which made them vulnerable to the ferocious storms that ripped up and down the American coasts. In the 17th and 18th Centuries, as the power of the Spanish and Portuguese Empires declined and the number of galleons sailing across the Atlantic diminished in proportion, East Indiamen—stout, bluff, and highly seaworthy ships manned by English or Dutch crews—took the galleons' place and carried the commerce between the Old World and the New. As the 19th Century approached, ships began to be more specialized, their size, hull forms, and sail plans adapted to specific roles, be they carrying cotton or tobacco, tea or coffee beans, passengers to Europe or emigrants to the United States or Canada—or given over to darker tasks, rum-running, and slaving.

And they carried mail. In this age of electronic media and the capacity for instant communications which they provide, it's difficult in the extreme to comprehend the importance of the mail to every level, every aspect of society in the days before the telegraph, telephone, or television. There was, literally, no other way to communicate between cities, states, or nations. Individuals holding close to ties with friends and family far away; businesses trading or seeking trade overseas; governments waging war, negotiating peace, pursuing allies, or subjugating new colonies, all were dependent on the mail to accomplish their ends. Yet even at the best of times a letter being posted from New York to London would take four weeks to arrive at the desk of its addressee, while the reply might take as many as eight weeks to make the return journey.

As frustrating as such a torpid pace of communication might be to businessmen and private citizens, the political implications of such delays were portentous. To be given the post of a nation's ambassador, today an appointment reduced in stature to a figurehead position with little real authority, most often a sinecure for civil servants who have distinguished themselves in some minor way, or a reward for political services rendered, was once an office almost omnipotent in the range of powers it could exercise. Ambassadors were literally their governments personified, and could, as their nation's representative to a foreign capital, and if their best judgment and the limited instructions they would receive from the mother country so ordained, declare war, sign peace treaties, establish trade agreements, or annex whole territories on their own authority. This was because the only means of communicating with their sovereign, prime minister, president or foreign secretary was via slow, erratic, and sometimes errant dispatches sent through the mail, often arriving with information and instructions hopelessly inaccurate or out of date because the document had been written as much as three months before it reached its destination. As a result, an ambassador could unknowingly commit his country to policies and courses of action that were contrary to the desires of the government at home. Sometimes the slowness of the communications would cost lives: the Duke of Wellington ordered a British army to storm the city of Toulouse in the south of France, in late April 1814, two weeks after Napoleon Bonaparte had abdicated, for news of the Emperor's downfall hadn't yet reached him; in January 1815 the Americans and British fought a bloody, pitched battle outside New Orleans, because neither commander yet knew of the peace treaty ending the War of 1812 that had been signed almost a month earlier.

The custom was for a ship sitting alongside a wharf to advertise the space she had available for cargo or passengers. Once her holds were full, she would take on whatever mail had accumulated while she was waiting, and set sail, arriving—hopefully—four, six, even eight weeks later at her destination. It was a system that had worked, after a fashion, since the days of the Hanseatic League of Baltic seaports in the 16th Century, but it clearly left much to be desired. Passengers might have to wait days, even weeks, for their crossing to commence, while the goods that businessmen wished to see sold overseas sat in the port's warehouses, earning them nothing. If the goods were perishable, they had little recourse but to accept whatever losses they incurred while waiting for the ship to sail.

On October 27, 1817, all that changed. New York newspapers that day carried advertisements for a newly formed shipping company that was proposing the most novel idea: their ships would sail monthly at a specified day and time, regardless of how full their holds may be. Similar announcements in Liverpool declared that the ships would "positively sail, full or not full." The New York Packet Company, soon to be known on both sides of the Atlantic as simply "The Black Ball Line" because of the emblem carried on the ships' foresails, was proposing to bring a degree of regularity to shipping on the North Atlantic that no one had before imagined.

The first announced sailing date was January 10, 1818, when the *James Monroe*, a relatively small ship of the type known as a packet or packet-boat, only 118 feet long and 424 tons burthen, would set sail for Liverpool at 10:00 A.M. The idea of a ship sailing according to a schedule seemed preposterous to most of the maritime community of New York, and yet when the appointed morning came, the *Monroe*'s captain, James Watkinson, was found supervising the last minute details of getting his ship ready for sea. As ten o'clock neared, her topsails were unfurled, but not yet set. Along with some miscellaneous cargo there were a handful of passengers aboard, but they were far outnumbered by the crowd of curiosity seekers who lined the length of the wharf, most of them still not really believing that the *Monroe* would depart as advertised.

Yet, as a nearby church bell struck ten o'clock, men began scurrying across the *Monroe*'s deck in response to Captain Watkinson's shouted orders, lines were cast off, the ship was warped away from the wharf, and as the topsails were sheeted home the little packet began to pull away. Within minutes she had cleared the East River piers and was soon lost to sight in the gently falling snow. Twenty-eight days later she arrived at Liverpool, a very respectable crossing time. Her sister ship, the *Courier*, was still driving hard westward, having left Liverpool the same day the *James Monroe* left New York. Working against contrary winds and winter storms, that crossing would take six weeks. Nevertheless, the ships had sailed as promised. The age of the Yankee packets had begun.

The ships themselves were not particularly remarkable. Though handsome enough, they had none of the lithe grace and sleek lines of the clipper ships of the 1840s and 1850s. Instead, they resembled nothing so much as the stout frigates of the United States Navy—not a demeaning comparison by any standard, for those ships had earned a reputation for speed and durability by defying the might of Great Britain's Royal Navy in the just-ended War of 1812. A three-masted square-rigged ship, the typical packet had a graceful "fiddle" bow, so-called because its shape resembled the outline of a violin, that gave way to a clean-lined, robust hull, a bit thicker in the waist and fuller than a frigate's. Roughly half of the packet's useful internal volume was given over to cargo holds, for carrying cargo made as much, if not more money than carrying passengers. Above the hold, in a poorly lit, poorly ventilated area called the "'tween decks," was steerage, the area where the packets made the most money on their westbound crossings: this is where the immigrants were quartered. They slept in rickety bunks secured to the decks and the overheads (ceilings) and were responsible for cooking their own meals. Sanitary arrangements were rudimentary—chamberpots that had to be emptied over the sides every morning. Steerage was foul-smelling, cramped, and gloomy; fortunately it was an experience that nearly all of the emigrants only had to endure once. (There was always a small percentage that decided to return to the "old country" after having tried to make a go of it in America or Canada, but they were few and far between). On eastbound crossings, the steerage decks were given over to additional cargo space—sometimes livestock—which did little to improve the conditions on the westbound voyage. By contrast, the cabin passengers were relatively comfortable. They were given two-person staterooms, located on the aft half of the upper deck (the area that would be called the quarterdeck on a man-o-war); while not particularly spacious, these cabins were a vast improvement over the claustrophobic 'tween decks of steerage. Meals were served to cabin-class passengers in their own dining saloon, while those traveling on newer packets were able to dispense with the noisesome chamberpots and avail themselves of proper water-closets. Bathing facilities for either class were non-existent.

Even given such amenities as there were for cabin class passengers, however, while infinitely more comfortable than steerage, any ocean crossing in cabin class could hardly be considered luxurious. What was inescapable, regardless of class, was that within days of departure the voyage would become something where the monotony was only relieved by the boredom and tedium; where one day of rolling seas, gray scudding clouds, and strong breezes would blend unnoticed into the next; or where the succession of days would be suddenly interrupted by violent storms with screaming winds and crashing waves; or worse yet, the ship might be overtaken by interminable periods of flat calm, when neither the sea nor the air stirred.

The mot of Samuel Johnson, that an ocean voyage was much like being thrown into jail, with the added opportunity of being drowned, has been repeated often enough that it has become something of a weak joke. Yet in Johnson's day it was a profound, if acerbic, observation, and just as much so in the opening decades of the 19th Century. Not every packet that set out from New York, Boston or Liverpool arrived at its intended port, and unless by some fortunate chance another passing vessel was nearby to render assistance, a packet that found itself in distress was doomed to disappear without a trace. Such a fate overtook the *Ocean Queen*, with ninety souls aboard her in 1834; the packet *Driver* with 372 people aboard likewise vanished two years later; nor would steamships prove immune—in 1854, the Inman Line's *City of Glasgow* would vanish in mid-ocean, taking her 480 passengers and crew with her.

It's worth mentioning that not every sailing ship that carried cargo and passengers was designated a packet, although the term has been applied loosely over the decades. Ships that sailed only when the weather was fair and their holds full, and the majority of the ships putting to sea were just such, were properly known as regular traders. It was the ships that sailed to a schedule, full hold or no, passengers or not, and which were then driven as hard as humanly possible to make the fastest crossings that were entitled to be called packets.

The packets were skippered by tough Yankee captains from New England, who more often than not had grown up within sight of the sea, or came from a seafaring family. They were a special breed, these packet captains, and they had to be, for they accepted challenges that no skippers had ever willingly faced before—sudden, brutal storms that threatened to dismast or overwhelm the ship; uncharted rocks and shoals which could rip out a vessel's bottom in seconds; mutiny among the crew and riots among nervous passengers were all risks that were implicit in every crossing.

It was mutiny that was always the greatest threat, for the crew was always a dangerous lot. "Packet rats" they were called, the majority of them coming from Liverpool, the products of the slums and waterfronts. The best sailors, Yankee and British alike, found berths aboard the whaling ships that plied the South Atlantic and vast expanses of the Pacific Ocean—while they might never grow rich that way, it was always a better wage than the miserable $12 a month that a typical packet rat earned. Such men were uneducated, seldom of even average intelligence, and had led hard, coarse, brutal lives from birth, and expected little if anything more from their lot in life—a far cry from the professional seamen who would eventually come to characterize the British merchant marine. No strangers to violence, they were kept in line by officers who weren't afraid to crack a belaying pin across a recalcitrant crewman's skull in order to make himself obeyed. When it was said that a skipper drove his ship hard, it was the packet rats who were being driven. In the words of one packet captain, Samuel Samuels, the packet rats "were the toughest class of men in all respects. They could stand the worst weather, food, and usage, and put up with less sleep and more rum, than any other sailors. They would not sail in any other trade. They had not the slightest idea of morality or honesty, and gratitude was not in them. The dread of the belaying pin or heaver kept them in subjection...."

It took a distinctive breed of man to be able to maintain command of such brutes, while never losing the capacity to uphold the conventions of polite society among the passengers and his fellow officers. At once an intriguing combination of civilized gentleman and hard-bitten, hard-souled dictator, the captains drove their ships, their crews, and themselves with a relentless, single-minded dedication—to make the fastest possible crossing of the Atlantic, east-or west-bound, and make it regardless of the time of year, or the state of the weather or seas.

But for a successful packet skipper there were astonishingly rich rewards waiting that made all the risks worth taking. In the 1830s and 1840s the average salary of a packet captain was $3,000, or more than $50,000 today. While a respectable, if not exorbitant salary, there were additional incentives. The captain of a mail carrier typically received a "master's fee" of $1,500 annually, while a commission of 2½% on all freight carried was customary, along with any "gifts" or gratuities that the passengers chose to bestow on him. And often a master was a part-owner of the ship he commanded, so that he received a share of the profits from the passenger fares and freight charges. It wasn't unknown for a packet captain to make upward of $8,000 a year, equivalent to $150,000 today. Coupled with the economic prosperity such a command gave was the social cachet that being known as a packet captain conferred on those who held such a title. While they may be hard-souled and ruthless when standing on the quarterdecks of their ships, most of the captains of the packet ships came from respectable and respected New England families, and were well-versed in the manners and conduct of polite company. Lions themselves at sea, they were lionized by society ashore.

But no matter how successful a packet captain might become, there was always one fundamental fact of which he was always aware: no matter how fast he might have driven his ship on her last passage, he had no way to ensure that he could repeat that performance. He was always at Nature's mercy, still powerless to defy the dictates of wind and weather. A packet captain's reputation and career could be meteoric indeed: a few weeks' calm in mid-Atlantic could reduce last month's toast of Liverpool, Boston, or New York to little more than the status of an also-ran. To a tiny but growing community of foresighted individuals on both sides of the Atlantic, the answer was obvious: the future of transatlantic travel lay not with wind-powered ships, no matter how fiercely driven, but with ships driven by engines powered by steam.

The first tentative steps toward introducing steam-driven ships to the North Atlantic were taken in 1819, when the paddlewheel steamer *Savannah* set out from her namesake port in Georgia on May 24, bound for Liverpool, where she would arrive twenty-seven days later. In the decades to come, her partisans would claim the credit for her of making the first steam-powered crossing of the Atlantic Ocean. Purists, on the other hand, are quick to point out that while the *Savannah* did indeed have a steam engine aboard, it was run for barely more than eighty hours during the entire voyage—or roughly three hours a day—hardly qualifying the passage as a "steam-powered" crossing.

They have a point. The *Savannah* was a pretty little ship, just 318 tons, one hundred and three feet long, able to make 5 knots under steam, 10 knots under sail. But she had actually been built as a full-rigged ship, and only had her engine and paddles installed after she had been otherwise completed. The steam engine was never meant to be more than an auxiliary to the sails, added on the advice of her first owners. Nevertheless, while the passage of the *Savannah* may not have met the strict definition of a steam-powered crossing, it is noteworthy as a valiant first attempt.

Fourteen years would pass before there was another. The second try at bringing steam power to the Atlantic was made by a ship that, unlike the hybrid *Savannah*, was designed and built as a paddlewheel steamer, albeit one with a somewhat chequered history, the *Royal William*. Constructed in 1830 on the banks of the St. Lawrence River in Quebec Province, the *Royal William* was almost four times the size of the diminutive *Savannah*, and the brainchild of an ambitious (perhaps even over-ambitious) collection of some 235 stockholders who had formed the Quebec and Halifax Steam Navigation Company. (By odd chance, among them were three brothers from Halifax, Nova Scotia—Henry, Joseph, and Samuel—who shared the rather curious surname of Cunard.) As the corporate moniker implied, the *Royal William*'s task would be to provide regular mail and passenger service between Quebec City, at the mouth of the St. Lawrence River, and the Maritime Provinces.

It was by no means an unrealistic undertaking, as steamboats had been a common sight on the St. Lawrence for more than twenty years. By August 1831, she was ready for sea, and set about making three round trips from Quebec City to New Brunswick, Prince Edward Island, Nova Scotia and back. It was while she stopped in Halifax that Samuel Cunard was observed walking her decks, asking a multitude of questions. One feature of the *Royal William* in particular seemed to catch his fancy: her dining saloon was set in a deckhouse, separate from the rest of the passenger spaces.

The spring of 1832 proved to be the *Royal William*'s undoing: an immigrant ship from Ireland brought a cholera epidemic to Quebec City, and on her first passage of the year, it quickly became evident that she was carrying passengers who were infected by the time she reached her first stop in New Brunswick. Ultimately she would spend nearly fifty days in quarantine, her schedule in utter disarray and her owners deeply in debt. When she finally returned to Quebec City she was put up for auction and sat idle until the following spring. Long before that time, the Cunard brothers had given up on steamships as a bad business, and had sold their interest in the company.

In June 1833 the *Royal William*'s new owners sent her first to Halifax, then to Boston, hoping to attract some sort of work for her. As events turned out, she was the first British steamship to ever put into the port of Boston, and she was given a grand welcome—but no business. Desperate, her owners decided to turn their hand to the transatlantic passenger trade, and on August 4, set out from Quebec into the open Atlantic.

Twenty-five days later, she steamed into Gravesend and the Port of London "in fine style," as her captain, John MacDougal, later told it. Unlike the *Savannah*, which had run her engines only intermittently, the *Royal William* had made almost the entire crossing under steam. Because she used sea water to make steam in her boilers, she had to stop her engines every four days or so to clean the accumulated salt scale from the boiler tubes—a job that took as much as a day each time it was done, and which necessitated the ship proceeding under sail while the work was underway. Because of this, purists would still find cause to object to the *Royal William's* claim of making the first steam-powered crossing of the Atlantic. But in doing so they would miss a larger point: in the fifteen years since the *Savannah* had crossed the Atlantic, the power and reliability of steam engines had increased so dramatically that they were now dependable enough to drive a ship across an entire ocean by themselves. Sails need no longer be the sole, or even primary means of propelling a vessel—ships on the high seas need no longer be subject to the absolute tyranny of the weather. The problem of salt scale in her boilers that bedeviled the *Royal William* was a mere technical difficulty awaiting a solution, not an overwhelming obstacle barring further progress. Already an engineer in London, Samuel Hall, was working on what would become known as the "Double Vacuum Steam Condenser," which would enable ship's engines to use a limited supply of fresh water by recycling their own exhaust steam, eliminating the need to use seawater in the boilers.

The outstanding problem that the *Royal William*'s passage brought to light was the amount of fuel consumed on the crossing—twenty-five tons a day, or more than six hundred tons for the entire voyage. The space needed for bunkering that much coal, combined with requirements of her boilers and engines, left comparatively little room inside a ship's hull for cargo and passengers—placing sharp limits on her ability to make money. Until something could be done about that, steam-powered crossings would always be technically feasible, but they would hardly be economically attractive.

The solution to that problem came about as a consequence of yet another effort to introduce steam-powered ships to the North Atlantic. This venture began three years after the voyage of the *Royal William*, in 1836. It started out as a remark made during a meeting of the Board of Directors of the Great Western Railway in London, England. The topic under discussion by the board at the moment was the extension of the railway's western line all the way to Bristol on England's western shore. One of the directors voiced the opinion that a rail line extending all the way to Bristol would be far too long. Another member of the board immediately replied that on the contrary, the London to Bristol line would be far too short.

It was an odd comment, seemingly laughable at first blush, but one to be taken seriously when the man making it was Isambard Kingdom Brunel. Already hailed as a brilliant railway designer — he would eventually construct a total of twenty-five rail lines — he was also the outstanding engineer of his day, arguably the greatest engineering genius in history. Tunnels were one of his specialties: early in his career Brunel had supervised the construction of the Thames Tunnel, one of the first pedestrian and traffic tunnels to be built in the world, connecting the north and south banks of the Thames River in London. When the Great Western Railway was built from London to Bristol, he cut a two-mile long tunnel near Bath that had critics crying doom and gloom in the House of Lords, declaring that the tunnel would collapse due to excessive length; the tunnel still stands today, and is still in use. Brunel was also an early

Isambard Kingdom Brunel, railroad designer and shipbuilder, the most gifted engineer of his day.

and successful proponent of suspension bridge design, building five of them in England, along with one hundred twenty-five railroad bridges, and with many of those bridges still standing and still in use. He invented a form of refrigerated railway car, and in 1839 introduced railway telegraphy.

Nor did Brunel's talents end at the water's edge: he constructed eight piers and drydocks, and would eventually design and build three steamships, the *Great Western*, the *Great Britain* and the *Great Eastern*. The overly-ambitious *Great Eastern* would ultimately prove Brunel's undoing, being the one project that would exceed his genius, but before that happened, Brunel's influence on steamship design would be as great as any individual's has ever been, leaving behind a mark that is still visible in the shipping industry today.

Brunel was somewhat different than many of his contemporaries, in that he readily resorted to theoretical calculation in order to reduce the element of "cut-and-try" which typified so much of early Victorian engineering. This was his special genius, a characteristic described as "a zig-zag streak of lightning across the brain." It was this disposition that led Brunel to discover a curious but fundamental relationship between the size of a ship's hull and the size of the engines needed to power it.

One of the quirks of shipbuilding is that merchant ships have their size determined by a measurement known as Gross Registered Tonnage, which, despite how it may sound, is not a measure of weight, but rather volume. In the Middle Ages, when ships began trading between various European ports, a uniform system of measurement had to be instituted to regulate shipping charges. The measurement used was the "tun," a large barrel about the size of an English "hogshead"-type cask. The size of a ship came to be determined by how many of these "tuns" it could carry—its "tunnage." As happens so often with words imported into the English language, the spellings became corrupted to "tons" and "tonnage" though the meanings didn't change.

By the beginning of the 19th Century, a "gross ton" had come to be accepted as equal to an enclosed volume of one hundred cubic feet, a standard, that with minor variations, still holds good today. Thus, a ship with an internal volume of ten thousand cubic feet was said to have a gross registered tonnage of one hundred tons. Pondering what combination of dimensions would produce the optimum tonnage for the ship he proposed to build for the Great Western Railroad, Brunel made what, for the day, was a startling theoretical discovery.

The conventional engineering wisdom of the day held that any increase in a ship's displacement would require an equivalent increase in the power of the engines required to drive the ship at a given speed—e.g. doubling the tonnage would require doubling the engine power. What Brunel found amid his calculations and equations, though, was something quite different: as the size of a ship grows, its capacity grows as the cube of its dimensions, while the amount of power required to move the ship at a given speed increases only as the square of those dimensions. Brunel's discovery meant that far larger ships than had ever been built before could be constructed, requiring only modest increases in engine size and power. It would revolutionize ocean travel, as it meant that the design and construction of larger and larger ships would eventually only be limited by the structural strengths of the materials used. Of more immediate import, it meant that ships could be built of a size that could guarantee profits without having to devote exorbitant—and costly amounts of space to bunkering coal.

Meanwhile, what Brunel had in mind when he made his half-jesting remark about extending the railroad westward was that the service provided by the Great Western Railway should not end at the water's edge. In a curious foreshadowing of the success the great Canadian Pacific Railroad would enjoy with its fleet of ocean liners seven decades later, Brunel saw an opportunity to provide transportation for freight and passengers, not only to their port of departure from Great Britain, but all the way across the Atlantic, by introducing a fleet of ships that would meet the railroad's freight and passenger trains at dockside, swiftly transfer them aboard and whisk them away to the United States or Canada. It only followed that since the parent company of this venture would be a railroad, the ships would be paddlewheel steamers rather than square-rigged packets.

The rest of the Great Western Railroad's directors knew better than to dismiss Brunel's ideas out of hand, but they were a cautious lot, and were willing to take his concepts just so far — in this case only as far as building a single ship which would be called, predictably enough, the *Great Western*, to test just how feasible—that is, how costly or profitable—the whole idea could be. Their conservatism further extended to the size of the ship they authorized Brunel to build. The *Great Western* would be the first ship built specifically for the North Atlantic run: 212 feet in length, with a beam of 35 feet, and displacing 1,340 gross tons, she was a large and handsome ship, actually the largest ship in the world at the time, but a far cry from the ocean-going behemoth that was slowly taking shape in Brunel's mind. She would be propelled by paddlewheels that would give her an average speed of 9 knots, and she would provide remarkably comfortable, almost opulent, berthing for one hundred forty-eight passengers. Built in Bristol at the William Patterson shipyard, she was launched on July 19, 1837, and towed to London where the engineering firm of Maudslay, Sons & Field installed her engines. By late March 1838, the *Great Western* was complete and

The Great Western, *the first product of Brunel's shipbuilding genius.*

ready for her maiden voyage.

Actually, it was going to be more than just a maiden voyage, it was going to be a race. Another ship, barely half the size of the *Great Western*, was sitting in the Thames being hastily prepared for an Atlantic crossing of her own. She was the little *Sirius*, a 700-ton paddlewheeler that had been built for service between London and Cork, a route she had already been serving for over a year. She was really too small for the North Atlantic, and there were doubts that she could even carry enough coal to make it all the way across, but the men who were fitting her out were desperate: the grandiose plans of the British and American Steam Navigation Company had gone very much awry.

This company was the product of the ambition of one man, Junius Smith, an American-born businessman who now lived and worked in London, and who possessed two abiding passions in his life—one was to be granted a knighthood by Queen Victoria, the other was to bring steam-powered mail and passenger service to the North Atlantic. While he could do nothing but wait on Her Majesty's pleasure to attain the first, to achieve the second, he threw all of his enormous energy into the effort.

It was a determined undertaking: Smith knew full well the penalties paid by businessmen for cargoes delayed by contrary winds and weather that held sailing ships in their thrall. Having emigrated in 1820 from Connecticut to London, he set himself up in the import-export business, dealing in commodities such as hemp, cast iron, cotton, timber and turpentine. Almost from the first he began to experience the frustrations caused by delays in the arrival of shipments, sometimes having orders canceled for goods that were trapped in the holds of ships becalmed in mid-ocean. After traveling to America with his family aboard the packet *St. Louis* in 1832, Smith was more determined than ever to bring a change to the shipping business on the North Atlantic: the crossing took fifty-four days, a "humbling" experience, Smith would later describe it. Like several of his contemporaries, Smith was a practical businessman who was not entirely devoid of imagination, and he also saw that steam powered ships were the answer.

Originally he tried to interest New York's commercial community in the idea of setting up a shipping company formed around a quartet of steamships. By his calculations, Smith concluded, four steamers would equal twelve sailing packets simply by the amount of time they saved in making regular crossings without having to depend on favorable winds, and he formulated his proposal around them. But in a surprising display of mulishness, the New York businessmen rebuffed Smith, announcing that they were satisfied with the system that was presently in place. Disgusted, Smith returned to London, where he pressed his idea forward on anyone who might be willing to listen and invest. It wasn't easy, but at least the London businessmen didn't laugh him out of their offices.

By 1836, Smith had gathered together enough investors to form the British and American Steam Navigation Company, and placed an order for the first of his ships, to be called the *Princess Victoria*, with the shipyard of MacGregor Laird. Smith was thinking big: at 1,890 tons the *Princess Victoria* would be the largest steamship yet built. Once she was a going proposition, Smith planned to order a consort for her to be built in a British shipyard, while a similar pair would be constructed by American builders. This way, he believed, he could emphasize the international nature of his venture.

The problem Smith and his company ran into was that the *Princess Victoria* wouldn't be a going proposition anytime soon—in fact, she wouldn't be going anywhere. The firm of Claude, Girdwood & Co. had been contracted to provide the engines for the new ship, but two thirds of the way through their construction the company encountered financial problems which eventually led to bankruptcy, and all work on the engines stopped. In desperation, Smith turned to the famous Scottish engine builder Robert Napier, who immediately agreed to finish the engines, but the delays already incurred were sufficient to guarantee that the *Princess Victoria* would not be ready for sea in 1838 as planned. And yet other circumstances seemed to be working in Smith's favor. The summer of 1837 was one of the stormiest ever recorded, and ship after ship suffered delays in reaching port, with more than one vanishing in the middle of the Atlantic. Fortunes were lost and sometimes bankruptcies incurred because of the delays caused to cargoes coming into, and departing from Great Britain. It was as if Nature sought to provide a graphic lesson on the fundamental truth behind Smith's ambitions.

In order to salvage those ambitions, Smith and his investors had to be able to provide some sort of service across the Atlantic, come spring 1838. Their solution was to charter the small paddlewheel coastal steamer *Sirius* from the St. George Steam Packet Company. She was a charming little ship, all business and no pretense, but pretty for all that. Just 700 tons, with two masts and one funnel, her hull was painted black, her deckhouses green, while her masts were varnished wood and her paddlewheels were picked out in red. Her figurehead was a small non-descript dog holding a white star in its forepaws, representing the Dog Star, hence the name *"Sirius"*. The charter was signed in February 1838, and most of the month of March was spent fitting her out for the North Atlantic.

On March 29th 1838, the *Sirius* left London for New York. She reached Cork on April 3, where she took on additional passengers, mail—and as much coal as she could carry. Since the little steamer hadn't been built for ocean service, her coal consumption wasn't a serious concern while she paddled about the Irish Sea or along the English Channel, but her bunkers were clearly inadequate to carry enough coal for the *Sirius* to make her way across the Atlantic. Consequently, her crew found themselves storing coal in every part of the ship not given over to her passengers. When she left Cork Harbor the next morning there were even two large piles of coal heaped up on her foredeck.

The *Great Western*, meanwhile, left London on March 29, having suffered the indignity of a minor fire aboard as she was steaming down the Thames for the first time on her way to Bristol. Fortunately, there was very little damage, but her departure was delayed by twelve hours, time the *Sirius* was sure to put to good use. She reached Bristol three days later, and the remaining preparations for her maiden voyage were completed by April 8. At 11:00am she cast off her mooring lines and set out to catch the *Sirius*.

The captain of the *Sirius*, Richard Roberts, knew full well that the *Great Western* had a far more powerful engine than their own little ship, so he drove her as hard as he dared, keeping up steam round the clock. In mid-ocean, the *Sirius* ran into a storm far worse than any she had ever encountered in the Irish Sea or the Channel, and her progress was slowed drastically. Worse, in order to just make seaway, her engine had to be kept turning at full power, which caused the rate at which she consumed coal, to soar. Consequently, while she was still five days out from New York, her bunkers were empty. Conscious that they were still ahead of the *Great Western*, neither Captain Roberts nor his crew were ready to concede the race, and they scavenged the ship for anything and everything that could burn. Furniture, gratings, doors and even the ship's extra spars were all broken up and fed into the boiler. (The story later circulated, that even a child's doll, ripped from her arms by a ruthless crewman, had been fed into the maw of the firebox was quite untrue; it was the product of a vindictive reporter for a New York paper who felt that Captain Roberts had failed to show him sufficient deference.) Their efforts were rewarded, for when the *Sirius* arrived off New York at 10:00pm on April 22, the *Great Western* was nowhere in sight. To the little *Sirius,* indisputably, went the honor of the first Atlantic crossing made entirely under steam. It would earn her a deserved place in the history books, but her fame would be eclipsed within a matter of hours.

The *Great Western* arrived in New York less than twelve hours after the *Sirius,* having made her crossing in fourteen days and twelve hours—a full four days faster than the *Sirius'* passage. More important, when she encountered the same storm that had slowed down the smaller ship so dramatically, the *Great Western's* size allowed her to shoulder her way through the heavy seas and drive on. Just as important, her larger size meant that when she arrived in New York the *Great Western* still had more than two hundred tons of coal in her bunkers, enough for an additional four days' steaming. It was a point not lost on the shipping world.

Despite the rebuffs the New York shipping community had given Smith just three years earlier, the city went delirious with the near-simultaneous arrival of the two steamers. A twenty-six gun salute, one for each state in Union, greeted the *Sirius* and the *Great Western*, while thousands of people lined the shores, and various bands played "God Save the Queen," "Yankee Doodle," "Hail Columbia" and whatever suitably patriotic airs took their fancy. For the next week, as a seemingly endless round of celebratory dinners and receptions was given for the captains and crews of both ships, showing, in the words of the *New York Enquirer*, "the most irrefragable testimony of the practicability of steam navigation between the Old and New Worlds...visions of a future advantage to science, to commerce, to moral philosophy, began to float before the mind's eye". The rest of the New York press waxed equally lyrical over the potential for trade and prosperity that the dawning of the steamship age seemed to herald for the city.

Both the *Sirius* and the *Great Western* would begin their return passages to Britain within a few weeks, once the celebrations had run their course in New York. The *Sirius* would make only one more crossing of the Atlantic before her place was taken by the long-delayed *Princess Victoria*, which was now renamed the *British Queen,* upon the accession of Princess Victoria to the throne of Great Britain. The *Great Western* continued to churn her way across the ocean throughout the remainder of the summer and autumn of 1838 and all through 1839, always an object of public attention, even if she rarely sailed with a full passenger list. Between them, Smith and Brunel proved to the world that large steamers could be employed on a regular transatlantic service. And yet, because of mismanagement and bad judgment, neither company would succeed in establishing a regular steamship service between Great Britain and North America.

Instead, Fate would play its hand, and deny both Brunel and Smith the opportunity to become known to posterity as the man who would bring steam to the North Atlantic, to stay. Instead, through a combination of good timing, good business sense, and a generous helping of good luck, that honor would go not to a Briton, but to a colonial, a businessman from Halifax, Nova Scotia. His name was Samuel Cunard.

CHAPTER TWO

Samuel Cunard

At 2:00pm on Saturday, July 4, 1840, the wooden paddle steamer *Britannia* pulled away from the pier on Liverpool's waterfront and began churning her way down the Mersey River and into the Irish Sea, on her way to Halifax, Nova Scotia, and Boston, Massachusetts. She was the first of four sister ships, *Britannia, Acadia, Caledonia,* and *Columbia*, that would begin the first regularly scheduled transatlantic steamship service. This quartet of ships had been built for the newly-formed British and North American Royal Mail Steam Packet Company—an ambitious undertaking whose awkward name would soon be supplanted in the public mind by the name of the company's senior partner, and become known simply as the Cunard Line.

Samuel Cunard wasn't a seaman, he was a businessman; he wasn't looking to make history, he was looking to make money. Yet genius, as Otto von Bismarck once observed, consists of hearing the distant hoof beat of the horse of history and then leaping to catch the passing horseman by the coat tails. In the morning of the Industrial Revolution, the problem was deciding at which horse and horseman to lunge, since for every new concept and technology that would ultimately become successful and profitable, there were a half-dozen which would prove to be dead ends. Samuel Cunard was a case in point: steamships would eventually make his name a household word on both sides of the Atlantic, yet he originally had neither regard nor use for them, although his interest in the business of shipping was considerable.

Born in 1787 in Halifax, Nova Scotia, Samuel was the eldest son of Abraham and Margaret Cunard, British Loyalists who had moved to Halifax from New York in 1783, when the American Revolution finally ousted the Crown from the Thirteen Colonies. A master carpenter, Abraham worked as a joiner for the Royal Navy Dockyard in Halifax, which at the time was the most important British port in North America. Eventually he became a shipbuilder in his own right, becoming prosperous enough to form a small shipping company, Abraham Cunard & Son. The "son" was, of course, Samuel, who though he was not yet twenty-one, had already served as a civilian clerk for the local militia as well as worked for a ship brokerage in Boston for three years, where he sharpened his clerical and accounting skills and developed a good head for business.

Cunard, father and son, quickly took advantage of the ill-grace with which Great

Britain accepted the loss of her American colonies; actually the British were far from reconciled to the outcome of the Revolutionary War, and the Royal Navy turned a blind eye as British privateers preyed on Yankee shipping. One of the victims of this legalized piracy was an American square-rigger named the *White Oak*, brought to Halifax and sold to the Cunards at auction. Within a few months, she was sailing for London, carrying cargo and passengers, and turning a handsome profit for her new owners.

In 1812, the undeclared war between Great Britain and the United States finally became a declared one, but that proved to be no obstacle to Cunard. The company fleet was given a permit by the Lieutenant Governor of Nova Scotia to carry on trade with any port in the former colonies, while the Admiralty concluded a contract with Cunard to provide "conveyance by sailing vessels of His Majesty's mails between Halifax, Newfoundland, Boston and Bermuda." By the end of the War of 1812, Abraham Cunard & Son owned over forty ships, as well as one of the largest wharfs on the Halifax waterfront.

A few years later, Abraham Cunard retired and Samuel took over the firm, restyling it simply "S. Cunard and Company". Cunard continued to expand, first as the East India Company named Cunard as its agent for the Maritime provinces and began shipping consignments of tea to Halifax, as many as six thousand chests—over five hundred tons—arriving at one time, and then a bit later becoming agents for the coal fields of Cape Breton. At the same time, proving that his acumen wasn't limited solely to maritime matters, Cunard began successfully investing in brickyards, coal, fisheries, and timber. Cunard demonstrated early in his career a particular talent which would stand him and his businesses in good stead over the years. He discovered that if he paid attention to new ideas, listened to the advice of technical experts, and welcomed bright employees into his company who were well-paid and well-treated, the employees would reciprocate with loyalty and pride in their work, while the experts and their ideas would allow him to always stay abreast, and usually ahead, of his competitors. Cunard's particular talent in this respect was an impeccable sense of timing, an innate ability to determine when a new idea's hour had arrived.

It was in 1829 when the idea of Cunard becoming involved with steamships was first raised. A pair of Canadian entrepreneurs from Pictou named Ross and Primrose asked him to join in their venture which would introduce coastal steamship service to Nova Scotia. Cunard's reply to their approach made it clear that he had given little, if any, thought to the employment of steamships, and had little time to start thinking about them now. "We are entirely unacquainted with the cost of a steamboat, and would not like to embark in a business of which we are quite ignorant. Must, therefore, decline taking part in the one you propose getting up."

There were reasons for Cunard's conservatism: it went with the territory, so to speak, for by now Cunard was a well-entrenched member of the Halifax social elite. Appointed commissioner for Nova Scotia lighthouses, he was also a Colonel in the fashionable Second Regiment of the Halifax Militia, and, as a dedicated Tory, had a seat on the powerful Nova

Scotia Legislative Council, whose membership was made up exclusively of the province's most influential businessmen and bankers.

Yet it would be unfair to portray Cunard as a stereotypical 19th Century businessman, faceless and colorless, all ledgers and balance sheets and stodgy upper-middle class respectability. Not an imposing figure—he was once described as "a bright, tight little man with keen eyes, firm lips and happy manners"—he appeared to enjoy his wealth and influence, but was at the same time known as a modest, almost shy man, with a quiet manner. By all accounts he was a caring father to his nine children and a loyal and loving husband to his wife, Susan, a truth made tragic by the fact that by the time he was forty-two, he was a widower.

Samuel Cunard, the Halifax businessman who started it all.

While he certainly welcomed the advantages his fortune and social standing offered, there seems to be little of the affectation and stuffy self-importance about him that characterized so many of his peers and colleagues on both sides of the Atlantic, the type lampooned so mercilessly by Charles Dickens.

If in 1829 Cunard was "ignorant" of steamships and displayed no driving desire to alleviate that ignorance, by 1833 his attitude had changed remarkably. Exactly what caused him to reconsider his opinion is unknown—in 1831 he was briefly one of more than two hundred stockholders in the company that built the *Royal William*, but never evidenced an interest in the ship as anything more than another in his variety of investments—however, his change of heart was profound. At one point, he remarked that "steamers, properly built and manned, might start and arrive at their destination with the punctuality of railroad trains on land.... The day will surely come when an ocean steamer will be signaled from Citadel Hill every day of the year." Yet another five years would pass before Cunard would take any active step toward a direct involvement with steamships.

When he did, though, it was with the same methodical determination that would become a Cunard hallmark for the next half-century. In mid-January 1839, Samuel Cunard sailed for Great Britain aboard the British packet *Reindeer*. Choosing to cross the Atlantic in mid-winter was sufficiently indicative of how seriously Cunard regarded the undertaking he was about to embark upon, for January is the Atlantic's most unforgiving month, filled with storms, ice, and fog. When the *Reindeer* was halfway to Liverpool, a notice appeared in the Halifax newspaper the *Nova Scotian*, announcing a "Tender for Performing by Steam Vessels the Mail Service between England and Halifax and New York." The one proviso of this particular announcement that made it unique was the requirement that the service was to be provided exclusively by steamships—packets were no longer considered swift or reliable enough for the purposes of the Royal Mail.

Whether Cunard had somehow learned before he departed Halifax that this tender was to be made, or if the coincidence of his journey to Great Britain and the announcement were just happy happenstance, has been the subject of debate ever since. Certainly there had been some correspondence with William Edward Parry, the Royal Navy's Comptroller of Steam Machinery and Packet Service, the department of the Admiralty that awarded the Royal Mail contracts. Parry had at one time been stationed at the Royal Navy's dockyard in Halifax, where he became acquainted with Samuel Cunard and was an occasional visitor to the Cunard household. How much of the Admiralty's plans Parry may have communicated to Cunard is unknown—certainly Parry had been casting about Great Britain for prospective investors to take up the Admiralty's mail contract. At one point he contacted George Burns, part-owner of the City of Glasgow Steam Packet Company, which ran steamboats between Glasgow, Liverpool and Belfast, thinking that Burns' experience with steamships would stand him in good stead when setting up a transatlantic service. Burns declined, however, and it appears that at this point Parry approached Cunard, who was already in London, with the idea of taking up the Admiralty contract.

Whatever may have been the case, what is certain is that once he arrived in London, Cunard borrowed an office in Piccadilly and set about drafting a proposal in response to the Admiralty's tender: "I hereby offer to furnish Steam Boats of not less than 300 Horse Power to convey the Mails from a Point in England to Halifax and back, twice a month." He would have his ships ready, he declared, by May 1, 1840, and found the proposed subsidy of £55,000 acceptable. He also added the interesting proviso that, "should any improvement in steam navigation be made during [the contract's] continuance which the Lords of the Admiralty may consider as essential to the service, I do bind myself to make such alterations and improvements as their Lordships may direct." Given such assurances, the Admiralty agreed to a tentative contract on March 18, 1839.

In the meantime, Cunard demonstrated how clearly he had thought his way through all of the complexities of the new undertaking he was proposing. On the advice of his friend James Melville, he had contacted Robert Napier, a marine engineer from Glasgow, Scotland, and the senior partner in the Clydeside shipbuilding firm of Wood and Napier. Melville was the Secretary of The East India Company, and knew well the particular success that the Company's steamer *Berenice* was enjoying in the Indian Ocean, passing with almost clockwork regularity between Bombay and Suez. The *Berenice* was one of fourteen ships already in service with hulls built by John Wood and engines constructed by Robert Napier. Melville also informed Cunard that Napier's work was well known and highly regarded by the Admiralty.

Cunard immediately directed an inquiry to Napier about the requirements for designing and building a trio of ships which Cunard believed were necessary to meet the Admiralty's requirements. Despite his high repute in Admiralty circles, Napier was regarded by the intellectual snobs of London as a "mere provincial engineer" who cobbled together "country-made engines," but Cunard had chosen his man shrewdly. In addition to the solid performance of the *Berenice* giving testimony to the quality of his work, for more than five years Napier-engined paddle-wheelers had been reliably plying between Glasgow and the Isle of Man, proving the soundness and durability of Napier's designs and the excellence of his craftsmanship.

His commitment to quality steamships was long-standing. In 1833, not long after the *Royal William*'s voyage to Great Britain, he had written a London banker about the prospects, as he saw them, for the future of steam on the high seas. "I would have everything connected with the machinery very strong and of the best materials, it being of the utmost importance to give confidence at first, for should the slightest accident happen so as to prevent the vessel from making her passage by steam, it would be magnified by the opposition. But if, on the other hand, the steam vessels are successful in making a few quick trips and beating the sailing vessels very decidedly, then you may consider the battle won."

These were sentiments that closely echoed Cunard's beliefs, and consequently, the two men got on well with each other from the very beginning of their association. At a meeting between the two men in March 1839, Cunard proposed to have Napier build three ships of 800 tons each, powered by 300-horsepower engines, at a cost of £30,000 each. Napier agreed, though he observed in a letter to a friend that, "From the off-hand manner in which [Cunard] contracted with me, I have given him the vessels cheap, and I am certain that they will be very good and very strong ships."

Having second thoughts about just how cheap, Napier went back to Cunard and informed him that, in his opinion, the proposed designs were too small and too cheap. He worked out a series of enlargements and improvements to the proposed designs, all of which he deemed essential for the success of the ships and the transatlantic venture overall. The result was that the ships' design had grown to 960 tons with an engine power increased to 375 horsepower. Overall, these enlargements would add £2,000 to the cost of each ship.

Napier's motive was ambition, not greed. Not satisfied with just building small steamboats that paddled between the Western Isles or across the Irish Channel, Napier wanted to see his ships take to the open Atlantic. As with so many of his fellow Scots, within his heart a romantic visionary co-existed alongside a hardheaded, practical businessman, and he was able to imagine something of the potential that steamships offered if they were allowed the opportunity to take to the oceans of the world. At the same time, he understood that the designs put forward by Cunard were hesitant, still having something of the experimental about them, as if Cunard, despite the confidence he displayed to the

Admiralty, was as yet unsure of how viable was this proposed venture. What Napier wanted to achieve was not simply the introduction of steamship service to the Atlantic, but, harking back to the thoughts he had expressed six years earlier, to do so on such a scale and with such solid reliability that their presence would be permanently established.

Napier argued his position passionately, and Cunard began to see something of the future that Napier saw. But neither man was able to divorce himself from the practical considerations of such ambitious undertakings, and the problem of financing the four ships Napier wanted to build, soon loomed large. For while Napier was redesigning Cunard's ships, Cunard had been compelled to revise the boundaries of the service he wanted to establish. The Deputy Postmaster of Quebec province, J. N. Stayner, a longtime friend and associate of Cunard's, had written him a long, well-thought-out letter outlining the need for *four* ships to be able to comply with the terms of the Admiralty contract, particularly the stipulation requiring specified, regular departure dates from Halifax and Liverpool. Quite independently of Stayner, Napier had come to the same conclusion, that four ships, not three, were an absolute necessity.

The arguments of the two men, Napier and Stayner, were quite unanswerable and it didn't take long for Cunard to see they were correct. Nevertheless, the proposed changes in the business plan Cunard had originally drawn up created problems for him. Although an investment of £128,000 for four ships was certainly not beyond his means, it was a huge sum to risk on a technological venture that was still very much in the experimental stage, and Cunard hesitated to undertake it alone. Napier, however, had taken Cunard's measure as well as Cunard had taken his, and on May 10, 1839, at a dinner party at his house, Napier introduced the Canadian to two Scottish businessmen who might be willing to become investors in Cunard's proposed transatlantic steamship company.

George Burns and David McIver weren't newcomers to the steamship business: they were already customers of Robert Napier, partners in the City of Glasgow Steam Packet Company. There was actually a certain irony in the meeting, for this was the same George Burns who had earlier declined when the Admiralty's representative had approached him with the idea of setting up a transatlantic steamship service. Nevertheless, the dinner went well, all four men enjoying each other's company, and all equally fascinated by the idea of operating a transatlantic steamship line. But the innate Scots caution shared by all four men held sway, and nothing was decided that night. It was over breakfast the following morning that the four men came to an agreement: Cunard would put up £55,000 of his own money if the other three men could raise sufficient capital to cover the balance of the construction costs of the four ships. Burns, realizing that delays might jeopardize the standing of Cunard's contract with the Admiralty, said that if he and McIver could not find a sufficient number of investors in a reasonable amount of time, Cunard would be free to pursue other financial arrangements. Cunard responded by asking, "How long will it take to ascertain what you can do?" and Burns replied, "Perhaps a month."

Apparently Burns and McIver were very persuasive, or else there were quite a few Scots in Glasgow who had also envisaged such a venture, for within a week the two men had gathered thirty-one other investors, who together, subscribed a total of £215,000 to add to Cunard's investment, providing the fledgling company with a sound financial foundation. A contract was drawn up where Cunard took on Burns and McIver as partners; together Burns and McIver invested £25,000 of their own money, receiving a half-interest in the Royal Mail contract and the four steamships that would be built for the new company. Out of this half-interest they would in turn sell shares to the other thirty-one investors. The British and North American Royal Mail Steam Packet Company was now a going concern.

While all of this maneuvering was going on in Glasgow, a group of English investors got wind of the plans being laid by Cunard and his associates. Quickly they petitioned the Admiralty to give them preferential treatment when considering replies to the tender for the mail contract, arguing that proper Englishmen should be given the right to carry the Royal mail over some Canadian rustic. The Admiralty, however, remained impressed by the thoroughness and alacrity with which Cunard had made his plans and preparations, and the English businessmen were turned away empty handed. On May 4, 1839, a seven-year contract based on those plans and preparations, with some revisions to the original proposal, was signed by Samuel Cunard and the Lords of the Admiralty.

What the revisions entailed were changes in the size, number and cost of the ships to be built. After persuading Cunard of the need for four ships, Napier had then set about redesigning them yet again. The longer he studied them, the more the Scots engineer became convinced that even his original revisions would be inadequate to face the rigors of sailing year-round in the North Atlantic. What he now had in mind were four ships of roughly 1200 tons and 700 horsepower, nearly a quarter again the size and twice the engine power of the ships he had earlier proposed to Cunard, to be built at a cost estimated at £50,000 each. Their enlarged size would not only make them more seaworthy and durable, it would increase their steaming range, opening new possibilities for the fledgling company, allowing Cunard to go to the Admiralty with the idea of extending the Royal Mail service to the American port of Boston. The Admiralty, displaying a foresight that it has often been accused of lacking, immediately saw the advantages presented by all of Cunard's proposed changes, and agreed.

Hardly was the ink dry on the contract when Cunard placed the orders for his four ships, all of them with Clydeside shipyards. They would be as identical as peas in a pod, differing only in the details peculiar to each builder. Stretching 228 feet in length, they would have a draft of 17 feet, with a gross tonnage of 1,156 tons and a maximum tonnage of 2,050. The first, the *Britannia*, would be built by Robert Duncan of Greenock, while John Wood was given the *Acadia*, Charles Wood the *Caledonia*, and Robert Steele the *Columbia*. Robert Napier would build the engines for all four. They would be three-masted barques, that is with square-rigged sails on their fore -and main -masts, and fore- and -aft sails on the mizzens. Each would have the traditional clipper bow and square transom stern of a sailing ship, with a single tall funnel (smokestack) stepped amidships between the foremast and mainmast.

The colors sported by those funnels would become a story in and of themselves, as one charmingly enduring detail to come out of Napier's work on his engines—the creation of what would become the company's most widely-recognized trademark, the Cunard-red funnel. It was designated that they be painted red for the lower four fifths of their height, the uppermost section being blacked out as a soot topping. Because of the heat created as the smoke and gasses formed in the boilers passed up a ship's funnel, it was necessary to provide some form of corrosion protection for the relatively thin metal. Ordinary paints were ineffective, as the searing heat would soon cause them to blister and peel off. After some experimentation, Napier came up with a mixture of buttermilk and fresh ochre, that when applied to a funnel actually took advantage of the heat to literally "cook" itself onto the metal, effectively sealing and protecting it. The process also caused the mixture to turn that unique shade of red-orange which would grace the funnels of Cunard ships for the next one hundred and sixty years. Of course, as paint chemistries developed, the buttermilk-and-ochre mixture would give way to more sophisticated compounds, but the shade, as unique as it was indescribable, would remain the same.

When word of Cunard's accomplishment reached Halifax, the city went wild: the prospects for business and commerce held forth by being the western terminal of the new steamship line were dazzling. New hotels were built, shipyards refurbished and expanded, and collieries set up to supply the expected steamships with coal. While not growing at anything like the pace that the population of the United States was expanding, Canada *was* growing, and Halifax was about to assume a primacy of place as the colony's busiest seaport, a claim it still holds today.

Boston, on the other hand, was openly resentful and appalled that it should be relegated to the status of a mere "feeder" to the primary service going to Halifax. The city of Boston has always been something of an enigma to the rest of the United States, and indeed to North America. For generations there had existed a smoldering enmity between Boston and New York, as each vied to become the financial and mercantile hub, first of the thirteen Colonies and then after the Revolution, of the young United States. Tracing the city's origins to the Puritan settlers who founded Plymouth Colony in 1621, wealthy Bostonians, forgetting the mercantile and sometimes agrarian origins of their own ancestors, adopted aristocratic airs and graces, and regarded New Yorkers, particularly those whose forebears were Dutch, as upstarts and parvenus, little more than a trumped-up peasantry. In their turn, the denizens of New York responded by coining a sobriquet that would be applied to Boston's self-proclaimed elite with varying degrees of venom and invective for the next two centuries, the "Boston Brahmins." Admittedly, the implication of the same hypocritical and snobbish self-righteousness that characterized the elite of India's caste-ridden society was to a surprising degree at once descriptive and demeaning. At the same time, New York's civic leadership, political and social, were hardly innocent of prejudice themselves, gradually adopting an attitude that regarded the rest of the United States in its entirety as merely an appendage to their city.

Cunard's first ship, the Britannia, *in icebound Boston Harbor.*

Whatever merits, if any, existed in the attitudes of the two populaces, one undeniable fact was on the side of New York: geography. However splendid a port Boston Harbor might be, New York Harbor was nothing short of magnificent, being both far larger and with better deep-water access than Boston. Those advantages, coupled with New York's closer proximity to the rest of the United States, and in particular to the capital, Washington D.C., which had no port facilities of its own, made the eventual eclipse of Boston as the major port of the United States, inevitable. It seems that on some level Boston's city father's realized this, which only made Cunard's decision to provide what amounted to only a secondary service, harder to bear.

Not that Boston didn't try everything within the city's power to influence Samuel Cunard. At one point a collection of merchants offered Cunard the use of a pier, dock, and any other necessary facilities for the loading and unloading of passengers and freight, free of charge, if he would make Boston his western Atlantic terminus, and run the feeder service to Halifax instead. Cunard declined, although he soon realized that the enlarged ship designs Robert Napier had created would give his vessels enough margin of speed and range to be able to extend their service through Halifax to Boston, which, once Admiralty permission to do so was secured, served to somewhat mollify the Bostonian's wounded pride.

Meanwhile, Cunard returned to Halifax via New York, making his crossing on the *Great Western*. It was an uneventful passage, if a bit rough, as the Atlantic in 1839 seemed to be almost as turbulent as it had been the year before. What was notable about this particular crossing by the *Great Western* was that it occurred simultaneously with that of another steamship, this one sailing from Gravesend to New York. She was the tiny *Robert F. Stockton*, a 35-ton schooner-rigged vessel a mere 78 feet in length and 10 feet in beam. Her claim to fame, and it would loom huge in the years ahead, was that unlike every other steamer then at sea, she had no paddlewheels. Instead, she was thrust along by a screw propeller, an invention conceived almost simultaneously by English engineer Francis Pettit Smith, and a Swedish captain, John Ericsson, whom the world would one day come to know as the father of the U.S.S. *Monitor*. Despite the *Stockton*'s success with this invention, it would be another decade and more before screw-propelled steamships began to dominate the North Atlantic—but the *Stockton* had shown the way.

Having arrived in New York as unaware of the *Stockton*'s accomplishment as the rest of the world, Samuel Cunard eventually made his way back to Halifax, where he arrived on August 28. There he was greeted as something akin to a national hero, which in a way, he was. The regimental band of the Eighth Militia played at dockside, where Cunard was met by a committee of prominent Haligonians. The committee had organized a public subscription among the population of Nova Scotia for the purchase of a set of silver plate, which was duly presented to Cunard with the requisite amount of speechifying suitable to such an auspicious occasion. Then, to everyone's great relief, especially that of Cunard, who particularly disliked public ostentation, the committee chose to dispense with the formal dinner that had been planned and adjourn to McNab's Island at the mouth of Halifax harbour for a clambake. By all accounts Cunard enjoyed himself immensely at this rather informal affair, but then it would be surprising if he hadn't, since those present later recalled that the wine and spirits flowed liberally, a total of at least thirteen bumper toasts being made over the course of the afternoon, the majority of them directed to Samuel Cunard.

While Cunard was literally becoming the toast of Halifax, he wasn't idle—that simply wasn't his nature. While his transatlantic paddle steamers would be connecting Liverpool with Halifax and Boston, there was still a need to serve the routes along the Gulf of St. Lawrence, as well as the St. Lawrence River and Quebec. Casting about for a suitable ship, he found one in service with his partner, George Burns. She was the little 700-ton *Unicorn*, who had been plying the west coast of Scotland between Glasgow and Liverpool for four years. A pretty little ship, she caught Cunard's eye, and he quickly bought her and sent her across the Atlantic as a sort of herald of the service to come.

Aboard her was his eldest son, Edward, along with twenty-three other passengers, leaving Liverpool's Clarence Dock on May 15, taking sixteen days to reach Halifax, where she stopped long enough to drop off the mail and a handful of passengers, and allow those who would be continuing on to Boston a chance to stretch their legs. Three days later the *Unicorn* paddled into Boston Harbor and tied up at the newly constructed Cunard wharf. Recognizing the little steamer as a symbol of things to come, the city celebrated with cannon salutes, ringing church bells, brass bands and thousands of cheering Bostonians. The celebrations lasted for three days with the usual round of banquets, speeches, and presentations, and with Edward Cunard standing in admirably for his father. At the end of the week, the *Unicorn* left Boston to return to Halifax, but the anticipation she left behind hardly died down, as it was known that soon Cunard's ships would be docking in Boston on a regular basis.

A better understanding of Boston's delirium can be gained by realizing that in the 19th Century, a city's stature was measured in great part by the volume of shipping that passed through its seaport, in much the same way that an airport's volume of air traffic would become a civic status symbol in the 20th Century. Trade and passengers meant revenue for the city, employment for the working class, and business for the merchants. There was far more at stake than mere bragging rights in the competition between Boston and New York — a city whose port went into decline soon followed it into decay, while a busy port meant growth and prosperity.

In the meantime, Cunard's four ships were taking shape along the Clyde in Scotland. Cunard had entrusted their construction to Robert Napier, who oversaw every aspect of shipbuilding with the same meticulous care that he put into his engines. The first to be ready for launching was the *Britannia*, which was sent down the ways of Robert Duncan's shipyard on February 5, 1840. A huge crowd of well-wishers and curiosity seekers gathered for the occasion, among them Samuel Cunard, who had made a special crossing from Halifax. The honor of naming the new ship was given to Robert Napier's niece Isabella.

The new ship was quickly fitted out and by June 16 was ready for service. While Cunard had little use for extravagance or ostentation, he knew well the necessity of making his passengers reasonably comfortable, and the interior appointments of the *Britannia* were sufficiently impressive to warrant comment in an article that appeared in the *Glasgow Courier* the day of her launching. After a lengthy description of the ship's dimensions and technical merits, the paper went on to say that "The accommodation of the vessel is provided on an improved and magnificent scale, the cabin below deck being fitted with spacious and well-ventilated staterooms. The dining saloon will be unique, and we may safely say that from the keel to the topmast, everything will be found substantial, and adapted to the course the vessel is to take." After a few trial runs up and down the Clyde to test her engines, the *Britannia* made her way down to Liverpool at the beginning of July, where she was made ready for her maiden voyage.

Why Liverpool? Because throughout the entire 19th Century, Liverpool was the largest and busiest seaport in Britain, which meant, by extension, the world. In 1840, Liverpool had already surpassed London, Southampton, Portsmouth and Bristol: protected by a massive granite sea wall eleven feet wide and forty feet in height from its foundations at the bottom of the river, the docks and wharfs of the Liverpool waterfront stretched along the eastern shore of the Mersey River for more than five miles, and were still expanding.

Situated in northwestern England, Liverpool was close to the growing industrial centers of Glasgow, Sheffield, and Birmingham, and was less than fifty miles from the sprawling factories of Manchester. Every day the docks were crowded with an amazing array of coastal traders, packets, steamships, clippers, tenders, and barges, collected from all over Britain, Europe and the United States.

Inevitably, the city reflected the maritime origins of its prosperity, though not always attractively. Crimps and longshoremen, sailors and beggars, rubbed shoulders with emigrants, ship owners, businessmen, and ships' captains, on crooked, narrow, muddy streets that were lined with shops, boardinghouses, chandlers, pubs, hotels, whorehouses, and factories. The numbers of people who passed through Liverpool on their way from Germany, Scandinavia or the British Isles on their way to the United States or Canada were staggering: in the forty years between 1815 and 1854, the total came to more than three million people.

Liverpool was not without its disadvantages: the mouth of the Mersey River, where it emptied into the Irish Sea, was constantly being dredged, as a sandbar, soon known simply as "The Bar," was constantly building there. At low tide the water over the Bar was only eleven feet deep — but a thirty-one foot rise at high tide allowed even the deepest laden ships to enter the port. As a consequence, the pace of life in the city moved with the tempo of the tides.

The first public notice in Britain of the new shipping line's transatlantic service came when the Liverpool *Mercury* published an announcement on the morning of July 3, 1840:

> British and North American Royal Mail Steamships of 1,200 tons and 440 horsepower each, Appointed by the Admiralty to sail for Boston and calling at Halifax to land passengers and Her Majesty's mails:
>
> > Britannia....................Captain Woodruff
> > Acadia........................Captain Edward C. Miller
> > Caledonia...................Captain Richard Cleland
> > Columbia....................
>
> The Britannia *will sail from Liverpool on the* 4th *July; the* Acadia *on the* 4th *August. Passage including provisions and wine to Halifax, 34 guineas; to Boston 38 guineas. Steward's fee one guinea.*
>
> *The steamship* Unicorn *plies between Pictou and Quebec in connection with the above vessels carrying the mails and passengers.*
>
> *For passage apply to G. & J. Burns, Glasgow, J. B. Ford, 52 Old Broad Street, London, or in Liverpool to D. & C. MacIver, 12 Water St.*
>
> *The* Britannia *goes out of Coburg Dock this morning (Friday) the* 3rd *inst., and all heavy baggage should be sent on board before that time. Tomorrow (Saturday morning) at 10 o'clock a steamer will be at the Egremont Slip, sound end of Prince's parade to take off the passengers.*

The captain of the *Columbia* hadn't yet been appointed when the notice was drawn up, but nonetheless, Cunard and his partners were taking a monumental step forward in the evolution of the passenger trade on the North Atlantic. For the first time, a fixed and regulated schedule of sailing dates was being implemented by an entire shipping line. They weren't simply putting a steamship line into service, they were introducing *regular* steamship service between Britain and America. The old practice of delaying a ship's departure until she had a full hold of cargo and a full complement of passengers was being thrown overboard by this ambitious trio—their ships would always sail whether the holds and cabins were full or not. It wasn't simply a minor innovation to the way things had always been done on the North Atlantic, it was an entirely new way of doing business. It may have been Isambard Kingdom Brunel who had the first glimmerings of the shape the future would take when he introduced the *Great Western* as a sort of sea-going extension of his railroad, but it was Cunard who was making Brunel's vision a reality: the first steps had been taken toward bringing the same sort of scheduled regularity and predictability that the railroads were bringing to travel on land, now to passage across the Atlantic.

No longer would a ship's master be at the mercy of fickle breezes and contrary weather, and the quality of his ship and his skills as a mariner negated by storms and contrary winds. The machinery that moved a steamship gave its captain an independence that had never been known at sea before, and opened up entirely new potentials for governments and businessmen alike. With the ship's speed now a known quantity, it was possible to calculate the number of days, even hours, that it would take to cross the Atlantic, and project established schedules.

Merchants and manufacturers could now anticipate exactly when their wares would reach their markets, or when their raw materials would arrive from overseas, allowing them to reduce stockpiles and inventories, cutting back overhead and increasing profits. Travelers could now plan the duration of their excursions abroad. That was no small consideration, for the uncertainties of crossing the ocean by sailing ship had daunted many a would-be traveler. The violin virtuoso Nicolo Paganini had once been offered a contract to tour the cities of North America, a proposition that would have netted the maestro nothing short of a fortune, but he declined, explaining that he couldn't afford to waste away the months required to make the voyage to America and back. Cunard was about to change all of that forever.

As advertised, the *Britannia* churned away from the Liverpool docks at 2:00pm on July 4, 1840, having loaded baggage and mails the day before, her passengers boarding her that morning, sixty-three all told, forty-eight of them bound for Halifax, fifteen for Boston. Among them were Samuel Cunard himself, along with his daughter Ann. It was a gray, wet, blustery day, but the *Britannia* took little notice of it and immediately began making good time, one sighting reporting her off the Welsh seaside resort of Llandudno around 6:00pm. She continued to make good time all the way across the Atlantic, despite the rough weather, and on her last day logged 273 nautical miles, a greater distance than any steamship had ever before traveled in a single day. She arrived in Halifax on July 17, three days ahead of schedule. Her arrival was greeted by a salute from the frigate *HMS Winchester*, a singular honor for a civilian vessel not carrying any government officials. After a stay of eight hours, she set out for Boston, arriving at 10:00pm the next day, having made her maiden crossing in fourteen days, eight hours.

The *Britannia*'s reception was a repetition of that given to the *Unicorn*, save on an even more lavish scale. Cunard himself received almost 1,900 invitations to dinners in the homes of prominent Boston families (never having overcome his shyness, he declined them all), and was presented with a 30-inch high silver loving cup, paid for by contributions from 2,500 Bostonians. (The cup is now on permanent display aboard the Cunard Line's *Queen Elizabeth 2*—minus its lid, which was lost when the cup was stolen for a brief period in the early 1970s). The climax of the events was a parade on July 21, followed by a public banquet attended by two thousand guests. A multitude of toasts and accolades were given, among the most memorable being one which ran, "Cunard's line of steam packets—the pendulum of a large clock which is to tick once a fortnight; the British Government has given £50,000 for one of the weights, and may the patronage of the public soon add another". Embarrassed by the attention—the banquet ran on for five hours—Cunard response was brief, as he declared that he could not find the language to express his gratitude.

There is, in that singular response of his, a lingering question about Samuel Cunard: why did he do it? The modesty of his response to the toasts of Boston was no sham—he never appeared to seek out the applause and approbation of the public. This is not to say that he had no ego—men and women who bring about great accomplishments are of necessity possessed of great egos, otherwise they would not see their ambitions through to completion. It is exactly because they have large egos that such people carry through their schemes and plans — they are convinced that not only is what they are doing important, but also that it is equally vital that they be the one to do it. So it was with Samuel Cunard.

And yet, by 1840 he was fifty-three years old, a widower and grandfather, who could have easily retired to enjoy the company and comforts of his family and fortune, and no one would have begrudged him that choice. Instead he threw himself into an enterprise more demanding of his time, his intellect and his resources than any he had ever before undertaken. Greed does not seem to be a motive, for he was already a wealthy man by any standard when he formed his steamship line, and there is nothing about his life to suggest that he was inordinately avaricious. Likewise, he was no spendthrift, casting about for ways to make new fortunes because he had exhausted the old ones. Perhaps he was lonely, perhaps he simply felt the need to continue to be productive, to feel useful. Perhaps, ultimately, the only valid answer to the question of why is simply because it could be done.

Whatever the reasons, the true magnitude of what Cunard was accomplishing had yet to be revealed, but the revelation would not be long in coming. A conjunction of talent, nearly unique in the history of commerce, had brought together the organizational skills and business acumen—which bordered on genius—of Cunard, together with the engineering talents of Robert Napier—which *were* genius, and combined them with the shrewd sense for investment possessed by Burns and McIver to produce, not just a method, but a *system* of transport that would revolutionize shipping. During their first calendar year in service, the *Britannia* and her three sisters made a total of forty Atlantic crossings without missing a sailing date. The impact of such regularity was demonstrated by the fact that although there were one hundred fifty sailing vessels on the Atlantic for every one steamship, one fifth of all the trade that crossed the ocean went by steamer. Like the pendulum of the Bostonian toast, Cunard's ships swung back and forth between Britain and America with almost monotonous regularity, and it was that regularity that was their greatest virtue. Now that they had established the standard, the challenge for Cunard and his partners was to see if they could maintain it.

CHAPTER THREE

Setting the Pace

Looking back from future decades, the significance of that first crossing by the *Britannia* from Liverpool to Halifax and Boston would loom much larger than it did at the time. While there were high hopes and higher ambitions for her success when she left Liverpool on July 4, 1840, to most people on both sides of the Atlantic, even those businessmen who stood to prosper if Samuel Cunard's ambitions were realized, there seemed to be little to distinguish the *Britannia* and her sisters from the likes of the *Royal William*, the *Sirius*, or the *Great Western* — laudable efforts all, but never quite fulfilling their potential for reliability or speed. What set the first Cunard ships apart from those other first attempts, however, were subtle differences easily overlooked by a casual observer. Perhaps most significant of those differences was that Samuel Cunard was singularly adverse to hyperbole: he refused to promise more than he believed he could reasonably deliver. This was a sharp contrast to Junius Smith, whose ambition led him to make extravagant claims on which he would then be unable to make good. (There is actually a legend within the company that Cunard deliberately underestimated the speed of his ships so that the public would be even more impressed when they proved faster than advertised). Cunard was also a far better businessman than Smith: the fiasco of the *Princess Victoria/British Queen*'s engines would have never been allowed to develop under Cunard's careful scrutiny, while the construction of the *President*, the second ship launched for Smith's British and American Steam Navigation Company, would not have lagged two years behind the introduction of the *British Queen*.

Also, Cunard had thoroughly thought out the details of what would be required to maintain a regular transatlantic service, something that Brunel and the rest of the directors of the Great Western Railway, for example, never seemed to do. The *Great Western* sailed alone, having no sister ships, and as a consequence, could only manage a single crossing each month. Such a schedule offered no real advantages over the sailings of ordinary packets, at least as far as delivery of the mails was concerned. This worked to the Great Western Steamship Company's disadvantage, for when Brunel and his colleagues responded to the Admiralty's request for tenders for a Royal Mail contract to be serviced by steamships, it appeared to the Royal Navy that the Great Western Steamship Company was little more than an adjunct to the Great Western Railway, and that despite the success their steamship had enjoyed, the hearts of the railway's directors really weren't in the effort to maintain a transatlantic steamship service.

Cunard, on the other hand, made it clear that he understood not only the need for regular sailings from Great Britain and North America, but also the need for relatively frequent crossings. Cunard was also wise enough to know when to heed the advice of experts. Robert Napier was able to persuade him that his original idea of fulfilling the requirements of the Admiralty contract with three ships was a false economy, and that the added cargo capacity of a fourth vessel would allow the additional ship to more than pay its way. Likewise, Cunard listened closely when Napier argued that the original design for his ships was too small and underpowered, and would suffer from the same shortcomings as the *Sirius*—insufficient bunkering for coal and almost no cargo space—and as a consequence approved the redesign that enlarged the *Britannia* and her three sisters, and made them a success from the outset.

They were barque-rigged ships; that is, they had three masts, the fore and main being square-rigged, the mizzen fore-and-aft rigged. They had clipper bows, square sterns, and two decks: the officers' quarters were on the upper deck, the passenger accommodations on the main deck, with separate quarters for servants. The four ships were each 228 feet in length, with a beam of 56 feet and a deep draught of 22½ feet. The machinery installation in each ship was identical: four boilers, each fed by three fireboxes, provided steam for a pair of side-lever engines, each with a single piston 72 inches in diameter. Together the engines produced seven hundred and forty horsepower, turning at a maximum speed of sixteen revolutions a minute, driving a pair of paddlewheels twenty-eight feet in diameter, propelling the ships at a designed speed of 8½ knots. Such figures soon became a fixture in the advertising for the new ships, and spawned a fascination among the public for the accumulation of statistics about steamships—eventually to become known as "rivet counting"—that would last as long as transatlantic service itself.

All that being said, there was still something of the experimental about what Cunard was attempting, and there were legions of observers on both sides of the Atlantic who fully expected his venture to fail. Steam power had moved well out of its infancy and into its adolescence, but it still had not completely supplanted sails, a fact that was borne out by the instructions given to the captains of the first four Cunard ships to make full use of advantageous winds whenever possible, both to increase speed and conserve coal. But steam promised dependability, something that sail could never promise, and dependability represented profits for businessmen with cargoes to ship across the Atlantic. This was a vital consideration for Cunard, for though the company would evolve into a passenger line with transporting cargo only a minor consideration, in its first decades Cunard's profits were made by carrying cargo: fully half of the internal volume of the *Britannia* and her sisters was given over to cargo holds.

When the *Britannia* set out from Liverpool on July 4, 1840, her passenger list included Samuel Cunard and his daughter, Ann, along with her friend, Laura Haluburton, the daughter of a Halifax magistrate. Other notable names on that list included the Earl of Caledon, the Bishop of Nova Scotia, two American consuls, and several senior officers of the British Army, who were traveling with their families. She was under the command of Capt. Henry Woodruff, RN, one of the stipulations of the Royal Mail contract being that Masters of the ships carrying the mail be officers of the Royal Navy. This did not mean he was above being admonished by his employers. One directive handed down to him and his colleagues declared that "It will be obvious to you that it is of the first importance to the Partners...that [the ship] attains a Character for Speed and Safety. We trust in your vigilance of this: good steering, good look-outs, taking every advantage of every slant of the wind, and precautions against fire are principal elements."

Certainly the *Britannia*'s maiden voyage established a number of long-enduring customs and traditions for the Cunard company, and laid the foundation of the reputation for caution and prudence that would become legendary on the North Atlantic. From the very beginning, routine and regulation were part of crossing on one of Samuel Cunard's ships, and passengers were reminded that "a cheerful acquiescence" with these regulations was expected. Notices were posted in each cabin announcing that stewards would begin sweeping out the staterooms at five o'clock each morning, then would empty the passengers' chamber pots (over the leeward railing!) while breakfast was being served. The bar would be opened at 6:00am, while proper dress was required at all meal times. Bed linens were changed every eight days, and passengers were admonished to keep the scuttles (portholes) in their cabins shut and extinguish all candles promptly at midnight. The cabins themselves were singularly unremarkable, usually being a room about eight feet by ten in dimensions, with space for an upper and lower berth, a settee, and a washstand. This was expected to accommodate two people, although experience soon taught travelers that it was an exceedingly cramped arrangement, more suitable for a single person.

All in all, the passengers were well fed and reasonably comfortable, but the accommodations of the public rooms, despite the presence of carved wooden paneling, tufted sofas, and handsome cut glass chandeliers—the standard fixtures of Victorian decor—these were not quite as plush as those aboard the *Great Western*. The Scottish shipwrights who built Cunard's first four ships took his instructions to heart: "I want a plain and comfortable boat. Not the least unnecessary expense for show." Still, even though the weather on the *Britannia*'s first crossing was a bit rough, no one aboard seemed particularly put out by it: one passenger, writing to a friend back in Britain, commented on having "a good steak, with a bottle of hock" for breakfast, then remarked: "There were too many good things for any man of taste to even think of sickness." Captain Woodruff ate with his passengers, and from the very beginning established the traditional—and still standing–hierarchy of the officers' mess: First Mate (or Officer), Second, Third, First Engineer, Chaplain, Surgeon, and "any respectable Second Class passenger."

Of course, favorable opinions of the comfort of traveling on one of Cunard's ships weren't universally held: one of the most memorable—and far from flattering—accounts of crossing the Atlantic on one of Cunard's early steamers came from a crossing made aboard the *Britannia* in January 1842 by one of the great figures of Victorian literature. It may not be accurate to say that people in the 19th Century were more literate than they are in the 21st, but certainly they *wrote* a great deal more on any given subject than do their great-great-grandchildren. Later generations are indebted to Charles Dickens for recording his experiences and impressions gathered aboard Cunard's *Britannia* on a crossing from Liverpool to Boston.

Dickens was going to America for a variety of reasons: first, he was outraged by the copyright laws of the United States, which did not guarantee reciprocity of royalties for writings published in America but written overseas. His stake in the matter was personal: none of his works published in the United States had earned him so much as one red cent. Second, he was anxious to actually see America with his own eyes, and stand, as he put it, "upon the soil I have trodden in my day-dreams many times and whose sons (and daughters) I yearn to know and be among." Taken with a small grain of salt, his recollections serve as a portrait of a typical steamship passage for most of the middle of the 19th Century.

Boarding the *Britannia* at Liverpool, along with his wife Kate and her maid, Anne, he watched the crew carefully preparing the ship for her departure. "...One party of men were 'taking in the milk', or, in other words, getting the cow on board [cows were a feature on almost every ship sailing the Atlantic—in the days before refrigeration it was the only way to provide fresh milk for the passengers]; and another were filling the icehouses to the very throat with fresh provisions; with butchers'-meat and garden-stuff, pale suckling-pigs, calves' heads in scores, beef, veal, and pork, and poultry out of all proportions; and others were coiling ropes and busy with oakum yarns."

While the stores were being loaded aboard, "...packing cases, portmanteaus, carpet-bags, and boxes are already passed from hand to hand and hauled on board with breathless rapidity.... In five minutes the packet is beset and over-run by its late [passengers], who instantly pervade the whole ship, and are to be met by the dozen in every nook and corner: swarming down below with their own baggage, and stumbling over other peoples'; disposing themselves comfortably in wrong cabins, and creating a most horrible confusion by having to turn out again; madly bent upon opening locked doors, and on forcing a passage into all kinds of out-of-the-way places where there is no thoroughfare; sending wild stewards, with elfin hair, to and fro upon the breezy decks on unintelligible errands, impossible in execution; and in short, creating most extraordinary and bewildering tumult."

All the while, up on the starboard paddle box, Captain Woodruff paced back and forth impatiently, speaking trumpet in hand, occasionally bellowing out an order to the crew.

Charles Dickens' cabin aboard the Britannia.

The reason for Woodruff's anxiety was that just as the Admiralty contract with Cunard specified financial penalties in late delivery of the mail to Halifax, it also provided for bonuses to be paid the ship's master for speedy delivery of the mails, and every hour of delay in departing Liverpool could ultimately cost Woodruff part of his bonus. By 2:00pm—two hours late—everything was aboard and stowed to Captain Woodruff's satisfaction and the *Britannia* got underway.

Meanwhile, Dickens had found his cabin, an "utterly impracticable, thoroughly hopeless, and profoundly preposterous box." He characterized his bunk as a kind of shelf with a thin mattress, covered by a single quilt: "nothing smaller for sleeping was ever made except coffins." Not that he would spend a great deal of time sleeping: seasick almost from the moment he stepped aboard the *Britannia*, Dickens spent the first night aboard out on the upper deck; having had enough of the cold and wind by midnight, he found his wife and maid huddled miserably together, equally seasick, in the main saloon. Unable to sleep, he tried to read the pocket edition of Shakespeare he'd brought for just such an eventuality, but was unable to concentrate, and once more "reeled on deck a little, drank cold brandy and water with unspeakable disgust...not ill, but going to be."

The first nine days of the voyage were rough, with weather and seas at times approaching gale-like conditions. For a poor sailor like Dickens, mealtimes offered no relief: the dining saloon itself he found off-putting, describing it as "a long narrow apartment, not unlike a gigantic hearse with windows." Lunches were a dismal offering of "pig's face, cold ham, salt beef" or a "smoking mess of hot collops." Dinner offered the prospect of "more potatoes and meat" followed by a "rather mouldy dessert of apples, grapes and oranges." When darkness fell and he returned to his cabin, Dickens found the candles that he and his fellow passengers were so firmly encouraged to extinguish promptly at midnight were set in an opening high up in the wall between two adjoining cabins, where its fitful light was meant to provide illumination for both. Summoning the services of a steward entailed stepping out into the passageway and bellowing for his attention.

The crossing took fifteen days, during which Dickens amused himself by playing endless games of whist with the *Britannia*'s surgeon; how his wife and her maid occupied themselves apparently escaped his notice. The ship rolled ceaselessly, smashing a small fortune in crockery, while the wind and waves made a shambles of the upper deck, reducing one of the ship's boats to flinders and carrying away part of the starboard paddle box. When she arrived at Halifax, the *Britannia* ran aground on a mud bank, but it wasn't a hard grounding and Captain Woodruff soon had her pulled free. After a seven-hour layover, she set out for Boston, where she arrived three days later. When he returned to Great Britain, Dickens chose to cross by sailing packet. Unfortunately, he chose not to record his experiences on the return voyage.

Whatever shortcomings Dickens decided the *Britannia* possessed, they did nothing to alter the fact the she and her sisters had made regular transatlantic service a reality. When the *Britannia* departed from Boston to return to Liverpool for the first time on August 1, 1840, the *Acadia* was preparing for her maiden voyage, departing Liverpool on August 4. The *Caledonia* went into service on September 9, while the fourth ship, the *Columbia*, made her first voyage on January 5, 1841. By mid-February, a Cunard ship was sailing from Liverpool and Boston every fourteen days.

The value of Dickens' recollections, even allowing for the embellishment and exaggeration that were so much a part of his style and made his novels such a delight for generations of readers, is that he caught the essence of an ocean passage perfectly. A transatlantic crossing in the 1840s *was* uncomfortable and inconvenient, and it was a voyage no traveler would undertake unless absolutely necessary. But the regularity that steam had introduced to the crossings was the beginning of the eventual transformation of ocean travel from odious necessity to luxurious convenience.

It's quite possible that Dickens' reminiscences were colored by the tragedy that was still looming over the Atlantic when he made his crossing to America; the disappearance of the steamer *President*. In August 1840, still determined to leave his mark on the North Atlantic trade, Junius Smith had introduced his consort to the *British Queen*, the *President*. There was more than just ego involved in Smith's decision—by the beginning of 1841, though there were one hundred-fifty sailing ships departing British or American ports for every steamship, steamers were carrying fully a fifth of all the cargo being shipped across the Atlantic. The *British Queen*, tubby and dumpy though she was, had been a moneymaker for Smith, and the *President*, in essence just an enlarged version of the *British Queen*, promised to be just as profitable.

The *President* made her maiden voyage in August 1840, just a month after Samuel Cunard's steamships began their service. It was not an impressive debut—she took more than sixteen days to make the crossing, a time that Cunard's *Acadia*, also on her maiden voyage, bested by three days. But she soon became a popular ship and usually sailed with a full or nearly full passenger list. The only persistent criticism of her was that her coal consumption was considered by some of her officers to be excessive, and on one occasion she had to turn back to avoid running out of coal in mid-Atlantic. On March 11, 1841, the *President* left New York with 136 passengers and crew aboard, and almost immediately was caught in a fierce gale. An American packet, the *Orpheus*, saw her two days later, "rising on top of a tremendous sea, pitching and laboring very heavily." She was never seen again. There were few clues to her fate, mostly scattered reports of wreckage found floating on the sea, but eventually the evidence was pieced together and Smith was forced to accept the inevitable—the *President* had sunk, taking everyone aboard with her. It was the end of Junius Smith's British and American Steam Navigation Company, and the end of his transatlantic ambitions.

The disaster badly frightened those travelers who had to make a transatlantic crossing, and they switched their bookings in droves from steamers to sailing packets, although it was never explained how the fact that the *President* was a steamship had contributed to her disappearance. Rigged as she was like any other steamer of the day with a full set of masts and yards, she should have been able to ride out almost any storm under sail, even if she were deprived of the power of her engines. What is most likely was that she encountered what at the time was a little-known phenomenon, one of the weapons that the Atlantic keeps at her disposal to teach respect to those who show her insufficient deference: the rogue wave.

All sailors know that waves travel in cycles, and that the height of the waves within a given cycle are remarkably uniform. They also know that when two different wave cycles meet, at some point the waves will coincide, and the resultant wave will be the *combined* height of the two cycles—for example, if two seven-foot high waves cycles coincide, the resulting wave will be fourteen feet in height— and will maintain that height for as long as the cycles are coincident. But what many sailors do *not* know is that it is possible for several wave cycles to coincide briefly—and the resulting wave is as high as the total height of *all* of the cycles combined. A half-dozen ten foot wave cycles coinciding for a single wave would create a monster as tall as a six-story building, containing millions of gallons of water, weighing tens of thousands of tons. Such a wave, breaking down over a steamship the size of the *President* would smash the ship to pieces in an instant, leaving few traces and no survivors behind.

The disappearance of the *President* was like a brooding presence that hovered over the Atlantic for a long time. Even a year later, the number of passengers making the crossing on steamships was barely half of what it had been before the *President* was lost. The situation became so desperate that the Great Western Steamship Company contemplated selling the *Great Western* in order to recoup their losses; Cunard was able to survive by virtue of the subsidy the company received from Her Majesty's Government. Still, by the end of 1842, Cunard's losses had totalled £63,954 for the company's first three years of operation, and it was solely by dint of an increase in the subsidy that Cunard was able to continue service.

Yet people began to notice that Cunard's four little steamers kept plying back and forth between Liverpool and Boston with almost metronomic regularity. A reputation for reliability and safety was slowly being built, and as the years passed and the ships made faster and faster passages, the company motto of "Comfort, Speed, and Safety" became a reality. Of the original quartet of Cunard ships, the *Britannia* and the *Acadia* eventually proved the fastest. In fact, their speeds actually improved with the passage of time, as their engines bedded in and their captains and engineers learned the limits of their boilers and pistons. The *Britannia,* in particular, proved remarkably swift for the day—when she made her maiden crossing in July 1840, she averaged $8^1/2$ knots on the run from Liverpool to Halifax. A month later she bettered that speed by more than two knots. The *Acadia* had made her maiden voyage averaging a full knot faster than the *Britannia* had done on her first crossing, yet two years later she would record her best speed ever by making an average of 11 knots for the entire Halifax to Liverpool run.

Such performances were a source of great satisfaction for Samuel Cunard, proving beyond any doubt the wisdom of his choice of engine builders; they were also a source of great pride for Robert Napier, as they effectively silenced the London skeptics who had regarded him as little more than a provincial iron-monger. Now, when anyone wanted to put an engine in a steamship, they no longer went to London, they went north to Glasgow to inquire when *Mister* Napier might be able to accommodate them. It was the beginning of the legendary Scottish love affair with seagoing steam that would last for more than a century and a half.

It would be no exaggeration at all to claim that the lion's share of credit for Cunard being able to make his concept of a regular steamship service a reality, was due to the engines Napier had built for his ships. It was their uncanny reliability which allowed the Canadian to make good on all of his claims for regular, scheduled sailings, that was the cornerstone of Cunard's success. While his association with Cunard would soon make Robert Napier's name synonymous with ocean-going steam engines around the world, Napier had worked long and hard to earn the recognition that eventually became his due.

The son of James and Jean Napier of Glasgow, he was born on June 21, 1791, with engineering already in his blood. His father and uncle John had a well-established partnership as engineers, blacksmiths and mill-wrights in Glasgow, while a second uncle was the estate blacksmith for the Duke of Argyll at Inverary. His

Robert Napier, progenitor of a century of legendary Scottish shipbuilders.

mother's family, the Deny's, would likewise become famous as shipbuilders and engineers just down the Clyde in Dumbarton. He was first introduced to steam engines at his father's works, where a steam-powered boring machine made cannon for the Royal Navy and the Royal Artillery.

The elder Napier had hoped Robert would enter the ministry of the Church of Scotland but it was soon evident that Robert's talents, as well as interests, lay in the family business, and at sixteen Robert became his father's apprentice. A move to Edinburgh broadened his experience, and when he had achieved Journeyman status he was able to secure a position with the great Robert Stevenson, the founder of another famous family of engineers and renowned as the builder of the Bell Rock lighthouse, one of the most remarkable engineering feats of the 18th Century.

By 1815, he felt confident enough of his abilities to go into business on his own, borrowing £50 from his father to rent a foundry floor in Glasgow. His early work was varied—there were orders on his books for pipes made for the Glasgow waterworks as well as a 12hp steam engine for a mill in Dundee, and before long he prospered; by 1818, business was good enough to allow him to marry his cousin Isabella, John Napier's daughter—the Scots being less priggish about such things than the English. He didn't get involved in building seagoing steam engines, though, until 1823, when a Dumbarton ship-builder and ship owner named James Lang gave Napier the engine contract for the paddlewheeler *Leven*. The engine he produced was so durable that it eventually found its way into another ship almost twenty years later, and still survives today in a museum outside Dumbarton.

In 1827 Napier's reputation was given a significant boost at the August Regatta of the Northern Yacht Club, when two boats with Napier engines, the *Clarence* and *Helensburgh*, took first and second place in a race for a twenty-guinea cup. For the first time the name Napier began to be heard outside of Scotland. By the early 1830s Napier was specializing in building engines for coastal steamers, then in 1835 the East India Company awarded him a contract to build the engine for their ocean-going paddle sloop *Berenice*. English engineers were critical of this choice, believing that, as they would later tell Cunard, Napier was little more than a provincial builder and tinkerer. They lapsed into a temporary silence, however, when on their maiden passages to India, the *Berenice* beat her English-engined consort *Atlanta* by 18 days.

When Cunard first approached Napier in 1839, he had already given a good deal of thought to what would be required for a transatlantic paddlewheel steamer. Although at first he accepted the design requirements that Cunard laid down, he soon felt that he owed Cunard the benefit of his experience and proposed the enlarged designs that Cunard eventually took to the Admiralty, which won for him the Royal Mail contract. A measure of his dedication to his work was his willingness, if Cunard agreed to build the larger ships, to cut his margin of profit in order to get Cunard to make the investment. What mattered most to Napier was maintaining his commitment to refuse to do any work he regarded as sub-standard in any way, writing of the engines he was building for Cunard, "...I cannot and will not admit of anything into these engines but what is sound and good."

That same devotion to principle led Napier, who had the vision to see "over the horizon" and grasp the potential of what Cunard was trying to accomplish, to become one of the group of Glasgow friends and business partners of Burns and McIver, who put up the balance of the capital Cunard required to float the British and North American Royal Mail Steam Packet Company. Napier invested £6,100 of his own money, as much as anything a measure of confidence in his ability to build engines of unsurpassed reliability: the Admiralty contract promised to be potentially lucrative for Cunard and his partners, but only if the mails were delivered on time—the penalty clauses for delay were severe.

The Admiralty was not a stranger to Napier: his first Admiralty contract actually preceded his association with Cunard. In 1838 he had been asked to build the engines for the paddle sloops *Vesuvius* and *Stromboli*, and though he had scrupulously observed every condition of the contract, the always-conservative Royal Navy preferred Thames-side builders and engineers, and no additional Admiralty orders were forthcoming. Napier would have the last laugh, however, when an inquiry by Parliament into original costs, repairs, operating expenses and down-time for steam vessels ordered between 1839 and 1843 proved that ships equipped with Napier-built engines were more reliable and less expensive than those from the English yards. A somewhat red-faced Admiralty, like much of the rest of the world, was soon going, hat figuratively in hand, to Mister Napier's office to acquire his engines for their ships.

Before 1841, Napier had been solely an engine builder, the hull contracts usually going to John Wood at Port Glasgow. On occasion Napier would act as a contract manager for his clients, but there seemed little reason for him to get into shipbuilding itself. However, demand for iron construction was growing fast and with it the need for iron shipwrights. It was inevitable then that Napier should expand his business. That was the year his brother James joined the company, while a year later their cousin, William Deny II, a talented draftsman, modeler and inspector came to work for the Napier brothers. This was the origin of the long-reaching influence that Robert Napier would have on Clyde shipyards: the next two generations of shipbuilders would be the greatest that history would ever see—the most talented, the most innovative, the most daring—and many of the outstanding designers, engineers and shipwrights of those two generations would train under Robert Napier, or would be at some point in their early careers, employed by him, while many a Clydeside yard would be run by old Napier men. And the close ties between Cunard and Napier that gave impetus to it all would endure long after both men had returned to dust: among the craftsmen employed by Napier was a leading smith named James Thomson, who with his brother George, (also once a Napier employee) would found the Clydebank shipyard of J & G Thomson, better known to the world by its later name of John Brown & Company, who would one day build Cunard's masterpieces; the *Lusitania*, the *Aquitania*, the *Queen Mary*, and both the *Queen Elizabeth* and the *Queen Elizabeth 2*.

Cunard's ships were not entirely able to escape mishaps of their own, although the company was able to avoid losing any lives. On the morning of July 2, 1843, as she was running down the Nova Scotia coast bound from Halifax to Boston, the *Columbia* encountered a dense fog bank as she was rounding Cape Sable, and ran aground. Unable to pull free under her own power, Captain Ewing ordered the *Columbia* abandoned, and the ship was eventually written off as a total loss. All of the passengers and crew were saved, however, as were the mails and cargo. By sheer good fortune, the brand-new *Hibernia* had joined the Cunard fleet three months earlier, so there was no loss of service or interruption of the mail contract.

The *Hibernia* and her sister ship *Cambria* were the first additions to the original quartet of Cunard's fleet. The *Hibernia* was the first to enter service, delivered by her builders Robert Steele and Sons of Greenock, at the end of March 1843. The *Cambria*, also built by Steele, did not come along until January 1845. They were virtually repeats of the *Britannia* and her sisters, some three hundred tons heavier, with the additional tonnage given over to cargo space. Like the first four Cunard ships, they were built with wooden hulls and propelled by paddlewheels.

This decision was made in defiance of all the experience gained by the Great Western Railway when it chose to introduce the ship that would be remembered as Ismabard Kingdom Brunel's masterpiece, the *Great Britain*. In July 1839, the keel was laid at Patterson's shipbuilding yard in Bristol for a new ship that was to be called the *Mammoth*. Originally, she was meant to be constructed of wood and propelled by conventional paddle wheels. The decision to change from wood to iron construction was made while she was still on the drawing board, but aside from the change in building materials, no substantial alterations were made to her design at that point. In May 1840, though, while the *Mammoth* was still on the stocks, a strange new ship steamed into Bristol, and once Brunel carefully examined her, what he found caused him to completely overhaul the design of the *Mammoth*, eventually changing almost everything about her, including her name. The new ship was the 237-ton sloop *Archimedes*; what made her so peculiar was that she had been fitted with a screw-type propeller invented a few years earlier by Sir Francis Pettit Smith.

Brunel was fascinated with what he learned. The screw or propeller proved to be much more efficient than the traditional paddle wheels, and Brunel immediately changed the plans for his new ship, redrawing them so that she would be fitted with a propeller instead. It was about this time that the board of directors of the Great Western Railroad approved the change of the *Mammoth*'s name to the *Great Britain*. In redesigning her hull to accommodate the change from paddlewheels to screw propulsion, Brunel stumbled on a hull form that approached hydrodynamic perfection, making the *Great Britain* one of the fastest, most economical ships of her day.

The leap forward in technology that the *Great Britain* represented was immense. While she wasn't the first iron-hulled ship, she was by far the largest ship built of iron. Just as significant was how Brunel reworked her interior subdivision, dividing her into six watertight compartments formed by five watertight bulkheads that ran laterally across her hull. Her engines were the most powerful installed in a steamship, with four 88-inch cylinders working at a pressure of 15l pounds per square inch, developing 1,500 hp which turned a single, six-bladed propeller. Launched on July 19, 1843, fitting out would take another two years, but when she was finally complete the *Great Britain* offered the most luxurious accommodations yet put to sea. Being the largest ship of her day, she had cabins for as many as 350 passengers. The public areas had received special attention, her decorators using mirrors extensively to create an impression of spaciousness.

On July 26, the *Great Britain* set out from Liverpool on her maiden voyage, arriving in New York fifteen days later, the first iron-hulled, propeller-driven ship to cross the North Atlantic. Critics—mainly tradition-ridden old shellbacks who were chary of any innovation—continued to insist that wood was the only material suitable for shipbuilding and that iron hulls had no place at sea, but the *Great Britain* was an immediate success with travelers on both sides of the Atlantic. In 1846 though, disaster struck and she came distressingly close to becoming a total loss. On September 22, she ran aground on the rocky coast of Ireland near Dundrum Bay—the result, her critics said, of deviations in her magnetic compass caused by her iron hull; the true cause, however, was defective charts. Unfortunately, the accident happened at high tide, causing the *Great Britain* to ground far enough inshore so that another year would pass before there was another tide high enough to float her off.

Ironically, though, it was this experience that once and for all silenced the nay-sayers of the wisdom of building iron-hulled ships. As the ship lay on the shore through the winter, she was repeatedly battered by gales and storms that would have reduced a wooden-hulled ship to matchwood. When the *Great Britain* was finally refloated on August 27, 1847, a team of naval surveyors subjected her hull to a thorough examination. It was found that aside from a handful of holes in her shell plating caused by the rocks where she grounded, her hull was structurally sound in all respects. By the following spring, the *Great Britain* was back in service.

But the accident had serious consequences ashore for the Great Western Steamship Company. Deprived of the *Great Britain*'s services for nearly a year — and the revenues she generated, the company had gone deeply into debt with the financial losses eventually becoming so large that the railway was forced into dissolution, and the ship was sold for a mere £18,000. The *Great Britain*'s career on the North Atlantic was over. But the *Great Britain*'s influence on shipbuilding was so great, and the rest of her career at once so incredible and wonderful, that the story deserves at least a brief recounting here.

Her new owners, Gibbs, Bright & Co., refitted her for the Australian emigration run, where she operated with success for the following three years. In 1855, the *Great Britain* was requisitioned for service as a troopship for the duration of the Crimean War, serving alongside several of her former competitors from Cunard and P&O. After two years of wartime service, the *Great Britain* was taken over by the Liverpool and Australian Navigation Co., and returned to the Australian run, where she would spend the next twenty years.

In 1876, after having completed 32 round-trip voyages to Australia, she was laid up in Liverpool, and sat idle until 1882, when she was again sold. Her new owners removed her engines and refitted her as a simple square-rigged ship, employing her as a cargo vessel, carrying Welsh coal and wheat "'round the Horn" from Liverpool to San Francisco. In 1886, she was forced to put into Port Stanley on the Falkland Islands after making her way through a particularly severe storm coming around Cape Horn. Badly damaged and no longer seaworthy, she was sold to the Falklands Trading Company and eventually converted into a floating storage hulk for coal and wool, a fate she would endure for the next eighty-four years.

Incredibly, though, the story of the *Great Britain* did not end in such obscure indignity. By sheer accident her hulk was discovered in 1968 by two rival, but ultimately cooperative maritime enthusiasts, one in the United Kingdom, one in the United States. A public effort to raise funds for her recovery proved hugely successful on both sides of the Atlantic, and on April 12, 1970, the *Great Britain*, borne up by a submersible pontoon, began an 8,000-mile journey back to the city where she had been built.

The trip took two months. On June 15, as more than one hundred thousand people lined the banks of the River Avon to welcome her home, the *Great Britain* was towed under a suspension bridge designed and built by Isambard Kingdom Brunel, on her way into Bristol. There she was eased into the very same dock where she had been built a hundred and thirty years earlier. Today, fully restored and returned to all of her original glory, the *Great Britain* remains a testament to the genius of Brunel and the romance of the early days of steam on the North Atlantic.

With the demise of the Great Western Steamship Company, the last serious British challenge to what was becoming Cunard's virtual monopoly on regular transatlantic steamship service, vanished. However, the *Great Britain*'s career had a profound influence on the history of the Cunard Line, and the history of the United States as well. The competition between Boston and New York to be America's primary port grew ever fiercer as the 1840s matured, and the *Great Britain* played a major role in deciding the outcome of that contest.

The Royal Mail contract awarded to Cunard initially called for direct service between Liverpool and Halifax, with a feeder line to Boston. The American city quickly overcame its resentment of having been relegated to the status of a mere feeder-line port, and the city fathers instead used every form of persuasion at their disposal to induce Cunard to extend his ships' direct service to Boston. But it wasn't until Robert Napier convinced Cunard of the wisdom of enlarging the ships he originally designed, and pointed out that their additional size would give them the bunkerage necessary to reach Boston without taking on additional coal at Halifax, that Cunard then proposed to the Admiralty that the terms of the contract be altered to provide direct service to Boston.

The benefits to Boston as a port were almost immediate, as the volume and value of goods brought into the United States through the city doubled within the first year of Cunard's service, and with that growth of trade came growing prosperity. The good citizens of Boston were determined to make sure that prosperity continued, especially when the *Great Western* continued its service to New York, the only steamship doing so at the time. This fact greatly rankled the merchants of New York. When the *Columbia* was lost on the rocks off Cape Sable, Nova Scotia, the New York press implied that it had been due to the fact that she had sailed from Boston and had to negotiate the extra "four hundred and fifty miles of rock, ledge, shoal, fog, and narrow intricate channels" that a ship sailing from Boston supposedly had to negotiate. Despite the growing reputation for reliability the Cunard ships were garnering, the loss of the *Columbia* not withstanding, the darling of the North Atlantic run was still the *Great Western*, and by making New York her western terminus, she drew ever more attention to that city and its harbor, causing some people, including some of Cunard's junior partners, to wonder why it wasn't Cunard's western terminus as well.

It was a challenge that Boston couldn't let go unanswered, and when Boston Harbor froze solid in February 1844, leaving the *Britannia* ice-bound and unable to make her scheduled departure, the city merchants and its citizens were put on their mettle. They responded admirably when Mayor Martin Brimmer chaired a hastily-called meeting of the city's leading citizens to decide on a solution. The upshot of the meeting was a succinctly worded contract which specified that "Mr. John Hill, in connexion with Messrs. Gage, Hittinger and Co. agree to cut a passage for the steamship *Britannia* to proceed to sea tomorrow night and to cut the passage from the Eastern Ferry as far as the India Wharf, the whole of the passage to be 200 feet wide at least; the whole to be accomplished within three days from the First Day of February at sunrise, and they agree to receive in full for their services the Sum of Fifteen Hundred dollars...to be paid when the work is accomplished and to receive no pay if they do not accomplish it as stipulated."

The amazing spectacle greeted Boston the next morning of horse-drawn ice plows cutting deep furrows along the route of the channel while gangs of workmen hoisted huge blocks of ice out of the water ahead of the *Britannia*. By the morning of February 3 a passage to clear water had been cut, and with reinforcing plates of iron bolted to her bow, the *Britannia* worked up to 7 knots and made a mad dash for the open sea, while thousands of Bostonians lined the docks and wharves of the waterfront and thronged out onto the ice itself as the Cunard ship was able to depart on schedule.

But the battle for pride of place as America's premier port was one that Boston was ultimately destined to lose: the incident where the *Britannia* had to be cut free of the ice highlighted the good will of the people of Boston, but it also drew attention to the fact that New York Harbor was never icebound. When the *Great Britain* entered service in 1845 as the *Great Western*'s running mate, the focus of attention of the shipping world on both sides of the Atlantic shifted to the mouth of the Hudson River. When the United States Congress announced that it would be offering a contract to carry the U.S. Mail similar to that given to Cunard by the Royal Navy, one of the provisions of the contract would be that the service originate in New York.

The winner of the contract was Edward Mills, a New York businessman whose knowledge of shipping was marginal at best. When he was unable to raise the money needed to build even two of the four ships specified by the contract, a consortium styled the Ocean Steam Navigation Company took it over. The new company struggled in its turn, but on January 20, 1847, launched the *Washington,* a 260-foot long, 1,750-ton behemoth powered by a pair of engines generating 2,000 horsepower. Her builders declared her to be the most beautiful steamship yet built, but less biased observers were not as charitable: the London *Times* declaring that she "looked like an elongated three-decker...about as ugly a specimen of steamship building as ever went through this anchorage. She did not appear to make much use of her 2,000 horsepower either, but seemed to roll along rather than steam through the water."

The reporter who wrote that article was a shrewd observer, for when she finally took to the water in the summer of 1847, the *Washington* proved to be an immense disappointment. She left New York on June 1 on her maiden voyage, bound for Southampton. Cunard's *Britannia* left Boston for Liverpool the same day, setting the stage for the first transatlantic "race" between steamships. In theory, it should have been no contest, as the *Washington* was larger, newer, and had engines with nearly twice the power of the *Britannia*'s. In the event, the seven-year old *Britannia* humiliated the *Washington*, having docked and unloaded her passengers and cargo in Liverpool two days before the American steamer was even spotted off the Isle of Wight.

The *Washington* never quite lived up to her promise, an embarrassment to her owners, the United States Congress, and the American people. She did, however, draw Cunard's attention even more sharply toward New York as both a passenger and mail terminus. As a consequence, Samuel Cunard went to the British Admiralty and proposed a new contract be drawn up, calling for mail and passenger service to run from Liverpool to New York one week, from Liverpool to Halifax and Boston the next. The new contract called for a total of eight ships to be in service by the beginning of 1848, with a ninth ship added within a year. Just as the original terms between Cunard and the Government specified that the company's ships were subject to requisition in wartime, as well as being capable of mounting heavy guns for defense, this new agreement contained the same requirements, along with specifications for compensation should the new vessels be utilized as troop transports or supply ships.

Despite the subsequent introduction of a running mate, the *Hermann*, the Ocean Steam Navigation Company never prospered, and by 1850 was defunct. Cunard refused to publicly gloat over his competitor's demise. His policy toward advancing the position of the British and North American Royal Mail Steam Packet Company was to build as much good will as possible—antagonisms were never to be exploited and controversy was never sought as a method of promoting the company's name or image.

Avoiding controversy was something that, for the most part, Cunard, both as a company and as a man, successfully accomplished. There were instances, however, when avoidance was simply impossible. One of the most unusual such occurrences arose in 1847, and it sheds an interesting—and not entirely flattering—light on one of history's most prominent black Americans. In 1845, Frederick Douglass, one-time fugitive slave, now a free man and a leading abolitionist, began a twenty-month long tour of Britain and Ireland, lecturing on slavery and the plight of Negroes in the United States. The British were particularly sensitive on this subject, having abolished the slave trade within the Empire more than forty years earlier, and they were still slavery's most outspoken opponents. He booked passage from Boston aboard the *Cambria*, as a steerage passenger, and at some point, some of the cabin class passengers invited him to deliver a speech on slavery to the passengers in the main dining saloon. He agreed, but when he attempted to speak was shouted down by other passengers—Americans—and a near riot ensued.

At the time, Douglass made no comment on the incident, and when his tour ended in 1847 he went to Cunard's London office to book his passage home, by coincidence again on the *Cambria*, this time requesting and paying for a cabin-class berth. A junior clerk, who knew nothing of Douglass or the earlier incident, issued the ticket without comment or condition, but when Douglass tried to board the *Cambria*, he was told that his berth had been given to another passenger. Douglass protested to Cunard's Liverpool agent, Charles McIver, and was told that the London agent did not have the authority to sell Douglass the ticket he'd purchased; Douglass would only be allowed back aboard the *Cambria* if he agreed to take his meals alone, not to mix with the cabin-class passengers, and accept a different cabin berth than the one he'd paid for. McIver was categorical in emphasizing that the issue was not Douglass' color but rather the incident his oratory had provoked on his earlier crossing: no one was objecting to his presence aboard the ship, but rather his penchant for arousing antagonisms among his fellow passengers. Cunard's sole responsibility, McIver made clear, was safely transporting *all* of its passengers, not catering to the political views of individuals.

Douglass was furious: he felt that the line's actions were motivated by his race—an experience with which he was all too familiar. McIver bluntly told him that while his race had nothing to do with it, the company had no intention of allowing another incident to occur like the one that marred Douglass' first crossing. Protesting bitterly, Douglass accepted the conditions and returned to the United States. There the matter might have ended had he then not chosen to engage on a very vocal and prolonged letter writing campaign involving newspapers on both sides of the Atlantic, and in doing so make claims about both incidents that were either exaggerations or outright fabrications. Most damaging to his credibility, he would claim he had been forced to take a berth in steerage on *both* crossings, not mentioning that he had purchased the steerage berth himself for the voyage to Great Britain, or that he *was* given a cabin-class berth on his return, just a different one than he had originally booked.

He also claimed that he had met McIver before booking his return passage, rather than after, and was assured by him that there would be no difficulties with his presence aboard the *Cambria*. Perhaps most significant of all is that at no time did Douglass acknowledge the greater responsibility Cunard had to see to the comfort and safety of all of the passengers: the consistent thread that would run through his correspondence on the incident was how his rights and freedoms had been suppressed, with little awareness or regard for the rights of his fellow travelers. Apparently it never occurred to Douglass that because his opinions, and even his presence, might arouse the antagonisms of some of his fellow passengers—passions that were utterly beyond Cunard's control—the consequences could easily threaten or actually harm other passengers who weren't involved at all.

What is more unfortunate is the way that Douglass suppressed some facts about the incident—and distorted others—in his effort to make as strong a case for discrimination as he could. While in a few years the entire episode would be lost in the looming shadow of the American Civil War, it long rankled Cunard, both the company and the man.

By the end of its first decade in business, Cunard's British and North American Ocean Steam Navigation Company had achieved what amounted to a virtual monopoly on the North Atlantic run, which was becoming known as the Atlantic Ferry. It had grown to a fleet of nine ships, which the *Liverpool Albion*, in February 1850, declared to be a "magnificent fleet which stands pre-eminent among ocean steamers." That was not hyperbole; it was a statement of fact. In that first decade, Cunard's ships had made four hundred and seventy crossings between Great Britain and the United States, and safely carried more than sixty thousand passengers. The volume of cargo that Cunard's steamers carried is impossible to estimate, although it is a matter of public record that almost $10,000,000 in duties were paid to U.S. Customs between 1840 and 1850. So thoroughly did those ships become identified with Samuel Cunard himself that, although the company was still styled the British and North American Ocean Steam Navigation Company—"Cunard" wouldn't become part of the corporate moniker for another three decades—it was known to the public on both sides of the Atlantic as simply "The Cunard Line."

Four new ships had been added to the fleet in 1848, the *America, Niagara, Europa,* and *Canada*. Advances in technology, however, were something in which Samuel Cunard wasn't particularly interested: establishing a corporate policy that would assume the stature of near-holy writ for the next four decades, Cunard eschewed adopting changes and innovations until they had been well-proven in service by his competitors, and only then, when the company's attachment to outdated technology threatened the company's revenues. Just as the *Hibernia* and *Cambria* had been simply enlarged versions of the *Britannia* and her sisters, the new quartet of ships continued the trend. Despite the urgings of Robert Napier, they were wooden hulled and propelled by paddlewheels, the lessons of the *Great Britain* completely ignored. Another decade would pass before Cunard would put its first iron-hulled, screw-propelled ships to sea, and in the meantime the line would bring the paddlewheel passenger steamer to its ultimate expression.

Of more immediate concern, however, was an American challenge thrown down to Cunard's dominance. Most American businessmen attributed the failure of the Ocean Steam Navigation Company to the fact that Edward Mills had no experience in the shipping world; consequently, they weren't ready to concede primacy on the North Atlantic to Cunard's steamships, and began clamoring in Congress to authorize a government-subsidized steamship line to carry the U.S. Mail, along with passengers on a run between New York and Liverpool. So closely had Samuel Cunard become identified with the transatlantic passenger steamer trade that he was denounced on the floor of the United States Senate, as legislators lined up to support a measure expressly intended to wrest the Atlantic trident from Cunard's grasp. It would take shape in the form of the Collins Line, the brainchild of one Edward Knight Collins.

CHAPTER FOUR

The Yankee Rival

The story of the Collins Line is the brief, glorious, futile, and ultimately tragic tale of the United States' one and only chance to achieve pre-eminence in the steamship service on the North Atlantic. It is one of the most inexplicable, yet undeniable truths of the annals of ocean travel that the United States, despite having a vast and rich seafaring tradition and a maritime history—going back to the earliest days of the Colonies—almost as long as that of the British, was never able to become a major competitor in the saga of the Atlantic Ferry. It is also ironic, as it was the Americans and not the British who really created the Atlantic Ferry with their hard-driven packet boats; the success of the British packet companies was due to their almost slavish imitation of the American example. Yet the talent that seemed to be most distinctly and distinctively American was for sail, not steam: Americans would continue to profitably build and sail square-rigged ships with a genius that would never be surpassed until the sailing ship itself became passé; the same degree of success in running a steamship line would constantly elude them.

No doubt the comparative degree of industrialization in the two countries was a factor. By 1850 Victorian Britain was the most industrialized society on the planet; in fact, the total output of British industry was greater than that of the United States, France, Austria-Hungary, Russia, and the various German states combined. It was also the fastest growing: at the time of the Battle of Waterloo in 1815 (one of the benchmarks of history that was a chronological touchstone for 19th Century Europeans), Britain's population was roughly thirteen million; by 1850, Britain's populace had almost doubled to twenty-four million.

Transportation was the key to this phenomenon, first on land, then at sea. It began with the railroad: prior to 1830, people and goods moved no faster over land than they had for the past four thousand years, limited by the endurance of human muscles or those of draft animals. In September of that year, the Liverpool & Manchester railway opened, and the transformation began. In its first year of operation, the railroad carried twice as many passengers between the two cities as had traveled by coach in the previous year; more important was that the volume of freight carried was more than tripled. Because at that time Liverpool was Great Britain's largest and most important seaport, and Manchester was Britain's most important manufacturing center, the advantages that the railroad opened up to Midlands businessmen were tremendous, allowing them to cheaply and reliably ship their goods, in particular cloth, to Liverpool, while at the same time having raw materials from overseas, most notably cotton from the United States, brought to Manchester with equal ease and economy.

The increased profitability that the railroad brought to Manchester industrialists did not go unremarked in other parts of Great Britain, and by 1850 more than five thousand miles of track had been laid across the British Isles. The consequences of the broadened domestic markets the railroads produced were soon apparent: even though profits actually rose between 1800 and 1850, the price of bread, meat, tea and coffee all fell, while the cost of coal was halved and that of cloth cut by four-fifths. The impact of the steam engine on Britain's economy and society was profound and pervasive. It was not surprising then that the British pioneered the steamship service on their most important shipping lane, the North Atlantic.

By contrast, the great influence of the railroad was yet to come in America. With an area of more than three million square miles, in 1850 the United States had barely nine thousand miles of railroad track, a density of one mile of track for every three hundred thirty square miles of territory, while that of Great Britain was one mile of track for every nineteen square miles. Consequently, the steam engine was far from common in the United States, so that the collective mentality of American businessmen was still attuned to the traditional methods of locomotion — muscle-power on land and wind-power at sea.

Not that Edward Knight Collins wouldn't do all he could to change that. Born on Cape Cod in 1802, his father was Captain Israel Collins, who commanded packets that sailed between Boston and Liverpool. From the beginning, Edward knew ships and the sea; he began his career in the shipping business while still in his teens, working for New York freighting companies that operated between several American coastal cities. He later worked as "supercargo"—a position that would eventually evolve into that of a ship's purser—for a New York merchant who traded in the Caribbean. When he was in his mid-twenties, Edward Collins went into partnership with his father and formed Israel G. Collins & Son, which operated packets between New York and Mexico. The elder Collins died a few years later and the firm became simply E. K. Collins & Co.

From the outset, Collins had a knack for appealing to the public, as well as maximizing the capacity of ships. His vessels were always smartly turned out whenever they were in port, which made them more attractive to prospective passengers than the weather-beaten appearance of so many of Collins' competitors. He also introduced a fundamental change to packet ship design, noting that vessels with a U-shaped hull not only sailed better but carried more cargo than one with a traditional V-shaped hull, making each of his ships individually more profitable.

Those profits allowed Collins to construct a second fleet of four packets, built primarily for carrying passengers rather than cargo, and as such their interiors were far more spacious and comfortable than conventional packets. Named after great theatrical figures, this quartet was soon popularly known as the Dramatic Line, and was inseparably linked in the public mind with Edward Knight Collins. These four ships, named *Garrick*, *Roscius*, *Sheridan* and *Siddon*, were the cream of the North Atlantic run throughout the 1830s and early 1840s.

But steamships had caught Collins' attention early. There are letters documenting his interest in forming an American steamship line as early as 1841. At the time, though, his vision was not shared by very many of his countrymen, and his first efforts came to naught. Five years later, the first abortive attempt by an American steamship company sent a massive (and massively ugly) American-built paddle-wheeler named the *Washington* from New York to London, but the ship was as slow

Edward Knight Collins, the man who almost took the Atlantic away from Cunard.

as she was homely, and it was obvious that she was doomed to be a dismal failure. By that time though, the idea of an American steam packet company was gaining some significant support in Congress, and Collins saw his opportunity. He sent a proposal to the Postmaster General, outlining a plan to carry the United States' mails between New York and Liverpool twice monthly in the spring, summer and autumn, and once a month in the winter—a total of twenty round-trips annually. This would require a guaranteed annual subsidy of $385,000, with which Collins would build and operate five steamers superior in all respects to any others then in service, and use them to establish the same sort of pre-eminence in steam that America already possessed in sail.

Collins' supporters were vocal and vociferous. The most outspoken of all of them, Senator James Asheton Bayard of Delaware, made no effort to disguise what was expected of Collins, or who was his intended target. Addressing the Senate in 1846, he declared, "I suggest cost must not be considered. I suggest, too, that Congress grant a carefully selected American shipping expert a completely free hand to proceed with the absolute conquest of this man Cunard!" Eventually Collins' proposal was accepted in November 1847, and a contract with the newly formed New York and Liverpool United States Mail Steamship

Company. Though four other partners, Elisha Riggs, W. S. Wetmore, and two brothers, James and Stewart Brown, joined Collins in forming and financing the new company, in the public mind it would forever be associated with Collins alone, and so become known as the Collins Line.

Portly, fleshy-faced and heavy-jowled, Collins resembled nothing so much as a walrus in search of its tusks and mustache. A happily married man, he was the proud father of a son, Henry Coit Collins, and a daughter named, as was his wife, Mary Ann. Like his rival Samuel Cunard, he was a shrewd businessman, but at the same time, again like Cunard, was never known for his devotion to the sharp practice. In short, he was an admirable man with great ambitions, and certainly didn't deserve the cruel future that Fate had prepared for him.

Collins' fleet would eventually consist of five ships, the first two, the *Atlantic* and *Pacific*, being launched on the same day, February 1, 1849, followed six months later by the *Arctic* and the *Baltic*, the fifth ship, the *Adriatic*, coming almost six years later. The first pair, the *Atlantic* and *Pacific*, were impressively large ships, 282 feet long and displacing 2,856 tons, bigger than anything else on the North Atlantic save the *Great Britain*. In appearance they were a radical departure from what had become the accepted form for a steamship. Gone was the sleekly raked stem that had characterized seagoing vessels for more than two centuries; in its place was a stark straight-up-and-down cutwater, while the bowsprit had been disposed of entirely. Instead of the graceful counter stern that was already the hallmark of all other transatlantic steamships—and would continue to be for the next eighty years—the Collins ships were abruptly, inelegantly rounded off, as if the shipwrights had simply run out of ship to build. They were blunt, almost pugnacious in appearance, as if from the outset Collins was determined to make it clear that his ships were distinctly different from every other passenger steamship on the North Atlantic run. The first to go to sea was the *Atlantic*, and when she set out on her maiden voyage on April 27, 1850, she created an immediate sensation among ocean travelers and sent shock waves through the shipping industry.

From the start, Collins' conception of what an ocean voyage should be like was a marked departure from Cunard's, or any of his other competitors', for that matter. Not only were Collin's ships as fast as Cunard's, they were markedly more comfortable. Public rooms were more spacious, cabins were larger, and steam heat was provided throughout the ship. Ventilation was improved as well, a feature much appreciated by passengers and crew alike, and the ships were equipped with large ice-rooms to provide for fresh food throughout each crossing. Each ship even had its own barbershop.

Inside, there was a profusion of expensive woodwork—satinwood, rosewood, mahogany and oak, delicately carved and finished, accompanied by yards of rich carpeting and brocaded wall hangings. Admittedly, though, a good bit of the elegance for which Collin's ships were soon known was as much for show as it was for the comfort of the passengers. When one of the Collins ships was in port, the interiors were displayed in all their finery, the better to attract customers. Once at sea, however, the carpets and hangings gave way to cocoa matting and canvas covers, the better to resist the rigors of rough seas and queasy passengers—the carvings stayed put, of course.

Not that Collins' passengers would have had much opportunity to notice: in contrast to the rather plain mealtimes which had become the standard fare on Cunard ships, the offerings on a Collins liner would have made an epicurean blush. On a typical dinner would be found the following:

Soups—Green turtle, Potage au choux
Boiled—Hams, Tongues, Cold corned beef, Turkeys (oyster sauce), Fowl (parsley sauce), Leg of mutton (caper sauce)
Fish—Cod (stuffed and baked), Boiled bass (Hollander sauce)
Roast—Beef, Veal, Mutton, Lamb, Geese (champagne sauce), Ducks, Pigs, Turkey, Fowls
Entrées—Macaroni au gratin, Filet of pigeon au Cronstaugh, Croquet de poisson à la Richelieu, Salmi de canard sauvage, Poulets (pique, sauce tomato), Cotelette de veau à la St.Gara, Fricandeau de tortue au petit pois, d'Oyeis en cassis, Epigram d'agneau (sauce truppe)
Vegetables—green corn, green peas
Salads—Potato and plain
Pastry—Baked vermicelli pudding, Apple fritters (hard sauce), Almond cup custards, Red currant tartlets, Apple tarts, Open puffs, Cranberry tarts, Coventry puffs, etc.
Desserts—Fruit, Nuts, Olives, Cakes, etc. etc. Coffee, Lemonade (frozen)

Collins' single most enduring and outstanding contribution to the passenger steamship was the introduction of the smoking room. Actually, it wasn't much of a room: it was little more than a rather cramped, poorly lit deckhouse in which nicotine addicts could indulge their cravings. But it was the forebear of what would evolve into an ocean-going institution, and ultimately become the home of some of the most magnificent interiors ever seen. By the turn of the century, the smoking room would become a carefully orchestrated assembly of carved mahogany paneling, leaded glass panels and etched-patterned mirrors, massive leather-covered armchairs, and an unbreachable bastion of masculinity.

All in all, the *Atlantic* was unlike anything that had ever before been seen on her namesake ocean. From the outset the American press had been uniform in trumpeting her features and attractions, while Collins himself had expended considerable sums of money on publicity for his new ship. It was something of a surprise then, when she departed New York on her maiden voyage that she sailed with only a hundred passengers on board, less than half the number she was designed to carry. What should have been a triumphal procession across the Atlantic proved to be anything but triumphant. Hardly was she out of sight of land when she ran into a low-lying ice field that played havoc with her paddle-wheels, and her top speed was sharply reduced. Six days later her condenser broke down, leaving her without power for forty hours. Eventually she steamed into Liverpool on May 10, looking bedraggled and forlorn. The British press took every advantage of the *Atlantic*'s misfortunes to heap scorn on her, her owners, and the American steamship industry in general. It was an unwise move, for once repairs were made, the *Atlantic* roared out of Liverpool on May 29, 1850 and stormed back to New York in record time—10 days, 16 hours, fully twelve hours faster than Cunard's *Canada*. She had vindicated Collins, the confidence placed in him by his supporters in Congress, and the faith of the American people in their maritime traditions.

Cunard, though, wasn't about to let the Collins ships have it all their own way. In late spring of 1850, the line added the sister-ships *Asia* and *Africa* to its fleet, built as all other Cunard ships with hulls of British oak and hearts of Scots-built steam engines by Napier. They would be among the last paddlewheel steamers built for Cunard, and also two of the loveliest. It may have been due to nothing more than the old man's innate conservatism, but Cunard's ships still echoed the graceful lines of the packet boats, avoiding any echo of the blunt and bluff hulls of Collins' ships. With each sporting a single tall, slender funnel and three modestly raked barque-rigged masts, the *Asia* and *Africa*, their lines and proportions neatly balanced, looked swift; certainly they weren't slow, as their cruising speed was 12½ knots, easily as good at the *Atlantic*'s best.

Nor were the Cunard ships already in service idle while Collins' ships were creating their sensations on the North Atlantic. Just a month after the *Atlantic*'s record crossing, Cunard's *Europa* cut her crossing time by four hours, although the *Atlantic* took the record back ten days later. But she in turn was trumped in October by the newly-launched *Asia,* by five hours, and in December the *Asia* bettered her own time by another five hours, accomplishing the crossing from New York to Liverpool in just over ten days.

But in the long run the Collins ships proved the faster: in May 1851, the *Pacific* made an eastbound crossing in 9 days, 20 hours-an average speed of 13 knots, the first ship to cross the Atlantic in less than ten days. It was a performance that the *Baltic* would improve upon the following year, with an average of 13.17 knots. A few months later the *Arctic* would make a crossing where she averaged 13.25 knots. Try as they might, the *Asia* and *Africa* couldn't hope to keep up with such a pressing pace, and for a few meteoric years the Collins Line eclipsed Cunard.

While he had not quite accomplished what Senator Bayard had demanded—"the absolute conquest of this man Cunard!"—he had certainly earned pride of place for the American merchant marine. The once-derisive British press soon changed its tune, a defining bit of doggerel appearing in Punch declaring of the *Atlantic* (to the tune of "Yankee Doodle"):

A steamer of the Collins Line
A Yankee Doodle notion
Has also cut the quickest brine
Across the Atlantic ocean.
And British agents no way slow
Her merits to discover
Have been and bought her—just to tow
The Cunard Packets over!

Yet the signs were there for those perceptive enough to see them that not everything was going Collins' way. While the line was carrying more passengers than Cunard, and Cunard was forced to cut its freight rates from £7 10s ($30) to £4 ($16) a ton, the British company was carrying more than three times the amount of mail than was the American line. Since the Collins subsidy was tied to the amount of mail the line carried, this was a significant deficit. In fact, the company was losing an average of nearly $17,000 (£4,250) a voyage, a hemorrhage of cash that could not continue. Consequently, Collins went to Congress for an increase in his subsidy that would cover the deficit.

His supporters in Congress were as vocal and strident as ever. Senator Bayard continued to bellow, declaring "Speed! Speed against which these British can never hope to compete. Speed of such magnitude as the Government of Britain and its chosen instrument, this man Cunard, ever visualized or could hope to achieve against America!" Representative Olds from Ohio sounded a similar note: "We have the fastest horses, the prettiest women, and the best-shooting guns in the world, and we must also have the fastest steamers! The Collins line must beat the British steamers. Our people expect this of Mr. Collins and he has not disappointed them."

When Collins' request was passed, over stubborn opposition from the Southern states, who liked being able to ship their cotton to Britain for only $16 a ton—it was applauded in the North and along the Atlantic coast as a far-sighted decision. The New York *Daily Times* declared, "Right and national pride have overruled a false and narrow economy. The supremacy of our steam marine has not been sacrificed to local and personal jealousies or to the insidious influence of a Foreign rival." The contest would continue unabated.

Cunard was prepared to do better than it had. Just two years after the *Asia* and *Africa* entered service, the Robert Steele shipyard of Greenock, on the Clyde, began work on another new ship, the *Arabia*. A beautiful, balanced design, at 2,400 tons she was still a bit smaller than the Collins liners, but her appointments were easily the equal of any of her Yankee competitors, and some of her features were particularly foresighted. In particular was her dining saloon, which featured a raised cupola with stained glass panels in the skylights, the precursor to the raised domes and ceilings that would be the centerpieces of the decor of many future liners. It was also the beginning of the proliferation of deckhouses which would gradually evolve into the superstructure. Two small libraries and a nursery for the littlest passengers were amenities that had no equal on any ship in the Collins fleet.

The *Arabia*'s power plant was more powerful than that in any of the Collins liners, and when she made 15 knots on her trials, it seemed that Cunard was poised to come racing back to the fore on the Atlantic. It wasn't to be so, however, for reasons her designers and builders never anticipated: her hull, as handsome as it was, had been built of oak, and her power plant was too powerful for it, threatening at times to shake the ship apart. Trials were one thing, but the prolonged stresses of actual service were quite another, and as a result the *Arabia*'s engines were rarely run full out, and she seldom reached the speeds she attained on her trials.

Of course, the company refused to acknowledge that it was in an out-and-out race with the Collins Line, nor would it entirely give in to that craving for innovation and novelty which seemed to characterize Collins and his ships. It was apparently a costly choice, for in the beginning of the 1850s, half again as many passengers crossing the Atlantic were carried in Collin's ships as were carried in Cunard's, as the dash and glamour—and occasional hint of rashness—of Collins' ships gained in popularity and appeal. What Samuel Cunard regarded as prudent business practices were beginning to look like little more than the stuffy conservatism of a man whose own industry had passed him by.

Yet, there was more to Cunard's policies than met the eye. The capitalist of the mid-19th Century was not the chairman of a board who fretted over a few cents per share lost on a quarterly earnings report—a deficit to be made up later in the year. His concern was literally economic life or death: there were incredible sums of money to be made by the fortunate few with the foresight to seize exactly the right opportunity at precisely the right moment; conversely, an industrialist or businessman could fall into ruin virtually overnight through making one wrong choice. Unless he had huge reserves of capital, and few did, such an individual had to play a canny game, not, as some have characterized him, like a gambler who wins big and then leaves his winnings on the table for the next wager. Instead, to continue the analogy, he had to know when to fold, when to bluff, and when he had a winning hand. Cautious and reckless, circumspect and bold by turns, a man like Samuel Cunard—or Edward Knight Collins, for that matter—had to calculate the potential consequences of every move he made. One false step could, and often did, spell disaster and ruin for many of their contemporaries.

Fortune, though, seemed to continue to smile on Edward Collins. A golden opportunity for him to establish a near-monopoly on the Atlantic came in the autumn of 1854, when Great Britain went to war with Imperial Russia and began a punitive campaign against the Tsar near the port of Sebastopol on the Crimean Peninsula. Almost the whole of Cunard's fleet was removed from the North Atlantic, throwing the line's operations into total disarray. Eleven of Cunard's sixteen ships—and for a brief period a total of fourteen of them—were pressed into service as troop transports when the British Admiralty exercised the provision of its Royal Mail contract, which allowed it to requisition Cunard's ships in wartime.

For Collins, the gap in the service on the North Atlantic caused by the absence of Cunard's ships should have been the opportunity for him to establish such a dominant position that even when his competitor returned he could not be challenged. Instead, hardly had the Cunard ships been recalled to Royal Navy service when a disaster overtook Collins, professionally and personally, that would mark the beginning of the end of the Collins Line. On September 27, 1854, the speedy *Arctic*, the finest ship in Collins' fleet, six days out of Liverpool and about sixty miles south of Cape Race, Newfoundland, was caught in a heavy fog and rammed by the small French steamer, *Vesta*. At first the damage to the *Arctic* seemed slight, but it soon became obvious that the flooding was rising faster than the ship's pumps could cope with it. The *Arctic*'s captain, James Luce, steered his ship toward Newfoundland, hoping to run her into shallow water and save her.

But while she was still some twenty miles short of her goal, the rising water quenched the fires in the *Arctic*'s boilers and she lost all power. With the ship's situation now hopeless, Captain Luce ordered the passengers, who included Edward Collins' wife, son, and daughter, into the lifeboats. In what was one of the saddest chapters of the history of the American merchant marine, the *Arctic*'s crew, abandoning all pretense of discipline, commandeered the boats—in some cases physically throwing passengers out—and rowed away, leaving those still on board to their fate. Shortly the ship sank, taking with her almost four hundred lives, leaving only forty five survivors. Among them was Captain Luce, but not Mrs. Knight, her son, or her daughter. Luce, who was desperately trying to save his crippled son, lost sight of Mrs. Knight and her children when he was pulled under by the sinking ship. No one ever saw any of the three again. Luce managed to get clear of the wreck, only to have his boy swept out of his arms as he came to the surface. For two days he clung to a section of wreckage before being picked up by, ironically, one of the few Cunard ships still on the Atlantic run, the *Cambria*.

It took two weeks before word of the disaster reached New York, and when it did the entire city was stunned. An unusually quiet and abbreviated meeting of the Council of Aldermen adjourned after passing a resolution to fly the city's flags at half-staff for three days, while the city's business centers were remarkable for their inactivity, the Merchant's Exchange actually closing upon receipt of the news. Collins himself, devastated, went into a prolonged seclusion. When he emerged, he was as dedicated as ever to seeing that his line continued to prosper despite the tragedy; even so, there was now a constant, unmistakable aura of melancholy surrounding Collins that would never leave him.

His task was not an easy one—public confidence in the Collins Line was badly shaken, and both passenger bookings and cargo carriage dropped off drastically. Conversely, although Cunard had only four ships in the North Atlantic service at the time, they were almost always sailing full. In some ways Collins was a victim of his own reputation for brashness, for though neither the *Atlantic* nor Captain Luce were to blame for either the collision or the despicable conduct of the crew, the perception of the general public was that somehow Collins *was* responsible for both. At the same time, he was also the victim of a great deal of hypocrisy, for no sooner had word of the disaster reached New York than the American press, which had echoed the strident voices in Congress that once clamored for the construction of fast American steamships to take control of the North Atlantic run, suddenly began decrying the "wicked recklessness of speed."

The careful game Cunard had been playing now started to reveal itself. It's unlikely that he had been counting on such a dramatic turn of events to take place, but he had clearly anticipated some sort of misstep by Collins, and now he intended to take as full advantage of it as possible, given the limited circumstances now present in his own line. The company's officials were quick to make the public aware of a court case in London (to which Cunard was not a party) where it was entered as evidence that between 1840 and 1854 the company had made seven thousand crossings of the North Atlantic, carrying more than 100,000 passengers, and in that time "not a single passenger had been lost nor a pound of baggage damaged." It was the beginning of the boast that would be the foundation of the line's reputation for the next fifty years—"The Cunard has never lost a life."

Unfortunately, the war in the Crimea continued, and the company was in no position to fully exploit Collins' vulnerability. It wasn't until the beginning of October 1855, with a peace treaty signed and Cunard's ships carrying away the last of the British troops from the Crimea and returning them to their garrisons, that the company was able to announce its intention "to resume in January 1856, the weekly sailings of the steamships of this Company from Liverpool to the United States. The British Mail steamships will thereafter be dispatched from Liverpool every Saturday as formerly, alternately to Boston (calling at Halifax) and to New York direct."

Isambard Kingdom Brunel's *Great Britain* had proven that ships made of iron would not only float, but had a strength and durability that wood could never equal, but his achievement was tainted somewhat by the misfortunes which the ship suffered, and most of the steamships that were built after the *Great Britain* were still made of oak. But the ever-increasing size of those ships—-ocean-going vessels now attained lengths of 300 feet or more—finally reached a point where their structures were larger than wooden keels and frames could safely support. Cunard, intending to surpass the Collins Line in every possible way, acknowledged this reality by commissioning the Scottish shipbuilders Robert Napier & Sons Ltd to build the line's first iron-hulled ship. The result was the *Persia*, one of the most beautiful steamships ever built, and at 360 feet in length and 3,400 tons displacement, the largest ship in the world. While at first glance switching from a wood hull to one made of iron seems a gigantic step for the ultraconservative Cunard, in fact it demonstrated how well and truly perceptive was old Samuel. Let others waste time and money on new technologies and gadgets—only when they were proven in service would the Cunard Line adopt them. The consequence of this was not only economy for Cunard, as others would spend their money—not his—on developing these new ideas, but also, because of the line's reputation for safety and reliability, there would be no question in the public mind of the absolute dependability of the innovation, further burnishing the company's image.

The *Persia*'s iron construction also marked the demise of a curious restriction that had governed the construction of new ships. When iron hulls began making their debut on the Atlantic, the Admiralty had specified that none of the Cunard ships were to be built of iron, as it was believed they would be of no value in wartime, the ability of iron hulls to resist gunfire being then suspect. Yet it was inevitable that Cunard build iron ships, as the size of passenger steamers began to exceed the structural capabilities of wood, and as the Royal Navy's own experience with iron hulls as well as ironclads belied the assumptions about their vulnerability, the restriction was lifted, and Cunard was able to proceed with the design of the *Persia*.

In appearance she was a very traditional-looking ship—a clipper bow, three masts, and a pair of tall, slender funnels, one forward and one aft of the paddle-boxes set amidships. As events would turn out, the *Persia* would be the Cunard Line's last paddle wheeler, save one; here Cunard's conservative nature won out, for despite the fact that the screw, or propeller, had proven to be both faster and more efficient than paddlewheels, the public still had more faith in paddles, preferring to see what made the ship move rather than trusting the forces of an unseen mechanism at the stern. Even so, with two Scotch boilers producing the steam for her engines, which were rated at 950 horsepower, she had a designed speed of 13½ knots, and achieved over 15 knots on her trials, faster than any of Collins' ships. The iron hull, far stronger than the oak hull of the *Asia*, withstood the strain with ease, and so Cunard was prepared to not only return to the North Atlantic, but to do so with a flourish.

By January 26, 1856, the *Persia* was ready to set out on her maiden voyage from Liverpool to New York. By purest chance, the then-fastest ship on the Atlantic run, the Collins Line's *Pacific*, had left Liverpool just three days before with forty-five passengers and one hundred forty-one crew aboard. Although the captain of the *Persia*, C.H.E. Judkins, was firm in his protests that there would be no "race" to New York between his ship and the *Pacific*, the public certainly anticipated such a contest. Certainly there was much belching of smoke and furious churning of paddlewheels when the *Persia* pulled away from the Huskisson Dock that morning, but unknown to those watching her depart or those aboard, there would be no record crossing for the *Persia* on this voyage. Five days out of Liverpool, making well over 11 knots, she ran headlong into a field of ice. Her bow was damaged—sixteen feet of her hull plating had its rivets sheered off—and her starboard paddlewheel and its housing were crushed and crumpled. Her speed reduced by more than half, down by the head, nevertheless the *Persia* pressed on to New York, her iron hull having withstood an impact that would have shivered one of her wooden-hulled predecessors.

When the *Persia* limped into New York on February 9, there was no sign of the *Pacific*—she had literally vanished without a trace. As more and more ships made port in New York and Boston and reported the extent of the ice field that the *Persia* had encountered, it became clear what had most likely happened to the *Pacific*. Running at 11 knots or better, she had driven into the ice field, and the impact which the *Persia*'s iron hull had been able to absorb had overpowered the wooden keel and frames of the *Pacific*, sending her to the bottom with everyone aboard. It would be more than a century before her wreck was ever found—in the same waters where the *Persia* had rammed the ice flow.

Curiously, the collision had no effect on the *Persia's* popularity, partly, no doubt due to the fact that she had survived. She had the capacity to carry two-hundred fifty passengers in a degree of comfort that rivaled anything the Collins side could offer, while her safety features were reassuring—in addition to her eight lifeboats, she had a series of watertight bulkheads which divided her hull into seven watertight compartments, including a special "collision bulkhead" in her bow. Her holds had a capacity for 1,100 tons of cargo, for despite the supremacy on the Atlantic that the *Pacific* disaster had given Cunard, the line was still as dependent on freight as on passengers, to earn a profit.

The loss of the *Pacific* was, for all practical purposes, the end of the Collins Line. Edward Collins did his best to put a brave face on the situation—company advertisements quickly shifted from emphasizing the luxury of the ships' accommodations to the thoroughness of their safety features. What could not be glossed over was the fact that despite the increased government subsidies, the line continued to lose money on every crossing. In truth, the Collins Line had never operated in the black, which added weight to the arguments of Collins' opponents in Congress that the subsidies be ended. They resented the fact that a handful of powerful New York business interests had received what seemed to many to be preferential treatment. Collins, they said, had come to regard his access to the public purse as unlimited, and while his accomplishments had been considerable, they were too expensive to be allowed to continue.

Collins fought back bravely, even though his fleet had been halved in the space of sixteen months. Stretching his resources to their absolute limit, he built the *Adriatic*, the ship which he believed—he hoped—would turn his company's prospects around. At 353 feet in length she was seven feet shorter than the *Persia*, but with a displacement of 3,760 tons she was the largest ship afloat, with a capacity of 376 passengers, 316 in First Class and 60 in Second. Her sixteen lifeboats were mute evidence of Collins' new attention to safety. Launched in April 1857 she sat idle for almost eight months as problems with installing her machinery caused her entire fitting-out to be delayed. When she was finally ready for her maiden voyage in November of that year, only thirty-eight passengers were aboard. The British press declared the *Adriatic* to be "the finest and fastest steam vessel built up to that date" but the damage to the Collins' reputation by the *Arctic* and *Pacific* disasters was too great an obstacle to overcome, and she returned to New York with fewer passengers than when she had departed.

The *Adriatic* made one more voyage, in February 1858, but by then it was a case of too little, too late. Congress had already cut its subsidy by more than half, from $858,000 to $385,000 annually, a hopelessly inadequate amount, and the numbers of passengers the line could attract were pitifully few. That same February, the *Atlantic* and *Baltic*, all that remained of the line's original quartet of ships, tied up at their New York berths alongside the *Adriatic*, and were shut down. Six weeks later the rag-tag little fleet was auctioned off for a mere $50,000, and the Collins Line was no more.

The whole, or even a majority of the blame for the failure of the Collins Line cannot be laid on Edward Collins, for he demonstrated before and after the adventure of the Collins Line that he was an astute and gifted businessman. While he would never again have anything to do with ships or the sea, he was very successful in the coal and timber industries, to which he devoted the remaining twenty years of his life. Had he been able to hold on for a few years longer, he might have achieved the success he had pursued with such fervor and dedication, and brought the line into profitability and prosperity. Samuel Cunard proved that success begat success on the North Atlantic, and even allowing for Collins' propensity for opulence, the excellence of service to which the Collins Line aspired—and frequently delivered—may well have garnered for his company the sort of reputation and loyal patronage that had accrued to Cunard.

Instead, events conspired against him, tragedy striking not once but twice, and at such an interval that public confidence, which was being carefully restored after the first disaster, was shattered beyond all recovery by the second. Rarely has the description "meteoric" been so well merited as by the career of the Collins Line: in the span of exactly eight years it burst on the scene of the North Atlantic; rose to supremacy in speed, service, and style; then vanished as if it had never been. Another hundred years would pass before the United States would again challenge the Cunard Line for pride of place on the North Atlantic, and by then it would prove to be a hollow victory. In the century between the demise of the Collins Line and the emergence of another American challenger, the United States would only be able to play the role of spectator to the race on the North Atlantic.

CHAPTER FIVE

The Struggle for Supremacy

The great opportunity to gain preeminence on the North Atlantic that Edward Knight Collins had gained and then squandered, came about when Samuel Cunard was called upon to fulfill one of the clauses of the Royal Mail contract he had been awarded in 1839. Eleven of his sixteen ships were called to the colors to serve as troopships carrying reinforcements to the Black Sea, and into what history would call the Crimean War.

The war had its roots in a dispute between Russia and France over the Palestinian holy places, when France challenged Russia's claim to guardianship in 1852 and won concessions from the Ottoman Turks. Russian counter-demands were turned down and in October 1853 after Russian occupation of Ottoman lands, the Ottomans declared war. In March 1854, England and France, in truth more concerned with preventing Russia from seizing the Bosporus and Constantinople than in defending Ottoman sovereignty, decided to make common cause against the Tsar of Russia, and declared war on Russia as well.

For reasons that still seem hopelessly muddled to this day, the French and British chose to land troops on the Crimean Peninsula. The Crimea was the garden spot of the Russian Empire, with its rolling, fertile hills, covered with acres of grain or dotted with grazing sheep and cattle, that gradually rose into the vineyard covered slopes of the Crimean Mountains. The strategic focus of the campaign was the fortified port of Sebastopol, the main naval base of Russia's Black Sea fleet. A combined Anglo-French naval force blockaded the port while a force of 26,000 British, 30,000 French and 5,000 Turkish troops was assembled to be landed at the mouth of the Balaklava Valley, with the intent of capturing Sebastopol.

From the outset, the war was marked more by incompetence and inefficiency than by any degree of intelligent direction. While all armies experience reductions in manpower and weaponry in peacetime, economy-minded politicians in Britain had cut away a lot of muscle while trying to trim the fat from the Army's ranks, leaving it under strength and ossified. The result was that the British Army was still trained and equipped to fight the Battle of Waterloo (so were the French and Russians, for that matter); and though the soldiers—'other ranks' in British military parlance—fought with unshakable courage, leading one observer to comment that "the British Army was made up of lions led by asses," the strategic leadership was notable only for its ineptitude.

Certainly the British commander-in-chief, Lord Raglan, could be justifiably accused of trying to re-fight Waterloo: he had actually fought in that battle, serving as an aide to the Duke of Wellington and losing an arm in the process. He had an annoying habit (annoying to his allies, the French) of referring to the enemy as "the French" rather than the Russians, and spent more time aboard his private yacht moored off the Crimean coast than he did ashore with his troops.

There the men were suffering in ways that would have triggered one of the Duke of Wellington's rare but justifiably famous explosions of temper. Despite the onset of winter, there was little winter clothing available for the other ranks, no provisions made for winter quarters, and the supplies of food were inadequate and often inedible. The British Commissariat, responsible for supplying the Army's needs, had completely broken down. It was an unforgivable situation, for the Commissary at one time had been brought to a high degree of perfection by Wellington, who, as befitting the greatest soldier of his day, understood the fundamental need for proper supply, shelter, and medical arrangements for the troops. Raglan clearly had learned nothing from his late commander-in-chief, and during that first winter in the Crimea, fully half the British troops became casualties due to inadequate clothing, shelter and food. The number of dead from disease exceeded that of those killed in battle, and the pioneering work of Florence Nightingale forcibly brought to the public's attention the ordeals the British soldiers were undergoing, most pointedly how utterly pathetic were the medical services.

It was the need to transport those troops to the Crimea, as well as make good the Army's losses with replacements and reinforcements, that brought about Cunard's involvement in the Crimean War. The Royal Navy, like its Army counterpart, had suffered severely at the hands of the cheese-paring politicians after the Napoleonic Wars. Its strength was sharply reduced from two hundred fifteen ships-of-the-line in 1815 to just fifty by 1854. The numbers of support vessels had suffered accordingly: when the war in the Crimea began, the Royal Navy had *no* troop transports available. Hence, the call to Cunard.

Transporting troops was not a difficult or arduous task, but it was a vital one. In addition to fresh battalions sent to the Crimea directly from Britain to reinforce the regiments already engaged, garrisons from as far away as India and the Cape Colony were recalled, borne to the Black Sea and landed outside Sebastopol. Replacements were in constant demand and continually being shipped out to Crimea; within a few months, a steady stream of transports was shuttling back and forth between Great Britain and the Black Sea. From the outset the Cunard ships gained a reputation as being the most reliable, best-maintained ships in the Royal Navy's service. It was the beginning of what would become a close and enduring relationship between Cunard and the British government, which would span almost a century.

But patriotism doesn't always equate to good business, which Cunard discovered in short order. By the end of 1854, eleven of the company's ships were serving with the Royal Navy, the remaining five being the absolute minimum the line required to be able to fulfill the mail contract. In September there were actually fourteen Cunard ships serving as transports, but the line quickly pointed out the absurdity of the situation: two ships weren't sufficient to carry the mail according to the schedule the Admiralty had specified, which meant it would lose the contract—which in turn would allow it to withdraw its ships from Royal Navy service. The Navy hastily gave three ships back to the line.

The first casualty of the attrition was the service to Boston, which was terminated in the fall of 1854, and would not resume for another two years. The most significant consequence of this decision was to permanently reduce Boston to the stature of a secondary port for Cunard, with New York assuming an undisputed place as the company's main American terminus.

With the Collins Line essentially out of the picture and the Crimean War over, Cunard methodically set about solidifying its place as the premier passenger line on the North Atlantic. The strength of the position which the company already occupied was amply demonstrated by the services between Europe and North America, offered in an advertisement in the *New York World* in 1856; it also shows the importance that the steamship lines still placed on shipping cargo:

British and North American Royal Mail Steamships
Appointed by the Admiralty
To Sail Between
Liverpool and New York (Direct)
and Between
Liverpool and Boston,
The Boston Ships only Calling at Halifax to land and receive
Passengers and Her Majesty's Mails.

Arabia *C.H.E. Judkins*   Africa *Wm. Harrison*
Persia *Alex. Ryrie*   America *W.J.C. Lang*
Asia *Edwd. G. Lott*   Niagara *John Leitch*
Canada *James Stone*   Europa *Neil Shannon*
Cambria *Captain W. Douglas*

The under-noted or other Vessels are appointed to Sail

From Liverpool:
Canada *For Boston Saturday, the 22nd July*
Arabia *For New York Saturday, the 29th July*
America *For Boston Saturday, the 5th Aug*
Europa *For New York Saturday, the 12th Aug*
Niagara *For Boston Saturday, the 19th Aug*
Africa *For New York Saturday, the 26th Aug*

From America:
Europa From New York Wednesday, 12th July
America From Boston Wednesday, 19th July
Asia From New York Wednesday, 26th July
Niagara From Boston Wednesday, 2nd Aug
Africa From New York Wednesday, 9th Aug
Canada From Boston Wednesday, 16th Aug

The Passengers and Goods for New York are intended to be landed at Jersey City, within the jurisdiction of the Custom-house of New York.

Chief-Cabin Passage to Halifax and Boston, £25.
Second-Cabin Passage, £15.
Chief-Cabin Passage to New York, £30.
Second-Cabin Passage, £20. These Rates include
Steward's Fee and Provisions, but without
Wines or Liquors, which can be obtained on Board.

Dogs charged £5 each.

These Steamships have accommodation for a limited number of Second-Cabin Passengers.

Apply, in Halifax, to Samuel Cunard:
in Boston, to S.S. Lewis;
in New York, to Edward Cunard;
in Havre and Paris, to Donald Currie;
in London, to J.B. Foord, 52, Old Broad Street;
in Glasgow, to G.and J. Burns; and
in Liverpool to D. and C. MacIver, 14, Water Street.

Note:-All letters and newspapers intended to be sent by these Vessels must pass through the Post Office, and none will be received at the Agents' Office.

The Owners of these Ships will not be accountable for Gold, Silver, Bullion, Specie, Jewellery, Precious Stones, or Metals, unless Bills of Lading are signed therefor, and the value thereof therein expressed.
Passengers will be charged Freight on their personal Luggage when it exceeds Half-a-Ton Measurement.

To prevent disappointment or difficulty, Passengers are respectfully informed that Packages of Merchandise will not be allowed to be shipped as Luggage, or with their Luggage.

Passengers are not permitted to go on board by the Steamer that takes the Mail.

Parcels will be received at the office of the Agents here until Six o'clock on the Friday Evenings previous to Sailing.

The Canada, for Halifax and Boston, will start on Saturday next, the 22nd instant [July, 1854]. The Steam-tender Satellite will leave the Landing-Stage, opposite the Baths, George's Pier, at Eight o'clock, morning, of that day, with the Passengers for the Canada. Cargo for the Alps is now being received at the Huskisson Dock, according to priority of arrival. Steam To New York And (via Jamaica) To Chagres. The undernoted or other first class Screw Steamships will sail From Liverpool For New York, Once a Month until further notice, the extended service being Twice a Month, when the Ships now building are completed:

Andes Capt. Moodie   Jura Capt. Douglas
Alps Capt. Wickman   Aetna Capt. Little
For Boston And New York

Alps Wednesday next, 19th July

Passage Money to Boston, beyond which Port Passengers cannot be booked, £18, including Provisions and Steward's Fees, but without Wines or Liquors, which can be obtained on board.

Freight on Fine Goods to America, £3 per Ton Measurement; other Goods by Agreement. Freight will be collected in America at the rate of $4.80 to the Pound Sterling.

Apply in Halifax to Samuel Cunard; in Boston to S.S. Lewis; in New York to Edward Cunard; in Havre and Paris to Donald Currie; in London to J.B. Foord, 52, Old Broad Street; in Glasgow to George and James Burns; or in Liverpool to D. and C. MacIver, 14, Water Street.

As soon as Goods are going for Canada, and any quantity offer for Portland, these Vessels will call there.

However, the other steamship lines were not about to let that happen without a struggle. A young Englishman named William Inman was quietly reshaping the steamship industry as a whole. Cunard, Collins, Guion, and the Great Western Steamship Company, had all concentrated their efforts on providing transportation for the cabin class traveler, leaving the hundreds of thousands of emigrants who were queuing up in European ports from Bremen to Queenstown to make their way to America aboard sailing packets. Inman recognized the potential market the emigrants represented and decided that the time had come to take advantage of the opportunity.

Inman was born in Leicester in 1825. When he was thirteen his family moved to Liverpool, and after spending three years at the Collegiate Institute he began an apprenticeship with Richardson Brothers, provisioners who supplied linen and foodstuffs to the packets that sailed from Liverpool to Philadelphia. Before long he became the manager of their shipping department, and by the time he was in his early twenties, was made a partner. As he gained experience he began to devote more attention to the actual shipping operations, and found himself paying particular attention to an iron-hulled screw-powered steamer called the *City of Clyde*. He persuaded the Richardsons to buy her in 1854 and put her to work in their own service to Philadelphia. Two similar ships, the *City of Manchester* and *City of Philadelphia*, were acquired within a few years, along with the *Great Western*, an orphan, now that her parent company had gone under.

Four years later, Inman found himself in the position to be able to buy out his partners and set up his own shipping line. The Richardson brothers were confirmed Quakers who firmly adhered to the organization's doctrines of non-violence, and so found themselves caught in a moral dilemma when the British Admiralty attempted to requisition their vessels as troopships. Inman made them an offer which they quickly accepted, and at twenty-nine, William Inman was sole proprietor of a new shipping line that bore his name.

From the outset, Inman was determined to be different from the other passenger lines on the North Atlantic. Instead of catering to wealthy travelers, he sought out the business of the lowly emigrant, especially the Irish. Rather than compelling those emigrants to cross the Irish Sea to embark at Liverpool, he began embarking them at Queenstown. The ships he put them in were different, as well. Just how much Isambard Kingdom Brunel's *Great Britain* influenced him is unknown, but from the beginning he recognized the absolute superiority of iron-hulled, screw-propelled ships, and ordered one, the *City of Glasgow,* as the first new ship built for his company: while Cunard's paddlewheel steamers consumed an average of seventy-five tons of coal a day, the *City of Glasgow* burned a mere twenty; the space saved in bunkering was turned over to cargo, allowing the *City of Glasgow* to carry 1,200 tons of cargo compared to the typical Cunard ship's 500 tons. Inman was determined to have only such ships in his fleet.

Inside, Inman's ships were different as well. His wife took on a very active role in determining the decor of the ships as well as their sailing schedules. She also made it her business to look after the welfare of Inman passengers. On one occasion she disguised herself as an emigrant on the passage from Liverpool to Queenstown in order to experience firsthand the conditions that the steerage passengers endured.

For the sum of £6 ($30), an Inman ship would carry an emigrant from Liverpool to Philadelphia, and provide him or her with a clean berth, fresh linens and soap each morning, and three meals a day: arrowroot with sugar and milk, oatmeal porridge and molasses at breakfast; a mix of salt beef and fresh beef at dinner; tea and gruel for supper. Bland and monotonous, but a genuine improvement over the offerings of the packets, where emigrants were expected to provide their own food and prepare it during the voyage. Little wonder then, that impoverished Irish families flocked to the Inman offices in Dublin and Queenstown.

The Inman Line did not get off to a particularly auspicious start, however. In March 1854, the *City of Glasgow* disappeared without a trace in mid-Atlantic with 480 passengers and crew aboard. Six months later, the *City of Philadelphia* ran up on the rocks at Chance Cove, Newfoundland, and although all of her passengers and crew were saved, the ship was a total loss. But Inman's skill as a businessman allowed him to maintain a bi-weekly service with just the *City of Clyde* and the *City of Manchester*, with the aging *Great Western* kept in reserve. He also had little difficulty financing the construction of a pair of new ships, the *City of Washington* and *City of Baltimore*. The line grew rapidly after that, and in the next decade added fourteen more steamers, all iron-hulled, all screw-propelled. Expansion was the order of the day for steamship lines in the 1850s. Cunard had begun the decade of the 1850s in fine style, introducing in quick succession the *Africa, Asia, Andes* and *Alps*. The first two were introduced in 1850, and continued the progression that had begun with the *Britannia* and her sisters. They were wooden-hulled paddlewheel steamers, slightly larger than their immediate predecessors, the *America, Europa, Niagara* and *Canada*,

Life in Steerage, soon to be known as Third Class, in the 1860's.

the only immediately recognizable difference being that they were barquentine rigged, rather than barque-rigged, meaning that only the foremast was square-rigged, the main and mizzen being rigged for fore-and-aft sails. They were the largest Cunard ships yet.

Although engineers had been urging the use of iron in the construction of ships' hulls since 1830, and superiority of the the screw propeller over the paddlewheel had been established for several years, it wasn't until 1852 that Cunard felt confident enough in these new technologies to incorporate them into any of his ships. In that year, four iron-hulled screw-powered steam ships were ordered from William Deny and Sons, of Dumbarton—the *Australian, Sydney,* the *Andes* and *Alps*. The *Australian* and *Sydney* never went into service with Cunard, instead they were sold to the Australian Royal Mail Steam Navigation Company while still on the stocks. The *Andes* made her maiden voyage from Liverpool to New York on December 8, 1852, but when she returned to Liverpool, she had to be taken out of service briefly when she developed problems with her engines. The *Andes* and the *Alps* were taken over by the Royal Navy in 1854 for use as transports in the Crimean War, and didn't return to the North Atlantic until 1856, when the war ended.

When the Cunard Line came back to the North Atlantic, it did so with a vengeance: nothing more dramatically illustrated the company's determination to beat back the threat of the Collins Line and resume what it felt was its rightful place as the premier steamship line on the Atlantic Ferry, than the introduction of two new steamships, the *Persia* and the *Scotia*. They were regarded by many as the most beautiful paddlewheel steamers ever built, combining power, elegance and grace as few other ships ever have. They were also the last paddle wheelers built for Cunard.

Ever since the first screw-propelled ship had crossed the Atlantic, the debate over which propulsion system was superior had been hotly contested. In order to settle the issue once and for all, the Royal Navy conducted an experiment in April 1845, when two small steamers were chartered for a simple tug-o-war. The two ships—the *Rattler* and the *Alecto*—were identical in size at 880 tons and had equally powerful engines. Their only significant difference was their means of propulsion: the *Rattler* had a single propeller and the *Alecto* was equipped with traditional paddle wheels. On a calm sea with no wind, the two ships were chained together stern-to-stern, and both vessels steamed at full power in opposite directions. Her paddlewheels churning furiously, the *Alecto* found herself being towed backwards by the *Rattler* at a speed of 2.8 knots. That should have settled the question of the propeller's superiority once and for all, especially as service experience with propellers demonstrated that the screw-propelled ships were more economical to operate.

Equally important, the machinery arrangements required in a paddle steamer were not very practical. The engines occupied almost all the space amidships, which forced the boilers and their coal bunkers to be awkwardly located fore and aft of the engine room, and left little room for steerage quarters. During the 1850s, the rapidly growing emigrant trade imparted a new importance to the amount of space available for carrying steerage passengers. In spite of these seemingly convincing facts, Samuel Cunard ordered the new *Persia* to be built as a paddle steamer. Admittedly, there was more involved than the old man's innate conservatism: the company's original Admiralty contract specified that any Cunard ships engaged in carrying the Royal Mail must be powered by paddlewheels. Of course, that provision had been made in 1839 when screw propulsion was still very much in the experimental stage, and had never been modified. Given how successful his paddle wheelers had been, Samuel Cunard saw no reason to change, and so never drew the Admiralty's attention to the fact that this particular provision was obsolete. The early experience with the *Andes'* faulty engines may have influenced his thinking as well, reinforcing his innate prejudice against propellers. Although her hull design and construction were as modern as any ship on the Atlantic, the *Persia* was built with paddlewheels. Laid down in early 1855 at Robert Napier and Sons, she was launched in October that same year, and set out on her maiden voyage from Liverpool to New York on January 26, 1856. Three months later, she had captured the Blue Ribband of the Atlantic, making a succession of record crossings in the summer months that year. Not only was the *Persia* the fastest ship on the North Atlantic, she was also the largest vessel in the world, 360 feet long, 45 feet in beam and displacing 3,400 tons.

Cunard originally planned to build a sistership for *Persia*, as she had been designed to compete directly with the ships of the Collins Line. But when the *Arctic* was lost in 1854 and the *Pacific* vanished without a trace with over 180 people on board two years later, the Collins Line collapsed and the immediate need for a running mate for the *Persia* was no longer needed. Five years would pass before a companion vessel for the *Persia* was ordered, and when the new ship was completed, she would be regarded as the epitome of paddlewheel steamship design.

On June 25, 1861, the new vessel was launched and christened *Scotia*. Like her older sister, she was a paddle steamer with two funnels and two masts. The two ships were not identical, since *Scotia* was slightly larger and longer. Her internal arrangements were particularly sophisticated for the day, with her hull being divided into seven compartments by six transverse, watertight bulkheads; she had a double bottom as well, and was considered by many maritime engineers to be the strongest ship yet built. Her exceptional strength had been achieved by using very heavy frames, seven to ten inches in cross-section and spaced only twenty-one inches apart. On her sea trials the *Scotia* reached 13.5 knots, and hinted that she would reach even higher speeds once her engines had been properly run in; she was also exceptionally maneuverable, easily turning around in the Mersey within her own length.

Because she had been built as a paddle steamer, *Scotia* had no space for steerage quarters; she was a one-class ship, with all of her passenger cabins located on the main deck. On the upper deck was a promenade reaching from stem to stern. Amenities featured on the *Scotia* that had never before been seen on a ship included a bakery, a butcher, a surgeon's office, and an icehouse. The *Scotia*'s public rooms were as large and lavish as anything that Edward Knight Collins had offered on his ships: the forward dining saloon was forty-five feet long, twenty feet wide and eight feet high, while the main dining saloon shared the same width and height, but was sixty-two feet in length. The most intriguing feature in both was the arrangement of alternating panels of plate glass and woodwork, creating a bright and spacious atmosphere for the passengers at mealtimes—a far cry from Dickens' "long narrow...hearse with windows."

A year after she was launched on May 10, 1862, the *Scotia* was ready for her maiden voyage, under the command of Captain Judkins, Commodore of Cunard Line, departing from Liverpool for New York as flagship of the Cunard fleet. When her engines had finally been run in, she was able to pass the *Persia*'s westbound speed record in July of 1863, and her eastbound record the following December, both times averaging more than 14 knots. At that time, none of the other steamship lines had any vessels that could rival Cunard's ships for speed, and the *Scotia*'s records remained unchallenged for another six years.

However, no matter how fast and luxurious she was, the fact that she was a paddlewheel arrangement was somewhat of a burden to *Scotia*. She was expensive to operate, using almost four times the amount of coal that a screw-propelled ship would have consumed, and the fact that she only had First Class accommodations meant that she unsuitable for the growing emigrant trade. On some of her crossings, Cunard actually lost money on her. In short, she was not a financial success. But the *Scotia* and the *Persia* were among the most popular ships of their day, and as a result they attracted a very loyal following among wealthy travelers for themselves, and for Cunard. Eventually though, her technological obsolescence caught up with the *Scotia*, and in 1869, she lost the Blue Ribband for eastbound crossing to the Inman Line's *City of Brussels*—a 3,100 ton, single-screw steamer. She was able to hold on to the westbound record for another three years, but in May 1872, the brand-new White Star liner *Adriatic* took it from her. Though she was still a handsome ship, the *Scotia*'s paddlewheels made her look old-fashioned and dated, while the *Adriatic*'s sleek hull, long, low superstructure and gracefully raked funnels gave her a look every bit as modern as she was. It would be another thirteen years before the Blue Ribband was reclaimed by a Cunard ship.

After she lost the Blue Ribband, the *Scotia* stayed in service for another four years, but by 1876 time had run out for Cunard's last paddle steamer, and in May 1876 she was laid up. But her story was far from over: in 1879 she was purchased by the Telegraph Construction & Maintenance Company, and was sent to the Birkenhead yards of Laird for the extensive refit for laying cable. When the work was complete, she was a completely different ship: the sleek and graceful hull was the same, but the paddle wheels were gone, replaced by two propellers, and one of her funnels had been removed when she was re-engined. And so the *Scotia* settled into a second career, not as glamorous as the North Atlantic passenger trade, but also not without drama. In 1896 she was sixty miles off the Eddystone Light when she suffered an explosion in a compartment where anti-fouling paint for the cable was stored, and caused serious damage to the *Scotia*'s bow. Thanks to her watertight compartmentation, she stayed afloat and was able to reach port, where she was quickly repaired. Sold again in 1902 she was used to repair cables in the Pacific Ocean, but eventually time caught up with the old ship, and on March 11, 1904, she ran aground on the Spanish Rock near Guam.

If there had ever been any questions about the durability of a "Clyde-built ship," the *Scotia* silenced them forever: grounded hard amidships on the reef, her iron hull held together until everyone on board had been rescued. Eventually she began to break up, and finally sank during a storm two weeks after she ran aground. In 1910, a salvage team recovered all of her engine machinery, with the exception of the crankshafts, and afterwards the hull was blasted flat from midships forward. Lying in thirty feet of water, the remains of the *Scotia* are sitting upright, still recognizable today: the double bottom is still there, as well as one boiler and her counter stern.

The success—that is, the profits—which the Inman Line was enjoying from the emigrant trade did not go unnoticed by Samuel Cunard. The same year that the *Scotia* went into service, Cunard introduced the propeller-driven steamer *China*. Slightly smaller than the *Scotia*, she was essentially identical in hull form, save for the fact that she was screw-propelled, and so the pair was the perfect seagoing experiment to compare performance. After both ships had been in service for some time, it was determined that the *China* was a significantly superior ship, as all the comparisons favoured her. Even old man Cunard had to face it: if the company was going to continue to be the dominant shipping line on the North Atlantic, it had to adapt to changes in technology as readily as it adapted to changes in the business world. As a consequence, a flurry of orders for screw-propelled ships flew out of Cunard's Liverpool offices. Cunard began service to the Mediterranean in the mid-1850s with the *Taurus* but expanded it rapidly in the next decade as the company began to tap into the emigrant trade and introduced a regular run from Trieste to New York. Six ships, the *Balbec, Damascus, Kedar, Aleppo, Olympus* and *Palestine*, all iron-hulled and screw-propelled, were built for the Mediterranean service.

The performance of these ships, along with the *China*, finally convinced the British Admiralty to remove the provision from its mail contract with Cunard that specified only paddle wheelers might carry the Royal Mail. With this restriction out of the way, the company quickly ordered a big new steamer for the North Atlantic run that would become the company flagship. This was the *Russia*, constructed in Glasgow by J. & G. Thomson Limited, forerunner of the great John Brown and Company shipyard. Fitted with a clipper bow, three raked masts and a single funnel with a matching rake, but without the bulky paddlewheels and boxes mounted amidships, she looked sleek and fast.

The *Russia* was designed as a single-class ship, accommodating 235 First Class passengers, but with no provision for steerage passengers. To many observers inside the company and out, this seemed an inordinately small number of passengers for a ship of the *Russia's* size, and after some time in service showed that her operating costs exceeded the revenue she was creating, so the stateroom area was expanded to accommodate 430 passengers. She set out on her maiden voyage from Liverpool on June 15, 1867, and five months later took the Blue Ribband for the eastbound crossing, averaging 14¼ knots. It would be the only time the *Russia* would make a record crossing, for as soon as she went into service the *Russia* found herself competing with the Inman Line's *City of Paris*, which had debuted on the

North Atlantic a year earlier. The two ships were almost identical in size, although the *Russia* had more powerful engines, and their competition was fierce, the difference in their speed of crossing often coming down to a matter of a few hours. Certainly the attention their competition drew to their respective companies was good business for both.

It was particularly good for Inman, for by 1870 it was carrying more passengers than any other steamship line on the North Atlantic. American immigration figures for that year showed that Inman ships had made sixty-eight crossings to New York, carrying 44,100 passengers; the Guion Line had carried 28,569 people on fifty-five crossings. Cunard found itself ranked fifth, carrying barely half the people that Inman had transported; 24,509 brought over on seventy passages. The business of steamships was growing, responding to an ever-increasing demand: for the year of 1870, the top five passenger lines, Inman, National, Guion, Anchor, and Cunard, made a total of 323 crossings to New York, carrying a total 157,955 passengers. What was perhaps most significant about those numbers is that 16,467 of those passengers were First Class, while 141,287 were steerage. What had been a trickle of emigrants was rapidly becoming a stream, and within another two decades would turn into a flood.

For Cunard, the figures for the same year were revealing of how far the company had descended from the days of the early 1850s, when it had achieved an almost virtual monopoly on the North Atlantic. While it had carried almost as many First Class passengers as its four closest competitors, it was only the fifth largest passenger carrier. This was a vulnerability of which the line's competitors were poised to take full advantage, while two companies new to the North Atlantic entered the lists, ready to battle for the lion's share of the passenger trade, France's Compagnie Generale Transatlantique, popularly known as the French Line, and Germany's Hamburg-Amerika Line.

It was as the 1850s were coming to a close when Isambard Kingdom Brunel reappeared on the shipbuilding stage to construct the ship that would literally loom over the transatlantic trade for the next two decades. Brunel built only three ships in his career, but the evolution of their design and construction was a remarkable testimony to his amazing genius. The first, the *Great Western*, was very much an ordinary paddlewheel steamer, conventional in every way; the second, the *Great Britain*, with her iron hull and screw propulsion, was very nearly the most perfect ship that the technology of the mid-19th Century could produce, and pushed contemporary shipbuilding to its limits; the third and last, the *Great Eastern*, finally exceeded those limits. Brunel's genius had outpaced the technology of his day and conceived of a ship of such capabilities and proportions that only the science and technology of five decades hence would be able to make a success of them.

The idea of the *Great Eastern* came to Brunel in 1855, and it was brilliantly simple: she was intended to make voyages from Great Britain to India and Australia without stopping for coal, dominating the emigrant as well as mercantile trade. This dictated her size: as he explained it, "To make long voyages economically and speedily by steam, vessels must be large enough to carry the coal needed for the entire voyage.... Vessels much larger than have previously been built could be navigated with great advantage from the mere effect

The Great Eastern, *the ship in which the reach of Brunel's genius finally exceeded his grasp.*

of size." Consequently, size, on the *Great Eastern*, was everything.

The ship Brunel designed was in every sense of the word a monster: forty years would pass before her length of 693 feet was exceeded by the White Star Line's *Oceanic* in 1899, while her 22,500 tons wouldn't be matched for four years after that, by White Star's *Baltic*. When completed she would have berths for four thousand passengers, a number never exceeded by any transatlantic passenger liner ever built. But the *Great Eastern*'s immense size, meant to be her most valuable attribute, proved to be her greatest liability. For once, Brunel's genius exceeded his means of execution: there simply were no powerplants large enough to propel such a behemoth. Brunel's solution was a curious hybrid installation, with three sets of engines; two driving a pair of 58-foot paddlewheels, and a third turning a 24-foot propeller. Together the three engines generated the then-unheard-of total of eleven thousand horsepower. Six masts capable of carrying 6,500 square feet of canvas augmented the engines, but even with their aid the *Great Eastern* would always prove to be an outsized giant with a stunted heart. Brunel's best friend, W. L. Lindsay, had a sense of this flaw when he remarked during her construction, "You're premature. The world hasn't grown up to her. Send her to Brighton, dig a hole in the beach and bed her stern in it. She will make a substantial pier and her decks a splendid promenade."

From the very beginning she was intractable and deadly. Built parallel to the River Thames in London because she was too big to be launched stern first, she claimed a half-dozen lives during her construction. Her launching was a fiasco, and through a combination of bad luck and poor planning, it took almost three months to move the *Great Eastern* the hundred feet necessary to get her into the Thames and properly afloat. Two workmen were killed during the first attempt, and the cost of getting the ship into the water caused the company that owned her to go broke. New backers were found, her machinery and interiors were completed, but while on her sea trials a boiler exploded, killing five crewmen. This latest tragedy was too much for Brunel: already lying in bed paralyzed, his health broken by overwork and the mental strain of trying to finish what he had hoped to be his masterpiece, the news overwhelmed him and he died the same afternoon he was told of it.

The *Great Eastern* made her maiden voyage, not to Australia as she had been designed to do, but rather to New York in the summer of 1860, her new owners believing that she could make a fortune for them carrying emigrants to America in vaster numbers than any ship ever had before. It was an absurd idea, for the great flood tide of emigrants from Europe was still some thirty years in the future, and there simply were not enough passengers to fill her immense bulk. Wandering about her immense upper deck, known as "Oxford Street", or through her white-enamel and gilt public rooms, the few souls who sailed on her felt themselves dwarfed by their surroundings.

Infatuated as always with anything big, the American public loved the *Great Eastern*, and every time she docked in New York sightseers flocked aboard. It was well that they did: charged $1 to be allowed to roam about her all day, tourists were her only reliable source of income. She continued to sail with only a fraction of the passengers she was meant to carry, incurring huge losses for her owners. In 1862 she struck an uncharted rock off Long Island, tearing a huge gash in her bottom, but her double hull—the first one ever built—saved her. While divers were repairing the damage they reported hearing a mysterious tapping sound, as if someone were beating on the inside of the hull with a hammer. Rumor quickly spread that the noise was caused by the ghost of a riveter who had been accidentally sealed up alive inside the double hull when the *Great Eastern* was being built, and whose spirit had cursed the ship ever since. Later, though, loose underwater tackle was found to be the source of the strange tapping.

Redemption of a sort finally found the *Great Eastern* from 1865 to 1873, when she was employed laying telegraph cables between Great Britain and North America, as well as lines from Aden, at the mouth of the Red Sea, to India. Her interior, gutted of her once-lavish furnishings, served as storage "tanks" for the cable, while the great open stretches of her upper deck were perfect for the working spaces needed by the workers to prepare the cable as it was paid out. But there wasn't enough such work to keep the *Great Eastern*, and in 1874 she was tied up in Liverpool, ending her days as W. L. Lindsay had predicted, as a pier and a sideshow. It was a sad demise for such an ambitious undertaking—though in truth it had been overly-ambitious. She went to the breakers in 1889, and despite legends that the skeleton of the doomed riveter who had haunted the *Great Eastern* throughout her career was found when her hull was opened up, no official record of any such discovery exists.

The death of Brunel and the fiasco of the *Great Eastern* marked the end of an era in the North Atlantic steamship trade. No longer would the marine engineer and naval architect play a dominant role in steamship design, dictating to the owner the size and specifications of the ships he would build. The age of experimentation was over—no longer did anyone question whether regular steamship service across the North Atlantic was possible or practical. Equally settled were the basics of design and propulsion.

As ships became more reliable and schedules more dependable, the directors of the steamship lines began to determine what capabilities they wanted for their vessels, and instructed the builders to produce ships to meet their expectations. One fundamental change in the way the passenger accommodations were laid out was introduced by all of the steamship companies within a matter of a few years, compelled by the almost universal adoption of screw propulsion. Since medieval times it had been an unwritten—and therefore all the more inviolate—rule that the wealthy and titled be permitted to travel in the most sheltered, and consequently, most comfortable part of the ship. Naturally, this was the stern, and the elaborate stern galleries that had graced Spanish and Portuguese galleons, and their less ornate counterparts on Dutch and British East Indiamen had evolved into the handful of passenger cabins found on every sailing packet. When steam engines appeared, they imposed no significant design changes to those packets: space was simply made amidships for the paddlewheels, engines, and coal bunkers. The stern paddle wheeler remained essentially a phenomenon confined to the coastal and inland waters of North America.

As long as the means of propulsion were located amidships, as they were on a paddle wheeler, the traditional location of the passenger cabins presented no problem, for the premium cabins were located in the stern, as far from the noise, heat, and vibration of the engines as possible. With the advent of the screw, all that changed, as the engines were gradually moved aft and the screw itself—which could only be located in the stern—imparted a whole new set of noises and vibrations, suddenly making what had once been the most desirable real estate aboard ship far less attractive to the moneyed passengers paying First Class fares.

The solution was to move the First Class accommodations to the center of the ship, and relegate the steerage passengers to the ends of the vessel. The result was a transformation in the appearance of steamships that would take place over the next two decades. The sailing-ship lineage and heritage of the *Persia, Scotia,* and *Russia* clearly showed in their clipper bows, flush decks and counter sterns, in their bowsprits and square-rigged masts. But soon the internal changes imposed by the screw propeller began to exert an influence on the appearance of passenger steamers. With only a handful of exceptions—in particular the truly beautiful ships of the Inman Line—the clipper bows would give way to straight stems, the bowsprits would vanish, and the masts become shorter until they were reduced to mere vestiges, no longer an aid to propulsion, but solely as an emergency measure. The flush decks would disappear as raised forecastles and afterdecks were added to improve seakeeping. The deckhouses would gradually blend into one long, connected structure that ran from the fore to the after deck, and which would then eventually evolve into the wedding-cake superstructures that were among the hallmarks of the transatlantic liner at the turn of the 20th Century.

While this was happening, the means by which the steamship lines would appeal to the potential ocean traveler were changing as well. Whereas the advertisements for transatlantic steamers in the 1840s and early 1850s had striven to allay the prospective voyager's anxieties with reassurances as to the soundness and security of the ships, as well as the thoroughness of the lifesaving arrangements, by 1860, the emphasis was being placed on the amenities and advantages that transportation on a particular vessel or steamship line could offer, in particular those features found in steerage. Inman's enticements were typical: "Three thousand miles at a halfpenny a mile, and this nourishment thrown in for nothing! Emigration made easy! Luxurious would be a better term." The inducements went on, demonstrating that hyperbole and thinly-veiled falsehoods weren't the exclusive domain of 20th Century Madison Avenue hacks: "Our emigrants march to the railway depot, enter the cars, and—Go West! In a few brief months the almighty dollar rolls across the pond, and the dear ones left behind follow in the footsteps of the pioneers!"

Cunard, though, would have none of this; as far as the owners of the line were concerned, it was sufficient to simply commend the prospective passenger's attention to the regularity and dependability of the company's ships to attract their business. The motto of the Cunard Line had always been "Speed, Comfort, and Safety," and while as long as old Sir Samuel—he was knighted in 1862 by a grateful Queen Victoria in recognition of the sterling service his ships had given the Empire during the Crimean War—was alive, the emphasis was always on the latter. It was a point of commendable pride with him that his company could declare with complete honesty that, "The Cunard has never lost a life."

Certainly that wasn't a claim the other steamship lines could make: the Inman Line, for example, while not discernably negligent, suffered losses of ships and lives in the first quarter-century of its existence that would have made Edward Collins blush. The first loss, of course, was the *City of Glasgow*, vanishing with all 480 of its passengers and crew in March 1854, followed by the loss of the *City of Philadelphia* six months later; fortunately no lives were lost when she was wrecked off Newfoundland. Ten years would pass before another disaster befell an Inman ship: in 1864 the *City of New York* was wrecked, but fortune still smiled on Inman, as again, all of her passengers and crew survived. The next year the *Glasgow* burned at sea; a passing steamer was able to safely take off everyone aboard her. The *City of Boston* sank off the coast of Ireland in 1870, taking 177 lives with her; the *City of Washington* was written off as a total loss three years later. It seemed that the Inman Line's run of bad luck was over, but when the *City of Brussels* was wrecked in the River Mersey on January 7, 1883, ten crewmen lost their lives, and the financial losses would finally become so severe that Inman would be forced to sell out to the American International Navigation Company.

The Guion Line had a similar unfortunate history of losing ships, although it wasn't as marred by loss of life. The company was formed in 1866 by Stephen Guion, an American citizen living and working in England, as the Liverpool & Great Western Steamship Company Limited, and it immediately settled into the Liverpool to New York via Queenstown route. The company named most of its ships after American states, and built a fleet of fast ships that were soon making crossings of the North Atlantic in less than seven days. But two years after the Guion Line began service, the *Chicago* was wrecked near

Queenstown, in January 1868. The *Colorado* sank after a collision with the *Arabian* in the River Mersey in December 1873—this time six lives were lost, the only fatalities ever suffered by the Guion Line. In May 1877, the *Dakota* came to grief on the Welsh coast at Anglesey, while the year after that the *Idaho* was wrecked on the Irish coast, and the *Montana* ran aground at Anglesey, North Wales in March 1880, near the spot where the *Dakota* had met a similar fate. While salvage crews were able to re-float her, she was a total loss and had to be scrapped. The cumulative effect of these losses was to create a burden of debt which the company could never overcome, and in 1896 the Guion Line would dissolve in bankruptcy.

But all of this was in the future when the true end of an era overtook the Cunard Line in 1865. In late March Sir Samuel Cunard suddenly took ill, and on April 28 he died. His had been an amazing career spanning seven decades, in which he had gone from serving as an apprentice in his father's shipyard to forming and directing the first successful regular transatlantic steamship service, ultimately guiding it to the position where it was the most reliable passenger line on the North Atlantic, and in the process, earning a baronetcy in recognition of the service his ships had performed for the British Empire.

With Sir Samuel's passing, the Chairmanship of the line devolved onto George Burns, who was soon to be created a baronet in his own right, and his son, also named George, who would become the first Lord Inverclyde. The elder George Burns was an almost stereotypical Scot: cautious, conservative and canny. While not always as conservative as Cunard had been—when Sir Samuel refused to abandon the paddlewheel in favor of the screw, which Burns quickly accepted as a vastly superior means of moving a ship, the row between the two men had been spectacular—he was perfectly content to generally follow the unpretentious policies that Sir Samuel had set down. It's difficult to fault him, as the success of not only the *Persia*, *Scotia* and *Russia*, but also the more modest members of the Cunard fleet was sustaining the line: where the more ambitious steamship companies were falling into debt and sometimes dissolution due to the cost of the amenities they offered, Cunard always found a way to turn a profit, always able to pay respectable—and sometimes handsome—dividends to its shareholders.

But conservatism can sometimes lead to inflexibility, which develops an inertia all its own, and in turn becomes stagnation. Such a fate was about to befall Cunard, and it couldn't have arrived at a worse time, for a new name was about to make itself known on the North Atlantic run. It was a steamship company whose name, reputation, and stature would soon come to rival that of Cunard's, before it was eclipsed in disaster. That new rival was the White Star Line.

CHAPTER SIX

White Star Rising

The name "White Star Line" first appeared in 1845, when two Boston businessmen, Henry Threlfall Wilson and John Pilkington, formed the White Star Line of Boston Packets. The name was slightly misleading, for the new company owned no packets at all, but rather a single ship, a barque called the *Iowa*. Equally odd was the fact that Pilkington and Wilson advertised their shipping firm in the Liverpool newspapers: at the time the White Star company only served a handful of ports along the eastern American seaboard. Whatever shortcomings they may have suffered over geography, the two men were certainly competent businessmen, for within five years the line had become profitable enough for them to begin casting about for other routes to which they could expand their service, the only question being where.

The issue was decided when gold was discovered in Australia in 1850. The resulting outbreak of "gold fever" rivaled the California Gold Rush, and soon thousands of fortune hunters were clamoring for transportation "down under." This was the perfect opportunity for the five-year-old White Star Line of Boston Packets, and the company put their ships into the Australian trade, building a small fleet of clippers that included the *Ellen*, the *White Star*, and the legendary *Red Jacket*, and in 1852 the company's name was changed to the White Star Line of Australian Packets. The clippers maintained a route between Liverpool and Melbourne, carrying would-be prospectors and adventurers to the goldfields, and returning to Britain laden with wool, whale oil, sealskins, and gold. In 1863 Pilkington left the company and his place was taken by James Chambers, who introduced steamships to the White Star Line, beginning with a ship called the *Royal Standard*. It should have been a masterstroke, for the *Royal Standard* cut the passage time to Australia to under 70 days, better than even the fastest clipper could do.

It didn't work out the way Wilson and Chambers had planned, though: White Star joined forces with two packet companies, the Black Ball and Eagle Lines, to form the Australian and Eastern Navigation Company Ltd in 1864, but financial problems plagued the new conglomerate. The company went seriously in debt while trying to enlarge its fleet. In 1866 the company's assets were then taken over by the Royal Bank of Liverpool, but when the bank failed in October 1867, White Star was forced into bankruptcy, having an outstanding debt of £527,000. In January 1868 Thomas Henry Ismay, a thirty-one year old shipowner from Liverpool, bought the line for £1000.

Ismay had been a partner in the shipping firm of Nelson, Ismay & Company, and had been keeping an eye on the White Star Line for some time. An informal business relationship had developed between the two companies as they frequently cooperated in expediting each other's shipments, allowing both to prosper. When mismanagement caused White Star to founder, Ismay saw his chance: he was shrewd enough to realize that, rewarding as the Australian trade had become, there were far greater profits to be made in the transatlantic passenger service, bringing emigrants from the Old World to the New and shuttling wealthier passengers back and forth between the two. When White Star was offered for sale he moved quickly to acquire it, and renamed it The Oceanic Steam Navigation Company. He kept the house flag, a red swallowtail burgee sporting a single large white star, and the company continued to be known to the public as the White Star Line.

Almost immediately Ismay set about creating a niche for the White Star by drawing up plans for liners that would be fast, and by the standards of the day, extraordinarily luxurious. In 1870, Ismay formed a partnership with William Imrie, and created a holding company called Ismay, Imrie and Company. One of their first business transactions was to contract with the Belfast shipyard of Harland and Wolff to build a fleet of iron steamships for the White Star Line. It was to be a happy union.

The origins of Harland and Wolff dated back to the 1840s, when the dredging of a deep-water passage in the section of the River Lagan known as the Victoria Channel, created Queen's Island in the middle of the channel. Robert Hickson built a shipyard on the new island and began the construction of iron ships there in 1853. Edward J. Harland came to the yard, then known as Hickson and Company, as a manager in 1854 and bought it outright from Hickson in 1859. Gustav Wolff was a silent partner when he first joined Harland in 1861, but by 1862 the yard was known as Harland and Wolff.

Gustav Wolff was the nephew of Gustavus Schwabe, a Hamburg financier who had relocated to Liverpool some years before. It was Schwabe who had loaned Harland the £5,000 he needed to buy Hickson's shipyard, and because Schwabe also owned a substantial interest in the Bibby Line, a small North Atlantic steamship company, he was in a position to assure himself that his investment in Harland paid off: of the more than 1,500 orders for ships on Harland and Wolff's books in the yard's 140-year history, the first three were for ships for the Bibby Line.

While it was true that being the nephew of Gustavus Schwabe had much to do with Harland's decision to take Wolff on as a partner, the yard itself bore the unmistakable stamp of one man only—Edward Harland. His talent for engineering, which bordered on genius, led Harland to make three lasting contributions to shipbuilding. One was purely aesthetic, but the other two were revolutionary. First, he eliminated the unnecessary clutter of sailing ships from steamship design: bowsprits, jib booms, figureheads, and their associated rigging. This made the ships cleaner and more distinctive in appearance. Next, he squared off the bilges on the ships' hulls, at once making them more efficient cutting through the water, so that engine size would not have to be increased to increase speed, and also enlarged the carrying capacity of any given hull size. Finally, he replaced wooden upper decks with decks of iron. This turned the hull into a giant box girder of immense strength, allowing far larger hulls than ever before, to be built.

Curiously enough, Ismay was able to buy the White Star Line because of financial assistance he received from the same Gustavus Schwabe who had backed Edward Harland. It was a carefully calculated move on Schwabe's part, similar to what he had done with the Bibby Line, as it protected his investment in the shipyard, for hardly had Ismay acquired White Star than he realized that the line would need an entirely new fleet of ships for the transatlantic service. As he prepared the specifications for a quartet of new liners, he was shrewd enough to throw out conventional ideas of shipboard accommodation and passenger comfort. The White Star Line would establish a new standard of luxury at sea when it introduced the new ships, giving Ismay a head start in the looming race between British, German, and American shipping lines, to build faster, more comfortable ships for the North Atlantic run. It would also lay the foundation for White Star's reputation for unrivaled elegance, which the line would not relinquish for another half a century.

Thomas Ismay, who transformed the White Star Line from an Australian immigrant carrier into the paragon of luxury on the North Atlantic.

The first White Star vessel ordered from Harland & Wolff was the *Oceanic*, her name an allusion to the line's corporate name. Launched on August 27, 1870, the *Oceanic* was the first of four nearly identical sisters. The next was the *Atlantic*, launched three months after the *Oceanic*, and was followed in quick succession by the *Baltic* and *Republic*. All-steel construction did not become standard in the shipbuilding industry until the mid-1880s, so all four were constructed almost entirely of iron. The *Oceanic* was a large ship for her day, 420 feet long and displacing just over 3,700 tons. With her unparalleled accommodations and stunning appearance—"more like an imperial yacht than a passenger liner" wrote one observer — the *Oceanic,* in a stroke, established the White Star Line as the arbiter

The Oceanic, *the White Star Line's first ship built for the North Atlantic run, whose appearance transformed passenger lines.*

of comfort on the North Atlantic, and in both appearance and amenities set the standard for all the White Star ships to follow. Lying long and low in the water, sporting a straight stem, a single, gracefully raked funnel, and four hollow cylindrical iron masts, the *Oceanic* and her sisters made their contemporaries look positively dowdy by comparison. Their staterooms were larger and brighter than those of any other ship, and were equipped with electric bells for summoning stewards; taps for hot and cold running water (fresh or salt) instead of the traditional pitcher and basin; lighting came from adjustable oil lamps instead of guttering candles (an experimental system of gas lighting was quickly replaced when it was found that the lines leaked when the ship flexed in heavy seas); and each cabin was provided with steam heat.

By the summer of 1871 the quartet of ships was complete, as in quick succession three identical sisters, the *Atlantic, Baltic,* and *Republic,* were added to the White Star fleet. That same year two more ships of slightly higher gross tonnage, the *Celtic* and *Adriatic,* were ordered. Originally, the *Celtic* was to be named the *Arctic,* but when it was recalled that the Collins Line steamer with that name had been sunk in 1854 with a terrible loss of life, White Star reconsidered the idea, and chose *Celtic* instead (all White Star ships had names ending in *-ic*).

All these ships were constructed by Harland and Wolff, and soon the Belfast shipyard found itself the exclusive shipbuilder for the White Star Line. Building the finest ships possible, Harland and Wolff had an unusual "cost plus" agreement with the line, billing White Star for the expense of construction plus a fixed percentage for a profit. By all accounts this arrangement was eminently satisfactory, for while it assured White Star of ships built by a yard whose reputation for quality and probity were already becoming legendary, it guaranteed the shipyard a reasonable return for its investment in time, labor, and material.

This is not to say that the *Oceanic* was an immediate, unqualified success, however well constructed: on her maiden voyage, departing Liverpool on March 2, 1871, she developed problems with an engine bearing, and her sailing had to be postponed by two weeks. A few months in service revealed a number of shortcomings, which White Star moved quickly to correct. From the first she was a very "wet" ship forward, with a propensity for shipping large amounts of water over her foredeck in even moderate seas—her forecastle was enlarged and a breakwater added to keep the front of the ship relatively dry in rough weather. Steam pressure was raised and two boilers added to increase the power of her engines, while her masts were shortened to cut down her top-weight and reduce her tendency to roll—a habit that her passengers hardly found endearing. Similar modifications were also made to the *Oceanic*'s sisters.

Several features introduced on the *Oceanic* proved so popular that they immediately became the standards for transatlantic liners. She was the first ship which had the first class accommodation placed amidships instead of aft, which allowed for larger cabins. She also introduced a covered promenade deck that ran the length of the superstructure, and at the same time did away with the old solid bulwarks that lined the upper decks, with open railings replacing them. This gave the *Oceanic* and her sisters a sleeker, less ponderous look, one that was instantly copied by every new ship then being built. The last significant innovation was found in her dining saloons, where the old bench seats were replaced by individual chairs for each passenger.

While the *Oceanic* was an immediate commercial success, she would never be a record-breaker—that was a distinction that went to the *Adriatic*, which took the Blue Ribband on her maiden voyage in May 1872, with an average speed of 14.41 knots. The following January the *Baltic* made a Blue Ribband crossing with an average speed of over 15 knots, the first time that such a sustained speed had been achieved. The public's response was overwhelming, and the demand for passage on White Star ships soon exceeded their capacity.

The old adage that imitation is the sincerest form of flattery has never held truer anywhere on earth than on the North Atlantic. The first company to copy the best features of Ismay's ships was the Inman Line, working hard to move out from under the shadow cast by the disappearance of the *City of Boston*, a shadow that lengthened when the *City of Washington* ran aground on the coast of Nova Scotia near Point Sable in 1873. However, as Inman had carried more than a half-million passengers across the Atlantic in the previous twenty years, a strong reservoir of public confidence in the company still existed, so Inman resolved to order a steamer to be called the *City of Berlin* from the Greenock yard of Caird and Company. The ship the Clydebank builder delivered was a remarkably beautiful vessel: with a clipper bow, a long, low hull that swept up into a counter stern, and topped by a compact superstructure set squarely amidships with a single funnel and three masts. In appearance, the *City of Berlin* combined the grace of a clipper with the power of a steamship. She was the first of a succession of Inman ships whose aesthetics would never be surpassed, and only equaled when the White Star Line introduced the *Olympic* class thirty-five years later.

That the *City of Berlin* was as fast as she was beautiful was proven when, six months after she entered service in September 1875, she took the Blue Ribband away from White Star's *Adriatic,* with a Liverpool to New York crossing of seven days, fifteen hours, averaging almost 15½ knots. The Inman Line, which had been built around serving the emigrant trade - the *City of Berlin* remained true to her company origins, for while she had accommodation for 202 First Class passengers, she could carry no less than 1,500 in steerage—suddenly found itself the most popular line on the North Atlantic, proving that a large portion of the traveling public would always follow the fast ships, regardless of which house flag they flew.

Of course, Inman's prospects were given a considerable boost by the fact that White Star had gone into temporary eclipse. On the last day of March 1883, the *Atlantic* ran at full speed up onto the rocky coast of Nova Scotia, some twenty miles west of Halifax; 585 out of 952 passengers and crew aboard were lost. It was the worst maritime disaster of the 19th Century. The findings of the subsequent inquiry reflected poorly on White Star, as it was learned that the ship had been forced to divert to Halifax because she was running short of coal, and that her master had been asleep in his cabin at the time of the wreck, forgotten by the Fourth Officer who had been given orders to awaken the captain as the ship neared the Nova Scotian coast. An added grisly detail, though no fault of the White Star Line, was that scores of scavengers lining the shoreline, rather than aid the helpless victims who were drowning within sight of land, systematically looted and plundered the dead and dying. The story was a newspaper sensation for months.

The loss of the *Atlantic* was a setback for that the White Star Line struggled to move beyond for more than a year, though the company gradually recovered its popularity. Building on the success of the *Oceanic* and her surviving sisters, as well as the hugely popular *Adriatic* and *Celtic*, Ismay ordered a pair of new 5,000-ton ships from Harland and Wolff in 1874, the *Britannic* and *Germanic*, both capable of reaching 19 knots and crossing the Atlantic in less than seven and a half days. They were also an unabashed attempt to regain the Blue Ribband for the White Star Line. It was, appropriately enough, the *Germanic* which took the prize from the *City of Berlin*, making a record east-bound crossing at a speed of 15¾ knots in February 1876. The *Britannic* then took the honors on the westbound route in June that same year, giving the White Star Line the first record-holding "pair" of liners in the history of the North Atlantic ferry. They would routinely trade the speed record between themselves for the next three years.

As a result, during those years the White Star Line's dominance of the North Atlantic went uncontested. Cunard was caught in the grip of a corporate and technological lethargy it couldn't seem to shake off, the Inman Line had run into financial problems and was unable to repeat the success of the *City of Berlin*, and the two German companies, Hamburg-Amerika and Norddeutscher-Lloyd, were still very much in the second rank among Atlantic steamship lines. The challenge, when it finally came in 1879, was from an entirely unexpected quarter; the hitherto conservative Guion Line, a Liverpool-based, American-owned company that had its origins in the old Black Star Line of sailing packets in the 1840s.

The challenger was named the *Arizona*. The Guion Line took a page from the Inman book, and frankly imitated White Star's *Britannic* and *Germanic* when they built the *Arizona*, much as the *City of Berlin* had copied the *Oceanic* and her sisters. The ships even looked alike, with straight stemmed bows, counter sterns, a four mast barque rig and two closely spaced funnels; even the *Arizona*'s dimensions and displacement were all but identical to those of the famous White Star pair. What set her apart was her machinery and engines: seven boilers with thirty-nine furnaces fed steam to a compound engine driving three crankshafts which generated a then-awesome 6,300 horsepower. She made a top speed of well over 17 knots on her trials, then proved that was no quirk when she went into service in the summer of 1879. Within two months she captured the Blue Ribband with a crossing that averaged just a shade under 16 knots.

However, the *Arizona*'s speed played only an incidental part in the liner's most memorable moment in the spotlight. In November 1879, homeward bound from New York, she ran into a dense fog in the Grand Banks off Newfoundland, and moments later smashed headlong into an iceberg. Her forward collision bulkhead held, and she was able to limp into Halifax, where the sight of her crushed and crumpled bow drew stares of disbelief. A false wooden bow was hastily fabricated and fitted, and the *Arizona* then stormed across to Liverpool in six days and seven hours. The subsequent inquiry held her captain to be at fault, but perversely, the accident made the *Arizona* the single most popular ship on the North Atlantic: the incident seemed to confirm the invulnerability of iron hulls to damage that would have shivered a wooden hulled ship. Guion promptly capitalized on this perception by advertising the *Arizona* as the "strongest and safest ship afloat!" It was the origin of a complacent delusion that would only be dispelled one cold April night thirty three years later....

Two years later, the *Arizona* acquired a running mate, the nearly identical *Alaska*, which became the first ship to make the crossing from New York to Liverpool in less than seven days. A year after that, an even larger ship, the *Oregon*, was built for Guion, but she only made a half dozen round trips between America and Great Britain as a Guion ship. Financial mismanagement forced her owners to return her to her builders in May of 1884, where an opportunistic Cunard line, seeking to add a Blue Ribband holder to its fleet, would snap her up.

In 1889 the White Star Line trumped every other shipping company on the North Atlantic by introducing the *Teutonic* and *Majestic*, enormous ships of nearly 10,000 tons each—more than twice the *Oceanic*'s displacement of less than twenty years before—with a designed speed of 20 knots, and every bit as handsome and sleek as their forebears. But these ships represented a point of departure for the White Star Line, as Ismay began to dramatically reshape the role the company would play on the North Atlantic.

The same year that the *Teutonic* and *Majestic* put to sea, Ismay's son, J. Bruce, entered the family business. Born in 1862, the younger Ismay was educated at Elstree and Harrow, though he never acquired a university degree. After the year-long "world tour" that was customary for young men of Ismay's social station in that day, he went to work for the White Star Line. His first day was to be an illuminating experience, highlighting as it did the elder Ismay's character as well as the nature of the relationship between father and son. Having left his hat and coat in his father's office, the younger Ismay was startled to hear his father, in a voice loud enough for everyone in the office to hear, tell a subordinate to instruct the new office boy to leave his hat and coat elsewhere. So dominating was Thomas Ismay's character, that despite his son's carefully cultivated air of arrogant self-assurance, which seemed to go hand-in-hand with his six-feet four-inch stature and handsome features, in truth, Bruce Ismay could never quite move out of his father's shadow to become his own man, or follow comfortably in his footsteps. It was a character flaw that one day would have dreadful consequences for the White Star Line.

Meanwhile, Thomas Ismay had taken a long, hard look at the North Atlantic passenger trade and concluded that it was becoming too expensive for White Star to continue to pursue unrivaled speed *and* unparalleled luxury. Of the two, Ismay decided, speed was ultimately more costly, because it was more perishable: today's Blue Ribband holder was tomorrow's also-ran. Amenities and accommodations within a ship could always be improved upon, while increasing a vessel's top speed was virtually impossible once she was completed. In the future then, the out-and-out race for the Blue Ribband would be run without the White Star Line. The line's ships would continue to be nearly as fast as its competitors', but since luxury had made White Star's reputation, it would be luxury that would continue as White Star's hallmark.

From the beginning, the challenge which White Star had thrown down to Cunard was unmistakable, and the company would let it go unanswered at its own risk. Cunard had actually begun the 1870s in fine style, when two new sister ships, the *Abyssinia* and the *Algeria*, went into service in May and September of 1870, respectively. Three hundred and sixty feet long, forty-two feet in beam, displacing 3,400 tons, they were large, comfortable ships. They were not quite identical, as the *Algeria* had accommodation for two hundred First Class passengers compared to the *Abyssinia*'s one hundred twenty, but both could carry almost eleven hundred passengers in Third Class. On February 2, 1870, the keel was laid for what was to be the Cunard fleet's finest ship yet; launched on September 10 that same year, she was christened the *Parthia*. Bearing strong resemblance to her immediate predecessors, the *Algeria* and the *Abyssinia*, the *Parthia* was flush-decked, had an open bridge, three square-rigged masts, and a single funnel.

Though she was actually slightly smaller than the *Algeria* and the *Abyssinia*, the *Parthia* had been designed to be a significant improvement over both. On the technical side, she was fitted with compound engines, which were considerably more powerful and efficient, and required only half the coal than the single-acting engines previously used on Cunard ships. The most notable feature of her passenger accommodations was that she was the first liner to come equipped with bathtubs—two of them—one each on the port and starboard sides of the berthing areas. She immediately proved to be very popular, and even though she was not quite as fast as the *Persia*, an admittedly curious circumstance, as the *Parthia* was screw-propelled and the *Persia* was driven by paddlewheels, Cunard's directors had every reason to believe they had three of the finest, most modern ships on the Atlantic run. But when the White Star Line introduced the *Oceanic*—which surpassed the *Parthia* in size as well as in comfort—in 1871, the entire Cunard fleet was outclassed.

Cunard's response was predictable. Though Sir Samuel had been gone for some years by this time, his dead hand still unquestionably had hold of the company's helm: in the closing years of Sir Samuel's life, the old man's devotion to the corporate motto, "Speed, Comfort and Safety," had gradually devolved to where only the latter of the three mattered to him, while the first two were becoming more and more important to the traveling public. Sir George Burns and David McIver, Samuel Cunard's original partners, were still alive and if not exactly kicking, were nonetheless able to exert a baleful influence on the company's policies: Burns had stepped into the chairmanship of the company when Cunard died, McIver working closely with him. At one point, not long after the *Oceanic* made her debut on the North Atlantic run, it was brought to McIver's attention that the service in the Cunard dining saloons was so sparse that it didn't even offer napkins for the passengers. McIver's response was to point out that going to sea was a hardship, and the company made no attempt to make it out to be anything other than that—if passengers wanted to wipe their mouths at dinner, they could use their pocket handkerchief!

The line's proudest boast was still "The Cunard has never lost a life," which was trotted out as the unchallengeable response whenever critics pointed out the disparity between the amenities offered by Cunard and the company's competitors, especially the White Star Line. But when White Star introduced the *Oceanic* and her sisters, that response began to look more than a little threadbare. Drastic measures would have to be taken if the company's luster was to ever be restored.

By 1880, they had been. Sir George Burns' son (also named George) succeeded him as chairman of the board, and at the same time the line underwent a radical change. The first step was to do away with the clumsy corporate moniker—the British and North American Royal Mail Steam Packet Company gave way to the Cunard Steam-Ship Company. There were more than just cosmetic changes, though, as next came a reorganization of the company's ownership. In the 1840s, Cunard, Burns and McIver had bought all of the outstand-

The first large ship built of steel and lit by electricity, the Servia *was the Cunard Line's first response to the White Star challenge.*

ing shares held by the company's original slate of junior partners; now the decision was made to raise the capital needed to build four new liners by putting £800,000 worth of those shares on the open market. They were snapped up within days, as investors, not as impressed by flash and fancy as the traveling public, still perceived Cunard as a solid investment.

The first fruit of these efforts was the *Servia*, launched in 1881. She was the first large ship on the North Atlantic built entirely of steel, the largest built since the *Great Eastern*, and the first ship to be lit by incandescent electric lamps. She was 510 feet long, with a beam of 52 feet and a displacement of 7,400 tons. Powered by three compound engines driving a single screw, she was capable of 16 knots—not a record breaker, but fast enough to be competitive with the White Star Line's best ships. What distinguished the *Servia* was an undefinable but unmistakable air of comfort that she wore: spacious, quiet, handsomely decorated—she had the most impressive grand staircase yet seen on a steamship—and with none of the frantic bustle that seemed to accompany so many of her competitors. A running mate, the *Aurania*, entered service two years later, and when they were joined by a trio of smaller but equally appealing ships, the *Pavonia*, *Catalonia* and *Cephalonia*, all three dedicated to the recently-revived Liverpool to Boston run, the company was ready to battle for pride of place again on the North Atlantic. Within their first year of service, all five ships proved to be money-makers for Cunard, and before long the company decided that it could afford to make an outright bid to take the Blue Ribband. This led to one of the more bizarre episodes in the company's history, the purchase of the *Oregon* from the Guion Line.

When she was launched in the spring of 1883, the *Oregon* was the largest steamer on the North Atlantic: 520 feet long, with a beam of 54 feet, although at 7,375 tons her displacement was slightly less than the *Servia* and *Aurania*. She was spectacularly fast for her day, with a designed speed of 18 knots. She wasted no time in proving her capabilities: on her third crossing from Liverpool to New York, in November 1883, she took the Blue Ribband from her half-sister *Alaska*, and five months later, in April 1884, she took the eastbound record as well.

But that was her last voyage as a Guion liner: the *Arizona* and *Alaska* were expensive ships to operate (their machinery installations were so large that they left comparatively little room for steerage accommodations) and the line found itself unable to afford to keep three ships in service. In order to reduce their burden of debt, her owners returned the *Oregon* to her builders, Fairfield Shipbuilding and Engineering, in May 1884. Cunard, seeing an opportunity to instantly enter the Blue Ribband stakes, bought her a month later.

The *Oregon* proved to be as popular in service with Cunard as she had been with Guion, breaking even her previous records on subsequent crossings. For Cunard it had been an inexpensive investment—her selling price of £616,000 was only half of her original cost—and it proved money well spent, not only for the attention the *Oregon* garnered for the line, but also in what the line learned from her popularity. She had accommodations for 340 first class, 92 second class, and 1,110 steerage class passengers. She was built with extensive watertight subdivision below the waterline, and lit entirely by electricity (electric lighting had been introduced on Cunard ships with the *Servia*, but there had been many areas in the ship, particularly in steerage, that were still illuminated by oil lamps). The grand saloon of the *Oregon* was sixty-five feet in length and fifty feet in width, stunningly illuminated by a stained-glass dome twenty feet in height. The floor was covered by parquet, the walls paneled in satinwood, and the pillars carved and turned from walnut. This elegance was continued throughout the ship: her interior was fitted with elaborate, expensive furnishings and ornate woodwork made of virgin timber from the state of Oregon.

Curiously enough, Cunard retained the liner's original name—which, as events turned out, would work to the company's benefit—while the cachet of having the fastest ship on the North Atlantic brought Cunard squarely back into the center of public attention. It was a fortunate coincidence, for as events would have it, the *Oregon* wasn't destined to remain in service with Cunard for long.

In the early morning darkness of March 14, 1886, near the Fire Island Light off Long Island, carrying 896 passengers and crew, the *Oregon* was rammed by a schooner that suddenly loomed out of the night and then disappeared again. Though she was never positively identified, it is commonly believed that the schooner was the *Charles H. Morse*, a three-masted coaster out of Maine. If that was so, the encounter was fatal for the *Morse*, for she was never seen again.

The collision created three large holes below the *Oregon*'s waterline, causing flooding in both of her boiler rooms. The watertight doors wouldn't close and the ship began to slowly fill.

The officers quickly mustered the passengers in the upper deck and started loading them into the lifeboats. In an ugly scene reminiscent of the disgrace aboard the Collins liner *Arctic*, the black gang suddenly came rushing up from below, and roughly shoved the officers and passengers aside, commandeering the first boats to get away from the sinking ship. But there were more than enough boats remaining, and the evacuation proceeded without further incident. The proximity to New York meant that help was not far off, and four hours after the collision a schooner, the *Fannie A. Gorham*, and the pilot boat *Phantom* appeared alongside the *Oregon* and began taking aboard the passengers from the lifeboats. About two hours after that, the Norddeutscher-Lloyd steamer *Fulda* arrived and relieved the smaller ships of the nearly 900 passengers and crew, and took them to New York. Meanwhile, the *Oregon* began settling bow first, her stern rising high out of the water as she slowly settled in 130 feet of water. While the loss of the *Oregon* was a blow for Cunard's plans for a three-ship express service across the Atlantic, the line's incredible run of luck continued, for the whole incident occurred without the loss of a single life. Nor did the company's prestige suffer, for by some perverse twist of public perception, while she was in service the *Oregon* was regarded as the premier ship of the Cunard Line, but when she was lost she was inseparably associated with the speedy, but badly mismanaged Guion Line.

The same month that Cunard acquired the *Oregon*, the line's two newest ships were launched—the *Umbria* and *Etruria*. Their design proved that, whatever her ultimate fate might have been, the purchase of the *Oregon* was nothing more than a stopgap measure taken until Cunard's own fully-realized replies to the White Star Line were ready. The two new ships also proved conclusively that Cunard has learned its lessons from White Star.

Built in the same yard that produced the *Oregon*, John Elder & Co. of Glasgow, the *Umbria* and *Etruria* were as alike as two peas in a pod. In size, they continued the trend of introducing ever-larger ships, being 520 feet in length and 57 feet in beam, with a displacement of 8,120 tons. They were powered by a complex set of three triple-cylinder compound engines connected to a single propeller shaft. Events would cause them to be the last single-screw ships in Cunard service.

In their appointments, the *Umbria* and *Etruria* became the epitome of transatlantic snobbishness for their day: they were the ships that ushered in the idea of the "floating hotel" on the North Atlantic. Outside, they could have easily been mistaken for one of White Star's ships, with their long, open fore-and after-decks, low superstructure and twin funnels placed amidships. Inside, they brought the essence and excess of the Victorian lifestyle to sea: stained glass cupolas and windows, overstuffed chairs and lounges covered in brocade and trimmed with tassels, heavy and heavily-carved tables and sideboards, velvet curtains and wall hangings, the inevitable piano in the music room, with an organ to keep it company, and the inescapable bric-a-brac tucked into every nook and cranny. Several of their staterooms were laid out *en suite* so that wealthy passengers with their families or entourage in tow could travel together. It was the beginning of a trend which would find its ultimate expression thirty years later in the *Aquitania*; the desire to bring the style and substance of an English country home aboard ship.

It was also the beginning of the era of the professional passenger, ushered in by Thomas Cook. The story of the Thomas Cook organization began in June 1841 with a 32-

year old cabinet-maker from Market Harborough, near Leicester. Thomas Cook, a religious man who believed that most of the social ills of Victorian Britain could be cured if the working classes drank less and were better educated, arranged for a "day trip" for about five hundred passengers on the Midland Railway Company for a shilling each, an event that was a great success. During the next three summers Cook arranged similar trips between Leicester, Nottingham, Derby and Birmingham, allowing thousands of people their first experience of traveling by railroad.

By the end of 1850, Cook had organized trips to Wales, Scotland and Ireland; in 1855 Cook seized the opportunity presented by the Paris International Exhibition to set up a "grand circular tour" that began and ended in London, and included stops in Brussels, Cologne, the Rhine, Heidelberg, Baden-Baden, Strasbourg and Paris. Europe had seen its first "tourists." Tours of Switzerland began in June 1863, in Italy in the summer of 1864.

The people comprising these tour groups now came mainly from the rapidly-growing middle class, and so expected better accommodation than the working-class customers with which Cook had begun his business. He set out to provide his clientele with the best possible inns and hotels at reasonable prices, and as these clients were the very embodiment of middle-class respectability, the innkeepers and proprietors were happy to have his business. The relationships that Cook formed with these businessmen allowed him to introduce two important innovations to international travel: the hotel coupon, introduced in 1868, which was used by Cook's customers to settle hotel and meals bills in place of cash; and his "circular note," first issued in 1874, a primitive form of traveler's check.

Building on his successes in Europe, Cook then moved beyond Europe in 1865, setting up tours which covered over 4,000 miles of railway in the United States and Canada. Four years later, he chartered two steamers and sponsored the first Nile river cruises. At this point his own personal travels became so frequent that his son, John Mason Cook, essentially took over the operations of the business, and did so with such a degree of success that by 1878 Thomas Cook left the company entirely. John expanded the business international interests even further, publishing a newspaper about the services it offered, *The Excursionist*, in such far off places as France, Germany, America, the Far East, India, and Australia. So thorough were the arrangements which the company made that a traveler merely had to provide one of Cook's agents with his preferred itinerary, and the company would see to all of the details, from purchasing rail and steamer tickets to booking accommodations and guides to providing food and beverages in places where the local offerings might be considered unsuitable.

Probably the best example of Cook's capable ability to organize came in 1884, when the British Government asked Cook to organize the supply of a relief column of troops to be sent up the Nile to rescue General Charles Gordon from the city of Khartoum in the Sudan. Ultimately, arrangements were made for moving and supplying 18,000 troops, an effort that required nearly 40,000 tons of supplies, 40,000 tons of coal and 800 whaleboats, carried a distance of 1700 miles through some of the most unforgiving desert terrain on earth, using the carrying capacity of twenty-eight large river steamers and 13,000 railway cars. Although Khartoum was destined to fall, and Gordon to be killed three days before the relief column arrived in January 1885, so thorough were Cook's arrangements that only a single British soldier was lost through lack of proper supply.

It was this sort of organizational resource that now brought thousands of Englishmen and their wives and children to the United States beginning in the 1880s, to observe how the quaint and rustic Americans lived. Clearly, they lived quite well, having given up their log cabins and buckskins for all of the civilized amenities that Europeans took for granted, and had prospered sufficiently to be able to send droves of their own families eastward across the Atlantic for summer holidays, it having become the popular notion that a season spent in Europe was culturally and socially edifying for the children of socially prominent, and socially ambitious families. Consequently, in the 1880s the steamship business, in all classes, was booming.

If this was the era of the professional passenger, it was also the golden age of the ocean liner's captain. In a few short years the wireless would suddenly permit the home office to be able to stay in constant contact—some captains would have said "constant interference"—with him, depriving him in some small but discernable degree of the absolute autonomy that had been a master's privilege and provenance since man first put to sea. But in the last two decades of the 19th Century, that authority was still unsullied and undiminished, and the captain was a figure of some certain mystique and awe to the majority of his passengers. Their appeal came from what one of their number once described as a combination of "great seamanship, ruthless conservatism, blasphemy and strange inarticulate warmth." From the mysteries of taking a noon sighting from the bridge, fiddling with his sextant and dividers to work out a position and course, to the way he would walk the deck in the worst weather without misplacing a step, seemed nothing short of arcane to most passengers.

His was a dual role, for not only was the captain the master of his ship, responsible for every decision made regarding the ship's navigation, speed, and safety, he was also the social arbiter of his passenger list. A ship at sea is a community—in the 19th Century it was a small kingdom: under British law, the master of a British-registered ship carried the same legal authority and jurisdiction as a magistrate, with the power to perform marriages (though far fewer took place than romantic imaginations would like to believe), issue a death certificate should someone aboard expire in the course of a crossing, or place a passenger or crewman in irons if he believed it necessary for the safety of the ship. He also had a far more ephemeral, but equally intimidating power as well—social reputations could be made or broken by the reception a captain gave his passengers.

An invitation to dine at the captain's table was sought by every First Class passenger. Often wealthy businessmen and members of the aristocracy took it as their due, while less well-known travelers hoped that they would, in some way, come to the master's attention and earn an invitation. To be invited to dine with the Captain implied that a person was someone of note, and worthy of the other passengers' attention. Certainly more than one social career, as well as business and financial career, was given a boost by a seat at a captain's table.

Many of them found this dual role to be a burden; while the duties of a ship's master were gladly accepted—that was the life they had chosen—those of shipboard social patriarch were particularly taxing. One captain, whose disdain for passengers was matched only by his skill as a seaman, would solve the dinner guest dilemma by taking his place in the dining saloon on the first day out of port, then loudly instructing the stewards to remove the rest of the chairs about the table. Another, who would later rise to become Commodore of the Cunard Line, recalled that on every crossing there would be at least one passenger who would ask the same four questions: "Does Cunard pay for your uniforms? What time do you get up in the morning? Do you know a reliable tailor in London? Why are the deck lights left burning all day?" (He was known to reply to this last, with a perfectly straight face, that it was in case they passed through a tunnel.) Another Cunard skipper who began his career in the last decade of the 19th Century and was known among his peers as "'Aughty Bill," was once peremptorily ordered by a female passenger sitting in a deck chair to take away her tray. Suddenly becoming very erect and proper, the captain loudly asked her, "And just what the deuce do you suppose, madame, that the Captain looks like?"

Perhaps the most memorable was the captain, known for suffering fools not at all (a common characteristic among his colleagues), who had a prepared recitation that he would gleefully deliver in an ever-accelerating and increasingly loud voice to any over-inquisitive passenger, declaiming:

> I have crossed the Atlantic four hundred and twenty-two times this will be my four hundred and twenty-third I have not been shipwrecked or cast away on a desert island or been burnt at sea or marooned or shanghaied or caught by sharks and I don't want to be the ship is doing fifteen knots and could do more if she were going faster you will be able to go ashore as soon as we are alongside the jetty and not before and if you have anything you want to smuggle I don't want to know about it and I don't know the best way to get it ashore without paying duty I hope to retire from the sea some day *Is there anything else you would like to know?*

That they were a breed apart is indisputable. Their sometime irascibility was matched by their superb seamanship. Their stamina was legendary: Commodore Bertram Hayes once spent sixty-nine consecutive hours on the bridge of the *Majestic* as she negotiated her way through one of the worst fogs ever encountered. When in a fogbank, a captain would remain on the bridge until the ship steamed into clear weather: he would perch himself on a swivel chair mounted on one of the bridge wings, and focusing all of his concentration, would listen for the faint murmur of water swishing against a hull, the barely-perceptible thumping of engines, or sometimes for something as obscure as the rattle of an anchor chain to warn him of an unseen ship lurking ahead. At times they even seemed to sense the presence of another vessel, abruptly giving helm or engine orders that made no sense until a black painted hull suddenly loomed out of the mist on what would have been a collision course.

And then there were the moments that called for nerves of iron. One dark night off the Grand Banks of Newfoundland, William Murdoch, the First Officer of the White Star Line's *Oceanic*, was surprised to hear the second officer call for hard turn to port—the man had seen the running lights of a fishing trawler almost dead ahead. Just as the quartermaster began to spin the ship's wheel, Murdoch shouldered him aside and held the helm steady—he had seen the masts and running lights of a square-rigged ship off the *Oceanic*'s port bow, and a turn would have carried the liner straight into her. For a tense minute, Murdoch held the *Oceanic* on her course, running down through the narrow ribbon of open water between the two vessels. Once they were safely clear, Murdoch ordered both the men on the bridge not to breathe a word of what had almost happened.

Of course, not every such incident had such a fortunate ending, and it was with dismaying frequency that the morning watch would find a cluster of spars and tackle-blocks strewn across a liner's foredeck, the only memento of an unseen, unheard encounter in the night between a becalmed fishing trawler and a speeding liner. The trawler, of course, would never be heard from again. No one would ever know how many such incidents there were, for unless the victim left some evidence behind of its passing, there would rarely be any witnesses to such an encounter, the crunch of the fishing boat's splintering hull drowned out by the noise of the liner's pounding engines, the cries and screams of the doomed crew swallowed up in the wake of the bigger ship. For decades the Grand Banks fishermen cursed the "ram you, damn you" liners that cut across their fishing grounds and blindly ran them down in the night.

Such accidents, tragic as they were, had become inevitable—these were the days before radar, before wireless, before any form of communication—save for signal flags and Morse lamps which would have been of only limited utility—that might have given the liners warning of the presence of a flotilla of fishing boats ahead. The increasing number of ships that were crossing the Atlantic every week simply increased the likelihood of such incidents: an advertisement in the New York Times for May 25 and 26, 1887, illustrates just how extensive was Cunard's service alone. It also gives an excellent idea of the cost of traveling across the Atlantic in the late 1880s.

Cunard Line
New-York to Liverpool via Queenstown.
From Pier 40 North River
Fast Express Mail Service
Etruria.... Saturday, May 28, 9 A.M.
Aurania.... Saturday, June 4, 4 P.M.

Umbria.... Saturday, June 11, 9 A.M.

Servia..... Saturday, June 18, 3 P.M.

Service from Boston to Liverpool

Sailing Thursdays,

Catalonia.... June 23, July 28, Sept 1, Oct. 6

Pavonia.... May 26, June 30, Aug. 4, Sept. 8

Cephalonia.... June 9, July 14, Aug. 18, Sept. 22

Scythia.... June 16, July 21, Aug. 25, Sept. 29

Bothnia.... June 2, July 17, Aug. 11, Sept. 15

Cabin passage, $60, $80, and $100; Intermediate, $35.

Steerage tickets to and from all parts of Europe at very low rates.

For freight and passage apply to the company's office,

99 State St., Boston, or 4 Bowling Green, New-York.

Vernon H. Brown & Co., General Agents

A sailing day in the last decade of the 19th century was an unforgettable event. The weekday that saw the greatest number of departures was Saturday, which was favored by Cunard, the French Line, the Anchor Line, Holland-America Line, and Norddeutscher-Lloyd, whose ships also sailed on Tuesdays and Thursdays, while Hamburg-Amerika favored just Thursday, in addition to Saturday sailings. The American, the Red Star, and the White Star Lines sailed on Wednesday. The amount of ceaseless activity and noisy bustle—almost a sort of controlled chaos—that always surrounded a ship in port was amazing, and peaked as she prepared for departure.

On a ship such as the *Etruria*, for example, making ready to sail from Liverpool, the first and most obvious sign that she was coming to life was the black smoke that would begin rising from her funnels into the early morning sky, as one by one her boilers were relit and steam was raised. After a few hours, the hull would begin to almost imperceptibly tremble as her machinery was warmed up and tested. For the better part of the preceding six days, her boiler and engine rooms had been the site of an astonishing amount of hard work that had to be repeated each and every time the *Etruria* crossed the Atlantic.

Earlier that week, as soon as the ship tied up at the dock in Liverpool, her engines were stopped, the fires in the grates drawn, and the main boilers allowed to cool. One or two small donkey boilers would then be fired to provide steam for working the ship (hence the term "donkey" boiler) while the passengers' baggage was unloaded, along with the cargo. As soon as the main boilers reached a workable temperature—which could still be well over one hundred degrees Fahrenheit—more than three hundred men set to work cleaning scale from the interior surfaces of the boiler casings, replacing worn fire-grates, dumping ash and clinkers, and working on the engines. Two thirds of them were crewmen, the rest were dockside laborers hired for the task. Cleaning out the interior of the boilers took two to three days during which time the engineers would begin stripping the engines. Bearings were separated, cleaned, and if need be, replaced, while spindle-guides and connecting rods were trued, coupler flanges realigned, and crosshead-gibs tightened.

While the "black gang" worked on the boilers and engines below decks, the crew of the navigating department, sixty quartermasters, trimmers, able bodied seamen, and ordinary seamen, went to work topside. Decks would be scrubbed, spots of rust on the superstructure scraped, primed and painted, and the hull touched up as necessary. Lamps and deck lights were checked and trimmed, rigging tightened, and various pieces of deck machinery and equipment—winches, ventilation fans, fair roller leads and capstans—given whatever attention they required. Brasswork was polished till it shone, and handrails buffed to a high luster. Overseeing all these tasks would be the ship's junior officers, or sometimes the bosun, the senior seaman among the crew, who would often take the opportunity to teach the younger officers some of the finer points of not only caring for the ship, but also dealing with the crew.

And while all this is going on, some 15,000 pieces of linen—sheets, pillowcases, tablecloths, napkins and dish covers—were taken ashore where they were laundered and pressed, to be brought aboard again ready for use in four days time. It was a task that required a special laundry with a permanent staff of forty men and women. The fresh linen, carefully folded, would be stored ashore until the ship had finished coaling.

A ship the size of the 7,800-ton *Etruria* would require some twenty-four hundred tons of coal for the seven-day run across the Atlantic, and bringing it on board was the single, most unpleasant task performed during a turn-around. Within hours of the last passenger's departure, every vent cowl, window, door, air louver and aperture opening to the outside would be closed and covered in canvas. Then the ship's carpenter and his assistants would go over the sides and undo the bolts—usually between eight and twelve each—that held the covers in place over the coaling ports. There were a dozen such ports in each side of the *Etruria*; on later, larger ships such as the *Mauretania* or *Aquitania*, that number would double. The covers were hinged at the bottom so that they swung outward to act as chutes for the incoming coal.

As soon as all the coaling ports were open and ready, a succession of coal barges would pull alongside both sides of the ship. Steam derricks mounted on the barges would lift great quarter-ton buckets of black bituminous coal into the chutes leading into the ship's bunkers, but there was always spillage, and inevitably a cloud of grey-black dust, gritty, foul-tasting and fine as talc, would gradually envelope the ship. Down below inside the bunkers, trimmers would be shoveling the coal away from the scuttles at the mouths of the loading chutes as rapidly as it descended, lest the incoming coal block the scuttles and then pile up into an immovable mass. On the decks, crewmen scurried back and forth to catch the worst of the spillage and reduce the damage done to the freshly scrubbed and cleaned decks and upperworks, to a minimum.

After the last bucket of coal had been brought aboard, the carpenter closed and resealed the covers on the coaling ports, and the clean-up began. For the deck crew it was a relatively easy task, for although almost every square inch of deck and superstructure would be covered with a fine, ash-like powder, it was readily hosed away, and within a few hours the ship was once again spotless. Inside the ship it was a different story. No matter how hard the stewards and stewardesses tried to block up doors, windows, ports, and vents, coal dust always seemed to find a way to get into the ship, and the next two days would be spent mopping, dusting, and sweeping the whole of the passenger accommodations and public rooms clean of the offending black powder.

Once coaling was complete, the process began of loading cargo, along with the provisions required for the crossing. The *Etruria* had some 1,500 tons of cargo space available, and as one of the fastest steamers on the North Atlantic, usually carried perishable goods along with cargoes that had the highest demand in the United States. In addition to the cargo, the steamer would carry up to ten tons of mail along with as many as 3,000 pieces of baggage. She had a capacity of 550 First Class, 160 Intermediate or Second Class, and 800 Third Class passengers, all of whom had specific limitations on the amount of baggage they could bring aboard. It's interesting to note that the limitations were on the space the baggage occupied rather than its weight. The First Class passengers were each allowed forty cubic feet of baggage, Second Class and Third Class twenty cubic feet each.

In many ways, a passenger ship had ceased to be just a mode of transportation and had acquired many of the features of a luxury hotel, in its size as well as its appointments, service, and cuisine. The passengers had to be fed, and providing their provisions was the responsibility of the shore steward. A "seven-day boat" would carry food and beverage for twelve days, while staple and non-perishable provisions for a month or more would be available in case of accident or delay.

When the ship docked, the Chief Steward would submit a list of requirements for the ship's larders and pantries, and the shore steward, who dealt with local suppliers, merchants, and mongers, placed the orders. In volume as well as value, such orders were considerably more extensive than those of hotels ashore, not only because the number of people to be served was larger than any hotel's guest list, but also, while hotels could place orders daily, the ship had to carry all of its provender with it. The competition for these orders was fierce, since there was a great deal of money at stake: the expenses of a single crossing by a vessel of the size the *Etruria* could run between £11,000 ($50,000) and £22,000 ($100,000), depending on the number of passengers.

On the bridge and at the stern, the officers and crew were busy checking mooring lines and gangways, testing engine and helm controls. Somewhere a Board of Trade inspector was nosing about, checking the lifeboats, lifebelts, signal rockets, and flares, determining that the ship did indeed, as her master would inevitably claim, fulfill every requirement of the Board's regulations. The "blue peter", the signal flown by a ship making ready to put to sea, was hoisted from the bridge, while the Stars and Stripes, the colors of the country of destination, were run up to fore-truck; at the main was the house flag, while the Red Duster, the ensign of the British Merchant Marine, flew at the jackstaff at the stern. (If the ship was under the command of an officer of the Royal Navy Reserve, the Blue Ensign of the RNR could be flown instead.)

All morning long passengers arrived at the pier, their carriages and cabs burdened with bags, rugs, and steamer trunks, along with all the accumulated trappings of ocean travel. Other carriages, wagons, and trucks milled about trying to complete last minute deliveries of foodstuffs, supplies and a surprising number of floral arrangements. Invariably there were gifts sent by some thoughtful individual to wish a friend "Bon Voyage", and some of them were amazingly elaborate pieces. They were delivered to the main saloon, where the stewards would then carry them to the recipients' staterooms. Later, as the passengers grew bored with them—or sometimes overwhelmed by the scent, often in the case of those inclined to seasickness—the stewards would be asked to dispose of the floral arrangements, who would then toss them over the side of the ship. Thoughtful stewards, however, would often save a spray of tea roses or a cluster of orchids and use them to decorate the dining saloon tables during mid-crossing.

Once deposited at the pier by whatever conveyance brought them, the First and Second Class passengers made their way aboard as quickly as possible, where friends were often waiting, and soon small knots of people were clustered about the ship, either on deck or in their cabins, wishing friends and family who were sailing "god speed and a safe voyage." In the meantime, their baggage was being brought aboard, anything tagged "NWV" ("Not Wanted on Voyage") being summarily hustled to the baggage holds, while the remainder was sorted by deck and cabin or berth number, to be brought along later, when the crowds of passengers, friends, and servants who were filling the saloons, decks, and companionways had cleared out.

At a quarter to noon, the steamer's whistle gave a great blast, and stewards made their way down the decks and corridors, ringing handbells and announcing, "All ashore who are going ashore!" The last hurried goodbyes would be said, sometimes tearful embraces exchanged, and then a steady stream of well-wishers would make their way down the gangway to the pier, where they would congregate and wave frantically to their friends aboard. (Almost invariably one or more of these visitors would take too long to make their farewells and get caught aboard the ship as it pulled away from the pier. These benighted souls would be taken off the ship by the pilot boat at the mouth of the Mersey.)

Meanwhile, the passengers would line the deck rails, waving hats and handkerchiefs to the crowd on the pier below, often able to seek out and find those familiar faces that had come to see them off. Often a last minute bit of drama was played out as a rumble of wheels and clatter of hoofs announced the arrival of a late mail coach, driven at breakneck speed from the Post Office to catch the steamer before the gangways were withdrawn. A line of porters formed behind the mail wagon and the mailbags quickly passed to them; within minutes the entire contents of the mail wagon was on its way to the mail-hold.

At precisely twelve noon, a great long bellow sounded from the steamer's whistle, and the ship prepared to pull away from the pier. Gangways were withdrawn, mooring lines eased off, and bells would jangle on the bridge and at the stern as engine orders were rung down to the engine room by the big brass telegraphs, while winches and windlasses gave off a ratcheting rattle as the hawsers were taken in. The propellers began to turn, churning up a froth of mud and water at the stern, and the tugs made fast to each end of the ship began pulling her slowly from the side of the pier. Spring lines were cast off last, and the ship began easing out into the Mersey. At this, the crowds on deck and the pier went into a renewed frenzy of goodbyes and best wishes shouted back and forth, but in the cacophony of chugging tugs, venting steam from the boilers, clanking deck machinery and the various whistles being sounded, they often went unheard.

Forward, a pair of tugs, their hemp-buffered bows pressed against the steamship's side, swung the ship into mid-channel, and as her captain ordered "Slow Ahead" she began making her way toward the Bar, the St. George's Channel, and the open sea. The last of the tugs would cast off its lines and return to the docks, while the watching crowd on the pier, having pressed to every conceivable vantage point, would be rewarded by the sight of the liner, now in its proper element and no longer bound to the shore, presenting a memorable image of power and grace.

Unfortunately, that power and grace could sometimes desert a ship, and in the case of both the *Umbria* and *Etruria*, it did. Not surprisingly the *Umbria* was the first victim: she had already had more than her fair share of minor but annoying teething troubles as she settled into service. Sailing from Liverpool on December 17, 1892, the *Umbria*'s propeller shaft suffered a complete fracture in mid-Atlantic, leaving the ship to wallow about for days until temporary repairs were completed, allowing her to reach New York on December 31. More extensive work was done there, and on February 4, 1893, the *Umbria* finally returned to Liverpool, where the final repairs were completed; it wouldn't be until April 1 that the ship was able to return to regular service.

Broken propeller shafts weren't a new phenomenon: in the 1890s metallurgy was still a dimly-understood science, and metal fatigue and stress fractures were only vague concepts, so that shipbuilding engineering still contained a fair amount of the cut-and-try of Isambard Kingdom Brunel's day. Nonetheless, the incident was an acute embarrassment for Cunard, as the *Umbria* was then the premier ship of the company's fleet. With only a single screw, a fractured shaft meant that the ship was utterly helpless; the auxiliary masts that had characterized steamships since the days of the *Britannia* and her sisters had begun to shrink until they were hardly more than vestigial remnants with little practical value, at least as a means of moving a ship in an emergency. It would be seventeen years before a similar accident would overtake the *Etruria*, but its shadow constantly loomed over her, and as a consequence, she and her sister were the last single-screw ships built for Cunard.

They certainly served the line well, though they actually began their careers in the service of the Admiralty. In early 1885 tensions had once again grown to near the breaking point between Britain and Russia when the Russians extended a railway to the border of Afghanistan, triggering British fears of a Russian offensive launched through that desolate country into India. Consequently, the Admiralty once more invoked the clauses in its mail contract with Cunard and requisitioned both sisters for use as either troopships or armed merchant cruisers. Fortunately, war was avoided, allowing the *Etruria* to begin her service with Cunard in April 1885, though as a precautionary measure the *Umbria* was retained for a bit longer.

Once they were in service, the sisters emulated the White Star Line's *Germanic* and *Britannic* of a decade earlier, passing the Blue Ribband between them for the next three years. Both ships had exceeded twenty-one knots on trials, but eventually the *Etruria* proved to be slightly the faster of the two, establishing a new benchmark for speed on the North Atlantic in May 1888 with a crossing that took six days and one hour, the first ship to break the twenty-knot barrier for her average speed.

The performance of both sisters was watched with keen interest on both sides of the Atlantic. As strange as it may seem a century and a quarter later, public scrutiny of the accomplishments of transatlantic steamships was intense: the fascination that the Victorians exhibited with machinery and technology permeated all levels of society—every steamship line had its proponents, every vessel her partisans. So hungry was every segment of society for details about the latest entry into the North Atlantic stakes that when the *Campania* and *Lucania* were being built for Cunard, journalists actually complained that the builders, the Fairfield Company, weren't as forthcoming with information about their construction as they might have been. Of course, the owners and operators of the steamship lines were quick to downplay any suggestion that any particular line was deliberately seeking to win the Blue Ribband. In a memorable moment aboard the *Etruria* on July 4, 1890, at a banquet commemorating the fiftieth anniversary of the Cunard Line's inaugural service from Liverpool to New York, the company's chairman, David Jardine, declared, "I do not believe that either on our Cunard steamers or on those of any other Line which sail from Liverpool, there is such a thing as racing. So far as Cunard commanders and engineers are concerned they are instructed that so far as racing is concerned they are not to recognize the fact that there are other steamers on the Atlantic. I believe it is the same in other companies, for the responsibility is too great to allow any racing to be run".

However sincere Jardine's comments may have been, the truth was that they were so much hogwash. An incident a little more than a month later belied the truth of his pronouncement when, on August 7, the Inman Line's *City of New York*, sister-ship to the current Blue Ribband holder *City of Paris*, departed from Liverpool an hour before the White Star Line's *Teutonic*. The ships' departures were reported to American as well as British newspapers, as was the *City of New York*'s clearing Queenstown thirty-five minutes ahead of her rival. When the *Teutonic* arrived in New York on August 13, four hours ahead of the *City of New York*, it made headlines on both sides of the Atlantic.

It was inevitable that these ships, which were in so many ways the physical embodiment of the accomplishments—for weal and woe—of the Victorian world, should be the objects of so much public attention. In many ways, the steamships of the late 19th

The First Class Dining Saloon aboard the Lucania, *proving that she was as luxurious as she was fast.*

Century had become the secular equivalent of medieval cathedrals. They were the source of endless pride to the communities and nations that built them, and were just as much an expression of men's hopes and dreams of technical perfection as the great churches had once been of hopes for spiritual purity; and as in the days of the cathedrals, each level of society contributed to the great seagoing structures' creation and upkeep. The upper classes endowed them by paying for their most elaborate and expensive accommodations; the burgeoning middle class supplied their material needs by being purveyors of the foodstuffs and cellars, linens and cutlery, fuel and furnishings which each vessel required in prodigious amounts; and the working classes built them, investing a level of craftsmanship and attention to detail not seen since the raising of Salisbury or Winchester.

So it was that the public eagerly anticipated the White Star Line's inevitable response to Cunard's speedy sisters. It wasn't long in coming, as Harland and Wolff began construction of the *Teutonic* and *Majestic* in 1887. These two ships, as identical to each other as the *Umbria* and *Etruria* had been, were a milestone in the development of passenger steamships. Externally they dispensed with the last trappings of the days of sail—the trio of masts each sported were devoid of yards, their function reduced to serving as kingposts for cargo derricks and anchors for signal hoists; their superstructure ceased to be glorified deckhouses, rising three levels above the main deck; while their funnels were spaced wider apart than ever before, and moved away from the squarely mid-ships position that a ship's funnels had occupied since the days of paddle wheelers. Their clean, flowing lines, the product of marine architect Alexander Carlisle, introduced a "look" for the White Star Line that would reach its culmination in the *Olympic* and *Titanic* twenty-five years later.

Inside, the *Teutonic* and *Majestic* introduced what became known as the "period" style of decor in their public rooms. The woodwork in the smoking room was dark mahogany, with the leather of the chairs and couches stained to match, as were the embossed leather panels covering the walls. On those panels were paintings depicting a succession of ships from the Middle Ages, with the entire effect meant to suggest an exclusive Pall Mall club. The First Class dining saloon was done in a Renaissance style, complete with gold and ivory accents. The whole effect of these ships' interiors was so potent that when Kaiser Wilhelm II was heard to mutter when given a tour of the *Teutonic* in 1889, "We must have some of these," it would prove to be a fateful remark.

Their machinery was as impressive as their appointments. Twelve boilers provided steam for a pair of triple expansion engines that each drove a separate propeller shaft. Their designed speed was 20 knots, which both ships easily exceeded on their trials. They were also the first liners to exceed 10,000 tons in displacement.

The *Teutonic* set out on her maiden voyage between Liverpool and New York on August 7, 1889, taking the place of the original *Baltic* in White Star's schedule, but set no records. That honor went to her sister, the *Majestic*, which took the Blue Ribband from the *City of Paris* on her maiden voyage in 1890. The following spring the *Teutonic* made an even faster crossing and took the Blue Ribband for herself with an average speed of 20.25 knots; she would better this performance later that same year with an average speed of 20.5 knots,

The Lucania, *which along with her sister the* Compania, *held the Blue Ribband for over four years as the fastest liners on the North Atlantic run.*

and retain sole possession of the Blue Ribband for the next two years.

Cunard would have last word, however, in the rivalry with the White Star Line. Two new ships, the *Campania* and *Lucania*, were launched by Lady Burns, the wife of Cunard's chairman Lord Inverclyde, in 1892 and 1893 respectively. They carried the evolution of steamships even further than had the *Teutonic* and *Majestic*. The Blue Ribband-holders at the time, Inman's *City of New York* and *City of Paris*, while undeniably fast and unquestionably beautiful, had actually been a step backward, with their clipper bows and quartet of masts rigged for sail. The new Cunard ships, in contrast, had a very modern, imposing appearance, with a barely raked, knife-like stem, long forecastle, and high superstructure, atop which sat a pair of massive, almost ungainly looking funnels, nineteen feet in diameter. In profile the bridge was unusually prominent, as it sat one deck higher than the rest of the superstructure, allowing the men at the helm an unobstructed view forward over the bow, a feature that would be imitated on every subsequent passenger ship. One other feature that the two ships shared would become a trademark of every Cunard ship for the next forty years: a forest of cowl ventilators clustered about the funnels and the upper decks.

Two dozen boilers fed steam into two ten-cylinder triple-expansion engines. The *Campania* and *Lucania* were the Cunard ships fitted with twin screws, and when the *Campania* slipped her moorings and set out on her maiden voyage from Liverpool on April 22, 1893, it was expected to be a record crossing. But the new engines needed time to get bedded-in, and could not beat the *City of Paris'* 20.7-knot westbound record. However, on the return from New York, the *Campania* showed what she was made of, and crushed the *City of New York*'s eastbound record of 20.1 knots with a speed of 21.33 knots, the first time a ship had averaged more than 21 knots for an entire crossing. Two months later, the westbound record was hers with a nearly identical average speed, and the Blue Ribband was again back in Cunard's hands. The *Campania* and *Lucania* actually got faster the longer they were in service, and for the next four years the two sisters passed the record back and forth between them almost at will, although as always, one sister proved to be slightly faster in the long run, in this case the *Lucania*.

This pair of Cunarders was the last straw for Thomas Ismay: for the White Star Line at least, the costs of building and operating ships that were exemplars of speed as well as paragons of luxury were simply becoming prohibitive. Consequently, when Ismay chose to abandon the race for the Blue Ribband after the White Star Line built the *Teutonic* and *Majestic*, it appeared that Cunard's monopoly on the Blue Ribband would go uncontested. But it would last only until 1897: a new contender was preparing to enter the lists, one that would present the greatest challenge to Cunard's dominance of the North Atlantic since Edward Knight Collins had thrown down the gauntlet a half-century before. However, this time the challenge would not come from across the Atlantic, instead it would come from across the North Sea.

CHAPTER SEVEN

The German Challenge

When the *Lucania* captured the Blue Ribband in 1894, the title had been in British hands—with the exception of the years from 1850 to 1856 when Edward Collins' ships had ruled the North Atlantic—for a half-century, and there seemed to be no reason to believe that the pre-eminence of British built-and owned ships wouldn't continue. Marine engineers, naval architects, and shipbuilders from all over the world—places as diverse as the United States, Germany, Japan, Russia, China, and South America—made pilgrimages to the British shipyards at Jarrow, at Belfast, on the Tyne, and most of all along the Clyde, to sit at the feet of the masters and learn the newest, most advanced techniques in steamship design and construction, and then take those secrets back to their homelands.

The Germans were particularly apt students, none more so than Robert Zimmerman, who spent eleven years as a designer with a succession of shipyards at Jarrow, Barrow-on-Furness and Greenock. He developed a particular eye for the aesthetics of steamship design, having worked with William John on the Inman Line's *City of Rome*, one of the most beautiful liners ever to sail the North Atlantic. In 1894, Zimmermann left the British shipyards behind to take the position as chief naval architect at the Vulkan Shipyard in Stettin, a Prussian seaport on the Baltic. His first assignment was to design and build a ship for Norddeutscher-Lloyd that would take the Blue Ribband away from Great Britain.

German ships were no sudden newcomers to the North Atlantic: in 1856, the embryonic Hamburg-Amerikanische Packetfahrt Aktien Gesselschaft (quickly and mercifully shortened to Hamburg-Amerika or HAPAG) began regular packet service between Hamburg and New York, while in Bremen the rival Norddeutscher-Lloyd line had begun passenger service to New York just a year later. Both companies concentrated on serving the immigrant trade with a fleet of modestly appointed, moderately fast, medium-sized ships. They were respectably, if not spectacularly, profitable, conservative, unassuming, and certainly nothing to be viewed as a potential rival by the great shipping lines of the North Atlantic—a reflection in many ways of Germany herself in the middle of the 19th Century.

All that was transformed in the wake of the Franco-Prussian war, however, when in 1871 Prussia created the German Empire out of what had been a motley collection of German states. The popular image of Germany as a nation of well-educated bumpkins, not unlike Professor Bhaer, Jo's charmingly inept suitor in *Little Women*, changed abruptly to that of the land of spike-helmeted soldiers and industrial behemoths, as the newly-created Teutonic empire began flexing its economic and political muscle across the continent of Europe.

In 1877, a new managing director was appointed at Norddeutscher-Lloyd; Johann Lohmann, who had for almost two decades been carefully watching the careening fortunes of Inman, White Star, Guion and Cunard. What struck him most notably was the rise in prestige—and consequently the number of passengers carried—of any particular line once one of that company's ships gained the Blue Ribband. That, combined with the rising expectations of First and Second Class passengers for ever more luxurious surroundings, convinced Lohmann that leisurely speed and the *gemütlicheit* atmosphere of Norddeutscher-Lloyd's current flotilla of ships were hopelessly out of date. The line would acquire an entirely new fleet that combined safety and speed "with special comfort and elegance during the voyage."

In 1880, putting word into action, Lohmann ordered twelve new ships, all named after rivers in Germany, all to be built in British shipyards; indeed, no German shipbuilder as yet had the skills or capacity to construct any of them. They were all between five and six thousand tons displacement, with top speeds of seventeen knots or so. This made them just a shade smaller and slower than their British contemporaries, but it was their interiors that quickly caught the attention of even the most jaded Atlantic traveler. Lohmann had invited the foremost interior designer in Germany, Johannes Poppe, to add his distinctive touch to the decor of the new fleet.

The result was a seagoing baroque collage of high ceilings, massive pillars, gilded balustrades, trumpeting cherubs, and gigantic statuary. It marked the beginning of what John Malcolm Brinnin characterized "as a period of steamship history when the landscapes of Valhalla enscrolled on the walls and ceilings of grand saloons would all but collapse under their own weight, as well as a period when Teutonic efficiency united with matchless engine power would give Germany all the honors on the northern seas. Then, when the wits of the first decade of the [Twentieth] Century began to say something was 'hideously' or 'divinely' 'North German Lloyd' they meant, according to one American contemporary, 'two of everything but the kitchen range', then gilded."

Though time has somewhat softened the sharper corners and muted the worst excesses of Wilhelmine Germany, what is still readily apparent is that Poppe's interiors were a physical expression of the pomposity and bombast of the bourgeois German Empire. Unlike Great Britain, whose five centuries of history and tradition allowed Victoria to wear her crown with a quiet self-assurance, the German Empire was very much the *arriviste* among the Great Powers of Europe, the fact of which the German Emperor, Kaiser Wilhelm II, was painfully self-conscious. He once remarked to King Victor Emmanuel of Italy that "in all the long years of my reign, my colleagues, the Monarchs of Europe, have paid no attention to what I have to say."

It's hardly surprising that the other European powers treated Germany as a parvenue—prior to 1871 "Germany" wasn't even a nation, but a geographical concept describing the checkerboard of petty Teutonic states which straddled Central Europe. Between 1865 and 1871, however, the kingdom of Prussia, under the guidance of King Wilhelm I and his ambitious and astute Chancellor, Otto von Bismarck, had fought a series of short, sharp, successful wars with Denmark, Austria, and France. The result of these "wars of unification" was that the collection of thirty-eight small kingdoms, duchies, principalities, and free cities were amalgamated into the German Empire, with Wilhelm I crowned as its first Emperor, or Kaiser. These feats of arms gave the newborn empire military and political supremacy in Central and Western Europe, while a penchant for hard work and efficiency allowed German workers and industrialists to spawn an economy that was second only to that of the British Empire.

Yet, despite these achievements, as well as their accomplishments in science, medicine and music, the Germans still felt the other European powers weren't giving them their due respect. When Wilhelm himself complained that when the British aristocracy toured the continent, they would flock to Paris and shun Berlin—never comprehending the vast appeal which the vibrant, decadent French capital had over Germany's stuffy and straight-laced chief city—he was only giving voice to a slight shared by all of his countrymen. The philosophies of Nietzsche and Treitschke, the *Übermensch* and the arch-nationalist, fed a growing belief among the Germans that Teutonic blood *was* superior, and that, by right, Germany was entitled to primacy of place in the world order.

It was an attitude guaranteed to alienate rather than endear, and the more overtly it was displayed, the more Germany's neighbors began to believe that one by-product of the Fatherland's easy victories of 1865, 1866, and 1871 was a nationwide form of arrogant self-delusion. When the Boxer Rebellion broke out in Peking in 1900, the German troops dispatched by Wilhelm to relieve the besieged European embassies there were charged by the Kaiser to model their conduct on Attila's ancient Huns when they met the Chinese in combat. (It was a poor choice, as "Hun" became a pejorative that would haunt the Germans for nearly a century.) Clamoring for their "place in the sun" when Germany entered the last mad scramble for colonies in Africa and the Far East, ultra-nationalistic societies such as the *Alldeutscher Verband* (Pan German Union) and the Navy League believed that the other European powers were obligated to concede to Germany on demand what those nations had acquired through outpourings of blood and treasure. German diplomacy became characterized not by endeavors at cooperation and conciliation, but by outright threats and blandishments of force intended to extract concession through intimidation. Barbara Tuchman put it this way: "In German practice [Theodore] Roosevelt's current precept for getting on with your neighbors was Teutonized to 'Speak loudly and brandish a big gun.'"

Johannes Poppe's interior designs then were simply extensions of this same national attitude. When passengers stepped aboard one of Norddeutscher-Lloyd's ships, they weren't merely surrounded by Teutonic vanity and bravado posing as luxury, so much as they were bombarded with it. A sort of Valkyrian megalomania prevailed, where kitsch and classicism existed side-by-side, half beer-hall, half Wagnerian opera, as the traditional *gemütlich* familiarity of German ships attempted to assert itself over endless vistas of marble panels, gilt scroll-work, and elaborate mirrors.

Whatever they may have been called, it's undeniable that Poppe's interiors, coupled with other improvements in the service and speed of the German ships, had a definite appeal to a significant portion of the traveling public. In the decade between 1881 and 1891, the White Star line carried over 371,000 passengers from Europe to New York, while Cunard had brought 323,000 across the Atlantic, the Inman Line just a thousand fewer than Cunard, and the Guion Line carried some 273,000. But in that same period of time Norddeutscher-Lloyd's Hamburg-based rival Hamburg-Amerika had brought over an incredible 526,000 passengers, and Norddeutscher-Lloyd itself had carried an unbelievable 738,000 passengers, more than twice as many as their closest British competitor.

Nor were the Germans content with merely besting the British in numbers of passengers carried, for they were now ready to put to sea in ships built in German shipyards, demonstrating that they could construct liners whose quality rivaled any of those built in British yards. The Vulcan Shipyard in Stettin was the first to do so, building the immediately popular 7,600-ton *Augusta Victoria* and 8,400-ton *Fürst Bismarck* for Hamburg-Amerika. The yard quickly followed these successes with three ships for Norddeutscher-Lloyd, the *Kaiser Wilhelm II*, *Spree*, and *Havel*. The last two had top speeds of 19 knots or more, which, while not yet the fastest ships on the North Atlantic, were among the fastest, and as a consequence, became quite popular.

By 1895, Lohmann decided that if Norddeutscher-Lloyd vessels were setting the style on the North Atlantic, they should also set the pace—and do it in German-built ships. Approaching the Vulkan works in Stettin and the Schichau Shipyard of Danzig, they had a simple proposal: "Build us the fastest ship in the world and we'll buy it; anything less and you can keep it". It was a daunting task, but one that both yards felt capable of accepting.

The Schichau offering was the three-funneled *Kaiser Friedrich,* a handsome and graceful but ultimately disappointing ship. From her maiden voyage it was clear that she was no record-breaker, barely able to sustain an average of 19.5 knots. After a half dozen crossings it was obvious that the best she could ever do was just a shade over 20 knots, and she was withdrawn from service.

The story was quite different with the product of the Vulkan work's efforts, where Robert Zimmerman was given the task of building the potential record breaker. He quickly proved that the years spent in British shipyards had not been wasted and that the lessons of the British shipwrights had been well-learned. Sleek, imposing, and unmistakably German, *Kaiser Wilhelm der Grosse* fully looked the part of an ocean-going thoroughbred. She clearly projected an aura of power, from the sweeping sheer-lines of her hull to the four buff-colored funnels set in two pairs atop her low superstructure. She was the first of the great four-funneled transatlantic liners, ushering in a new fashion on the North Atlantic, as a quartet of funnels immediately became the hallmark of the elite among Atlantic steamships.

Nor was their presence a mere pretension, as they furnished the necessary draught for the twelve double-ended boilers which provided the enormous head of steam that drove the *Kaiser Wilhelm*'s huge engines. These were a pair of quadruple (that is, four-cylinder)

Norddeutscher-Lloyd's Kaiser Wilhelm der Grosse, *the best-known of the succession of fearsome German greyhounds that monopolized the Blue Ribband for nearly a decade.*

triple expansion steam engines, turning two propeller shafts with a combined power of 31,000 horsepower, intended to drive the *Wilhelm* at a top speed of over 22 knots. There was far more to the *Kaiser Wilhelm der Grosse*, though, than simply powerful engines and the promise of high speed. Private suites, private dining rooms, a nursery and play room for the littlest passengers, and such amenities as writing and reading rooms, all of which would become standard features for every subsequent transatlantic liner, made their debut aboard the *Wilhelm der Grosse*.

At 627 feet in length and displacement of 14,350 tons, she was not only the most luxurious but also the largest passenger ship in the world. The only question remaining was whether or not she was the fastest. The answer was not long in coming. Although she broke no speed records in her maiden voyage in September 1897, with sustained speeds of nearly 22 knots, the *Kaiser Wilhelm der Grosse* left no one in doubt that the Blue Ribband would soon be hers. By November those expectations were fulfilled, as the *Wilhelm der Grosse* took the Ribband with a crossing where she maintained an average speed of 22.35 knots.

Great Britain was aghast. "In that jubilee year, England was not feeling modest", wrote Humphrey Jordan. "She despised all foreigners without troubling to conceal the fact; she recognized herself with complete assurance, as a great nation, the head of a mighty empire, and the ruler of the seas. But with the jubilee mood still warming her citizens with a fine self-satisfaction in being Britons, England lost, and lost most decisively, the speed record of the Atlantic ferry to a German ship. The *Kaiser Wilhelm der Grosse* was a nasty blow to British shipping; her triumphant appearance on the North Atlantic came at a moment particularly unacceptable to the English public".

Not content in merely besting the British, the Germans proceeded to embarrass them. Hamburg-Amerika, under the direction of Albert Ballin, one of the most gifted businessmen to ever sit at the head of the board of a steamship line, had the Vulkan yard build an even larger, faster liner, the *Deutschland*. In many ways she was an enlarged version of the *Wilhelm der Grosse*, even repeating the layout of having her four funnels set in pairs; the *Deutschland* was every inch an Atlantic greyhound. Yet there were differences between the *Deutschland* and the *Kaiser Wilhelm der Grosse* that reflected the fundamental differences in the business priorities of their respective owners. The *Wilhelm der Grosse* carried 332 passengers in First Class, and 343 in Second, but her capacity of 1,074 in Third Class demonstrated that Norddeutscher-Lloyd still regarded emigrants as its greatest source of profits. By contrast, the *Deutschland* carried 700 passengers in First, 300 in Second, and only 280 in Third Class, showing that under Albert Ballin, Hamburg-Amerika was shifting its priorities toward catering to the more affluent North Atlantic travelers.

In the whole history of the North Atlantic steamship trade there have been few figures as charming and interesting as Albert Ballin. Born in Hamburg almost within sight of the city's great harbor, his whole life was intertwined with shipping. It was almost inevitable, as Hamburg's proud, five-hundred year tradition as a seafaring Hanseatic city and the economic gateway to central Europe made it the pre-eminent city in the cluster of petty Teutonic states which would one day be welded together into the German Empire.

Ballin began his career working for a tiny company that acted as a booking agent for emigrants departing from Hamburg, but soon became fascinated by the intricacies of operating ships themselves. In his early twenties he went to work for the Carr Line, a highly undistinguished fleet of six small rusty steamers devoted to the emigrant trade, and before long he was able to form a combine with two other small Hamburg shipping companies—the American Line and the Union Line. Good management allowed Ballin's little combine to become such a serious competitor to the Hamburg-Amerika Line that they bought him out. It was the most significant decision in the history of Hamburg-Amerika: originally the managing director of the Passenger Division, two years later, at the age of thirty-one, Ballin's talents had propelled him to the directorship of the entire line, the *Wunderkind* of the entire shipping world. By this time Hamburg-Amerika was the largest shipping firm in the world, and while the line's ships lacked the glamour and cachet of those of Cunard or White Star, Ballin was carefully creating a style for the line that was distinctively its own.

What Ballin did was put the stamp of his own unique personality on the company: born a Jew, he rose above the pervasive anti-Semitism of Imperial Germany and transformed himself into the very picture of European cosmopolitanism. His wife, a Protestant woman several inches taller than Ballin, adored him and he doted on her. When they adopted a daughter after eleven years of marriage, they lavished endless attention on her. Always elegantly dressed and elegantly mannered, Ballin believed that Hamburg-Amerika ships should be equally elegant and mannered. He traveled frequently on his ships, moving among the passengers, asking their opinions, always keeping an eye open for flaws and lapses in service, making notes that would be transformed into memorandums when he returned to his office: one crossing to New York found him jotting down such observations as, "Notices on board to be restricted as much as possible; those which are necessary to be tastefully framed—no room for portmanteaux and trunks—towels too small—soiled linen cupboard too small—butter dishes too small—toast to be served in serviette *hot*." It was a practice that the managing director of almost every other shipping company was imitating within a few years: the results of such personal involvement were soon evident for all to see. By 1899 Hamburg-Amerika's growth had given it a combined tonnage greater than any other company in the world; it was actually larger than the entire merchant marine of any nation on earth save for those of Great Britain and Germany.

The change in Hamburg-Amerika's focus of service—appealing to the First and Second Class Atlantic traveler instead of concentrating on the emigrant trade—was a consequence of Ballin's philosophy, and placed his line more squarely in competition with White Star than with Cunard. In some ways the two German companies complemented each other, and corporate relations between them were always cordial, again a consequence of Ballin's urbanity.

Certainly the *Deutschland*'s speed added to the appeal that Ballin's influence had produced for potential passengers. Sixteen boilers provided steam for her two sets of six-cylinder quadruple-expansion engines, which provided over 33,000 steam hp. Her designed speed was 23.6 knots, which she attained easily on her trials. More important to Hamburg-Amerika was that she was able to sustain average speeds of 23 knots or faster when she began crossing the Atlantic in July 1900 and take the Blue Ribband away from the *Kaiser Wilhelm der Grosse*. The only criticism that could be leveled at the *Deutschland* was that when she was running all-out her entire structure shook with the vibration created by her immense engines. It was a problem that was inherent in reciprocating engines, and one for which the German engineers had no effective solution: the best the Vulkan works could hope to do was reduce the vibration by stiffening the hull as much as possible.

The *Deutschland*'s pre-eminence was to last less than a year as Norddeutscher-Lloyd responded with the new *Kronprinz Wilhelm,* which set a new record at 23.5 knots in September 1901; the year after that the *Kaiser Wilhelm II* proved a shade faster still. This Teutonic monopoly on the Blue Ribband was more than Great Britain could stand: a head to head showdown was approaching between these upstart Germans and the established maritime power of the British. France and the United States, once serious contenders, were soon left in the wake of these two great rivals.

The threat—"problem" is too weak a word—that this German pre-eminence posed to the British shipping lines, and in particular to Cunard, was very real. Almost overnight it seemed, Cunard's entire fleet seemed dated, obsolescent, a collection of dowdy, frumpy old ladies whose staid conservatism, which had once seemed to be part of their appeal, was now seen as quaint, homely—and hopelessly passé. Even the vaunted claim, "The Cunard has never lost a life," which had been invoked with suitable gravity for more than half a century any time a newcomer to the North Atlantic appeared to challenge the line, now lost its potency: the Germans could make the same claim with equal veracity, and still offer these fabulous new ships. That the Germans were each carrying roughly twice as many passengers as Cunard was bad enough, but because of the sensation these new ships were creating for Norddeutscher-Lloyd and Hamburg-Amerika, along with the accompanying publicity, they were attracting even more passengers. Even if a traveler wasn't able to make his or her crossing on one of the German speedsters, the cachet of sailing on one their stablemates was still attractive. And because Cunard, like Norddeutscher-Lloyd, still relied on the emigrant trade to make its profits, any decline in the number of fare-paying passengers carried, had serious financial consequences.

But what was setting the German ships apart from their British counterparts wasn't just speed. When Mark Twain made a crossing aboard Norddeutscher-Lloyd's *Havel* in 1895, his experiences illuminated exactly what the Germans had done to gain their pre-eminence on the North Atlantic:

> One curious thing which is at once noticeable in the great modern ship is the absence of hubbub, clatter, rush of feet, roaring of orders.... A Sabbath stillness and solemnity reign... I observe stateroom doors three inches thick, of solid oak and polished. I note companionway vestibules with walls, doors, and ceilings paneled in polished hardwoods...all dainty and delicate joiner work.... I find the walls of the dining saloon upholstered with mellow pictures wrought in tapestry and the ceiling aglow with pictures done in oil. I find great panels filled with embossed Spanish leather, the figures rich with gilding and bronze. Everywhere I find sumptuous masses of color—color, color—color all about, color of every shade and tint and variety; and as a result, the ship is bright and cheery to the eye, and this cheeriness invades one's spirit, and contents it.

Another passenger on the same ship remarked that, "It is pleasant to be summoned to one's meals, not by a barbarous gong, but by a civilized and inspiring bugle. Only musicians are employed as second class stewards, and an excellent band plays on deck every morning...." The German ships were offering not only high speed but also a degree of comfort which the British lines were going to be hard-pressed to equal, let alone exceed.

Not that the Germans were resting on their laurels. If Norddeutscher-Lloyd seemed to have committed its ships to holding the edge in speed, with theirs Hamburg-Amerika was setting even higher standards for interior appointments and service. Albert Ballin, Hamburg-Amerika's managing director, had an eye for detail, whether on one of his ships or that of a competitor. Traveling from Hamburg to New York and back, he would fill entire notebooks with comments, criticisms, and suggestions for improvements. At breakfast, the toast must be served *hot*, while the butter dishes should be larger; the bouillon served at 11 o'clock tea was fine, but would be better if Westphalian ham sandwiches were served with it; the stewards serving dinner were competent, but should be uniformed in jackets cut like those of the White Star Line, which were at once more handsome and more practical. Back in his cabin, he devised ways of rearranging its furniture to create more usable space for luggage, and insisted that the pillows be made larger and softer. This sort of attention to detail paid off in ever-increasing numbers of First and Second Class passengers, many of whom were frequent travelers and who transferred their allegiance (along with their dollars and pounds sterling) to Hamburg-Amerika.

Nor were such details the extent of Ballin's involvement. In 1901, Ballin contracted with Harland and Wolff to build a new ship, even larger than the *Deutschland*, to be called the *Amerika*. Choosing to stylistically distance Hamburg-Amerika somewhat from the overwrought Wilhelmine pretensions of Johannes Poppe, Ballin asked pre-eminent architect and interior designer of the day, Charles Mewés, to create the new liner's interiors. The result was a symphony of 18th Century styles, ranging from Robert Adams to Louis XVI, all carefully harmonized throughout the ship. The key to Mewés style was a light touch: he assiduously avoided the massively gilded baroque of Poppe. Mewés masterstroke was the reproduction of the restaurant of the Ritz-Carlton hotel in London, aboard the *Amerika*. This *a la carte* restaurant, run by Cesar Ritz as a concession, was Ballin's masterstroke—offered to First Class passengers as an alternative to the dining saloon, it was a feature immediately copied by every other steamship line. Another novelty in First Class that was immediately copied was an elevator, the first such apparatus to be installed in a ship. Taken together, these features made the *Amerika* the most fashionable ship on the North Atlantic run.

It all proved too much for Thomas Ismay, who decided that the expense of pursuing unrivaled speed *and* unparalleled luxury was beyond the White Star Line's resources. Instead, since luxury had made White Star's reputation, luxury would continue to be White Star's hallmark. The Line's ships would continue to be nearly as fast as its competitors', but the out-and-out race for the Blue Ribband would now be run without the White Star Line.

What motivated Ismay's decision was not a lack of resolve, but a lack of money. Buried in the endless recitations of speeds, horsepower, boilers, and triple—and quadruple—expansion engines, was a stark reality: building and operating ever-larger and faster ships was an expensive proposition. Higher speeds demanded larger engines; larger engines required more boilers to provide steam, which in turn required more coal and more stokers and trimmers to feed the furnaces. All of this had to be fitted into hulls that had to be constantly built larger to accommodate them. Larger hulls were more expensive to build and maintain, and while a larger hull could carry more passengers, there was no guarantee that enough could be carried to cover the ship's operating costs, let alone show a profit.

For the two German giants, such concerns did not loom as large as they did for the British steamship companies, because they were being substantially underwritten by the German government. In 1889, at the Royal Navy's annual review at Spithead, Kaiser Wilhelm II was piped aboard the White Star Line's appropriately named *Teutonic*, which was serving as a reviewing platform for the assembled royalty and other dignitaries. The Kaiser spent an hour and a half exploring the ship from boat deck to keel, remarking on everything from the *Teutonic*'s barbershop, to her engines, to her graceful profile. When he was finished, he was overheard to casually remark, "We must have some of these." Later, writing to his mother, he would describe the impression that the British ship had made on him: "Any man who, standing on the deck of a ship with the starlit firmament of the Almighty as his canopy and the boundless seas as the only object of his vision, takes occasion to question his conscience, to weigh his responsibilities, and to contrast them with his inclination to do good and keep in the path of righteousness, will not hesitate to pronounce a sea voyage a salutary thing for himself and those depending upon him".

Of course, just as Wilhelm was becoming at once covetous of, and inspired by Great Britain's liners, both Hamburg-Amerika and Norddeutscher-Lloyd were drawing up plans to construct ships that would rival those of their British competitors. Royal patronage certainly wouldn't hurt when both lines approached the German government for financial assistance, nor did it. Just how extensive were the government subsidies for Hamburg-Amerika and Norddeutscher-Lloyd is difficult to determine after so many years have passed, for all parties involved appear to have kept more than one set of books, but it is clear that each company was receiving upward of $750,000 annually (roughly equivalent to $750,000,000 today), in addition to the payments being made to carry the German mails.

This was the sort of financial commitment which the British government was loathe to make to the likes of Cunard or White Star, and it gave the two German companies a hidden strength when a challenge to their independence arose, a challenge that would overwhelm many of the British shipping companies, including the White Star Line, and threaten the existence of Cunard. The demands of operating a fleet of steamships was fast becoming something the financial resources of most of the shipping firms could no longer sustain; raising fares to cover costs was merely a stop-gap, for while the passengers traveling in First and Second Class might be willing to pay, the price of a Third Class ticket would soon rise beyond the ability of those wanting to emigrate, and for all of the splendor of the new generation of liners, the emigrant trade was still the foundation of the steamship lines' prosperity.

The looming challenge came from across the Atlantic in the form of an American named J. Pierpont Morgan, who had the green gleam of money in his eye. Morgan, the greatest of a generation of trust builders, had conceived of a vast freighting monopoly which would control the shipping rates of goods and the fares of passengers being transported from Europe, from the moment they left the Old World until they arrived at their destination in the New. Since the American rail barons, and especially Morgan, had already monopolized the U.S. railroads, all that remained for Morgan's dream to become reality was to gain control of the North Atlantic shipping lines.

At least that is how Morgan is usually depicted, and given the reputation for greed and acquisitiveness that has come to be synonymous with his name, it's understandable. The truth behind the legend is, however, somewhat different—and far less malicious. While it's quite true that Morgan intended to profit—and profit handsomely—from the cartel's operations, there was more than just greed at work in his maneuverings and machinations. What Morgan was attempting was to bring the same sort of rationalization to the Atlantic shipping industry that he had brought to the American railroads and the steel industry. His formation of the Pennsylvania Railroad and United States Steel, for example, had eliminated a lot of competitors, it was true, but it also eliminated a lot of wasteful competition, both for resources and markets, with the result that both industries grew in size, capability and prosperity to statures that were far beyond what would have been possible, if left in the chaotic conditions in which Morgan found them.

He saw a similar situation in the North Atlantic passenger trade: it seemed nothing short of absurd to him to have two or three crack passengers liners from as many competing lines all departing New York for Liverpool on the same day, each ship vying for the same passengers. By spreading the sailings out during the week so that a first-class steamer would be departing New York each day of the week, not only could travelers have their choice of ships, but also their choice of departure days—a situation that, as Morgan saw it, would ultimately work to benefit all of the lines. At the same time, the fierce rate wars which were plaguing the shipping industry could be eliminated by regulating and rationalizing fares.

In early 1898, Morgan approached two American ship owners: Bernard Baker, who had formed the Atlantic Transport Company in 1882 and which had acquired the failing National Line based in Liverpool, in 1896; and Clement Griscom, owner of the American Line. Griscom also had connections to the International Navigation Company based in Philadelphia, which owned the Belgian-flagged Red Star Line. International Navigation had also acquired the Inman Line, which by 1886 had fallen on hard times following the death of its founder, William Inman. His successors lacked both his drive and his business acumen, and despite the mail subsidy provided by the British government, the Line was no longer profitable. International Navigation reorganized the Inman Line as Inman and International, and would become the corporate nucleus around which the giant Morgan combine would eventually be formed, an idea that at the outset apparently originated with Baker and Griscom, with Morgan providing the financial backing.

It was Baker who actually made the first move toward the formation of International Mercantile Marine, by offering to merge the Atlantic Transport Line with Griscom's International Navigation. It was a calculated move, intended to provide capital for the construction of new ships for Atlantic Transport. It was at this point that J.P. Morgan entered the picture, for when the merger of Atlantic Transport and International Marine was made public in December 1900, it was also announced that the financial backing for six new ships would be provided by Morgan, who had become a partner in International. Buried in the announcement was a notice that two additional steamship companies would soon be added to the merger.

The first of these was the Leyland Line, or correctly, Frederick Leyland and Company, the Liverpool shipping firm which operated the largest fleet of freighters on the North Atlantic. The line had been run by John R. Ellerman, who at 36 was one of the towering figures in British shipping by virtue of his position as Chairman of the Leyland Line; however, he was a businessman through and through, and had none of the sentimental attachment to the steamship business that the Cunards, Burns, or Ismays possessed. So in the summer of 1901, when Morgan, who by now was a partner in International Navigation instead of just the company's financier, offered Ellerman $11 million in cash for the Leyland Line, Ellerman didn't hesitate to accept. Morgan's next move was to take over the Dominion Line in early 1902. Formally known as British and North Atlantic Steamship Company, Dominion ran a service of moderate size and profit between Liverpool and Boston.

Thomas Ismay, somehow sensing what Morgan was about to do, attempted to form a consortium of British ship owners who would buy the Inman line back from International Navigation and thus deny the American company its foothold in the British shipping industry, but the attempt fell apart because too few of Ismay's colleagues believed Morgan was serious. It was one of the few failures in Ismay's career, and he rued it until his death in 1899, foreseeing a fierce rate war on the North Atlantic instigated by Morgan that could spell the ruin of the White Star Line.

He was right. Morgan began cutting fares until his lines were offering a Third Class passage to America for as little as £2, rates that were ruinous for the two big British shipping companies. J. Bruce Ismay, who succeeded to the director-ship of the White Star Line after his father's death, was every bit as determined as his father to resist Morgan, but Morgan received help from an unexpected ally: Lord Pirrie, the Chairman of the Board of Harland and Wolff, the huge Belfast shipyard that was the exclusive builder of White Star's ships. Pirrie was also, after Ismay himself, the single largest shareholder of White Star stock. Realizing that Morgan's rate war would leave White Star with little capital for building new ships, and having made Harland and Wolff heavily dependent on White Star for new construction, Pirrie began to pressure the younger Ismay to accept Morgan's offer to buy the line. Thomas Ismay would have told Lord Pirrie to be damned and fought the "Yankee pirate" tooth and nail, but though Bruce Ismay was his father's son in many ways, he did not possess the innate ruthlessness his father had. Rather than stand up to Pirrie, the younger Ismay eventually caved in, and in late 1902 Morgan's shipping combine, now known as International Mercantile Marine (IMM), acquired ownership of the White Star Line.

Cunard would soon skillfully exploit Morgan's purchase of White Star, and ultimately wring considerable concessions from the British government in order to keep the company in British hands. Meanwhile, Morgan's combine began making overtures to Norddeutscher-Lloyd and Hamburg-Amerika. The American's first move was to approach Hamburg-Amerika's chairman, Albert Ballin, with a proposal to acquire control of fifty-one percent of the company's shares, while still allowing Hamburg-Amerika to operate with a considerable degree of autonomy. Within a week a similar offer was made to Johann Lohmann at Norddeutscher-Lloyd. The terms were carefully calculated to appeal to the German companies, as Morgan realized that the German government's subsidies made them far less financially vulnerable than their British counterparts. Certainly he knew he wasn't dealing from the same position of strength as he had been with the British, and instead of attempting to gain outright ownership of Hamburg-Amerika and Norddeutscher-Lloyd, he merely sought a controlling interest in both.

Ballin's first impulse was to accept Morgan's offer, as it would virtually institutionalize German supremacy on the North Atlantic. However, in a quiet demonstration of the influence the German government exerted on the Hamburg-Amerika and Norrdeutscher-Lloyd, Ballin was informed within a matter of days that the Kaiser had expressed his dissatisfaction with the terms of the agreement and was prepared to intervene to prevent the sale of the shares. Specifically, Wilhelm was concerned as to what extent IMM would affect Hamburg-Amerika's actual control of its ships; at the same time he wanted to be sure that the same guarantees being made to Hamburg-Amerika would also apply to Norddeutscher-Lloyd. While always fierce competitors, professional relationships between the two companies had always been cordial, and now in the face of the growing strength of IMM, that cordiality served them well. The two firms had discussed the terms of the offers made to them by IMM, and so Ballin was able to assure the Kaiser that Norddeutscher-Lloyd's ships would also remain under that company's effective operational control. Satisfied with Ballin's reassurances, and after suggesting a few minor changes, Wilhelm gave his consent to the agreements.

Wilhelm's concerns were due to the fact that there were still other fascinating attributes of the swift German liners in addition to their speed and luxury; aspects of their construction invisible to the layman but readily discernable to a naval architect, and features invisible to all but those in the German government who had access to the rolls of the officers and ratings of the Imperial German Navy. In essence, they had been built to serve not only as passenger liners, but also as warships, in the guise of auxiliary cruisers.

Auxiliary cruisers were a slightly addle-brained fad that enjoyed considerable vogue in most of the world's larger navies in the last part of the 19th Century and the early part of the 20th. Essentially they were fast ocean liners that had been built with reinforced platforms for mounting a number of medium-caliber guns (some as large as 6"), along with compartments that could easily be converted into magazines and powder storage rooms, along with shell hoists, handling rooms and special mountings for range finding and naval signaling equipment. In the event of a declared war, a belligerent navy would bring these fast liners into dry dock, mount their guns and load their ammunition. They would then be manned with crews of reservists leavened by a handful of regular seamen and petty officers, while their officers would all be reservists. Their mission would be to go out onto the high seas and hunt down enemy shipping, using their superior speed to catch enemy merchant vessels or, if cornered by proper warships, run away.

These fast German liners, the *Kaiser Wilhelm der Grosse, Deutschland, Kronprinz Wilhelm, Kaiser Wilhelm II*, and the *Kronprizessin Cecile*, in their wartime guise represented the equivalent of an entire squadron of cruisers, and were regarded by the Royal Navy as a clear and present danger to British merchant shipping should war break out between Britain and Germany. At the time, Britain's only available response would be to deploy large numbers of the fleet's cruisers for the task of hunting down the German auxiliaries, which would be costly in terms of men, resources and money, and tie up ships indefinitely that might be desperately needed for other duties.

(One indication of how seriously the British regarded the potential threat represented by the German auxiliaries was the effect they had on the Royal Navy's construction programs. In February 1905, the same committee that had designed HMS *Dreadnought* produced the design for HMS *Invincible,* the first battle cruiser. The specification for a maximum speed of at least 25 knots for these ships was motivated by the need to be able to catch the swift German liners should they ever appear in their cruiser guise.)

At this point, with most of its competitors either absorbed by, or cooperating with the new cartel, Cunard was under tremendous pressure to make a dramatic response or be permanently eclipsed. The new German ships completely outclassed anything in the Cunard fleet, and the innate conservatism of the British ship owners and shipbuilders assured that there were no new British ships readily forthcoming which could compare with their Teutonic rivals. At the same time, the drastic fare cuts that Morgan was using as leverage to try to compel Cunard into acquiescing to a takeover by IMM were, as intended, threatening Cunard's solvency.

The obvious solution was to level the playing field, and allow Cunard the same advantages that gave the Germans the ability to retain their independence—in short, have the British government subsidize Cunard. Admittedly, Parliament had been alarmed at IMM's acquisition of the White Star Line, and had frantically passed a bill requiring White Star's ships to remain under British registry, so there was a certain sympathy within the House for the idea of government intervention to keep Cunard out of Morgan's hands. However, it had traditionally been the policy of the British government to offer no form of subsidy or underwriting for any steamship company apart from the payments specified in the Royal Mail contracts, and as always with the British, that tradition would be overcome only with considerable difficulty.

Given the strength of the government's antipathy toward subsidies, Cunard was taking no chances: Lord Inverclyde, grandson of one of the line's founders, George Burns, and its current chairman, stayed true to his Scots heritage and played a canny game. When Morgan's representatives approached Cunard with an invitation to either join the combine or let IMM purchase a controlling interest, Inverclyde countered with the proposal that IMM buy the line outright, and suggested that IMM make an offer. What Morgan's people didn't know was that Inverclyde was keeping the British Government informed of every new turn in the developing negotiations, determined to play one side against the other. At first it appeared that his strategy had backfired, for despite the sympathy that existed among some members of Parliament for Cunard, the Government itself, under the guidance of Prime Minister Arthur J. Balfour, took the position that the decision whether or not to sell out to Morgan was purely Cunard's affair.

Now, Lord Inverclyde was a genuinely patriotic Briton, but he was first and foremost a businessman, with an obligation to create the best possible situation for Cunard and the company's stockholders, so he was careful to make sure the Government understood that if they chose not to subsidize Cunard, he was not bluffing when he stated that he was quite willing to accept Morgans's offer—as long as the price was right and Inverclyde had decided it was in the best interests of the company. He made it perfectly clear that he believed only the Government possessed the resources necessary to keep Cunard out of Yankee hands. At the same time, however, Inverclyde wasn't simply playing the role of Morgan's unwitting dupe: he studied IMM's initial offer of £18 per share for 55% of the company stock, and decided it wasn't generous enough. When he informed the Government of this, Balfour and his Cabinet thought they had Inverclyde's measure—he was merely trying to raise the level of any possible government subsidies—and blandly reiterated their position that the decision to join or not join Morgan's combine was entirely Inverclyde's decision.

Balfour, whose status and stature both as a statesman and politician were greater than his talents and abilities warranted, seemed almost dismissive of the whole affair, as if it were beneath him. It was not an uncommon attitude of Balfour's, who maintained intellectual pretensions about art, philosophy, music, literature, and science, but of whom it could be safely said that there was far more breadth to his intellect than depth. Indeed, in the Commons he seemed to take more interest in the style of any particular debate than the substance of it, delighting in complex dialogues where much was spoken, but little actually said. Henry Campbell-Bannerman, who succeeded Balfour as Prime Minister in 1905, took Balfour's measure when he described his dedication to "the same airy graces, the same subtle dialectics, the same light and frivolous way of dealing with a great question.... They are utterly futile, nonsensical and misleading".

Balfour seemed to think that he was dealing with an intellect of the second rank in Inverclyde, when in truth he was facing someone more intelligent and ruthless than himself. He was dealing with a Scot, and Inverclyde let him know it. In a letter to Lord Inverclyde, Lord Selborne, the First Lord of the Admiralty—which was still in charge of Royal Mail contracts and so was the Cabinet minister with whom Inverclyde communicated—outlined three possible courses of action that Balfour's Government believed available to Cunard, and the line was free to choose from any of them. They were 1) allow Cunard to join or be bought by IMM; 2) remain independent of IMM and fight Morgan's fare war with Government assistance; and 3) join a British anti-combine designed to counter IMM. As Lord Selborne outlined it, the Government was adamantly opposed to the first, less than enthusiastic about the second, and very favorably disposed to the third.

Lord Inverclyde in turn decided that the time had come to get tough, and made it clear that if the government were not willing to assist and underwrite Cunard in a manner similar to that which the German government underwrote Norddeutscher-Lloyd and Hamburg-Amerika, he would sell the line outright to Morgan, and the Government could face the political consequences of his decision alone. Publicly he let it be known that Cunard faced either "absorption or annihilation" if government assistance were withheld.

He was equally blunt with both Balfour and Selborne, writing to them that "I think the time has come when you should say what you intend to do with regard to the Cunard Company and not continue on the present indefinite course. If you do not intend to make any arrangement with us, but prefer to work with somebody else, I would much rather that you say so and let us know where we are. In any case, a time is coming when I must let my shareholders know what has been going on, so that they may judge for themselves whether their interests have been properly looked after, and moreover, the Directors of the Company cannot longer put off certain arrangements which they have had in view, but which latterly have been held in abeyance, to give you time to make up your mind whether you would do anything or not."

The impasse was broken by the sudden and unexpected intervention of the British Admiralty. The Royal Navy was suspicious of the motives of IMM's near-simultaneous acquisition of controlling interests in several of Britain's shipping companies, as well as Norddeutscher-Lloyd and Hamburg-Amerika. To the admirals it seemed there might be collusion between Morgan and the Germans to deprive the British of a significant proportion of their merchant marine, should war break out between Germany and Great Britain, by removing the ships from the British registry, bringing them instead under American jurisdiction and laws. Consequently, the Admiralty pressured Parliament into forbidding the transfer of IMM's newly acquired White Star ships from the British to the American registry, while at the same time forcing increases in the naval budgets and some rudimentary subsidies to the larger shipping lines.

That was not enough to satisfy the Royal Navy however, and when it began to press its own case for fast British liners that could be used as auxiliary cruisers to counter the German auxiliaries, given the popular sentiment of the day there was no way for Parliament to resist. When H.O. Arnold-Foster, Secretary of the Admiralty and a respected defense expert, presented a paper to the Cabinet declaring that the posture of the German navy was one of aggressive intent toward Great Britain, and emphasizing that the fast German liners were specifically designed for swift conversion into auxiliary cruisers so they could be sent out to prey on British shipping, the Government began to rethink its position with Cunard.

Meanwhile, the British press, with a few helpful nudges from Lord Inverclyde, was having a field day with the story of how Morgan was trying to acquire Cunard, rousing public sentiment against the "Yankee pirate," wondering if there was no end to the man's avarice. Before long the issue took on a life of its own, as on street corners in London and Glasgow "Licenses to Remain on Earth" were being sold for a penny each—they came complete with a reproduction of J.P. Morgan's signature. Over and over editorials asked, Who was to rule the waves—Morgan or Britannia? After he had taken control of the Atlantic, it was postulated, Morgan would begin stripping Britain of her national treasures and reducing the island empire to insignificant vassalage to the might of his omnipotent dollars. In *The Sway of the Grand Saloon,* John Malcolm Brinnin summed up this sublimely hysterical situation this way: "Its hands and wrists fettered, its beautiful white body tied to the tracks while the glinty-eyed locomotive from Wall Street came bearing down the line, Cunard cowered and blinked in the mock terror of those who know they are going to be snatched to safety."

He was right. Realizing that the sentiment of not only the public but also that of the Royal Navy was now on his side, Lord Inverclyde pressed home his case with the government in the autumn of 1902. Members of the Royal Institute of Naval Architects were, at the Admiralty's request, invited to help Cunard form the basic outlines for the design of a pair of new liners which would surpass anything afloat in size, luxury, and most of all, speed. The Admiralty expressed a desire to have these ships be capable of sustained speeds of 24 to 25 knots, in order to be able to catch the German liners. To be able to do so would require a power plant larger than any that had ever before been installed in a ship. This in turn necessitated a longer and larger hull than had ever been built, which would carry naval architecture and design far beyond its existing limits. Likewise, the cost of building these ships would be greater than anyone had ever imagined: each liner would cost well in excess of £1,200,000 each, while the annual operating subsidy would be on the order of £200,000.

When confronted with these figures, Lord Selborne balked, but Inverclyde again reiterated his position that it was simply a matter of "annihilation or absorption" for Cunard if the government did not intervene, and that the government could take it or leave it, and deal with the consequent uproar in the House of Commons and across the nation. The upshot of the whole affair was an almost total capitulation by His Majesty's Government; Balfour knew when he was beaten. Under the terms of the agreement between the government and Cunard that was signed in October 1902, the Admiralty would finance the construction of two new ships at a cost of nearly £2,600,000, the sum to be repaid over a ten year period at 2.75% interest, while an annual subsidy of £75,000 would help defray the operating expenses. In return, Cunard guaranteed that control of the line would never pass from British hands—thus thwarting IMM in one deft stroke—and further pledged that in wartime the company's ships and resources would be placed at the disposal of the Royal Navy; in peacetime, a certain percentage of their new ship's crews would consist of Naval Reservists, who, should they ever be needed, would form the nucleus of their wartime complements. Lastly, the contract reaffirmed that Cunard would receive Admiralty assistance in designing the two new liners.

Thus the stage was set for a showdown between Cunard and the two German companies, one that Cunard would win so decisively and convincingly that the line would attain a pre-eminence on the Atlantic Ferry, and while it would be challenged in the future, it would never be entirely relinquished. The instruments with which that triumph would be achieved were to be, of course, the two new ships, vessels that would usher in a fresh era on the North Atlantic, revolutionizing ocean travel, technologically and economically, forever. They would become the archetypes of the classic transatlantic liner: their profiles would become synonymous with the Golden Age of ocean travel, their appointments and interiors in all classes setting standards for style and comfort to which all subsequent ships would aspire, but rarely surpass. They were the *Lusitania* and the *Mauretania*.

CHAPTER EIGHT

Cunard Ascendant

When the 20th Century opened, the Cunard Line confronted the gravest crisis of its history, for it was facing not just oblivion, but a fate far worse: obscurity. The company was unable to sustain the energy and momentum that had driven it to so many successes in the 1880s, and the decade between 1895 and 1905 was not one of the line's finest hours. Only six new ships had been launched in the whole of the 1890s, and by the turn of the century the majority of Cunard's fleet was made up of ships that were small, slow, and rather pedestrian: the average age of the company's ships was thirteen years, the oldest member of the fleet, the *Servia*, had been launched in 1881. While for sixty years Cunard had been symbolic of safe, well-founded vessels that crossed the Atlantic reliably, if not always spectacularly, the new standards for speed and comfort set by its British and German competitors meant that safety and reliability were no longer enough. The choices of the traveling public made it clear that they *wanted* to be sped across the Atlantic and coddled as they did so, a capability that Cunard was manifestly lacking. That the *Lucania*, the last British ship to hold the Blue Ribband in the 19th Century was a Cunard ship was a happy coincidence, but not the consequence of a deliberate policy on the part of the line.

Despite the spending spree in the 1870s which followed the death of Sir Samuel Cunard, and resulted in some of the most luxurious ships the company had yet built, along with some rather daring technical innovations in the 1880s, the power and potency of the old man's personality still overshadowed the company: the innate caution with which Samuel Cunard had brought the line to a dominant position on the North Atlantic in the 1850s, had ossified into an institutional conservatism with a massive inertia all its own. The reliability and safety that had been the company's hallmarks under Sir Samuel had achieved the status of corporate icons, and indeed it was an immense and yet perverse point of pride that the line could boast—in complete truth—that "Cunard had never lost a life." Doubtless, there was a distinct and definite appeal to certain transatlantic travelers in such reassurances: it was with as much truth as wit that Mark Twain summed up Cunard's attitude when he observed, "The Cunard people would not take Noah as first mate until they had worked him through the lower grades and tried him for ten years or such matter.... It takes them about ten or fifteen years to manufacture a captain; but when they have him manufactured to suit, at last they have full confidence in him. The only order they give a captain is this, brief and to the point: 'Your ship is loaded, take her; speed is nothing; follow your own road, deliver her safe, bring her back safe—safety is all that is required." For more than two decades after the demise of the Collins Line—and the public never really forgot the spectacular tragedies that had brought about Collins' downfall—it seemed that for Cunard safety *was* all that was required: the sort of disasters and accidents that beset Cunard's British and American rivals never seemed to come Cunard's way.

That didn't mean the Cunard ships were free from accidents: In July 1900 the *Campania* was involved in a serious collision at sea. Returning to Liverpool from New York, she ran into a thick fog about two hundred miles west of Queenstown. She was able to reach Roches Point, but was forced to wait for it to lift before attempting to enter Queenstown Harbour. Just as the fog was beginning to clear and the *Campania* got underway, she collided with the *Embleton*, a barque out of Liverpool, and sliced clean through her. The forward half of the sailing ship sank instantly, while the aft section swung around and struck the *Campania*'s starboard quarter, damaging it slightly. The *Campania*'s crew put lifeboats in the water within minutes, but were only able to save seven of the *Embleton*'s crew of eighteen. The *Campania* reached the Mersey without further incident and after some minor repairs set sail for New York again on 28 July.

The *Campania* also figured in the first incident where the Cunard line suffered the first loss of life among its passengers. In October 1905 in the middle of the Atlantic, a rogue wave hit the ship broadside—five steerage passengers were swept away and another twenty-nine were injured. Three years later the *Etruria* was only four hours out of New York when she was struck by a similar freak wave, fifty feet high, that smashed guardrail stanchions and carried away part of the forebridge, killing one passenger as it passed. In 1907 two of the *Etruria*'s crew would be killed while trying to secure the starboard anchor during rough weather.

In succession, the Inman Line, the Guion Line, the White Star Line and the German companies proved that, although Cunard had taken as an article of faith the public's continued estimation of safety and reliability over speed and luxury, the public were a fickle lot, and soon the opulent offerings of Hamburg-Amerika, Norddeutscher-Lloyd and the larger British lines made such serious inroads on the number of passengers the Cunard ships were carrying, that Cunard was compelled to start casting about for any means of making money which might come to hand.

The truth was that Cunard was out of touch with the closing years of the Victorian Era. The success and growth the line had experienced in the 1860s and 1870s had throttled creative thinking at the rarified atmosphere of corporate management. What the line needed was an exploiter, someone who could bring the company's services into line with what the paying customers were expecting, and beginning to demand. Yet, despite the challenges from both British and German competitors, there was no one on the Board who was capable of accomplishing such a task.

Actually, it isn't difficult to understand why this was so. The men who made up the board of directors were all, to some degree, protegées of Samuel Cunard and his original band of partners, and so were reflections of their values. However, those were values tied to the industrial era of the mid-19th Century, not the beginning of the 20th. The world of 1901 was as vastly different from that of 1850 as 1850 had been from 1801, but in their most conservative circles this truth was far from self-evident.

It was a peculiar myopia, although it is one that has an echo in the present day. Reflecting on the opening years of the 20th Century from the perspective of the opening years of the 21st, it is still stunning to look upon the twilight of the Victorian Era, at a world which seems so far removed from the present it is often difficult to believe that only in the last decade did it really cease to be a living memory. It also reveals a reality that is extraordinarily difficult for many modern sociologists, historians and political observers and commentators to grasp: this was the world that gave birth to the present one. What makes it so difficult for them is that the values, beliefs, motives, the very pace of life a century ago seem nearly incomprehensible today. Barry Pitt, in his introduction to John Keegan's *August, 1914*, caught the essence of this seeming unreality when he wrote:

> Dimly can be perceived a life which seems to bear no relation to the present one, conducted apparently to a different rhythm, by a different species of being, reacting to a totally different scheme of behavior. Bewhiskered monarchs write stiff family notes to each other before going out to shoot stag or bird, tiara'd queens whisper behind their fans, frock-coated statesmen hurry from capital to capital and debate in solemn enclave (occasionally one is shot), while the tight-collared and cloth-capped masses alternately riot or cheer, fortified the while on ale, wine, or porter, at a penny a pint. Away in a far corner, a square of British infantry in blue and scarlet repels cavalry charges or hordes of fanatical natives. Perhaps the most astonishing aspect...is that the sun seems to have been shining all the time.

Yet, except for the privileged minority of the upper classes it was not the Golden Age or *Belle Epoque* that the rose tinted lenses of a hundred years' distance has caused many to believe it was. Class defined the Victorian era, and its successor, the Edwardian world. Defining class distinctions was sometimes a question of nationality—it was decided more by birth than wealth in Great Britain, just the reverse in the United States; but the boundaries were usually quite clearly delineated no matter where they were set: they were always particularly clear when distinguishing between "we" and "they." Almost universally, society was divided into three classes—the working, or lower class; the middle class; and the upper class, or aristocracy. There were none of the shadings of upper-middle or lower-middle or similar variations that would become so popular among late 20th Century sociologists. Mobility, especially from the middle to the upper class, was discouraged and restricted, usually by tradition and occasionally by law, although the line between the lower and middle classes blurred occasionally.

It would be going too far to describe the turn of the 20th Century as a turbulent era, but it was not a time of unbridled stability, security, innocence, comfort, or peace—although it has often been portrayed as such. Certainly these qualities were present, but in an ongoing state of flux. People had confidence in their standards and ideals, were secure in their values, and believed in Progress and Science as good things. But they weren't entirely free of doubts about the future, worried by the tangled skein of European military alliances coupled with a seemingly endless arms race. There were demonstrations and protests–sometimes violent ones—over grossly inadequate wages of the lower classes as well as the appalling working conditions and hours under which they worked; strikers and strike-breakers clashed in street brawls while anarchists and nihilists carried out a haphazard rash of bombings and assassinations. A new form of hatred and fear that became known as "terrorism" manifested itself in bloody confrontations between British police and the IRA, or Austro-Hungarian authorities and Serbian pan-nationalists, or Russian soldiers and Russian revolutionaries.

Yet while there is a real temptation to depict the first decade of the 20th Century as closely resembling that of the 21st —and superficially it may—there was one fundamental, yet subtle, difference: for all the tensions and upheavals that were shaping those years, there was a constant note of confidence running though the times. A perceptive, vocal, and eloquent minority of all social classes readily acknowledged the problems existing in society—where they differed was in the solutions and their methods of application; all agreed that it was only a matter of how and when they would be found. It was that sense of confidence, quite possibly unique in the history of the human race which made the last years of the Victorian Era and the decade of the Edwardian Era so dazzling to later generations.

Significantly, these were the years of composers like Richard Strauss and Igor Stravinsky, philosophers of the mold of Friederich Nietzsche and Henri Louis Bergson, artists such as Cezanne and Seurat, writers like Emil Zola and Bertrand Russell—compelling, forceful, and dynamic, almost revolutionary, artists and thinkers. They thoroughly transformed the external expressions of their disciplines in a breathtaking expression of art imitating life.

A hundred years of the most rapid and massive change in society and technology that mankind had ever known, culminated in the first decade of the new century. In 1800, transportation, communication, production, and manufacturing methods were still powered by muscles—human or animal— augmented by wind and water; 1900 was the high water mark of the Steam Age, with its steam engines, steamships, and steam-powered machinery. Electric power, lighting, and communications were rapidly ceasing to be mere novelties, though as yet domestic electricity was common only in the cities, and then only in the middle and upper-class areas. Trucks, lorries, and motorcars powered by internal combustion engines were beginning to compete with horse-drawn hansom cabs, carriages, wagons, and drays as a means of transport.

And the pace of change was continually accelerating. In 1900 there were less than 8,000 automobiles in the entire United States, but by 1910 there would be close to a half-million. The first flight of a heavier-than-air craft would take place in 1903, last 12 seconds, and cover 852 feet; by 1909 the French aviator Louis Bleriot would fly across the English

Channel, a distance of twenty-six miles. The electric light, motion pictures, wireless telegraphy, the original Kodak "Brownie" camera, turbine-powered steamships, the phonograph, heavier-than-air flying machines, would all be introduced in the years between 1900 and 1910—and all of them as reliable apparatus rather than mere technical novelties.

Such inventions were the products of the careful and systematic application of science to industry. Science was being transformed from a dalliance for eccentrics into a systematic discipline, becoming the foundation of industry. The Victorian-Edwardian world would witness revelations in medicine where the secrets of vitamins, genes, and hormones would be unlocked; in the psychology of Jung, Freud, Pavlov, and Adler; in the physics of Roentgen's X-rays, Marie Curie's radium, and Einstein's $E=mc^2$.

Yet, while these changes were being wrought in technology, at the same time they began an unintended erosion in the millennia-old faith in God as the source of all certainty and stability. No longer would the authority and infallibility of the Bible be universally regarded as absolute—and with that loss of absolution the heretofore solid core of religious doctrines and dogmas that had bound Western civilization together, began to slowly crumble. New, unexpected pressures were created as prosperity and poverty lived cheek-by-jowl, spawned by the industrial society which created and supported these innovations. Growing populations and densely crowded cities created new antagonisms between classes, new problems for industry owners, new opportunities for radicals and rabble rousers, while questions were raised about social values that the once-staunch pillar of the established order, the church, could no longer answer convincingly. Far from wallowing in its own decadence, as is all too often depicted, the twilight of the Victorian world was a dynamic, even exciting, time: driven by the momentum of centuries of accumulated tensions and energies of industry, economy, and society, it created extremes of wealth and poverty, opulence and indigence such as no society had ever known before. It was this era that Mark Twain christened the "Gilded Age."

It was this era with which, as the slow realization dawned, Cunard was finding itself increasingly out of touch. The company wasn't blind to new technologies: the *Servia* had been the first ship to be lit by electricity, back in 1881, and in 1901 the *Campania* became the first vessel to be fitted with a Marconi Wireless Telegraph. Experiments were already in hand to determine the suitability of marine turbines for passenger ship service and would soon offer amazing results. But the overall impression created by the Cunard fleet was that of a company rapidly falling behind the times.

If Cunard was to have any chance to remain competitive on the North Atlantic, it was imperative that she build new ships. The alternative was to accept being consigned to the second rank of shipping companies.

Cunard's ultimate response to the German challengers was yet to come, but a handful of more modern, if somewhat modest liners were already under construction. The first step taken toward refurbishing the fleet was an order placed for three liners, two to be built by C. S. Swan & Hunter and one by the John Brown shipyard. The first two would be the

Ivernia and *Saxonia*, followed two years later by a ship that would be neither the largest nor the fastest ship in the line's service, but would ultimately become one of the most famous in the whole history of Cunard, the *Carpathia*.

Built in the Swan Hunter yard, the *Ivernia* was launched in late 1899, and entered service in April 1900. At close to 14,000 gross tons, she was the largest Cunarder yet built, but she would hold that honor for little more than a month, as the next ship to enter service, the *Saxonia*, was even larger. Built by the John Brown shipyard on Clydeside, the *Saxonia* was launched on December 16, 1899, with a gross tonnage of over 14,200 tons. By mid-May, 1900, her fitting out was complete, and she set out on her maiden voyage from Liverpool to Boston on May 22. She was equipped with a pair of quadruple expansion engines, which turned two propellers. Not yet ready to challenge the Germans head-to-head, Cunard priority with the three sisters was size, not speed, and the *Saxonia*'s machinery gave her a service speed of 15 knots.

The appearance of the *Ivernia* and *Saxonia* was in its own way as distinctive as the four-funneled look of the German speedsters. A long, black hull with a graceful sheer sported a low, well-balanced superstructure and four masts. Atop the superstructure stood a single funnel with the extraordinary height of 106 feet. As awkward as this arrangement may sound, as a whole the proportions worked together to create a look that was at once purposeful and handsome. It's believed that the *Ivernia* and *Saxonia*'s funnels were the tallest ever installed on any passenger liner.

This class of ships had been designed with both passengers and cargo in mind. The four masts were no affectation added for appearance—they acted as kingposts for the booms that were used when loading or unloading cargo. The cargo spaces were quite large, and as a consequence the passenger accommodations were not as extensive or luxurious as might be expected of the largest ships in the Cunard fleet. There were accommodations for two hundred Second Class passengers and fifteen hundred Third Class, but no First Class accommodations at all: these ships had been built as money-makers, not for prestige. Their dual roles as cargo *and* passenger ships were confirmation, if any were needed, of Cunard's straitened circumstances: the line could no longer depend on ships built exclusively for passengers for its revenues, but was once again looking to freighting to enable the company to stay solvent. In the first few years of the 20th Century, under pressure from both the Germans and J. P. Morgan, Cunard had to earn every pound it possibly could.

The *Carpathia* joined the *Ivernia* and *Saxonia* in 1903. Her keel had been laid down on September 10, 1901 at the Wallsend shipyard Swan & Hunter, and she was launched on August 6, 1902. An interesting sidelight to her construction was that while the *Carpathia* was taking shape in one of the yard's gantries, at the other end of the shipyard archeologists had begun excavating the recently-discovered eastern end of Hadrian's Wall, the ancient Roman boundary between Britannia and Alba—Britain and Scotland—a fascinating juxtaposition of the ancient world and the modern. As the *Carpathia* was just barely larger than 14,000 tons, the *Saxonia* remained the largest ship in Cunard service until the

Caronia made her appearance in 1905. The *Saxonia* stayed on the Liverpool to New York run until 1911, when she was transferred to the Mediterranean service, crossing between Trieste and Boston, where she would continue until the beginning of the Great War.

In her role as a cargo carrier, the *Carpathia* was a bit more specialized than her two sisters. Designed to carry refrigerated food, in particular, meat, she had been built with three large refrigerated holds, as well as one for her own provisions. Her power plant was identical to that of the *Ivernia* and *Saxonia*, a pair of ten-cylinder quadruple expansion engines turning her two propellers, which gave her a top speed of about 14 knots.

Like her two sisters, the *Carpathia* was originally designed to carry just Second and Third Class passengers. Despite the absence of First Class, the standard of the accommodation was remarkably high: Third Class features included a smoking room, a bar, a ladies' sitting room and a dining saloon large enough to serve 300 people at one sitting; Second Class had similar amenities as well as a library. All told, the *Carpathia* could carry 1,700 people—200 in Second Class and 1,500 in steerage.

While the term "steerage" was still used more-or-less interchangeably with "Third Class," the circumstances that greeted Third Class passengers in the first decade of the Twentieth Century were a far cry from the dank 'tween decks of sixty years before. The culmination of the trend begun by William Inman a half-century earlier, the accommodations aboard the Carpathia were typical of a new consciousness of the value of Third Class passengers to the Cunard Line.

A great many myths have built up around the flood of emigrants that flowed to the shores of the New World at the end of the 19th Century and the beginning of the 20th, aided by a spate of romanticized reporting, photographs, and artwork from the period. All too often the steerage passengers were portrayed as "tired, poor...huddled masses"—babushka- and shawl-beclad mothers gripping the hands of small, wide-eyed children, or young men in ill-fitting clothing clutching their few belongings in loosely tied bundles, all hoping to find their fortunes in such exotic locales as New York, Pittsburgh, or Chicago.

The truth, as with so many subjects of the journalism of that day, was a good deal more mundane. Despite the increasing numbers of central and southern Europeans emigrating to America, the majority of those leaving the Old World for the New were still Anglo-Saxon. Many were Germans, whose Fatherland was undergoing a bewilderingly rapid transformation from an agrarian society to an industrial juggernaut, with all the attendant social dislocations; many others were Britons, often skilled or semi-skilled workers, sometimes craftsmen, occasionally members of the professions, forced to seek employment in America as Britain edged toward her slow decline, industrially and economically. To these people a ship was transportation, its sole purpose to take them from Liverpool (or Southampton or Cherbourg or Queenstown) to Halifax, Boston, or New York. Passengers like these were not influenced by such luxuries as Grand Staircases, electric elevators, or swimming baths. Their interests lay in clean quarters and decent food. In this respect, the Cunard Line served them not only admirably, but with the German lines' new emphasis

Deck space for Third Class, making do among the machinery and rigging.

on opulence, better than their competitors.

Third Class berthing on a ship like the *Carpathia* was spread out along the lower three decks of the ship, the superstructure being the exclusive preserve of Second Class. The quarters were divided into sections for single men, single women, married couples, and families were berthed forward. There was a near-Puritanical streak at work in the layout of these sections, peculiar to the morals and morality of the day, which made sure single men and women wouldn't have cabins anywhere near each other. The cabins themselves were spacious, spotless, and if a bit austere, were by all reports comfortable enough. The unmarried men or women would share a room with three to five other passengers of the same sex, while married couples and families had rooms to themselves.

The Third Class galley provided a fare that, though unspectacular, offered good food and plenty of it; in some cases, especially those from the more impoverished Irish counties, the steerage passengers ate better aboard ship than they ever had at home. All in all, it was a good deal more than most would be expecting when they paid for their passage.

Nothing better illustrates how far steerage had come in the past six decades than do the terms and conditions outlined in the ticket issued to each Third Class passenger, such as the one issued by a Cunard agent in Trondheim, Norway:

CONTRACT

Between

THE CUNARD LINE

And the passenger listed below regarding transportation to

[the passengers final destination would be listed here, followed by his or her name.]

I, OLAF H. SOLEM, *agent in Trondhjem, hereby commit myself to transport the said person, by 3rd class or Steerage, from Trondhjem to the destination which is likewise specified herein, for the sum of 244.00 crowns, which I acknowledge I have received as full payment.*

Trondhjem, 5 June 1913

/s/ Olaf H. Solem

Specifications - The passengers are to be transported below deck by a steamship that is sailing on 5 June 1913 from Trondhjem to Hull, from there by 3rd class railroad car to Liverpool, with the first ordinary train after customs inspection. From there they will be transported by Cunard Steam Ship Company Limited, Liverpool, owners of the Cunard steamships, on one of their steam-ships to New York or Boston. For the duration of the whole journey to New York or Boston and during the time they are delayed in any place whatsoever regardless of the cause, the passengers will be provided with suitable lodging and will receive good and properly cooked food, served thus:

Breakfast and evening meal. Tea or coffee, sugar, fresh bread and butter, etc.

Midday meal. Alternately soup, meat, pork, fish, potatoes, bread, as well as pudding on Sundays.

Each person over 12 years old can take along free of charge 10 cubic feet of baggage on the steamship and 150 pounds on the train in America, half of that for children from 1 to 12 years. The emigrants will be met and transported further by the Company's own employees in Hull, Liverpool, New York and Boston.

Should an emigrant's departure be prevented by illness, he will be allowed to leave with a steamship departing later, and should the police prevent his departure, his money will be returned or handed over to the police.

Without responsibility for the baggage that the passengers have in their own custody on the trip.

In truth Cunard was just marking time with the *Ivernia, Saxonia,* and *Carpathia*—they were essentially time servers, certainly nothing spectacular, but in their own way handsome and comfortable enough to attract a clientele sufficiently respectable in numbers and manners which would keep Cunard from drifting into desuetude. With a mighty infusion of cash from the Exchequer, Lord Inverclyde was not about to squander what was a once-in-a-lifetime opportunity simply building ships to match the German efforts. What he intended was not to just trump the Germans, but crush them, and do it so decisively that in the future it would be the Germans who would be compelled to play catch-up with

Cunard. In the meantime, the ships already in service were asked to hold the line against the German challengers until the *Lusitania* and *Mauretania* were ready to put to sea.

The design brief for the two new ships was given in the summer of 1903 to a combined civilian and Admiralty design team, headed by Leonard Peskett, Cunard's senior marine architect and designer. Peskett and his staff were faced with a herculean task, for while the ships had to meet the requirements laid down by the Admiralty offices in Whitehall, they also had to be able to create a profit for Cunard. As the Admiralty outline ran, these ships had to be capable of sustained speeds of up to 25 knots, carry an armament of not less than twelve 6-inch guns, and have their vital machinery spaces protected on a scale similar to the cruisers of the Royal Navy. Peskett then had to find a way to provide accommodations for enough passengers to keep the ships operating in the black. As if that was not enough, Cunard compounded the poor man's problems by decreeing that the accommodations in all three classes were to exceed in comfort and convenience anything ever seen before on the North Atlantic. The short of it was that Peskett was faced with the challenge of creating what amounted to a floating hotel, capable of holding 2,300 passengers and 900 crew, which could double as a warship if needed. What he and his team of architects and designers produced was a work of genius.

In one bold swoop the plans for the *Lusitania* and *Mauretania* moved ship construction into what was virtually *terra incognito*. The designs were so revolutionary that they deserve to be examined in some detail. While the sheer size projected for the two ships would push naval architecture and marine engineering well beyond the bounds of anything yet tried, that in itself wasn't particularly remarkable—successive generations of steamships had been growing steadily larger for the past sixty years. What was at once so daunting and yet so thrilling was the application of new technologies which, though hardly unproven, had never been applied on such a scale before, meaning that Peskett and his fellow designers could not always depend on past experience as a guide for solving new problems. That they succeeded at all is remarkable; that they succeeded as well as they did is a tribute to their considerable talents.

The result of their two years of design work was a *tour de force* in naval architecture and an aesthetic nightmare. The ships would have a long, narrow hull, 768 feet in length and with a beam of only 88 feet, while their fully laden draft was projected to be 33 feet. The designed displacement of these ships was 41,400 tons fully laden, making them the first ships to pass the 40,000-ton mark in size; or, to put it in perspective with their potential rivals, these ships were to be almost 70 feet longer, 16 feet broader, and nearly 18,000 tons heavier than the largest of the German liners they were meant to best, the *Kaiser Wilhelm II*. Some indication of how rapidly ships were growing in size can be gained by recalling that the last British ship to hold the Blue Ribband, Cunard's own *Lucania*, had a total displacement of 18,000 tons—only ten years earlier!

Perched atop this huge hull would be a ventilator-cluttered superstructure which bore more than a passing resemblance to a Queen Anne's mansion, with an after-section that

One of the Wilhelm der Grosse's *six-cylinder reciprocating engines. A sense of how immense were these engines can be gained noting the man standing at the center of the two cylinder blocks.*

looked like an afterthought. Towering above it all were four massive, ungainly funnels that vented the huge boiler rooms below, the whole creating a not incorrect impression of top-heaviness. The *Lusitania* and *Mauritania* would be the largest and most powerful passenger ships yet built; they would be undeniably impressive, but there was no way they could honestly be called beautiful. Taken overall they created a sense of ponderous bulk, as opposed to the slim grace of the two ships that would be the White Star Line's eventual reply, the *Olympic* and *Titanic,* or what would be the stately majesty of Cunard's own *Aquitania,* which would follow in 1913.

Their less-than-inspired aesthetics in no way detracted from the magnitude of Peskett's achievement, however. The outstanding feature of their design was their power plants: the choice of high-speed turbines for propulsion was a decision that marked the beginning of a new era in passenger ship construction. What made them so remarkable was the complete and utter contrast that a turbine presented when compared with a reciprocating engine.

Reciprocating engines were made up of a series of cylinders, ranging from as few as two in number to as many as ten, inside of which heavy steel pistons were moved up and down by steam pressure. A connecting rod attached to a crankshaft converted the piston's vertical motion into rotary motion, which then turned the propeller shaft. This meant that every time the shaft made a single revolution, the piston had to be moved downward, its momentum stopped, then moved upward and have its momentum halted again at the top of the stroke—the whole process being repeated sometimes as many as 120 times a minute, if the engine was turning that fast. The pistons, rods, and shaft were subjected to a constant, extraordinary pounding, compounded by the number of cylinders in the engine. The brass bearings carrying the loads between piston and connecting rod, and connecting rod and crankshaft, required constant attention and adjustment—it was not unknown for a hose to keep a steady jet of water playing on an overheating bearing during prolonged high-speed run. The vibration created was bone-shaking, the noise deafening, and the clouds of steam the engines emitted were blinding; a reciprocating engine room was a dangerous place, the decks slick with oil and water, making footing treacherous, and as the machinery was open, falling into the maw of a thrashing collection of connecting rods and crankshafts was a constant peril. The din made carrying on normal conversation difficult, and hearing orders shouted down from the bridge through a voice tube or over a telephone was often a dicey proposition.

The contrast of the engine room of a turbine-driven ship with that of one powered by reciprocating engines was astonishing. Turbines were far quieter, they caused no clouds of steam to fill the engine spaces, and the vibration they created was remarkably mild compared with the pounding of the great masses of metal being shunted back and forth in a reciprocating engine. Even more significant was that the rotor of the turbine was connected directly to the propeller shaft, so steam acted directly on the shaft, resulting in very little wasted motion or loss of power, and vastly reduced stresses on the moving parts.

There was another significant advantage that turbines offered over reciprocating engines: smaller size. The only way to significantly increase the power output of a reciprocating engine was to make it larger, either by increasing the size of the cylinders and the length of their stroke, or by increasing their numbers. There were practical limits, though, to this process; increased cylinder size and length of stroke meant increasing the height, which took up volume inside the ship which would normally be given over to passenger accommodations. Increasing the number of cylinders simply increased the overall length of the entire engine. Already there were engines that stood almost forty feet tall and eighty feet in length, with cylinders more than eight feet in diameter. Any dramatic increase in the horsepower produced by such engines would require a corresponding increase in size; there was the real possibility that the engines might actually become too big for the hulls they were meant to be driving.

For turbines, the key to increased power was an increase in the number of blades attached to the turbine rotor. While this could be done by increasing a given rotor's diameter, it was more easily and efficiently accomplished by simply lengthening the rotor, increasing the number of rows of blades. By eliminating the need for pistons, connecting rods, and crankshafts, turbines could be built that were much smaller than a piston engine with a similar power output; as a rule of thumb, a turbine required roughly half the space of its reciprocating counterpart. This meant smaller engine rooms and more available space for passengers.

While all the theoretical advantages seemed to lie with turbines, Cunard was still nervous about committing itself to putting them in the two new ships. True, the Royal Navy already had a pair of turbine-powered destroyers in service, *Viper* and *Cobra*, and the decision had been made to install turbines in the revolutionary new battleship *Dreadnought*. But even so, she would be barely half the size of the *Lusitania* and *Mauretania*, and the service demands of a warship and a passenger liner were far different. While the engines of a battleship might be periodically called upon to deliver very high speeds, the engines of a crack liner on the North Atlantic run had to be capable of being reliably run all-out all the time. Cunard decided that they had to have a body of practical experience with a large ship in service to examine, from which the line could draw the proper conclusions, as well as learn how to service and maintain a turbine-driven ship.

A Parsons turbine, with the casing opened to show the seven sets of rotor blades.

The result of that decision was the construction of the *Carmania* and the *Caronia*, two ships that externally and internally were as alike as two peas in a pod—with one exception: one would be fitted with reciprocating engines turning two screws, and the other with turbines turning three propellers. Cunard was fortunate in that the two ships were already building at the Clydebank firm of John Brown & Company when the debate over turbines *versus* reciprocating engines reached a critical stage, and were at a point in their construction where the *Carmania* was able to be quickly modified to accept a turbine powerplant. The *Caronia* was the first of the two ships to go down the ways, launched on July 13th 1904. With a displacement of 19,524 tons, she was the largest Cunard ship ever built at that time. The proportions of her superstructure and funnels differed somewhat from earlier Cunarders, which caused her funnels to be divided into four equal bands instead of the five that had been the tradition to this time. Being the biggest ship in the Cunard fleet, the *Caronia* was naturally put on the Liverpool to New York run. While she would never be a record-breaker—she wasn't designed to be one—she could easily maintain a service speed of 18 knots, which surprising numbers of passengers would find both comfortable and convenient.

The *Carmania* was launched on February 21, 1905, just four days before the *Caronia* set out on her maiden voyage. Ten months later, the *Carmania* created a tremendous stir in the Cunard offices when she had easily exceeded her sister's top speed by more than two knots. As successful as the *Caronia* had been, the *Carmania* was even more so: the *Carmania* proved to be both faster *and* more economical than *Caronia*, and as she was much quieter and vibrated less noticeably than her sister, it was hardly surprising that she should quick-

The first Caronia, *which together with her sister the* Carmania, *made up the duet known as the "Pretty Sisters."*

ly become the most popular ship in the Cunard fleet. Dignified and balanced, with two tall funnels that were carefully proportioned to the ships' superstructures (Cunard would never again make the kind of aesthetic blunder that led to the railway tunnel-like funnels perched atop the *Campania* and *Lucania*!), the *Carmania* and *Caronia* were soon known as the "Pretty Sisters", and this duo began encroaching on Hamburg-Amerika and Norddeutscher-Lloyd's near hegemony on the North Atlantic.

In the meantime, with the issue of the propulsion systems to be installed in the *Lusitania* and *Mauretania* finally resolved, work on them forged ahead. The first of the sisters to be laid down was the *Lusitania*, her builder the John Brown & Son works on the Clyde below Glasgow. In the last quarter of the 19th Century and the first of the 20th, the River Clyde was the center of world shipbuilding, gaining such a reputation for quality engineering and construction that simply declaring a vessel to be a "Clyde-built ship" was sufficient testimonial to her soundness, and the *Lusitania* would prove to be no exception. With all the appropriate fanfare, her keel was laid on September 20, 1904. Over the next eighteen months, as the world watched in anticipation, the hull was framed and the shell plating went up, then the engines, shafts and screws were installed. Yet for Cunard there would be a small, dark cloud hovering about the *Lusitania* as she was being built, as tragedy struck the company a little more than a year after her keel was laid. At the age of forty-four, vigorous, dynamic, and at the height of his powers, Lord Inverclyde was struck down by a heart attack and died on October 8, 1904.

It was a blow that the line felt keenly, for aside from old Samuel Cunard himself no one had ever exerted a greater influence over the fortunes—present and future—of the

Cunard Line than Lord Inverclyde. The second John Burns and the second Lord Inverclyde to sit in the Chairman's seat on Cunard's Board of Directors (his father was the first of both) he was the grandson of George Burns, who had been one of Samuel Cunard's original partners. With a business acumen as sharp as any of his colleagues or competitors—British, American, or German—and of a stronger character than any of the American robber-barons, Inverclyde had been the quintessential right man in the right place at the right time when the challenge from IMM had been thrown down to Cunard. He had succeeded to his title and the chairmanship on the elder John Burns' death in 1901; his own tenure at the helm of Cunard lasted just three years, but what he accomplished in that time saved the company from absorption and obscurity. The impact of his decisions would be felt within Cunard for another six decades, while the *Lusitania* and *Mauretania* would be his memorials, testament to his leadership and vision.

The *Lusitania* was the first of the two sisters to be ready for launching; the date was set for June 7, 1906. When that morning came, a concerted effort by all concerned effectively dispelled the pall that had faintly but unmistakably shrouded the *Lusitania* since the death of Lord Inverclyde. The event was regarded as something approaching a national holiday, and the shipyard was crowded with an amazing array of distinguished personages from the Empire as well as the scientific and maritime communities. Representatives from Germany, France, Russia, Italy, and Japan were invited; no official envoy from the United States was present—whether this was an oversight or an indirect snub at Morgan and IMM has never been determined. Among the notables present were Sir Charles MacLaren, chairman of John Brown and Company, who would preside over the launching ceremonies, along with the rest of the directors of the shipyard; William Watson, Cunard's new chairman, accompanied by the other members of the board; Leonard Peskett; the chairman, director, and yard manager of Swan Hunter of Tyneside, where the *Mauretania* was being built; several members of the Board of Admiralty; the Provost of Glasgow; and curiously enough, Lord William Pirrie, chairman of Harland and Wolff, the Belfast shipbuilders. All in all, some twenty thousand invited guests packed the balconies and grandstands surrounding the slipway where the *Lusitania* waited.

A crowd of over a hundred thousand people watched from both banks of the Clyde. All eyes were focused on the slender figure of Mary Burns, Lady Inverclyde, the widow of Cunard's late chairman, as she stepped up to a rostrum at the foot of the *Lusitania*'s forepeak, and at precisely 12:30pm pressed a button that released a bottle of champagne to break across the ship's bow. Simultaneously, workmen began knocking away restraining blocks and balks of timber that had been holding the great hull in place, and after those first few anxious moments that accompany every launch, when the ship seems to refuse to budge and sits motionless on the ways, the *Lusitania* began moving, and within a half-minute was afloat on the River Clyde.

The next thirteen months were spent fitting her out in the Clydebank Shipyard Basin, as her boilers and uptakes were installed, her interior completed, her superstructure finished, her hull and upperworks painted, and her funnels and masts stepped. As Sir Charles MacLaren had observed in a toast at the formal luncheon that followed her launch, the *Lusitania* exceeded any other vessel ever built in length, beam, draught, and tonnage. By the end of August 1907, she was ready for a week of intensive sea trials which would prove whether all of the time, effort, and money invested by Cunard and the Admiralty were well spent—or were hopelessly wasted.

Four sets of Parsons turbines would power the *Lusitania* and *Mauretania*; each set, which included one forward and one reverse turbine, driving one propeller shaft, the total output of the four being over 68,000 shaft horsepower (shp), nearly double that of the *Kaiser Wilhelm II*. The turbines were remarkable engineering achievements, each rotor nearly fifteen feet in diameter and weighing ten tons, containing hundreds of thousands of individual vanes or blades, each meticulously positioned and balanced, machined to tolerances measured in thousandths of an inch, and spun at such high speeds that a drop of water striking one of the blades would shatter it. There would be a combined total of more than three million such blades in the four sets of turbines installed in each ship. Gone were the huge pistons, connecting rods, crankshafts and valve gear of the reciprocating engines, along with all of their pounding and vibration.

Installing a turbine was a major engineering challenge. Unlike reciprocating engines

The control room of a turbine-powered ship. The telegraph in the foreground rang down engine orders from the bridge, while the large wheels on the bulkhead behind the engineering offices controlled the flow of steam to the turbines.

which could be erected section by section in a ship's engine room, turbine rotors could only be installed as complete assemblies. In the machinery shop where they were assembled, the ten-ton rotors were hoisted onto flatcars and slowly wheeled to the dock where the ship was being fitted out. Once the flatcar was in position, a floating crane would hoist the rotor away: this work was always done on windless days to minimize the movement of the crane, the ship, or the rotor as it was being moved; no other work took place on board the ship on these days as well. The crane would lift the rotor seventy feet or more into the air, then once it was poised above the access hatch on the upper deck, it would stop and allow teams of riggers holding onto lines attached to each end of the rotor to carefully dampen any oscillation that might have been induced by the lifting. Then in movements measured in inches—in fractions of inches as the rotors were actually being eased into their casings and bearings—the entire assembly was lowered into the hatchways. The need for such care was paramount—should any of the turbine blades be damaged, they could throw the entire rotor and shaft out of balance and destroy the turbine the first time it was spun up to speed.

While adopting a turbine power plant saved weight and space in the engine room, huge amounts of steam were still needed to spin those turbines, more steam than had ever been generated aboard a ship before. Twenty-five coal-burning boilers, divided between four boiler rooms, numbered 1 through 4 from the bow aft, provided the steam. Twenty-three of the boilers were double-ended, that is, they had fireboxes at each end of the boiler casing, while two were single ended. Each end held four fireboxes, so that the *Lusitania* had a total of 192 furnaces, each of which had to be constantly fed coal, one shovelful at a time—almost a thousand tons of coal a day, more than 3,000 tons on each crossing, in order to generate the steam necessary to speed the ship at over 26 knots.

With the possible exception of the lot of a galley slave, it would be difficult to conceive of a task more demanding and demeaning, more backbreaking and more soul-breaking, than feeding the furnaces of a coal fired boiler on a steamship. The confines of the hull meant that none of the bulky automated feeding mechanisms that fired boilers ashore could be installed in the ship. Instead, the entire chore was accomplished through sheer human muscle power. The task began with the trimmers, who had to carry the coal from the bunkers to the foot of the firebox, using wheelbarrows to deliver great lumps of coal measuring as much as twenty inches in length and eight inches thick. At the start of the voyage, with full bunkers, it was a relatively easy job, but toward the end of the crossing, as the bunkers began to empty, it was fiercesome work, for by then the coal might be a hundred-fifty feet or more from the scuttle where it was loaded in the barrows, and for every trimmer carrying a load to the furnaces, there was one *inside* the bunker shifting coal. Despite the fact that the trimmers were at the very bottom of the hierarchy of the Engineering department, there was a certain degree of skill required in their job as well—it was their responsibility to see that the coal was used in uniform amounts from each bunker, so that the weight of the remaining coal wouldn't unbalance the ship, upsetting her trim—hence the name "trimmers." Their world was an eerie one, poorly lit, poorly ventilated, where temperatures ranged from the searing heat of the furnace door to the chill reaches of the farther bunkers. Once the coal was delivered to the firebox, the stokers took over.

Looking back at them and their work, there is something akin to an arcane science, or more appropriately, a black art, to the task of a stoker. If there was ever a physical embodiment of Dante's *Inferno*, it would have been found on the floor of a 19th Century steel mill or the boiler room of a coal-fired steamship. Usually working stripped to the waist, their torsos, arms and faces covered in coal dust, the stokers were eerily illuminated by the glow of the flames in the fireboxes and the flare of clinkers and slag as they went through an elaborate and exacting ballet of muscle and sweat.

A stoker's first task was to break up the large lumps of coal brought by the trimmers into something more manageable, so using their shovels and slice bars, they would reduce the larger pieces into fragments roughly the size of a man's fist. Next, timing his movements to the pitch of the ship, the stoker would swing open the door to a firebox and quickly thrust home his slice bar along the fire-grate, working it back and forth four times, once for each track of the grate, to improve the draft across the burning coals by breaking ashes and clinkers loose. These were quickly raked into the pit below the firebox and the fire-door swung closed again. On double-ended boilers the stokers worked in tandem so that doors at the opposite ends were never open at the same time; this conserved heat in the boiler, but more important, it prevented back-drafts that could blow the fire out into the stokers' faces.

Then the fire-door would be opened again, and the stoker would shovel a layer of coal across the grate—a skilled stoker would usually feed in no more than four shovelfuls of coal, spreading them over the grate at a uniform depth of four inches. At the same time, the water tenders would keep a close eye on the gauges, careful to keep a level of two inches in the boiler, a combination that maximized the amount of steam each fire-grate could produce.

The whole routine moved to the inexorable ringing of Kilroy's Patent Stoking Indicator, a mechanical timer that could be set for intervals between eight and thirty minutes. The higher the speed of the ship, the lower the interval between rings on the Indicator; the amount of time for which the Indicator was set was the total allotted to performing the entire cycle of breaking coal, slicing, clinkering and stoking. In express liners such as the *Lusitania* and *Mauretania* were expected to be, the usual settings would be between eight and ten minutes. At the end of each four-hour watch the stokers would finish by raking the ashes and clinkers out of the pits, hosing them down to cool them, then shoveling them into hoppers that mixed them with seawater and then ejected them out scuttles near the ship's waterline.

It's little wonder that, given the endless monotony and the sheer mindlessness of the work, that the trimmers and stokers were a hard, sometimes brutal breed. Barely educat-

The "Black Gang" at work. Some ships consumed almost a thousand tons of coal each day at sea, all of it fed into the furnaces one shovelful at a time.

ed, with little if any prospect of advancement from their station in society or aboard the ship, they were valued only for their strong backs. Despite the revolution effected by the turbine in engine design, the roles of the stoker and trimmer had altered very little since the days of the *Britannia*, and would remain essentially unchanged until the advent of oil-fired boilers.

Although the *Lusitania* and *Mauretania* were first and foremost passenger liners, their potential role as auxiliary cruisers was a very real consideration, and in addition to the high speed provided by their turbines, there were several features of the design of the *Lusitania* and her sister that were mandated by the requirements of the Admiralty contract which were not found on most passenger liners. There would be twelve specially reinforced platforms, six on each side of the ship, eight on D deck, and four on C deck that would serve as the mounting points for the guns, should the *Lusitania* or *Mauretania* ever be called upon to don their guise as an auxiliary cruiser. Specific compartments were designated for swift conversion into magazines and shell handling rooms, while other areas—including some passenger accommodations—were specified to be reserved for use exclusively by the Royal Navy in the event of a war or a national emergency. The moveable structure of each ship's rudder was located below the waterline to protect it from enemy gunfire, although their profile was contoured along the lines of the traditional ocean liner's counter stern.

While there were other technical concessions made to the Admiralty requirements, Lord Inverclyde made certain that Peskett and his colleagues never lost sight of the fact that the two new ships were first of all passengers liners. They were specifically charged to not only take the Blue Ribband away from the Germans, but also to draw enough pas-

The Caronia's *First Class Dining Saloon, a vista of white-enameled elegance.*

sengers away from the two German rivals as to return Cunard to a place of primacy on the North Atlantic. Swiftness alone would not assure bookings on Cunard ships—in addition to speed, the *Lusitania* and *Mauretania* had to offer prospective passengers comfort, convenience, and—a relatively new word in the Cunard lexicon—luxury on a scale that matched or exceeded anything that Norddeutscher-Lloyd or Hamburg-Amerika had to offer.

The *Carmania* and *Caronia* had been the forerunners of what was to come, for although they were never record breakers, they were reasonably fast and remarkably comfortable. With the *Lusitania* and *Mauretania*, however, the line was about to soundly trump the Germans and White Star on both counts. Consequently, it wasn't only necessary for Peskett's design team to produce an extremely fast ship—they also had to produce a fabulously luxurious one. The First Class public rooms demonstrated how well the design board fulfilled Cunard's requirements. They included a dining saloon, reception room, restaurant, lounge, reading and writing room, and smoking room and the verandah cafe, and were served by a pair of elevators—a novelty in 1907. *En suite* cabins were provided, as well as a pair of elegantly appointed "Regal Suites" that were clearly meant for the *creme de la creme* of transatlantic society. Each of these suites consisted of a dining room, drawing room, two bedrooms, a bath and toilet, as well as adjoining rooms for valets or maids. There was also a barber shop, a darkroom for photographers, a clothes-pressing room, a special dining room for passengers' personal servants, a lending library, even a telephone system that allowed passengers to place calls from one cabin to another. Simply put, everything had been done in fitting out the first class accommodation to make it more than equal to the finest hotels ashore in Europe or America.

The centerpiece of each ship's decor was the magnificent two-tiered First Class Dining Saloon, also known as the Grand Saloon, with its white enameled paneling, and its enormous gilt and alabaster dome, done in a Louis XVI style. It was the largest such room yet seen in a ship, over 90 feet in length, running the full width of the hull. With a 500-seat capacity, aboard the *Lusitania* it presented a vast sea of gilt-topped Corinthian columns, overstuffed swivel chairs and polished mahogany tables, set with glittering crystal and gleaming silver. The *Mauretania*'s Grand Saloon was similar in layout, but the gilding and alabaster gave way to oak, maple, mahogany, and walnut; this difference characterized the differences in decor throughout the two ships—and as far as the number of passengers carried was concerned, the traveling public's taste would prove to be evenly split between the two. The *Lusitania*'s partisans were as vocal in espousing the virtues of the white enamel-work of her corridors and the carefully subdued gilt-work of her public rooms as those of the *Mauretania* were in declaring the superiority of her warmly wood-toned interiors.

The First Class Smoking Room, located on A Deck, was an equally eloquent testimonial to the care and expense lavished on both ship's interiors. Sitting under a huge, ornate,

The Mauretania*'s First Class Dining Room, with the Captain's Table set under the open ceiling.*

The Mauretania's First Class Lounge, with its distinctive oval skylight.

wrought-iron skylight inset with leaded glass and etched-patterned panels, it was decorated in the style of the late Georgian period, a symphony of mahogany and walnut-paneled walls, handsomely carpeted flooring, and massive leather-covered armchairs, beside which sat exquisitely carved, marble-topped tables. The entire atmosphere immediately evoked images of silk waistcoats, gold watch chains, expensive cigars, and the deep baritones of rail barons, shipping magnates, international publishers, and millionaire businessmen.

The staterooms and suites for the First Class passengers were, of course, on a scale in keeping with the other First Class amenities. Instead of the usual bunk or berth typical of the transatlantic liner of the day, each stateroom had its own full-sized, wrought-iron bedstead, as well as a washstand with hot and cold running water. If a passenger was willing to spend the extra money, whole suites of three, four, or five rooms could be booked, in decor that included several Louis (XIV, XV, and XVI), Georgian, and Regence (as the British insisted for years on spelling "Regency").

The craftsmanship and meticulous construction were carried over fully into Second and Third Classes as well. Indeed, Second Class rooms, public and private, could have been mistaken for First Class on almost any other ship on the North Atlantic, including the Dining Saloon, Smoking Room, and Library, and while the Second Class dining saloon may not have been as grand as that of First Class, it was still an exceedingly handsome structure.

Third Class berthing was concentrated in the forward end of the ship, with arrangements made for single men and women, married couples and families. The Third Class accommodation included a large number of permanent cabins as well as large sections of berths formed by movable wooden partitions, so that the numbers and sizes of the cabins could be adjusted to the number of passengers, and the unused space given over to open common areas, a touch that was much appreciated by the steerage passengers when the weather was rough and going out on deck was out of the question.

There was one particularly pleasing element of decor that was used consistently throughout the ships, which more than anything gives an idea of the thought and care that went into the design of the *Lusitania* and *Mauretania*'s interior furnishings. In many of the public rooms, wherever columns were used, their capitals were always done in the elaborately detailed Corinthian style in First class, the more subdued but still elegant Doric style in Second class, and in Third they were done in the clean and simple Ionian motif. It was the sort of touch that set the interiors of the two ships apart from the heavy-handed baroque effects of Johannes Poppe or the sometimes ambiguous designs of Charles Mewés: the *Lusitania* and *Mauretania* were each distinctive, yet unmistakably British.

Her fitting-out complete, the *Lusitania* was ready for sea trials at the end of July 1907. They lasted for three days, and at their conclusion it was clear to everyone that the *Lusitania* was a marvel: she exceeded every expectation that anyone held as to her ability to better, and better decisively, the best speeds the German liners could produce. In four runs from Gourock, Scotland to Land's End in England, made between July 29 and August 1, 1907, she averaged nearly twenty-five and one half knots, and at one point passed the twenty-six and one half knot mark. However, her sea trials were not an unqualified success: inadequate structural bracing in her stern caused the entire after section of the ship to shudder violently at high speed. To one observer it was a sort of "violent convulsion" that rattled through the keel and frames to shake the decks, shell plating, and fixtures. It was so bad that much of the stern section was declared uninhabitable due to the vibration. The *Lusitania* went back to the shipyard where she was pulled into dry dock and her entire stern section was completely gutted, including 142 Second Class cabins. Strakes, columns, reinforcing frames and brackets were all added to reinforce and stabilize the stern. The results proved to be satisfactory, although vibration in her after sections would plague the *Lusitania* throughout her career—Second Class passengers would often be overheard remarking about the vibration being particularly noticeable in the Second Class Dining Saloon, as if, one of them said, "it had been built right over the screws."

The next month was spent finishing preparations for the *Lusitania*'s maiden voyage from Liverpool to New York. The results of her sea trials were hardly a secret, and it was only a question of by how much would she beat the *Kaiser Wilhelm II*'s record, not if she would. When she departed Liverpool with a full passenger list and under the command of Captain J. B. Watt at noon on September 8, 1907, a crowd of more than 200,000 people

The Lusitania, *making up in power what she lacked in grace, preparing for her maiden voyage in September 1907.*

lined the waterfront to watch her steam down the Mersey. Bad weather held her back and when she arrived off Sandy Hook seven days later, she had missed taking the Blue Riband away from the Deutschland by less than six hours. But she wouldn't be long denied, as on her second westbound the *Lusitania* had returned the Blue Riband to Great Britain, becoming the first liner to cross the North Atlantic in under five days, her time from Queenstown to New York just four days, 19 hours and 52 minutes. On the return to Liverpool she promptly took the eastbound record as well.

Now it was the *Mauretania*'s turn. If it was possible, her launch created just as much excitement as the *Lusitania*'s. When September 20, 1906 dawned bright and clear, a crowd as large as the one which had gathered along the Clyde, formed on the banks of the Tyne near the Swan Hunter yard. The collection of notable personages assembled for the launch was virtually identical to those who had gathered at the John Brown yard. The Dowager Duchess of Roxburgh, sister of Lord Tweedmouth, the First Lord of the Admiralty, did the honors, formally naming the *Mauretania* before pressing the switch that released the last restraints on the great hull and sent it sliding down into the Tyne.

While the *Lusitania* and *Mauretania* were being built, arrangements were being made in Liverpool and New York for mooring and docking them. Neither port had ever been called upon to accommodate such huge hulls, and shortly after Cunard announced the construction of the two ships, the company began negotiations with the port authorities of both cities. The Princes Landing Stage in Liverpool wasn't deep enough for the new liners' proposed deep-laden draught of thirty-seven feet, so more than 200,000 tons of rock, mud, and sand were dredged away to deepen the channel. In New York a similar undertaking was underway, despite the usual protests from some business circles who felt that Cunard was receiving preferential treatment; Cunard always had the trump card to play of threatening to move its main American terminus to either Boston or Philadelphia, a ploy that worked every time. In Liverpool, the Canada dry dock was modified to allow berthing for the *Lusitania* and *Mauretania* when they were undergoing refits or overhauls.

The sea trials of the *Mauretania* were even more extensive than those of her sister, as several small but significant modifications had been made to her power plant. The diameter of her turbine rotors had been increased, along with the diameter of her screws, which also had their pitch altered. For five days she ran up and down the North Sea along the English coast, through the English Channel and up the Irish Sea to the waters of the Western Isles, at several points working up to speeds well over 26 knots. In every respect she was pronounced more than satisfactory, and in the first week of November was handed over to Cunard. On November 16, 1907, she set out from Liverpool on her maiden voyage.

The dark, cold and blustery weather wasn't enough to keep fifty thousand people from lining the Liverpool waterfront to watch her go. A late-arriving Boat Train delayed her departure until 7:30pm but finally, ablaze with light from bow to stern, the *Mauretania* pulled out into the river and headed out to sea. Just as happened to her sister, the weather grew foul, and while she struggled valiantly to maintain the pace for a record crossing, finally just off Sandy Hook a heavy fog closed in, forcing the *Mauretania* to anchor until it cleared. When she finally docked at the Cunard Pier, she had missed beating the *Lusitania*'s time by less than six hours. But also as her sister had done, the *Mauretania* took the Blue Ribband on her second voyage, and for the next seven years the two ships would trade the Blue Ribband between themselves, a monopoly that no other pair of sister ships had never achieved on the North Atlantic. Eventually the *Mauretania* would prove to be slightly the faster of the two, but the *Lusitania* always remained popular and had a staunchly loyal following among Atlantic travelers.

From the beginning, though, there was something special about the *Mauretania*, as for reasons that were as undefinable as they were real, she generated an affection that few other ships have ever been given. "She was, as men say of a horse, all quality," was the way that Humphrey Jordan put it. "She did not wallow in a seaway, although she might be wet in one; in good weather and in bad she had a grace of action which made

The Mauretania, *showing her slender lines and immense height.*

most other ships look like laboring tugs. That was her primary distinction; even the sea-timid and the sea-careless recognized it at once. To that, she added speed, comfort, reliability and her own atmosphere." Franklin Delano Roosevelt was the Assistant Secretary of the United States Navy when he crossed on her in 1908, declaring that she "always fascinated" him with her "graceful, yacht-like lines, her four enormous black-topped red funnels, and her appearance of power and good breeding.... Not for one minute did I ever fail to realize that if there ever was a ship which possessed the thing called a 'soul,' the *Mauretania* did.... Every ship has a soul, but the *Mauretania* had one you could talk to....she had the manners and deportment of a great lady and behaved herself as such."

There was no doubt that she and her sister brought a distinctly dignified tone to the North Atlantic, an almost deliberate note of protest to the stridently operatic excesses of the German liners. Even Charles Mewés became susceptible to overstatement, as his designs for the interiors of the *Kaiserin Auguste Victoria* made clear. While Albert Ballin had enlisted Mewés to give Hamburg-Amerika's ships a less overbearing atmosphere than the heavy-handed gilt offerings of Johannes Poppe had brought to the ships of Norddeutscher-Lloyd, the German love of the massive and ponderous, physical expressions of the Teutonic infatuation with order and regularity, subtlety overtook his work. The *Kaiserin* was not a pretty ship—her superstructure seemed to ramble and her funnels looked oddly out of place, as if they had been made for a smaller ship. This of course, was none of Mewés' doing, but inside, while she lacked the "castle on the Rhine" massiveness of the Norddeutscher-Lloyd ships, she still suffered from an overabundance of marble, stone, and bronze; she lacked the sort of understatement that characterized the *Mauretania* and *Lusitania*, an atmosphere that one observer was moved to deem "a silent sermon in good taste."

The extraordinary attention with which the *Lusitania* and *Mauretania* were examined and scrutinized by the public on both sides of the Atlantic—but in particular among the British—was the product of a variety of different impulses. Most obvious, of course, was the promise they held out for returning the Blue Ribband to Great Britain, thus offering confirmation of what most Britons instinctively felt: the superiority of British shipbuilding over any, and all challengers. Alongside that, and much related to it, was Britain's long maritime tradition, which meant that any ship built in a British shipyard was liable to close examination.

But on a deeper level, the hopes that were pinned on the *Lusitania* and *Mauretania* went farther. Although the British Empire had yet to reach its flood tide—it would go on expanding until 1923—Great Britain's economic and industrial strength had already begun a slow, but ultimately irreversible decline when compared to other nations, particularly Germany and the United States. Perceptive Britons, and there were more than a handful, began to suspect that while the sun had yet to set on the Union Jack, it was beginning to get a bit low on the horizon. The two giant liners were to be as much an assertion of Britain's determination to maintain her primacy as they were to be the rejuvenation of the Cunard Line; their unprecedented size and revolutionary technology were notice to the world that despite whatever technical and scientific innovations with which the Germans had dazzled the world, British engineering was still a force to be reckoned with.

That the British were feeling the looming German presence is undeniable. In 1905, despite attempts by Germany in 1899, and again in 1901 to form an alliance with Great Britain, the Reichstag, responding to the megalomaniacal goading of Admiral Alfred von Tirpitz, would pass a law authorizing the construction of a High Seas Fleet that would challenge the supremacy of the Royal Navy, a threat to which Great Britain could never be reconciled, nor could she ignore.

Beguiled by their own bluster, neither the German people nor their leaders understood the antagonisms their actions and attitudes provoked. Of course, the continued hostility of France, a consequence of her bitter defeat in the Franco-Prussian War, was taken as inevitable. What was inexplicable to the Germans was how such dissimilar nations as republican France and autocratic Russia could formulate an alliance—or how Great Britain could achieve an *entente* with both of her traditional foes in order to focus her energies on defending against what was perceived as the greater Teutonic threat. Even while German bombast was driving such unlikely partners into understandings, the only explanation that seemed acceptable to the Kaiser and his people was that the nations surrounding Germany were formulating a policy of political and military encirclement (*Einkreisung*) of Germany, in order to deny the Germans their rightful place as masters of the world.

Nowhere did this seem so obvious to the Germans as in the attitude of the British toward the German merchant marine and the German navy. By the turn of the century Germany possessed the second largest merchant fleet in the world, ranking behind only Great Britain's: its total tonnage was greater than all of the smaller merchant navies combined. Yet at the same time, Germany possessed a navy that numerically only ranked fifth—even Italy had a larger fleet—and almost all of its ships were old, slow, and obsolete. As a consequence, should a war involving Germany break out, a not unlikely possibility given the Kaiser's provocative nature and taste for brinkmanship, the German merchant marine was pitifully vulnerable to any belligerent fleet. For decades the Germans had relied on the goodwill of the Royal Navy and the unspoken understanding that it would protect their merchant ships, a role the British fleet gladly undertook as those ships were often carrying British goods and cargoes, but as Germany's ambitions and arrogance grew, that once-cordial relationship deteriorated into something approaching outright confrontation. The issue came to a head in 1900 during the Boer War, when three German merchant ships, the *Bundesrat, Herzog* and *General*, were seized by the Royal Navy in international waters on suspicion that they were carrying supplies and munitions for the Boers, with whom the German people and government sympathized. Lacking any kind of fleet that could pose any credible threat to the British, the Germans were unable to do any more than lodge diplomatic protests at what they believed, with some justification, to be a gross violation of international law. When the three ships were searched, it was discovered that their cargoes were entirely innocuous, and they were released, but the damage had been done.

A wave of Anglophobia, which had been building before the incident, broke across the German people who fumed at their impotence. The Kaiser declared that Germany would demand her "place in the sun" and that "Germany's future lies on the water." Admiral Alfred von Tirpitz, seeing the chance to actually acquire the battle fleet for which he had been agitating for nearly a decade, seized the opportunity presented by the incident and pushed an ambitious program of naval expansion through the Reichstag. He couched his aims in reasonable, even modest terms, but there could be no mistaking his intent: in presenting his proposals to the German legislature, he declared, "To protect Germany's sea trade and colonies in the existing circumstances there is only one means—Germany must have a battle fleet so strong that even for the most powerful naval adversary, a war against it would involve such dangers as to imperil that Power's position in the world." The meaning was obvious—Germany was going to build a fleet that would be capable of challenging the Royal Navy.

It was a monumental blunder, perhaps the greatest in history, for it antagonized Britain in a way that no other threat or bluster ever could. Sea power was the lifeline of the British Empire, and to challenge British sea power was to threaten Britain's very existence. Winston Churchill, First Lord of the Admiralty in 1912, put the case bluntly but succinctly when he declared, "The British Navy is to us a necessity and, from some points of view, the German Navy is to them more in the nature of a luxury."

In Germany, the Reichstag, press, and people howled in protest—the word "luxury" translates into German as *Luxus*, an extravagance, and Churchill's use of the word was regarded as a slur. But the point had been made—Prime Minister Asquith said that Churchill had made "a plain statement of an obvious truth": in wartime, Britain could not survive without her merchant marine, and without the Royal Navy, the British merchant marine could not survive; Germany, as events would eventually prove, could well survive without a merchant navy at all, making the need for a High Seas Fleet moot.

Relations between the British and German shipping lines remained cordial, as well as those among the officers and crews of their ships, but a certain frostiness had descended on the North Atlantic that had nothing to do with the weather. When the *Mauretania* went to sea in November 1907 and proved to be even faster than the *Lusitania*, the humiliation of the German shipping world was complete: for all of its vaunted and self-proclaimed superiority, German technology was incapable of building a ship that could equal either of the new Cunarders, let alone surpass them. It would take more than five years for a German reply to the *Lusitania* and *Mauretania* to take shape, and even then Teutonic bombast could only find its outlet in trumpeting how new German ships had surpassed the

British ships in pompousness and pretense.

While the *Lusitania* and *Mauretania* would long remain the fastest liners on the North Atlantic—the reign of the *Mauretania* would last for over twenty years—the luxury of their accommodations was a challenge which the White Star Line could not ignore. Before his death in 1898, Thomas Ismay had made a deliberate decision to make luxury the hallmark of his company, and soon a new class of vessels planned by White Star would exceeded the Cunard duo in both opulence and size. Conferring over cigars and brandy on a summer evening in 1907, Bruce Ismay, now the Chairman of the White Star Line, and Lord Pirrie, Chairman of Harland and Wolff, produced a sketch pad and began doodling, roughing out the dimensions and proportions of the ships that would become White Star's response to the *Lusitania* and *Mauretania*. The only concession that White Star would make was in speed: the Admiralty expertise that had gone into the design of the big Cunard ships' turbines was beyond Harland and Wolff's experience. As a result, the ships that Lord Pirrie's yard would build would be at least a knot or two slower than Cunard's two speedsters. Beyond that, the *Lusitania* and *Mauretania* would have to be beaten at their own game. If Cunard wanted to build big, White Star would build bigger; if Cunard wanted to offer luxury, then White Star would offer luxury on a scale never before seen on the North Atlantic.

It was necessary, Ismay decided, to have three ships, all built to the same design, so that the White Star Line could offer weekly sailing east- and west- bound; in doing so, the line could maintain a cargo and passenger capacity that was nearly double that of the two Cunard ships. As the two men continued to talk, the doodles and sketches became more defined, and by the end of the evening Pirrie and Ismay had outlined the trio of ships that were to become the *Olympic*, *Titanic*, and *Gigantic*.

In the remarkably short time of six months, ideas from that night had started to become reality, and in December of 1907 the keel of the *Olympic* was laid in the newly designated Slip No. 2 at Harland and Wolff. The new liners were so huge that the space previously used to build three hulls was devoted to the construction of two of the new giants. The *Olympic* was laid down first, followed a few months later by the *Titanic*. Once the *Olympic* was launched, the *Gigantic*'s keel would be laid in her old slip. The new liners were projected to be ready to go into service in the spring of 1911, 1912, and 1913 respectively.

At 45,000 tons displacement and a length of 882 feet each, White Star's trio would dwarf the *Lusitania* and *Mauretania* by nearly 12,000 tons, and though they would not be as fast, their appointments would make those of the two Cunard ships pale in comparison. The *Olympic* went into service as scheduled in 1911, and immediately proved immensely popular with the traveling public. Eleven months later, the White Star Line sent her sister, the *Titanic*, out on her maiden voyage, anticipating an even greater success than the *Olympic*'s. But Fate intervened in the shape of an iceberg, and White Star's plans, along with the company's reputation, was left in tatters. The White Star

Line would never really recover from the loss of the *Titanic*, and never again be a serious threat to Cunard. Ironically, the White Star Line's tragedy would be Cunard's hour of glory.

CHAPTER NINE

The Glory Years

At 11:40 pm on the night of April 14, 1912, the *Titanic* struck an iceberg in the North Atlantic and began to sink. A little more than half an hour later, she began sending out a distress signal by wireless, calling for the assistance of any ship close enough to come to her aid; some thirty minutes after that she began to fire white distress rockets, eight in all, trying to summon help from any ship close enough to see them. The *Carpathia* was 58 miles away from the *Titanic* and heading in the opposite direction when her wireless operator, Harold Cottam, heard, purely by chance, the *Titanic*'s distress calls. He raced up to the bridge, reported to the First Officer, who had the watch, and then ran down to the captain's cabin, where he threw open the door and blurted out the news that the *Titanic* was sinking and required immediate assistance.

That Captain was Arthur Rostron. Forty-three years old, Rostron had spent the last thirty of them at sea, the first ten in sail. He had joined Cunard in 1892 and had risen steadily, if unspectacularly, up the company ladder. (Cunard captains are expected to be conscientious and circumspect—never spectacular.) He was an experienced mariner, known and respected throughout Cunard as "the Electric Spark" for his decisiveness and boundless, infectious energy. He was also noted for his piety; he neither smoked nor drank, was never heard to use profanity, and in a day and age when recourse to the Almighty was not regarded as quaint or a sign of weak-mindedness, was known to turn to prayer for guidance.

He was given command of the *Carpathia* in January 1912. This cold April morning she was three days out of New York on her way to the Mediterranean, carrying just over 800 passengers in three classes, on what had been up to now, an uneventful crossing. In all of Rostron's years at sea, he had never been called upon to carry out a rescue. This was to be his first real test.

At first, indignant when Cottam and First Officer Dean burst in—people were expected to at least knock before barging in on the captain, after all—the reprimand died on his lips when a clearly anxious Dean told him about the *Titanic*. Rostron swung his legs out of bed and then seemed lost in thought for a few seconds as he digested the news. The first words he spoke showed the stuff he was made of.

"Mr. Dean, turn the ship around—steer northwest, I'll work out the course for you in a minute." As Dean sped back to the bridge, Rostron turned his attention to Cottam. "Are you sure it's the *Titanic* and she requires immediate assistance?" he asked.

"Yes, sir."

"You are absolutely certain?"

"Quite certain, sir."

"All right, tell him we are coming along as fast as we can."

After dressing, Rostron made a quick trip up to the bridge to give the helmsman the new course—North 52 West—then called down to the engine room to order "Full Speed Ahead." At the *Carpathia*'s top speed of 14 knots she would cover the distance between herself and the *Titanic* in four hours, which was not good enough for Rostron. Now he swung into action.

Returning to the chartroom he called for Chief Engineer Johnstone. Speed, he told Johnstone, he wanted more speed than the old *Carpathia* had ever mustered. Call out the off-duty watch to the engine room; get every available stoker roused to feed the furnaces. Cut off the heat and hot water to passenger and crew accommodations; put every ounce of steam the boilers made into the engines.

Next he spoke to First Officer Dean and gave him a list of things to be done: all routine work knocked off, the ship prepared for a rescue operation; swing out the ship's boats; have clusters of electric lights rigged along the ship's sides; all gangway doors to be opened, with block and tackle slung at each gangway; slings ready for hoisting injured aboard, canvas bags for lifting small children; ladders prepared for dropping at each gangway, along with cargo nets; forward derricks to be rigged and topped, with steam in the winches for bringing luggage and cargo aboard; oil bags readied in the lavatories to pour on rough seas, if needed.

Captain (later Commodore) Arthur Rostron, proudly displaying the medals he earned while commanding the Carpathia in her rescue of the Titanic's survivors.

Dean set-to immediately and Rostron turned to the ship's surgeon, Dr. McGhee: the three surgeons aboard, McGhee, an Italian physician and one who was Hungarian, were to be assigned to specific stations—McGhee himself in First Class, the Italian doctor in Second, and the Hungarian doctor in Third. All three were to be supplied with stimulants and restoratives, and first aid stations to be set up in each dining saloon.

To Purser Brown: see that the Chief Steward, the Assistant Purser and the Purser himself each covered a different gangway to receive the *Titanic*'s passengers and crew; get their names and classes and see to it that each one went to the correct dining saloon for a medical check.

Chief Steward Henry Hughes received an additional set of instructions: every crewman was to be called out; coffee was to be available for all hands. Also, soup, coffee, tea, brandy and whiskey should be ready for those rescued; the smoking room, lounge, and library were to be converted into dormitories for survivors. All the *Carpathia*'s steerage passengers were to be grouped together; the extra space would be given over to the *Titanic*'s steerage passengers.

His instructions issued, Rostron quickly reviewed everything he had ordered, trying to think of what he had overlooked. There did not seem to be anything, so he quickly strode to the bridge and began posting extra lookouts. He was determined that the *Carpathia* was not about to meet the same fate as the ship she was rushing to aid. Rostron had an extra man posted in the crow's nest, two lookouts in the bow, extra hands posted on both bridge wings, and Second Officer James Bisset, who had especially keen eyesight, posted on the starboard bridge wing.

Now having done all he could do, Rostron faced the toughest task—waiting. But there was one last detail Rostron did not overlook. Second Officer Bisset noticed it first, then so did the others on the bridge—the Captain standing toward the back of the bridge holding his cap an inch or two off his head, eyes closed, lips moving in silent prayer.

Down in the boiler room it seemed as if the entire "black gang" had suddenly been infused with Rostron's energy: the extra hands began shoveling coal into the furnaces of the boilers like they had never shoveled coal before. First, the safety valves were closed off, then the engineers began to systematically shut off steam to the rest of the ship, ducting it instead into the reciprocating engines. Up, down, up, down, up, down, the pistons pounded, as the Chief Engineer watched the revolutions steadily increasing. Faster and faster the ship drove ahead—14½ knots ...15½...16...16½...17 knots.... The old *Carpathia* had never gone so fast.

Chief Steward Hughes gathered all his stewards in the main dining saloon and quickly, quietly, he told about the *Titanic*, explained how the rescue was up to the *Carpathia*, then pausing dramatically, and eyeing each man directly, he solemnly intoned: "Every man to his post and let him do his duty like a true Englishman. If the situation calls for it, let us add another glorious page to British history." The stewards immediately set to work, determined that when they arrived at the *Titanic*'s side, they would be ready for anything.

What they found were twenty lifeboats, many of them only half filled, scattered across five square miles of ocean. Dawn was just breaking as the *Carpathia* arrived, and it took nearly four hours for all the survivors to be brought aboard, as one by one the *Titanic*'s

The Carpathia, *a 14-knot ship that Captain Rostron pushed to nearly 17 knots in the race to reach the survivors of the* Titanic *disaster.*

lifeboats made their way to the *Carpathia*'s side. Thirteen of the boats were hoisted aboard the ship, the rest were abandoned. There were just 705 survivors. The rest were lost with the *Titanic*.

Later, as accolades and testimonials poured in, and he was hailed as a hero on both sides of the Atlantic, Rostron remained self-effacing, refusing to take credit he didn't believe was his due: when he recalled the *Carpathia*'s mad dash to the north, Rostron observed that, "Surely some other Hand was on the helm that night other than my own." In the years to come, Rostron's resolve and decisiveness, as well as his willingness to risk his own safety and that of his ship to rush to the aid of others in distress, would become the yardstick by which all other ship's master's would be measured, while the *Carpathia*'s heroic dash through the icy waters suffused the entire Cunard fleet with a faint nimbus of glory. In little more than a decade, Cunard had rushed back from the brink of obscurity to once again assume the role of the premier passenger steamship line on the North Atlantic. And it must be said that it did so with the unspoken, but unmistakable assumption that such a place was the company's rightful position. In the eyes of the traveling public on both sides of the Atlantic, Cunard seemed to possess the finest ships, skippered by the bravest captains, and providing the best service of any steamship line. It was an image that the officers and crew, as well as the staff and agents ashore, carefully cultivated and burnished, going about their duties with a confidence that bordered on the arrogant. The handful of years remaining before the cataclysm of the Great War fell upon Europe would be a Golden Age for Cunard.

That Cunard's confidence stopped just shy of the arrogance which White Star had embraced, may have been due to a handful of incidents that overtook Cunard ships in the first decade of the century which, while none of them resulted in catastrophe, may have well served to remind the company that for all the power and pretense of the grandly named and appointed cockleshells it sent out into the Atlantic, they were still only ships, nothing more. First came the freak wave that smashed into the *Campania* in 1905 and took the lives of five passengers; three years later, a similar incident aboard the *Lucania* cost the life of a crewman. The most frightening incident came in January 1910, in a shattering demonstration of the power of the Atlantic Ocean.

The *Lusitania* was two days out of New York, bound for Liverpool, when just after midnight a rogue wave rose up in front of her and crashed down on her bow. It pounded some of her lifeboats to flinders, and tore the canvas covers off the rest as it swept the length of the ship. The wheelhouse, eighty feet above the *Lusitania*'s waterline, was flooded as the wave stove in the face of the bridge and smashed the heavy plate glass windows. The officers and quartermasters were injured by flying splinters and shards of glass, although none of the injuries were serious. Far more serious was the discovery that the *Lusitania*'s wheel came unshipped, and for forty critical minutes she had no helm control. Back in the public rooms, corridors, and passengers cabins, there was an interesting assortment of bumps, bruises, and minor cuts, but fortunately there were no fatalities. Repairs to the *Lusitania* would take the better part of the week she spent in turnaround when she reached Liverpool. The entire incident was an awesome demonstration of the power and fury of which the Atlantic was capable: the hand of the Almighty may have guided the *Carpathia*'s helm in the early hours of April 15, 1912, but it was not always so benign.

All the while, though, the endless game of one-upmanship on the North Atlantic continued, although the *Lusitania* and *Mauretania* had fundamentally changed the rules: so complete was their victory over the German ships—and any others that might have come along—that speed had become a secondary consideration for everyone but Cunard. The new watchword was luxury, and the impetus was to build ships that would outdo competitors' offerings for comfort, elegance, opulence and sheer extravagance. The results would be the epitome of the "floating palaces."

The *Titanic* was still sitting on Slipway Number 3 in Belfast when Cunard made the decision in 1911 to build a third ship for the Liverpool-to-New York express service. She was to be named the *Aquitania,* and she was also meant to be as much a response to the efforts of Cunard's competitors, particularly the White Star Line's *Olympic* and *Titanic*, as she was to be running mate for the *Lusitania* and *Mauretania*—not quite as fast but with interior appointments that would surpass even those of the White Star Line's finest ships.

Once again Cunard turned to Leonard Peskett to do the design work, while the contract to build her was given to John Brown & Company. Peskett drew heavily on the *Mauretania* for inspiration, and though he had no intention of producing what was simply an enlarged version of the older ship, the resemblance was unmistakable. Like the *Lusitania* and *Mauretania* she had a long slender hull with four equally spaced, functional funnels, though her extra length—a hundred and thirty feet greater than that of the *Lusitania* and *Mauretania*—allowed her a far less ponderous and top-heavy appearance. Unique among Cunard ships, she was fitted with Frahm's anti-rolling tanks, an ambitious but not-quite-successful system of water tanks designed to dampen the motion of a rolling ship: Cunard meant for the *Aquitania* to be a comfortable ship, much closer to the White Star Line's *Olympic* than the Cunard greyhounds. All the same, like the *Lusitania* and *Mauretania*, reinforced gun platforms and compartments which could be readily converted into magazines and shell handling rooms were worked into the design, so that the ship could be quickly converted into an armed merchant cruiser in wartime.

The *Aquitania*'s keel was laid in December 1910, and she was ready for launching by April 1913. The unusually long construction time was a consequence of the *Titanic* disaster: Cunard made significant changes to the original design in the interest of improved safety. The most expensive and time-consuming modification was the introduction of a double hull, while details in the arrangement of her watertight bulkheads were re-worked. The most visible change was the increase in the number of lifeboats she carried.

One of the greatest tragedies of the night the *Titanic* was lost was that she carried lifeboats for barely half the number of people aboard. What was even more frightening, in retrospect, was that her full complement of boats would have been sufficient for less than a third of the total number of people she was capable of carrying. What made this all so outrageous was that when she sailed, the number of lifeboats the *Titanic* carried actually *exceeded* the total required under the regulations of the British Board of Trade. Those regulations had been laid down in 1894 for ships that were barely a third the size of the *Titanic*,

The Aquitania, *showing to advantage her origin in the design of the* Mauretania *as well as the influence of the White Star Line's* Olympic *and* Titanic.

but as steamships grew in size, the regulations remained unchanged. That oversight was quickly remedied, and when she was ready for sea the *Aquitania*'s complement of boats had nearly tripled from the sixteen originally specified, to forty-six, capable of holding more people than the *Aquitania* could actually carry. Two of the boats were specially equipped with motors and had their own wireless sets.

The underlying causes of the *Titanic* disaster were not so easily resolved however, for they were symptomatic of the times, and highlighted a flaw in the Edwardian world that would soon be a major factor in its destruction. For all of its technological progress—sophistication would be too strong a word—the world that existed before 1914 was remarkably naive and astonishingly ignorant of its own capabilities: while it embraced with varying degrees of enthusiasm the newest advances in technology, it rarely paused to consider the implications of what that technology has wrought. The optimism which characterized the Edwardian world was at once its greatest strength and its Achilles heel: it gave the shipping world the confidence to build leviathans like the *Lusitania, Mauretania, Olympic* or *Titanic*, but blinded them to their inherent vulnerablities. It would allow marine engineers and architects to design ships that would survive any foreseeable accident, yet denied them the vision to understand that there could well be unforeseen disasters lurking.

The sinking of the *Titanic* was the first scene in the last act of a drama that had slowly unfolded for centuries. The same energies that powered the Edwardian Age would, like a flywheel spinning too fast, ultimately tear it apart. When the waters of the North Atlantic closed over the *Titanic*'s stern that cold April night, something changed in the Western world, though no one knew it at the moment. Attitudes, beliefs, and values which had endured for hundreds of years were shaken, overnight as it were, and would still remain unsettled almost a century later.

Most profoundly disturbed was mankind's belief in technology. The engineers and scientists of the early 1900s were viewed as benefactors, their products as benevolent gifts that could only improve humanity's lot. The construction of the *Olympic* and *Titanic* were thought to represent the first sure steps in mankind's eventual, inevitable, triumph over the elements. But after the loss of the *Titanic*, scientists and engineers would no longer be unhesitatingly hailed as modern-day saviors, their works greeted as panaceas for the assorted ills of mankind, or their efforts the repository of humanity's confidence. Confidence was probably *the* single outstanding characteristic of the Edwardians, confidence—faith—in the future and in the belief that, no matter how profound the problems, there *were* answers to all of society's ills, and that they *would* be found. And nowhere had that faith been given greater expression than in the advances made by science and technology. Science, and its handmaiden, Progress, had in the previous century steadily eroded a faith in God, or *Gott*, or *Dieu*, which had sustained men for two thousand years, until it seemed that the Millennium would be ushered in not by theology but by technology. Yet suddenly what had appeared to be the ultimate accomplishment of Science and

Progress, the very pinnacle of technological achievement, was shown to be helplessly flawed and deadly fragile.

Similarly, Privilege would never be the same. As never before, death was perceived as the great leveler it had always been. Forty-two hundred dollars might buy passage in the most opulent suite on board the *Titanic*, but it could no more purchase a seat in a lifeboat than could the thirty-six dollars paid by the lowliest steerage passenger. It would take the cataclysm of the First World War before the barricades of class and privilege would begin to crumble, but their foundations were irreparably weakened that April night.

It would be going too far to say that the sinking of the *Titanic* marked the end of an era: the Edwardian Age and the Victorian Era could not be disposed of so easily—but in a way it sounded their death-knell. Certainly it loomed like a brooding presence over the North Atlantic for the few remaining years of peace, and when the *Aquitania* put to sea, she would sail, figuratively, in the doomed White Star liner's shadow.

The *Aquitania* was launched on April 21, 1913, by the Countess of Derby. Cunard had made a great play during her building that the *Aquitania* would be the largest liner yet built in Great Britain, so it was no surprise when nearly one hundred thousand people lined the banks of the River Clyde to witness her launch. The fitting out began immediately, and took some thirteen months, and the results showed that it was time well spent. The *Aquitania*'s marvelous interiors were then considered by many to be the most thrilling ever installed on a passenger liner. The *Lustiania* and *Mauretania*, while comfortable and luxurious in their own right, had been built with speed as their first priority—the *Aquitania* focused unashamedly on passenger luxury.

Arthur Davis, a Fellow of the Royal Institute of British Architects (and incidentally a partner of Charles Mewés, the chief interior designer for Hamburg-Amerika), was engaged by Cunard to create an interior that was nothing less than magnificent for the new liner. Many years later he recalled the design brief that Cunard gave him, as well as the company's method of persuading him of the wisdom of that brief.

> When I was first engaged...to start this work...I said to the directors of the company that employed me: "Why don't you make a ship look like a ship?"... But the answer I was given was that the people who use these ships are not pirates, they do not dance hornpipes; they are mostly seasick American ladies, and the one thing they want to forget when they are on the vessel is that they are on a ship at all. Most of them have got to travel and they object to it very much. In order to impress that point upon me, the Company sent me across the Atlantic. The first day out I enjoyed the beautiful sea, but when we got well on to the Atlantic, there was one thing I craved for as never before, and that was a warm fire and a pink shade. The people who travel on these large ships are the people who live in hotels; they are not ships for sailors or yachtsmen or people who enjoy the

sea. They are inhabited by all sorts of people, some of whom are very delicate and stay in their cabin during the whole voyage; others, less delicate, stay in the smoking room all through the voyage.... I suggest to you that the transatlantic liner is not merely a ship, she is a floating town with 3,000 passengers of all kinds, with all sorts of tastes, and those who enjoy being there are distinctly in the minority. If we could get ships to look inside like ships, and get people to enjoy the sea, it would be a very good thing; but all we can do, as things are, is to give them gigantic floating hotels.

As a result, the *Aquitania* would prove to be the high-water mark of the "country home at sea" era of ocean liner decor, and for many people her interiors were never surpassed by any other ship. The sad truth about the *Aquitania*'s history is that somehow this fabulous ship would always be overshadowed by another. First there was the tragedy of the *Titanic*, which delayed her appearance on the North Atlantic by almost a year. Then, no sooner would she enter service than all Europe would plunge into the mad frenzy of the First World War, in which the *Aquitania* would serve with distinction. After the war the public would be enamored with the romanticized career of the *Mauretania*, and finally the sheer size and majesty of the *Queen Mary* would relegate the *Aquitania* to the status of just another pre-war liner on the North Atlantic run. She deserved better, and was worth a closer look.

At 901 feet in length, a beam of 97 feet, and a displacement of 45,647 tons, her dimensions made it clear that the *Aquitania* was meant to compete directly with the White Star Line's *Olympic* class ships. She was fully 130 feet longer, ten feet wider and more than 12,000 tons larger than the *Lusitania* and *Mauretania*. The additional size allowed her to carry over eight hundred additional passengers more than her smaller running mates. It also freed her designer, Leonard Peskett, from the need to build as high in proportion as he did with his previous two ships, and the *Aquitania*'s profile, while never quite matching the balance and grace that Alexander Carlisle achieved with the *Olympic* and *Titanic*—but then, no other ships ever did—had none of the top-heavy, ponderous, appearance which the *Mauretania* and *Lusitania* displayed.

Like the *Lusitania* and *Mauretania*, the *Aquitania* sported four tall, equally-spaced funnels, but again the new ship's additional length worked to her advantage, for while the funnels were the same size as those on the earlier pair of liners, they were smaller in proportion, giving the *Aquitania* a more elegant appearance. Of course, like all ships of her day, her upper decks were festooned with a forest of ventilator cowls, but once more, size was the ally of aesthetics, and they didn't dominate the *Aquitania*'s profile the way they did that of the *Mauretania*.

Passengers traveling aboard the *Aquitania* were afforded all the luxuries of a land-based hotel. The styling throughout was harmonious and comfortable, and her handsome and distinguished appointments earned her the sobriquet "the ship beautiful."

The unvarnished truth is that the interior of the *Aquitania* was the most handsome, opulent, and distinguished that ever appeared in any ship ever built. One particularly popular feature was the Garden Lounge, shamelessly cribbed from the Café Parisien aboard the *Olympic* and *Titanic*, situated outside the public rooms on both port and starboard sides of A-Deck. The decor was meant to recreate the atmosphere of an old English garden by means of natural teak trellis covered in climbing flowers and ivy on walls tricked out to resemble dressed stone, while the chairs, settees and tables were wicker. Large windows along the sides and at the after-end of the Garden protected the passengers from the elements.

The First Class Smoking Room was an adaptation from, of all places, Greenwich Hospital, but it worked magnificently. The style was from late in the reign of Charles II. Seventy-six feet in length and fifty-two wide, it had a high-ceilinged central section dominated by two large decorative painted panels representing the *Embarkation of St. Ursula* and a *Seaport with Figures*. Five adjoining rooms featured oak beamed ceilings and window treatments that echoed the Admiral's Walk on an old battleship. Throughout the room were hand-carved representations of coats-of-arms and military motifs, much of it done in solid oak, copied from the style of Grinling Gibbons. Carrying the general nautical theme further, the electric light fittings were copied from old Dutch ships' lanterns.

The Aquitania's *First Class Smoking Room, a tour-de-force of craftsmanship that would never be seen again.*

The epitome of opulence at sea: the First Class Lounge aboard the Aquitania.

Louis XVI gave the *à la carte* restaurant its style and flavor, with mahogany paneling on the walls, along with recreations of the works of various 18th Century masters, the whole accented with carved ornamental woodwork, pilasters and columns. On the ceiling of the great central well in the First Class dining saloon—a sort of sea-going rotunda—was a recreation of the *Triumph of Flora*, and the well itself was surrounded by an elaborate wrought iron balustrade, with motifs forming panels representing the combined monogram of Cunard and the ship.

In the First Class Lounge, the decor was inspired by the work of Sir Christopher Wren. The color scheme of the room was executed in wine red and grey, and in the center was an original painting on canvas, signed by Van Cuygen. Large Georgian windows overlooked the Garden Lounge. At each end of the room were arched spandrels, flanked by hand-carved wooden panels representing the Four Elements—Earth, Fire, Water, and Heaven—copied from Jean Baptiste Van. A semi-circular stage or platform was planned at one end of the room, and was decorated with a fine, coffered vault, under which appeared a reproduction of the famous Mortlake tapestry representing the Battle of Solebay. Completing the room was an oak parquet dance floor.

The First Class Drawing Room echoed the best of the Brothers Adam, circa 1780. The most striking feature of the entire room was its ceiling, which was an oval dome with accented lunette-styled leaded-glass windows. The walls were hung with blue tabourette silk, while on all sides of the room there were bookcases made from Cuban mahogany. This rare wood was also used for the doors and the accents of carefully carved, interlacing moldings on the door panels, as well as the console tables scattered throughout the room.

The Grill Room would become one of the most popular features aboard the *Aquitania*. Its Early Jacobean decor was taken from an elaborately carved, oak-paneled room from the Palace at Bromley-by-Bow, which dated from the beginning of the 17th Century, and was located at the Victoria and Albert Museum. Blue Delft china ornaments accented the room, while the curtains, which reproduced an Elizabethan needlework pattern, helped to complete the scheme.

The period chosen for the Salons was that of an old French chateau from the reign of Louis XVI. Embroidered silk curtains in purple and old gold quietly harmonized with camel-colored carpet and Persian rugs dominated by grey and gold. Reproduced Bergère chairs, settees, occasional chairs and writing tables were scattered throughout, while a large, recessed mirror was placed in between two large reproductions of paintings by Hubert Robert, a style taken from the palace at Fontainebleau. In a particularly subtle touch, the rooms were illuminated by cut-glass dish electric lights identical to those in the Gainsborough Suite, the style of which would have been contemporary with that of the Salons.

The mock-Tudor private suites aboard the *Titanic* were the most exclusive feature of her accommodations, and served as the impetus for a whole series of suites aboard the *Aquitania*, the best known being the Gainsborough Suite. Carved mahogany Chippendale furniture was set against French windows, with finely carved architraves, which led on to the private verandah, the *Aquitania's* reply to the private promenades aboard the *Titanic*. Dominating the suite was a magnificent white marble fireplace over which hung antique mezzotint reproductions of pictures by Gainsborough. There had never been anything like it aboard any ship, nor has there since.

It was said of many ships of the period, usually with more hyperbole than fact, that their Second Class accommodations were the equal of First Class on most other ships, but in the case of the *Aquitania* this was nothing short of the truth. The Second Class Dining Saloon was a room of magnificent style; the staircase leading into the saloon was copied from an example by the Brothers Adam, while the dome over the Saloon was accented with a plaster frieze, surrounded by a wrought iron balustrade copied from an old Brothers Adam balcony. The ceiling itself was supported by four Ionic columns copied from an old house in Fitzroy Street, London, and was composed of large panels of alabaster with carefully moulded details, while the walls were decorated with allegorical paintings adapted from works of Giovanni Battista Pegolesi.

Antique mahogany Hepplewhite furniture, a dome supported by fluted Ionic columns, a rich, moulded plaster frieze, and two finely executed wrought iron skylights dominated the Second Class Drawing Room. Again the late 18th Century style of the Brothers Adam was repeated, in particular the Georgian windows, which were used to minimize the suggestion that a passenger was actually in a room on a ship rather than in a house on shore. Finishing the room was a beautiful marble fireplace and chimneypiece, to which was fixed a gilt mantel. Just as their First Class counterparts had done with their Smoking Room, the Second Class passengers made their Smoking Room one of the most popular parts of the ship. As it adjoined the Veranda Café, which offered a magnificent view over the *Aquitania*'s stern, some travelers felt the Second Class passengers actually had the better part of the bargain. Kensington Palace, with its oak-paneled walls, provided the inspiration for the room, while comfortable chairs and settees copied from originals at Kensington set before a beautifully carved fireplace, gave it a quiet and dignified atmosphere. Reproductions of old Georgian columns and pilasters with carved caps supported the ceiling, while the floor was covered with subdued black and grey linoleum tiling.

All in all, the interiors on the *Aquitania* were executed on a scale at once lavish and restrained that had never before been seen at sea—and would never be seen again. Even before she was completed she was being called "the Ship Beautiful," which was nothing more than an accurate description. All that remained to be seen was whether her performance would be on a par with her appearance.

In May 1914, the *Aquitania* was ready for sea trials, which she passed flawlessly. Company officials were particularly pleased when she made 24 knots over the measured mile, fully a knot faster than expected, and her maiden voyage was set for May 30. The usual gala atmosphere of a maiden voyage departure was muted somewhat by the news that reached Liverpool just hours before her departure: the night before, the Canadian Pacific Line's *Empress of Ireland* had collided with a collier in the St. Lawrence River and sank in ten minutes with the loss of over 1,400 lives. Despite the tragedy, it wasn't long before those aboard settled into the comfort and luxury of the new ship.

They were aided in this none-too-arduous task by their stewards and stewardesses. The decade before the Great War was the apogee of stewardship aboard transatlantic liners, that unique combination of tact, understatement and professionalism in which the British crews seemed to excel, and which would one day become the stuff of legend. Often, employment as stewards aboard a crack liner like the *Aquitania* was a sort of family tradition, with fathers bringing their sons into the service, and they in turn, brought their sons aboard. Being a good steward was an exacting job: while perhaps not as physically demanding as the work of a stoker or trimmer, the hours were long, beginning well before 7:00am and usually not ending until after 10:30pm. Meals were usually taken standing up, often a mouthful or two at a time quickly wolfed down in the steward's "glory hole"—the little cubby from which he worked—and any personal needs, cleaning or mending a uniform, for example, were taken care of only after the last passengers had finally retired.

The prerequisites for a good steward were patience and tact; the latter was particularly vital, as by the nature of their work, stewards were often privy to incidents or conver-

The Lusitania*'s Boat Deck, as she rolls her way through rough seas.*

sations, which could have been acutely embarrassing or compromising to their passengers. Consequently, successful stewards quickly learned when to turn a blind eye, a deaf ear, or a mute tongue to a particular situation. There was also more to their shipboard role than to simply be at passengers' beck and call to fetch and carry: they were also invaluable in advising inexperienced travelers of the various nuances of social etiquette, in particular those Americans whose newfound or newly-made fortunes thrust them into social strata for which the circumstances of their birth had never prepared them. From making certain that a young gentleman's evening clothes were properly turned out before he went down to dinner, to carefully offered advice on which fork to use with which course, to a word of caution about which young ladies were and were not eligible, a conscientious steward did his best to make certain his charges were never an embarrassment to themselves or to him. It was this professionalism that so enamored Theodore Dreiser when he was aboard the *Mauretania* in 1912:

> On shipboard I noticed for the first time in my life that there was an aloofness about the service rendered by the servant which was entirely different from that which we know in America. They did not look at one so brutally and critically as does the American menial; their eyes did not seem to say, "I am your equal or better," and their motions did not indicate that they were doing anything unwillingly. In America—and I am a good American—I have always had the feeling that the American hotel or house servant or store clerk...was doing me a great favor if he did anything at all for me. However...when I went aboard the English

ship...I felt this burden of serfdom to the American servant to be lifted. These people did not seem anxious to fight with me. They were actually civil. They did not stare at me out of countenance; they did not order me gruffly about. Yes, and it was so in the dining-saloon, in the bath, on deck, everywhere, with "yes, sirs," and "thank you, sirs," and two fingers raised to cap visors for good measure. Were they acting? Was this a fiercely suppressed class I was looking on here? I could scarcely believe it. But as to manner: Heaven save the mark! These people are civil. They are nice. They are willing. "Yes, sir! Thank you, sir! This way, sir! No trouble about that, sir! Certainly, sir! Very well, sir!" I heard these things on all sides and they were like a balm to a fevered brain.

The stewards' rewards for these efforts came in the tips passengers gave their stewards at the end of the crossing. Actual wages were low, just over £5 a month, but a good steward could make as much as ten times that each way in tips.

The years before the Great War were also the glory days of the ocean-going gambler. Such individuals were, and continue to be, fixtures on passenger ships; most were known to the pursers and assistant pursers on the larger liners, but as long as the stakes never went too high, the games did not appear to be rigged, or no one seemed to be victimized by their losses, the gamblers' activities were largely ignored. Cunard did take the precaution of issuing a warning, inserted in the passenger list, that professional gamblers might be aboard and discouraging "Games of Chance, as being likely to afford these individuals special opportunities for taking advantage of others." Admittedly, this warning was more for the self-protection of the company than the welfare of the passengers, to keep the Line from being implicated should anyone lose too heavily. What's most intriguing about the pre-War professional gamblers was that for the most part they were honest card players, not card-sharps, thieves, or swindlers: the day for that ilk would come in the 1920s and 1930s.

Unable to build ships that could compete with the *Lusitania* and *Mauretania*, the Germans—specifically Hamburg-Amerika—felt compelled to respond to the White Star Line's *Olympic*-class ships. In a way, they had no choice, as for more than seventy years success on the North Atlantic had been built upon the image a company presented to the traveling public: superlatives meant money. If the British were allowed to have the largest, fastest *and* the most luxurious ships on the Atlantic Ferry, the German lines would quickly go into eclipse. Taking the Blue Ribband from the *Lusitania* and *Mauretania* simply wasn't possible, as German shipyards lacked the experience and technical expertise to produce turbines powerful enough accomplish the task. The alternative was to introduce ships that were even more handsome and luxurious than those of Cunard and the White Star fleets.

It was Hamburg-Amerika which made the effort, and though the company strove valiantly, it failed miserably. In what was meant to be Albert Ballin's moment of triumph, it was announced that a trio of new ships, the *Imperator, Vaterland,* and *Bismarck,* would be introduced in three successive years, beginning in 1913. Almost from the very beginning, however, they proved a source of endless discomfiture for Hamburg-Amerika, as it became obvious to even the most casual observer that their designers' sole concern was exceeding the British liners in any way possible.

It seemed as if all the bluster of Wilhelmine Germany came to be embodied in these ships. The result was an aesthetic nightmare that made the ponderous proportions of the *Lusitania* and *Mauretania* seem elegant in comparison. Viewed from almost any angle, the lines of this new class never appeared to be *right*, lacking balance and proportion. A raised forecastle on the forward deck gave the bow a cluttered, unfinished look, while the stepped face of the superstructure was oddly reminiscent of a wedding cake. The spacing of the three funnels on the superstructure was awkward (the brief heyday of the four-funneled ship was over), as the forward one was set too far back from the front and the aftermost appeared to be too close to the aft end, giving the superstructure a truncated look; their height made them seem, correctly as it turned out, somewhat oversized and top-heavy. Looking for ways to add to the ships' overall length, the architects gave them an unusually long overhang for their counter sterns, which in turn were rather blunt, creating the impression that they had been designed for smaller ships and somehow were grafted onto the larger hulls. A sense of the pretentiousness of this new class could be obtained from the massive amount of gilding used inside and out, even to the point of adding ornamental gold scrollwork to the stern overhang, of the kind long dispensed with on British liners.

Inside, the ships were equally overdone: where a British liner would be unashamed to sport a Café Parisien, openly, even cheerfully suggestive of a French street café, no such Gallic venues were allowed on the wholly Teutonic *Imperator*: its place was taken by a Continental Grill meant to suggest a German *biergarten,* overdone with heavy mahogany furniture and false brickwork. In each of the First Class staterooms, the lavatory fixtures, including the bathtubs, were all carried out in heavy Purbeck marble. More marble found its way into her public rooms, which, in what was meant to be an innovative design, were all concentrated on the two upper decks.

The *Imperator* was the first of the trio to enter service; launched by Kaiser Wilhelm II on May 23, 1912, she was finished late in the spring of 1913 and set out on her maiden voyage on June 13. Instead of the triumph that Hamburg-Amerika had expected, it was something of an embarrassment for the line. While certainly the largest—and by some standards the most luxurious passenger liner in the world, her seakeeping qualities were poor, so much so that even the passengers became alarmed at times: she was sluggish in responding to her helm, something of which only the crew would be aware, but there was no disguising the fact that she rolled badly, and had a tendency to "hang onto a roll," that is, once she heeled over, she would take a long time to begin recovering. It soon became obvious that the *Imperator* was distinctly top heavy, so much so that she would take on a slight list even while sitting at pier side, a consequence of the designers' decision to place all of her public rooms high up in the superstructure, as well as the pretensions of her decor.

Hamburg-Amerika's solution was to shorten her funnels by nine feet, as well as remove all of the heavy decorations—including the bronze bust of the Kaiser in the Social Hall. The Continental Grill's mahogany and marble fixtures were torn out, replaced with a *wintergarten* decorated in light woods, ivy, and wicker, while in the First Class cabins all of the marble bathroom fixtures were torn out. In a final effort to lower the ship's center of gravity, some 2,000 tons of concrete were poured into her double bottom. These measures helped somewhat, but the *Imperator* would always remain distinctly tender. As one of her captains put it, "She was a ship of gloomy paneled majesty, hard to handle, clumsy and Teutonic, a creation of industry without pretensions to beauty."

But what the world focused on was not the *Imperator*'s lack of stability, over-wrought interiors, or slightly skewed profile, but rather her absurd figurehead. In order to assure the *Imperator*'s place as the longest ship in the world, her designers had fashioned an ornament of the sort not seen on an ocean liner since the clipper-bowed ships of the Inman Line more than two decades earlier: an eagle with outstretched wings, squatting on a globe representing the Earth, with a banner stretched across the equator bearing the motto *"Mein Felt ist die Welt"* (My Field is the World). Perched on the eagle's head was a dinky little crown, symbolic of what no one seemed to know. The figurehead looked more than faintly ridiculous and did nothing for the *Imperator*'s profile, but fortunately, it didn't remain in place for long. On her third crossing a large wave rose up in front of the *Imperator* and broke down over her bow. When the water shipped away, the eagle—globe, dinky crown and all—was gone. Some semblance of sensible taste asserted itself in Hamburg-Amerika's front office and a replacement for the figurehead was never ordered, nor was the feature repeated on the *Imperator*'s sister ships.

One large part of the *Imperator*'s interior that did not live up to the standards of Hamburg-Amerika's competitors was her steerage accommodation. The Third Class dining room was far forward in the bow, an unusual position that had been abandoned by the other steamship lines many years before. The tables were long, which wasn't unusual, but they were closely spaced, and instead of the deck-mounted swivel chairs that had become standard on almost every other ship on the North Atlantic, long benches flanked the sides of each table, the same sort of arrangement that had been found on Samuel Cunard's *Britannia* seventy-five years earlier. The berthing for Third Class in the *Imperator* was cramped and crowded, while on the decks, a plethora of lifeboats and rafts took up most of the deck space that would ordinarily have been the province of the steerage passengers.

The immense number of the lifeboats carried by the *Imperator* was a consequence of the *Titanic* disaster, of course. New American safety regulations were simple and direct—there would be lifeboats for every person, passengers and crew alike, that a ship could carry. For the *Imperator*, this translated into a total of eighty-three boats, for Hamburg-Amerika had designed this new class to carry more than 5,100 people. This almost institutional vastness ultimately worked against the *Imperator* and her sisters, for they were never able to match the warmth and intimacy of the *Olympic* or the *Aquitania*. Their differences were much the same as the difference between Richard Strauss' *Ein Heldenleben* and Edward Elgar's *Enigma Variations*. One was brash and loud, all pretense, bombast and pomposity, the other subtle, ingenious and engaging.

In 1914, the second of Ballin's trio entered service, the *Vaterland*. With a gross tonnage some 2,000 tons greater than the *Imperator* and thirty-one feet longer, she assumed the mantle of the largest ship in the world. That same year the third ship of the class was launched, her intended name to be the *Bismarck*, but before she could be finished, Europe would be swept by war, and when it was over, the German merchant marine would have ceased, at least temporarily, to exist. When the *Bismarck* would finally put to sea, she would not be wearing the colors and bearing the name of Hamburg-Amerika, but ironically, of the White Star Line.

The almost barracks-like accommodations for Third Class in the new German ships was mystifying, for even more than any of the British steamship lines, the success enjoyed by Hamburg-Amerika was due to the immigrant trade. While Cunard and White Star were providing more space and more amenities for steerage, the *Imperator*'s furnishings were almost a throwback to conditions of a generation before. Certainly, the fact that she had space for almost twenty-seven hundred emigrant passengers—more than any other liner on the North Atlantic—showed that Hamburg-Amerika's executives hadn't lost sight of the money-making potential of the emigrant trade; what it seemed to express was a sense that since those carried across the Atlantic in steerage represented little if any opportunity to become repeat customers, there was no reason to offer them anything but the bare necessities.

Certainly if Hamburg-Amerika wanted to concentrate solely on those passengers who would be making a one-way, one-time-only voyage, the numbers were there to ensure that the *Imperator* and her sisters would sail full. In the last four years before the Great War, some 4,133,131 immigrants were admitted into the United States, the vast majority of them coming ashore in New York and Boston. Cunard had recognized the importance of Boston as an immigrant port when the *Cephalonia*, *Pavonia*, and *Catalonia* were built specifically for that route back in the early 1880s. In 1904, seeking to expand its role in the immigrant trade, Cunard successfully negotiated a contract with the Austro-Hungarian government to operate a service from Fiume to New York; soon, several other shipping lines petitioned Vienna to be allowed to set up operations similar to Cunard's, which in turn resulted in a fierce competition among them to offer the most attractive fares and accommodations.

The *Cephalonia*, *Pavonia*, and *Catalonia* had remained in service until they were replaced between 1900 and 1903 by the *Saxonia*, *Ivernia*, and *Carpathia*. Sailing monthly

The Aquitania *bound for New York in a heavy seaway.*

from Trieste in Austria-Hungary to Boston, they could each carry as many as 1,500 steerage passengers. The Mediterranean route was also served by some of the line's older ships: in 1904 the *Ultonia* had been converted from a cargo ship with berths for just 675 Third Class passengers to an immigrant ship with accommodations for 102 Second Class and 2,100 Third Class passengers. The *Slavonia* and the *Pannonia* were acquired by Cunard from the Furness Line specifically to cater for the Hungarian and Italian emigrant trade. On westbound voyages the ships would be filled with emigrants heading for the New World, while on the return voyage from New York they would carry mostly First and Second class passengers, many of them former immigrants who had achieved a measure of success which allowed them to go back to visit their former homes. And of course, on every eastbound crossing there was always that small number of returning immigrants, for whom, for whatever reason, life in American had not turned out as they had hoped.

The numbers of emigrants seeking passage to the United States and Canada had grown to such proportions that in 1911, Cunard's board of directors decided to acquire a controlling interest in the Anchor Line, a Glasgow-based steamship company which had a strong presence on the Mediterranean run, as well as a respectable and popular fleet serving New York, Boston, and Halifax. It was a happy union for both companies, as they had a long history of informal cooperation. The Anchor Line had begun in 1856 as a steamship service between Glasgow and New York; in the 1860s routes were introduced running from the Mediterranean to both Scotland and North America, while in

1875 the company Line established its other major route, this one running from Glasgow and Liverpool to Bombay and Calcutta. In 1902, the directors of the Anchor Line took courage from Cunard's defiance of J.P. Morgan's combine, and likewise refused to join International Mercantile Marine, which drew the two lines even closer together. The overlapping interests and routes between Britain, the Mediterranean, and the New World, coupled with the still-rising numbers of emigrants, made the union of the two a perfect match.

On the Liverpool to New York route, which of course included a stop at Queenstown, even the "Pretty Sisters," the *Caronia* and *Carmania*, which remained the darlings of a surprising number of affluent and titled passengers, were carrying as many as two thousand emigrants on each crossing. Meanwhile, the flow of emigrants to Canada had become a flood, so that at the same time Cunard acquired control of the Anchor Line, the company decided to introduce an entirely new route of its own, running from London to Southampton and then to Montreal; in the winter when ice closed the St. Lawrence River, the route would run to Portland, Maine, instead of Montreal. This route would be the first regularly scheduled Cunard service to sail out of Southampton. So anxious were the company's directors to begin this new service that they refused to wait for new ships to be built for it, and instead purchased a trio of liners from the Thomson Line, the *Ascania, Ausonia,* and *Albania*.

A year after the service to Montreal began, a trio of liners built specifically for the Canadian run were ordered from Scotts Shipbuilding & Engineering, the *Andania, Alaunia,* and *Aurania*. The three ships were virtually identical, and at 540 feet in length, 64 feet in beam and displacing 13,900 tons they were almost the same size as the *Saxonia* and her sisters, but with more handsome profiles, the tall, almost ungainly single funnel of the *Saxonia* being replaced by a pair of shorter, broader funnels. The new trio of ships carried only Second and Third Class passengers, but did so in a degree of style: taking a cue from the White Star Line, Cunard did away with the old dormitory style berthing in Third Class for single men and women and replaced then with four or six-berth cabins.

While these glory years were filled with success for Cunard, they weren't without their share of drama. On June 3, 1909 the *Slavonia* left New York bound for Trieste, and seven days later was near the Azores when she encountered thick fog; at 10:30am she ran hard aground two miles west of Flores Island. The rocks opened up the hull and the engine room quickly flooded, eliminating any chance of the *Slavonia* being able to pull free. The ship immediately began sending out a distress signal, but it wasn't until the next day that Cunard's *Batavia* and Norddeutscher-Lloyd's *Prinzess Irene* were able to reach the stranded ship, but once they did, they immediately began taking off the passengers and crew. It was soon clear that the *Slavonia* was a total loss; a salvage ship, the *Ranger*, owned by the Liverpool salvage firm of Risdon-Beazley Ltd., was sent out to try to salvage some of the ship's cargo but was largely unsuccessful, and the *Slavonia* was soon broken up by heavy Atlantic seas.

In October 1913, while on her way from New York to Liverpool, the *Carmania* picked up a distress call from the emigrant ship *Volturno*, part of the Canadian Northern Steamship fleet. The *Volturno* had been traveling from Rotterdam to America carrying 22 First Class and 539 steerage passengers, along with a crew of 96, and a cargo of barium oxide and industrial chemicals. As she was making her way through an autumn gale, a fire, whose source was never adequately explained, broke out in the forward cargo hold. An explosion then tore through the forward part of the ship, claiming the lives of between eighty and ninety of the crew who were fighting the fire, among them some of the *Volturno*'s officers. Soon the blaze was completely out of control and the only hope for those aboard was for someone to respond to the *Volturno*'s distress calls.

The *Carmania*'s Captain, James Clayton Barr, proving that the example of Arthur Rostron was no fluke, immediately altered course as soon as the *Volturno*'s SOS was picked up, arriving four hours after she first received the burning steamer's distress signal. The weather was so severe, though, that when she reached the *Volturno*, the *Carmania* was forced to heave to and stand helplessly by all night, as the high winds and rough seas made it too dangerous to launch the ship's boats. When the tanker *Narragansett* arrived early the next morning, she was able to pour oil on the storm-torn water, calming it enough for the boats from the *Carmania*, as well as the half-dozen other ships which had come to the *Volturno*'s aid, including Norddeutscher-Lloyd's *Grosser Kurfurst*, to be safely launched. Even so, the seas were still powerful enough that four of the *Volturno*'s own boats were crushed and swept away when the remaining crewmen tried to launch them. Four hundred ninety-nine passengers and crew were saved from the burning ship—one hundred and thirty three lost their lives in the fire. Fittingly, several awards for gallantry, both official and private, were made to the officers and crew of the *Carmania*.

Drama was not the sole domain of Cunard in those years: it came to the Hamburg-Amerika line as well—but the dramas that befell the two German lines had been of the genuinely tragic kind. On her fourth voyage to New York, the sheer number of passengers the *Imperator* had brought across the Atlantic overwhelmed the U.S. Customs officials and the debarkation of eighteen hundred steerage passengers was delayed overnight. At 4:00am, a fire was detected in a storeroom in the ship's bow, which began filling the forward part of the ship with smoke. The remaining passengers aboard were quickly roused and hustled off the ship while the crew rushed forward to fight the fire, which was quickly contained, though it resisted their best efforts to extinguish it. One of the *Imperator*'s officers was overcome by smoke, and died while leading some of the crew into the burning compartment.

Meanwhile, a pair of fireboats had pulled alongside the liner and began spraying the burning bow with water, while twenty teams of New York City firefighters rushed aboard, trailing hoses behind them, and soon they were enthusiastically pouring water on the flames. The weight of the rapidly accumulating water was doing nothing for the *Imperator*'s already delicate stability, and soon she was listing sharply, rapidly approaching the point where the list would become irrecoverable and the liner would roll over onto her starboard side. Fortunately, the blaze was put out before the critical point was reached, but it had been a close-run thing.

The cause of the fire was never discovered, although faulty electrical wiring was suspected. Shipboard electrical fires were hardly a new phenomenon—they are still quite commonplace, for that matter—given the amount of flexing, bending and twisting to which a ship's hull would be subjected through its career. Insulation on cables would chafe away where they passed through bulkheads, fittings at junction boxes would fracture creating shorts, and mounting screws and bolts would work loose over time. It's particularly ironic, though, that while German electrical engineering was the most sophisticated in the world in the years before the First World War, the electrical systems on German ships seemed to suffer a higher number of failures than those of any other nation.

The memories evoked by the fire aboard the *Imperator* had nothing to do with electrical systems however, but rather harked back to a tragedy that had begun at that same pier some thirteen years before. On June 2, 1900, a cargo of cotton bales, always a highly inflammable cargo, caught fire while stored in Norddeutscher-Lloyd's Ocean Terminal at Pier 3, and the flames quickly spread to three liners tied up alongside, the *Saale, Main,* and *Bremen*. Their mooring lines burned through, and the three ships began drifting down the Hudson River, ablaze from end to end. The *Main* and *Bremen* drifted aground off Weehawken, but the *Saale* stubbornly remained floating in mid-channel, the trio a tragic spectacle to thousands who lined both banks of the Hudson, watching in vain as crewmen aboard the doomed ships struggled in vain to escape the flames though portholes too small for a man or a woman to fit through.

Eventually the fires were brought under control but the three ships were total losses, and Norddeutscher-Lloyd's Ocean Terminal was burned to the waterline. Even worse was the death toll, which climbed to over two hundred. The sole positive consequence of the entire tragedy was a new American shipping regulation that required all portholes in passenger ships be enlarged to a diameter of eighteen inches, large enough, it was believed, to allow an average person to squeeze through in the event of a similar emergency ever recurring.

Fortunately, there were no future holocausts awaiting the transatlantic liners, but an even greater conflagration was looming in the high summer of 1914. On June 28, in a street in Sarajevo, Serbia, a young man named Gavrillo Princzip shot and killed the Archduke Franz Ferdinand, heir to the throne of Austria-Hungary, along with his wife. The assassination served as the trigger which released tensions that had been building in Europe for nearly a century. A little more than a month after the shootings, a tragedy of errors saw Russia, Germany, Austria-Hungary, France and Great Britain go to war. The Great War would eventually claim over 10,000,000 lives, and leave more than twice that number wounded and maimed. A vicious war at sea would send more than 25,000,000 tons of shipping to the bottom of the world's oceans. When it was over, Cunard's fleet of liners would be decimated—Germany's merchant marine would have ceased to exist.

CHAPTER TEN

The Great War

Late on the night of August 4, 1914, wireless sets in Royal Navy ships all over the world began sparking with the dots and dashes of a fateful message:

>
> Admiralty to all HM Ships
> and Naval Establishments
>
> Signal
> 4 August 1914
> 11 pm   Admiralty
>
> COMMENCE HOSTILITIES AGAINST GERMANY

The warships receiving this instruction were patrolling the waters of the North Sea, steaming up and down the English Channel, or roaming the waters of the Mediterranean, the North and South Atlantic, or the vast reaches of the Pacific, searching for German vessels. The dreadnoughts of the Grand Fleet waited with steam up on their anchorage at Scapa Flow, should the German High Seas Fleet sortie into the North Sea, while the Battle Cruiser Squadron was making ready to patrol off the German coast. Reserve ships were manned and ready for action, while auxiliaries were steaming toward British ports where they would undergo the transformations that would make them part of the fleet. Nowhere did the Germans achieve surprise against the British, either strategic or tactical. Any chance Germany may have had of winning the naval war against Great Britain vanished in those first hours of the war, as the Royal Navy stood tall while the German fleet dithered.

The Royal Navy's incredible state of readiness was the result of the prescience of the First Lord of the Admiralty, Winston Churchill. July had found the Royal Navy in the middle of its annual maneuvers, part of which was a practice mobilization of the entire fleet, including reservists. Churchill kept a careful watch as the crisis on the Continent precipitated by the assassination on June 28 of Archduke Franz Ferdinand, heir to the throne of Austria-Hungary, grew and expanded until it seemed that war might sweep across the whole of Europe. When the maneuvers ended on July 25, Churchill sent only the second-line reservists home, and rather than disperse the fleet, he kept the battle squadrons of the Grand Fleet concentrated in the waters of the North Sea.

By contrast, the German Navy's preparations for war were so incompetent as to be almost comical. Admiral von Tirpitz wanted to convert Germany's fast liners into their merchant cruiser guise as swiftly as possible and send them out into the sea lanes to prey on British shipping; the Kaiser refused to consent. Next, Tirpitz urged that the High Seas Fleet be ready to put to sea at any moment so that it might take advantage of any strategic opportunities which might present themselves should Great Britain come into the conflict. Again he was denied. Tirpitz, caught in a purely administrative office with no actual operational control over the navy he had created, could only fume impotently, while the Naval Chief of Staff, Vice-Admiral Hugo von Pohl, a man whose dilatory tendencies approached cowardice, counseled prudence to the Kaiser, which in his eyes meant avoiding a clash with the Royal Navy, at all costs.

Such a clash had not been inevitable. Until German troops crossed the border of Belgium in conscious and deliberate violation of an international treaty signed in 1839 which guaranteed Belgian neutrality, there was no reason for His Majesty's Government to become involved in what essentially was a quarrel in Eastern Europe. However, once the *feld grau* flood began flowing across the Belgian plains, and Britain's demand that it be turned back was rejected, Britain's declaration of war on Germany swiftly followed and orders went out dispatching the British Expeditionary Force, (the B.E.F.), to ports on the Channel coast of France, there to take up positions to meet the German juggernaut.

The main body of the B.E.F. began shipping across the Channel on August 12. Every day for the next week, an average of thirteen ships sailed from Southampton to Le Havre or Boulogne, among them Cunard's *Ultonia*. One hundred and forty thousand men were safely transported, the largest movement of troops in history, up to that time. Germany's only chance of winning a swift, decisive—and relatively bloodless—victory in the opening weeks of the war was to intercept these convoys and do as much damage as possible. Instead, the Kaiser's timorousness left the High Seas Fleet riding at anchor in Wilhelmshaven and Kiel. Not a single British soldier lost his life being transported to France; it would be Germany's single greatest blunder of the entire war.

To the German *Generalstab* (General Staff), the B.E.F. was so small as to be almost not worth consideration—indeed Kaiser Wilhelm II had referred to it as a "contemptible little army," giving rise to the nickname which the officers and rankers of the BEF adopted as a badge of honor, "The Old Contemptibles". German derision notwithstanding, those seven divisions were the finest troops Europe had ever seen or would ever see, and when they met the oncoming waves of field-grey on August 22, they handed the advancing Germans setback after bloody setback for the next month, retreating only when their exposed flanks were threatened, their numbers slowly but irrevocably dwindling, as the supporting French armies, bleeding and demoralized, reeled from the shock and surprise of the German assault.

What the courage and tenacity of the B.E.F. achieved was to inflict fatal delays on the

The Mauretania *in one of her many wartime guises, this one being the dazzle-paint she wore during her service as a troopship.*

unforgiving timetable of the German's schedule for advance, known as the Schlieffen Plan's, and when the German Army was within sight of Paris, a hastily assembled French army, not letting the time bought so dearly by the BEF go to waste, launched a devastating counter attack that threw the now-weary Germans back some forty miles, with the exhausted armies finally coming to a halt on September 22.

By the end of the year, after a series of sidesteps called the "Race to the Sea" had ended, two thin, snake-like lines of opposing trenches, growing more and more elaborate with each passing week, had been dug from the Swiss border to the Channel, depriving each side of the opportunity to maneuver, as the armies began looking for a way to break the enemy's lines. A slightly discordant note began to slip into the strains of *Die Wacht am Rhein,* or the *Marseillaise,* or "Tipperary" as the *soldaten, poilus,* and Tommies left for the front, when it slowly dawned on the generals and politicians alike, and even more slowly on the general public, that something had gone terribly wrong in the calculations that had been made and the assurances given, before the troops marched off to war.

It would all be over in six weeks, eight at the most, they had believed; the troops would be "home before the leaves fall." But when the leaves fell, they only covered the fresh graves of the dead, or swirled into the newly dug graves of those still dying. Then the cry was that the war would be over before Christmas, but Christmas came and went and there was no end in sight, either of the war or the casualty lists.

Soon entire military traditions were being overthrown, as it began to dawn on the Germans and French that neither intellect nor elan were about to deliver a quick victory, and the British saw that their magnificent but tiny BEF, decimated in the first four months of combat, could never be resurrected.

What was developing, and what would become the lasting memories of the Great War, were methods of living and dying that could only find parallels in the darker passages of writers like Edgar Rice Burroughs, Jules Verne, or H. G. Wells. Trenches evolved into sophisticated systems of defensive positions, listening posts, dugouts, bunkers, and communication cuttings. The Allies were faced with the task of forcibly ejecting the Germans from occupied Belgium and France, a bloody and rather hopeless undertaking, as time and again the French and British armies surged forward against the waiting German defenses—and each time found some hellish new innovation that cut them down by the thousands. Machine guns proliferated behind huge entanglements of barbed wire, which appeared with barbs the size of a man's thumb, the better to catch on uniforms, accouterments, and flesh, pinning the hapless victims long enough for the chattering Spandaus to find them. Mine-throwers made their debut, as did flame throwers and poison gas.

Soldiers learned that sounds were dangerous—the steady mechanical rattle of the Spandau machine gun; the hissing roar of the *flammenwerfer*; the unforgettable "click-clack, clack-click" of a round being chambered in a Lee-Enfield rifle; the short, sharp scraping of the primer cord being drawn from the handle of a potato masher hand grenade. And always the shells—whistling, warbling, chugging like freight locomotives, or whining like banshees. And there was always the sound you never heard—the one that got you.

Even colors were perilous: red Very lights at night signaling corrections to artillery bombardments; green or yellow mists snaking along the ground, the terrible tendrils of phosgene or mustard gas; white on a man's gums or blue on his feet announcing the presence of trench mouth or trench foot; black on a wounded soldier's body declaring that gangrene had already set in.

It was an article of faith that the enemy always suffered the worst—the French in particular refined their talent for self-deception, somehow formulating the absurd idea that for every two Frenchmen who died in action, three Germans had been killed, but the truth was that the slaughter was appalling for both sides. In the First Battle of Ypres in October 1914, where wave after wave of German infantry, many of them university students advancing arm-in-arm singing patriotic songs, were cut down by the deadly accurate British rifle fire; one German division lost over 9,300 men out of strength of 12,000—*in a single morning*. Later, when the Allies were on the offensive, time and again the Tommies and *poilus* would clamber over the top of their trenches after an artillery bombardment that had lasted for hours, sometimes days, or even weeks, as the second-hands of their officers' watches touched zero hour, and and begin their methodical advance, the British to the sound of the officers' whistles, the more romantic French to bugles blaring the *Pas de Charge*, across the shell-torn mudscape that stretched between the opposing lines of trenches and became known as No Man's Land. The Germans, having weathered the barrage in the relative safety of their deep dugouts, would emerge to assume their prepared positions and bring down a withering hail of rifle, machine gun, and artillery fire on the advancing troops. The results were inevitable: more often than not, there wouldn't be enough soldiers left alive among the attackers to take the objective and hold it, or if the Allied troops did reach their goal, the cost was prohibitive—one advance of barely 700 yards took three weeks at a cost of nearly 30,000 lives. Even on days when the public communiques would read "All quiet on the Western Front," nearly 5,000 men were being killed by sniper fire and random shelling. The British, with methodical callousness, referred to such losses as "normal wastage."

In the post-war years, the commanding generals on both sides were pilloried as mindless brutes who could conceive of no alternative but to feed endless masses of men into a vast killing machine, in the hope that the enemy would run out of troops first. In fact, the generals, much maligned as incompetents as they are, and many of them deservedly, really didn't intend to slaughter the finest generation of young men their nations would ever produce. Certainly none of them ever enjoyed it, no matter what the slanderers might say in later years. The hard, painful truth was that they were unprepared for the war they found themselves given the responsibility of fighting. For years it had been a tenet of military faith, and correctly so, that the day of the frontal assault was over—the American Civil War and the Franco-Prussian War had first demonstrated that, and the Russo-Japanese War of 1905 and the Balkan War of 1912 had only reinforced the lesson. Modern firepower made frontal assaults too costly, for infantry in even a hastily prepared defensive position could hold off several times their number of attacking troops, inflicting unacceptable losses in the process. So for decades the emphasis had been placed on conducting wars of maneuver, which gave an army the opportunity to turn a foe's flank, and achieve a decisive result in battle without having to resort to the terrible waste of frontal attacks. What they never anticipated was a war where maneuver would be impossible, where there would be no flanks to turn, and the dreadful frontal assaults the only option remaining to them. The result was a slaughter the like of which had never been seen before, or since.

And yet, somehow, there is still a rose-tinged nimbus of romance that surrounds the Great War. It was the songs—"Keep the Home Fires Burning," "Pack Up Your Troubles," "Till We Meet Again," and everyone's favorite, "Tipperary." It was the magnificently anachronistic traditions—French cuirassier regiments and squadrons of German *uhlans* who looked as if they had just stepped out of a Phillipoteaux painting of the Napoleonic Wars; the Germans' wearing faintly absurd spiked *Pickelhauben* helmets; in England, a tradition harking back to the Hundred Years' War found newly commissioned subalterns visiting an armourer to have their swords sharpened before leaving for the front. It was the grandeur of an age that was, in fact, its shroud. France and Germany had armies of conscripts, it is true, but conscription had been a national institution for generations—what made these conscripts conspicuous was how few tried to evade their responsibility. In Great Britain the situation was even more astonishing: not until 1916, when Britain would be compelled to field the largest army the Empire had ever mustered to carry out the Somme Offensive, would the British Army have to resort to a draft to fill its ranks. These young men, rightly called the flower of European youth, were the most idealistic the world would ever see, untainted by the cynicism and affected, postured disdain of later generations. Instead, they steadfastly believed in *Ein Kaiser, ein Volk, ein Reich*, or *Liberte, Egalite, Fraternite*! and *Vive le Republique*!, or fighting for King and Country. What Europe was killing, no matter how willing the victims, was the vitality that would leave later generations listless and disillusioned: the fire that had driven the Continent for a thousand years was being quenched forever.

By contrast, the war at sea would be just as vicious and just as brutal, as the one being fought on land, but it would never be cloaked in the romantic nonsense that made the Western Front at once so fascinating and so repulsive. Instead, it was far more methodical and deliberate, and for the British at least, far more successful than most of her efforts on land.

It was in Captain Alfred Thayer Mahan's work, *The Influence of Sea Power Upon History*, one of the most influential books written in the last two hundred years, that the concept of "sea power," long intuitively understood by the navies of the world, was articulated in a clear and coherent form. Mahan defined sea power as a nation's capacity to use the world's oceans to transport the flow of raw materials and finished goods necessary to sustain a nation's economy in peacetime, as well as transport troops and supplies in wartime, while simultaneously denying that capability to the enemy. No nation has more thoroughly understood or expertly executed that concept throughout its history than Great Britain.

Probably the most convincing demonstration of that understanding was the results produced by the flurry of orders and deployments issued by the Admiralty in the first week of the war. By the end of August, of the forty-two liners Germany had planned to convert to auxiliary cruisers to prey on British shipping, seventeen had been bottled up in neutral harbors while British warships cruised just offshore in international waters, keeping a watchful eye on them. Another fourteen were still tied up in German ports, trapped by the Grand Fleet and rendered impotent by the Kaiser's indecisiveness and von Pohl's timidity. Of the five remaining at large on the high seas, only one was armed when the war began, the *Kaiser Wilhelm der Grosse*; it was her misfortune to meet HMS *Highflyer* on August 26—she was sent to the bottom in less than half an hour. The remaining four would be hounded by the Royal Navy for the next four months, and one by one would be sunk or interned in neutral ports.

It was during the hunt for these remaining four fugitives that one of Cunard's most popular ships, also converted to merchant cruiser guise, became the only auxiliary cruiser ever to engage another such ship in combat on the high seas. The handsome *Carmania*, one of the "Pretty Sisters," had been requisitioned by the Admiralty on August 7, 1914, and underwent conversion to an Armed Merchant Cruiser (AMC) in Liverpool. It was a considerable task: no sooner had she tied up at dockside than scores of painters began applying a coat of Royal Navy grey to her hull and upperworks, while ordnance officers were mounting eight 4.7-inch guns, four to a side, on her upper deck. Armour-steel plates were riveted over her vitals, while hundreds of sandbags and thousands of feet of heavy hemp cable were used to protect her bridge and superstructure. Inside, various compartments were converted into magazines, shell handling flats, and hoisting rooms. Meanwhile, all of the *Carmania*'s peacetime furniture and furnishings had to be removed, including everything flammable, and all of her woodwork—the splinters created by a bursting shell shattering wooden doors, partitions, or decorations could be as lethal as fragments from the shell itself. Linen, mattresses, candelabra, tableware, crystal, china, pianos, carpets, bedsteads, dressing tables, and leather chairs all went ashore to be put in storage until the day arrived that peace returned, and the ship could be restored to her former glory.

Under the command of Captain Noel Grant, RN, with Captain Barr as his First Officer, the *Carmania* sailed from Liverpool on August 14, and arrived at Bermuda a week later. The German liner *Cap Trafalgar*, one of the Hamburg-Amerika fleet, had been sighted off the island a few days earlier and was now believed to be headed for South Africa. The *Cap Trafalgar* had meanwhile made a rendezvous with the gunboat *Eber*, taken the smaller ship's guns aboard, and began haunting the waters around Trinidad. In a twist of incredible irony, the crew of the *Cap Trafalgar*, in an attempt to disguise their ship, had altered her appearance so that she would closely resemble one of the "Pretty Sisters." (Though it would be later said that the *Carmania* had also altered her appearance so that she might be mistaken for the *Cap Trafalgar*, there is no truth to the claim.) The *Carmania* set out to find her, and on the morning of September 14, she spotted the German liner. The two ships turned toward each other and began a desperate sea battle unlike any before or since.

The two ships were roughly the same size and neither one had an appreciable margin of speed over the other. The *Carmania* had the advantage in armament, though, for the *Cap Trafalgar* only mounted a pair of 105-mm (4.1-inch) guns, along with a half-dozen machine guns. Her commander, *Kapitan* Julius Wirth, kept trying to close the range, hoping to board the *Carmania*, while his two popguns kept up a steady fire, eventually scoring a total of seventy-nine hits on the British ship. But despite the fact that the German 4.1-inch shell was only slightly more than a half-inch smaller in diameter than its British 4.7-inch counterpart, it weighed barely half that of the British round, and did far less damage.

The gunners on the *Cap Trafalagar* kept raking the *Carmania's* upperworks with machine gun fire, causing a considerable number of casualties and setting the superstructure on fire. Soon the *Carmania's* bridge was swept by flames and Captain Grant had to shift his command to the auxiliary bridge on the stern. But the trained gunners aboard the *Carmania* had been steadily pumping round after round into the *Cap Trafalgar*'s waterline, and little more than an hour after the action had started, the German liner began to list dangerously to starboard. When her decks were awash, Wirth, mortally wounded, gave the order to abandon ship, and a little more than ten minutes later, the *Cap Trafalgar* slid beneath the waves, having fought, however odd the circumstances may have been, with a dignity and honor that would desert the German Navy a few months hence.

The well-punctured *Carmania*—the seventy-nine hits had caused 304 holes in her plating—had lost nine dead in the action, with an additional twenty-six wounded. Her upper decks were a shambles and her interior scorched and pitted by fire. Escorted by the cruiser HMS *Bristol* to Gibraltar, she remained there for eight weeks while repairs were done. She would remain in the waters off Spain and Portugal until May 1915, when she was sent to the Aegean to serve as a troopship in the Gallipoli campaign. Later that year her crew would be called upon to assist in quelling a mutiny aboard the British steamship *Maristan*. In May 1916, the *Carmania* was returned to Cunard, although still in His Majesty's service: she spent the remainder of the war on trooping duty between Halifax and Liverpool.

For all of its surreal nature—there is something admittedly absurd about the idea of a pair of ocean liners disguised as warships pummeling each other to a shambles in the middle of a tropical sea—the battle between the *Carmania* and the *Cap Trafalgar* in a sense rang down the curtain on an era of naval warfare. Just as was happening on land, the notions of what did, and did not constitute civilized behavior in warfare at sea, was undergoing a fundamental transformation. Even as the *Carmania* and the *Cap Trafalgar* slugged it out off Trinidad, the demands of 20th Century warfare began imposing themselves on Great Britain's armed forces, Royal Navy, and in turn, on Cunard Line. When the rest of Europe was confidently declaring the war would end in a matter of weeks, Field Marshall Lord Kitchener, the Secretary of State for War, in a moment of terrifyingly profound insight, declared that the war would last three or more years, and that the reserve stocks of ammunition, guns, and equipment would be woefully inadequate. Kitchener had urged that the Cabinet take steps to procure the materials needed before the reserves on hand ran dangerously low. As a whole, the Cabinet disagreed with Kitchener, but Sir Walter Runciman, the President of the Board of Trade, felt that the Field Marshal's arguments had merit, and decided to act accordingly. Realizing very quickly that it would be several months before Britain's industry would be able to supply the demand of Britain's armed forces, he could only see one alternative: purchase the materials needed from manufacturers in the United States. Consequently, he set up an organization that would work through the "old boy network" to acquire supplies and equipment for the British Army. Runciman sat on the board of the Bank of England, and so he approached one of his fellow directors at the bank, George Booth, and asked him to assist in setting up what became known as the Committee on War Purchases.

In addition to the contacts in the financial world that Booth's position as one of the director's of the Bank of England provided, George Booth was the cousin of Alfred Booth. Alfred Booth was the chairman of the shipping and import/export firm of Alfred Booth and Company, a Liverpool business started by his father. The Company owned one shipping line outright, the Booth Steamship Company Ltd., as well as tanneries, factories, and construction companies in Brazil, the United States and Great Britain; it had financial ties to several other shipping firms, as well as having holdings in a number of storage and wholesaling businesses. Alfred Booth and Company was also the single largest stockholder in Britain's single largest shipping line, Cunard, and Alfred Booth sat as Cunard's chairman of the board.

Runciman and D.F. Wintour, the Director of Army Contracts for the Board of Trade, asked George Booth to inquire of Alfred Booth if the Company would be willing to arrange the financing of British munitions purchases in America, as well as act as the overall coordinator of the British purchasing missions to the United States. Alfred Booth agreed, realizing that not only was he doing his patriotic duty, but that since all transactions were to be conducted as private business affairs, it was good for business as well.

Certainly there were risks involved, despite the fact that the German surface raiders had effectively been eradicated. On October 20, 1914, naval warfare entered an entirely new era when the *U-17*, cruising submerged fourteen miles off the Norwegian coast, surfaced alongside the British merchant ship *Glitra* and ordered her to stop. After the *Glitra*'s crew had safely taken to the lifeboats, the *U-17*'s crew opened the ship's seacocks and scuttled her. It took twenty minutes for the *Glitra* to sink, and while no lives had been lost, it was a turning point in naval warfare—she was the first merchant ship ever sunk by a submarine.

For all of its implications for merchant shipping, the event was overshadowed in both the public and the Royal Navy's consciousness by a more terrifying incident that had taken place a month earlier. On September 22, 1914, like ducks in a shooting gallery, three British armoured cruisers, *Hogue*, *Aboukir*, and *Cressy*, were torpedoed and sunk by the *U-9*, which was commanded by *Kapitan-Leutnant* Otto Weddigen. They were not the first British warships to be sunk by a German submarine—that unhappy distinction belonged to H.M.S. *Pathfinder*, a light cruiser torpedoed and sunk in the North Sea on September 3 by the *U-21*. But the implications, as well as the magnitude of the disaster that befell the three cruisers far overshadowed the loss of a single light cruiser. Assigned to, of all things, an anti-submarine patrol in a section of the North Sea known as the Broad Fourteens, the three cruisers were big (12,000 tons), and heavily armed with twelve 6-inch guns each, but they were all nearly fifteen years old, slow with nearly worn-out engines, and very poor, almost non-existent underwater protection. Within the space of two hours, all three cruisers were sent to the bottom, taking with them more than 1,400 British sailors and the legend of British naval invincibility.

The Royal Navy was stunned. Suddenly the Grand Fleet began to believe it was seeing submarines everywhere, even in Scapa Flow alarms were being raised there on at least three different occasions, the climax coming on October 17, when the entire fleet put to sea as destroyers dashed about, firing guns at anything that resembled a U-boat. Not that the German Naval High Command was particularly quick on the uptake in understanding the significance or the potential of the *U-9*'s exploit. The strategy, planning, and doctrines of the German Navy were so firmly fixed on the idea of one great cataclysmic clash of fleets, that the Germans were at first oblivious to the fact that Weddigen had given them the key that could release German naval power from its North Sea prison.

For it was an unavoidable reality that, despite all the confidence, ability, and quality of ships and crews they commanded, the German Naval High Command was utterly unable to force the Royal Navy to do battle. The whole balance of naval power had been determined by two overriding factors, one industrial, and the other geographic. In both instances, Germany came out second best.

First of course, was Britain's enormous numerical superiority in capital ships, coupled with the industrial capacity to maintain it. Britain boasted nearly twice as many slipways capable of building battleships as Germany, while maintaining a huge standing army was a burden that Great Britain's foundries and arsenals never had to bear.

The second, a geographic factor, was in some ways even more fundamental to the impotence of the High Seas Fleet. Great Britain sat astride the only two routes that the German navy had to the North Atlantic, through the English Channel or up through the North Sea and around Scotland. Neither proved to be practical, since the Channel was a natural choke point, easily sealed off by Royal Navy mines and submarines. Meanwhile, the Grand Fleet, moored at Scapa Flow in the Orkneys, sat at the entrance to the North Sea, waiting for the High Seas Fleet to steam into its grasp. As Grand Admiral Karl Doenitz, a destroyer captain in the Great War, would write in his memoirs, "The High Seas Fleet was denied its normal radius of action—to steam into the North Atlantic, where alone a decision was possible. Our fleet presented no danger to the British Grand Fleet only when it was in the North Sea. The Royal Navy then had but to put into operation the war plans envisioned before 1914."

Doenitz was referring to the fact that the Royal Navy wholeheartedly embraced the concept of the blockade as the definitive expression of sea power. By sealing off the Channel and the North Sea, it cut off all imports into Germany—most important, food, since Germany was not able to produce enough for her own needs, and nitrates, which were essential to the manufacture of explosives, of which Germany possessed no natural sources. The Germans devised stratagems for countering the Royal Navy's original plans, where cruisers and destroyers would cruise a few miles outside German waters, while the van of the fleet would keep station over the horizon, but the British Admiralty threw a spanner into the works of the High Seas Fleet even before the war broke out, when it realized that the Grand Fleet only need prevent the Germans from breaking out of the North Sea. By stationing the Grand Fleet at three distant anchorages in Scotland, the Royal Navy effectively sealed off the North Sea, catching, as the Duke of Wellington would have put it, "a damned big rat in a damned small bottle!" That the Grand Fleet would have ample warning of any sortie by the High Seas Fleet only made the task easier. That it was the Germans themselves who were unwittingly providing the warning was probably the best kept secret of the war; and thereby hangs a tale, for the British ability to read German ciphers would have a decisive effect on the course of the war.

In the early hours of 4 August, 1914, a British cable ship, the *Telconia*, dredged up five underwater telegraph cables from the waters near Emden, where the German and Dutch borders meet at the North Sea. These were the German transatlantic cables, Germany's secure links with her overseas embassies and consulates, and one by one, they were cut. Now Germany would be forced to rely on wireless to communicate with her agents and diplomats overseas, counting on the security of her codes and ciphers to prevent prying enemy ears from listening in. In an incredible string of bad luck for the Germans in the first three months of the war, the British were able to recover copies of three of the most widely used German codebooks: the diplomatic cipher, the zeppelin cipher, and the greatest prize of all, a copy of the German High Seas Fleet naval cipher, captured by the Russians when two of their cruisers destroyed the German light cruiser *Magdeburg* in the Baltic.

The cipher books were rushed to Room 40, Old Building (Rm 40 OB), the cryptographic department of the Office of Naval Intelligence (ONI). With the three codebooks in its hand, the ONI had the capability to decode and read German communications just as quickly as the recipient. All the while, the Germans remained blissfully ignorant that their signals were compromised, and so continued to chatter merrily over the airwaves to one another, while British listening stations faithfully copied each message. The results allowed the Grand Fleet several hours', sometimes days' notice when the High Seas Fleet planned a sortie, so that the Royal Navy was never taken by surprise.

It was a vital advantage for Britain's war effort, for her very existence depended on the steady flow of food, goods and materials from overseas. Any interruption of Britain's shipping lanes would be devastating; if they were cut, it would be fatal. In the early months of 1915, the war at sea took a new and nasty turn as the number of British merchant ships being sunk by German U-boats began to increase alarmingly. What Great Britain now faced was not just a crisis, but the beginnings of a threat to her survival.

What had happened was simple: on February 15, 1915, Germany issued a declaration which not only changed the course of the war at sea, but also changed the basic nature of warfare forever. The German Foreign Office had sent a cable to every neutral capitol in Europe, as well as every country in North and South America, that read:

> "The waters surrounding Great Britain and Ireland, and including the whole of the English Channel, are proclaimed to be a War Zone. On and after the 18th of February 1915, every enemy merchant ship found in the said war zone will be destroyed without it always being possible to avert the dangers threatening the crews and passengers on that account. Even neutral ships are exposed to dangers in the war zone, and in view of the use of neutral flags ordered on January 31st by the British government and of the accidents of naval war, mistakes may not always be avoided and they may be struck by attacks directed at enemy ships."

Accompanying the declaration was a list of safe zones in which neutral ships could travel to Europe, none of which, of course, led to a British port.

Simply put, the British had pushed the Germans too far. Beginning in October 1914, a steady stream of orders had issued forth from the Admiralty to British merchant captains regarding their conduct if, and when they were attacked by a German U-boat. First, it was made a criminal offense for a captain to stop his ship if ordered to do so by a German submarine, then merchant skippers were given orders that required them, if they were challenged by a U-boat, to not only refuse to stop, but to attempt to engage the submarine with whatever armament the merchant ship had, or if it were unarmed, to attempt to ram the U-boat. Finally, all British merchant ships were ordered to paint out their funnels colors and names, and to fly false flags whenever possible to make identification as difficult as possible.

The Germans learned of these orders entirely by accident, when *U-21* stopped the *Ben Cruachan* on her way to Liverpool on January 31, 1915. A prize crew from the *U-21* found the orders along with the ship's papers before sending the *Cruachan* to the bottom. The German government's reaction was so sharp and so swift because the Admiralty orders were making a mockery of the German navy's attempt to carry out its submarine campaign, according to the dictates of the Cruiser Rules.

The Cruiser Rules were a naval etiquette dating back to the days of Henry VIII in the early 1500s that governed a warship's conduct toward merchant shipping. A warship was expected to order an *unarmed* merchant ship to halt by firing a warning shot across the merchantman's bow. Once stopped, the merchant crew was obliged to allow the warship's crew to search the vessel without threat of harm or interference in any way, while in turn the searchers could not threaten or use force against the crew except in self-defense. If the merchant ship belonged to a neutral, it was to be allowed to proceed untouched, even if it were bound for a port belonging to a hostile power.

If the freighter belonged to a hostile power, then the warship had two options available: a prize crew could be put aboard the merchantman, or if that proved to be impractical, then both the vessel and cargo could be destroyed—after the crew and any passengers were given time to take to the lifeboats. It was a very clearly defined and very civilized method of waging war.

However, the protection the Cruiser Rules offered to ships, cargo, passengers and crew applied only to *unarmed* freighters and merchant ships. Any show of resistance, including attempting to run away or simply refusing to halt when so ordered, allowed the warship to resort to force. So did opening fire on the warship with a deck gun, trying to ram, or assaulting the boarding party. Finally, any attempt to signal for help allowed the warship complete freedom of action. Obviously, this whole convention was obsolescent by 1914, especially in the case of submarines. U-boat crews were small, making capturing enemy freighters impractical, while the advent of wireless made a call for assistance by a merchant ship ordered to heave to a virtual certainty. Such a call was dangerous for the submarine, since it would invariably include the U-boat's position and would bring any nearby anti-submarine forces rushing to the scene.

Most critically, though, was the fact that by January 1915, many British merchant ships were "defensively" armed as a measure of protection against submarine attack, usually with a pair of twelve-pounder guns, as the British called their 3-inch gun, although some ships carried guns with calibers as large as 6-inches. A single hit from a twelve-pounder could cripple a U-boat, while a hit from a 6-inch shell would blow the submarine out of the water. Surfacing and challenging a ship carrying such an armament left the U-boat dangerously exposed to an attack itself, to which the U-boat would have no reply but to torpedo the merchantman.

The defensive armament had originally been a measure intended to provide a degree of self-defense against surface raiders, the threat that dissipated when the fast German lines were all sunk or interned in the first few weeks of the war. But when the U-boats began sinking merchant ships in late 1914, and a number of armed merchantmen used their deck guns to force the U-boats to break off their attacks, the Admiralty realized that the guns were very effective defenses against submarines. With typically Teutonic passion for legality, the U-boat crews had been very scrupulous in observing the Cruiser Rules in the first five months of the war: the U-boats' favorite method of sinking a merchant ship was to surface alongside her, order the ship to stop, then wait for the crew to take to the lifeboats before using their deck gun to blow holes in the merchant ship's waterline, saving their torpedoes for warships.

However, the thought of surfacing amid a flurry of 3-, 4-, or even 6-inch shells whistling past their ears did not appeal to the U-boat crews, who began to attack without warning. Learning that even unarmed freighters were expected to try to ram U-boats on sight caused the U-boat commanders to argue that the British measures had made further adherence to the Cruiser Rules a practical impossibility, and any attempts to do so would needlessly lose boats and crews. They wanted to be able to sink British ships on sight, without warning, and they wanted neutrals warned that they sailed in British waters at their own peril. The solution was to declare the waters around the British Isles to be a war zone, much like Britain's announcement of the North Sea as a "military area" in October 1914. The Kaiser himself endorsed the idea, and the appropriate memoranda were drawn up and sent out to the German embassies around the world on February 5.

The U-boats wasted no time in putting the proclamation into effect. Between February 18 and March 28, twenty-five ships were sunk by U-boats, sixteen of them torpedoed without warning. Of a total of 712 crewmen from those sixteen ships, 52 were killed, though not a single passenger out of 3,072 involved was even injured. It was a not unenviable record but it couldn't last forever.

On March 28, 1915, the 5,000-ton steamer *Falaba*, bound for Liverpool, was torpedoed

The U-20, *nemesis of the* Lusitania.

The Lusitania, *leaving New York on her last voyage.*

by *U-28* after refusing to obey the U-boat's order to halt. The ship's cargo of explosives blew up in sympathetic detonation, sending the ship to the bottom in minutes. Among the 104 lives lost was Leon C. Thresher, an American citizen, the first American to be killed in the war at sea. That incident seemed to act as a sort of trigger because the conduct of the U-boats suddenly underwent a transformation from gentlemanly to barbarous in a matter of days. A whole series of neutral ships were sunk in March and April—two Norwegian ore carriers, the *Regin* and *Nor*; a Swedish freighter, the *Hanna*; and the *Duoro*, a Portuguese coastal freighter. On April 10, the 6,000-ton steamer *Harpalyce*, boldly marked with the words "Belgian Relief Commission" and flying a prominent white flag was torpedoed without warning; the ship sank so rapidly that seventeen members of her 44-man crew were trapped and drowned before they could reach the lifeboats.

All of this was leading up to the single most barbaric act of the war, the destruction of the *Lusitania*. Since she had been returned to Cunard in September 1914, she had been maintaining regular monthly sailings from Liverpool to New York and back. The war had reduced the number of passengers to a trickle, and even that abbreviated schedule was causing Cunard to lose almost £1,000 each crossing, so as an economy measure, six of her twenty-five boilers were shut down. This reduced the *Lusitania*'s top speed from 26 knots to barely more than 21, but since that was half again the top speed of a U-boat, it seemed more than sufficient to offer her a measure of protection. For reasons which were never adequately explained, the Admiralty ordered Cunard to paint all four of her funnels completely black and the lower half of her superstructure buff, as well as paint over her name and port of registry.

Her departure from New York on the morning of May 1, 1915, was remarkable only for its relative normality—it could have almost been mistaken for a peacetime sailing. There was one discordant note, a warning issued in the name of the German Embassy in Washington D.C. appeared that morning in the travel section of several New York newspapers, advising all passengers crossing the Atlantic on British vessels that they did so at the risk of being sunk without warning. In one of the papers, the *New York Sun*, it actually appeared right next to the advertisement for the departure of the *Lusitania*. Some people would later attach a sinister significance to that arrangement, but as it turned out, the placement had been the result of pure chance.

That the notice was nothing more than a harmless warning seemed to be borne out by the lack of incidents on the first six days of the crossing. On the morning of the seventh day, however, the *Lusitania*'s captain, William Turner, had the lifeboats uncovered and swung out as a safety precaution and posted extra lookouts in the bow and the crows' nest. Rather than swing in close to the southern coast of Ireland and run along just a mile or two offshore, Turner stood away from the coastline, maintaining a distance of ten miles.

Captain William Turner, the Lusitania*'s first, and as Fate would have it, last captain.*

Just before noon he received a signal from the Admiralty that he was expected to enter Liverpool without stopping at the Bar for the pilot, lest a U-boat lying in wait be presented with a stationary target. Knowing that he would only be able to cross the Bar at high tide because of the *Lusitania*'s enormous draft, Turner plotted a course that would require very careful navigation in order to arrive outside of Liverpool at the right time and place. He needed to know his position down to the yard, and so began taking a fix known as a "four point bearing."

What Turner didn't know was that he and his ship were being watched. Through the monocular eye of the periscope of the submarine *U-20*, *Kapitan-Leutnant* Walther Schwieger was tracking the *Lusitania* as she steamed past the promontory of the Old Head of Kinsale at a steady 18 knots. These waters had already been rich hunting grounds for Schwieger—on the previous day he had sunk a pair of 5,000-ton freighters. Now he was looking at the largest target he had ever seen.

The profile of the *Lusitania* was unmistakable, but Schwieger chose to fire a single torpedo at her. It struck the ship on the starboard side, abreast of her first funnel. Within seconds, the ship took on a sharp list, then was shaken from stem to stern by a violent internal explosion deep within her bow. Steam lines burst in the boiler rooms and engine rooms, depriving the motor of the power to turn the rudder, and denying Turner the chance to beach the ship on the nearby shore. But the momentum of the 33,000-ton liner still making 18 knots, continued to drive her forward, pushing her bow deeper into the water and making it all but impossible to launch the lifeboats.

The boats on the *Lusitania*'s portside were useless in any case, the list becoming so severe within minutes of the torpedo's impact that they couldn't be swung out far enough to clear the ship's side. The situation on the starboard side was chaotic: many of the crewmen panicked and mishandled the boats, the most experienced seamen having been trapped below decks by rising water as they struggled to save the ship; passengers rushed to and fro trying to find a way to safely escape the sinking liner, and all the while the list increased ominously, as if the *Lusitania* were going to capsize before she sank.

Eight hundred yards away, *Kapitan-Leutnant* Schwieger peered through his periscope and examined the sinking ship. Although he couldn't hear the cries for help or the din of the sinking liner, some sense of the awful spectacle before him impressed itself on his mind, for he would record in his log:

"...The ship was sinking with unbelievable rapidity. There was a terrible panic on her deck. Overcrowded lifeboats, fairly torn from their positions, dropped into the water, as desperate people ran helplessly up and down the decks. Men and women jumped into the water and tried to swim to empty overturned lifeboats. It was the most terrible sight I have ever seen. It was impossible for me to give any help: I could have saved only a handful...."

Stepping back from the eyepiece, Schwieger gave the order for the *U-20* to dive to twenty meters and proceed on a course to the

Kapitan-Leutnant *Walter Schwieger, Commander of the* U-20.

southeast. His work here was finished.

The *Lusitania*'s stern began to lift out of the water, exposing the four great screws, still slowly turning. Suddenly the ship gave a shudder that ran her entire length as her bow struck the bottom some three hundred feet below. Almost lying on her beam ends, her four funnels almost parallel to the water, she began to settle very quickly. Hundreds of people still crowded her decks, clutching desperately at whatever they could to maintain their balance against the list; hundreds more were struggling in the water, trying to find something buoyant to which they could cling. With a long moan of tortured metal, the *Lusitania* slipped beneath the Irish Sea, just eighteen minutes after she had been struck by the *U-20*'s torpedo.

A flotilla of fishing boats and small coastal steamers set out from nearby Queenstown, intent on rescuing the survivors, summoned by the distress signals the *Lusitania's* wireless operator had been able to send before her power failed. No one had any idea of how many survivors there might be: many of the ship's lifeboats had been launched while still half empty, while others had been damaged while they were being lowered into the water, spilling their occupants into the sea; several of the lifeboats had been carried to the bottom by the *Lusitania*—she sank so quickly there had been no time to load or launch them. Most of the collapsibles had floated free of the wreck, although many of them were damaged as well. As a result, hundreds of people were clinging to bits of wreckage in the hope that help would soon come. As the afternoon passed and the sun began to set lower in the sky, the temperature dropped and the water began to grow colder. One by one, the people clinging to an upturned boat, an oar, a deckchair or a section of planking, began to slip off, as their strength gave out before the fishing boats arrived from Queenstown.

The sun was low on the horizon when the first rescue vessels reached the survivors, and when they arrived the rescuers found the water littered with debris, human and otherwise, for nearly a mile in every direction from where the *Lusitania* went down. While the lifeboats and collapsibles were fairly easy to see, spotting a swimmer or some poor soul clinging to a bit of wreckage, became increasingly difficult as daylight faded. It took less than an hour for the rescue vessels to pick up all of the lifeboats and collapsibles. Now the challenge was to find the people still adrift in the twilight. The survivors were exhausted—often too far gone in fatigue to even wave an arm or call out to an approaching boat. No one will ever know how many survivors were lost in the rapidly dwindling twilight, unconscious, unable to even call for help, they went unseen by sailors desperately straining their eyes for some sign of life.

One sight repeated over and over again was the number of people in the water who had been drowned because they had put their lifebelts on backwards, and instead of having their heads supported out of the water, had them held beneath the surface instead. And then there were the bodies of the children, over a hundred of them. Especially pathetic were those little ones who were too small to be able to wear one of the special small-sized

A dazed Captain Turner wandering the streets of Queenstown the day after the Lusitania *died.*

children's lifebelts. All too often these "babes in arms" were exactly that, held close to their mothers' bosoms, where they died together.

When the final totals were tallied, out of 1,959 people on board, passengers and crew, 1,198 had been killed, 128 of them Americans. The news of the *Lusitania*'s destruction was devastating to Cunard. "To all of us in the Company the moment we first learned of our loss will remain the most awful moment of our lives—the moment when God Himself seemed to forsake us", was how one member of the board recalled that day.

For the Germans it was cause for national celebration: in Berlin, the Kaiser declared a national holiday, although despite Allied propaganda which some historians have perpetuated to this day, there were no masses of people crowding the streets of the German capital in celebration. Rather, the prevailing mood was that of a job well done. An editorial in *Kolnische* (Cologne) *Volkszeitung* summed it up when it said, "With joyful pride we contemplate this latest deed of our navy"—harsh sounding in translation, but in intent, more of a "Well done, lads!" than outright gloating.

The rest of the world, however, was aghast at the news of the sinking. The *Lusitania* was not some obscure tanker or merchantman that had been torpedoed by accident. She was arguably the most famous and in some ways the best-loved ship in the world. It would be impossible for Germany to claim that this was anything other than a deliberate act. How America would react to the sinking, and how Germany would explain it, riveted the attention of the chancelleries and foreign offices of the nations of the Central Powers, and the Allies alike.

In Great Britain, the news of the *Lusitania*'s destruction was a bitter blow to the entire nation. In Liverpool and London, riots broke out as mobs savaged German-owned businesses—or even those with merely German-sounding names. Many naturalized British citizens of German birth were forced to seek police protection, as were some nationals of neutral countries who were mistaken for Germans in the hysteria: several were accosted and beaten bloody in the streets of the British capitol.

News of the disaster began to spread in the United States in mid-afternoon on May 7. Soon extra editions of all the New York newspapers hit the streets, and the story was quickly picked up by newspapers up and down the East Coast, followed by those further inland. By the end of the day, the word had spread from one end of the country to the other that the *Lusitania* had been sunk by a German U-boat. For the next six weeks, the *Lusitania* was *the* front page story in every American daily. There was talk in some circles of war between America and Germany, but the Wilson Administration, for all of the noble and high-minded rhetoric it had directed toward the Allied and Central Powers, was not prepared to defend the humanitarian principles it so loudly espoused, largely due to the Machiavellian maneuverings of Robert Lansing, the Assistant Secretary of State. Still, though Lansing may have prevented the destruction of the *Lusitania* from becoming a *causus belli* between the United States and Germany, it was clear to observers on both sides of the Atlantic that American tolerance had been pushed to the limit.

Suddenly—and rather hypocritically—appalled at what had been done in his name, and rightfully fearful of the reaction of the American people, Kaiser Wilhelm called off his undersea dogs, issuing an imperial decree to the U-boat commanders to strictly observe the Cruiser Rules, and in any cases of doubt as to the identity of a target to err on the side of caution and break off an attack. It was not long, though, before the U-boats themselves gave the lie to the Imperial posturing.

On August 19, the 16,000-ton White Star liner *Arabic* was sixty miles out of Liverpool, headed up around the north coast of Ireland bound for New York, when she was sighted by the *U-24*, commanded by *Kapitan-Leutnant* Rudolf Schneider. Knowing that the *Arabic* was an unarmed passenger ship, Schneider put a torpedo into her anyway. She sank in a little over ten minutes, taking forty-four of her passengers and crew to the bottom with her, three of them Americans. The next victim to follow the *Arabic* was another liner, the *Hesperian*, sunk on September 4, also in direct defiance of the Kaiser's orders not to attack passenger liners. Thirty-two lives were lost; the submarine responsible was the *U-20*, still under the command of Walther Schwieger. In a macabre twist, the *Hesperian* was carrying one of the last victims of the *Lusitania* to be recovered and identified—an American—back to the United States for burial.

On November 7, 1915, the *U-38* stopped the Italian liner *Ancona* with the traditional warning shot across her bow. It was the only concession to the Cruiser Rules the U-boat would make that day. Once the *Ancona* had stopped, and while the terrified passengers and crew were frantically trying to take to the lifeboats, the submarine's gun crew calmly began indiscriminately shelling the ship, hitting the hull, decks, and superstructure with little regard for the civilians aboard who were desperately trying to save their lives. The ship sank in less than an hour: 208 passengers and crew were killed.

That the *U-38*'s actions weren't a mere aberration of German naval policy or the product of an unusually cruel commander was driven home to the world by two further incidents, when in April and July 1917 the crews of the *U-55* and *U-44* methodically set about shooting survivors in the water who had escaped ships they had sunk—the steamers *Torrington* and *Belgian Prince*. What many observers around the world came to regard as the worst atrocity of all, in some ways surpassing even the sinking of the *Lusitania* in its cold-blooded ruthlessness, happened on June 27, 1918, when the *U-86* sank the hospital ship *Llandovery Castle*. Much like Schwieger on the *U-20* when he stalked the *Lusitania*, the *U-86*'s skipper, *Oberleutnant-zur-See* Helmut Patzig, had identified the *Llandovery Castle* as a hospital ship before he made his attack run; as she went down, he ordered his U-boat to ram the life boats and shot the survivors. By a stroke of luck there were no wounded aboard the *Castle*, but out of a crew of 258, which included more than forty nurses, only 24 survived. Patzig and his officers were charged with war crimes, tried and found guilty by a military tribunal in Leipzig after the war, but as it was a German court trying German officers, predictably they were given extraordinarily light sentences—a mere four years imprisonment each.

At the same time, the same German tactics of terror were being applied with an equally heavy hand in the occupied portions of France and Belgium. The actions of the Germans in August and September 1914 had been reprehensible enough: German records captured after the war showed that systematic execution of civilian hostages began as early as August 4, and in one of the most horrific examples of "frightfulness" on August 21 and 23, 1914, the Prussian 101st Grenadiers, one of the "elite" units of the German Army, carried out a series of systematic executions in the city of Dinant; a total of 639 civilians were killed in cold blood—seven of the victims were less than two years old, the youngest of them three-week old Mariette Fivet, who died in her father's arms. The "offense" against the Germans which had provoked the massacre was never revealed. A year later, on September 22, 1915, four French civilians were shot for assisting French prisoners of war to escape. Two weeks later, in an act that outraged the whole of the Western world, 49-year old British nurse Edith Cavell was executed by firing squad for helping captured British soldiers escape. *Schrecklicheit* (frightfulness—terror) was the official German policy, reprisals the standard response to any show of defiance or resistance.

The rot had evidently gone to the very top—or else had started there: legality had replaced morality, and even the cruelest acts were acceptable as long as they could be wrapped in the mantle of a legal justification. It appears that it never occurred to the Kaiser, his Ministers, or his generals and admirals, that while such actions might be acceptable to the German people, with their passion for adhering to legal niceties and correctness, it was only serving to harden the hearts of the British and French, with whom they might some day have to negotiate a peace settlement, and alienating the Americans, who could provide the Allies with the manpower and industrial capacity to overwhelm Germany, if they were provoked to war.

Certainly German ruthlessness was taking its toll on the Cunard Line. Almost the entire "A" class, some of the company's newest medium-sized ships, was wiped out during the war. The *Alaunia* and her sister ship, the *Andania*, were requisitioned in mid-August 1914, and were immediately put to use as troop ships carrying Canadian soldiers across the Atlantic. In the summer of 1915, both ships were sent to the Mediterranean to carry troops from Alexandria to the Aegean in support of the Gallipoli campaign; later that year the *Alaunia* was transferred to the Indian Ocean, and carried the Indian Army troops from Bombay to Suez.

In the summer of 1916, she was brought back to Britain and once again found herself transporting Canadian troops from Halifax to Liverpool. On October 19, 1916, she struck a mine two miles off the Sussex coast, and despite attempts to first beach the ship and then tow her to shore when two tugs appeared, the order to abandon ship finally had to be given. All the passengers and 163 of the *Alaunia*'s crew were taken off safely, but two of the crew, a steward and a trimmer, had been killed by the blast of the mine. Shortly after she was abandoned, the *Alaunia* sank.

When she was first transferred to the Mediterranean, the *Andania* had carried two of the finest Irish regiments in the British army, the Royal Inniskilling Fusiliers and Royal Dublin Fusiliers, to Cape Helles, where they formed the landing force that attacked Suvla, part of the Gallipoli operations. When her sister, the *Alaunia,* was sent to the Indian Ocean in June, 1915, she remained in the Mediterranean for a year, returning to the Atlantic and once again transporting Canadian troops in the summer of 1916. Later that year the *Andania* was returned to Cunard and put back into service on the Liverpool to New York route.

On January 26, 1918, the *Andania* left Liverpool for New York, with forty passengers and a crew of around 200 on board, taking the route around the northern coast of Ireland. Two days later she was hit by a torpedo fired by the German submarine *U-46*, and immediately took on a sharp list to starboard. She sank quickly, but fortunately everyone on board was saved, except for seven crewmen who were killed outright by the torpedo.

The *Aurania*'s career with Cunard was tragically brief. Laid down before the war began at Swan Hunter, the same shipyard that built the *Mauretania*, she was launched in July 1916, and was immediately fitted out as a troopship. Her shakedown cruise was a voyage in March 1917 from the Tyne to New York, returning to Liverpool, and the British government subsequently kept her in service on the North Atlantic, transporting supplies and munitions from the United States. On February 3, 1918 she left Liverpool and the following morning, when she was about fifteen miles off the coast of Donegal, she was hit by a torpedo fired by the *UB-67*. Nine crew members were killed in the explosion. A trawler responded to the *Aurania*'s distress signals and tried to take her in tow but the towline broke and she ran aground near Tobermory on the Isle of Mull. Spring gales quickly began to break the *Aurania* up and she was declared a total loss.

The *Aurania*'s sister ship *Ausonia* remained on the North Atlantic when the war broke out, sailing under charter from Cunard with the Anchor-Donaldson Line between Glasgow, Melville, and New York from August 1914 to July 1915. Requisitioned as a troopship she served in the Mediterranean until she was returned to Cunard in May 1916. On June 11, 1917 the *Ausonia* was on her way from Montreal to Avonmouth when she was torpedoed off the southern coast of Ireland. The damage, while serious, was not fatal and she was able to reach port under her own power. The remainder of her service was uneventful until May 30, 1918 when she was torpedoed without warning some 620 miles west of Fastnet. Eight stewards were killed by the explosion with the rest of the crew taking to the lifeboats. About forty-five minutes after the initial attack, the U-boat that had fired the torpedo surfaced and finished off the *Ausonia* with shell fire, but left the crew adrift in five boats. They weren't found until June 8, when two destroyers, one British, the other American, happened across them, after the boats had drifted nearly 900 miles. Though forty-four of the crewmen died of exposure, the rest were saved by the actions of their skipper, Capt. R. Capper, who was subsequently awarded the Distinguished Service Cross for his leadership.

The Gallipoli operation—also known as the Dardanelles Campaign—was one of the few truly brilliant strategic concepts of the war, and one that, like so many other brilliant schemes in history, failed to achieve its potential through flawed execution. In October, 1914, Germany skillfully exploited the distrust and repeated insults that France and Great Britain had visited on the Turks throughout the 19th Century, and concluded a military alliance with Turkey. Suddenly all French, and especially British possessions in the Near East were vulnerable to attack by Turkish armies, but even more disastrous for the Allies was that by joining the Central Powers, Turkey now closed the Straits of the Bosporus and the Dardanelles, the only access from the Mediterranean Sea to the Black Sea. Even more important, this was the only route by which Britain and France could send supplies to Russia during the winter months, when ice closed Russia's northern ports.

For Russia, this was critical: in the first three months of the war she had lost over a million men, new recruits were being sent to the front without rifles because all the existing prewar stocks had been issued, while troops at the front who had rifles often had no ammunition for them. Artillery units were rationing their shells, some guns being limited to firing three rounds a day. Without the material support of France and Great Britain, Russia's war effort would collapse in a matter of weeks—Russia's industrial capacity was still far too small to be able to meet more than a fraction of her armies' needs. In turn, it was vital to France and Britain that Russia continue fighting, for she was tying down huge numbers of German soldiers that, if they were suddenly available for service on the Western Front, could allow the Germans to overwhelm the Allies by sheer weight of numbers. The Allies were left with no alternative: to keep Russia in the war they had to reopen the supply route through the Black Sea, and they could only do so by actually seizing the Straits of the Dardanelles.

The site chosen for the Allied landing was the Gallipoli peninsula, a barren, rocky promontory on the southern, or Asia Minor, shore of the Dardanelles. Planning went swiftly, and the staff work was completed by early December, with a target date for landing operations to begin in March, 1915. Considerable naval resources were allotted to support the landing force, no less than sixteen French and British battleships, including the brand new *Queen Elizabeth*, at the time the most powerful warship in the world, taking part in a series of bombardments against the Turkish defenses all along the Dardanelles, which began on February 18 and continued intermittently through March 22.

The Turkish defenses were all but obliterated, as most of their heavy guns were destroyed, along with most of their reserves of ammunition. Had they but known it, the Allied warships could have sailed up to Constantinople and demanded Turkey's surrender, literally at gunpoint. Not that the warships had gotten off unscathed: several were damaged to greater or lesser degrees by the Turkish guns before they were silenced, and two battleships, the French *Bouvet* and the British *Irresistible*, were lost to mines, but these were older ships, not first-rate units, and the Admiralty had been willing to risk their loss. Unfortunately there was no way for those aboard the Allied warships to realize that their shelling had succeeded beyond all expectations, and so when they completed the bombardment, they sailed back to their base in the Aegean off the island of Lemnos, prepared to support the Army's landing force.

The problem was that the landing force was far from ready. Despite repeated urgings from Churchill to make haste and strike as hard and as quickly as possible, the commander of the landing force, General Ian Hamilton, proceeded with all deliberate speed. Churchill's fear was that every day the army tarried in getting troops ashore on the Gallipoli peninsula was another day gained by the Turks to recover from the mauling they had received from the navy. He was right, of course, although there were personal reasons for his anxiety. The Dardanelles operation was his brainchild, and while the operation had been endorsed by the whole of the War Cabinet, he had become inextricably linked to it, so he was acutely aware of who would be compelled to shoulder the blame should anything go wrong—consequently, his repeated pleas to the army to hurry. Hamilton demurred and asked Churchill to defer to his greater experience: the Turkish guns were silenced, that was all that mattered. There would be little if any opposition to the landings, since without artillery support the Turks would never be able to put up an effective defense. Despite considerable misgivings, Churchill backed down and the army continued its preparations.

Of course, when the British forces finally did land (actually they were ANZACs, the justly famous Australian-New Zealand Army Corps) on April 25, they met with fierce resistance that caused heavy casualties and made the landings a shambles. Instead of being able to sweep up the length of the peninsula, the ANZACs were forced to dig in on their beachheads, sometimes barely a dozen yards from the water's edge. What had happened was exactly what Churchill had feared. Under the advice and leadership of the German general Otto Liman von Sanders, who was as energetic as Hamilton was languorous, the Turks had reorganized and reinforced the Gallipoli garrison and turned the rubble of their coast defense fortresses into defensive strong points, bristling with machine guns. They didn't need artillery support, since the ANZACs had no way of bringing their own guns ashore and no effective means of coordinating with the naval forces offshore to provide fire support, so Turkish rifles and machine guns were sufficient to contain the ANZAC beachheads. Within days, the Allied position on the peninsula began to look like a microcosm of the Western Front, as the ANZACs began to earn their nickname of "Diggers" by frantically excavating trenches to protect themselves from the constant Turkish fire.

Consequently, the whole Gallipoli campaign turned into a disaster. Had the execution of the landings been as bold as their planning, there can be little doubt that the entire operation would have succeeded brilliantly, fundamentally altering the strategic balance—and outcome—of the war. That the landings failed was in no way due to a lack of courage, dash, or determination on the part of the ANZACs—they possessed those qualities in overabundance, and were they all that had been required for victory, the issue would have been decided within days. It was the lack of those qualities in the higher echelons of command, in particular General Hamilton and Admiral De Roebeck, which caused the delays and hesitations that gave the Turks time to prepare their defenses, and in so doing threw away Britain's one chance at winning the war at a single stroke, and saving the lives of millions. Instead, eight months after it began, the Gallipoli campaign ended, not with a bang but a whimper, as the Australian and New Zealand troops were withdrawn. The Turks, content with their victory, let them depart unmolested. Out of 479,000 Allied troops engaged on the Gallipoli Peninsula, 252,000 had become casualties.

Even after the Gallipoli Campaign wound down, the Mediterranean, or the "the Med" as the British called it, remained a very dangerous place for the Cunard ships that had been taken into government service. The *Ivernia* had been requisitioned as a troop transport during the first week of the war, and immediately began ferrying troops between Canada and various Mediterranean ports. On January 1, 1917, she was on her way from Marseille to Alexandria, escorted by the destroyer HMS *Rifleman*, when she was torpedoed by the *U-47* sixty miles southeast of the Greek coast near Cape Matapan. It took less than an hour for the *Ivernia* to sink, and though most of the crew were saved by *Rifleman*, along with a handful of trawlers that were nearby when she was struck, thirty-six crew members and eighty-four troops were killed in the explosion.

At the start of the war the *Franconia* continued her regular service between Liverpool to New York, but in February 1915 she was called up to serve as a troopship, and after her conversion work was done, she was sent to the Mediterranean to support the Dardanelles campaign, carrying wounded troops from Gallipoli to Alexandria. On October 4, 1916, still working in "the Med" but now plying between Alexandria and Salonika, she was torpedoed by the *UB-47* while two hundred miles east of Malta. Although there were no troops aboard—she could carry as many as 2,700—twelve crewmen were lost. The survivors, some 302 in all, were picked up by the hospital ship *Dover Castle*.

In January 1917, to make up for some of the losses already suffered among troopships, the *Cameronia* was taken over by the government. She began by working the route from Devon to the Mediterranean, but was later based in Marseilles. On 15 April traveling from there to Alexandria carrying 2,650 troops, she was torpedoed by the *U-33*, and sank in 40 minutes. Some of the survivors were picked up by the escorting destroyer, HMS *Rifleman*—something that was becoming rather a habit for this ship—but with the U-boat still lurking about, the destroyer offered too tempting a target, so the rescue had to be abandoned, and the rest of the survivors weren't picked up until the following morning, when a sloop out of Malta came for them.

Carrying the munitions and materials that supplied Britain's war effort occupied several of Cunard's ships, sometimes in unusual circumstances. A curious interpretation of America's neutrality laws by the U.S. State Department forbade the purchase of war materials by official government agencies, but permitted their acquisition by private individuals and businesses. Consequently the food, guns, ammunition, chemicals, explosives, accoutrements, and other goods and materials could not be shipped in government-owned vessels. Another restriction imposed by the Americans was that no munitions could be transported on passenger vessels.

The British, desperately needing every bit of tonnage space available to carry the supplies purchased in the United States—Great Britain's industries wouldn't be fully mobilized into a wartime economy until 1916, and even then American production would remain a vital part of the British war effort until the end of the conflict—developed a clever, if ethically questionable, evasion of this obstacle. There was a loophole within the regulations which they were quick to exploit. Every ship sailing from an American port was required to file a copy of her sailing manifest—a listing of all cargo being carried—along with a record of provisions and supplies purchased for the voyage, to be filed with the Collector of Customs at the Port Authority. Almost invariably, a passenger or cargo ship would make last-minute purchases of perishable food, particularly fresh vegetables, at dockside before departing. Since these purchases had to be accounted for as well in the ship's sailing papers, a "supplementary manifest" would be filed by the shipping agent after the ship sailed. The British began filing very brief, innocuous manifests which made no mention of any munitions or explosives in order to obtain sailing clearances. Once the ships in question were safely at sea—or in some cases even after they had reached their destination—a supplemental manifest listing the full cargo would be filed.

One particularly strange incident resulted from this British manipulation of these rules in January 1915. Two of Cunard's ships, the *Transylvania* and *Ausonia*, were each used to transport a pair of 14-inch guns for the Royal Navy from New York to Liverpool. (Some sources claim that entire turrets were being shipped, which is highly unlikely, as the complete weight of such a turret and guns would have been around seventy tons, a weight beyond the capacity of the ships' derricks or those at the Cunard Pier in New York.) The guns were apparently too large to fit in the cargo holds of either ship, and so sat on their foredecks for the entire voyage. If so, the *Transylvania* and *Ausonia* were the only passenger ships to ever mount battleship guns, however briefly!

In May 1915, with the rising numbers of Canadian troops and the demands of the Gallipoli campaign straining Admiralty resources to the limit, the *Transylvania* was taken over by the British government to serve as a troopship. Converted to carry 200 officers and 2,860 "other ranks" (as the British call enlisted men), she was sent to the "Med" where she was first used to carry troops to the Dardanelles, and then after that unhappy operation had wound down, to Salonika and the Middle East. Her service was uneventful until May 1917. On May 3rd she left Marseilles for Alexandria with a full complement of troops aboard, escorted by the Japanese destroyers *Matsu* and *Sakaki*. (Japan, sensing an opportunity to expand her Pacific empire at Germany's expense, declared war on the Central Powers in August 1914, and after snapping up all of the German colonial possessions in the Pacific, had sent a few token naval forces to the Mediterranean.) The day after she sailed, the *Transylvania* was off Cape Valdo in the Gulf of Genoa, when she was torpedoed by the *U-63*. While *Sakaki* circled the area in an effort to prevent another attack by forcing the submarine to remain submerged, *Matsu* came along side the *Transylvania* and began to off-load the troops. But the skipper of the *U-63* was patient, and taking advantage of a brief opportunity when *Sasaki* was steaming away from the U-boat's position, he put a second torpedo into the *Transylvania*, which then sank almost immediately. While most of the troops and crew had been safely transferred to *Matsu*, not everyone got away, and a total of 414 lives were lost. The *U-63* escaped unharmed.

The *Laconia* was turned into an armed merchant cruiser in 1914. She was based at Simonstown in the South Atlantic, which she patrolled until April 1915; after that she was used as a headquarters ship for the operations to capture Tanga and the colony of German East Africa (Tanzania). Four months later she returned to the patrolling of the South Atlantic. The *Laconia* was handed back to Cunard in July 1916.

Another Cunard ship lost while carrying troops was the *Tuscania*. Actually, she belonged to the Anchor Line, in which Cunard owned a controlling interest, but had been taken over by Cunard for the service between Liverpool and New York. Her wartime career was an eventful one. While on her way to New York in September 1915, her lookouts spotted a ship on fire nearby—it was National Greek Line's ship *Athinai*. The fire was out of control and the *Athinai*'s captain was forced to give the order to abandon ship— the *Tuscania* took off all of her 339 passengers and 70 of her crew. Another ship, the *Roumanian Prince*, had also spotted the burning liner and gone to her aid, taking off the remaining 56 crewmen.

The government called up the *Tuscania* a year later, and in September 1916 she began carrying Canadian troops from Halifax to Liverpool. In August 1917, she carried one of the first contingents of American soldiers sent to France. The United States, having been provoked beyond tolerance by Germany's declaration of unrestricted U-boat warfare–essentially a license to kill for the submarines, giving them permission to sink any ship on sight regardless of nationality, and without warning—as well as the diplomatic blunder of the Zimmermann telegram, which sought to initiate a war between the United States and Mexico, had declared war on Germany in April 1917. The *Tuscania* brought 1,236 officers and men of the 16th Regiment of Engineers from New York to Liverpool, proof to the increasingly war-weary British and French that the Yanks really *were* coming.

The *Tuscania* left Hoboken, New Jersey, on what would be her final voyage on January 24, 1918, under the command of Capt. Peter McLean OBE, carrying 2,013 American troops and a crew of 384. She joined a convoy, *HX-20*, at Halifax, bound for Le Havre. On February 5 the convoy was seven miles north of the Rathlin Island lighthouse when it was sighted by the German submarine *UB-77*. The U-boat fired a spread of torpedoes at the convoy, one of which hit the *Tuscania*. Immediately a well-rehearsed lifeboat drill was underway, and in little more than an hour all the ship's boats had been safely launched. However, there were more men aboard the *Tuscania* than there were boats for them and some 1,350 were still on the ship. The convoy escorts came alongside the sinking liner one by one to take as many of those remaining as they could, a highly dangerous undertaking with the U-boat still prowling about. Ultimately the effort proved successful, for when the *Tuscania* sank four hours after being struck, everyone who was still alive had been taken off. Two hundred thirty American soldiers and British sailors were dead.

The *Tuscania* was the first ship to be sunk while carrying American troops, and while her sinking was by any interpretation a legitimate act of war, public opinion in the United States regarded the attack as an outrage, confirming America's decision to take up arms against the "barbarous Hun." After the war, a monument to the American dead was raised by the American Red Cross on the Isle of Islay, where many of the victims had been buried. Later, most of the victims were re-interred at the American War Cemetery at Brookwood, or returned to the United States for burial on American soil.

One of the last losses suffered by Cunard during the war was one of the most modest and at the same time best-known ships of the entire line, the *Carpathia*. When World War I broke out in Europe, she remained in service with Cunard, at one point being the source of a minor *contretemps* for the company: on September 5th, 1914, the Italian government levied a fine against her for carrying immigrants without a license. In early 1915, she was requisitioned by the British government and converted to a troopship. The refitted *Carpathia* could now carry more than 3,000 officers and other ranks, or alternatively, a thousand cavalry mounts and troopers, along with a thousand tons of supplies.

On July 17, 1918, the *Carpathia* was part of a convoy bound for Boston, 120 miles west of Fastnet, when two torpedoes fired by a German submarine slammed into her starboard side, and she immediately began to sink. Five crewmen were killed in the explosions, while the rest of the crew immediately saw to the safety of the fifty-seven passengers aboard, getting them away in the lifeboats. A third torpedo struck the ship, but despite the severe damage she had taken, the *Carpathia* remained afloat long enough for the rest of her officers and crewmen to escape. She went down at 12:40am, and her survivors were picked up a few hours later by H.M.S. *Snowdro,* and taken to Liverpool.

Not all of Cunard's losses were due to enemy action. In 1918, *Ascania* ran aground off Cape Ray, five days after the *Ausonia* was torpedoed. Heavy seas broke her back and the wreck had to be destroyed by gunfire from Royal Navy destroyers; and one of the strangest losses suffered by Cunard was that of the venerable old *Campania*, which was sunk—albeit accidentally—by the Royal Navy itself.

At the outbreak of World War I, the *Campania* was bought by the Admiralty for conversion into a seaplane tender. Despite its somewhat stuffy, hidebound reputation, the Royal Navy was one of the most innovative naval services in the world, and was the first to recognize the potential of the airplane, and the first to introduce an air service, the Fleet Air Arm, which had its beginnings in the Royal Naval Air Service (RNAS), formed in 1912. After conversion at Cammell Laird, Birkenhead, the *Campania* was commissioned as HMS *Campania* on April 17, 1915. She was given not only facilities for handling seaplanes, but also a wooden flight deck, some 160 feet long that could accommodate ten aircraft. On April 30 she left the Mersey to join the Grand Fleet in Scapa Flow. Soon after her arrival at the northern anchorage, *Campania* made history by being the first ship to launch aircraft while under way.

Campania returned to Liverpool later that year to have her flight deck lengthened and her interior arrangements further modified. Her massive forward funnel was removed and replaced with a pair of narrower uptakes sitting side by side, the after end of the flight deck running between them. She returned to Scapa Flow in the spring of 1916, but an engine failure caused her to be left behind when the Grand Fleet steamed out of Scapa on the sortie that climaxed in the Battle of Jutland on May 31, 1916. The rest of her service was spent in and out of Scapa Flow, as her aircraft provided anti-submarine patrols for the Grand Fleet. In October 1918, her base of operations was moved to Burnt Island in the Firth of Forth. On the morning of 5 November, during strong winds, she began to drag her anchors, and the winds drove her into the side of a battleship anchored nearby, HMS *Royal Oak*, which in turn was driven into the large cruiser HMS *Glorious*. The collision tore a gaping hole in *Campania's* port side, and despite the best efforts of her crew, her pumps could not stay ahead of the inrushing seawater. She began to sink by the stern, and just a little more than three hours after she collided with the *Royal Oak,* she sank.

Ironically, the *Campania* was lost just six days before Germany signed an Armistice with the Allied Powers, and the fighting ended. Over ten million soldiers had died between 1914 and 1918, bloodletting on a scale that had once been unthinkable and unimaginable; as a consequence, the world that would emerge from the Great War would be unrecognizable, physically and morally, as the one that entered it. At sea, the material cost had been astronomical: world-wide, more than eleven million tons of merchant shipping had been sunk, over half of it British. The human cost had been equally high: 14,959 civilians, including women and children, lost their lives at sea. When casualties among crewmen were included, the number more than doubled. It had truly been, as the U-boat skippers called it, a "Killing Time." Now, it was up to the survivors to determine if the peace was worth the price that had been paid.

CHAPTER ELEVEN

Collapse

When the guns fell silent on November 11, 1918, Cunard quietly reassumed its position as the dominant presence on the North Atlantic. It was hard to believe, in a way, for Cunard's fleet had been decimated by the German U-boats: eleven ships had been sunk—the *Lusitania*, of course, was the most famous victim, but also lost were the *Franconia, Alaunia, Ausonia, Carpathia, Ascania, Ultonia, Aurania, Laconia, Ivernia,* and *Andania.* Almost all of Cunard's flotilla of intermediate-sized liners had been wiped out. But the line still had the *Aquitania* and *Mauretania*, along with the "Pretty Sisters," the *Caronia* and *Carmania*, as well as what was left of the Anchor Line's fleet; Anchor hadn't been as hard-hit by the U-boats as had Cunard, losing only the *Cameronia* and *Tuscania*. What made the situation such an opportunity for Cunard was that, as badly as the company had suffered during the war, its competitors had fared even worse.

The loss of the *Titanic* in 1912 had hurt the White Star Line badly, but the loss of the *Britannic* to a mine in the Aegean Sea while she was serving as a hospital ship in November 1916 was a crippling blow from which the company would never really recover. With two of the three *Olympic*-class ships gone, the plans for a weekly express service between Southampton and New York were hopelessly shattered. German U-boats and raiders accounted for the loss of ships like the *Laurentic, Georgic, Arabic, Cymric, Delphic,* and *Afric*, and the war had intervened before White Star's plans for a class of medium-sized liners comparable to Cunard's "Pretty Sisters," meant to replace the aging "Big Four"—the *Baltic, Adriatic, Celtic* and *Oceanic*—could be realized, leaving White Star with a fleet that was old and slow.

Another factor hampered the White Star Line's recovery, one which was a burden Cunard didn't have to bear: White Star was still part of IMM, and one of the consequences of the "rationalization" the combine imposed on the shipping lines that composed it, was that the individual companies were forced to coordinate and dovetail their services and schedules, which in turn dictated the size and number of new ships each line could order. White Star did not have the freedom of action that Cunard enjoyed to decide for itself what new construction was called for, but had to secure permission from the parent company to place new orders.

Cunard's board of directors, in the meantime, while pondering the designs and specifications for the ships that would replace the line's wartime losses, was scrambling to put together a scratch fleet to maintain its North Atlantic service. Ships were chartered from the Union Castle Line, Pacific Steam Navigation, and Lamport & Holt to make up the lost tonnage until replacements were built; at one point even a Dutch ship, the *Princess Juliana*, was under lease to Cunard. Most of these stop-gap charters sailed under their original houseflags and colors, and retained their original names, although in the case of P&O's *Kaisar-I-Hind* the name was changed to its English translation, *Emperor of India*, as "Kaisar" was a little too similar to "Kaiser" for comfort, so close to the end of the war.

There was a curious irony to Cunard's search for ships to augment its fleet, as the demand for space was urgent, yet the actual number of passengers crossing the Atlantic had dropped dramatically from pre-war totals. The dreadful casualty lists of the Great War had included a disproportionately high number of rich or titled names, along with a huge toll taken from the middle class, as the British officer corps had been more than decimated during the War; they were the very men who, along with their families, would have been occupying the First and Second Class cabins. What created the shortfall in available passenger berths was the sudden absence of the German liners. The simple truth was that while the British merchant marine had suffered desperate losses during the War, Germany's merchant fleet, once the second-largest in the world, had, for all practical purposes, ceased to exist. In the first three months of the war, those German merchant ships not safe in German harbors were quickly interned in neutral ports or hunted down, and either sunk or captured by the Royal Navy. Norddeutscher-Lloyd alone lost sixty-three ships, while Hamburg-Amerika, which in 1914 was the single largest shipping company in the world, saw more than one hundred of its vessels either sunk or seized. The handful of ships left to either line meant that it would be a long time before either company was again a major presence on the North Atlantic. The sudden and complete disappearance of their fiercest competitors was a golden opportunity the British shipping lines were anxious to exploit—if only they could find the ships with which to do so.

The answer was obvious and soon apparent to everyone on both sides of the Atlantic: it was the Germans who had started the Great War—at least so the story was told among the victorious Allied powers—so the Germans would be made to pay for the costs of the war. If the gaps in the ranks of the British merchant fleet were created by the mines and torpedoes of the German Navy, then the Germans could make good those losses: those gaps would be filled with ships seized from the German merchant marine.

The Americans had already taken the initiative in that direction. Immediately upon America's declaration of war on Germany, the United States government seized as the prizes of war all of the German shipping that had been interned in American ports and harbors, including the pride of the German merchant navy, the fast transatlantic liners. Aside from a few of the ships that had been used as armed merchant cruisers, such as the *Cap Trafalgar* or *Kaiser Wilhelm der Grosse*, almost all of Germany's fast liners had been instructed to make for American ports when the war broke out. Once there, they were duly interned, but as no one had expected the war to drag on for four years, it seemed at the time to be an ideal choice for protecting such valuable ships. But when the United States declared war on Germany in April 1917, one of the first acts taken by the American government was to seize all of the German ships interned in American ports. The seizures were fully justified under international law, and not even the German government could protest that the United States wasn't acting entirely within its rights, although many Germans in and out of office in Berlin rued the use to which the Americans put the ex-German liners. Calling them "the fleet the Kaiser built for us," the Americans quickly adapted the *Vaterland* (now the U.S.S. *Leviathan*), *Kronprizessen Cecilie* (*Mount Vernon*), *Kronprinz Wilhelm* (*Von Steuben*), *Amerika* (*America*), *Grosser Kürfurst* (*Aeolus*), *George Washington*—her name remained unchanged—and *Kaiser Wilhelm II* (*Monticello*) for trooping duties. When the shooting was over, they remained in American hands, giving the United States a presence on the North Atlantic passenger routes that it had lacked for more than a half-century. Unfortunately, the Americans would prove to be just as inept in running a successful—that is, profitable—steamship company in the 20th Century as they had been in the 19th.

When the Treaty of Versailles was signed in May 1919, it merely formalized what was already a *fait accompli* for the fate of the German merchant fleet. Save for some minor adjustments, each of the Allied nations was permitted to keep whatever German ships it had seized or captured. The greatest prizes were, of course, the three Hamburg-Amerika giants. The United States was allowed to keep the *Vaterland*, which retained her wartime name *Leviathan*; as reparations for the loss of the *Britannic*, the White Star Line was given the still-unfinished *Bismarck*, which would eventually sail as the *Majestic*. To compensate Cunard for the destruction of the *Lusitania*, the line was given the *Imperator*, which joined

The Berengaria, *formerly the* Imperator, *a prize of war, Cunard's ostentatious Teutonic stepchild.*

the Cunard fleet as the *Berengaria*.

While the big German liners went a long way toward making good the lost passenger capacity of Cunard and White Star, and gave the United States a presence on the North Atlantic it had lacked for decades, they were far from truly successful. The years of neglect while they sat rusting in American ports or German shipyards had taken a toll on them, while their crews had often sabotaged every possible system aboard before the ships were turned over to the Allies. Despite the best efforts of British and American engineers, they were often never able to completely return the ships to their original condition. Strangely enough, though German excellence in the field of electrical engineering had long been an acknowledged fact, the three giant liners' electrical systems were frequently faulty and prone to minor fires. At the same time, British and American designers and decorators fought a losing battle to rid the ships' interiors of their Teutonic flavor, something which they could never quite divest, making them less than popular with a large number of would-be passengers.

Meanwhile, those liners which had put aside their opulent furnishings and donned warpaint, returned to their home ports where they were taken in hand and refurbished. Carpets were unrolled down corridors; furniture, paintings and sculptures were trundled out of warehouses and ensconced once more in their accustomed places in smoking rooms, lounges, and dining saloons; beds, wash stands, and wardrobes were replaced in cabins; crates of china, crystal, and silverware were brought aboard, and their contents carefully stored in cabinets to await the first dinner hour of peacetime.

While the passenger areas were being restored to their pre-war glory, deep inside the ships, fundamental changes were being made. The experience gained by the Royal Navy with oil-fired ships, particularly the huge *Queen Elizabeth*-class dreadnoughts, the most powerful warships in the world at the time, had proven that oil-firing was not only less expensive, but more efficient than coal-firing. Oil burns at higher temperatures than does coal, creating more steam, which in turn increases the pressure in the head of steam that spins the ship's turbines, raising the vessel's top speed. Coupled with this improved performance came economies in operating costs, as boiler room crews could be drastically reduced, and scores of stokers and trimmers could be done away with, reducing the ranks of the "Black Gang" on a ship the size of the *Mauretania* from three hundred to less than sixty.

Even the term "Black Gang" was reduced to an anachronism, as oil made the grit and grime of the boiler rooms a thing of the past, relieving the stokers and trimmers of being coated with a layer of coal dust every time they worked a watch; nor would every surface of every bulkhead, deck, and machinery be encrusted with years of accumulated soot. Finally, the ordeal of coaling at the end of each crossing was banished, much to the relief of the entire crew, the stewards and stewardesses in particular. The first two Cunard ships to undergo conversion were predictably, the *Mauretania* and *Aquitania*, followed by the *Caronia* and *Carmania*. The newly-acquired *Imperator*, re-christened the *Berengaria*, was converted to oil firing while she was being refitted to Cunard specifications.

The *Mauretania*'s conversion was carried out in a French shipyard in St. Nazaire (the Chanteliers d'Atlantique, who would one day build the *Queen Mary 2*), as a workers' strike at the Swan Hunter works threatened an unacceptable delay to her return to transatlantic service. Legend has it that when the grand old liner's turbines were being overhauled, the *Mauretania*'s chief engineer, a stereotypical dour Scot, fussed over them like a mother hen watching over her brood of chicks. When the time came for the turbines to be spun up for a low-speed dynamic test, he was seen crawling over their casings with a stethoscope, listening intently. Suddenly his hand flew up, making a "stop" motion, and he ordered the turbines shut down; when the casing on the turbine rotor in question was opened up, out fell a collar button. Had it been allowed to remain inside the turbine, it would have stripped the blades off the rotor shaft when the turbine was spun up to full speed, destroying the engine. It was incidents like this that made the relationship between Scottish engineers and their engines, their beloved "wee bairns," reach mythical proportions as the years went by.

The *Berengaria*'s position in the line was unique—and not always comfortable. She was the first ship in the Cunard fleet to have been built and operated by a foreign shipping line, and the first named—despite the customary "*-ia*" suffix—for a person rather than a geographic territory. (The real Berengaria was the wife of Richard the Lionhearted.) The transformation from German to British liner was more than just cosmetic, although new funnel colors, new nameplates on the bow and stern, and a new company flag were the most readily visible changes. Inside, the Ritz-Carlton restaurant, once the *Imperator*'s most distinctive feature, was done away with, being transformed into a ballroom, while the winter garden, an obligatory on any German liner, was transformed into its British equivalent, the palm court. However, there were still small but noticeable reminders of the *Berengaria*'s Teutonic origins: the cigar holders in First Class staterooms still bearing a little plaque engraved with the word *Zigarren*, the drains in the bathtubs *Auf* and *Zu*, the taps marked *Heiß* and *Kalt*.

While hardly a matched set, the *Mauretania*, *Aquitania*, and *Berengaria* would soon become known as Cunard's "Big Three," and maintain the line's weekly service between Southampton and New York. As befitting the oldest of the trio, the *Mauretania* had the most loyal following, perhaps the most loyal of any liner on the North Atlantic. As one Cunard advertising copywriter observed in a company brochure, "she holds the passionate allegiance of whole families of America's highest type, who would rather miss Ascot or the first day of grouse shooting than cross in any other ship afloat but the *Mauretania*." Yet despite the fact that she would assume the mantle of the "dowager queen of the Atlantic," during the 1920s she proved to be the most popular ship among younger travelers. As a result, the same brochure declared,

> ...her clientele are very gay, always very chic; her sailings are gala nights, with the Junior League at its most junior visible all over the lot... You will find her decks

populous with young girls and young men who more nearly, than any other flesh and blood young girls and young men, look like the drawings in Vanity Fair and Vogue. Girls "just out," sophomores on vacation, whole families of sons and daughters going abroad for the summer or for school. People you've seen on the beach at Southampton or Newport... on the trails at Hot Springs... or at the polo matches at Meadowbrook in the fall. Dancing at dinner in the restaurant, the floor looks like the Ambassador Grill during Christmas vacation, and Tea in the lounge, like a coming out party at the Colony Club.

The *Aquitania*, on the other hand, as befitting the handsomest ship afloat, at least as far as her interiors were concerned, seemed to draw her passenger lists from the ranks of those with Old Money, Old Titles, or both. The same copywriters tell that:

The Aquitania's passenger lists tend slightly towards Burke and Debrett. The country family sort of atmosphere...predisposes in her favor people of social consequence, people of title, people who like their transatlantic crossings to taste of that rather formal sub-division into hierarchies—social, political, hereditary—which mark their lives... If a ship may be like a house, the *Aquitania* is like some Georgian house of weathered brick that looks through the mist toward the fairy tale outlines of Windsor Castle. A house quiet and beautiful with age without, and inside as modern, as perfectly appointed, as some tower apartment on Park Avenue that has sprung up overnight to forty stories... The people who cross in her are people you might meet at an important Thursday to Monday, where blood and achievement both count... By day, Harris tweeds...Chanel jerseys...indolent conversation and energetic sport. By night, a sudden increase of tempo...a blaze of jewels...the gleam of ivory shoulders...gowns, rose, gold, green...Men and women both wearing formality, brilliance, with the perfect ease that is the distinction and delight of aristocratic English life. The same sharp contrast of the extremes of informality and ceremony that makes English country life so stimulating is part of the charm of life, day by day, night by night...

Clearly the obvious, almost arrant snob appeal of this brochure was meant for consumption by an American audience, as any true British aristocrat would have never responded to such blandishments. Rather, he or she would have been mortified to find themselves so described, no matter how accurate the description may have been!

Predictably, when the *Berengaria*, the ostentatious Teutonic stepchild, entered service, she immediately attracted a far flashier crowd. The same brochure makes no effort to disguise this fact:

The *Berengaria* is accustomed to move through the night brighter than the

Milky Way with the cluttered constellations aboard her... The Queens who cross in the *Berengaria* are the more conspicuous Queens...the more debonair Mayors choose her. A *Berengaria* sailing is tempestuous with the exploding of flashlights, the pursuit of reporters... Everything about the *Berengaria* is on the grand, the opulent, scale. She is sensational. Sensational people board her...Her passenger lists are electric with great names. Great enterprises of finance are flung back and forth across her tables...

Not all of the claims made in such advertisements were exaggerated or specious. Among the prominent, if not always distinguished names that sailed on Cunard ships, were the heavyweight boxer Jack Dempsey, former Prime Minister David Lloyd George, Vincent Astor (the son of John Jacob Astor, who had died on the *Titanic* six months before Vincent was born), various Vanderbilts, the legendary ballerina Anna Pavlova, the Sultan of Jahore, the usual assortment of British aristocrats, and of course film stars such as Mary Pickford and her husband, Douglas Fairbanks, Tallulah Bankhead, Charlie Chaplin, Clara Bow, and Stan Laurel and Oliver Hardy. On one crossing in 1924, the *Aquitania* carried five Roman Catholic cardinals who were attending a Eucharistic Congress in New York.

Sometimes a passenger didn't even have to be living to attach a certain amount of celebrity to his or her presence aboard ship. When Edgar Wallace died in Hollywood in 1930, where he had been earning $3,000 a day writing the script for *King Kong*, his body was shipped back to England aboard the *Berengaria*. Her flag flew at half-staff when she docked in Southampton. The obverse of that experience can be found in noting how obscure have become the names of so many of the then-prominent passengers: Leonore Ulrich, film and stage star of the decade; Jimmy Walker, onetime mayor of New York; Madge Bellamy, an immensely popular actress in her day; Aline Bernstein, mistress of author Thomas Wolfe.

The decade of 1920s, in addition to being the first in which the tinsel-behung "glamour" of film stars graced the transatlantic route, was also the heyday of the shipboard swindlers who often, but not always, tried to dignify their profession by passing themselves off as professional gamblers. They were crooks, pure and simple, but until and unless someone lodged a formal complaint or brought charges, there was little that could be done to prevent them from plying their "trade" aboard ship. Some captains tried: aboard the *Aquitania*, when Captain Sir James Charles would order the assistant purser to walk through the lounges at various times, announcing, "Ladies and gentlemen, we have reason to believe there are card sharpers aboard." In 1927, the captain of the *Franconia* had a cluster of "gamblers" brought to his cabin where he confronted them with the choice of being turned over to the police, or returning all of their ill-gotten gains to the passengers they had fleeced. The gamblers chose to return the money.

But in truth, unless a passenger made a fuss, gamblers were regarded as essentially harmless: they were never violent, never did anyone any bodily injury, and were always careful to never hit up a mark for more than he or she could afford, something of which the victims themselves seemed to have been aware. Some of these professional gamblers were such frequent travelers—always under pseudonyms—that stewards and pursers got to know them by sight, sometimes greeting them with a sardonic, "What name this time, sir?" It should be noted that the gamblers were usually very good tippers, which kept the stewards happy, and of course, prevented them from giving the game away. Charles Spedding, the purser aboard the *Aquitania* during the 1920s, recalled one famous crook who had actually become wealthy by investing the profits from his gaming days, and eventually repented of his ways and gave up shipboard gambling and swindling altogether: in those years, the man would often be approached by fellow passengers for a friendly game of cards, simply so they could tell their friends that they had shared a game with him. Then there were the two retired British Army officers who never played a dishonest hand in their lives, but still made a comfortable living simply through their formidable skills at bridge-whist.

The role of a ship's purser was much like that of the manager of a large hotel ashore, and required many of the same talents: a good head for business; tact, charm, and diplomacy for dealing with temperamental passengers; and the ability to delegate authority without relinquishing responsibility among subordinates. He also had to be the very soul of discretion, as well, as he was often the confidant of passenger and crewman alike. Frequently the Purser's Table in the First Class Dining Saloon was as popular as that of the captain, for a good purser always seemed to know everybody and everything, from the latest shipboard gossip to the current stock market tips.

Captain Arthur Rostron was once heard to comment that all Cunard ships have three sides—port, starboard, and social, and that the captain must be the master of all of them. Certainly in the 1920s, ships captains came to the fore: while their social standing had been rising for decades, they were now approaching the pinnacle of their power and fame. A popular captain who gained a reputation for being a good host, entertaining storyteller, and discerning social arbiter quickly attracted a loyal coterie of passengers, almost invariably wealthy and socially prominent, who would follow him from ship to ship, or if he preferred, as did many Cunard captains, to stay with one vessel, would travel exclusively on that ship. Both for the money they spent and the attention they attracted, this entourage of passengers were worth their weight in gold to Cunard.

Not all captains liked the social side of their responsibilities. William Turner, known as "Bowler Bill" for his habit of wearing a bowler hat while on the bridge, was the first captain of both the *Lusitania* and the *Mauretania*; he was also the master of the *Lusitania* when she was sunk by the *U-20*. Turner detested most passengers, regarding them as overblown bores and busybodies, and vastly preferred the company of his officers and the surroundings of his bridge to that of the Captain's Table in the First Class Dining Saloon. Because of his skill as a mariner, Cunard created the position of Staff Captain, a second captain subordinate to him, qualified in every way as a ship's master, who would relieve Turner of some of the burden of the administrative details of the ship's operations, and take over the odious duty of entertaining the passengers. Apparently, it was a successful solution all around, for the position of Staff Captain became a permanent fixture on Cunard's larger ships, even though most Captains found presiding over their own table at dinner in the Dining room to be one of the more pleasant aspects of their job.

In contrast to the taciturn Will Turner, there were few personalities, be they captains, staff captain, pursers, or otherwise, as popular as Sir James Charles, K.B.E., R.D., R.N.R., long-time captain of the *Aquitania*, and commodore of the Cunard Line. If ever the phrase "legend in his own time" befitted anyone, that person was Sir James. He was quite possibly the most debonair captain ever to stand on the bridge of any liner: square-jawed, handsome, and dignified in his double-breasted jacket with its four bands of gold braid on the cuffs and two rows of decorations on the left breast, Charles looked and acted every inch the part of a master of the most popular ship on the Atlantic. He was renowned for the cultivation of his palate, presided over an unparalleled table, and his devotion to the strict observance of the rules of proper dress was legendary. Guests invited to his table were expected to appear at the appointed hour given on their invitations, in the dress specified (and laid out by the stewards in advance to avoid mistakes); any departure from form or failure to comply was met with an icy glare and instant dismissal to the nether reaches of the dining room.

Commodore Sir James Charles, a North Atlantic legend among passenger ship masters.

Not that Charles was a pompous, overbearing bore who enjoyed having passengers, however wealthy or titled, dance to his tune: he was charming, affable, and guests at his table could expect to be regaled with endless tales, well told, of his years at sea. Like most of his contemporaries, he had started young, going to sea in 1880 at the age of fifteen as an apprentice, and like every other Cunard master, had worked his way through the ranks, earning all of his certificates in both sail and steam. He had commanded the *Aquitania* throughout the Great War and received a knighthood in acknowledgment of his services. Recognized throughout the shipping world as an outstanding seaman, Sir James' attachment to the *Aquitania* was so strong that he said he could never conceive of himself in command of another ship.

Prophetic words, as it turned out, for in July 1928, on his seven hundred and twenty-eighth crossing, just as he brought the *Aquitania* into Southampton, he collapsed on her bridge. He had just been given a commemorative plaque in New York to honor his pending retirement, and on the way back to Southampton the weather was so fine that Charles remarked to a passenger that it was the most perfect he could recall in forty-nine years at sea. Rushed ashore, he died quickly and peacefully; it was said by more than one friend that he had really died of a broken heart, not being able to bear the thought of being separated from his beloved *Aquitania*. More to the point, just what sort of man Sir James Charles had been was demonstrated by the fact that an entire trainload of Cunard officials came down from Liverpool to Southampton to attend his funeral. The crew of the *Aquitania*, meanwhile, voluntarily walked the six miles from the Southampton docks to the church in Netley to be at the service—eight of them served as pallbearers for the coffin, which was draped in the Union Jack and the Cunard house flag. As commodore of the Cunard Line, Sir James was succeeded by Sir Arthur Rostron, one-time captain of the *Carpathia*, now in command of the *Mauretania*.

At the beginning of the decade, while the *Mauretania* and *Aquitania* were returning to their regular service, and the *Berengaria* was being converted for her new owners in 1919 and 1920, Cunard had set about building an entirely new intermediate-sized fleet, drawing up plans for an even-dozen liners. At the same time, the line shifted the British terminus for its New York express service, the most prestigious run on the North Atlantic, from Liverpool to Southampton. It was not a decision made easily, since Liverpool had been Cunard's homeport since the first voyage of the *Britannia* in 1840, but it was a necessity. The presence of the Bar across the mouth of the Mersey already meant that the *Mauretania* and *Aquitania*, each with a draught of thirty-six feet, could only cross it at high tide, while the new *Berengaria*, which drew thirty-nine feet, would risk running aground even at flood tides. Liverpool would be served by the new flotilla of intermediate-size liners, as would the London route.

The first of these new intermediates was the *Scythia*, which was laid down at Vickers-Armstrong in late 1919, at 624 feet in length, 74 feet wide, and with a displacement of just under 20,000 tons. Not designed as a fast ship but rather a comfortable one, she had twin screws that gave her a top speed of 16 knots; passenger accommodations in three classes totaled 2,206 people: 337 in First Class, 331 in Second, and 1,538 in Third. Her design reflected the realities of the North Atlantic passenger trade as Cunard's directors understood them in the first years of the 1920s, which they believed would remain fundamentally unchanged from those before the war.

But incidents during the *Scythia*'s construction could have given Cunard warning that things were changing, and the world that emerged from the First World War was far different from the one that had entered it. A series of paralyzing strikes and complete work stoppages at the Vickers yard—unknown at those works before 1914—forced Cunard to

The handsome Laconia *was one of Cunard's first trio of post-war intermediate liners.*

have the ship towed to a yard in Rotterdam in order for her to be completed on schedule, something that had never before happened to Cunard. Across the Atlantic, a seemingly-obscure piece of legislation called the "Emergency Quota Act" made its way through the United States Congress in 1921; it would be two or three years before its full consequences were appreciated, but when they were, it would permanently transform the transatlantic passenger trade.

The *Scythia* was joined by two identical-looking sisters, the *Samaria* and *Laconia*, in 1921. All three were boxy, high sided ships with a short, purposeful-looking single funnel set squarely amidships. The derricks and kingposts set about the fore - and main-masts reflected that, to some degree, Cunard had recognized the requirement for these new ships to be of a dual nature: they were meant to carry goods as well as passengers—almost a quarter of their displacement was given over to cargo space. One feature that set them apart from their competitors was the provision for private bathrooms in most of the Second Class cabins, a feature not always found in First Class on ships of other lines. The *Laconia*, while outwardly almost indistinguishable from her sisters, was a special ship in her own right: given an even more lavish interior than her sisters, her main lounge was decorated in a Queen Anne style, the writing room in the manner of the Brothers Adam and echoing the decor of the *Aquitania*, while the smoking room was laid out to resemble an English inn—complete with working red-brick hearth and fireplace. This trio of ships soon proved extremely popular with Atlantic travelers, though the numbers of passengers were a shadow of what they had been before the Great War. The *Samaria* attained a particular distinction when, in the summer of 1925, she carried Mrs. Thomas Winthrop of Boston, to Liverpool and back. It was Mrs. Winthrop's seventy-fifth transatlantic voyage, all of them aboard Cunard ships, her first having been made in 1865, on the old paddlewheel steamer *Europa*.

The basic layout and design of the *Scythia* class was then reworked into a new class, the superstructure in particular significantly enlarged, eliminating the *Scythia*'s prominent break between the bridge and the passenger accommodations, while the overall level of luxury in the appointments was raised. The result was the *Franconia* and *Carinthia*. The new pair were, in a way, the successors to the "Pretty Sisters" *Carmania* and *Caronia*, which were aging and due to be retired at the end of the decade. Some features were in a way typical and to be expected: the decor of the smoking rooms in both ships was done in a style that copied the residence of the 15th Century Spanish painter El Greco, while the popular open hearth of the *Laconia*'s "English inn" smoking room was copied for both of the new ships. But there were also some amenities that were not only entirely new but particularly novel, such as a chocolate shop, a health spa, and a racquetball court. While they were not fast ships—their service speed was only 17 knots—with such attractions it wasn't long before the *Franconia* and *Carinthia* were among Cunard's most popular ships, as passengers began to appreciate their more relaxed and sedately paced shipboard life.

The company continued to exploit the potential of the *Scythia* class, as further reworking of the design resulted in the "A" class, a series of six ships built in two sets of three between 1922 and 1925. The first trio was the *Antonia, Andania,* and *Ausonia,* the

The first ship of a six-vessel class of comfortable, economical intermediates, the **Ausonia**.

Originally a pre-war design, the Lancastria *was one of Cunard's most popular ships in the years between the World Wars.*

second trio the *Aurania, Alaunia,* and *Ascania*. The similarities in profile between the new class and the *Scythia* made their origins obvious, but they were almost a hundred feet shorter in length and eight feet narrower in beam, with a displacement of only 14,000 tons. Their appointments were a bit more austere, with only two passenger classes, First and Third, and a greatly enlarged cargo capacity, a design philosophy that echoed that of the *Saxonia* and her sisters from a generation earlier. Often lost in the glamour of the big express liners were the economic realities of running a profitable steamship line. Even as the numbers of passengers were growing to fantastic levels before the war, the flow of goods and materials back and forth between the Old World and the New had grown as well, and while the demand for passenger space had diminished, the need for cargo space was even more critical, as the losses suffered by British and American shipping at the hands of the German navy had created a circumstance where there was more cargo to be shipped than there were bottoms to carry it. Consequently, the cargo holds of the *Scythia* class and the "A" class, were consistent money-makers for Cunard.

The twelfth ship of Cunard's new post-war fleet of intermediates was something special. Though she bore a superficial resemblance to the *Scythia*, she was in fact an entirely different design. Her plans had been drawn up before the war, and shared much with the *Cameronia* of Cunard's subsidiary, the Anchor Line. Originally called the *Tyrrhenia* when she entered service in 1922, for some reason that name proved unpopular with just about everyone, passengers and crew alike, and in 1924, she was re-christened the *Lancastria*. It was said about her that "Everything glowed that was meant to glow, everything shined that was meant to shine." A two-class ship, her appointments in both First and Third were considered outstanding, and she quickly established a reputation for being a comfortable ship with impeccable service.

The twelve ships of Cunard's new flotilla of intermediate-size liners were handsome, they were well appointed, and they were comfortable, but when they set sail, even though they were among the most popular ships on the North Atlantic, they sailed almost half-empty with their Third Class accommodations nearly devoid of passengers. It wasn't just Cunard's ships that were deserted, it was a malady being suffered by every steamship company on the Atlantic. An act passed by the United States' Congress in 1921 forever altered the North Atlantic run, and in many ways brought about its doom. Called the Emergency Quota Act, it was popularly known as "The Three Percent Act", as it implemented a restrictive system of quotas on immigration that allowed only three percent of any nation's population, based on the 1903 census, to be admitted into the United States. Immigrant traffic immediately plummeted—-in the calendar year immediately following the implementation of the act, 230,000 fewer passengers crossed from Europe to the United States. By the mid-1920s, the annual number of immigrants to the United States was less than a third of what it had been before the war.

This hit the steamship companies hard, as they had built their liners to accommodate that immigrant trade: some ships had devoted as much as seventy-five percent of their cabin space to immigrants. What had been a reliable and rewarding source of income for the steamship lines had vanished almost overnight, and there was literally nothing they could do about it: the United States government had spoken, and that was that. Travel agents and shipping executives alike scrambled to find solutions.

The one that seemed to hold the most promise appears to have occurred more or less simultaneously to almost all the shipping lines. The answer was to improve what had been the Third Class areas of their ships, adding amenities and appointments, and quietly drop the word "steerage" from the corporate lexicon. Third Class became "Tourist Third," while Second Class was transformed into "Tourist," and First Class became simply "Cabin" class, innocuous labels that no longer implicitly stated a passenger's social or economic status. Advertising brochures were suddenly filled with colorful copy detailing how crossing on one of the great North Atlantic steamships was no longer just a means of travel, but was now an integral part of the experience of journeying abroad.

Of course there was a good deal more involved in changing "Third Class" to "Tourist Third" than just changing names: it would have been impossible to simply pretend that the "Tourist Third" areas had never been steerage—the traveling public knew better. But there were improvements to be made that would demonstrate that while the spaces may have been the same, the accommodations were noticeably improved. For starters, more toilets and bathrooms were added, although the days when every cabin had its own private facilities were still in the future, while the number of people assigned to each cabin was reduced by half, giving everyone a great deal more room. On the *Berengaria*, for example, the space originally given over to more than 2,100 steerage passengers when she had been the *Vaterland*, now had berths for only a thousand. The menus for all meals were improved significantly, and tailored specifically to American taste. Cunard then very deliberately courted what it considered to be the "right" sort of people to fill these cabins, aiming its advertising squarely at teachers, college professors, students and the like, as well as businessmen traveling on limited expense accounts, and emphasized the economy of a Tourist-Third passage—a round trip ticket could cost as little as $150 aboard the *Aquitania*, as compared to $1,500 for a First Class passage aboard her. The company also campaigned very actively and successfully among civic and professional organizations to secure their business: in 1927 alone, thirteen of Cunard's ships were chartered to carry American delegates to conferences in Europe, among them the American Legion in Paris, the Rotarians in Ostend, and the American Guernsey Association in Guernsey, one of the Channel Islands.

One of the charms of traveling Tourist Third, according to Cunard brochures, was the fact that a passenger's traveling companions were sure to be simple and unostentatious folk, a joy to get to know. They may have had a point: the passenger list for Tourist Third on one ship in 1923 included 470 college students, forty-six college and university professors, three university presidents, and 205 school teachers; the professions were represented by nine physicians, six dentists, and seven lawyers; the clergy accounted for eight Protestant ministers and nine Roman Catholic priests. The level of intellectual achievement among the passengers listed was equally impressive, including as it did some thirty-seven members of Phi Beta Kappa, ninety-five PhD's, and four writers of international reputation. Even the business community was represented, as seventy-three American businessmen were aboard in Tourist Third.

Where the steamship lines got lucky with the whole Tourist Third concept was in the fact that Americans *wanted* to travel: there was more than just a minor ring of truth in the popular lyric *"How ya gonna keep 'em down on the farm, after they've seen Paree?"* More than two million American doughboys had been shipped to France between 1917 and 1919, and to them Europe was no longer the stuff of myth and legend: it was real and it was fascinating. It was also very affordable—a dollar would go far in post war Paris. Consequently, just as the westbound flood of the immigrant trade virtually dried up, the sons, grandsons and great-grandsons of those immigrants were now making eastward passages, not seeking new lives as had their forebears, but rather seeking new experiences and broader horizons.

For a while it worked, and worked well. Almost inevitably the segment of American society among which the concept was most popular was the middle class, as thousands of families exploited the new-found affluence offered by the economic boom of the 1920s, and intrigued by the Europe described by the returning doughboys, filled the cabins of the Tourist Third spaces. By 1925 it was estimated that almost 80% of the passengers crossing the Atlantic were Americans. It was a change that was not always appreciated in every corner of the North Atlantic. John Malcolm Brinnin tells of a woman who had been a frequent traveler on the North Atlantic before the war, who reflected rather ruefully on the changes she observed in shipboard behavior in the years following the war.

"Everything about an ocean voyage is now changed," she lamented. "The boats are not shipshape; the whole idea is to make them as much as possible like hotels... The restlessness..is unceasing; no one can take the shortest nap, there is such a universal 'doing something noise.' Games of all kinds are arranged each day to 'amuse' the passengers: 'Potato races for children, 'egg and spoon races for ladies and children,' 'international tug of war,' etc., etc.... The drinking on the outgoing boats is another calamity. The men begin as soon as they cross the three mile limit, and never cease until they are nearly insane...."

The heavy drinkers to which this dowager traveler referred were Americans, their behavior a consequence of one of the more absurd episodes in American history, Prohibition. Properly known as the Volstead Act, it passed into American law as the Eighteenth Amendment, and forbad the manufacture, distribution and sale of alcoholic beverages anywhere on American territory of any description. (Curiously, the one thing the Volstead Act didn't prohibit was the actual consumption of alcohol.) Since American-owned and -registered merchant ships were considered American soil, this meant that American vessels were "dry." This also meant that while foreign-owned vessels would have their liquor cabinets securely locked the moment they crossed into American territorial waters, those same cabinets were unlocked on the outbound passage as soon as the vessels crossed the twelve-mile limit and were in international waters. American ships, however, were never able to serve their passengers anything stronger than club soda during the entire voyage. Would-be passengers avoided them as if they were plague-ships.

The career of the former *Vaterland*, now the *Leviathan*, was a microcosm of the failure of the latest American effort to maintain a first-rate passenger service on the North Atlantic. Refurbished and rehabilitated at the then-prodigious cost of eight million dollars, the *Leviathan* set out on her American maiden voyage in July 1923. She never had a chance. Her gargantuan size was her first obstacle: it had become customary to build pairs, or even a trio of ships in order to maintain regular, simultaneous east- and westbound schedules, an important consideration for passengers seeking round-trip bookings. The lack of a running mate of comparable size meant that the United States Lines had to schedule two, sometimes three ships to sail opposite the *Leviathan*, creating additional operating expenses that the line could ill afford. Her greatest handicap was the same one that afflicted every other American ship: she was "dry." With Americans flocking to sail on foreign vessels and so escape the restrictions of Prohibition, there was little about the *Leviathan* to attract any significant numbers of passengers; consequently, she was never able to operate at a profit, and dragged the rest of the company down with her. As one of the directors of the United States Lines observed, "The *Aquitania* is the most popular ship in the world and it cost us nine million dollars to find it out."

It was in the mid-1920s though, in part a consequence of Prohibition, that the French became a major presence on the North Atlantic, exploiting Germany's absence and America's ineptness. France, and in particular the Compagnie Generale Transatlantique (CGT), more commonly known as simply the French Line, already had a long tradition of offering ships that were slightly smaller, slightly slower than their British or German counterparts, but on which the comforts and service were always of the highest standards, and which always had a distinctly Gallic air about them.

The French managed to produce one ship every generation that seemed to embody the essence of France, or at least what the popular conception of what France was. Before the war it had been the *France*, four-funneled, graceful-looking, known on both sides of the Atlantic for the excellence of her cuisine and the severity of her rolling. Her most outstanding feature was a collection of six-room suites, which had no counterparts for size and elegance on any other ship on the North Atlantic. While never a record setter, nor ever a contender for the Blue Ribband, she attracted a distinct and loyal following who appreciated what one observer recalled as being her "high style and efficient ease."

In 1927, the French Line introduced a ship that would almost instantly become the favorite of the self-proclaimed "smart set," the *Ile de France*. A genuinely handsome three-funneled ship of 43,000 tons that rejoiced in being all things French in her decor, appointments, and amenities, which her designers had hoped would show "all the richness and all the imagination of French decorative art," according to one company brochure. A unique feature of that concept was that no two of her 439 First Class cabins were identical. She certainly attracted the patronage of the leading men and women of art and letters during the last years of the "Roaring Twenties," and remained a favorite with the stylish and famous throughout the years between the wars.

But even while the *Ile de France* was entering service, plans were being drawn up for a successor that would be almost twice her size and would capture the hearts and imaginations of tens of thousands of people on both sides of the Atlantic, the *Normandie*. About this same time, Norddeutscher-Lloyd announced that Germany would be returning to the North Atlantic, by introducing two new giant liners, to be named the *Bremen* and *Europa*.

While the egalitarian revolution that abolished the traditional passenger class structure was overtaking the North Atlantic trade, a revolution in how passenger ships could be employed in making money for their owners was underway as well, as Cunard discovered the fiscal joys of cruising. The concept apparently first occurred to Cunard's directors sometime in 1922, the *Laconia* becoming the first Cunard liner to make a world cruise the next year. It lasted just over four months and called at twenty-two ports, and was such a smashing success that it was repeated the following year. The lesson was quickly learned, and when the *Franconia* and *Carinthia* were being designed and

The Carinthia, *which, together with her sister the* Franconia, *continued the tradition of elegance established by the ships they replaced, the* Carmania *and* Caronia.

built, their accommodations were designed for rapid and efficient conversion to a cruising configuration, especially in the winter months when the numbers of passengers crossing the Atlantic always fell off precipitously, allowing Cunard to use the ships profitably year round—some cruises making as much as $800,000 for the line. Lean and graceful, painted white overall save for the famous red-and-black funnels, they resembled nothing so much as huge yachts, as each autumn they set out on expensive and exclusive world cruises.

These voyages, sometimes arranged for as few as four hundred passengers, were a far cry from the glitzy, glittery passages that would be the hallmarks of cruising in the late 20th Century; lacking were the casinos, stage shows, sports bars, sun decks, and shopping malls of modern cruise ships. Instead, they were characterized by a relaxed atmosphere centered around the simple experience of being at sea. Even the advertising copy is charming in its simplicity when compared to the hyperbolic offerings of present-day cruise lines, as illustrated by a 1925 brochure for the *Carinthia*:

> You'll want the best! The Raymond-Whitcomb Round the World Cruise. Sails from New York, October 10th 1925; from Los Angeles, October 25th; from San Francisco, October 27th. Visits Cuba, Panama, Hawaii, Japan, China, the Philippines, New Guinea, New Zealand, Australia, Java, Singapore, India, Egypt, Italy, France, and England; European termination March 1st 1926, New York on March 10th. All on

board the new 20,000-ton *Carinthia*. The route: the admittedly superior westbound course—sailing from the 51st degree north of the Equator to the 45th degree south—38,000 miles—149 days of cruising—visiting 51 ports and places of prime interest in 21 countries and colonies. The ship: the brand new *Carinthia*, finest of the Cunarders—launched in 1925—unique equipment—instantaneous hot water in every room used—beds six inches wider than on other ships—exceptional deck space—squash court and pool. All for $2,000 upward.

The pool mentioned was a rather interesting contraption, a temporary arrangement rigged up solely for cruising. Ships on the North Atlantic run had no need of outdoor swimming pools—the North Atlantic can be a cold and blustery place even in July—but when cruising through the tropics, a pool was a necessity. A collapsible canvas pool roughly twenty five feet in length and twelve feet wide was designed. It would be erected in the after well deck, and filled with salt water, passengers then being invited to splash and paddle about to their hearts content. It would be another decade before swimming pools would be introduced as permanent installations on passenger ships on the North Atlantic, and then only on the Mediterranean run—by the Italian Line.

It was the summer of 1929 when the Germans finally made their presence known again on the North Atlantic. The *Europa* had been badly damaged in a fire while she was fitting out, spoiling Norddeutscher-Lloyd's plans for simultaneous maiden voyages, but when the *Bremen* sailed from her namesake port on July 16th, she created a tremendous stir all by herself. Gone were the aesthetic nightmares of the *Imperator* class liners: the *Bremen* and *Europa* were handsome ships with low, sleek hulls, and carefully proportioned superstructures topped by a pair of large, but balanced-looking funnels. Though any resemblance was ephemeral, they possessed the same sort of powerful, authoritative look that had been so much a part of the mystique of the *Kaiser Friedrich der Grosse*, *Kronprinz Wilhelm* or *Kaiser Wilhelm II*. Inside, the gilt-and-marble bombast of Wilhelmine Germany gave way to the wood, wrought iron, and glass of the Bauhaus school, which unashamedly and also without acknowledgement borrowed heavily from the Scottish architect Charles Rennie Mackintosh. Each ship's geared turbine engines turned four screws that were meant to drive the new German liners at average speeds of more than 27 knots. On her maiden voyage, the *Bremen* quickly gave notice that she could not only meet, but exceed her designers' expectations. When she entered New York harbor on July 21, she had taken the Blue Ribband, making the westbound crossing in 4 days, 17 hours, 42 minutes—an average speed of 27.9 knots—more than two and one-half knots faster than the previous record holder. On her return, the *Bremen* set her seal on the eastbound record as well, the first new Blue Ribband liner in twenty-two years.

Sadly, the old record holder was the gracious and beloved *Mauretania*. She had been the epitome of marine architecture when she had been built in 1907, but two decades of

The Mauretania at her most elegant, wearing cruising white.

technical progress had overtaken her, and innovations in the *Bremen*'s hull form, engines, and construction gave the new German ship a two-knot margin of speed over the Cunard liner, a gap that the dowager queen of the Atlantic could never hope to overcome. Not that the *Mauretania* would bow out before giving a final flourish of her own. Her captain, James MacNeil (Sir Arthur Rostron had assumed command of the *Aquitania* after Sir James Charles' passing), may have paid a courtesy call to Captain Ziegenbaum of the *Bremen* to congratulate the German skipper on his new liner's accomplishment, but MacNeil was determined to show that the old lady could still pick up her skirts and run. On August 3, 1929, the *Mauretania* left Cherbourg, arriving in New York four days, 21 hours and 44 minutes later, for an average speed of 26.85 knots. The return crossing was made in four days, 17 hours, 50 minutes, giving an average speed of 27.22 knots, the best crossings the *Mauretania* ever made. Capt. Ziegenbaum, acknowledging such a remarkable accomplishment by such an old ship, sent MacNeil a telegram of congratulations. The astonishing run of the *Mauretania* was over—she had held the Blue Ribband for twenty-two years—but the legend was still very much alive.

Such flourishes and accomplishments served to draw further public attention to the transatlantic steamship lines, and inevitably, more business as well. Bookings were increasing every year, and with them lifted the corporate profit margins. It was more than the steamship companies had dared to hope for, and as their revenues once again rose, they began to consider building ships that were larger and faster than ever. As their balance sheets improved, something of the old pre-war arrogance and cockiness came back to the boardrooms, while the fiscal caution that had been their collective watchword in the early twenties went by the wayside; they had no idea of the collapse that would soon overtake them.

By the late 1920s it had become clear to Cunard and White Star that not only were their German prizes a disappointment, but their prewar liners were nearing the end of their useful service lives. It would be pointless to replace them on a one-for-one basis, as the actual costs of operating a large ship was only marginally greater than that of a medium-sized vessel, so another quantum leap in size similar to that made at the beginning of the century would be necessary, allowing a single hull to take the place of two or three smaller, older ships. Liners displacing 80,000 tons or more, and over a thousand feet in length—ships that had been the stuff of fantasy before the war—would have to be built.

White Star was the first line to venture in those uncharted waters of steamship design. In 1921, when White Star was still part of International Mercantile Marine, the company's board of directors reflected on the changes the war had wrought on the passenger trade on the North Atlantic, and issued a statement declaring that "the building of further steamships of the monster type in the near future is rendered problematical...special consideration will be given to steamers of the cabin and third-class type -increasingly popular in these democratic days." But by 1928 the White Star Line was no longer under the thumb of IMM, which had begun to break up, but instead was now part of the wholly-British Royal Mail Group led by Lord Kryslant. While Cunard had launched an even-dozen new ships in the early 1920s, White Star had only been able to introduce three new ships in those years, the motor vessels *Britannic* and *Georgic*, and the 35,000-ton steamer *Homeric*, originally a German liner built for Norddeutscher-Lloyd and turned over to the White Star Line as war reparations. While the company's finances weren't quite as secure as they had been before the Great War, the fortunes of White Star were sufficiently bright to cause the line, looking to replace some of its rapidly aging pre-war fleet, to place an order with Harland and Wolff, the Belfast shipyard that had been building White Star ships for nearly sixty years, for a ship that was to be called the *Oceanic*. Designed to be over a thousand feet in length, with a displacement of roughly 80,000 tons, she would be the heir to all the traditions of the White Star Line that had begun with the original *Oceanic* of a half-century before, but with none of the aesthetic grace. The physical and structural requirements of such an enormous hull required a much larger, more massive hull than had ever before been built.

About this same time the French Line (more correctly known as CGT—*Compagnie Generale Transatlantique*) decided to assert its presence on the North Atlantic in a way it never had before, by building a ship as large and as fast as any of its potential British or German competitors, and began work on what was to become the *Normandie*. Even the Italian Line got into the act, introducing the *Rex* and the *Conte di Savoia*, two smart, fast ships approximately the same size as the *Bremen* and *Europa*, which would prove the most popular vessels on the Mediterranean run.

Cunard began work on its own superliner a year after Harland and Wolff began construction of the *Oceanic*, laying the keel of Hull Number 534 at the John Brown works on

December 1, 1930. It was a dark, murky, typically Scottish winter day, but it was bright with promise for the Clyde and for scores of communities for miles around. Cunard had decided in the late 1920s that two fast, powerful super-liners, larger than any ever built, would be able to provide a regular, weekly transatlantic service—something that heretofore had required three ships. Each ship would be expected to make the crossing in five days, then spend two days in "turn-around," where fuel, provisions, fresh linen and all the other supplies required for the next crossing would be brought aboard, and set out on the return crossing with almost clock-like punctuality. As far back as 1840, Sir Samuel Cunard had dreamed of a time when a weekly service between Great Britain and North America could be maintained by just two ships. Now it seemed that his prescient vision would be realized.

Alas, it was a vision that would quickly fade, as the financial disaster that swept across Wall Street on October 24, 1929, wiped out the passenger lists of the transatlantic liners almost overnight. At the time, more than 80% of the liners' passenger lists were comprised of Americans, most of them from the middle class. When the Crash came, it wasn't just the great financiers and tycoons who saw their fortunes dwindle: huge numbers of middle-class Americans had invested in the stock market and lost their life's savings. Suddenly for many of them, there was no longer any question of being able to afford a trip to Europe on a steamship—now the issue was survival. Almost overnight, as it were, not only did the shipping companies' capital reserves dry up, but their single largest source of income vanished as well.

The financial collapse that became known as the Great Depression has become indelibly associated with one locality and one date: Wall Street, October 24, 1929, the day known as Black Thursday. But it wasn't limited to just October or simply to Wall Street. It actually began in Austria on March 25, 1929, when the Kredit-Anstalt, Vienna's largest bank, closed its doors. This was the first domino, as a series of bank failures then spread across Europe, and then jumping the Atlantic, triggering a series of small crashes and recoveries over the next six months. The summer of 1929 was actually fairly prosperous, as many economists—who should have known better—thought the cycles of crash and recovery were symptoms of a market adjusting itself, as it certainly appeared to be relatively stable.

It was on September 3, though, that the roller coaster began its final descent. A hopelessly tangled skein of interlocking loans and credit deals proved to be the system's undoing, as one bank after another began failing, when trying to cover shortfalls on financial deals of their own they called in their outstanding loans, only to find themselves left with bad debts. Often the loans had been made to companies and individuals who were purchasing stocks on margin. This meant buying stocks by putting cash down on a "margin" of their value—usually 10%—and putting the rest on credit, using the stock itself as collateral, counting on the rising value of the stock to have exceeded the balance of the loan when it came due, thus making a nice profit in the process. But when the loans were called in early, the money necessary to pay them simply wasn't there, and stocks which had their values artificially inflated by the buying frenzy of the previous years were suddenly found to be worth only a fraction of that value, making repaying the loans impossible. Hundreds of thousands of shares of stock were catastrophically devalued, many to the point of worthlessness, and as a consequence, the financial underpinnings of the market were torn away. The result was Black Thursday, October 24, 1929, when at the end of the day, the New York Stock Exchange had dropped to less than half of what its opening level had been that morning. The Crash of 1929 had begun.

The immediate consequence for Cunard of the Wall Street Crash was the loss of revenue created by the suddenly-vanished American passengers. While certainly a cause for concern, it wasn't seen as a reason to panic: no one yet had any idea how long the depression—it wasn't yet the "Great Depression"—would last; after all, President Hoover was reassuring the people of the United States almost daily that a return to prosperity was "just around the corner." If Hoover was right, it might be possible to carry on business as usual, relying on cash reserves to cover any temporary shortfalls, until the American economy returned to something resembling normal. Work continued on Hull 534, and the regular schedule of sailings to and from the United States and Canada was maintained.

But New York and London were the twin lynchpins of the world's financial system in the years between the two World Wars, and what affected one would inevitably affect the other; in this case, when one part collapsed, the strain proved irresistible and ultimately fatal for the other. Dramatic economic changes take time to make their way across continents and oceans, and Europe had actually begun a modest recovery from the debacle that followed the fall of the Kredit-Anstalt in the spring of 1929. But by the summer of 1930, shockwaves from the American disaster hit Europe, and the minor gains made in the last year were wiped out.

The bottom fell out in 1931, when the values of securities and investments fell to barely 11% of their pre-Crash worth. A vicious downward spiral began, as retail sales plummeted, forcing manufacturers to dismiss "surplus" workers; each new round of layoffs only meant that there were even fewer people able to make purchases, causing sales to drop still further, resulting in even more employees finding themselves out of work. A ruinous run on British banks was only narrowly averted—at one point more than £25,000,000 were withdrawn from the Bank of England in a single day—and Great Britain plunged into the depths of a chasm-like depression from which British industry would never fully recover.

Hit especially hard was the White Star Line: passenger lists rapidly dwindled, the company's reserves of capital dried up, and the company began to slowly sink into a sea of red ink. Work on the *Oceanic* was suspended in early 1930 for lack of money; shortly thereafter, the whole project was canceled completely, as White Star found itself struggling for survival. The French Line was able to keep its ships in service by virtue of hefty government subsidies, but the future of the still-building *Normandie* was in doubt. Only the German and Italian companies continued to show a profit, but Norddeutscher-Lloyd and Hamburg-Amerika were being propped up by Berlin, being underwritten by the Weimar Republic until 1933, and by the National Socialists after that. In Rome, Benito Mussolini's Fascists found it politically expedient to maintain a facade of "business as usual," even though the Italian Line's ships were frequently sailing almost empty.

By the end of 1931, Cunard's operating deficit approached £5,000,000 ($20 million), and work was suspended on the 534 less than a year after it had begun, taking with it all the hope of returned prosperity for the Clyde. What had promised to be four or five years of steady work building the two new ships (they were to be so large that they could only be built one at a time—John Brown's slipways weren't large enough to allow them to be built together) turned to ashes, as Cunard, faced with continually shrinking passenger lists and growing deficits, slowly ran out of money to pay for the new ship. By the end of the year, the line's finances were barely in better shape than White Star's, and the possibility of dissolution was looming on the horizon.

With the desperate economic straits in which Cunard found itself, the iron grip of the Great Depression was slowly strangling the Clydeside, that stretch of the River Clyde that reaches west of Glasgow toward Gourock and the Western Approaches. For almost a century the banks of the Clyde had been the home of the finest shipyards in the world, so much so that the phrase "a Clyde-built ship" had become an assurance that any vessel so described was sound, sturdy and built to last. But as the world's economy descended into a stagnation that seemed to offer no hope of relief, so trade and travel between nations steadily declined, and with it went the demand for ships to carry cargo or passengers across the world's oceans. One by one the shipwrights' hammers were being stilled in the Scottish shipyards along the river, as the orders for new ships dwindled, then vanished.

And finally, that stillness came to the yard of John Brown Ltd. One of the greatest, proudest shipyards on all of the Clyde, indeed in all of Great Britain, John Brown Ltd. had built dreadnoughts for the Royal Navy, freighters by the hundreds that sailed to all corners of the globe, and some of the greatest ocean liners the world had ever seen, including the magnificent *Lusitania* and the majestic *Aquitania*. But on December 11, 1931, when the whistle sounded "down tools," the silence in the John Brown works was more than deafening, it was frightening. Thirty-five hundred workers were suddenly unemployed, with little prospect of soon finding other work. Many a basher and fitter wondered apprehensively if they would ever work again.

Towering over the yard, its brooding presence soon to become a constant reminder of all the glories there had been on the Clyde and might never be again, was the huge gray mass of the unfinished, un-launched Hull 534. The 534 was supposed to have been as great a triumph of British shipbuilding as the *Lusitania* had been a quarter century before, but now it was nothing more than an empty shell, unpainted, unfinished, lacking engines, its decks open to the wind and rain, sitting desolate and empty. It would have been wrong to refer to the 534 as "she"—after all it wasn't really a ship yet. It didn't even have a name.

By the end of 1932, Cunard faced a threat unlike any it had ever known. What the line confronted now was not the challenge of some ambitious upstart like Edward Knight Collins in the 1850s, or the determined advance of the German shipping companies in the 1890s. Nor was the threat simply absorption by a giant American shipping combine, or being reduced to the second rank of North Atlantic passenger lines; what Cunard was facing now was nothing short of extinction.

CHAPTER TWELVE

Return to Glory

It was the worst of times.

Echoing scenes found along the Bay of Biscay, in Belfast, and on Germany's Baltic coast, shipyards up and down the Clyde sat empty. In the John Brown yard the giant new ship that had been ordered in the bright days of early 1929 now sat empty and unfinished—there was no money to pay for it, no way to pay the men who were to have built it. "For more than two years," recalled David Kirkwood, a Clydeside labor leader, "the Clyde had been like a tomb—not a tomb newly made, but a tomb with a vast and inescapable skeleton brooding over its silence." The vise-like grip that the Great Depression had gained on the industries of America and Europe only grew tighter as time passed, and more and more factories, mills, and shops closed their doors completely, or eked out an existence with their work-rolls reduced to a bare minimum.

Slowly at first, but with growing conviction, the comprehension dawned that only massive intervention by the national governments would save, not only the unfinished ships, but the steamship companies themselves. The French were the first to bite the bullet. Hardly had work stopped on the *Normandie,* when officials from the Compagnie Generale Transatlantique approached the French government with the idea of a massive loan to fund the completion of the new ship and recapitalize the line. Despite heated, sometimes rancorous debate within France's National Assembly, where Socialist deputies demanded that the money be spent on social programs and welfare relief for unemployed Frenchmen, the loan was swiftly approved and work resumed on the *Normandie* with only the briefest of interruptions.

In Germany, where the Weimar Republic huddled and muddled as the power of the once-upstart National Socialist German Workers Party began to threaten the stability of the government, the program of subsidies for Norddeutscher-Lloyd and Hamburg-Amerika that had begun under Kaiser Wilhelm II continued and was even expanded. National prestige was at stake, and the Weimar politicians deemed it vital to the ongoing redemption of Germany's international reputation that her ships continue to ply the seas. Consequently, though in practical terms it could ill-afford the cost, the German government underwrote the two great German shipping lines. When the Nazis finally came to power in January 1933, there was no question but that the subsidies would continue: few men have been as conscious of the importance of international symbolism as Adolf Hitler. He may have had only a limited understanding of sea power and ships, but on some instinctive level he knew they were important, so the German liners sailed on schedule.

A similar arrangement seemed to be the only solution to Cunard's debacle. The company tried hard to avoid resorting to such action, hatching all sorts of money-making schemes, some which worked and some which didn't. But they were never enough, and in the end Cunard went, hat figuratively in hand, to His Majesty's Government, hoping the politicians would be sympathetic. It had to be acknowledged that there were powerful arguments in Cunard's favor—after all, in this case it wasn't just national pride or the prosperity of the company that were at stake. Literally thousands of jobs were on the line: workers in the yards and the factories which would build the ship and her equipment; chandlers who would supply the necessities for day-to-day operations; joiners and carpenters who would complete the interiors; and of course, the stewards, stewardesses, waiters, cooks, galley hands, stokers, engineers and seamen who would make up the crew. With the welfare roles growing weekly, the idea of putting the many thousands of men to work who would build and serve the new ship had an undeniable appeal. Cunard's board of directors approached the one man who had the means and authority to provide the solution to their dilemma—Neville Chamberlain.

History has not been kind to Neville Chamberlain, and justifiably so—his tenure as Prime Minister was unarguably the most disastrous in all of Great Britain's existence. However, he *was* a businessman *par excellence*, and so was admirably suited to the position he occupied in 1933, that of Chancellor of the Exchequer, the keeper of the British government's purse strings. He welcomed Cunard's overture for government assistance, for with a shrewd merchant's eye he perceived the shared plight of Cunard and White Star as an opportunity to bring an end to what he regarded as an unnecessary competition between the rival steamship companies. "My own aim," he would record in his diary, "has always been to use the 534 as a lever to bring about a merger between the Cunard and White Star Lines, thus establishing a strong British firm on the North Atlantic trade." He called the managing directors of both steamship companies to a series of meetings in London in December of 1933: the terms of the Government's offer, as he outlined them, were generous, but Chamberlain's delivery was blunt. He made it perfectly clear that neither White Star nor Cunard would be able to survive independently, while His Majesty's Government was in no position to support both. The only way the Government would loan the money to complete the 534 would be if the two rival shipping lines merged.

Both Cunard and White Star had struggled to find ways of generating income in the first two years following the Crash of '29, hoping to discover some formula that would fill the yawning emptiness of their ships and allow them to maintain their independence. Nothing seemed to work—cutting fares was pointless, as few people were able to afford extended holidays abroad, spending as much as a week aboard ship traveling to their destination, staying abroad for an indefinite period of time each way, and then spending another week on the return crossing. What holidays people were now able to enjoy were short, often of only a few days duration, sometimes just a single day. The challenge to the steamship lines was to find a way to get these people aboard during such brief periods of time.

It's not exactly clear who came up with the idea of sending idle or under-booked passenger liners away on cruises as a way of making money for the cash-strapped shipping companies. It could be argued that the father of modern cruising was Albert Ballin, who, rather than see the 8,000-ton *Augusta Victoria* laid up for the winter months of 1890, sent her on a sightseeing jaunt about the Mediterranean. Certainly the idea of cruising wasn't new: groups of wealthy travelers had been chartering small and medium sized ships for exclusive jaunts for more than seventy-five years. However, the idea of regular and organized cruises with set itineraries and fixed schedules seems to have been an innovation of the 1920s. Certainly Cunard's *Carinthia* and *Franconia* were among the first ships to be given over to cruising the tropics in the winter months, and it was a lead that the White Star Line soon followed, as did the French. The Italian Line never wholeheartedly embraced the idea, but then the southern route across the Atlantic from New York or Boston to the Mediterranean was a far different creature than the usually cold, often vicious northerly route to Southampton or Liverpool. Indeed, the southerly route was so comfortable and balmy it could be said that it was a cruise in itself, and many travelers booked passage on it for that reason.

But ships that were built for, and operated, on the northern route often found themselves idle or running a reduced schedule between November and February, and this was something of which Cunard had taken advantage with the *Franconia* and *Carinthia*. The two intermediate liners' ample cargo capacity also made cruising a practical undertaking, as they could earn their keep transporting goods at the same time they were carrying passengers to exotic tropical ports of call. Somewhere along the line, some unsung genius took that idea and stood it on its ear: instead of voyages to specific destinations, why not offer trips to nowhere? Why not have ships simply depart from a given port, sail about the Caribbean or the British Isles for a few days, then return the passengers to the port from which they had originally sailed? Moreover, why not make them relatively inexpensive—or to be blunt about it, cheap? The four-month long cruises made by the *Franconia* and *Carinthia* had cost upward of £420 ($2,000) per passenger, a sum clearly out reach of all but the wealthiest passengers even in the best of times. But £10 ($48) per head for a week steaming down the Atlantic coast and back was a different proposition altogether.

The result was a schedule of cruises out of New York and Boston that sailed down the American coast to Cuba or the Caribbean islands and back, taking a week to make the round trip. Cruises out of British ports would call at the Canary Islands, Portugal, or the Mediterranean; Norway and the Baltic Sea also became particularly popular destinations. Before long, such ships as the *Mauretania, Laconia,* and *Lancastria* found themselves painted white to ward off the tropical heat and were puttering about West Indies. The *Olympic* was reduced at times to taking £1-a-day Bank Holiday vacationers on cruises about the

British Isles, or making three-day excursions from New York to Halifax and back. On February 3, 1932, she left New York for a two week excursion about the Mediterranean, then followed it up with cruises on the New York to Bermuda route, as well as another trip to the Med later that year. In November she underwent an extensive reconstruction of her passenger accommodations, as First Class was reduced to 650 persons, while the cabins in Tourist (formerly Second) Class were enlarged, though the actual passenger capacity in that class was reduced to 600; Tourist Third Class (the old Third Class) was altered to accommodate 950 passengers. Meanwhile, all of the public rooms were refurbished, and a theatre was added. For the next six years the *Aquitania* would continue to offer a combination of transatlantic service and tropical cruises.

A less-than-glamorous offshoot of these excursions was the three day excursion to Halifax and back that became known as the "Booze Cruise." Conceived solely to circumvent Prohibition, a Booze Cruise would sail from New York or Boston into international waters, and then steam northeast past New England and the Maritimes to call at Halifax long enough to permit some sightseeing and shopping—such as there was—before returning to New York. Once back in American territorial waters, the liquor cabinets would again be locked, but until then, the whisky and gin flowed freely, until an imbiber ran out of money or consciousness. Sometimes charging as little as $5 for fare—the rest of the costs were made up by the margins on the sales in the ship's bars—the Booze Cruises were definite money-makers for Cunard and the other steamship lines, however tawdry they may have seemed in concept. Sadly, even such fine ships as the *Mauretania* found themselves periodically doing stints on this duty. The *Berengaria*'s reputation was so soiled by her stint on this run that she became known to dockworkers, never the most reverent or respectful bunch to begin with, as the "Bargain Area."

But using passenger liners as cruise ships, a role for which they were manifestly unfit, was a stop-gap measure at best, and everyone knew it. Eventually even the Booze Cruises wound up losing money for the steamship companies, and by the end of 1933, both Cunard and White Star were compelled to accept the wisdom of Chamberlain's proposal. Admittedly, it was not that difficult an idea to sell—the management of both companies also realized that the only way either would survive was to become the Cunard White Star Line. The Government was offering the new company a total of £9,500,000 ($47,000,000)—£3,000,000 to be used to complete the 534, £1,500,000 for working capital, and £5,000,000 to be set aside for the construction of a future sister ship for the 534. The offer was accepted with almost indecent haste, and by the end of January 1934, the North Atlantic Shipping Act was approved by Parliament.

It took a couple of months to work out the definitive terms and complete the final arrangements for the merger, but in April 1934, while massed pipes played and thousands of voices sang Scottish national songs, the workforce at John Brown and Company, Ltd. returned to work on the 534 and the shipyard came to life again—and with it, the towns and factories for miles around. Although no one had actually worked on the hull for near-

Hull 534, sitting empty and all but abandoned at the John Brown shipyard on the banks of the Clyde.

ly two and one half years, the workers were astonished to find that all they needed to do was pick up where they had left off. Instead of a deteriorating hulk that would require months of refurbishing before new work could even begin, they found the 534's scantlings, frames, shell plating, decks and machinery in first class condition: the relative handful of workers who were retained at John Brown after work had been suspended had justified their employment by looking after the 534 with the same attentiveness a father pays to his smallest child. No rust was allowed to build up, no dirt accumulated, each piece of machinery was carefully oiled and maintained.

Just how well those men had done their job was shown to the world when, just six months after work on the 534 resumed, she was ready for launching. It was even fitting to call the 534 "she" now, for the newly formed Cunard White Star Line had agreed on a name for her. In the past, Cunard had followed the tradition of giving its ships names ending in "-*ia*" while White Star had a similar tradition of names ending in "-*ic*." In order to avoid any deliberate association with either of the parent lines and demonstrate a clean break with the past, the two component lines of the new company agreed to name the new ship the *Queen Mary*.

The story is often told of how Cunard's board of directors had brooded over the name to be given to the new liner, finally settling on the *Queen Victoria*. One of their number, Lord Royden, was then dispatched to Balmoral on a shooting holiday to seek the Crown's approval for using the late monarch's name. When the somewhat flustered envoy broached the subject of the new vessel to King George V, the monarch remarked, "I say,

Royden, just how *is* that ship of yours coming?" Lord Royden replied that it was coming along very well indeed, and then put the question to the King, reportedly phrasing it, "Your Majesty, we wish to name the new ship after Great Britain's greatest queen," thinking his meaning—Victoria—would be obvious. The King, whose wife was, of course, named *Mary*, promptly replied, "Splendid! That's the greatest compliment that has ever been paid to my wife! I'm sure she'll be very pleased!" Nonplussed, Lord Royden made no further comment—after all, correcting the Crown is simply *not* done! - and the company, caught in a quandary, gave in and accepted that the new ship's name would be the *Queen Mary*. The story is so charming that it's easy to wish it were true, but alas, it isn't.

There was one genuine problem with the name *Queen Mary* which Cunard White Star had not anticipated: there was already a ship on the Registry of the British Board of Trade by that name! The owners of a small Scottish coastal steamer, assisted by a cash bonus from Cunard, allowed themselves to be persuaded to rename their little ship the *Queen Mary 2*, and that obstacle was overcome.

The *Queen Mary* was launched on September 26, 1934. In what should have been Scotland's most beautiful month, the notoriously fickle Scottish weather brought a day full of wind and drenching rain, but nothing could dampen the spirits of nearly a quarter-million cheering Scots who had gathered to watch, as for the first time in history, the reigning King and Queen presided over the launch of a merchant ship. This was not just the launching of a ship, the London *Times* reminded its readers in an editorial run that morning, it was an event in the life of the nation. "It is customary," the article said, "for Great

Hull 534, now proudly bearing the name Queen Mary, *slides down the ways on September 26, 1934.*

Britain to construct from time to time such ships as are necessary to maintain her ancient predominance on the seas." It went on to say that Cunard had shouldered the burden and the splendour of the Empire in a way that only a handful of private companies had ever done in all of Great Britain's history, the Merchant Venturers, the East India Company, and the Bank of England. In other words, in the building of the *Queen Mary*, Cunard had made itself a national institution. The spirit of the day was probably best expressed in the special booklet issued by Cunard to commemorate the launch: it quoted the words of Sir John Burns, Chairman of the Cunard Line, and son of George Burns, Sir Samuel's original partner, spoken at the launch of the *Etruria* on 20 September 1884: "I have been told that it is an anomaly in shipping to talk of bad times and yet to build such immense ships . . . but I believe that . . . the Company which reduces the time in crossing the Atlantic . . . will ensure success in the long run. There is no courage in entering upon great enterprises in prosperous times, but I have faith in the future, and confidence that the Cunard Company will hold its own upon the Atlantic."

Built alongside the ship's starboard bow was an enclosed platform, some thirty-five feet above the floor of the slipway, where King George V and Queen Mary would have shelter from the rain. There was an elevator for their use, but they chose to mount the platform via an open walkway, sharing for a few minutes at least, the sodden discomfort of their subjects who were waiting patiently for the ship to be launched. Earlier that morning, in the offices of John Brown, company officials had made a special presentation to Her Majesty, a small commemorative casket made of gold and silver, with a delicately detailed map of the North Atlantic etched on the lid. In mid-ocean was a representation of the new liner's profile, her wake extending all the way back into the English Channel. The Queen was visibly delighted, breaking into one of her rare smiles.

King George V, wearing the uniform of an admiral of the Royal Navy, addressed the assembled throng, and his speech was carried worldwide by the BBC. He was best known as a rather dull speaker, but on this day he seemed inspired as he spoke with obvious pride of the new ship. "Now, with the hope of better trade on both sides of the Atlantic, let us look forward to her playing a great part in the revival of international commerce. It has been the nation's will," he declared, "that she should be completed, and today we can send her forth, no longer a number on the books, but a ship with a name in the world, alive with beauty, energy and strength." It fell to him, he said, to perform "the happy task of sending on her way... the stateliest ship in the world." The Queen used a pair of golden scissors to cut the cord holding back a bottle of Australian champagne, which promptly broke against the bow of the ship, at the same time making the traditional announcement, "I name this ship *Queen Mary*! May God bless her and all who sail on her." Then, not realizing that the microphone was still live, she turned to her husband and in a stage whisper asked, "Shall I press the button now?"

Receiving an affirmative answer, the Queen pressed the button that triggered the hydraulic ramps that would set the new liner in motion. For a fraction of a second it

Scottish pride! The builder's plate of the Queen Mary, *mounted on the face of her bridge.*

seemed as if the ship would not move, but then the white-painted hull began to tremble, and slowly gaining momentum, slid down the ways toward the waiting waters of the Clyde. There was a brief tongue of flame under her keel as the weight of the hull scorched the stocks supporting it. Drag chains attached to the launching cradles rattled and roared, but the crowd remained strangely silent. An anxious minute passed as the hull continued to gain speed, causing some watchers to wonder if she would bury her stern in the opposite bank of the river, then suddenly there she was, what Poet Laureate John Masefield called "a rampart of a ship" floating high and proud on Scotland's most famous river.

Instantly the crowd broke into deafening cheers. No longer a forlorn hope, a painful reminder of what might have been, a stillborn giant that could have given testimony to the greatness of British shipbuilding, the *Queen Mary* was real and alive. At last the hull of the 534 tasted water, she had been christened by a queen, and she had a proper name—finally, she was a ship. Surely it was the best of times.

And what a ship she was! Advertising shills for the shipping lines had been pushing the limits of hyperbole for decades, seeking to impress and over-awe prospective passengers with the size, speed, splendor, or some combination of the three, of each successive generation of steamships. In the case of the *Queen Mary*, their artifices eventually reached the level of the inane, offering such absurdities as comparing the power of the *Mary*'s four turbine engines to the muscle power of seven million galley slaves, or announcing that her displacement was 22,000 tons greater than that of the entire Spanish Armada. The First Class lounge was to be so spacious, it was said, that nine double-decker buses could be placed inside, with three Royal Scot locomotives placed atop them, with room to spare. The ship was described as "long as a street and lofty as a tower, loftier and wider than many a country church."

In truth, her dimensions were staggering enough without such embellishments. From end to end she measured 1,019 feet, with a beam of 118 feet, and an average draught of 39 feet. She displaced 80,677 tons. Compared to the largest warship in the world at the time, H.M.S. *Hood*, the *Queen Mary* was one hundred fifty feet longer and twelve feet wider in the beam, with twice *Hood*'s displacement. (In fact, the *Queen Mary* would dwarf any warship ever built until the American aircraft carrier U.S.S. *Enterprise* entered service in 1963.) Over ten million rivets were used in constructing her hull, which contained over two thousand portholes. The distance from the keel to the top of her forward funnel was one hundred eighty-one feet, while her Boat Deck (also called the Sun Deck) was seventy-five feet above the waterline. She had ten decks, four in the superstructure, the uppermost being the Sports Deck, running down through the Sun Deck and the Promenade Deck to the Main Deck; the six below that were lettered from A Deck down to G Deck; the very bottom deck, where the boiler rooms and engine rooms of the power plant were found, was the Orlop Deck.

That powerplant was probably the finest such installation to ever be put inside a ship. Cunard was determined to recapture the Blue Ribband for Great Britain as swiftly and decisively as the *Lusitania* had done three decades earlier. The *Queen Mary* was driven by four screws powered by four sets of Parsons Single Reduction Steam Turbine Engines. There was one forward and one reverse turbine on each shaft, the turbines being turned by the steam produced by a total of 24 water-tube boilers, divided between three boiler rooms. The boilers were oil-fired, each heating steam at 700 degrees Fahrenheit and at a pressure of 400 pounds per square inch. All told, the *Queen Mary*'s engines produced 160,000 shaft horsepower. It was believed that she would be capable of speeds up to, or even exceeding 32 knots.

She spent the months from September 1934 to March 1936 fitting out in the Clyde and conducting her sea trials. Her superstructure was completed along with the remainder of her machinery installation, and the funnels stepped; her galleys, laundries, and cold rooms installed; her public rooms and passenger cabins finished. The hull was painted satin black, her upperworks gleaming white, while her three funnels were traditional Cunard orange-red topped by a black soot band on the upper quarter of each. Most of the month of March 1936 was spent in extensive sea trials. There was an anxious moment when the *Mary* ran aground as she steamed out into the Clyde for the first time under her own power, but the soft river bottom did no damage to the hull, and the ship soon pulled free. Once out of the mouth of the Clyde and into the waters of the Western Approaches, she began three weeks of testing, running at varying speeds up and down the western coast of England and Scotland. There were prolonged high speed runs, dashes along measured miles, and tests for maneuverability and stability. When all of these were completed, she was ready to head for Southampton, there to begin taking aboard all the provisions, supplies and necessities that were required for her to fulfill her role as a passenger liner.

As she steamed into Southampton for the first time in May 1936, the sight of her was literally breathtaking. Towering over the Ocean Dock where she was moored, there was no question but that she was epitome of traditional British shipbuilding. Her gracefully raked stem and gently flared bow gave way to the rounded bridge and superstructure front that would be a hallmark of Cunard ships for the next half century. Fully enclosed, the superstructure itself ran unbroken for nearly three quarters of the ship's length, eliminating the fussy, cluttered look that had characterized the *Mauretania* and *Aquitania*, while the *Mary*'s three red-and-black funnels, gently decreasing in height from fore to aft, were carefully proportioned to bring a sense of balance to the ship's appearance, giving her a purposeful, thrusting look without creating an illusion of top-heaviness.

The Queen Mary *arrives in Southampton for the first time on March 25, 1936.*

At the same time, Cunard avoided the worst of the aesthetic pretensions which beset the ship that would be the *Queen Mary*'s closest rival, the *Normandie*. The *Normandie* inside and out embodied the ideal of pure Art Deco, her French decorators applying their knowing skill in the manner that initially created the Art Deco style. Unfortunately this style didn't always work: her sharply raked clipper bow contrasted bizarrely with her conventional counter stern, while her three funnels looked outsized in proportion to her hull, giving the *Normandie* a squat, almost bloated look. Cunard was far more traditional in its approach to the Art Deco style, and in the *Mary*'s décor, utilized over fifty different exotic and rare woods, collected from all over the British Empire, in places where the *Normandie* was given over to crystal, chrome and glass. The result was a distinctly British atmosphere, a combination of the traditional and the modern that was considered too sedate by some critics of the 1930s. On the other hand, it could be said that the rather understated style was perfectly in keeping with the manners of royalty: when the *Queen Mary* put into Southampton for the first time, the royal family came down from London to visit the ship. The Queen toured her namesake from bow to stern, and by all accounts enjoyed herself immensely. At then at the end of the day when she had returned to London, she confided to her diary: "Toured the new *Queen Mary* today. Not as bad as I expected."

Aboard the *Queen Mary*, passengers were never left unaware that they were on a ship. The *Normandie*'s designers tried to disguise her interiors as a Paris hotel. Cunard openly rejoiced in the fact that the *Mary* was a ship. Round portholes were proudly exposed rather than hid behind false window sashes, while nautical touches, ranging from mementos of other Cunard ships to signal flags to simple informational signs that unashamedly used words like "port," "starboard," "fore," and "aft" were found in every part of the ship. One observer best quantified the disparity between the two with the remark, "The French built a remarkable hotel and put a ship around it. The British built a beautiful ship and put a hotel inside it."

Nowhere was that difference more readily brought home than in the *Queen Mary*'s First Class Lounge. While its two-deck height and huge pillars might have made it too imposing a space in which most people could feel comfortable, the half-dozen working fireplaces with little clusters of leather wing chairs and tables about them, along with the numerous corners and nooks those same columns created, ultimately gave the lounge a coziness that the *Normandie*'s lounge, too reminiscent of a hotel foyer, could ever match.

Certainly the centerpiece of the *Queen Mary*'s interior was the First Class Dining Saloon. The White Star Line's *Olympic* and *Titanic* had been the first to introduce small tables for four or eight dinner guests, eliminating the long tables that had been found on all ocean liners previously. The *Queen Mary* copied that excellent idea, allowing the guests to seat themselves in whatever numbers and combinations they wished at tables covered in snow-white linen, set with spotless crystal and sterling tableware, surrounded by gleaming oak and mahogany paneling and polished brass fixtures. On one wall was a giant map of the North Atlantic—an indicator showed the exact position of the *Queen Mary* during

The Queen Mary's *First Class Dining Room, where art deco met traditional British style.*

each transatlantic voyage. (When the *Queen Elizabeth* entered service, a similar map was installed in her First Class Dining Saloon, with indicators showing the positions of both *Queens*, so that passengers could see when they would meet.) One of the most popular features was the small and exclusive Verandah Grill, found at the aft end of the superstructure, just below the main mast. The *Queen Mary*'s design allowed her to carry 776 passengers in First (or "Cabin") Class, 784 in Second ("Tourist") Class and 579 in Third (Tourist Third) Class, a total of 2,119, with a crew of 1,035.

When the *Normandie* set out on her record-setting maiden voyage on May 29, 1935, the French had been extremely secretive about whether or not she would attempt to take the

Blue Ribband away from the Italian liner *Rex*. By contrast, when it was announced in May 1936 that the *Queen Mary*'s maiden voyage would take place in July, it was no secret that Cunard intended for her to snatch the Blue Ribband away from the *Normandie*. On July 1, 1936, the *Queen Mary* left Southampton on what would be a crossing marked by remarkably fair weather and very high speed. As the *Mary* approached the American shore, it became clear to her passengers and crew alike that the Blue Ribband was in her reach. Almost at the last moment, though, the *Queen Mary* found herself surrounded by fog barely a day out of New York. Her captain, Commodore Sir Edgar Britten, cut her speed back to barely more than steerage way, rightly being more concerned with the ship's safety than with the record. Once the fog had lifted, he pushed the *Queen Mary* as hard as he dared, averaging just over 32 knots for the rest of the voyage, arriving in New York in four days, twelve hours and twenty minutes after she left Southampton. The time lost in fog had been crucial, for *Normandie*'s record-setting crossing had been just 38 minutes faster. Her performance had left no doubt, though, that the Blue Ribband was the *Queen Mary*'s for the taking.

That it had not been a record crossing made little difference to the Americans, as New York seemed almost delirious with the celebration of the *Queen Mary*'s arrival. A flotilla of fire ships spraying water hundreds of feet in the air surrounded her, as hundreds of pleasure craft followed in the great liner's wake as she steamed up the Hudson River. Tens of

Coronation march—the **Queen Mary** *arrives in New York on her maiden voyage on June 1, 1936.*

thousands of people lined the waterfront, while untold thousands more watched from windows in the skyscrapers overlooking New York Harbor. They had never seen such a ship! The *Normandie* had been impressive, but from the very first, there was a sense of majesty, a "presence," about the *Queen Mary* that inspired a sense of near-awe in those who saw her. It would be a presence that the *Queen Elizabeth* would share with her, but would never again be duplicated.

While the *Mary*'s performance made it clear that the Blue Ribband was within her grasp, before any record setting crossing could take place, there was the usual assortment of teething problems found in any new ship that needed to be corrected. At high speed the *Queen Mary*'s stern shook violently, and in heavy seas she would develop a pronounced corkscrew motion. She also had a marked tendency to roll in almost any kind of seaway (it would not be cured until gyroscopic stabilizers were installed in 1956). As far as the passengers were concerned, the most annoying problem was that smoke from the funnels would drop soot and drops of oil on the after promenade decks. The interior structure of the stern was stiffened to better resist the vibration and corkscrewing, while a switch from three-bladed to four-bladed screws eliminated the worst of the vibration. The problem of soot dropping on the passengers was solved by the installation of special ventilators in the funnels.

The worst of her teething problems remedied, the *Queen Mary* had another go at the Blue Ribband on August 31, 1936. Arriving in New York on September 3, she had made the crossing in three days, 23 hours and 57 minutes - the first time the crossing over the Atlantic had been made in under four days, her average speed being an amazing 30.63 knots. Though the *Normandie* would take the Ribband back the next year on March 1937, the *Queen Mary* would finally prove the faster in August 1938, with an eastbound crossing time of three days, twenty hours and forty minutes—an average speed of 31.69 knots. The Blue Ribband had returned to Great Britain. Surely, it was the best of times.

Part of the *Queen Mary*'s charm, which she never lost in any of her guises, was the way she seemed to bridge the gap between the old and new generations of transatlantic liners. The Germans, French, and Italians all seemed absolutely determined to make a complete break with the traditional decor—and appearance—of ocean liners for half a century. When the *Bremen* and *Europa* were introduced, they brought the stark simplicity of Germany's new Bauhaus school of design with them; in the *Ile de France* and *Normandie*, the French line overwhelmed its passengers with the pretense and self-conscious chic of Art Deco; the Italians were probably the most successful, giving their new liners handsome, rakish lines without affectation, and bringing a distinctly Mediterranean flavor to their interiors. The German twins and the French *Normandie* were praised among the self-proclaimed "smart set" of the day, and appealed to the sort of frantic, self-promoting minority that always fears not being seen to be part of the cutting edge of a new trend. However, it was instructive of the tastes and preferences of the overwhelming majority of the traveling public that, after the *Queen Mary*, the most popular ships of the day were the *Rex* and the *Conte di Savoia*.

The First Class Smoking Room of the Queen Mary.

This was the most telling indicator of how clearly the *Queen Mary* established her supremacy over her closest—and only—rival, the *Normandie*: passengers of all nationalities, save, predictably, the French, heavily favored the British ship. The *Normandie* rarely sailed with a full booking of passengers, while the *Mary* frequently had a waiting list. In 1937, her first full year of service, the *Queen Mary* carried 56,895 passengers, almost twice the number carried by the *Normandie* that year. While it was probably inevitable that the British aristocracy would prefer the *Mary* over the *Normandie*, it did take the French by surprise when ordinary businessmen and American tourists passed on their fashionable, trendy ship with its cold, pretentious interiors to book passage on the *Queen Mary* instead. Obviously, despite what the critics thought, the unique combination of traditional decor with touches of Art Deco produced a far more welcoming and comfortable atmosphere for everyone aboard.

In the *Queen Mary*, Cunard possessed a ship that combined tradition and innovation in a way that brought out the best in both. Tradition has had a stronger influence, both positive and negative, on British society than on possibly any other in the world. Nowhere was that influence more strongly felt than on British ships: several classes of British battleships in the late 19th and early 20th centuries, for example, had the officers' quarters stationed at the extreme stern of the ship, probably the single most uncomfortable spot on the whole vessel, simply because that was where officers' quarters in sailing vessels had traditionally be placed.

In the last half of the 1930s, the *Queen Mary*'s primary running mate was the old

Aquitania, the last of the four-funneled liners and the last British liner to actually enter service before the Great War began. With her straight up-and-down stem, counter stern, fussy superstructure, busy—almost cluttered—upper decks, and quartet of tall stovepipe funnels, each with its octet of round, cowl-shaped ventilators clustered at its base, she was the epitome of the traditional British ocean liner. The *Queen Elizabeth*, when she eventually entered service, would sport a raked stem and cruiser stern, an astonishingly clean superstructure, clear, open upper decks, and a pair of massive oval funnels, with their intakes built into their bases, eliminating the need for ventilators at all. The *Aquitania*'s interiors were dim, heavy with dark wood paneling, overstuffed leather chairs and settees, leaded glass and elaborate carvings. The *Elizabeth*'s would be open and airy, bright with polished metals, etched glass and lightly tinted veneers. The two ships were a generation and a world apart.

The *Queen Mary* somehow bridged this gap, and in doing so became the best-loved ship ever to sail the North Atlantic. She had her problems, of course: she rolled, and rolled heavily, in anything more than a moderate seaway, breaking several fortunes' worth of crockery in her lifetime. But there was something in her lines that harked back to the tradition of the *Aquitania*, while it looked forward to the future of the *Queen Elizabeth*; how her interiors embraced the Art Deco style without becoming enslaved to it; the way her funnels echoed but didn't copy the profile of the *Aquitania*, and served as the models for those of the *Elizabeth*; the lines of her superstructure foreshadowed the clean sweep of the *Elizabeth*, while her upperworks still hinted at the same fussiness and clutter of the *Aquitania*. She was unique in that, unlike any other ship afloat, she spanned the lost era of elegance and the new era of modernism.

Probably nothing sums up this apparent contradiction, nor demonstrates how well it worked in practice, than does something as mundane as the flooring used on the decks of the *Queen Mary*'s public arcades, lounges, and passageways. A unique linoleum-like material called "Korkoid" was laid down, each room being given a distinctive, stylish pattern. Daily, these floors were buffed to a mirror-like shine, but rather than make a great show of this new material and draw the passengers' attention to its newness and novelty, as would have been done on one of the French or German liners, parts of the decking would then be covered with large woven oriental rugs or area carpets, similar to the treatments given to hardwood floors ashore. This sort of homeliness, while lacking any appeal to the critics, was attractive to passengers, who felt comfortable with such familiar touches.

It was this atmosphere, at once relaxing and exciting, that made the *Queen Mary* the toast of the North Atlantic, and assured a waiting list for almost every crossing she made. So successful was she that Cunard was actually able to pay installments in advance on the loan the government had made for the construction of the two *Queens*. While the nature of the passenger trade on the North Atlantic had changed beyond all recognition from what it had been before the Great War, it had become as profitable as ever.

That there *were* passengers aboard was due to a remarkable rise in the number of peo-

RMS Queen Mary—*King George V called her "the stateliest ship afloat."*

ple who were crossing the Atlantic in all classes. After having declined steadily—and sometimes plummeting—for five years, in 1935 the number of passengers the steamship lines carried to and from the New World and the Old actually began to rise. The economies of Europe and the United States had begun to recover from the worst depredations of the Great Depression, though by no means had they returned to their pre-Crash prosperity. At the same time, one of the realities of the Cunard-White Star merger began to assert itself: the new company simply had too many ships. Cunard already had fifteen liners and White Star had ten when the merger went through. It was time to start retiring the oldest ships, as well as those that were perpetually losing money.

One of the first to go was, sadly, the *Mauretania*. Departing New York for the final time on September 26, 1934, ironically the same day that the *Queen Mary* was launched, her passing would become almost a national rite of mourning in Great Britain. While there was a strong element of nostalgia in the sentiment, especially in that so many of those mourning had never even seen her, let alone sailed on her, there was a genuine sense of loss among officers, crew, and those passengers who had been regulars on the grand old ship.

"Legendary" is an adjective that is badly overused in reference to steamships, but in the case of the *Mauretania* it was unquestionably deserved. Her astonishing run as the Blue Ribband holder for twenty-two years of active service would have been sufficient to qualify her as "legendary": no other ship would ever come close to matching that accomplishment. But the genuine affection that she generated among her officers and crew, not to mention her passengers, would rarely be equaled and never surpassed. It was as if Franklin

Roosevelt's observation, that "if ever there were a ship which possessed the thing called 'soul,' the *Mauretania* did," had become fact.

Her last years, it must be said, had not been as happy as her earlier career. As Cunard struggled to make ends meet in the early 1930s, she had been variously consigned to duties on the "Booze Cruise" circuit and in the West Indies as a tropical cruise ship, service for which she was particularly unsuited. Yet even there, her magic never quite deserted her. The story is told of how each time her unmistakable profile would steam past one particular insignificant scrap of an island over which the French claimed sovereignty and on which they had posted a small colonial station, she would be challenged with the signal, "What ship are you?" Without fail, and with devastating aplomb, the *Mauretania* would respond, "What island are you?" The story may be apocryphal, but somehow, given that the French insist on being French, it has the ring of truth to it. But eventually it had to end: there was little else Cunard could do—the company was desperately trying to make or save every honest pound or dollar it could. In her decline she began to suffer the malady that afflicts every aging ship sooner or later, electrical fires, while on her hull and superstructure patches of rust had taken hold that even the most dedicated efforts with scrapper and paintbrush could not overcome. But what never gave out, or even faltered in the slightest, was her heart—those magnificent, revolutionary turbines that had driven her across the Atlantic as no other ship had ever been driven before.

After being tied up at Southampton's Berth 108 on the far west end of the waterfront, in April 1935 an auction was held a month later and the *Mauretania*'s fittings and interiors sold off. Ordinarily these events attracted little attention outside the ranks of interior decorators, but in this instance hundreds of buyers showed up, ready to purchase anything that wasn't riveted in place. The end finally came on July 1, when she left Southampton bound for the Firth of Forth. When she arrived at Thomas Ward, the breakers' yard in Rosyth, she was met by a piper in full Highland regalia, and as "Finished with Engines" was rung down on her bridge telegraph for the last time, he played "Flowers of the Forest," the traditional Scottish lament for those who have departed this world. It was the end of an era.

Time ran out for the *Olympic* as well. During the 1920s she had been the most popular of all the ships of the White Star Line, hinting at what might have been had the *Titanic* and *Britannic* not been struck down. During the Great War, she served as a troopship and even rammed and sank the *U-103* in May 1918. When peacetime returned and she went back into passenger service, so regular were her crossing times and so dependable had she become that she was affectionately dubbed "Old Reliable." But by 1934, bad luck began to plague her. On some of her crossings she carried as few as five hundred passengers, consequently running up huge operating deficits. A series of minor electrical fires signified that her wiring was beginning to develop faults, and sometimes interfered with her sailing schedule, never a good sign for an older ship. The decision to take the *Olympic* out of service came in May 1934, after she rammed and sank the Nantucket lightship in a fogbank, killing all seven crewmen aboard that hapless vessel. Withdrawn immediately after the accident, she was broken up in 1935, with many of her interior fixtures and decorations sold at auction and finding their way into houses and pubs in Liverpool, Southampton, and London.

The *Majestic* followed shortly after that, as did all of White Star's pre-war fleet: the *Adriatic* (her sisters *Baltic* and *Cedric* had been scrapped by White Star in 1932), the *Doric*, *Albertic*, and *Calgaric*. In better times the handsome *Homeric*, originally built for Norddeutscher-Lloyd and only taken into service in 1921, might have survived, but her operating costs were considered to be too high, and so she went to the breakers as well. Only the relatively new motor-ships *Georgic* and *Britannic* were retained in the revamped Cunard-White Star fleet.

In a few years, these discarded ships would be followed by the *Berengaria*. Never the happiest ship in the Cunard fleet, ill-luck seemed to follow her. Twice during the early 1930s she went aground coming up the Solent to Southampton, and although she suffered no significant damage, a cloud began to gather over her. She underwent a major renovation in 1933, with particular attention paid to upgrading her interiors, and in 1934 and 1935 she actually had some of her most profitable crossings. She also had some remarkable memories about her, the most notable being the night in the early 1930s when she was tied up in Southampton and thought to be all but deserted. Suddenly Captain Thelwell, standing watch on the bridge, heard ragtime coming from the ballroom. When he made his way down there he was greeted by the sight of a jazz band called the Blackbirds playing in time to the beat conducted by the Prince of Wales, who would soon become King Edward VIII, and then later the Duke of Windsor. When His Royal Highness had finished, thanked the band, and assured them that cheques would be sent to them in the morning (they were), the officer respectfully inquired of the Prince just what had been going on. "It was very convenient, of course," the Prince explained, "and—well I thought we shouldn't be disturbed.... Sometimes, you know, it's very hard to find a place where you can be alone." It was an illuminating moment: posterity hasn't always treated the memory of the Duke of Windsor well, and to those who knew him, the incident spoke volumes about his almost painful shyness, and how inadequate and unprepared he felt for the role thrust upon him by his birth. He would come to have a long-standing relationship with Cunard, and fortunately for him and the line, it was always a happy one.

But for the *Berengaria*, as it had for the *Olympic* and *Mauretania*, time had run out. In 1936, a fire broke out in the First Class cabins on the starboard side of the ship during an overhaul at Southampton. The fire was quickly brought under control, but not before it had caused considerable smoke and water damage. The cause of the fire was determined to be defective wiring, the bane of many an older ship. It would ultimately prove the *Berengaria*'s undoing, as over the next two years she suffered an increasing frequency of small, but annoying electrical fires.

The end came in March 1938. After she had arrived in New York on March 3, a fire sprang up in the First Class lounge that took the crew and a gang of firemen brought over from the pier, more than three hours to bring under control. Again faulty wiring was the culprit. New York Port Authority officials inspected the ship immediately afterwards and decided on the spot that they could not give her a sailing clearance to carry passengers. The next day she sailed back to Southampton on what would prove to be her final Atlantic crossing.

Once back in her home port, she was inspected again, this time by Cunard officials, who determined that the cost of renovating her electrical system was prohibitive given the *Berengaria*'s age, so on March 23, 1938, it was decided to take her out of service altogether. She lay idle in Southampton until her furniture and fittings were auctioned off in January 1939. She was then towed to Jarrow on Scotland's North Sea coast where she was gradually dismantled over the next seven years. Of the pre-war giants in White Star's and Cunard's fleets, only the *Aquitania* remained, and she was already slated for retirement in 1940, when the *Queen Mary*'s new consort would go into service.

Over the years, much has been said and written about how some, or all of these ships were retired too early, before their usefulness had truly been used up; other critics have commented on the apparent ruthlessness with which Cunard disposed of the White Star fleet once the merger became a fact: some have attributed it to a sort of corporate vindictiveness, a chance to eliminate the last vestiges of a hated rival. Nothing could be further from the truth. In point of fact, all of the ships that Cunard sent to the breakers were too old, slow, or expensive to operate. Almost of them were essentially pre-war construction; certainly all of them were of prewar design. Their passenger accommodations were no longer adequate to the demands of the transatlantic traveler, while their technologies were badly outdated; hull forms, boiler design, turbine construction, all had made tremendous advances in the past twenty years, and in doing so they had made the grand old dames of the North Atlantic obsolete. While some passengers might have wished to see them remain in service out of sentimental attachment, sentimentality could not pay crew wages or fuel costs. The ships that were eliminated may have been beautiful, but they were hopelessly out of date.

Yet even while these venerable old ships were passing away, passenger lists were growing again, and as revenues increased Cunard found itself in the enviable position of having to consider adding new ships to the fleet, and expanding its transatlantic service even further by reviving the moribund London to New York route. Plans were drawn up for the addition of a handful of smaller liners, all of them at around 35,000 tons, slightly less than half the size of the *Queens*. These would replace the aging prewar ships that Cunard had discarded, as well as the retired White Star fleet. The first of these new ships—and as events turned out, the only one completed before war once again swept across Europe—was the second *Mauretania*, built by Cammel Laird and launched on July 28, 1937. She was a handsome ship with a long, open foredeck, rounded bridge face, and a superstructure that was nicely balanced with her hull, topped by two large, but not oversized funnels, that gave her a profile which bore more than a passing resemblance to the forthcoming *Queen Elizabeth*—in fact the new *Mauretania* would look very much like a smaller version of the

The second Mauretania, *seen here in tropical cruising colors.*

newest *Queen*. It was also a look that demonstrated how well Cunard's designers had mastered the ability to strike that balance between the traditional and the fashionable. Despite her name, the new *Mauretania* would be no record breaker—her designed speed was just over 23 knots, but she was comfortable and popular, with room for fourteen hundred passengers—"guests" in the new parlance of the North Atlantic—in three classes. Her maiden voyage came on June 17, 1939, when she sailed with a full passenger list. The praise for the new ship when she arrived in New York was unanimous, proving that despite the recent hard times, the Cunard magic was back.

By the end of 1937, while the new *Mauretania* was fitting out, the still growing number of passengers on the North Atlantic showed every sign of being a permanent revival of the trade, and so Cunard decided that the time was right to avail itself of that £5,000,000 that Parliament had earmarked for the construction of a sister ship for the *Queen Mary*. Everything that the line had learned from the experiences of the *Mary*, the *Normandie*, and the German and Italian ships, would be incorporated into the new design. The announcement was made that the new ship would be built in the same yard as the *Mary*, John Brown and Sons, Ltd. Her name was to be the *Queen Elizabeth*.

While the *Elizabeth* was often referred to as being the *Mary*'s sister ship, it's probably more correct to refer to her as the *Queen Mary*'s running mate, for while there were many similarities between them, they weren't built from the same original design. Cunard hadn't ignored the *Normandie*, but had carefully noted that the public clearly preferred the *Queen Mary*'s more conservative atmosphere over the artistic pretensions of the French ship, and decided to work the best aspects of traditional British shipbuilding into the *Queen Elizabeth* while adopting many of the Gallic ship's better features. The most immediate difference between the two *Queens* was in their appearance: from the *Elizabeth*'s more sharply raked bow, to the far fewer vents and cowls on her upper decks, to the reduction of the number of funnels from three to two, the *Elizabeth* was distinctive.

She was also slightly larger than the *Queen Mary*. Her length was 1,031 feet, while her beam (118 feet) and deep draught (39 feet) were the same as the earlier ship. Her displacement of 83,673 gross tons made her the world's largest passenger ship, a distinction she would hold for sixty years. Her power plant was almost identical to that of the *Queen Mary*, though it never quite matched the older ship in total power output, and like the *Mary*, she had four sets of Parsons turbines driving four screws. Her designed service speed was 28.5 knots, which she would easily surpass—in practice she would prove to be almost, but not quite, as fast as the *Queen Mary*. She was designed to carry 2,283 people with a crew complement of 1,100.

The *Queen Elizabeth*'s keel was laid on October 6, 1936 and work on her was given absolute priority at the John Brown yard. So important was this new project considered (she was given the hull number 552, but unlike the *Mary* was never known by it) that work on her hull went on around the clock, something almost unheard of among British shipbuilders in peacetime. But as the *Queen Elizabeth* grew, so did a sense of unease that slowly covered all of Great Britain. Although most Britons thought of Adolf Hitler as hardly more than an ill-educated, ill-mannered little man with a ridiculous moustache and an over-inflated sense of his own importance, events were unfolding across Europe that suggested that this coarse little person, loud mouth, bad cowlick and all, was actually a rather dangerous fellow. He might be readily lampooned, but dismissing him was not so easily done. Hitler's announcement that Germany would repudiate the terms of the Treaty of Versailles in 1935, followed a year later by the reoccupation of the Rhineland, had alarmed some Britons, while many others regarded them as acts of redress against a far too punitive peace. There was a certain amount of truth in that idea, but what gradually became more and more disturbing to the British people was that righting old wrongs didn't seem to be sufficiently satisfactory to the German *Führer*. His requests evolved into demands, and were presented with a temerity—even insolence—that would have made even the most arrogant of the old Imperial German diplomats blush. Though the British Government, personified in the Prime Minister, Neville Chamberlain, tried it's best to placate and satisfy Hitler (Chamberlain's name for this policy was "appeasement") it began to dawn on the British people, (though the Prime Minister was never to share in this enlightenment) that the real "Mr. Hitler," as Chamberlain referred to him, was a far cry from the figure of caricature and mockery seen in the music halls. Instead, he was a very frightening individual: here was a man who wanted, indeed craved, a war. More frightening still, he possessed the means of waging one, whether his neighbors were willing or not. Less than two decades had passed since the end of "The War to End All Wars," and the man who was the absolute dictator of a rapidly re-arming Germany, whose mental and emotional stability were questionable, who in another time and place would have been dismissed as simply a sore loser with delusions of grandeur, was preparing to fight the whole thing over again. It was a terrifying thought.

But it was not a thought that the new Queen choose to dwell upon. King George VI came to the throne following the death of George V in 1936 and the brief interregnum of Edward VIII. When the *Queen Elizabeth* was ready to be launched on September 27, 1938, Cunard White Star requested the presence of the Royal couple and George VI adopted the same protocol as his father: his wife, Elizabeth, would actually launch the ship. With the graciousness that would mark her whole life, Queen Elizabeth chose to speak of peace instead of war. As she prepared to break the bottle of champagne against the ship's bow, sending her on down the ways, she declared to a listening world, "We proclaim our belief, that by the grace of God, and by Man's patience and good will, order may yet be brought out of confusion, and peace out of turmoil. With that hopeful cry in our heart, we send forth upon her mission this noble ship." Barely more than a minute later, the *Queen Elizabeth* was floating high and proud in the River Clyde, and was quickly towed to the fitting out basin. But the threat of war loomed over the shipyard, for despite Neville Chamberlain's triumphant return from Munich three days after the *Queen Elizabeth*'s launch, declaring "Peace in our time!" the triumph soon soured and Britain began to look to her defenses. The needs of the Royal Navy took precedence in every shipyard in the country, and work on the *Queen Elizabeth* was slowed as manpower and materials were allotted to the warships awaiting refits and modernization that began to queue up along the banks of the Clyde.

Though the war clouds were clearly gathering over Europe in the months following her launch, the *Queen Elizabeth*'s completion was given absolute priority at the John Brown yard, and workers continued to labor on her around the clock. There was always a chance that war could be averted, and Cunard still had hopes of making a reality of its plan for a two-ship transatlantic service, so the Line and the shipyard were putting their best efforts in her. By being the first ship to exceed a thousand feet in length and eighty thousand tons displacement, the *Queen Mary* had been called "the inevitable ship"—the *Queen Elizabeth*, in turn, being longer and larger than her consort, as well as the French Line's *Normandie*—was soon dubbed "the ultimate ship."

Certainly, she was an engineering marvel: over 7,000 experiments using scale models in a test tank were conducted before the final shape of her hull was determined. In their travels from one end of the tank to the other, these models traveled over 1000 miles, as each configuration was studied to find the optimum combination of resistance, flow, and wake form. In her construction, over 10,000,000 rivets were used. Her power plant was similar to the *Queen Mary*'s, consisting of four sets of single reduction geared turbines capable of developing 160,000 horsepower. Each one of the 257,000 individual blades on each turbine (there were a total of eight—one forward and one reverse on each shaft) was tested and fitted by hand. The ships' four manganese-bronze propellers were each machined from a single casting and weighed thirty-two tons apiece.

Differences in appearance as well as similarities between the two *Queens* were immediately noticeable. The *Elizabeth* was distinctive with her more sharply raked bow, which flared into a long, unbroken, flush main deck, eliminating the small well deck forward of the *Mary*'s superstructure. Her upper works were less crowded with ventilator cowls (of which, in fact, there were very few) or deck houses, instead offering long expanses of open deck space for the passengers. The huge air intakes for the boilers and engine room vents were carefully worked into the superstructure, a styling cue that had been adopted from the *Normandie*. But the *Elizabeth*'s designers went the *Normandie* one better, reducing the number of funnels from three to two, creating even more deck space. Overall, her cleaner lines and thrusting bow gave the *Elizabeth* the appearance of a fast ship, which she was, although ultimately, the *Mary* would prove to be slightly faster.

Even though the three ships were almost exactly the same size, the impressions their individual appearance made was quite different. The *Queen Mary* was the most traditional, big and powerful, four-square looking, imposing from any angle; the *Normandie*, with the elliptical lines of her superstructure, strangely short foredeck, and oddly outdated counter stern could, in turn, appear yacht-like from one angle, squat and dumpy from another. The *Queen Elizabeth* was perhaps the most beautiful of the three: the long foredeck, unusually clean superstructure and sweeping lines of her hull and upper works created a sense of grace and power that no other liner ever matched, before or since.

Her interiors were somewhat different from the *Queen Mary*'s as well, again reflecting a certain amount of influence exerted by the *Normandie*. While never abandoning the "English country home" atmosphere that had been the hallmark of British passenger liners for more than a half-century, the *Queen Elizabeth* designers did shy away from the walnut and mahogany of the *Mary* in favor of lighter woods. For example, the main lounge was paneled with a veneer of Canadian maple burl, which had a warm beige-pink tone, and highlighted it by mixing it with panels of light blue, pale grey, and beige leather. The Captain's cabin in particular received a special treatment. The paneling was literally unique: the wood had been taken from Rock elm piling that had been driven in the Thames River for the original Waterloo Bridge in 1911, and removed in 1936 when the bridge was replaced. The waters of the river had worked a chemical reaction on the wood, creating a subtle, handsome shade of light grey that could be found nowhere else in the world. Art Deco motifs were found throughout the ship, though not with the stridency that they sometimes confronted the *Normandie*'s passengers. One particularly graceful theme carried throughout the ship echoed the way the *Queen Mary*'s designers had acknowledged, rather than concealing the fact that she was a ship: motifs and panels in staircases, over fireplaces and along the *Elizabeth*'s passageways were variously made from steel, copper, bronze, white metal, aluminium, lead, and glass—all materials used in the construction of the ship. It was an aesthetic tour-de-force that would never be equaled.

At least that was the vision the designers had for the *Elizabeth*, and thankfully it would one day be realized, but the likelihood that it would accomplished in the near future began to fade almost as soon as she was launched. Despite the joy and celebration that marked the launch of the *Queen Elizabeth* on September 27, 1938, and the enthusiasm that the workers were putting into her completion, a growing air of foreboding was spreading over Great Britain. The Munich Crisis had passed, war being narrowly averted when British Prime Minister Neville Chamberlain and French President Edouard Daladier sold Czechoslovakia down the river to a gleeful Adolf Hitler, but an awareness was growing among the British people that all was not right in Europe, and that the price paid by their Prime Minister was probably too steep. They were right: though Chamberlain had declared that the Munich Agreement had brought Europe "Peace in our time," within six months of its signing, Hitler had trampled all over the accord. Belatedly, Britain began to look to her defenses, and refitting and modernizing the ships of the Royal Navy became a growing priority in every British shipyard.

Consequently, the focus of the work at the John Brown yard began to shift away from the *Queen Elizabeth* as work gangs were reassigned to military jobs. Starved of funding for new ships by the skin-flint (parsimonious is too kind a word) Governments of Stanley Baldwin and Neville Chamberlain, the Royal Navy was forced to increase its numbers of active warships by drawing out of Reserve a large number of worn and aging—and in some cases antiquated—ships, mostly of First World War vintage, modernize them as best it could, and send them out to the Fleet. Sometimes this meant simply upgrading or modifying a ship's armament and equipment, which was fairly easily accomplished. Other times it meant extensive reconstruction to a ship's hull or superstructure, always a long and often difficult process—usually the task was somewhere in between the two. In any case, it became clearer with each passing month that the *Queen Elizabeth* was most likely going to become an expensive luxury, and though the work on her never stopped, the number of work gangs dwindled weekly as the Royal Navy demanded more and more of John Brown's resources.

One of the reasons for this was the newly-launched battleship, *Duke of York*. A 35,000 ton behemoth armed with ten 14-inch guns and a battery of sixteen 5.25-inch anti-aircraft guns, she was one of the most modern battleships in the world, and was being readied to take her place with the Royal Navy's Home Fleet at Scapa Flow. A decision would have to be made, and made quickly, as to which of the two—*Queen* or *Duke*—was to be finished first.

The whole issue became moot, of course, when Hitler's *Wehrmacht* smashed into Poland on September 1, 1939. Neville Chamberlain suddenly discovered a backbone no one suspected he had (he was soon to lose it again) and honored Great Britain's alliance with the Poles, issuing an ultimatum to Germany to withdraw from Polish soil within forty-eight hours or face war with the British. Hitler ignored the ultimatum (he felt he had the measure of Chamberlain and the British people—he was right about the first and fatally, for him, wrong about the second) and for the second time in two decades, war swept across the Continent. Now, more than ever, it was the worst of times.

CHAPTER THIRTEEN

The Second World War

On August 30, 1939, the *Queen Mary* had left Southampton for New York, carrying a record number of 2,332 passengers, on what would be her last commercial voyage for the next eight years. When, four days after her departure, she received the chilling but not entirely unexpected news that Great Britain was once again at war with Germany, her captain, acting on the orders of the First Lord of the Admiralty, Winston Churchill, laid out an impromptu zigzag course and steamed a hundred miles south of the standard shipping lane in order to allow the liner to avoid any German U-boats that might be lying in wait for her. Meanwhile, stewards hastily rigged blackout curtains throughout the ship and checked the readiness of her lifeboats, providing the *Queen Mary*'s passengers with an adventure they never expected.

Once she safely reached New York, the *Mary* was ordered to remain there—the Admiralty wasn't willing to take the chance of bringing her back to Britain just yet. She was berthed alongside the French liner *Normandie*, which likewise had been sent to the United States for safety, but unlike the French ship whose future was uncertain, there were definite plans for the *Queen Mary*—she was going to war.

That the danger to the *Queen Mary* had been real was revealed for all the world to see, along with the true nature of the foe confronting the British Empire, the same day that war was declared. At 7:45 in the evening of September 3, the *U-30*, lurking some 250 miles off the Irish coast, spotted the liner *Athenia*. The submarine's commander, Leutnant Julius Lemp, tracked her, and despite the fact that he had identified her as a passenger ship before he gave the order to fire, put two torpedoes into her side. Among the 112 dead were twenty-eight Americans. Two British destroyers and a Swedish yacht picked up the survivors, officers and crew aboard all three later signing affidavits stating that the *U-30* had surfaced and circled the sinking *Athenia* twice without offering any assistance. The *Athenia* was the first, but not the last passenger ship to be lost in the great conflict to come.

The world had expected the war to be a reprise of the high drama of the autumn of 1914, when French and British troops, fighting shoulder-to-shoulder, first stopped and then turned back the German invader. What it got was something far different. The Germans, not yet ready to attack in the West, overran Poland and then bided their time. France, long on brave words and short on action, fell into a timorousness that would be her trademark for the rest of the century, refusing to take action for fear of German reprisals. And despite the growing belligerence of the British people, Neville Chamberlain was still deluded by the hope that Hitler would negotiate a fair and lasting settlement. The result was an early flurry of bold words between Germany and the Allies, soon replaced by a dull routine popularly dubbed the "Bore War".

Winston Churchill had returned to the Admiralty as First Lord on the same day that Britain declared war on Germany, and he was painfully aware that regardless of whatever happened on land, the war at sea was going to brutal, bitter, and ultimately decisive. In 1939 the Royal Navy was far from the "somnolent service" Churchill had discovered it to be in 1911—the problem was that it was being stretched to near the breaking point by its responsibilities. Churchill, though, had confidence in the men he was to lead, and they had confidence in him: when word of his appointment as First Lord was announced, the signal was flashed throughout the fleet, "WINSTON IS BACK!" The morale of the officers and ratings was good, their competence unquestioned, their dedication unchallenged. The problem faced by the Royal Navy was not with its human elements, but rather with its ships.

While supremacy of the Home Fleet's capital ships would never be seriously challenged during the whole course of the war, in 1939 the gravest danger lay in the lack of lighter units, particularly light cruisers and destroyers, the ships that would be required to escort and protect the convoys on which Britain's survival would depend. Even as it was drawing heavily on the reserve fleet, the Royal Navy was hard pressed to provide adequate protection for all of its charges. Within days of war being declared, the "pocket battleship" *Deutschland* was prowling the Western Approaches, the waters to the north and west of Scotland's Western Isles, while her sister ship, *Graf Spee*, was patrolling the South Atlantic, threatening the sea lanes that tied Great Britain to South Africa, India and South America. In the great German naval base at Kiel, *Scharnhorst* and *Gneisenau*, a pair of battleships masquerading as battlecruisers, were preparing to put to sea. And even though Admiral Karl Doenitz, the commander of Germany's U-boat fleet, possessed only a fraction of the U-boats he felt would be required to wage a successful submarine war against Great Britain, he had every submarine he could muster infesting the waters surrounding the British Isles, and they were soon taking a heavy toll on British shipping. Just as dangerous were the swift raids of the squadrons of torpedo craft— *Schnellbooten,* or S-boats (the Allies knew them as E-boats)— that would strike hard at the British shipping that had to steam down the North Sea or up the English Channel to reach the Thames Estuary and the Port of London.

Every destroyer, every light cruiser that was seaworthy, or could be made seaworthy, was pressed into action. Consequently, the shipyards of the River Clyde were desperately needed to refurbish the older ships drawn out of reserve, build new ships for the Royal Navy, and allow bomb and torpedo damaged merchantmen and warships to be repaired, so work on the *Queen Elizabeth* stopped entirely, and she sat idle at her fitting-out basin— a large dry dock—at the John Brown yard.

For Cunard, Britain's declaration of war meant yet another call to the colours. Within days of Britain going to war, several of the smaller ships—the "Intermediates" that had proven so popular in the 1920s—were requisitioned as either troopships or Armed Merchant Cruisers, and it certainly didn't require a crystal ball to see that the Royal Navy would be needing even more ships in the future. The company's biggest concern was the safety of their quartet of large liners, the new *Mauretania*, the grand old *Aquitania*, the awesome *Queen Mary*, and of course, the as-yet-unfinished *Queen Elizabeth*. With the *Berengaria* and *Majestic* gone, these were the four largest ships in the British Merchant Navy—fat targets for German submarines, but vital hulls for Britain's war effort. With the *Queen Mary* safely on her way to New York when the war broke out, Cunard quickly sent the *Aquitania* and the new *Mauretania* packing off to join her, and then turned its attention to the knotty problem of what to do with the *Queen Elizabeth*.

Clearly, the need for a new passenger liner was long past, and completing any more work on her would mean diverting time, materials, and workers from badly needed warships. And while scrapping her might be a painful, even wrenching, task for the Scottish shipwrights who built her, the strategic value of the thousands of tons of steel in her hull was undeniable. On the other hand, it seemed that *something* could be done with her—the Elizabeth's boilers and engines were complete and most of her superstructure finished, including her two funnels, though she was still a long way from being ready for sea.

The fate of the *Queen Elizabeth* was left in the hands of the Admiralty—Cunard could not do anything with her at this point. Much of Cunard White Star's fleet had already been requisitioned for service with the Royal Navy, and most of the line's officers—who were Royal Naval Reserve—were already in service with the Navy, while almost all of the company's administrative staff were busy coordinating the movements of their ships to meet the needs of the Royal Navy. Heated debates took place at the highest levels of the British Government over how the liner could best serve the needs of the Empire. The Germans wouldn't ignore her forever, no matter how phony the Phony War seemed to be. Some serious thought was given to the idea that the *Queen Elizabeth* should be sold to the United States in her unfinished state in exchange for war supplies. With the shipyards along the River Clyde desperately needed for the warships of the Royal Navy, work on the *Queen Elizabeth* had been halted: completing her would mean diverting time, materials, and workers from those warships, and so she was left to wait at her fitting-out basin, her very existence a threat to her survival. She became an obvious target for the *Luftwaffe*, as the German bombers struck hard at Britain's shipyards. The Royal Navy tried to envision a role in which she could best serve the needs of the Empire and various plans were put forward. At one point there was some talk of cutting away her superstructure and converting her into an aircraft carrier, but although a few design studies were begun to test the feasibility of the idea, no actual work on such a conversion was ever put in hand.

Finally, common sense prevailed and Churchill, at this time still First Lord of the Admiralty, decided that the *Queen Elizabeth* would be best employed as a troopship, and on November 2, 1939, the Ministry of Shipping issued urgent orders to complete the work necessary to make the liner ready for sea. Workers once again swarmed over the liner, finishing what was determined to be the essential work. It is interesting to note that, in what was defined as essential and what wasn't, the *Elizabeth* would sail with part of her launching cradle still attached to her bow. All of the navigational systems were installed, but all of the working up, testing, and corrections that would normally have been part of the *Queen Elizabeth*'s sea trials would have to be done on one mad dash to safety. In a sort of silent acknowledgment of what might happen, all of the lifesaving equipment—including a full complement of lifeboats—-was installed, and most important, the power plant was completed in all respects. Inside she might be little more than a big empty space, but she would go to sea as a proper ship.

There was no way that the preparations for the *Elizabeth*'s movement could be concealed, but if the British couldn't hide the fact that the *Queen Elizabeth* was getting ready to put to sea, they could mislead the Germans about her destination. A carefully detailed cover story was worked out to keep the Germans and their agents looking in the wrong direction: word was leaked out that the *Queen Elizabeth* would be taken to Southampton to finish her fitting out. Elaborate, but false preparations for her arrival were made—crates with furnishings and fixtures for the *Elizabeth*'s interior were delivered to Southampton, carefully worked-out docking plans for her mooring were drawn up, and orders were placed for foodstuffs and supplies, with just the right amount of secrecy to keep the Germans from suspecting a ruse. That the Germans swallowed the tale hook, line, and sinker was proven by the swarms of *Luftwaffe* bombers which appeared over Southampton on the afternoon of March 3, the earliest that the *Queen Elizabeth* could have arrived, and every day for the next three days—until the Germans realized they had been had.

February 26 dawned gray and bleak, with threat of rain, typical weather for a Scottish winter, and perfect for moving the *Queen Elizabeth* unobserved by German reconnaissance planes. The crew aboard *Queen Elizabeth* were told the day of sailing that a secret and dangerous mission was soon to come, and the opportunity to leave the ship was granted: all but thirty of the 428 crewmen chose to stay aboard. (As events turned out, they may have regretted not making the crossing, as the crewmen who did were paid an extra £30 "inconvenience money" in addition to their regular wages!)

On the morning of March 2, 1940, the *Queen Elizabeth* sat in the mouth of the Firth of Clyde where she had conducted a series of engine and compass trials after a tense but uneventful passage down the Clyde. A King's Messenger stepped onto the bridge with a set of sealed sailing orders, and within minutes, the *Elizabeth* was underway, accompanied by an escort of four destroyers and an umbrella of aircraft. Ten hours later, when the flotilla was two hundred miles past of the Western Isles, the destroyers and aircraft departed in a flurry of lamp signals wishing the *Queen Elizabeth* "Good Luck!" leaving the liner on her own. She was to make for New York.

The *Queen Elizabeth* had three factors offering her protection against German submarine or surface attack: her speed and maneuverability, the secrecy surrounding her departure, and the bad weather. Always dreadful in mid-winter on the North Atlantic, the weather was windy, filled with squalls and heavy seas, and made for poor visibility, which drastically reduced the chances of any German warship spotting the liner. The ship maintained strict radio silence, while the British worked hard to maintain the deception that she was actually bound for Southampton. Even the Cunard officials in New York were unaware that she was coming until the day before she was due to arrive, kept in the dark by the Admiralty.

On the morning of May 7, a Trans World Airlines DC-3 flying forty miles east of Fire Island on its way into New York was astonished to see a huge grey ship zig-zagging furiously toward New York harbor. The *Queen Elizabeth's* dramatic, unannounced appearance created a sensation in New York. The *New York Post* captured the moment vividly:

As she slowly made her way up the river, she was accorded the tumultuous welcome befitting the most distinguished representative of maritime royalty ever to reach America's shores. Thousands of spectators thronged the windows and tops of West Side buildings. More than a dozen planes circled overhead and dipped time and time again in salute, while scores of tugboats churned the water on all sides of the great grey Majesty with whistles and sirens wide open. The waterfront personnel took to the piers en masse to watch her pass.

The *New York Times* called the *Queen Elizabeth* the "Empress Incognito," remarking that "Many sagas of the sea have begun and ended in our harbor, but can the old-timers remember anything to compare with the unheralded arrival of the biggest and fastest liner in the world, after the most daring of all maiden voyages?"

With the arrival of the *Queen Elizabeth* at Pier 90, the gathering of Cunard's four largest ships was complete. Alongside the *Elizabeth* was, of course, the *Queen Mary*, next to her was the *Mauretania*, which carried on the name of the great Blue Ribband holder, and the *Aquitania*, the last of the great four-funneled liners, and the only liner to serve in both World Wars. The future of the Cunard ships had already been decided—the *Aquitania* had already been requisitioned as a troop transport on 21 November 1939, and on March 1, 1940, His Majesty's Government had informed Cunard that the rest of the company's fleet was being requisitioned for the duration of the war for service with His Majesty's Armed Forces. American intelligence officers feared that German agents would plant bombs aboard the British ships to prevent them from being used by the Allies; consequently, armed guards patrolled their decks as well as the pier, while at night powerful searchlights kept them illuminated.

In *The Influence of Sea Power Upon History*, Captain Alfred Thayer Mahan described "sea power" as a nation's capacity to use the world's oceans to transport the flow of raw materials and finished goods necessary to sustain that nation's economy in peacetime, as well as transport troops and supplies in wartime, while simultaneously denying that capability to the enemy. No nation has so thoroughly understood or expertly executed that concept as Great Britain, to which the service of the ships of the Cunard Line gave proof throughout the

Painted in "Light Sea Grey" and dubbed "the Empress Incognito" by the New York Times, *the* Queen Elizabeth *enters New York Harbor after her daring secret dash across the Atlantic.*

war, being used to exercise sea power in ways that Britain's enemies could never effectively counter. What the Cunard fleet offered the Allies was the means of combining Mahan's theory with General Nathan Bedford Forrest's homely dictum for victory, "Gettin' there the firstest with the mostest." Though Britain's land and air forces were small compared to the huge numbers that Germany had mobilized, the resources of the Empire were still vast, and the manpower that the British could call upon from India, Australia and Canada could prove decisive. When the United States entered war in 1941, those resources became near-overwhelming. The challenge for Great Britain and the Allies would be to bring their immense strength to bear in the places where it would do the greatest damage to the enemy.

It's important to underscore one essential fact, one that is often overshadowed by the sheer volume of post-war German apologia and Soviet propaganda: the strategic key to the Second World War in Europe was the island kingdom of Great Britain. As long as she continued to resist Germany, Britain would serve as the base for the increasingly destructive Combined Bomber Offensive, allowing the Royal Air Force and the American Army Air Corps to attack key German industries, sap the strength of the *Luftwaffe*, and cause valuable resources to be diverted from new construction to rebuilding bomb-damaged factories and towns. Equally important was the continued British presence on the periphery of the Nazi empire, a constant threat that drew men, tanks, trucks and supplies away from the fighting fronts to defend vulnerable points along a perimeter that stretched from Narvik, above the Arctic Circle, down to the Mediterranean coast of North Africa. Most crucial of all, as long as Britain stood, she could serve as the staging ground for the Allied invasion of Western Europe, the Second Front, that would spell certain doom for Nazi Germany.

While it's true that most of Germany's manpower and the majority of her tanks and artillery were posted to the Russian Front, which in terms of sheer numbers was the largest war ever fought, Great Britain's continued defiance of Hitler meant that Germany never had the luxury of turning all of its resources against the Soviet Union. The men, vehicles, fuel, materiel, aircraft, artillery pieces and supplies that the Germans were forced to deploy in Norway, the Low Countries, France, Italy and even within Germany itself, were denied the over-stretched and exhausted *Wehrmacht* units on the Eastern Front. They were needed to either defend against an invasion which might come at any time, in any place, or to protect the Reich from the Allied bombers that everyone knew would come nearly every day and every night; it was Great Britain's belligerence that would make possible the huge Soviet victories at Stalingrad and Kursk, and the Red Army's crushing rout of the *Wehrmacht* in the summer of 1944.

Nor was it difficult for the strategists of the German high command to realize the potential threat that Great Britain posed to the Third Reich's hopes of victory, especially after December 1941. While the British Empire posed a threat to Nazi Germany, the manpower and industrial strength of the United States combined with Britain's strategic advantages could well prove fatal to those hopes. So it was that the German armed forces threw themselves into the Battle of the Atlantic with a fury rarely seen elsewhere in the war. The

North Atlantic was simultaneously the lifeline by which Britain survived, and to which the Allies brought their mounting offensive power to bear against the Axis, and was also the hunting ground of two of the Allies' always tenacious, often brilliant, and sometimes ruthless foes: the German Luftwaffe and the German *Kriegsmarine*.

There were several dangerous airplanes in the *Luftwaffe*'s arsenal, ranging from the Ju-87 Stuka divebomber to the Heinkel He-111 torpedo bomber, but strangely enough, the aircraft that was the most dangerous to the Allied convoys was never designed to be a war plane. The Focke-Wulf Fw-200 *Kondor* was a huge, four-engine aircraft that bore a more than passing resemblance to the Douglas DC-4. Originally built as an airliner, in 1937 it made headlines around the world by flying nonstop to several distant cities, including New York and Tokyo. These flights brought the aircraft to the attention of the *Luftwaffe*, and though there were initially no plans for the aircraft to be put to any military use, when the Germans suddenly realized in 1940 that it had no long-range reconnaissance aircraft capable of ranging out over the Atlantic, the obvious answer was the Fw 200C. A modification of the basic *Kondor* design was made that allowed it to carry a bomb load as well as cannon and machine guns for attacking shipping. Compared to British and American four-engine heavy bombers, the Fw 200C was a modest performer—hardly surprising since it was essentially only a lash-up and not a purpose-built aircraft. Only 278 were built in all.

The *Kondors* could range far out into the Atlantic and shadow convoys for hours, guiding German bombers, warships and submarines to the location of the hapless Allied merchant ships. These aircraft became such a fixture over the Atlantic convoys in the first three years of the war that communications between patrolling *Kondors* and the convoys

The enemy above: the Luftwaffe*'s Focke-Wulf 200c Kondor served as a long-range observation plane and bomber.*

they shadowed were not unknown: on more than one occasion the crew of a *Kondor* circling above a convoy bluntly asking it for its position—the reply invariably consisted of very precise set of longitude and latitude figures that placed the convoy firmly on the other side of the world. There were several variations of the story where a convoy signaled to the aircraft overhead, "Please circle the other way round, you are making us dizzy!"

In the simplest possible terms, the surface fleet of Hitler's *Kriegsmarine* (Navy) was an unmitigated failure. When the war began, nearly six years before the target for the completion of Admiral Raeder's "Z Plan," the numerical strength of the Royal Navy over the *Kriegsmarine* was nearly overwhelming. In 1939, the German navy possessed only a handful of modern ships: just three "pocket battleships" and two big battle cruisers. There were two battleships still building, that when finished would be bigger, faster, as heavily armed and armored as any ship in the British fleet, but neither would be completed before 1941. While it was arguable that ton for ton the German warships were superior to their British counterparts, the German Naval High Command seemed to have no real idea of what to do with them. Surface raiders like the *Admiral Hipper* or *Prinz Eugen*, with their main batteries of eight 8" guns and top speed of 32 knots, were always a threat to the Allied ships on the North Atlantic, and there were episodes like the chase of the *Bismarck* that gave the British quite a scare; the fact is that, in terms of its material effect on the war, the German surface fleet accomplished very little indeed.

That was, of course, in total contrast to the other arm of the *Kriegsmarine*, the U-boat fleet. The U-boat had nearly brought Great Britain to her knees in World War I. Admiral Karl Doenitz, the Commander-in-Chief (U-boats), envisaged eventually building a fleet of over three hundred submarines, which could deploy attack squadrons of fifteen to twenty submarines each—a concept that eventually evolved into the tactics of the "wolf packs"—which would decimate enemy convoys. When the war began in September 1939, Germany had just fifty-seven submarines, of which only twenty-two were fit for service in the Atlantic. Gradually the number of operational U-boats increased, but it was not until early 1942 that their numbers exceeded one hundred. Individual U-boats, however, operating with courage, skill and daring—and sometimes ruthlessness—made their mark from the first days of the war.

In the first four months of the war, 221 ships totaling more than 750,000 tons, were sunk by the U-boats. The period between July and October 1940 was even worse—known as the "Happy Time" for German submarines, it was during this time that the "wolf pack" tactics first began to be employed by the U-boats. An incredible toll of 217 ships were sunk and more then a million tons of shipping was exacted from the Allied merchant fleets during those months —in exchange for a loss of only six U-boats. And though the Allies didn't know it, that was only the beginning of the U-boat onslaught, for despite increasing numbers of escort ships that were protecting the convoys, in 1940 the U-boats would be sinking an average of 200,000 tons of Allied shipping a month; in 1941 the average rose to 211,000 tons a month, and in 1942 it was still more than 187,000 tons a month. It was a loss rate that the Allies couldn't make good, and in 1942, just as Cunard's

The enemy below: the Kriegsmarine's *Type VIIc U-boat was the scourge of Allied shipping on the North Atlantic.*

liners were about to begin the Atlantic runs, the outcome of the Battle of the Atlantic—and of the war—hung in the balance.

There is no denying that the German U-boat crews were good at what they did. At the same time, an image has come down through the years that they were little more than a bunch of efficient, hard, ruthless and sometimes cruel fanatics. Certainly the First World War had seen more than its share of ruthless U-boat commanders—was this next generation a collection of cold-blooded murderers, steely-eyed, dedicated Nazis who preyed on helpless merchant ships, striking unseen and undetected, killing without mercy or compunction? Yes and no. *Leutnant* Julius Lemp, commanding the *U-30,* torpedoed the *Athenia* on the third day of the war, with the loss of 112 lives, when there was no doubt in his mind that he was sinking an unarmed passenger liner. Significantly, even though it was done in contravention of the Führer's orders, there is no record of Lemp ever being disciplined or reprimanded for his action. And yet there were U-boat skippers who were as humane as Lemp was barbaric.

On Sept 12, 1942, the *U-156* under the command of *Kapitan Leutnant* Werner Hartenstein torpedoed a large ship in the South Atlantic. The ship was, as fate would have it, Cunard's *Laconia*, carrying four hundred eighty-four passengers and crew, along with eighteen hundred Italian prisoners of war. When he realized what he had done, Hartenstein sent out an uncoded radio signal, both to nearby U-boats and also to any other vessel close at hand, asking for help and promising not to attack any ship assisting in the rescue. Three submarines responded, and together the four U-boats rescued more than fifteen hundred survivors, delivering them to the care of the Vichy French, despite being bombed by an American B-24—which had picked up Hartenstein's signal but attacked the rescuing U-boats anyway—while on the way to the French African coast. Clearly, Hartenstein came from a far different mold than Lemp, but the aftermath said much about the U-boat service and the men who served in it. The incident prompted one of the most notorious instructions Admiral Doenitz ever issued: in what became known as "the *Laconia* order," Doenitz made it absolutely clear that under no circumstances were U-boats to take part in any kind of rescue operations of the crews of the ships they sank—the men were to be left in the water.

Doenitz's orders, while harsh, reflected the realities of the U-boat war from the perspective of the submariners themselves. If abandoning survivors from a sinking ship in the middle of a freezing ocean seems cruel, it was no worse a fate than they faced when the destroyers and corvettes escorting the convoys hunted them down. The German sailors had very little chance of rescue when their U-boats were sunk, their usual fate being a slow death by asphyxiation in a crippled submarine lying on a shallow bottom, or being smashed into a pulp when the hull of their sinking boat finally passed its crush depth and collapsed. It was a hard, cruel war they were fighting, with no quarter asked or given—the stakes were far too high for such niceties. So the German U-boat crews became efficient, hard, and sometimes cruel themselves. A measure of their determination can be gleaned from a few simple facts: between September 3, 1939 and May 7, 1945, German submarines sank nearly twenty-five hundred merchant ships, totaling almost thirteen million tons—more than half of all the merchant ships lost by both the Allies and Axis nations *combined* during the war. How many people died in those ships will never be known for certain; just Britain's losses, her Merchant Marine and the Royal Navy together, totaled almost 105,000 men.

If the U-boat crews were determined, they were also incredibly brave. Of the more than forty thousand young men who served aboard the German U-boats during World War II, fully three-quarters of them lie forever on the bottom of the Atlantic Ocean.

This was the war that the Cunard fleet was about to make its very own....

Though much of America and Britain's focus was understandably directed toward the two *Queens* now safely tied up together at Pier 90, and whose finest hours were yet to come, it had already been an eventful war for the Cunard Line. By the time the *Queen Elizabeth* made her daring run from the Clyde to New York, several of the line's ships had already been requisitioned by the government, even before the Admiralty order of March 1, and some had already seen action. There was a great deal more to come.

One of the first ships to be called to the colours was the *Carinthia*. When war was declared, she was just departing New York for Liverpool, and when she arrived she was immediately requisitioned as an Armed Merchant Cruiser. (Some ideas, no matter how absurd, die hard.) The conversion work took almost four months, most of her furnishings were removed, cabins were converted to mess decks, and the ship was armed with an assortment of obsolete naval guns. After undergoing trials off Liverpool in late December, she sailed down to Portsmouth to embark her crew and an assortment of last-minute equipment and supplies, then sailed back up to Greenock to join the Northern Patrol in January 1940. She made several patrols between the Western Isles and Iceland, and then in March was sent to Birkenhead for re-fitting.

Two months later the *Carinthia* was assigned to the naval forces patrolling the coast of Portugal, putting into Gibraltar on June 3 to take on stores. She began her patrolling duties two days later, and was about one hundred miles west of Lisbon when, at 2:00pm on June 9, she was struck by a torpedo fired by German submarine *U-46*. Several crewmen were killed by the explosion, which holed the engine room and two of the after holds. It seemed like there would be no chance to save the ship, which was flooding very rapidly. About half an hour after the ship was hit, a second torpedo was spotted in the water, which missed, and the gun crews, who had refused to abandon their weapons, fired on what they believed to be the submarine's periscope. Meanwhile, two other ships of the patrolling force had responded to the *Carinthia*'s distress signals and by 7:00 the following morning the ship was under tow. It was a valiant but vain effort, as the ship continued to take on water, and had to be abandoned. The *Carinthia* sank at 9:40pm on June 7.

Just a week later, another Cunard ship fell prey to a U-boat. This was the little *Andania*, which had joined the line in 1922, serving the London to Montreal route. Like the *Carinthia*, she was requisitioned by the Admiralty to serve as an armed merchant cruiser when the war began. Her conversion work was done at Cammell Lairds, in Birkenhead, and when she was commissioned on 9 November she was armed with eight 6-inch guns and a pair of 3-inch anti-aircraft guns. For a few months she and the *Carinthia* sailed together in the Northern Patrol, but while the larger ship was transferred to warmer waters, the *Andania* remained in the cold and dangerous waters off the Western Isles. On the morning of June 15, 1940, while on patrol off the northern coast of Ireland, a torpedo slammed into the *Andania*'s starboard side. Almost immediately the ship begin listing to starboard, but quick work by the engineers in shifting fuel oil to bunkers on the opposite side of the ship enabled them to right it. More serious was the fact that the blast put the rudder and main generators out of action, meaning that not only was the ship unable to be steered but also that there was no power for the pumps. Up on deck the crew opened fire on what they believed to be the periscope of the attacking U-boat. Whether it actually was the U-boat was never confirmed, but as the gun crews kept up their barrage a second torpedo, then a third and a fourth, went skimming past the ship, missing her by a wide margin. It seems that the *Andania*'s gunfire spooked the submarine, because despite the fact the ship was dead in the water, there were no further attacks. Meanwhile the engineers had assessed the damage and realized that, with all the pumps being out of operation and the widespread flooding, the water level was rising too fast to control. Around noon her captain gave the order to abandon ship, and the *Andania*'s crew was picked up by an Icelandic trawler, to be later landed at Scapa Flow—the only lives lost were four crewmen who were killed in the engine room when the torpedo struck. A few hours after she was abandoned, the *Andania* sank by the stern.

Just two days later, however, one of the worst tragedies of the entire war befell Cunard's *Lancastria*. In April 1940, the Royal Navy requisitioned the *Lancastria* for service as a troopship, and within weeks she went into action during the evacuation of British troops from Norway. She was scheduled to return to Liverpool, her homeport, on the 14th of June for dry-docking and a well needed overhaul, but the refit was cut short when she received urgent orders to make for the English Channel.

The military situation in Europe was catastrophic. The Nazis had swept across Holland, Belgium, Luxembourg, and the north of France in less than four weeks, utterly routing the French Army and driving the British Expeditionary Force into the English Channel. With the French forces on the verge of collapse, every available troopship was required to help in evacuating the few remaining pockets of British troops who had made their way to the coast, along with any French forces that were not prepared to surrender. As dawn broke on a bright, but cool morning on the 17th of June 1940, the *Lancastria* lay five miles off the port of St. Nazaire, France, where she would embark troops and refugees fleeing the advancing Germans.

Nazi tanks and infantry were advancing on the port, and because of the urgency of the situation, Captain Sharp and Chief Officer Grattidge were under orders to take aboard as many troops and refugees as possible. Several destroyers and smaller craft began bringing the troops out, and by noon the *Lancastria*'s decks were packed with thousands of troops and refugees.

A destroyer signaled for the *Lancastria* to get under way, but suddenly the air-raid siren sounded from the harbor at St. Nazaire and the skies were full of German aircraft. The *Oronsay*, another troop transport lying nearby, was the first ship to be attacked, and a bomb landed near her bridge. The explosion blew fragments and shrapnel against the hull of the *Lancastria*, causing some of the troops below decks to believe that she had been hit; they began making their way to the already crowded upper decks—most of them had no life jackets.

Suddenly, German bombers swarmed out of the sun, bomb doors open, and the *Lancastria* was under attack by almost one hundred aircraft. A stick of four bombs walked their way from the ship's stern to her bow, one of them exploding in the Number 2 hold, where some eight hundred Royal Air Force ground crew had been berthed. Thick black smoke and walls of flames poured out of the hatches—there were no survivors.

The second bomb struck near the base of the *Lancastria*'s funnel—some witnesses later said it actually went down the funnel—and took out the boilers and engine room, causing the ship to shudder and shake for her entire length and starting fires inside the hull and superstructure. On the bridge, officers frantically shouting down the voice tubes to the engine room received only silence as a response. Smoke began enveloping the forward half of the ship when the next bomb plunged through the hatch of the Number 3 hold, rupturing fuel bunkers and releasing fourteen hundred tons of fuel oil into the sea. The last bomb missed the *Lancastria*, but landed in the water close enough to blow a huge hole in her side and start more fires.

The liner began listing to starboard but Chief Officer Grattidge ordered those aboard

The Lancastria, shattered by bombs and sinking, while survivors clamber over her hull and into the water.

to move over to her port side, briefly bringing the ship back to an even keel. Next, Grattidge had the crew clear away the lifeboats, hoping to get them loaded and launched. There was no chance—the *Lancastria* had only minutes to live. Hundreds of men, women and children were thrown into the oil-covered sea, most of them soldiers of the British Expeditionary Force, the BEF. Hundreds, possibly thousands more—including most of the crew—were still inside the burning hulk of the *Lancastria*. The ship began a slow roll onto her port side, her propellers emerging from the water as survivors began clambering up her sides and onto her keel. Eerily, they began singing—the strains of "Tipperary," "Roll out the Barrel," and "There Will Always be an England" began to drift over the water, mingling in a bizarre cacophony with the crackle of flames, the scream of falling bombs, the wail of aircraft engines, and the cries of the victims.

Those people who were struggling in the water weren't singing: the oil from the ruptured bunkers covered the water with a thick scum that coated everything it touched. It burned into eyes, mouths, throats and lungs, choking men, women, and children who were struggling to keep from drowning. The torture didn't stop there: several of the German aircraft dove low over the water, strafing the survivors with cannons and machine guns. Others dropped incendiary bombs into the water, trying to ignite the oil which was pouring out of the doomed *Lancastria*.

It was over in just twenty minutes. Gutted, burning, and rent apart, the *Lancastria* disappeared into the waters of the English Channel. Many of the bodies scattered across the sea floated there motionless, the life jackets that now buoyed them up had killed them—many of them had jumped into the water from the upper decks, and when they plunged into the water, the collars on the life jackets snapped up and broke their necks. Others, burned by the oil or wounded by the bomb blasts, floated helplessly out to sea, beyond hope of rescue.

As the last of the German aircraft disappeared from sight, two destroyers, HMS *Highlander* and HMS *Havelock*, began plucking survivors from the water. On board other ships nearby, including the transports *Glenaffaric, Fabian, John Holt,* and the *Oronsay,* which surprisingly had survived the attacks made on her, the crews shook off the shock and horror of what they had just witnessed and began launching boats to save as many of the survivors as they could; scores of the men, women and children struggling in the water were seriously wounded and wouldn't live through the night.

The exact death toll that day would never be known—the Chief Purser stopped counting after more than 6,000 people were taken aboard the *Lancastria* that morning. Her usual compliment, including crew, was 2,180: it was later estimated that when she was sunk there were as many as nine thousand people aboard the *Lancastria*. Rescuers were able to save 2,447 people from the sea that day, among them Captain Sharp and Chief Officer Grattidge. The wreck of the *Lancastria* would be the worst disaster in Cunard's history.

Nineteen-forty was Great Britain's darkest hour, and it continued to be a very bad year for Cunard. Another ship was lost in November, the *Laurentic*. She had originally been built for the White Star Line, becoming part of the combined Cunard White Star fleet when the two companies merged in 1934. The *Laurentic* was something of an anachronism, being the last triple-expansion coal-fired Atlantic liner ever built. Launched in June 1927, she entered service in November of that year, and was soon part of the regular service between Liverpool and Montreal. Her career was a somewhat checkered one, as she was involved in two collisions, the second one being fairly serious—in August 1935 the *Laurentic* was rammed by the Napier Star, a Blue Star Line vessel, off the Skerries in the Irish Sea; six crewmen were killed in the collision. The ship was repaired but sat idle at Birkenhead until September 1936.

At that time she was used to carry a contingent of British troops to Palestine, but upon her return was immediately withdrawn from service again and laid up at Southampton, her future uncertain. The Second World War gave the *Laurentic* a new lease on life: in September 1939 she was converted into an armed merchant cruiser at Plymouth, her masts and derrick posts removed, and a battery of eight 6-inch guns and a quartet of anti-aircraft guns mounted on her decks. Just a few weeks out of drydock, on November 29, in the waters north of Iceland, she captured the *Antiochia*, a German merchantman being used to re-supply the surface raiders of the German Navy, a rare success for the armed merchant cruiser, whose worth was often more psychological than material.

Early in 1940 the ship ran aground during thick fog off Islay, an island off Scotland's western shores, but damage was minimal, and she was quickly repaired and returned to duty with the Northern Patrol. On the night of November 3, though, the *Laurentic*'s rather erratic luck finally ran out off Bloody Foreland in the North Western Approaches.

Purely by chance, the *Laurentic* was nearby when the 6,000-ton merchant ship S.S. *Casanare* was struck by a torpedo fired by the *U-99*. The U-boat was commanded by

Kapitan-Leutnant Otto Kretschmer, who was one of the most determined and daring submarine skippers in the German Navy, and who would become the highest scoring U-boat "ace" in history. With fires breaking out on board and her engines knocked out, the *Casanare*'s crew began abandoning the ship while her wireless operator frantically called for help. In addition to the *Laurentic*, there was another armed merchant cruiser nearby, the *Patroclus*, and both ships immediately went to the stricken steamer's assistance.

It was a golden opportunity for an aggressive commander like Kretschmer, and *U-99* quickly put a torpedo into the *Laurentic*, striking her in the boiler room and blowing an enormous hole in her side. But she was still afloat, although fires had broken out below decks all over the ship, and her wireless operator signaled that she was under attack and the crew had begun to abandon ship. *U-99* then fired another torpedo at *Laurentic*, which struck near the stern, this one also having no apparent effect on her. A thoroughly bewildered Kretschmer fired yet a third torpedo, putting this one in the hole made by the first, trying to break the ship's back. Now the *Laurentic* began to settle noticeably in the water. All during the attack, however, the gun crews (who would become legendary among the British Merchant Navy for their courage and determination to stay at their guns to the very last) had been firing star shells, illuminating the whole area, and then opened fire on the U-boat, driving Kretschmer off for a while.

Meanwhile the *Patroclus* was drawing closer, and when she reached the *Laurentic* she began the slow process of taking the sinking Cunarder's lifeboats aboard. Kretschmer waited until the *Laurentic*'s starshells burnt out, then turned *U-99* back to face the motionless trio of ships. The submarine closed to within 300 yards without being spotted, and fired a torpedo which struck *Patroclus* near the stern, directly beneath a loaded lifeboat. The lifeboat and the men aboard it vanished in a sheet of flame, and a huge section of *Patroclus*' was ripped apart. A second torpedo hit the *Patroclus* and the forward well deck disintegrated, taking with it several of *Patroclus*' crew. But there was still fight left in the *Patroclus*, and a flurry of shells from her guns splashed into the sea just a few yards from the submarine, which broke off the attack again.

By this time the *Casanare* had gone down, just two lifeboats full of survivors bobbing on the sea marking where she had been. A British Sunderland flying boat, bristling with machine guns and depth charges, suddenly appeared out of the darkness, barely 50 feet above the water—it had heard the *Laurentic*'s distress calls and came swooping down to her assistance. Kretschmer was no fool, and he gave the order to crash-dive.

Patiently waiting until the Sunderland flying boat left the area, the *U-99* surfaced once again at about 3:30am and made for the *Laurentic* and the *Patroclus*, which were sitting side by side like a pair of harpooned whales. All around the ships were the lifeboats and Carley floats from the *Laurentic*. A Royal Navy destroyer was just looming over the horizon.

Determined to sink both ships before the destroyer arrived, Kretschmenr brought the *U-99* to within 250 yards of the *Laurentic* and fired another torpedo. It blew off the ship's stern, setting off the depth charges she carried there. The blast hammered the *Laurentic*, which began sinking very rapidly, and shook *Patroclus* from stem to stern. Even the *U-99* was pitched over onto her side at a dangerous angle by the shock wave. The *Laurentic*'s bow rose into the air and the ship quickly slid beneath the waves.

The *Patroclus*, her crew as badly shaken as the ship, was at Kretschmer's mercy, and he wasted no time in putting another torpedo into her. Stubbornly, the ship still refused to sink, and the *U-99*'s deck gun opened fire, hitting the *Patroclus* amidships and aft, starting a fire in the aft well deck. Refusing to give up, the *Patroclus'* remaining deck gun fired back, forcing the submarine's gun crew off the deck.

Now a thoroughly frustrated Kretschmer fired his fourth and fifth torpedoes in quick succession, taking out the remaining deck gun and smashing two lifeboats, killing all who were aboard them. Finally, the *Patroclus* gave up the fight and began to settle, but not fast enough for Kretschmer, who fired a sixth torpedo into the ship, breaking her back. With an banshee-like screech of tearing metal, the ship split in two, the bow and stern then rose into the air, and as the few remaining crew scrambled to get off, finally sank.

Kretschmer ordered an emergency dive and *U-99* fled the area as quickly as possible. The approaching destroyer, HMS *Achates*, reached the scene moments later and immediately began picking up survivors from the three sunken ships. While the entire complement of the *Casanere* survived, forty-nine lives had been lost on the *Laurentic*, seventy-nine on the *Patroclus*. It was going to be a long and costly war.

But not every Cunard ship's wartime service would be so tragic, though there was certainly more than enough adventure to go around. An excellent example of this was the wartime service of the little *Aurania*, one of the four "A" class liners built in the early 1920s. Immediately after Britain declared war on Germany, she was called to serve with the Royal Navy and began conversion into an armed merchant cruiser. Like most of the other Cunard ships similarly requisitioned, she was armed with eight 6-inch guns and four 3-inch anti-aircraft guns, and was commissioned into the Royal Navy on 15 October. For nine months she served with the escort ships of the Northern Patrol and then joined the Halifax Escort Force in July 1941. In the middle of that month she was escorting a convoy bound for Reykjavik, Iceland when she ran into am enormous bank of thick fog. When she emerged from the fogbank, she found herself on the edge of an ice field, heading straight for a large iceberg. Her captain rang down for full reverse on the *Aurania*'s engines and put her helm hard over to starboard, but it wasn't enough to keep the ship from striking the berg bow on. The damage, while serious, wasn't fatal, but it did force the *Aurania* to return to Halifax for emergency repairs. From there she sailed to the U.S. Navy shipyard in Newport News, Virginia, where her permanent repairs were made, a task that took almost three months. By late September, she was back in service with the Halifax Escort Group.

On 13 October the *Aurania* sailed from Halifax, escorting a convoy bound for the Clyde. Eight days later, halfway to Scotland, she was struck by a torpedo. Immediately she began listing to port, but prompt action by her captain righted the ship. Although she was heavily damaged, the decision was made to try to reach the Clyde and the *Aurania* sailed on, reaching the Isle of Bute on 23 October. Repairs were complete by February 1942, by which time the Admiralty desperately needed heavy repair ships. The Royal Navy purchased the *Aurania* outright, and sent her to Devonport to be converted, work that was completed on 10 May 1944, when she was re-commissioned at Plymouth as HMS *Artifex*. After her trials she was sent to Trincomalee and remained in the Far East for the rest of the war.

On 26 August 1939, the *Samaria* made her final pre-war voyage from Liverpool to New York. Unlike many of the ships of the Cunard fleet she was not immediately requisitioned by the Royal Navy, but remained in service for Cunard for a further four months, making several unescorted transatlantic crossings. On December 16, a few hours out of Liverpool, she was involved in a collision with the *Aquitania*, which was part of an outbound convoy bound for Halifax. Both ships were blacked out, showing no lights at all, and the night was overcast, so it was only at the last minute that the two ships spotted one another, too late to avoid a collision. The *Samaria* struck the *Aquitania*'s port quarter, and suffered significant damage along her bow and forward superstructure, while the *Aquitania* had some of her shell plating stove in. It didn't take long to determine that neither ship had suffered critical damage and the *Aquitania* steamed off into the darkness on her way to Halifax. Meanwhile the *Samaria* returned to Liverpool for repairs.

In early 1940, she was chartered by the Ministry of Transport to serve as a troopship. Her first mission was to transport British children to the United States and Canada in the summer of 1940, part of the evacuation plan that the British government put into action to minimize civilian casualties should the Nazis invade the British Isles. By January 1941, the *Samaria* was carrying troops from Liverpool to Suez and by the end of 1944 it was still trooping in the Mediterranean. Her final wartime mission was in March 1945, when she sailed to the Black Sea port of Odessa and took aboard over a thousand Allied prisoners of war who had been liberated by the advancing Soviet Red Army.

As for the *Aquitania* herself, Cunard had planned to keep her in service only until the *Queen Elizabeth* was ready for her maiden voyage in the summer of 1940; these plans were shredded when the German panzers rolled into Poland on September 1, 1939. She had been sitting at the Ocean Dock at Southampton, her departure just a few hours away, when the news came that Britain and Germany were at war. It was too late to cancel the sailing; instead, hastily printed notices were posted throughout the Cunard terminal, announcing that the ship would depart as scheduled. In their hurry to get the notices posted, the company officials failed to notice the chilling echoes of the warning issued the day the *Lusitania* sailed on her last voyage in 1915: "American citizens are hereby advised that they are taking passage on a belligerent ship and are subject to sinking without notice."

The *Aquitania* did not suffer the *Lusitania*'s fate, though, and reached New York safely on September 9. She stayed there for the next two months before being requisitioned by the Royal Navy and converted to a troopship capable of carrying 7,800 of His Majesty's troops. For most of 1940, she stayed in the North Atlantic carrying Canadian soldiers and aircrews from Halifax to Gourock in Scotland. In the spring of 1941, she began carrying Australian and New Zealand troops from Sydney to the Suez.

A year later she was shifted back to the North Atlantic, and became a vital part of the fleet of troopships carrying millions of American and Canadian soldiers and airmen to Great Britain, building up the forces for the D-Day invasion of France. While she never received the glory that was showered on the *Queens*, the *Aquitania* was in her own way just as vital. Her capacity was only half that of either the *Queen Mary* or *Queen Elizabeth*, but what made her accomplishments so remarkable was her reliability: she was already a quarter-century old when the war began, and many marine engineers believed her boilers and engines were worn out. Yet between 1940 and 1945 she steamed half a million miles without a single major breakdown, and carried three hundred thousand Allied troops to Europe without suffering a single casualty. The last of the great four-funneled liners, she was the only troopship to serve in both World Wars. She was magnificent.

While the rest of the Cunard fleet was confronting dangers all over the globe, the great trio of ships—*Queen Mary, Queen Elizabeth,* and *Mauretania*—docked in New York in March of 1941, were being prepared to face perils of their own. But first they had to be transformed into ships suitable for carrying troops. Despite the fact that the *Queen Mary* and *Mauretania* had been sitting at the pier for nearly seven months, very little work had been done on them in preparation for trooping, aside from covering the black, white and red paint of their hulls, upper works, and funnels with a coat of paint in a shade the Royal Navy was pleased to call "Light Sea Grey". Admiralty lethargy wasn't to blame for the delay, however: painting the ship to make it less visible to prowling U-boats was a permissible step for Cunard to take, even if it was at Admiralty direction. More obvious changes and modifications, though, stood a good chance of running afoul of American neutrality

A collection of liners preparing for war in New York Harbor; from the top they are the Mauretania, Normandie, Queen Mary, *and* Queen Elizabeth.

legislation and the isolationist segment of the American population that was ever-anxious to enforce it. Some extra protection was added to the bridge, mostly in the form of sandbags, and a half-dozen 20mm Oerlikon guns, along with the same number of machine guns, were mounted for anti-aircraft defense, but any further modifications would have to be made in a British or Commonwealth shipyard.

The morning of March 20, 1940, saw the *Mauritania* pull away from Pier 90 on her way to the West Coast of Canada, where she would begin carrying Australian pilots, trained in Canada, back home "down under." The next day the *Queen Mary* left as well, also bound for Sydney, Australia, where the work to fit her out as a troopship would be done. It was an uncomfortable eight days' journey, as the *Mary* wasn't air conditioned—she had been designed for the North Atlantic, after all—and she was badly overcrowded. In fact, poor ventilation would plague all of the Cunard ships that were pressed into service in the tropics, but in particular, the *Queens,* as for the next two years they moved British and Commonwealth troops back and forth between the Far East and Suez, where the Tommies and Diggers were fighting the *Afrika Korps.*

It was a problem for which there was no solution, for though both *Queens* would undergo modifications in Sydney and Singapore to increase their berthing to accommodate more than 5,000 troops each, there was neither the time nor the means to install air-conditioning systems in either ship. As the liners would make their way across the Arabian Sea and up the Red Sea, the heat would defeat the ventilators entirely, turning the spaces below decks into something akin to vast ovens. Even for healthy, fit young men like the Australians and New Zealanders, the heat could be deadly, and nearly every such passage was marked by a handful of deaths among the troops, attributable to heat stroke or heat exhaustion. The crews of the two *Queens* did what they could, rigging salt water showers above decks, jury rigging extra fans, spreading awnings where possible, but the heat remained an oppressive enemy. Inevitably, something had to give, and did.

It happened on board the *Queen Elizabeth* as she was steaming toward Suez in July 1941. Tempers suddenly flared, and soon a fight broke out on one of the mess decks among the Australian infantry and the crew—no one ever found out what started it—and within minutes the brawl evolved into wholesale fisticuffs and thrown crockery. The crew had legitimate grievances; many had not been off the *Elizabeth* for nearly a year, their quarters were located in some of the hottest areas of the ship, and their diet—food is always a priority with sailors—had become bland and monotonous to the point of insult. The Australian brawl seemed to serve as a catalyst for all the pent-up resentments among some of the *Elizabeth*'s crew: where the Diggers had limited themselves to breaking knuckles and dishware on various parts of their collective anatomies, the crewmen quickly escalated to kitchen utensils, pans and pots of boiling water being hurled at one another, and at one point, a cook who was clearly in the wrong place at the wrong time was forced into his own—heated—oven. The senseless brutality of the act suddenly seemed to take the heart out of the rioters, and when a company of Royal Marines was hastily brought on board, they were quickly rounded up, arrested and

Below decks on a troopship, space was always at a premium. Here, hammocks are slung above the troops mess tables.

placed in detention. The unfortunate cook survived, although severely burned, and his assault was the basis for the charges brought against the crewmen. The ringleaders of this violent episode were eventually taken to England for trial and given long prison sentences.

But the episode cast a harshly revealing light on the conditions the essentially civilian crews on the commandeered Cunard ships had to endure for months on end. That such an incident should occur is understandable in hindsight; that there were no recurrences speaks volumes about the level of professionalism and dedication to duty those men possessed. Together, Cunard and the Admiralty took steps to alleviate as many of the causes of the crewmen's discontent as they could, although there was little they could do about the heat, of course.

The Suez was a dangerous place for ships as well as soldiers and crewmen. In May 1941, the *Georgic* left the Clyde as part of a convoy bound for Port Tewfik in the Gulf of Suez, to embark Italian internees being sent to Britain and Canada for the duration of the war. She had been requisitioned by the Royal Navy for trooping duties almost as soon as the war began, and had already seen action evacuating British troops from Norway in May 1940, and from Brest and St. Nazire in France a month later. She also carried Canadian troops to the Middle East via the Cape of Good Hope route around Africa.

The *Georgic* arrived at Port Tewfik on July 7. A week later, still riding at anchor in the harbor, she was attacked by the *Luftwaffe*. She was hit twice by bombs, which started fires that quickly became uncontrollable. Ammunition for the 6-inch guns mounted on the stern began exploding, wrecking the after part of the ship, and in a desperate attempt to save her, the *Georgic* was beached by her captain outside the port and the fires allowed to burn themselves out.

Although most of the ship was gutted by the fires, a naval survey crew found that her engines were still intact and her hull apparently still sound, so the decision was made to salvage her. In October, the *Georgic* was raised, and two months later she was towed stern first to Port Sudan where she was made seaworthy once again. In March 1942 she was towed to Karachi and then Bombay for further repairs, the *Georgic* finally sailing for Liverpool on 20 January 1943, and from there back to Belfast, and the Harland and Wolff yards a few months later, where she underwent a seventeen month long refit. When she emerged in December 1944, she looked like a different ship: gone was her fore funnel and after mast, and her foremast had been cut down almost by half. On December 16, she was returned to service and spent the last year of the war carrying troops to Italy, the Middle East and India.

Another Cunard ship that saw action in the Mediterranean was the *Scythia*. She had been requisitioned in November 1939, undergoing conversion to a troop transport in Glasgow. Her first service was to carry children from Liverpool to New York in 1940 as part of the Children's Overseas Reception Board evacuation programme. In November 1942, she was part of the fleet that supported the Operation "Torch" landings on the North African coast. It was during this operation while she was anchored near the southern entrance to Algiers harbour, that the *Scythia* endured a series of air raids by the *Luftwaffe*. After several near misses she was struck on her starboard side by a torpedo dropped from a Heinkel bomber. Brilliant damage control was able to limit the flooding to a few bunkers and void spaces, allowing the ship to reach her assigned berth; a terrible disaster had been narrowly avoided, as there were over four thousand troops on board. Temporary repairs were made to the *Scythia* at Gibraltar, then she was sent to the United States for permanent repairs, and spent the rest of the war carrying American troops to Europe.

Though many of Cunard's smaller ships would continue to serve in the Mediterranean and the Middle East, events would bring the *Queen*'s stifling passages between Australia and Suez, as well as the *Aquitania*'s and *Mauretania*'s crossings between Australia and the United States, to an abrupt halt. The Japanese attack on the United States' naval base at Pearl Harbor, Hawaii, on December 7, 1941, fundamentally changed the strategic balance of the war, bringing the full weight of American manpower, industry, and economic might into the conflict on the side of the Allies. The *Queens*, the *Mauretania*, and the *Aquitania* were all ordered to Cape Town to take them out of range of the advancing Japanese, while the *Mauretania* was sent through the Panama Canal and on to New York. In mid-December, Prime Minister Churchill and his military staff traveled to Washington, D.C. for a conference with their American counterparts. It was at this conference that the Americans and British decided on a "Germany first" strategy, rightly perceiving that Nazi Germany posed not only a greater, but also a more immediate threat to the Allies. It was also decided that the Americans would be responsible for the operations of both *Queens*, as well as the *Mauretania* and *Aquitania*—the crews would remain Cunard employees, but the costs of operating the ships would be paid by the United States government.

By March 1942, they were carrying American reinforcements to Australia, mainly artillery units and engineers, along with a large number of Army Air Corps personnel, the vanguard of some twenty thousand GIs they would carry to Australia in the next four months.

The *Queen Mary*'s first voyage carrying GIs began on February 18, 1942, when she left New York bound for Sydney via Trinidad, Rio de Janeiro, Cape Town, and Freemantle. U-boats were taking a heavy toll of American shipping in the Caribbean, and after she left Trinidad, the *Mary* had to briefly put into Key West, Florida, for safety before heading back out into the Caribbean and into the Atlantic again. Unknown to anyone, the *U-161* and *U-129* were following almost the same course. Just moments after the *Mary* cleared the Anageda Passage, a tanker was torpedoed ten miles away. Two days later, less than an hour after the *Mary* had cleared Rio de Janeiro, the Germans announced that she had been sunk by a U-boat—the first, but not the last time they would claim one of the *Queens* had fallen victim of their submarines.

The rest of the voyage was uneventful, and the *Mary* docked in Sydney on March 28, where she spent nine days refueling, restocking her storerooms, and recovering from the effects of carrying American troops for the first time. Overall, the GIs had behaved themselves, but one habit they brought aboard provoked an instant and imperious reaction from the *Mary*'s skipper, Commodore James Bisset. Bisset was something of a legend among Cunard captains and merchant skippers on the North Atlantic. Having spent thirty-five years with Cunard, he was now the senior skipper of the line. Thirty years before taking command of the *Queen Mary*, he had been the second officer on a small Cunard steamer called the *Carpathia* in the early morning hours of April 15, 1912, as she thundered at high speed through iceberg infested waters to rescue the survivors of the *Titanic*. On this voyage, Bisset was introduced to the wonders of chewing gum, one of the less notable American contributions to Western civilization. After the voyage was over, the *Queen Mary*'s crew had to use scrapers and caustic soda to remove the layers of discarded gum that the GIs had dropped on her decks. Bisset immediately forbade chewing gum aboard either *Queen*—it was a ban that would remain in force until the war was over.

Pacific service for the *Queens*, the *Mauretania* and the *Aquitania* came to an end in the middle of 1942 though, as all four were made ready to sail into the heart of the most bitter naval campaign ever fought, the Battle of the Atlantic. It wasn't going to be easy: while neither the Japanese navy nor air force ever really posed much of a threat to either of the *Queens*, or the *Mauretania* or *Aquitania* for that matter, they would be sailing into mortal danger when the ships were transferred to trooping duties in the North Atlantic. If they survived, they would change the course of history.

CHAPTER FOURTEEN

The Warrior Queens

While other ships such as the *Mauretania* and the gallant old *Aquitania*, along with the rest of the Cunard fleet, were invaluable to the Allies, and performed bravely throughout the whole of the war, the jewels in the crown of the Allied effort were beyond doubt the *Queen Mary* and the *Queen Elizabeth*.

When the *Queen Mary* and *Queen Elizabeth* were transferred to the Atlantic, they were faced with a whole new set of priorities. In the last week of December 1941, when Prime Minister Churchill and his military staff came to Washington, D.C. for a conference with American and British military leaders, the United States Army Chief of Staff, General George C. Marshall, raised the question of possibly further modifying the *Queen Mary* and *Queen Elizabeth* to drastically increase their capacity to carry troops to as many as ten thousand soldiers each—the equivalent of an entire division—at one time. If it could be done, it would give the Allies the capability to rapidly build up the forces needed for the inevitable invasion of continental Europe—what would be the most complex and difficult military operation ever attempted. And it had to be accomplished as soon as there was a reasonable chance of success, for the longer the Germans were allowed to retain their grip on Europe, the more formidable their defenses would become.

Marshall, who had what amounted to a genius for logistics, had conceived of a plan, Operation Bolero, which was to be the most colossal logistical effort in history. It wasn't just necessary to get the soldiers and equipment to the British Isles, but once there, they had to be fed, clothed, and housed. Not only that, but tens of thousands of tanks, trucks, armored vehicles and artillery pieces had to be brought over and stored—not to mention the thousands of bombers, fighters and other aircraft required by the Army Air Corps, the RAF and the RCAF—which meant that every open field in Great Britain was a potential parking lot.

Eventually more than sixty-nine hundred vessels were involved in bringing more than five million tons of supplies to Great Britain, along with over one and one half million men. When the invasion was finally launched, the support forces included six battleships, twenty-two cruisers, hundreds of destroyers, landing craft and support ships, as well as more than ten thousand aircraft of all description. But the centerpiece of this effort would be the *Queens*.

Moving a whole division on one ship in one voyage was a feat never before attempted or accomplished, and choosing to try it was not a decision that was easily reached: if one of the ships were to be torpedoed and sunk, the casualties would be beyond terrible. Each ship's compliment of lifeboats could hold more than three thousand people, and it would be easy enough to bring additional rafts and floats aboard to raise the lifesaving capacity to eight thousand. But Marshall, though not a seaman, was astute enough to realize that these figures were only at best a theoretical ideal, and that the chaos aboard a sinking ship would inevitably result in thousands of lives being lost. The question that Marshall had to answer for himself—and for the Allied planners—was if the strategic opportunities offered by the *Queens* were worth such risks.

Marshall, never one to mince words, bluntly put the question of whether or not to take the risk, to Churchill. Churchill, with equal bluntness, replied, "I can only tell you what *we* should do. You must judge for yourselves the risk you will run. If it were a direct part of an actual operation we should put all on board that they could carry. If it were only a question of moving troops in a reasonable time, we should not go beyond the limits of lifeboats, rafts, etc. It is for you to decide."

Marshall didn't immediately respond, but a few days later he visited the *Queen Mary* when she was in New York, and was taken around the ship by Harry Grattidge, the liner's Staff Captain. Clearly, what Marshall saw and learned impressed him, and the orders went out within a matter of days for work to begin on both of the *Queens* to prepare them for carrying troops to Europe, using every available bit of interior space aboard the two ships. Work on the *Queen Elizabeth* would be done in San Francisco at the same time the *Queen Mary* was taken in hand in New York. While not quite identical conversions, they were very similar in most respects.

The work done earlier in Australia to convert the *Queens* to troopers had increased their capacity to fifty-five hundred people. While the Australian shipwrights had installed rows of fixed wooden triple-tiered bunks in the liners' cabins and used some of the public rooms for slinging hammocks, the Americans had an entirely different concept in mind. The American plan hinged—quite literally—on a device called a standee bunk. This was a rectangular frame of tubular steel, mounted on hinges and bolted to a bulkhead. Its arc of travel was limited by snubbing chains at both ends of the frame, so that it could lay horizontally. Within the frame, laced tautly to it, was a fitted length of heavy canvas. The standee bunk's occupant slept on this. It was an ingenious design, easily cleaned, reasonably comfortable, and since it could be folded up and out of the way when not in use, it allowed for more room to move about than did the fixed bunks used by the Australians.

Another difference between the Australian and American approaches was the sheer ruthlessness of the American conversion. The *Aquitania,* also transferred to the North Atlantic where she would be used to transport Canadian troops from Halifax and New York, was allowed to make do with the conversion work done in Australia, which gave her a capacity of just over four thousand troops, but left much of her original interior intact. Aboard the *Queens* it was an entirely different story. No place on either ship, aside from the crews' quarters and the engineering spaces, was considered sacrosanct. The absence of many of the *Queen Elizabeth*'s interior furnishings and almost all of her decor meant that greater use could be made of her large public rooms, and modifications were considerably simpler to those decks that were given over to staterooms. On the *Queen Mary,* the First Class Smoking Lounge was converted to a hospital; the tourist-class cocktail bar became a pharmacy; the cabin-class restaurant was filled with mess tables and benches; the Observation Lounge and the Midshipman's Bar were unceremoniously filled with bunks; Austin Reed's tailor shop became a detention center and the headquarters of the military police detachment permanently stationed aboard. Standee bunks went *everywhere*—a stateroom originally designed for four people could be converted into sleeping space for as many as twenty-one GIs. Not even the swimming pool was spared: bunks were mounted in there *seven* high! The installation of the bunks would create some lasting images of their own. Soldiers who sailed aboard the *Queens* would later liken the appearance of some of the larger public rooms with their rows upon rows of standee bunks to the shelves of a supermarket.

Working round the clock, it took less than two weeks for all of the additional bunks, latrines, and storerooms to be installed and finished. When the conversion was complete, each ship had bunks for more than 12,000 troops.

Standee bunks aboard one of the Queens; *in some places aboard the ships they were stacked seven high.*

In a tacit acknowledgment of just how dangerous the Atlantic had become, it was decided then that each ship should carry a defensive armament equal to that of a light cruiser, so the number of 20mm anti-aircraft guns was increased to twenty-four, while ten 40mm guns in five twin mounts were added. Additionally, six 3-inch guns in high angle/low angle mounts were emplaced, similarly disposed on both liners, with two guns in front of the bridge and the other four mounted on the after decks. Finally, the 4-inch popguns originally mounted on the stern of each ship for defense against submarines were replaced with far more imposing—and effective—6-inch weapons. While certainly not meant to allow either of the *Queens* to slug it out with a conventional warship larger than a destroyer, it was an armament heavy enough to discourage any raider or surfaced U-boat that might mistakenly want to try conclusions with the liners.

That some measure of self defense was required was due to the fact that the *Queen Mary* and *Queen Elizabeth* would almost always sail alone: their best defense, in fact, their only real defense against U-boats, was their speed. Making a steady twenty-eight to thirty knots, while following carefully designed zig-zag patterns, they could easily outpace any submarine the Germans had. Even if a U-boat skipper were, by chance, lucky enough to draw a bead on one of the *Queens*, the target wouldn't be in range long enough for him to make any corrections to his initial approach or line up for a second shot—he would have one chance, and one chance only to get his torpedoes off, and if his calculations weren't perfect, he'd never get another. That same speed, though, also meant that the *Queens* were much, much faster than any other merchant vessel afloat, and faster than many escorts.

There was always the chance of a carefully set ambush, with U-boats lying in wait for the approach of an unsuspecting *Queen*. That possibility was prevented by having the liners follow a zig-zag course as they crossed the Atlantic, a seemingly random series of course changes that would prevent any ship trying to carry it out, from staying on any one bearing long enough for a submarine to target and fire its torpedoes. Of course, there was nothing random about it at all, as the zig-zags were arranged in such a way that their cumulative effect was to keep the ship traveling on its base course, at a constant relative speed.

Elaborate measures were taken to keep the date and time of the *Queens'* departures secret—or at least not general knowledge—while the ships themselves were heavily guarded at all times to prevent sabotage. When either of the *Queens* was preparing to sail from New York, their captains were informed of the exact time of departure only twenty-four hours in advance. A set of sealed orders would be handed to the captain at the Shipping Office on Cunard's Pier 90, which he was not to open until the ship was past the Ambrose Light. At that time, he would open his instructions and inform the navigating officer and helmsman of the course and speed, as well as the zig-zag pattern to be followed. A half dozen of the U.S. Navy's most modern destroyers would accompany the liners until they were one hundred and fifty miles out of New York, with Navy patrol planes or blimps

Passing out of New York Harbor, the Queen Mary *sets out on her first voyage as a troopship.*

some distance further. Once the last escort turned back for New York, the *Queens* would be on their own until they were met by their British escorts north of Ireland. Only a handful of people on either side of the Atlantic knew when they would arrive at their destinations. It was during these solitary passages that the *Queens* would sometimes loom swiftly and unexpectedly out of the mist, sweeping past a solitary patrol vessel or fishing trawler, only to disappear back into the mist moments later, earning them the nickname "The Grey Ghosts."

The possibility of a German attack from above, on, or below the sea, was always a constant and real fear for the crew and troops alike aboard the *Queens*. Daily gunnery drills were held to keep the skills of the gun crews sharply honed, with prizes sometimes being awarded for particularly smart performance. Admittedly, these drills also did a lot to sustain the morale of the troops, who would be essentially helpless aboard the ships if they were attacked, something the troops were acutely aware of. The rattle of the various machine guns, the strings of staccato barks from the 20mm and 40 mm anti-aircraft guns, the bangs of the 3-inch guns, and finally the thunder of the 6-inch stern mount, were reas-

Bristling with anti-aircraft guns, the Queen Mary *is greeted by an RAF Catalina flying boat as she enters the Western Approaches.*

surance that if need be, the *Queens* could always bite back—*hard*.

What every GI aboard looked forward to, and every sailor, as well, no matter what ship they were aboard, was the rendezvous with the British escorts. Usually the first to appear was a Sunderland or PBY flying boat, part of the RAF's Coastal Command, responsible for patrolling the waters around the British Isles. The first patrol planes would appear while the *Queens* were roughly six hundred miles from the northern Irish coast. A squadron of a half dozen destroyers and a light cruiser would show up a few hours later, the destroyers sweeping the seas for submarines, the cruisers staying close to the liners to protect them from aircraft.

It wasn't always easy. The Royal Navy had more tasks to accomplish than it had ships to accomplish them, and even with a large part of the American fleet serving in the Atlantic, there were not always enough modern destroyers or cruisers to go around. Even before the war began, the Royal Navy became acutely aware that its fleet was badly unbalanced, for while its capital ship strength was sufficient to overwhelm any possible European foe, the numbers of lighter units—cruisers and destroyers—were barely enough to meet the requirements of peacetime. Trying to make up for the shortage, the Royal Navy had gone to the Reserve Fleet, a collection of ships that, because of age or design limitations were no longer suitable for front-line service, but still could be useful in secondary and support roles. As the likelihood of war grew at the end of the decade, they were reactivated and refurbished, most of them being modified with up-to-date weapons and range finding equipment, along with such new inventions as radar.

No amount of modification could make up for the fact that many of them were showing their age and sometimes were not up to the rigors of the North Atlantic: many had been designed to protect the Empire's sea lanes in the more temperate climes of tropical and sub-tropical colonial service. But when the crisis came in 1939, the Royal Navy had no choice but to return these ships to service. There was little that could be done about aging hulls and engines—but that did not prevent their crews from doing their level best to carry out their duties with as much dedication and professionalism as any of the newer ships in the Royal Navy. The officers and ratings knew they were performing an incredibly important task protecting the *Queens*. In May of 1942, the *Queen Mary* brought 9,880 American troops to Gourock: along with the eight hundred seventy-five crewmen aboard, this was the first time over ten thousand people has been carried aboard a single ship; within a few weeks the *Queen Elizabeth* was carrying similar numbers. Even greater feats were to follow: on her first crossing in August of that same year, the *Mary* carried 15,125 GIs, the entire 1st Infantry Division, the first time one complete division had ever been transported on a single ship.

From their very first Atlantic crossings, the *Queens* proved the wisdom of the decisions made by Churchill and Marshall. Commodore Bisset, who commanded the *Queen Mary* on nearly three-quarters of her Atlantic crossings during the war, was in a unique position to judge how useful they really were, and concluded: "Together they were equal to a fleet of twenty normal troop transports. That calculation takes into account their high speed, which enabled them to make more voyages in a given time than ordinary liners could make."

Their safety and survival soon transcended all other considerations, something Captain Gordon Illingworth sought to drive home to those aboard the *Queen Mary* in October 1943, when he addressed the passengers and crew.

> I call upon all officers and men to obey my orders to the letter. I have but one task. It is the job of bringing this ship safely to port, and that job, God willing, I *will* do. It is not important that you, numbering some 15,000, arrive safely in the Firth of Clyde, but it is important that the ship be brought safely to anchor there. Remember that. You and I are not indispensable to the successful prosecution of this war, but the ship is. You will keep in mind, therefore, that all your thoughts during the crossing will be directed to her security. Enemy forces will be at work, and the Hun will try every device in his power to bring the "*Queen*" to harm. Submarines will trail us and aircraft will harass us. They have done it before and we have every reason to believe they will do it again.

But the "*Queen*" will take care of herself. From now until the moment you debark, think in terms of the ship. Treat her gently and do not abuse her. She stands ready to do for you what she has done for thousands who have gone before. Keep her confidence and do not betray her by carelessness or misdeed. Do these things and the ship will bring us to the mouth of the Clyde on Tuesday next—so help us God.

Certainly the Germans shared Captain Illingworth's estimate of the *Queen*'s importance to the Allied war effort. Not long after the two liners began ferrying troops across the Atlantic, the German Führer Adolf Hitler, offered a reward of RM 1,000,000, the equivalent of $250,000, to the U-boat skipper who sank either of them, though no one ever collected. Three times Winston Churchill crossed the Atlantic on the *Queen Mary*. The first was in May 1943, when the Prime Minister and his entourage took passage to New York on their way to the Trident Conference in Washington D.C. The next were for the Quadrant Conference in August 1943 and the Octant Conference in September 1944, both of which were held in Quebec.

By some sort of strange juxtaposition, while the *Queens* were carrying thousands of Allied troops to Europe on every eastbound crossing, when they were westbound there were thousands of German and Italian soldiers aboard. They were prisoners of war, being shipped to detention camps in the United States and Canada, and their transport added just one more dimension to the wartime careers of the Warrior *Queens*.

The Germans weren't the only threat the *Queens* faced, however—sometimes the sea itself was just as dangerous. In one of the most frightening episodes on all of her North Atlantic crossings, the *Mary* was struck broadside by a rogue wave that was so large and powerful, it almost caused her to capsize. On December 13, 1942, while carrying more than ten thousand GIs and a crew of nearly a thousand, the *Mary* was steaming through heavy, but not unusually rough seas while still some seven hundred miles west of Scotland. The sky was overcast and there had been intermittent rain all day—in other words, a typical winter day for the North Atlantic. At approximately 2:30 that afternoon, without warning, one monstrous wave reared up and smashed into the ship's port side. The wave was so huge that it stove in boats on the Boat Deck and smashed windows on the bridge—ninety-five feet above the waterline. As the weight of the wave bore down on the ship, she heeled over to starboard, beginning a roll from which many on board thought she would never recover. Over she went, past thirty degrees, past forty, past forty-five, past fifty, until she finally reached an angle of fifty-two degrees. The wave held her there for some seconds, the starboard lifeboats and Boat Deck railings awash, nothing but green seawater visible though the portholes and windows on the starboard side of the ship. Then with an agonizing slowness, she began to recover, regaining an even keel some minutes later.

Below decks was chaos. Since there had been no warning for either troops or crewmen, people had been thrown out of bunks, tossed around machinery spaces, flung across decks, galleys and mess halls. There were broken arms and legs, cracked skulls and concussions, but amazingly no fatalities. Even more amazing, no one topside was swept overboard—if they had, they would have been lost, since both of the *Queens'* standing orders forbade her stopping or altering her course. For the men in the anti-aircraft gun positions, it was a particularly terrifying experience—normally sitting well over a hundred feet above the water, the men at the portside guns had the awesome prospect of this mountainous wall of water threatening to break down over them at any moment, while those on the starboard guns had the equally frightening vision of the sea rushing by only a few feet below them.

It was later calculated that the *Queen Mary* had come within three degrees of capsizing. If she had, not only would it have been a huge loss for the Allied war effort, but it would have become one of the great mysteries of the sea, as it's quite likely that she would have sunk without a trace—there would have been little chance for anyone below decks to escape, while those above decks who were lucky enough to get away would have succumbed to the cold of the sea within a matter of hours. What would have been the greatest maritime disaster in history had been avoided by the slimmest of margins. It was a chilling reminder that the sea was an ally to no one, and a constant danger.

And sometimes the *Queens* themselves were the danger....

On an uncommonly bright morning in late autumn 1942, in waters just off of Bloody Foreland, northwest of County Donegal, Ireland, seven ships were steaming eastward in a loose, ever-changing formation toward the Western Isles. They were the *Queen Mary*, with over ten thousand American soldiers and a crew of more than eight-hundred fifty aboard, and six escorts—five destroyers and the World War One-vintage light cruiser *Curacoa*. It was just on ten o'clock that morning when the liner and her escorts made their rendezvous, and the cruiser took up a position roughly five miles ahead of the huge liner, with the two ships weaving back and forth in an intricate pattern of zig-zags. Almost immediately a series of incidents and circumstances, invisible

Built during the First World War, HMS Curacoa *was cut in half by the* Queen Mary, *a tragedy not made public until the end of the war.*

at the time, began to fall into place which would lead to the moment when, at fourteen minutes past two in the afternoon of October 2, 1942, the 81,000-ton *Queen Mary* would run down the 4,400-ton *Curacoa*, knifing the cruiser in two and killing three quarters of her crew.

How it happened is the kind of mystery that haunts ships at sea and causes captains to have nightmares. Visibility was excellent and both ships had the other in full view the entire time they were approaching the instant of collision. Both captains were aware of the other ship's speed and course, as well as what each ship's movements, as dictated by the zig-zag pattern, should be at any given moment. Both ships' officers and crew did everything right, both did everything wrong. It was almost as if the collision was preordained from the moment the *Queen Mary* and *Curacoa* sighted each other.

HMS *Curacoa* was a "C" class cruiser of First World War vintage, launched in 1917. She was 451 feet in length, with a beam of 43 feet; her displacement was 4,300 tons. Relegated to the Reserve Fleet between the wars, in June 1939 she was reactivated and modernized. All five of *Curacoa*'s 6-inch guns were removed, and replaced by eight 4-inch guns in four special High Angle/Low Angle twin mounts. In addition, a multiple pom-pom (four 2-pounder guns) was mounted forward of the bridge, and six 20-mm Bofors guns were installed to port and starboard about the funnels. On January 1, 1940, *Curacoa* was placed back in commission and rejoined the fleet.

She saw action in Norway in April 1940, where she was struck by three 250-pound bombs. Damage was serious, and casualties were severe—forty-five dead and thirty-six wounded. Repairs took five months, and when she returned to service in September 1940, *Curacoa* was assigned to escort duties in the North Sea and the waters around northern Scotland, then on August 1, 1942, was transferred to the Western Approaches to serve as anti-aircraft escort for convoys sailing to and from Gourock, Scotland. This was a tricky assignment, as the anti-aircraft cruisers had to stay fairly close to the Queens to protect them, requiring that both ships keep a careful eye on the movements of the other. Certainly it was a task that demanded the attention of a first class officer in command on each bridge.

The man in command of HMS *Curacoa* was Captain John W. Boutwood, RN, a career officer who had joined the Royal Navy in 1917. While no single command had marked him as an exceptional officer, that he was more than simply competent was demonstrated by his promotion to Captain in early 1941, a rank not lightly bestowed in peacetime or war.

The man on the bridge of the *Queen Mary* that day was Captain Cyril Gordon Illingworth. Like Boutwood, he took over his new command in June 1942, and like Boutwood, he spent most of his adult life at sea. He was member of the Royal Naval Reserve, serving on active duty during the First World War, while in the 1920s and 1930s he held a succession of commands for Cunard, where he was respected within the company as being a conscientious and careful officer. It has been said that he was disliked by the officers of the Royal Navy, although it's impossible to determine at this remove whether or not that animosity was due to the collision with *Curacoa* or predated it. No doubt some of it stems from the traditional rivalry—rarely friendly—that always existed between the Royal Navy and the British Merchant Marine. It's difficult to seriously question Illingworth's competence as a captain, since Cunard had entrusted him with the pride of their fleet—a responsibility compounded by the sheer number of lives she was carrying on each of her wartime crossings.

Yet, in spite of their experience, on the morning of October 2, 1942, both captains made critical errors of commission and omission. HMS *Curacoa*, accompanied by the destroyers *Bulldog, Skate, Saladin, Bramham, Cowdray,* and *Blyskawica*—this last being a Polish ship with a fearsome combat record—steaming steadily to the west roughly forty miles off the north coast of Ireland, met the liner off Bloody Foreland at just past 10:00am. Inexplicably, both Boutwood and Illingworth failed to pass critical information to each other—both men made certain assumptions about their own ships and each other's that, had they made those assumptions clear to one another, might have averted the tragedy that was about to unfold. The *Queen Mary* was using Zig-zag Pattern No. 8, and Illingworth apparently assumed that Boutwood knew this, but Illingworth never confirmed that.

Also, the two commanders were working from different interpretations of the Rules of the Road, each assuming that the current circumstances dictated that their ship would have the right of way. This was no trivial consideration, since the handling characteristics of the two ships—the *Queen Mary* being big, ponderous and clumsy, slow to answer her helm compared to the light and nimble *Curacoa*—differed so vastly that in the event of an emergency situation such as an air attack or a U-boat threat that might require swift and violent maneuvering by *Curacoa*, it would be vitally important for each captain to know what was expected of his ship, as well as the other.

Ultimately, though, it would all come down to a question of speed. The cruiser could only do a maximum of 25 knots, but the liner was making just over 28 knots, and even following her zig-zag pattern, her rate of advance was still an inexorable 26½ knots: four hours after *Curacoa* took her position some six miles ahead of the *Queen Mary*, the liner would overtake the cruiser, and because no one aboard the cruiser had plotted the *Mary*'s course in advance, Captain Boutwood lacked the information that would let him know exactly where the liner would be when that happened. As the time passed and the ships began to draw abreast of each other, Boutwood wouldn't know when the *Mary* was due to change course, or what that change would be. If his ship were in the wrong place when that happened, there might not be time or room enough to get out of the way....

And so it was that at 2:00pm, in the wheelhouse of the *Queen Mary*, Quartermaster John Leydon relieved Quartermaster John Lockhart at the helm. No sooner had he done so than the wheelhouse clock chimed, indicating that it was time for a twenty-five degree turn to starboard. First Officer Wright confirmed the course change and the *Mary* began to swing to the right. *Curacoa* was about two cables (800 yards) distant from the *Mary*'s starboard bow, on a course that would take her in front of the liner. Wright was concerned by how close the cruiser seemed to be, and mentioned it to Captain Illingworth. The captain, believing that the cruiser knew the liner had the right of way, reassured him, saying, "He will keep out of your way." A few moments later, Senior First Officer Robinson relieved Wright. Robinson also was convinced that the cruiser would give way if the two ships got too close.

But a few moments later, after confirming the change in course with Leyden, Robinson returned to the bridge to look for the cruiser. What he saw was terrifying: she was so close now that when she rolled he could see down her funnels. The two ships were still closing. There was less than a cable between them. Turning toward the wheelhouse, Robinson yelled, "Hard a-port!" and Leydon spun the wheel as fast as he could, but the sheer bulk of the *Queen Mary* meant that she would turn too late. A lifetime too late. More than three hundred lifetimes too late.

It was over in barely a second. At 2:14pm the *Queen Mary* struck *Curacoa* 140-150 feet forward of her stern, at an angle somewhere between twenty and forty degrees. Impacted by the incredible momentum of 81,000 tons of steel moving at 28½ knots, the cruiser never stood a chance. The liner knifed through the belt of 3-inch-thick armor as if it weren't there, split the cruiser's hull wide open from side to side, crushed through decks, bulkheads, machinery and crewmen as if they were little more than tissue paper, then shunted the two halves of the ship aside and continued to thunder on, her speed not abated a whit.

The impact rolled *Curacoa* over on her starboard side so far that it seemed she would turn turtle. The crash of the collision was instantly followed by the screech of tearing metal and the scream of escaping steam as every steam line in the ship gave way and a huge cloud of vapor and smoke surrounded her. The stern section did roll over completely, the cruiser's two bronze propellers spinning lazily as that half of the ship quickly sank. The forward part righted itself momentarily, but then quickly began to sink.

On board the *Queen Mary*, Captain Illingworth felt a bump and asked the quartermaster, "Was that a bomb?"

"No, Captain," Leydon replied, "we hit the cruiser." Below deck and in the engine room the collision was felt as hardly more than a bump as well, as if the *Mary* were butting through a large wave. A quick inspection showed that there had been no noticeable damage to the liner.

Illingworth now had to make what was probably the most agonizing decision in his life. No true seaman will willingly leave another to die in the water, but Illingworth had to put the safety of his ship and the eleven thousand men aboard her ahead of the four hundred thirty-nine men of *Curacoa*'s crew. He ordered the escorting destroyers to turn about and pick up any survivors they could find, then made the best possible speed for Gourock.

It was almost two and one half hours after the collision when the destroyers *Skate*, *Bramham*, *Cowdray* and *Saladin* reached the survivors. Of the four hundred thirty nine men of *Curacoa*'s crew, only one hundred one were saved. No one would ever know how many went down with the ship, though doubtless scores died in the collision itself, with many more lost to the cold of the sea or washed off into the encroaching darkness, beyond the vision of the searching destroyers. Of the three hundred thirty-eight who died, the bodies of twenty-one eventually washed ashore, either on the Isle of Skye or the Scottish coast. The sea held onto the rest.

The news of the collision and the sinking was suppressed in Great Britain until the war was over. Inquiries and lawsuits against Cunard by families of the crewmen lost aboard *Curacoa* would drag on for five years, but something seems wrong in allowing attorneys and judges to have the last word on the *Queen Mary*'s royal tragedy. The gulf between the abstractions of a warm, dry, quiet courtroom in peacetime, and the realities of the bridge of a warship on the high seas in wartime is almost beyond imagination. Ultimately, the terrible responsibility rested on the two captains—one of whom went on to be knighted and become commodore of the Cunard Line, the other to win the Distinguished Service Order and command minesweepers in the Mediterranean. Yet neither man ever completely shook off the burden of grief over the tragedy they each would bear for the rest of their lives.

The phrase "converted to a troopship" is somewhat deceptive. It conveys none of the complexity involved in the work that was undertaken, to say nothing of the painstaking

Demonstrating just how crowded life could be aboard the Queens, *this group of American airmen are engrossed in what is most likely an illegal craps game.*

planning that was done before the work begins. Nor does it hint of the meticulous organization that had to be implemented once the conversion work is complete, so that the ship can function properly and actually meet the needs of the troops it's meant to carry.

Given the sheer size of the *Queens*, it was an immense task. After setting up several thousand bunks and hammocks throughout the ships, arrangements for the facilities required for the troops' hygiene—toilets and showers certainly, laundries in some circumstances—had to be installed, while shipboard galleys had to be able to produce enough meals to feed the men at least twice a day, and space for the men to be able to sit down and eat their meals had to be found.

A routine of access to the ship's facilities, mess halls, and decks had to be worked out, along with a means of coordinating and directing the men's movements. The crews, ranging from eight hundred fifty to a thousand men, depending on the time of year, were divided into four departments: the Engineering Department, which was responsible for the engines and machinery aboard the ship; the Catering and Purser's Department (sometimes called the Victualing Department), which had the primary task of feeding the troops; the Deck Department, which took care of the navigation, handling, and operations of the ship; and the Permanent Military Staff, which was responsible for loading and unloading the troops to be embarked, as well as all discipline aboard.

The Catering and Purser's Department had probably the busiest role of any of the departments on either of the *Queens*. Feeding fifteen thousand soldiers (and nearly a thousand crewmen) two meals a day required a lot of planning and preparation, as well as hard work. The typical load of stores brought aboard for a six day crossing would include 155,000 pounds of meat; 124,000 of potatoes; 76,000 pounds of flour; 53,000 pounds of eggs, butter, and powdered milk; 31,000 pounds of canned fruit and an equal amount of coffee, tea, and sugar; 29,000 pounds of fresh fruit; 20,000 pounds of bacon and ham, as well as a similar amount of jams and jellies; and 4,600 pounds of cheese. Sixty-five hundred tons of fresh water were pumped aboard (water usage was strictly rationed) and to stock the nine troop canteens scattered about the ship where soldiers could buy personal items, fifty thousand bottles of soft drinks, five thousand cartons of cigarettes, four hundred pounds of candy and varying amounts of razor blades, soap, shampoo, shaving cream and other toiletries were brought aboard as well. No chewing gum was sold aboard either ship, of course.

The methods created to load, house and feed fifteen thousand men for the six days of the crossing was nothing less than a work of genius, a demonstration of that peculiarly American talent for organization and application of assembly-line techniques to human resource problems. Each ship was divided into thirds, the sections labeled from bow to stern "Red," "White," and "Blue." Every GI embarked on the ship was given a button in one of these three colors, to be worn at all times, and they were restricted to their designated area of the ship.

The GIs would start boarding the ship the day before she sailed. Each man brought with him his rifle, helmet, canteen, cartridge belt and webbing, field pack and a duffel bag with his spare uniforms and any personal belongings he chose to bring along—a burden of just over a hundred pounds for each man to carry. The experience that 19 year-old Jerry Cerrachio had aboard the *Queen Mary* was typical. Cerrachio was from Elizabeth, New Jersey, and had enlisted in the Army Air Corps six months after the attack on Pearl Harbor. By December 1942, having been promoted to sergeant, and completed the Air Corps radio operator training program at Madison, Wisconsin, he was assigned to the 459th Air Transport Command, one of several units scheduled to set sail aboard the *Queen Mary* on December 8. Boarding the night before the *Mary* sailed, Sergeant Cerrachio dumped his duffel bag in a section of the deck set aside for them, then made his way to his designated tier of bunks. As he zeroed in on the bottom standee bunks a friend called out behind him, "Don't take that one, Sarge—if one of the guys above you throws up, it'll wind up all over you!" Instantly seeing the wisdom of this observation, Cerrachio instead took the *top* rack—a bit more difficult to reach as well as get into or out of, but definitely safer!

Sergeant Cerrachio recalled that his weapon (he carried a .30-cal. M-1 carbine instead of the heavier, bulkier M-1 rifle) went with him everywhere he went, and that most of the men, particularly the infantry, did the same, which made movement rather difficult at times—but there is no separating an infantryman from his rifle! A system was put in place where starboard passageways were used only for forward movement, portside passageways for moving aft. Traffic control was the responsibility of the Military Police detachment, and probably their single most important function.

Once aboard, each soldier was given a copy of the ship's Standing Orders, which covered emergency procedures in the event of an air attack, abandon ship drills, and fire precautions, always ending with the reminder that "ignorance of these regulations will not be accepted as an excuse in any case of breach of discipline."

While each soldier was assigned a bunk, he didn't always have to sleep in it every night he was aboard, which could be as many as six or seven nights if he was one of those unfortunate souls whose unit was one of the first to board and the last to leave the ship. Since the total number of "standee" bunks aboard each of the *Queens* was only 12,500, when either of them was carrying a entire division of troops, some fifteen thousand strong, a rotation was worked out so that in the summer months each man would sleep "topside" on the open upper decks for two nights, twenty-five hundred men at a time. Far from being a hardship, a berth on the upper decks was coveted by many of the soldiers, and understandably so: in most places below decks, there was only about eighteen inches between one bunk and the next above it, cramped and claustrophobic by anyone's standards. Of course, sleeping on the upper decks was only allowed in the summer months—winters on the North Atlantic were far too cold.

The ship's staff, as well as the officers of the units being transported, did their best to find ways of keeping the men occupied. There were impromptu concerts put on by some of the more talented troops, and if there was a Canadian unit aboard, then a regimental band would give a series of concerts throughout the ship. There was a small library of films aboard both *Queens*, and movies would be shown several times a day. The limited number of choices made little difference to the soldiers, since none of them would be on board long enough to go through the entire catalogue of films carried aboard either ship, but the rather sparse selection did become something of a hardship for the crews: it is recorded that one crewman aboard the *Queen Mary* saw *Pride and Prejudice* one hundred twenty times.

There were always lectures of course: lectures on tactics, on equipment, on personal hygiene. There were lectures, to which most of the troops, to their credit, paid close attention, about getting along with the British, soldiers and civilians alike. Every soldier was given a copy of the U.S. Army Special Services Division's leaflet "A Short Guide to Britain," which articulated some of the most crucial "Do's" and "Don'ts" about everyday life in the British Isles. Among the more memorable passages was this collection of some very sound advice:

> You are higher paid than the British "Tommy." Don't rub it in. Play fair with him. He can be a pal in need. It isn't a good idea to say "bloody" in mixed company in Britain—it is one of their worst swear words. To say "I look like a bum" is offensive to their ears, for to the British this means that you look like your own backside. The British are beer drinkers—and they can hold it.

However entertaining the movies and lectures were, the most popular form of entertainment aboard either of the *Queens* was also the strictly forbidden: gambling. Barely had the troops found their billets aboard the ship than scores of poker, blackjack, and crap games would commence. A watchful eye was kept for wandering MPs who patrolled ship—there is a sense that a large part of the attraction of these games was the fact that they *were* illegal. Some of them would go on for the entire six days of the crossing, players drifting in and out as their fortunes were made or lost.

The officers and crews did their bit as well. Often the crewmen of the *Queen Mary* or *Queen Elizabeth* were the first "foreigners" that many GIs had ever met. For more than one young American, meeting a British sailor face-to-face brought the reality of the war home to him as nothing had ever done before, with the people who had been the targets of Nazi bombs and U-boats suddenly became very human indeed. Sometimes the crew were able to turn the tables on the Germans with a typically British display of humor. On one crossing by the *Queen Mary*, Commodore Bisset made an announcement over the ship's public address system, informing those aboard that the ship had just been sunk. A German propaganda broadcast to that effect had just been picked up, and Bisset had the unique pleasure of announcing his own greatly exaggerated demise on four successive days, as the Germans kept repeating their broadcast.

Two meals were served each day, breakfast in the morning, beginning at 6:00am and running until 11:00; and dinner, which began at 3:00pm and ran until 7:30. The men ate in shifts, each section being allowed forty-five minutes to get their meal, eat it and clean their mess kits. Schedules were so carefully set up and dovetailed that as the last men of one shift were leaving the mess, those of the next were just taking their seats. As the men left the mess, they passed by tables laden with ham-and-cheese or roast beef sandwiches, which they would take with them to fight off hunger pangs until the next meal.

While most of the units transported by the *Queens* were infantry, artillery and armored units, there were others, and not all of them were American. The buildup of Allied forces required not only tens of thousands of combat troops, but also tens of thousands of support personnel. In particular, the American air forces in Britain required thousands of ground personnel, crew chiefs, mechanics, armorers, and ordnance experts, who maintained the thousands of bombers and fighters that were savaging the Third Reich from the air. Large numbers of Royal Canadian Air Force personnel were carried to Great Britain aboard the *Queens,* also.

But regardless of where they came from, what their nationality, or what service they belonged to, these young men the *Queens* were carrying beyond the shores of their homelands for the first time in their lives, were on their way to what would become the great adventure of their lives. Like all adventures, there would be danger, laughter, boredom, fear, courage, tragedy, and triumph. Not all of them would return, and not all of those who returned would be whole. But they were about to become part of the greatest military force ever assembled, one that was gathering its strength and slowly clenching like a titanic mailed fist, poised to strike a devastating blow at the most evil regime the world had ever known. Those bored, hungry, lonely, seasick kids huddled aboard the *Queen Mary* and *Queen Elizabeth* were about to become men; the young soldiers and airmen who would achieve the Allied victory.

The great thunderclap of doom that burst over the Third Reich sounded on June 6, 1944, when Operation Overlord successfully landed one hundred seventy-five thousand soldiers and fifty thousand vehicles on the Normandy shores. They were supported at sea by a naval force of more than five thousand ships and in the air by more than eleven thousand aircraft. It was an operation that had taken two and one-half years of planning, entailed tens of thousands of hours of staff work, demanded the creation of new weapons and new tactics, and required endless days and nights of training for soldiers and airmen who would carry out the assault.

Twenty-six Allied divisions, two American air forces and two Royal Air Force commands were committed to the D-Day landings, their support and follow-up. It was a concentration of men and material the likes of which the world had never seen before, and which the Germans could never hope to turn aside. When the Americans broke through the German front at St. Lo in the beginning of August, the Allied armies were able to exe-

With almost 15,000 troops aboard, the Queen Elizabeth *sets out into the North Atlantic, bound for Gourock.*

cute a swift, sweeping war of movement and maneuver which turned what had been a stubborn and systematic withdrawal by the German Army into a rout. German units disintegrated as they ran pell-mell for the German border, allowing the Allied forces to roam almost at will across France.

The *Luftwaffe*, all but driven from the skies by the combined strength of the U.S. Army Air Corps and the Royal Air Force by August 1944, lost their advanced bases in France to the advancing Allied armies, so what little fighter and bomber strength it still possessed in the West, was pulled back into Germany to make a desperate and hopeless last stand. Though there would be bitter and costly fighting in the months ahead—the Battle of the Hurtgen Forest, Operation Market-Garden, the slow painful slog through Holland by the British and Canadian armies, and the epic fighting of the Battle of the Bulge - the defeat of Nazi Germany was made certain on those five Normandy beaches—Gold, Sword, Juno, Utah, and Omaha. It was the *Warrior Queens* that had made it possible. Statistics can sometimes be incredibly boring, but there are times when the sheer power of numbers can be staggering. Together, the *Queen Elizabeth* and *Queen Mary* brought to Great Britain, by April 1944, over four hundred thousand American and Canadian army and air force personnel. A simple comparison gives a sense of scale to the magnitude of this accomplishment: in early 1942 the United States Army's 34th Infantry Division was sent from New York to Belfast, the movement required a convoy of twenty-one ships and took eleven days. Eight months later, when the 1st Infantry Division was sent from New York to Gourock, one ship—the *Queen Mary*—accomplished the same feat in half the time. Of the twenty-six Allied divisions committed to the D-Day landing and its immediate follow-up, more than half of them had been brought to Great Britain aboard just two ships—the *Queens*. Each crossing the *Queens* made freed a score of other ships to carry vital supplies and equipment. Put another way, the thirty-eight combined crossings from New York to Gourock made by the *Queen Mary* and *Queen Elizabeth* between May 1942 and April 1944 was equal to the combined crossings of *eight hundred* ordinary transports and merchantmen.

After VE day, the *Queens*, along with the *Aquitania*, began carrying troops back across the Atlantic to the United States, where they would eventually be sent to the Pacific to fight the Japanese—a need that evaporated in early August 1945, when the Americans dropped atomic bombs on the Japanese cities of Hiroshima and Nagasaki, and the Rising Sun took a backward topple into the sea. Suddenly, the troops weren't just going back to the States to eventually face more fighting—they were going home! For the next eighteen months, the *Queen Mary* and the *Aquitania* were employed first in bringing home the tired but triumphant American and Canadian soldiers, airmen and sailors, and then they became an integral part of the "Bride and Baby Fleet," which in the course of the next year and half brought some fifty thousand war brides and their children to their new homes in United States and Canada.

The *Queen Elizabeth*, meanwhile, had been released from her wartime service and finally donned her civilian colors. Her interiors installed for the first time, she made her true maiden voyage on October 16, 1946. The *Queen Mary* followed a year later. It was with a touch of irony and yet somehow perfectly fitting, that in their first years back in service, so many of those making the crossing had only a few short years before made the same journey in those same ships, carrying rifles, wearing uniforms, with steel helmets on their heads.

Now with their new wives on their arms, and children in tow, they went back to Europe to reminisce with old friends, to drink beer in fondly remembered pubs, stroll in peace along streets where once they could only crawl in safety, gawk at cathedrals that they had only glimpsed through bombsights, gaze out across beaches still choked with burned-out hulks of tanks, trucks and landing craft, or spend a few silent moments in one of those vast fields of white crosses, saying a last farewell to buddies who would forever be left behind.

So the Cunard Line had come to the end of its second World War, with shouts of joy and a fanfare of trumpets. Oh, the shouts were real enough, and if the fanfare was more imagined than heard, it was all the more real for that. The surviving ships of the Cunard Line would spend the rest of their days proudly wearing their company colors, never again donning wartime grey or mounting guns. But they could rightly take their place alongside the great warships of history, because on their decks, history was made.

They never fired a shot in anger, never sank an enemy ship or submarine, never destroyed an enemy aircraft, never took part in an invasion fleet. But just the *Queen Mary* and *Queen Elizabeth* together were bringing an average of thirty thousand American and Canadian soldiers to Great Britain every month—and did so for three years! Ultimately Cunard's ships transported more than two million troops across the Atlantic—the greatest on-going mass movement of troops in history—and it changed the history of the world: Britain and the United States launched the invasion of Europe at precisely the right moment, when it would result in the beginning of the end of the Third Reich. The decisive battle of World War II in Europe—D-Day—could only have come about because of the yeoman efforts of the ships of the Cunard Line.

It meant the difference between a year's reprieve for the Nazis, who could have completed their new wonder weapons, reorganized and rebuilt their industries, and finished the defenses of the Western Wall. An Allied victory might only have been postponed, but it would have been a postponement that could have spelled death and destruction for millions more, innocent and guilty, civilian and combatant alike.

Instead, the British and American divisions who went ashore on June 6, 1944, had left the Thousand Year Reich lying in ruins eleven months later. It happened because the Allies had relied on the ships of the Cunard Line, who never let them down. Their place is well assured, not only in maritime history but also in military history. Though he was speaking of the *Queens*, the gratitude expressed by the man best suited to speak of their accomplishments could have been an accolade for the entire Cunard fleet, Sir Winston Churchill:

"Built for the arts of peace and to link the Old World with the New, the *Queens* challenged the fury of Hitlerism in the Battle of the Atlantic. Their sterling service allowed the war to be shortened by as much as a year. Without their aid, the day of final victory must unquestionably have been postponed."

CHAPTER FIFTEEN

Cunard Triumphant

Eventually the day came when the *Queens*, along with the other Cunard liners pressed into service as troopships, ceased their eastbound crossings of the Atlantic laden with soldiers destined for combat. By March 1945 the Third Reich was collapsing almost faster than the Allied armies could overrun it, and the *Queen Elizabeth* and *Queen Mary* made their last runs to Gourock with troops aboard. The westbound crossings carrying wounded and invalid soldiers would continue until June. In the meantime, the British and the Americans were drawing up detailed plans for using the *Queens*, the *Aquitania* and the *Mauretania* to bring American and Canadian troops back from Europe to the United States, where they would have a chance to rest, refit, and be trained to fight the Japanese in the Pacific.

The *Queen Mary* began this process on June 10, 1945, when she left Gourock for New York, with 14,777 GIs aboard, arriving in New York Harbor ten days later. She received a welcome on an order of magnitude more tumultuous than her maiden voyage. Decked out in flags from stem to stern, the *Mary* found herself surrounded by hundreds of harbor craft, from fireboats throwing up sprays of water to small powerboats and sailboats that looked like the tiniest of minnows next to the *Mary*'s greatest of whales. Every ship in the harbor sounded their whistles and horns in salute to the *Mary* as she passed, which she returned with almost continuous blasts on her horn. The troops crowded the upper decks, straining to catch a glimpse of the Statue of Liberty and the New York skyline. Overhead helicopters buzzed the ship, while a pair of blimps kept up a more stately escort. As the *Queen Mary* was eased against the Cunard Pier, thousands of people leaning out of the windows of skyscrapers along the Hudson River, along with other thousands lining the docks, cheered wildly. At the pier, a brass band played continuously, unheard among the din. The troops began to disembark almost immediately, to be swallowed up in a hero's welcome.

It wasn't to be a unique experience: New York accorded the same sort of welcome to the *Queen Elizabeth* later that month, as well as every other ship bringing GIs back to the United States. Similar welcomes awaited the Cunard vessels when they returned to Britain, for they brought with them tens of thousands of British expatriates who were returning home for the first time in almost five years, including thousands of children who had been evacuated to Canada during the dark days of 1940. It was altogether a very happy time on both sides of the Atlantic.

While all of this fuss was going on, the *Ascania, Samaria,* and *Scythia* were all busy plying back and forth between Great Britain, Suez, and India, carrying British veterans of the European Theatre to the Pacific Theatre to prepare for the final assault on the Japanese Empire. But the need for all of those soldiers to be sent to the Far East evaporated in early August 1945, when the Americans dropped atomic bombs on the Japanese cities of Hiroshima and Nagasaki. When the news of the Japanese surrender was announced on August 14, the *Queen Elizabeth* had just delivered twelve thousand GIs to New York, while another fifteen thousand were in the middle of embarking on the *Queen Mary* at Gourock. Suddenly, these troops weren't just going home only to be shipped out again to fight another foe in another war—they were going home to stay.

By October 1945, the *Queens* brought almost one hundred fifty thousand GIs home from Europe, an accomplishment that made the American public happy, but was a source of some bitterness among the British. While the war was still being fought, no one questioned the wisdom of allowing the *Queens* to remain under American control, but now that the fighting had ended, many Britons, in and out of the Government, began to wonder out loud why they were being used to transport Americans home from Europe, rather than bringing British soldiers home from India and the Far East. Prime Minister Clement Atlee (who had replaced Churchill at No.10 Downing Street in May) sent a cable to President Truman in October, bluntly telling him, "With so many of our troops overseas awaiting repatriation after nearly six years of war and separation from their families, I cannot justify to the British public the use of our three biggest ships [the *Aquitania* was also being used by the Americans] in the American service." Atlee went on to say that while he was not actually demanding the immediate return of the three ships, he did expect the United States to make a sufficient number of other ships available to the British to equal to capacity of the *Queens* and the *Aquitania*. Truman immediately ordered the Army Transport Corps to work out an equitable arrangement with the British Ministry of War Transport. Peacetime inertia hadn't yet set in for the bureaucracies involved (it's also easy to believe that Truman lit a few fires under bureaucratic backsides) and in less than a week it was decided that the *Queen Mary* would remain under American authority and continue to bring the GIs home from Europe, while the *Queen Elizabeth* and the *Aquitania* were immediately returned to British control.

The U.S. Army Transport Command reshuffled the assignments and routing of a large number of ships, allowing all of the GIs originally slated to return home aboard the *Queen Elizabeth* and the *Aquitania* to still be able to do so on other vessels. The intricacies of the operation were lost on the American public, who could only see that two of the three largest troopships being used to return the GIs from Europe were suddenly being taken out of American service and given to the British. Newspapers across the country echoed that perception, adding their own editorial bleatings about how unfair it was that the British were being given preference over American boys and wondering by what right the British would have the audacity to demand the return of their own ships! It was all very surreal, but fortunately the ruckus was a tempest in a teapot that rapidly blew over as it became apparent with each passing week that the original schedules were being maintained, even without the *Queen Elizabeth* and the *Aquitania*.

Ironically, the *Elizabeth* continued to sail between Gourock and New York until January 1946, but she was bringing Canadian troops home from Europe, rather than GIs. It didn't matter—the cheers of the crowds greeting her arrival were just as loud and long as if the soldiers had been Americans: the people were simply delirious with peace. Once the Canadians disembarked, they were taken to Grand Central Station where they waited for the trains that would take them to Montreal; from there they would be mustered out of the service and returned to their homes. American Red Cross volunteers working at the station plied them with coffee and doughnuts, and showed as great an interest in Newfoundland soldiers who were just returning from Italy, or a Winnipeg regiment coming home from a year's combat in the Netherlands and the Lower Rhine, as they did any American unit that had served with Patton's Third Army. These volunteers were fondly remembered for providing each soldier with a small khaki bag, nicknamed a "housewife," that contained shaving gear, a toothbrush and toothpaste, and a sewing kit, small treasures for which the soldiers were grateful, as they were used to make many a field uniform, as well as the man wearing it, look smarter in time for the last leg of the journey home. Some of the Canadian soldiers kept them for years afterwards.

When VE-Day arrived and the GIs who weren't required for occupation duties in Germany began to be shipped back to the States, another intriguing situation developed, one that had no previous parallels. It had its roots in the dark days of late 1942, when Allied plans and objectives were still in a state of flux, and as a result, units shipped to Great Britain often sat around idle, the troops' morale eroding as the war seemed to be passing them by. Even the Army Air Corps, which at least had the ability to strike at the Germans, was confronted with serious morale problems when casualties began rising to frightening levels in the 8th Air Force's bombing raids over Germany.

The British, while certainly not hostile, were understandably perturbed that many of their "Tommies" were off to Africa or Italy to fight the Germans, or India and Burma to fight the Japanese, while ever-increasing numbers of American soldiers appeared to be doing nothing but sitting in their camps. At least it could be seen that the American airmen were fighting. For the most part the British accepted the situation with their typical phlegmatic poise, touched by a dash of humor, but the undercurrent of strain was always there, encapsulated in the barbed gibe that "The problem with you Yanks is that you're overpaid, oversexed, and over here!". When General Dwight D. Eisenhower assumed command of the Allied forces in Europe in December 1943, one of his first directives was to immediately initiate a program of intense training for all Allied units, believing, with some justification, that training could be so strenuous that the troops would become convinced combat couldn't be any worse. The directive was greeted with something less than enthusiasm, as all it seemed to do at first was add to the overall misery of the troops. Field exercises in the notoriously fickle British weather left the GIs exhausted, muddy, wet, and wretched. Adding homesickness to the mix only made it worse—the Americans were thoroughly unhappy.

After a few months, though, that began to change. The troops became more fit than they had ever been, and as their skill and proficiency improved, they gained a confidence and poise that they had never known before. Disciplinary problems declined as they took more pride in themselves, and as their self-pity evaporated, they began to look around them at the beautiful country to which they had been posted, and discovered the wonderful people among whom they were living.

Suddenly it was a situation almost akin to an invasion by a friendly army of occupation. The Americans discovered local pubs, local dances, and local girls who had been living—courtesy of the German U-boat fleet—under an austere regime of rationing and doing without. If there had been the slightest hint of malice in the GIs' actions or motives, the entire Western Alliance might have collapsed, but the Americans represented themselves to be exactly what they were: lonely young men, many of them not even out of their teens, who were a long way from home who just wanted the company of a friendly face.

If that face happened to be female, young, and pretty, so much the better. The British girls could hardly be blamed for being overwhelmed by the abundance of candy, chewing-gum, cigarettes, and food from Army and Air Corps mess halls. The young ladies' parents no doubt had their worries about their daughters and the intentions of their "Yank" friends—though that rarely stopped them from accepting the gifts of canned ham or fruit, ground coffee, or other delicacies long vanished from wartime Britain, that the GIs brought along as a peace offering to "Mum and Dad."

And it wasn't just the American boys, it was also the lads of the First Canadian Army, nearly one hundred thousand strong, along with the tens of thousands of other young Canadians in the Royal Canadian Air Force who were flying Lancaster, Mosquito, and Halifax bombers from bases scattered across the British Isles. The advance on the hearts of Britain's young ladies was an international, two-pronged assault.

The results were inevitable: American and Canadian boys fell in love with English and Scottish girls left and right, and the local priests and clergy were soon making regular visits to commanding officers all over Britain with requests for permission to marry one of the local girls to one of the officer's young men. The officers knew that their charges were often caught up in the throes of wartime passion, but they also knew that the men were liable to get married whether permission was forthcoming or not, so many a Solomon-like interpretation of Army Regulations resulted. (Of course, it wasn't long before the "Yanks" were responding to the British barb with typical American cheek: "The problem with you Limeys is that you're underpaid, undersexed, and under Eisenhower!")

When the servicemen returned home, they were very vocal in demanding of their governments in Washington D.C. and Ottawa that their brides be allowed to join them—and quickly. Similarly, the anxious new wives were clamoring for His Majesty's Government to make arrangements for them to join their husbands in the United States and Canada. Before the Japanese surrender in September 1945, bringing these "war brides" and their children to their new homes was a low priority, for obvious reasons. By the end of 1946, though, when most of the American troops scheduled to return from Europe were back home, Congress and both Parliaments cooperated in setting up "Operation Diaper," which would bring sixty thousand war brides and their children to the United States and Canada.

The U.S. Army Transportation Corps took responsibility for the project, and in January 1946 announced that thirty ships would be taking part. The British Government, anxious to put both *Queens* back into passenger service as quickly as possible, at first resisted the idea of allowing either ship to be used for carrying the war brides and children to America and Canada, preferring that some of the older liners be used instead. The Americans were insistent, however, and eventually a compromise was reached with His Majesty's Government agreeing to allow the *Queen Mary* to remain under American control for another six months, while the *Queen Elizabeth* would return to Britain so that she could finally be finished as the passenger liner she was always meant to be.

Before she could become part of what the American press soon dubbed the "bride and baby fleet," the *Mary* required substantial modification from her troopship guise in order to make her a satisfactory transport for young wives and small children. On January 14, 1946, returning to Southampton from her final run to New York carrying returning GIs, she entered the King George V dry dock where she was the scene of sixteen frantic days of round-the-clock activity. First to go were the thousands of standee bunks, followed by the latrines and showers that had been temporarily installed throughout the ship. Next over the side went all of the military equipment and fittings: the splinter shields over the bridge windows, the thousands of sandbags packed around vital areas of the upper works, the gun mounts on the decks, the radar tower behind the bridge, the Gunnery Officer's position on the Verandah Cafe, the gun tubs atop the ventilators, all were removed as quickly as possible.

The Warrior Queens in Southampton: The Queen Elizabeth, *left, being readied for her maiden voyage as a passenger ship, while the* Queen Mary *soldiers on, carrying war brides and their families to Canada and the United States.*

The last of the barbed wire coils and barricades that were erected throughout the ship when she was carrying German prisoners of war went over the side. The degaussing coil remained in place, though, as there was still a danger from floating mines that hadn't yet been swept. The hull was scraped of marine growth and corrosion, and the engineers examined the boilers and engines, replacing any parts that were worn or in questionable condition.

While all this work was going on, crews were holystoning the upper decks, and scraping and polishing fittings all over the ship. Inside the *Mary*, the interiors were painted, decks refurbished, and in each of the staterooms six relatively comfortable bunks were installed. The ship's nursery was restored to its pre-war condition, playpens were set up in the smoking rooms, and the swimming pool on D Deck, once the standee bunks were removed, was strung with clotheslines, the pool being designated as an area for drying diapers. In anticipation of babies arriving in mid-ocean, call bells connected to the ship's hospital were set up in those cabins designated for expectant mothers. The dining rooms that had once been mess halls for thousands of soldiers became dining rooms once again, as the tables, chairs, linens and tableware were brought out of storage and returned to the ship. During the last year of the war, most of the interior furnishings—carpets, furniture, murals, glassware, dishes—that had been removed in New York in early 1940, had been shipped to Southampton in anticipation of the day when they would be restored to their rightful places, and that day had arrived.

By January 30, the *Queen Mary* was judged to be ready to join the "bride and baby fleet" and was eased out of the dry dock to a place alongside the Ocean Dock, where her pantries and refrigerated rooms were stocked, her stores replenished, and her bunkers topped off. On February 5, 1946, she set sail for New York, with 1,706 brides and their 604 children aboard, the first of six crossings the *Mary* would make to New York as part of "Operation Diaper." There were five of these Southampton-to-New York voyages by the end of April 1946 which, all told, brought 12,886 young British women and their children to the United States. For everyone aboard, passengers and crew alike, these were happy voyages.

The American and British governments tried to be as fair as possible in determining which women would have priority in being brought to the United States. A handful of women who were deemed "hardship cases" because of special circumstances were given preferential treatment, and allowed to come the United States before "Operation Diaper" actually began. One of ten such women aboard the *Queen Mary* when she left Southampton on December 29, 1945, was Mrs. Emily Glass, whose husband, Robert Glass, was a sergeant in the Army Medical Corps. Her special circumstances were named Shawn, Stephen, and Robert, Jr.—seven-month old triplets. Traveling with her were eighty-eight hundred men of the 82nd Airborne Division, who took up a collection of a dollar a man for the children, to be used as a college fund. All eighty-eight hundred GIs became instant uncles as well, Mrs. Glass recalled, saying that, "The American soldiers were so wonderful. They did just about everything." With one notable exception—like most men, the soldiers managed to find ways of avoiding laundry duty, leaving Mrs. Glass to wash thirty-six diapers every day.

Joyce Beck was crossing with her fifteen month old son, David, in July 1946. Not a good sailor—it was the first time she had ever been aboard a ship—she suffered greatly from seasickness. Her first meal aboard the *Queen Mary* was her most memorable—and her only one. What made it memorable was the white bread. After five years of eating bread that had been grayer in appearance every month as bleached flour became a wartime luxury, white bread became symbolic to Joyce—and thousands of other young British women who traveled on the "bride and baby fleet"—of not only the end of the war, but the amazing new country and new life she was sailing to. Joan MacKelden remembered not only the bread, but the oranges—a luxury unknown in Britain for over five years.

Joyce Beck wasn't the only one who was seasick on that crossing. In fact, most of the wives and children were—and it wasn't always the fault of the sea or the *Mary*'s notorious roll. Captain Charles Illingworth traced the source to something else: "The poor dears had been starved for chocolates. When they found the canteens loaded with sweets, I'm afraid they overindulged." It was a malady that would be repeated on subsequent crossings—no one had the heart to close the canteens.

These crossings were as much fun for the crew as they were a fascination for the young women and children. During the day, there would be lectures on life in the United States, as well as cooking and sewing classes, and instruction on childcare and nutrition. In the evenings there were dancing lessons, bingo games, and movies. (It isn't recorded if *Pride and Prejudice* was still being shown.) The ship's carpenter and his assistants built toys, rocking horses, and doll houses for the children, while their mothers were given tours of the ship and saw first hand how many of their husbands had come to Great Britain. The general consensus of the crew was that the children were noticeably better behaved than their fathers had been.

When the *Mary* arrived in New York at the end of her first crossing carrying war brides, the welcome she received was even warmer and louder than any of her arrivals carrying returning GIs. Every fireboat that could be spared escorted her into New York harbor, throwing up sprays of water in salute, while hundreds of smaller ships and pleasure craft surrounded the huge liner as dozens of aircraft buzzed overhead. Some tugs and larger boats had bands assembled on their after decks, playing the wedding march from Wagner's *Lohengrin*, best known as "Here Comes the Bride." Once the *Mary* was tied up at Pier 90, gangways were swung into place and a steady stream of young women and very small children began to flow down them. The immigration officials had set up what they thought was an efficient, sensible system for processing each of the young wives as they came off the ship. Each woman (and her children if she had them) was directed to an enclosure labeled with the name of the state which would be her ultimate destination; they would be processed in alphabetical order.

What the officials hadn't counted on was the reaction of the husbands, many of whom hadn't seen their wives for as much as a year, some of whom had never seen their children. The ex-soldiers and airmen soon ran out of patience, though, and began swarming over the enclosures, pushing past gates and barricades, breaking down doors, doing whatever it took to be reunited with their loved ones. Soon a happy chaos overtook the whole scene as officials gave up trying to maintain any semblance of order, and hundreds of couples and families were soon gathering each other up in loving embraces.

Sometimes, though, there wasn't a happy ending. Annie Smith was coming to America with her daughter, Joyce Elizabeth. She was one of the lucky ones who were able to secure passage on the *Queen Mary*'s first crossing "bride and baby" crossing in 1946—she celebrated her birthday on the second day of the voyage, February 6. Ultimately she was bound for Texas City, Texas, the hometown of her husband, Corporal Robert F. Smith. It was a "homecoming" tinged with sadness—Smith had been a tail gunner in a B-17 of the 535th Bomber Squadron, 381st Bomber Group, a plane nicknamed *Spamcan*. On May 24, 1944, *Spamcan* failed to return from a mission over Berlin. Initially Smith had been reported as missing, but by January 1946, the truth was known: he had been killed when his plane went down. Annie eventually reached Texas, where she met her late husband's family, who took her and little Joyce in, while she set about trying to build a new life in the shadow of what might have been. Sad as her plight was, in a way Annie was lucky: she had a family waiting for her. Many an English girl and Scottish lass waited in vain for a Yank bomber to return, or received a telegram informing them that their GI in France wouldn't be coming back, and who cried their quiet tears and then carried on, never seeing America, never meeting the families of the boys they had loved and lost.

While the *Queen Mary* was being kept busy with brides and babies, the *Queen Elizabeth* was undergoing a transformation inside and out. When she left New York on February 21, 1946, the American government returned her to Admiralty control, who then promptly "demobbed" (demobilized) her and turned her over to Cunard when she arrived in Southampton five days later. That same day the *Elizabeth* was guided into the King George V drydock which the *Mary* had vacated three weeks earlier, and a small army of dockworkers and shipwrights descended on her to bring her to the glory she would have known back in 1940, had the war not intervened. Hundreds of workers chipped away the layers of wartime grey and applied thirty tons of new paint to dress her in the Cunard livery that she had never worn before: black hull, white superstructure and Cunard-red funnels with black tops.

Fifteen hundred craftsmen came down to Southampton from the John Brown yard to finish the *Queen Elizabeth*'s interiors, among them one hundred and twenty women who had mastered the art of applying a french polish finish to fine woodwork. All of the furniture and furnishings that had been prepared for her, but had spent the last five years in storage, were taken out of the warehouses and brought aboard: fifteen hundred wardrobes and dressing-tables, four thousand mattresses, three thousand sets of curtains and bedspreads, forty-five hundred tables, armchairs, and settees, and more than six miles of carpets. When the work was finished, she had cabins for 823 First Class, 662 Cabin Class and 798 Tourist Class passengers.

One of the more hotly debated aspects of the project was the fate of the handrails throughout the ship. Countless thousands of GIs, Canucks, and Tommies had left reminders of their presence behind in those railings, in the form of names, initials, hometowns, regimental names and numbers, and bits of artwork carved into them with bayonet tips or penknives. Some thought they should be left as they were, as a reminder of the great service the *Elizabeth* had performed during the war. Cunard, on the other hand, felt that there were already enough reminders and remembrances of the war throughout Britain, and that their new flagship didn't need to be one more. The rails were either planed smooth, or when necessary, replaced entirely.

Of a more practical matter, the *Queen Elizabeth*'s power plant was given a thorough overhaul, her first in six years. While the dockyard workers were scraping the accumulated marine growth off the bottom of her hull, the *Elizabeth*'s engineers, along with a special team from John Brown, inspected her boilers, uptakes, turbines, and condensers, replacing boiler tubes, turbine blades, and shaft bearings wherever necessary. Her four great screws were removed and re-machined to restore them to their proper balance, while her propeller shafts were drawn out and inspected, along with the packing of the shaft housings.

The British Government had decided that getting the *Queen Elizabeth* into service as quickly as possible was to be a national priority. Understandably, there was some outcry among Britons, who were still living under wartime rationing six months after the war ended (rationing would continue in Britain for five more years), who resented the special exemptions the Government issued to Cunard for materials and workers, simply so the company could put a luxury liner to sea for the pleasure of the British aristocracy and American plutocrats. Cunard countered by pointing out that refitting the *Queen Elizabeth* would provide jobs for a battered British economy, while the fixtures and furnishings had all been acquired before the war began, so that nothing was being taken away from the needs of British citizens. The Government believed that a refurbished *Queen Elizabeth* would be proof to the world that Great Britain was prepared to resume her rightful place in world affairs and was successfully putting the war behind her.

On October 16th 1946, the *Queen Elizabeth* finally set out from Southampton on her maiden voyage as a passenger liner, with Commodore James Bisset in command. King George VI, along with his two daughters, the Princesses Elizabeth and Margaret, had paid a visit to the ship a few days earlier while she was running speed trials. Princess Elizabeth, dutifully manning a stopwatch, timed the ship along the measured mile, noting a time of 2 minutes 1.3 seconds, just a tick of the clock under 30 knots. For reasons known only to God and the laws of physics, despite having a theoretically better hull form and fractionally more power, the *Queen Elizabeth* would always be a shade slower than the *Queen Mary*. The King and his daughters spent the night aboard as the liner returned to Southampton and began final preparations for her long-delayed maiden voyage. The next morning, as he was leaving the First Class Dining Room after breakfast, the King was seen slipping a few of the whitebread rolls into a paper bag to take with him. During the war years, the Royal Family had chosen to live with the same rationing restrictions as the rest of their subjects, and white flour had been as hard to come by at Buckingham Palace as it had been in the East End.

There was one note of sadness present as the *Queen Elizabeth* departed Southampton that afternoon. Word reached the Cunard offices just as she was making ready to cast off that Sir Percy Bates, Chairman of the Board of Cunard, had died of a heart attack that morning. Taking over the chairmanship from Alfred Booth in the early 1920s, Sir Percy had been a driving force behind the line's survival in the worst years of the Depression and its remarkable recovery in the late 1930s. More than any other single person, Bates had been responsible for construction of the two *Queens*, determined to see a two-ship weekly service finally become a reality; it was he who had the courage to enter upon great enterprises in times of adversity. Though he didn't live to see his dream come to pass, he always had great faith in the future; there can be little doubt that the greatness that would accrue to the *Mary* and *Elizabeth* was nothing more than what he always expected of them, and for them.

Certainly the *Queen Elizabeth*'s first crossing as a passenger liner was promising: it was booked solid, and among those aboard were several people who had bought tickets eight years earlier for the maiden voyage that never took place. Two passengers in particular seemed rather out of place aboard her, at least they weren't the sort of passengers normally found in such monuments to capitalist decadence: Vyacheslav Molotov, the Soviet Union's Foreign Minister, and his deputy, Andrei Vishinsky, were bound for the first session of the newly formed United Nations. At one point during the crossing, Commodore Bisset invited Comrades Molotov and Vishinski to tour the bridge, where Molotov, grinning like a school boy on holiday, took a stint at the ship's helm. It was later reported that he steered somewhat to the left.

Certainly the two commissars had ample opportunity to sample the delights of western decadence. Though somewhat limited in comparison with the menus that would be offered on future crossings, the dinner served the first night out was positively Sybaritic, especially when contrasted with the bland fare to which Britons had become accustomed during the war:

> *Grapefruit au Kirsh*
> *Hors d'Oevres Variés*
> Soup:—*Consommé Royal, Cream of Mushroom*
> Fish:—*Red Mullet Meunière, Halibut, Sauce Mousseline*
> Entrées:—*Croquette of Duckling, Tête de Veay Vinaigrette*
> Joint:—*Leg and Shoulder of Lamb with Mint Sauce*
> Vegetables:—*Green Peas, Cauliflower*
> Potatoes:—*Boiled, Roast, Snow and Gaufrette*
> Relève:—*Roast Turkey, Chipolata Sauce*
> Grill:—*Devilled Ham and Succotash*
> Sweets:—*Orange soufflé Pudding; Coupe Monte Carlo, Macedoine of Fruit Chantilly*
> Ices:—*Vanilla, Strawberry, Lemon with Petit Fours*

Cunard, to forestall any awkward questions about whence these delicacies had suddenly appeared, quickly pointed out in a press release that all of the items on the menu had been purchased in the United States for express use on the *Queen Elizabeth*. There was a minor note of panic when Sir Hugo Cunliffe-Owen, a tobacco magnate and major power in the London Stock Exchange, collapsed after dinner the first night out, but the fears of investors were quickly dispelled when it was reported that Sir Hugo was merely a victim of his own overindulgence, and would make a full recovery. His system, still attuned to the monotonous diet of the war years, had simply succumbed to the richness of that first dinner. More than any other single malady, including seasickness, the consequences of overeating was the ailment that kept the ship's surgeons busy during that first crossing.

On October 2, 1946, two weeks before the *Queen Elizabeth* set out on her peacetime maiden voyage, the *Mauretania* was finally released from government service and returned to Liverpool, where she would be reconditioned by her builders, Cammel, Laird & Co. Like the *Elizabeth*, she went through a thorough overhaul, and it would be the better part of a year before she was ready for commercial service, leaving Liverpool on her first post-war crossing on April 26, 1947. Her first two roundtrips were from Liverpool to New York, but rather than return to the London to New York route, her home port was moved to Southampton. The London-to-New York route, its terminus on the Thames bombed into oblivion during the Blitz, was simply discontinued. The *Aquitania* was soon to be retired, leaving the *Mauretania* as the third-largest ship in the Cunard fleet; as such she became the "relief ship" for the *Queens* on the New York to Southampton run should one of them need to be temporarily taken out of service. But for the most part, her scheduling was distinct from that of any other Cunard ship, sailing every three weeks from Southampton to Cherbourg, Cobh (the former Queenstown), and New York, as she kept to her own unique routine. She immediately became an immensely popular ship, with a clientele that proved to be, in many ways, as loyal as that of the first *Mauretania*.

While the *Queen Elizabeth* and *Mauretania* were undergoing their refits, the *Queen Mary* was being kept busy with a Canadian version of the "bride and baby fleet." From the beginning of May to the end of September 1946, she brought a total of 16,883 young women and their children from Southampton to Halifax, Nova Scotia, as the brides who had wed Canadian soldiers and airmen were reunited with their husbands. While perhaps in keeping with the Canadian way of doing things, the reactions to the *Queen Mary*'s arrivals were a bit more subdued than those witnessed in New York, but the welcomes at Halifax were every bit as warm and heartfelt. When the *Mary* steamed majestically into Halifax Harbour, her presence created as much of a sensation as the precious cargo she was carrying: she had only stopped at Halifax once during the war, in September 1944, when she brought Prime Minister Churchill and his entourage to Canada for the Octagon Conference. On that occasion, arriving at nightfall, she was gone with the dawn the next day, and many Haligonians never knew she had been there. So when she arrived in May 1946, it was the first glimpse most of Halifax ever had of her, the largest ship the city had ever seen, or ever would see.

With the last of the British brides gone and the stores and fuel replenished, the *Queen Mary* bade farewell to Halifax for the last time on September 24. Captain Illingworth had been informed that the ship would be returning to civilian control as soon as he returned to Great

Britain, happy news which he gladly shared with the crew. Once the *Mary* reached open water, he rang down FULL AHEAD on all four engine telegraphs and left them there for the rest of the voyage—they were going home at last! Even the *Mary* herself seemed to sense that she was on her way back to the life for which she had been built, as she made her fastest crossing of the Atlantic ever—3 days, 12 hours, 40 minutes, a *sustained* speed of over 32 knots—a time that would stand as the second fastest crossing of the Atlantic by any passenger ship, ever.

On September 29, two days after she arrived in Southampton, the Admiralty officially handed the *Queen Mary* back to Cunard. During her service in "Light Sea Grey" she had traveled over 600,000 miles and carried nearly 800,000 people of all descriptions. In her turn, the *Queen Elizabeth* had traveled more than 500,000 miles and carried almost 700,000 souls. With none of the mid-winter refits and lay-ups that would have marked their civilian service, the two ships had steamed over a million miles without a major mechanical failure or breakdown. They never missed a sailing, never arrived more than a few hours late. If the quality, pride, or care John Brown's Scottish shipwrights put into their workmanship were ever questioned, here were the answers.

A ten month-long refit of the *Queen Mary* that was as comprehensive as that given to the *Queen Elizabeth* was undertaken at Southampton. Once again entering the King George V dry dock, her hull was scraped and inspected, while her wartime coat of grey was chipped away and replaced with her resplendent Cunard livery. A similar debate to that waged over the GI-scarred railings of the *Queen Elizabeth* broke out over those equally blemished railings on the *Queen Mary*. This time, the decision was made to repair or replace them immediately, but at least one of the yard workers, whose name has sadly been lost to history, decided to save some of the sections of railing, a thoughtful act for which future generations would be grateful, as they would one day be put on display for respectful gaze of those GIs sons, daughters, and grandchildren. One detail that was corrected, for which the urgencies of wartime had never left time, was a permanent repair to her bow. The concrete substitute that had been fitted after the *Mary*'s tragic collision with the *Curacoa* was removed and a new cutwater frame, forged in Glasgow and shipped down to Southampton, was fitted, along with new shell plating. All of her interior fittings and furnishings had been returned to Southampton from Sydney and New York, and soon the *Queen Mary*'s interiors were restored to their pre-war splendor. Some modifications were made to the passenger accommodations, allowing her to carry 711 First Class, 707 Cabin Class and 577 Tourist Class passengers, 1,995 in all. An added bonus was that air-conditioning was fitted throughout the ship, something which Cunard had overlooked for the *Elizabeth*, an amenity she would not have until 1950.

Just before the *Queen Mary* returned to Southampton, there was a red-faced moment for the *Queen Elizabeth*. On April 14, 1947, as she was steaming up the Solent, she ran aground and found herself stuck hard. A frantic effort to lighten her began immediately, and twenty-six hours later, with sixteen tugboats straining at their lines, she was pulled free. In the interim, an amazing assortment of people and goods were taken off, giving a detailed look at what a transatlantic liner was asked to carry. In addition to the 2,246 passengers, there were 8,992 pieces of stateroom luggage and 1,689 pieces of heavy baggage; 649 bags of mail and 34 diplomatic pouches; £13,000 ($63,000) worth of express cargo, 113 canisters of cinema film, 26 automobiles, and 479 gold bars, valued at £148,000 ($720,000). Not only were the *Queens* the most popular ships among Atlantic passengers, but their speed made their cargo spaces particularly valuable as well. The presence of the gold isn't surprising—the Queens were considered to be the safest means of transporting particularly valuable cargoes across the Atlantic; in 1946 the *Queen Elizabeth* was chosen to bring the Magna Carta, which the *Queen Mary* had carried to the United States in 1939 for the New York World's Fair, back to England.

While all the refurbishing activity was bustling about the two *Queens*, the gallant old *Aquitania*, now six years past the date when she had been scheduled for retirement, entered the last phase of her long and glorious career. Judged too old and worn out to warrant a complete restoration and overhaul, she spent her last years on what was called "austerity service" between Southampton and Halifax. The first two years were given over to mainly returning Canadian troops and their wartime families to Nova Scotia, then ferrying over refugees from Europe who had expressed a desire to emigrate and settle in Canada.

It was a vital process, for the chaos of post-war Europe had reduced what had once been the Third Reich and its subject territories into one vast displaced-persons camp. The forced labor programs of the Nazis had uprooted hundreds of thousands of men and women from the countries of Eastern and Western Europe and brought them to the industrial centers of the Reich, most of which were concentrated on the Rhine. Once the war was over, these workers, literally free of their shackles, were allowed to return to their homes. For those who were French, Dutch, or Belgian this presented little problem; most however, had lived in territories now occupied by the Red Army: Czechoslovakia, Poland, Hungary, or Yugoslavia. Any person passing into these Soviet-controlled lands from the West was immediately an object of extreme suspicion. Fearing that such people might have been contaminated with western ideas and ideology, the Soviets automatically sentenced many of them to long terms of hard labor in the gulags—the rest were simply executed out of hand. For many of the Third Reich's *Fremdarbeiter* ("foreign workers"—a thinly disguised euphemism for "slave") there could be no thought of returning to their homelands: consequently, when presented with the opportunity of creating a new life in a new country, one that was young, growing and filled with opportunity, it was a call that few such individuals could resist.

Even worse than the plight of the *Fremdarbeiteren* was that of the survivors of the German racial policies, in particular the Jews. Denied even the tenuous dignity of a euphemism, their status as *Untermensch* ("subhumans") and *Sklaven* ("slaves") was never in doubt. When the war ended, most of them had no homes to which to return: the Nazis had eradicated them and obliterated any trace of their existence. Consequently, for hundreds of thousands of such people, the chance to emigrate to the United States or Canada wasn't just an opportunity, it was a mercy.

A war-weary Aquitania *returns to Southampton in May 1945, the only liner to have served in both World Wars.*

As a result, *Aquitania* spent the last three years of her career carrying thousands of hopeful passengers to Canada. It may not have been a glamorous service, but certainly it was a noble one. Most of them had few, if any belongings other than what clothes were on their backs and whatever meager possessions they had collected since liberation, so it was possible to berth them six or eight to a cabin, much like steerage in the old days, and bring as many as five thousand across on a single voyage. Sadly, such service was all that the *Aquitania* was good for anymore: by the war's end the ravages of age were rapidly overtaking her. Her engines and boilers were worn out, her bulkheads and decks leaked and in some cases had begun to crack, her four funnels were pitted and eaten away by corrosion—in some places, there was more paint holding them together than metal. At one point, in late 1949, a ceiling gave way, sending a piano crashing through to the deck below, narrowly missing a group of Cunard inspectors. She was, literally, a shell of her former self. But she carried on.

She was assisted by the *Ascania, Scythia,* and *Franconia,* the survivors of Cunard's intermediate fleet. The repatriation and relocation service was continued until the end of 1949, but by December the vicissitudes of time caught up with the *Aquitania*, and she was sent to Southampton and tied up at Berth 108. Everybody knew what that meant: 108 had long been a sort of "death row" for liners about to be retired and scrapped. So it was for the *Aquitania*: on February 15, 1950, her house flags came down at last, the next month her interiors were auctioned off, and she was sent north to the Thomas Ward breakers yard at

Inverkeithing. By the following spring there was nothing left of her. She had been the last of the four-funneled "floating palaces;" the last great contemporary of the *Mauretania* and *Lusitania*, the *Olympic* and *Britannic*, and the German giants; the last link with the world of elegance, grace, and leisure that existed before 1914 and had vanished forever in the red mist of the Great War. It was, truly, the end of an era.

The *Queen Mary* at last returned to passenger service on July 31, 1947, sailing from Southampton to New York. The *Queen Elizabeth* left New York Harbor the following day, finally making the Cunard line's dream of a two-ship weekly transatlantic express service a reality. The next decade and a half would be a golden time for the century-old company, as the line had twelve ships in service, including the two greatest ships ever to sail the route, and completely dominated the transatlantic trade. Incredibly profitable during these years, the *Queens* were routinely booked solid on most voyages. With transatlantic commercial air travel very much in its infancy, the ocean liner was still, in John Maxtone-Graham's felicitous phrase, "the only way to cross."

Transatlantic travelers have always had a preoccupation with food, and in the years following the Second World War they proved to be no different. If possible, they may have been more enamored of food than any other generation of passengers, in view of the shortages and deprivations imposed by six years of war. In this, as well as all other areas of ser-

The Queen Elizabeth *steams up the Hudson River in the summer of 1946, a passenger ship at last.*

vice, Cunard was determined to live up to its prewar standards. Purchasers for the line scoured markets and suppliers in New York, Paris, Brussels, London, Liverpool, Southampton, and the Scottish Highlands for the finest provisions, at whatever the cost may be. Maine lobster, Angus beef, Florida oranges, California avocados, the finest Ayrshire potatoes, vintage wines from France and Italy, salmon from cold Scottish lochs, olives from dusty Sicilian hillsides, escargot, truffles, grouse, caviar, all made their way into Cunard holds and cold-storage rooms where they awaited preparation for, and consumption by, Cunard passengers. Jewish passengers could even count on a Kosher menu always being available, ranging from matzoh to heimische cucumbers to Kosher cheese, ice cream, margarine and cooking oil; all meats intended for the Kosher menu were carefully prepared under the watchful eyes of the Beth Din. Regardless of what class in which they traveled, at which table they sat, or even what dietary requirements they may have had, everyone aboard a Cunard ship knew they would enjoy culinary experiences without parallel, on their crossing.

There was also a puckish element to the degree of service provided aboard Cunard ships. The company still savors the story of the American oil magnate who ordered rattlesnake steaks for four one evening: the order was taken without question, and when his dinner arrived, it consisted of four eels served on a silver salver, accompanied by a pair of waiters gravely shaking rattles. Another story that centered around a Texas oilman involved a conversation between the tycoon and the captain of one of the *Queens*. (If the tale was being told aboard the *Queen Mary*, it had taken place aboard the *Queen Elizabeth*; if the venue was the *Elizabeth*, the *Mary* was the site of the story.) The millionaire apparently approached the captain with an offer to buy the ship, to which the captain replied, "Awfully kind of you, sir, but she's not for sale."

"Why not? My money's good!"

"Indeed, sir, but you see, she's part of a set."

One of the persistent charms of Cunard, which was at once the bane and envy of self-proclaimed egalitarians on both sides of the Atlantic, and of which echoes can still be heard today, was the subtle, yet definite snobbishness that permeated the line's day-to-day workings. The strictures and structures of British class-society exerted subtle influences throughout the ship, ranging from what sort of behavior would be tolerated from whom, to which passengers were given seats at the Captain's table or reservations in the restaurants. The unspoken, unwritten rule was that "Passengers must not be antagonized unless they antagonize others more valuable to the company than themselves." Thus the inebriated balladeering Lord Shuphlebotham in the First Class lounge would be tolerated, at least until the Dowager Duchess Rumpledore voiced a complaint to a passing steward. A word from the Captain or Chief Purser, or a discreet comment by the port office, would be enough to guarantee anyone who had embarrassed the company or the ship at some previous date, a quick, quiet, but unmistakable trip to Coventry. Passengers so designated, unaware of their particular status, would, for example, find themselves seated at a table next to the kitchen entryway in their Dining Room, or would learn that a reservation for two in the Verandah Grill was simply not to be had at any price at any time: "Dreadfully sorry, sir, but we're all booked up. Perhaps tomorrow night...." It was hardly fair, but it was a process, silent yet understood by all of the crew involved, that protected the aura of dignity with which the company surrounded itself and its ships.

And while it was dignified, life aboard a Cunard ship in the 1940s and 1950s was a far from stuffy or boring existence. Mornings usually began around seven—or whenever a passenger decided to arise from his or her bed—with a steward or stewardess bringing a steaming pot of tea on a tray. While it was certainly possible for passengers to take their meals in their cabins, breakfast in one of the dining rooms was an experience not to be missed: a menu offering over eighty dishes, from a traditional British mixed grill (including kippers), to American bacon and eggs, with scores of other choices available, as well as five kinds of toast, eleven types of cereal, and tea from India, China, or Ceylon. Breakfast was sure to be a leisurely affair spent reading the *Ocean Times*, a news digest printed in the early hours of the morning, a copy being delivered to each cabin.

Mornings would be occupied by taking turns around the Promenade Deck or visiting the gymnasium for a brisk workout with the weights or on the rowing machine, the stationary bicycle, the electric horses, or the electric camel. The later was a German-designed device, almost sadistic in nature, that moved in odd ways at high speed while the rider sat atop it. It was the cause of serious concern aboard the *Queen Mary* in 1953, when the Archbishop of Canterbury, returning from New York for the Coronation of Queen Elizabeth II, was pitched hard on his head from that particular machine. He made a full recovery and suffered no long-term ill effects, but Don Valenti, the former boxer turned gym instructor aboard the *Mary*, lost quite a few nights' sleep in worry over whether or not Her Majesty would be properly crowned.

Lunch was a mere five-course affair, followed by cards in the lounge or shuffleboard on the upper decks. Alternatives to shuffleboard were deck tennis, golf, or skeet shooting. Visits to the open decks could be adventures in themselves, given the wind and sea conditions on any given day—at some times of year they were impossible: access to the open decks would be strictly forbidden, as the risk of injury, or even being swept overboard, was simply too great. At noon the ship's whistle would give one tremendous, long blast, the signal for the officers to take their noon sightings, after which, when they had calculated the ship's position, the results of the previous day's run would be announced, along with the stakes' winner, if any.

The traditional betting pool on a ship's daily run, that is the number of miles she had covered since noon the previous day, dated back well into the 19th Century, and had eventually become a fixture on every ship on the North Atlantic. Actually, there were several different betting pools, at least one for each class as well as one for the crew. Some were simple affairs, consisting of nothing more elaborate than drawing a number from a hat: in order to win, the number had to match the last number of the day's run. Others were a bit more complex, the most difficult also offering the highest return, that one requiring the player to guess exactly how many miles the ship had progressed since noon the previous day. While the most difficult to win, it was also the most entertaining.

Another variation was the auction pool, where a range of twenty numbers were grouped around a ship's average daily performance for that time of year, usually around six hundred miles. Twenty passengers or groups of passengers would then be given, at random, one of these numbers, for which they had paid between £1 to £5 ($4 to $20). They were then free to retain the numbers if they chose, or turn them in to be auctioned off. The proceeds from the auction were split evenly between the general pool and the number's original owner: often players, having auctioned off one number, would decide to bid on another, swelling the pool yet further. The auctions would take place in the dining rooms, and the dining room stewards were kept busy holding the stakes and keeping track of the bidding. The stewards would also do their best to encourage the passengers to keep the bidding going as long and as high as possible: they pocketed ten percent of the proceeds, so they had a vested interest in seeing the numbers grow large. These auctions became famous for their entertainment value, as a good auctioneer, chosen from among the passengers, could inspire his fellow travelers to sometimes astonishing bids. At times, egos became involved as bidding wars sprang up between two headstrong competitors, so it wasn't uncommon for pools of hundreds or even thousands of pounds to accumulate. The all-time champion on the North Atlantic was a woman who crossed from New York to Southampton in 1933. For five consecutive nights she won the auction pool—her winnings totaled over £10,000. Ironically, she never won a betting pool again.

The hours between lunch and teatime, if not spent at the auction pool or in pursuit of athletics on deck, could be whiled away in the shopping arcade, the cinema, the Turkish bath (today it would be called a spa), or if a passenger was spiritually inclined, in the chapel or synagogue (both were available). Tea was a time-honored ritual, where immaculately turned-out stewards served piping hot pots of tea, along with scones, muffins, and tiny puff-pastries. Teatime was always a quiet time, disturbed only by the murmur of subdued conversation, perhaps the perfect reminder of just how soothing and relaxing an ocean voyage could be.

Dressing for dinner, save on the first and last nights out, was not an option, it was expected. A queue would form at the Purser's Office as the ladies recovered the jewelry they would wear that evening, while throughout the ship, bartenders would begin readying the tools of their trade in expectation of the groups that would congregate at various spots throughout the ship—each *Queen*, for example, had more than a dozen bars—for pre-dinner cocktails. Often there would be several small receptions given either in one of the passengers' cabins or in one of the lounges, sometimes by the Captain or one of his senior officers. Dinner itself was a nine-course *tour-de-force* in the culinary arts, and sometimes lasted more than two hours. Gorged to repletion, the passengers would then retire to the lounges, smoking rooms, or most popular of all, the Verandah Café for a few hours dancing, conversation, or bridge—occasionally a game of bingo would break out. When midnight had come and gone, singly or in pairs the passengers would begin to drift off to their cabins, the day ending with the ritual setting of watches and clocks, forward an hour eastbound, back an hour westbound.

It was a routine that appealed to unprecedented numbers of people in the late 1940s and throughout the 1950s. While the *Queen Mary, Queen Elizabeth, Aquitania* and *Mauretania* had survived the Second World War unscathed, as had happened in the First War, Cunard's fleet of intermediate liners had taken a beating, and an entirely new flotilla of ships had to be built to meet the demands of the skyrocketing passenger lists. This would be Cunard's finest hour, for through a combination of good management, good seamanship, and good luck, the line had continued to exist when almost all of its competitors had been forced into oblivion or reduced to mere shadows of their former selves. White Star lived on in name as part of the Cunard-White Star Line, but nobody ever called the company that—it was simply Cunard: White Star's presence had been reduced to just two ships, the *Georgic* and *Britannic*, and the *Georgic* was soon to go to the breakers. The CGT, the French Line, was left with just two ships, the pre-war *Ile de France*, still handsome and graceful but definitely aging, and the *Liberté*, which was nothing less than the Norddeutscher-Lloyd's *Europa*. Her sister, the *Bremen*, had been bombed into oblivion in her namesake harbor, but the Allied bombers missed the *Europa*, and she was handed over to the French. Extensively rebuilt, with entirely new interiors, a reworked superstructure, and two new and impressive funnels, she was meant to take the place of the lost *Normandie*. (One feat at which the French succeeded that had eluded the British was in eliminating the last Teutonic vestiges from their war prize—when *Liberté* entered service she felt French through and through, and only the most knowledgeable travelers had any idea that she had begun life as the German *Europa*.) The Italian Line had to start over from scratch: of its impressive and popular fleet of ships, only six out of thirty-seven survived. Many of them pressed into service as troopships, had fallen victim to Royal Navy submarines in the Mediterranean. Allied and German bombers took care of the rest. And while some American steamship lines, most notably the Matson Line, had been popular and profitable in the Pacific during the 1930s after the repeal of Prohibition (Americans had no ingrained aversion to traveling on American ships, just on *dry* American ships), the United States had no transatlantic liners capable of competing with Cunard's new "Big Three"—the *Queens* and the *Mauretania*—and so America continued to be a secondary presence on the Big Pond.

Some idea of just how big a business the North Atlantic passenger trade had once again become can be demonstrated by a few statistics. In 1902, the year before the flood tide of immigration began to flow, 205,000 passengers crossed the Atlantic. By 1929, just before the stock market crashed, the number was 1,069,000. Just two years later that number had fallen by almost half, to just 685,000, while in 1934 it bottomed out at a discouraging 460,000 passengers in all classes. Yet by 1950, the number would climb back to its 1929 level, and by 1958, the year when the most passengers ever sailed across the Atlantic, the total would be 1,200,000.

Consequently, Cunard's need for new ships was urgent and real. Chartering vessels from other steamship lines as the company had done after the First World War wasn't a practical alternative this time: there simply weren't enough ships left for any to be available for hire. Instead, Cunard resorted to a form of polite piracy for the first two additions to its second post-war fleet.

Actually, what took place was a good deal more civilized and good-natured than actual piracy: it was really just a form of corporate legerdemain and bureaucratic exploitation. Cunard controlled the Anchor Line, which in turn held a controlling interest in the Brocklebank Line. Brocklebank had two new ships building in 1946, a pair of big freighters with limited passenger accommodations. Cunard simply informed Brocklebank, via Anchor, that it was taking over the two new hulls. As construction was still at a point where the designs could be reworked without necessitating extensive rebuilding, the company was then able to have them completed to new specifications. The result was a pair of what are called "passenger freighters": the *Media*, which joined the fleet in August 1947, and the *Parthia*, which arrived a year later. With their principal dimensions of 531 feet in length, 70 feet in beam and a tonnage of 13,350, they were almost identical in size to the "A" class ships of the 1920s. The *Media* and *Parthia* never left their freighter origins far behind: the forest of kingposts, derricks and booms on their fore- and after-decks made it obvious that carrying cargo was as much a priority with them as was transporting passengers. Not that the passengers suffered: there were accommodations for 250 of them, all in First Class. And as was typical of the passenger freighter type, the accommodations were

New York Harbor, 1956. Among the Cunard ships visible are the Parthia, *the* Queen Mary, *and the* Mauretania.

as spacious and comfortable as any found aboard Cunard's big ships, and the food was considered to be just as good, if not better.

The passenger freighter has always been one of the best-kept secrets of the North Atlantic. A latter-day descendant of the original sailing packets, this type of ship made its living primarily by carrying cargoes, but also offered a limited number of berths for passengers, sometimes for as many as two hundred, others with space for as few as a dozen. "Berths" is actually a somewhat misleading term, for the cabins such ships provided were usually nothing short of luxurious: spacious and well-ventilated, each had its own private bath and toilet, still a somewhat novel concept, while many also had private sitting rooms. Despite the frenzy over the Blue Ribband that existed for decades and the persistent clamor for ever-speedier ships, there had always been a considerable number of passengers who actually enjoyed the experience of being at sea, and who didn't require an endless array of activities to be offered throughout the day for their entertainment, but for whom excellent food, a comfortable chair on deck or in the lounge, a cup of tea and a good book was their idea of traveling in style. The passenger freighter first became popular in the 1890s but truly began to flourish in the 1920s, as the cargo carriers grew more and more aware of the number of passengers who simply wanted to "get away from it all," or wished for more privacy than they could obtain on one of the big liners.

The *Media* and *Parthia* were paragons of the type, and before long had their own loyal following of passengers who would travel on no other ships. A sense of how important they were to Cunard can be gathered from the fact that when the company first entertained the idea of introducing gyroscopic stabilization in the mid-1950s, the first ships to receive such installations were the *Media* and *Parthia*, a distinct echo of the days of the "Pretty Sisters" at the beginning of the century.

The first ship actually built from the keel up for Cunard after the war was one of the most novel in the whole history of the line, the *Caronia*. She wasn't the largest or the fastest ship ever built for Cunard, but she was, in all the best sense of the word, unique. Originally meant to have been a sister to the second *Mauretania*, her construction hadn't even begun when the Second World War erupted. After the war ended and the *Mauretania* was settled comfortably into her own distinctive route and schedule, the company realized that the need for a running mate wasn't urgent, and instead recalled how popular—and profitable—had been the extended tropical cruises of the *Franconia* and *Carmania* in the 1920s and 1930s. Consequently, the decision was made to complete the *Caronia* as a dedicated cruise ship, the first in the history of the line.

She was a beauty. That she shared a common heritage with the *Mauretania* was obvious to anyone who had the opportunity to compare the two, but there were some significant differences. At 715 feet in length, the *Caronia* was 57 feet shorter, but had a greater beam, 91 feet vs. 89. At 35,655 tons, the *Mauretania*'s displacement was marginally greater by 1,500 tons. Both were twin screw, and could make a service speed of 22-23 knots. But the *Caronia* had a more sharply raked bow and a shorter foredeck, giving her an almost

The first addition to Cunard's post-war fleet, the elegant Caronia, *known round the world as "The Green Goddess."*

racy look, and instead of the *Mauretania*'s traditional arrangement of a foremast before the bridge and mainmast on the after superstructure, she had a single tall tripod mast stepped atop the bridge. In order to maximize deck space, a single massive funnel, raked at an angle identical to those of the *Queens* and the *Mauretania*, was set squarely amidships. Most distinctive of all, and immediately indicative of her intended role, the *Caronia* abandoned the black hull and white upperworks livery of the North Atlantic run, instead being painted in four—some sources say as many as seven—different shades of pale green. (The traditional Cunard-red and black funnel colors were retained, of course.) The overall effect was stunning, the *Caronia* looking more like an enormous yacht than a passenger ship. Inevitably perhaps, it wasn't long before she was dubbed the "Green Goddess," a nickname by which she would be known throughout her career.

The *Caronia*'s appointments were as distinctive as her appearance. She was the first Cunard ship to have an outdoor pool, and the first to have private toilets and either a bath or shower in each of her cabins, regardless of class. She was designed for various cruising configurations, either as a two-class ship, carrying 581 passengers in First Class and 351 in Cabin Class, or as an all-First Class ship, carrying just 600 passengers. There were even cruises where she was booked for as few as 300 passengers, all of whom were paying premium fares. But they didn't mind—they wanted it that way. Often older and invariably wealthy, the *Caronia*'s passengers liked the "world's largest floating country club" atmosphere such exclusivity created.

The main lounge was dominated by an enormous full-length portrait of then-Princess

Elizabeth and Prince Philip (it now hangs, appropriately enough, outside the Caronia Dining Room aboard the *Queen Elizabeth 2*). This was where tea was served at precisely 4 o'clock each afternoon by stewards resplendent in starched white jackets and impeccably creased black trousers; each of them having been specially selected to serve aboard the *Caronia*. The level of service was, even for a Cunard ship, extraordinarily high. Passengers grew accustomed to going ashore for an afternoon when the Caronia put into one of her ports of call, and upon returning to their cabins finding their favorite afternoon cocktail waiting on the sideboard, their dinner clothes laid out, and a warm bath drawn and waiting.

At dinnertime, it was considered unexceptional to abandon the menu completely and request dinner cooked entirely to order in one of the two restaurants aboard, the Sandringham or the Balmoral, each named for a royal residence. Touches like this led many passengers to comment that the service aboard the *Caronia* was actually superior to that in First Class aboard either of the *Queens*. Given the evidence, that hardly seems an overstatement.

As a result, the loyalty such service generated among the passengers was astonishing. There was always a waiting list for the *Caronia*, and many passengers returned year after year, often booking the same cabins. Friendships sprang up as frequent passengers became neighbors and would stay on board for months at a time. One woman sailed continuously on the *Caronia* for almost fifteen years, only leaving when it was necessary for the ship to go into drydock for overhauls and maintenance. It's been estimated that she paid over $4,000,000 in fares in that time—certainly she felt the money well spent. Such *esprit* made the *Caronia* arguably the most glamorous ship in the Cunard fleet.

These were the years when glamour didn't accrue to a ship by virtue of the celebrities she carried, but rather became attached to the passengers as a consequence of the ship on which they traveled. The litany of famous names who crossed the Atlantic on a Cunard ship—usually one of the Queens—reads like a *Who's Who* of politics, finance, the arts and literature, and film-making. Sir Winston Churchill and his wife Clementine always insisted on traveling to and from America aboard one of the *Queens*. So did Clement Atlee. So did Queen Elizabeth II, as well as the Queen Mother. Japan's Crown Prince Akihito once won a table tennis tournament aboard the *Queen Elizabeth*. The deposed King Peter of Yugoslavia was a frequent passenger. Writers as diverse as Aldous Huxley and Ernest Hemingway booked passage on Cunard liners. Hollywood was represented by the likes of Rex Harrison, Humphrey Bogart and Lauren Bacall, Spencer Tracy and Katherine Hepburn, Marlene Dietrich, Charles Boyer, Lana Turner, Greta Garbo, all of whom were careful to have their photograph taken while on board. Industrialists like Henry Ford II wouldn't travel on anything but a Cunard ship.

The result was prosperity the likes of which Cunard had never known. In their first three full years of service together, the *Queen Mary* and *Queen Elizabeth* made a combined operating profit of more than £10,500,000 ($50,000,000). Their popularity grew to such degree that in 1949, the Tourist berths on the *Queens* were sold out for a year in advance, Cabin class was booked solid for six months, First Class for two months; passengers want-

The New York skyline, as seen from the bridge of the Queen Elizabeth *in 1956.*

ing to book a particular cabin on a particular crossing were expected to put down a deposit six months in advance. Each ship was making a profit of over £50,000 ($240,000) on each crossing; for the year, Cunard's books showed a profit of £7,000,000 ($33,600,000).

In 1952, Colonel Denis Bates decided that the time had come to replace the four survivors of Cunard's pre-war intermediate fleet, the *Franconia, Samaria, Ascania*, and *Scythia*, which, though similar, were of three different sizes and designs. The Colonel was the brother of Sir Percy Bates, and had been appointed by the line's board of directors to the chairmanship of the line when Sir Percy died unexpectedly in 1946. The decision to build new ships was a shrewd move: a man of a particularly forceful and determined personality, he realized that Cunard couldn't depend on Europe to provide sufficient numbers of passengers to keep the company's ships full; consequently he decided to deliberately court North American travelers, and do so by offering passage aboard ships that were new and stylish. By the mid-1950s his efforts were remarkably successful—three-quarters of Cunard's passenger lists were made up of Americans and Canadians.

The quartet of new sister ships that the Colonel wanted to build, all virtually identical to each other, would serve the Liverpool to Montreal route, which had always proven to be popular and profitable for Cunard, but which was inaccessible to larger ships the size of the *Mauretania* or the *Queens*. Bates felt that it deserved ships as modern and comfortable as those serving New York. He had a point: Canadians have never forgotten that Sir Samuel Cunard was one of their own, and the line, despite its dominance by Scottish businessmen since Sir Samuel's death, never forgot his Haligonian origins either. As a consequence, Cunard had never regarded the Halifax or Montreal routes as the "poor cousins" of the New York run: while other lines ignored the Canadian market entirely, Cunard had dedicated some of its finest ships to serving it.

The result was the *Saxonia* class: *Saxonia, Ivernia, Carinthia,* and *Sylvania*. Though they were considerably smaller than the *Caronia*, it was clear that their design owed much to their glamorous sibling: it featured the same raked bow and clean, elegant superstructure, with a single mast stepped above the bridge. The most distinctive feature was a dome that improved the flow of stack gasses which topped the single large funnel set squarely amidships—it was a feature that was never repeated on any other Cunard ship.

Perceptive observers would have noted that the new *Saxonia*-class ships carried a quartet of kingposts forward of their bridge, and a matching set at the aft end of the superstructure. They were clues to the class' dual role as passenger-cargo ships. The design provided accommodations for 925 passengers—125 in First Class, 800 in Tourist—and six large holds for cargo. Once again the John Brown and Son shipyard was called upon to build ships for Cunard; the first one of the class, the *Saxonia*, entering service in 1954, with a new ship added each year until the last, the *Sylvania*, joined the fleet in December 1957. At 22,000 tons, their displacement was only two-thirds of the *Caronia*'s, while they were 608 feet in length, 80 feet in beam.

This new class was meant to be modern and up-to-date in every respect, and when the *Saxonia* and *Ivernia* were completed, their interiors reflected that intent. Open and spacious, the public rooms were done in pastel shades and blonde woods, giving them what Cunard hoped would be a softer, lighter appearance. But the legions of faithful Cunard passengers disagreed, many loudly expressing a desire to see a return to the darker, glossy

The Sylvania, *one of the Cunard's quartet of intermediate liners introduced in the 1950's, renamed the* Carinthia *after her conversion to cruising in 1963.*

woods that had been the hallmarks of Cunard ships for decades. The line's response was to complete the next two ships, the *Carinthia* and *Sylvania*, in a style more reminiscent of the older Cunard liners; aboard the *Carinthia*, for example, passengers seated in the First Class Dining Room were pleased to learn that the chairs in which they were sitting had originally graced the *Aquitania*.

Nineteen fifty-two was significant to Cunard for another reason, as well. In May, the United States Lines introduced a ship that was meant to assert American supremacy on the North Atlantic, once and for all; the S.S. *United States*. It had been a century since Edward Knight Collins had tried to establish an American steamship company as the preeminent passenger line on the North Atlantic. He had nearly succeeded, but his fall was every bit as spectacular as his rise, and in the intervening decades, the American presence on the Atlantic was never more than that of an also-ran. The United States Line was about to change that forever.

The *United States'* designer, William Gibbs, had long dreamed of designing what he called "the perfect ship." In it, he would incorporate every technological advance in materials and construction, as well as building what he considered to be the ultimate hull form. The American government, which was underwriting more than half the cost of the new liner, gave Gibbs *carte blanche* to produce his dream ship, no matter how costly, as long as she took the Blue Ribband, and did so decisively.

The experience Gibbs had gained designing the United States last pre-war liner, the S.S. *America*, along with the design work he had done on the United States Navy's *Essex*-class aircraft carriers and the *Iowa*-class battleships, helped him perfect his new design. The whole of the *United States'* hull was flush-riveted, with special aluminum-alloy rivets driven cold, to reduce underwater drag. Legend even has it that the hull was sanded smooth to lessen the resistance as it passed through the water. Gibbs then matched this ideal hull with a power plant and screw combination more powerful than any ever before built; to this day just how powerful is still debated, for official figures were never made public. (In fact, about the only dimensions that were never questioned were the *United States'* length of 990 feet and beam of 101 feet. As for the rest—draught, tonnage, shaft horsepower and the rest—no reliable numbers have ever been released.)

Whatever the truth about her design, when the *United States* left New York on July 3, 1952, on her maiden voyage, it was expected that she would take the Blue Ribband. Four days later, when she passed Bishop's Rock in the early hours of July 7, she had done it: her time of three days, twelve hours and twelve minutes gave her an average speed of 35½ knots—at times she touched speeds of more than 38 knots, a four knot margin over the *Queen Mary*'s best. A century had passed since the ship holding the Blue Ribband had been an American steamship; no one could have known it at the time, but there would never be another.

Yet, if the Americans thought that speed alone would suffice to allow the *United States* to supplant either of the *Queens* as the most popular ship on the North Atlantic, they were wrong. Much of the ship left passengers cold, as she seemed to lack character: despite the best efforts of some of the finest interior designers in America, everything about her seemed impersonal, at once pristine and superficial. The explanation wasn't difficult to find—every feature of the new ship's design was subordinated to the requirements of rapidly converting her into a troopship. The wartime accomplishments of the *Queen Mary* and *Queen Elizabeth* had left a lasting impression on the United States Navy, as the strategic capabilities that the *Queens* gave the Royal Navy were not lost on its American counterpart. As a result, features worked into her design to accommodate her wartime role left an impression on her design, from the layout of the decks to the furnishings of her interiors. In particular, fire had always been a phobia of William Gibbs', and he was determined to make his dream ship as fireproof as possible. Aluminum was everywhere, wood wasn't to be found at all, save for the butcher blocks in the galleys and the grand pianos in the lounges. Stainless steel ran rampant, from the staterooms to the lounges, even to the vases on the table in the dining rooms. Except for the linens on the beds in the passengers' cabins and on the tables in the dining rooms, every fabric was fibreglass, from the carpets to the draperies. But the result was that the veil of elegance the *United States* wore was transparent: she was a technological tour-de-force, but lacked the charm and warmth of the *Queens*—as more than one passenger was quick to remark that, for all her veneer of civility, it was never difficult to see that she was really just a warship in disguise.

Admittedly, some notable people, including the Duke and Duchess of Windsor, did switch their allegiance to the new liner—the Duchess never lost her penchant for social climbing, and her need to appear trendy was never sated—but that hardly made a dent in the waiting lists for cabins on Cunard ships. The threat to Cunard's near-hegemony on the North Atlantic would not come from the sea, but from the sky. Aviation had made huge advances during the Second World War, in particular in the areas of range and payload. Once the shooting stopped, it wasn't long before aircraft designers on both sides of the Atlantic began applying the lessons learned with Lancasters, Halifaxes, B-17s, B-24s, and B-29s bombers to Avro Tudors and Lincolns, Boeing Stratoliners, and Douglas DC-4s and DC-6s. By 1952, the first commercial jetliner, the DeHavilland Comet, was in service with British Overseas Airways, and though they were still some years away from production, design work was already underway on the first two great intercontinental jets, the Boeing 707 and the Douglas DC-8.

In the mid-1950s, transatlantic air travel had only one advantage to offer over making the crossing by ship: speed. If time were of the essence, the way to cross was by air, but it was hardly a comfortable experience, the trip taking twelve hours or more from New York to London; airfare could also be just as expensive as a passage on one of the *Queens*. But the jets would soon change that, cutting the travel time to less than eight hours and dramatically reducing costs.

Nineteen fifty-eight was the turning point. In that year more people than ever before crossed the Atlantic by steamship—1,200,000. But the next year the number began to noticeably decline. Still, Cunard wasn't worried—it still seemed highly unlikely that the airplane would ever become more than a supplement to the passenger capacity of the Atlantic Ferry. In its annual *Reports and Accounts*, issued in April 1955, Cunard took the official stance that "There is no freedom to fly in the air as there is freedom to sail the seas, and it is very doubtful that there will ever be such freedom in view of the way in which air traffic has grown up as a political pawn of the Government of every country."

Critics would later chide the shipping lines for failing to anticipate the eventual dominance of the airplane over the steamship, but such lack of prescience wasn't limited just to the ship owners. In January 14, 1957, *Newsweek* announced bids were being accepted for a sister ship for the *United States*, to be called the *America* (replacing the older, smaller ship of the same name), which could cost as much as $100,000,000. Nine months later, on September 9, 1957, an article entitled "More Ships for Busy Seas," appeared in the same magazine. It speculated that the North Atlantic passenger trade stood on the brink of an even greater era of prosperity, with a new French super liner, the *France*, under construction, plans being drawn up for the new American super ship, and 55,000-ton replacement for the *Queen Mary* being considered by Cunard. Yet the editors of Newsweek couldn't have been more wrong: the *France* would be plagued by strikes and cost overruns, delaying her appearance on the North Atlantic by more than two years, while the United States Congress failed to vote the appropriations necessary to build the *America*, and Cunard dithered between alternative designs for their new liner, resulting in no order for a new ship being placed at all. At the same time, though no one knew it, 1958 was the zenith of the transatlantic steamship trade: by the end of 1959, nearly two Atlantic travelers would be making their journey by air for every one that crossed the ocean by ship.

While the character of the passenger trade was undergoing this transformation, one of the greatest chapters of North Atlantic history was coming to a close. In December 1960, the *Britannic* put into Southampton for the final time, the last surviving ship of the White Star Line. Her sister ship, the *Georgic*, had been badly damaged by bombs and a fire during the Second World War, and although she was repaired, was never the same ship. When she was returned to Cunard-White Star after the war, the *Georgic*'s superstructure was considerably modified and one of her funnels was removed. She was considered to have been too badly damaged to be worth returning to her prewar appearance; instead she was given an all tourist-class interior and spent the last ten years of her life employed on charter service for tourists and emigrants, finally being withdrawn and scrapped in 1955.

Meanwhile, the *Britannic* had been returned to her prewar splendor, and quickly carved out a special place for herself on the North Atlantic, working a Liverpool to Cobh to New York route similar to that of the *Mauretania*. Like the larger Cunard ship, she had a certain "club" atmosphere about her, the product of a relatively small passenger accommodation, only 429 in First Class and 564 in Tourist, which endeared her to her passengers. Even though she wasn't air conditioned and had none of the deckside amenities considered essential to cruising, every January the *Britannic* embarked on a nine-week cruise through the Mediterranean. It was always booked solid, sometimes years in advance. Part of the popularity can be understood by a listing of her ports of call, a veritable litany of the romantic and exotic: departing Southampton, the *Britannic* would call at Madeira, Casablanca, Tangier, Malta, Alexandria, Haifa, Larnaca, Rhodes, Istanbul, the Dardanelles, Piraeus, Dubrovnik, Venice, Messina, Naples, Villefranche, Barcelona, Palma, Algiers, Malaga, Gibraltar, Lisbon, and Cherbourg, finally ending the cruise in London. Fares began at $1,275, and included a First Class return to New York aboard any Cunard ship.

Although Cunard had liquidated the last of the White Star Line's assets in 1950 and dropped "White Star" from the company name, the *Britannic* was allowed to wear her White Star livery—black hull and white superstructure separated by a thin gold band, buff-colored funnels with black tops—throughout her career. By the summer of 1960, though, that career was coming to a close. The *Britannic* was almost thirty years old, and wearing out. She spent most of that summer sitting tied up at the Cunard pier in New York, undergoing repairs. When they were far enough along that she could be declared seaworthy, the ship departed for Southampton, where on the last day of December, 1960, her house flag was lowered for the last time. All that remained of the White Star Line were memories.

The *Britannic*'s end came as a consequence of her age; what happened to the *Saxonia* and *Ivernia* was something else entirely. By 1962, the Canadian route had lost so many passengers that it could no longer support four ships in service year-round. Cunard decided to take the two oldest ships, the *Saxonia* and *Ivernia*, off the Montreal run and turn them into full-time cruise ships. They went back to the John Brown shipyard, where the conversion work was extensive: the *Saxonias* lacked the outdoor pools and open deck spaces that are the prerequisites of cruise ships, so the after cargo areas were eliminated and in their place a series of stepped lido decks were built and a kidney-shaped swimming pool installed. Inside, all of the cabins were given private toilets and showers, something that previously had only been found in their First Class accommodations. Their public rooms were completely redone and air conditioning was installed throughout the ships.

They emerged from the shipyard with new identities, the *Saxonia* becoming the *Carmania*, the *Ivernia* becoming the *Franconia*. Originally they were painted shades of light green reminiscent of the *Caronia*, but before long that was changed to an overall white. What all the paint and name changes couldn't hide, however, was the reason behind them. As the airlines took more and more passengers away, all of the steamship lines were falling onto hard times, but for Cunard the fall was more akin to a plummet. In 1962, the same year that the *Saxonia* and *Ivernia* were pulled from the shrinking Montreal route, Cunard announced a loss of £1,728,000 ($8,294,000); it was the beginning of the end. The days of Cunard's triumph were over.

The last great crisis of the Age of Cunard had arrived; when it would finally pass, little would remain of the Cunard Line but the name.

CHAPTER SIXTEEN

Decline and Fall

Nineteen fifty-eight was the last year in which more transatlantic travelers would cross by steamship than by commercial aircraft. By the end of the following year, the figures were reversed—1,500,000 passengers traveling by air against just 882,000 making the crossing by steamship. With each successive year the gulf between the two would continue to grow; in 1961, 2,000,000 passengers crossed the Atlantic by air, while 750,000 traveled by ship; by 1965 there were 4,000,000 airline passengers compared to only 650,000 who made the crossing by steamship. In 1967, the last year that both *Queens* would be in service, only one transatlantic passenger in twenty was aboard an ocean liner.

Yet it needn't have been that way, for the airline industry was having its own trials and tribulations. In 1961 there was only a marginal increase in the number of passengers traveling by air over the previous year, while the number of aircraft flying the North Atlantic rose by 45 percent. This surplus was expensive for the airlines, who were forced to cut fares in an effort to attract more passengers, which in turn ate into their profit margins, leaving many carriers actually operating in the red: British Overseas Airways Corporation, in particular, lost more than £12,850,000 ($36,000,000) that year; in a circumstance that would later loom large in Cunard's future, BOAC's Chief Financial Officer that year was a young chartered accountant by the name of Sir Basil Smallpiece.

This stumble by the airlines actually presented an opportunity that Cunard tried to exploit, as even after the fare cuts, it was still more expensive to fly across the Atlantic than to make the crossing by ship, the average airfare being £82 ($230) one-way in tourist class, against £72 ($201) for a tourist-class cabin on one of the *Queens*. Determined to emphasize how much more comfortable sea travel was in comparison with air travel, Cunard adopted a new advertising slogan, declaring that "Getting there is half the fun."

It was also in the summer of 1961 that Cunard's new chairman, Sir John Brocklebank, decided that getting there by ocean liner could be half the trip as well, as he made the first moves toward Cunard's acquisition of an airline of its own. Brocklebank, whose father and grandfather had chaired the Brocklebank Line that bore the family name, and which was now a Cunard subsidiary, by all accounts knew the shipping world inside and out. It may well have been that appearances were deceiving, however, for at several points during Brocklebank's tenure as Chairman at Cunard, the company missed golden opportunities to adapt itself to the evolving nature of international travel. Not that Sir John was blind to the changes being wrought by passenger aircraft: one of his pet projects, which he nearly achieved in 1961, was the formation of a Cunard-owned airline which would offer unique air-and-sea travel packages between Great Britain, the United States, and the Caribbean.

The idea of a Cunard-owned airline wasn't new: the company had originally planned to add an air arm in the late 1940s, but its efforts were preempted by another fit of nationalization by Clement Atlee's Labour Government, when in 1948 all of Great Britain's privately-owned passenger airlines were absorbed into two state-owned monopolies. They were British European Airways Corporation, soon known simply as BEA, which served domestic and European routes exclusively, and British Overseas Airways Corporation (BOAC), which provided all other international flights and services. Almost from the start, the nationalized airlines were operating in the red, and soon succeeding Governments, Conservative and Labour alike, quietly began developing policies that would gradually lead to the reintroduction of privately-owned, independent airlines, a process which culminated in the Civil Aviation Act of 1960, and

As she began her fourth decade in service in 1966, the Queen Mary *had lost none of her majesty.*

which presented Brocklebank with an opportunity to realize Cunard's ambition to get into the air travel business.

He set his sights on a modest air carrier that ran mainly between the Caribbean, Great Britain, and the United States' East Coast, called Eagle Airways. Originally a freight carrier, Eagle had been allowed to establish a few passenger routes that did not compete with Britain's state-owned airlines, and by 1961, had a regular schedule of flights between London, Bermuda, Nassau, and Miami, as well as flights from Bermuda to New York. It was these routes that made Eagle particularly attractive to Brocklebank, as they all served ports of call for Cunard ships. Another attractive feature was Eagle's flock of aircraft: three DC-6s, three Britannias, four Viscounts, and five Vikings, all fairly modern and comfortable turboprops, nearly as fast but far less expensive to operate that the latest jet-powered Comets, DC-7s and 707s. Not that Cunard was going to forego jet aircraft entirely— Brocklebank had plans to purchase a pair of brand-new Boeing 707s as soon as the deal between Cunard and Eagle was completed.

Brockelbank's idea was to offer a unique travel package where travelers would be whisked across the Atlantic one way, have their holiday abroad, then return home aboard one of Cunard's ships, or alternatively make their initial crossing by ship and return by airplane. It was an ingenious concept, another way for Cunard to put meaning into its new slogan "getting there is half the fun," and it might well have been quite successful had Cunard been able to put it into practice.

It didn't happen. In July 1961 Cunard received permission from the British government's Air Transport Licensing Board to pay £5,000,000 ($14,000,000) for a 60% share of Eagle, which was promptly renamed Cunard Eagle, but no sooner had it done so than BOAC appealed the decision to the Air Ministry. Peter Thorneycroft, the Minister for Air, unexpectedly ruled in favor of BOAC on the ground that BOAC, which was already hemorrhaging cash, would only suffer further losses at the hands of Cunard Eagle.

For the next eleven months BOAC blocked all of Cunard's efforts to get Cunard Eagle off the ground, while during this time the other airlines were gathering in more and more of Cunard Eagle's potential customers. In retrospect, given the comparatively modest numbers of passengers that Cunard's airline could have carried, BOAC's objections seem to have been motivated more by petty politics and jealousy than by genuine concern over a possible loss of business: the British airline objected to the presence of any British company other than itself in the international air passenger trade, and since BOAC couldn't attract enough passengers on its own to generate a profit, it wanted to acquire, by whatever means possible, any business Cunard Eagle might be able to create.

The impasse was broken by a compromise of sorts in June 1962 when Sir John Brocklebank and Sir Matthew Slattery, Chairman of BOAC, hammered out a deal. Cunard Eagle would continue to serve New York, Miami, and the Caribbean, but the airline's transatlantic routes would be taken over by a new joint effort formed as sub-

Like her sister, the Queen Elizabeth *possessed a special power and dignity.*

sidiary of Cunard and BOAC, called BOAC-Cunard Airways. It was a strange amalgamation, with 70% of the new company owned by BOAC—and by extension, the British government—while only 30% was held by Cunard. The creation of the new subsidiary was essentially a victory for BOAC, since its outright majority ownership allowed it to arbitrarily establish fares, routes and schedules with little, if any reference to Cunard's requirements or desires. The venture would carry on as a modest success for the next six years, but a window of opportunity had been closed for Cunard, as the chance to introduce thousands of potential passengers to the idea of air-and-sea travel had been lost to BOAC's petty intransigence.

Meanwhile, as passenger lists and revenues dwindled, Cunard began to cast about for ways to try to bring some measure of prosperity back to the fleet. Borrowing a page from the late 1920s and early 30s, the line hastily converted several of its ships to cruising, but with exceedingly mixed results. In February 1963, the *Queen Elizabeth* made a one-class, five-day cruise from New York to Nassau in the Bahamas. Fares were as low as £45 ($125), and the ship sailed with a full passenger list, but by this time the *Elizabeth*'s operating costs were so high that the entire excursion barely broke even. Even if it had been more successful, the idea of using the *Queens* for cruising had inherent flaws which would have doomed the effort in the long run: built for the North Atlantic rather than the tropics, neither ship was fully air-conditioned, while they both lacked outdoor swimming pools and the vast expanse of open deck space that were the most basic prerequisites for successful cruises.

The same deficiencies plagued the *Mauretania* when, in 1962, she was given a cosmetic make-over and sent on a series of week-long cruises in the Caribbean. Although her new pale green paintwork was meant to invoke the *ésprit* and charm of the *Caronia*, the success and popularity the *Mauretania* had once enjoyed on the North Atlantic didn't follow her into her rather abbreviated cruising career, nor when she was shifted to the Mediterranean in 1963 in an attempt to reopen Cunard's southern route, which had been so popular in the first decades of the century. In this case, the problem wasn't the *Mauretania*; it was the company's surprising lack of business acumen. Where once the line's fame had rivaled that of any of the Italian steamship companies in the ports of the Adriatic and Tyrrhenian Seas, Cunard had abandoned the Mediterranean after the First World War, and now its name was barely recognized in ports like Trieste, Naples, and Palermo. Since the Second World War, the ships of the resurgent Italian Line had become extremely popular with passengers traveling to and from the Med, both for their stylish good looks and their breezy, congenial, yet impeccable service. Cunard's traditional, almost stuffy, British standards of service, which had become the benchmark of the northern run of the Atlantic Ferry, were ill-suited to match the appeal of sunny Italian hospitality: it was an uphill struggle that Cunard was virtually preordained to lose.

Even the *Caronia* was beginning to fall on hard times. In a way, Cunard was a victim of its own success with the *Caronia* in the 1950s. The cruise passengers of the 1960s had become far more sophisticated creatures than their earlier counterparts, and demanded more from the ships upon which they bestowed their patronage. Now those passengers expected more than just lido decks and outdoor pools—casinos, discotheques, spas, and live entertainment aboard ship were now expected as part of the cruising experience.

While the line turned to cruising in an attempt to rejuvenate some of its ships, the decision was made to simply get rid of others. The first to go on the auction block were the *Parthia* and *Media*, both of which were sold in 1961. At the same time, in a chilling echo of 1929 when the loss of passengers after the Crash of '29 caused White Star to give up on the *Oceanic*, and compelled Cunard to suspend work on Hull 534, the same malaise now spelled the demise of a projected replacement for the *Queen Mary*, a 75,000-ton liner known as Project Q3, in 1963.

Hardest hit, though, were the *Queens* themselves. Service, the hallmark of British passenger liners for three quarters of a century, was suddenly falling off; just as detrimental, some services that were offered were no longer relevant or needed. The experience of John Rosselli, an English historian and journalist not given to exaggeration or flights of fancy, throws a harsh light on the realities of traveling on the *Queens*. In 1962, he took his family to the United States on holiday, crossing to America on the *Queen Mary*, returning on the *Elizabeth*, traveling in Tourist class both ways. It was a less-than-auspicious experience, but highly illuminating of how the *Queens*, and by extension the Cunard Line, had lost touch, not only with the realities of travel in the era of air travel, but with many of the expected standards of service on a steamship. Rosselli recounted, for example, how at dinner one evening, the wine steward claimed to have never heard of a carafe—they were listed on the menu—and the wine he and his wife did order with dinner didn't arrive at their table until the end of the meal. One passage, at once amusing and disconcerting, tells of bath time for his two small children: Rosselli wanted to bathe them himself, but the Bath Attendant for his deck (neither of the *Queens* yet had private baths in every cabin) was female, and regulations required the presence of a male Bath Attendant when a male passenger wanted to use the bath facilities. Consequently, Rosselli and his little ones were forced to go to the deck below, where a male Bath Attendant was on duty, in order to accomplish their mission! Such hide-bound adherence to tradition, even when it flew in the face of common sense, made the suggestions Rosselli brought forward in his article most pertinent: there was no longer a need for such people as bath attendants—passengers could open doors themselves—nor was it necessary to compel passengers to wait for their bar drinks to be brought by stewards. It would be better to have the cabin staff concentrate on keeping the accommodations fresh and tidy, assuring that the passengers' clothes were cleaned and pressed as required, and assuring a fresh supply of linens and towels was available. Simplified menus and fewer service and kitchen staff might allow the company to reduce overhead and divert its money into maintaining and refurbishing the ships.

While scaling back the culinary accomplishments of the *Queens'* galleys may have seemed little short of heresy only a decade before, it was a far from inappropriate suggestion. While veteran Atlantic travelers may have bewailed such measures, the truth was that even many of those crossing in First Class were no longer as discriminating as in years past, as the far simpler "steak and potatoes" appetites of the typical American traveler demanded a far less sophisticated menu. More telling of the overall decline in the quality of transatlantic passengers was revealed when the numbers of those who traveled in the old style dwindled at an even greater rate than the overall passenger lists. In the whole of 1963, only forty-two passengers in First Class crossed with a manservant or maidservant in tow, a fraction of the number that would have done so on a single voyage in the 30s and 40s.

These changes in the nature of the transatlantic travelers themselves had, in large part, been wrought by the airlines. Seemingly minor details had tremendous effects: weight restrictions compelled passengers to accept traveling with far less baggage than had been customary in the past; at the same time, the limited variety of services offered by the airlines caused those same passengers to become more self-reliant. The days of traveling with sixteen steamer trunks—along with one's own butler or maid—while having the cabin steward or stewardess cater to a passenger's every whim were replaced by two suitcases and one carry-on bag, as airline hostesses served in-flight martinis and soft drinks, and passed out pre-packaged meals.

It was in an attempt to come to terms with the new realities of air travel, that when Sir John Brocklebank retired in 1965, Cunard's board of directors deliberately sought out a new chairman who understood the airline industry. The thought was that someone from the industry might provide the line with an insight on how to draw passengers back aboard Cunard's ships. In their enthusiasm they may have gone too far: their choice was Sir Basil Smallpiece. A chartered accountant by training (the British equivalent of an American certified public accountant), Smallpiece was a strange choice for the role: he was as ignorant of the shipping world as Brocklebank had been familiar with it, and he openly reveled in the fact that he was an outsider in the industry. The apparently outstanding recommendation for his assumption of the chairmanship at Cunard was his tenure as BOAC's comptroller and managing director prior to his joining the Line. Yet even that experience was of questionable value, as under Smallpiece's financial direction the airline had suffered losses which dwarfed any yet experienced by Cunard. In 1962, when Cunard was posting a disheartening loss of £2,820,000 ($7,900,000), BOAC lost a staggering £13,000,000 ($36,400,000). Because the airline was government-owned, certain methods of financial sleight-of-hand known only to governments allowed the company to post marginal profits in the years following, creating the impression that Smallpiece had worked financial wonders, and in turn could be the savior for Cunard. However, *nomen est omen*. Smallpiece and his colleagues were guilty, in the American idiom, of "thinking small" and trying to salvage the company in bits and pieces. Cunard, and in particular the *Queens*, represented a Britain that was passing into history, and it was the company's misfortune to be led by men who lacked not only the ability to discover a way to exploit the appeal of that past, but also the perception to comprehend the present or the vision to perceive the future. In short, the company's leadership was floundering.

Upon assuming the chairmanship, Smallpiece issued a statement that was meant to sound progressive and forward-thinking, but instead grated arrogantly on the sensibilities of many Cunard employees, as well as a sizeable portion of the British public. "Cunard," he declared, "like so many British businesses, like Britain herself, had become ossified in patterns set by past success. They had been living precariously on their fat until suddenly the supply ran out." Yet his own methods were little more than a series of short-term band-aids, rather than of a long-term program that would bring both stability and prosperity back to the company. His favorite tactic, designed solely to generate revenue and enhance the bottom line, with which Smallpiece was obsessed, was to simply sell off the company's properties and holdings, and report the proceeds realized from such sales as profits.

The first move in that direction had actually come under Sir John Brocklebank, who sold off seven dockside warehouses in Liverpool in 1962, but that had been a common-sense measure: more and more of the company's operations, freight as well as passengers, were based out of Southampton, and the Liverpool warehouses were no longer needed. What Sir Basil undertook was an apparently willy-nilly program of selling off any part of the company that failed to show a profit of at least 15%. While such methods may have produced attractive short terms results, they did little for the company's long-term prospects for survival, let alone prosperity. A question that Smallpiece never answered, apparently because no one else asked it of him, was how the company could hope to be profitable when it had no assets left to sell. In fact, it could be argued that Smallpiece had no long-term plans for Cunard at all, but merely intended to whittle away the company's assets until there was nothing left of Cunard, at which time he would simply dissolve the firm.

There was no need for such shortsightedness. During these same years in which Cunard sought to cut costs by any means, reasonable or otherwise, the Italian Line introduced in quick succession the *Leonardo da Vinci*, *Raffaello* and *Michelangelo*, rakish, smart ships which attracted large numbers of passengers with their service, ambience, and decor. Certainly Cunard's board of directors gave every indication that they felt there was still a place for steamships on the North Atlantic: in 1966 the company decided to spend £1,000,000 on a refit for the *Queen Elizabeth*, expressing their certainty that she had "at least ten good years of service left in her." Their failure wasn't in their belief, but in the execution: they were unable to identify what made the Italian ships so popular—their blending of traditional standards of service with contemporary egalitarianism—and then find ways of adapting their success for Cunard.

Smallpiece's administration also appeared to suffer from a form of corporate schizophrenia: Cunard seemed unable to decide if it wanted to be a steamship line or a holding company. Here Smallpiece's unfamiliarity with the shipping industry was a definite handicap. He was unable to grasp the fact that a century and a quarter's accumulated habits and traditions, which despite the best efforts of Carnaby Street and socialism, were still powerful forces in the British business world, couldn't be undone and dispelled in just a few years. Nor did he have any real idea of the limits to which a shipping company could be made to adapt and change it ways. Sir Basil had concluded that steamships trying to compete head-to-head with aircraft as a means of transportation made no sense, instead deciding much as the Italian Line had done, that the future of passenger ships lay in their becoming "floating resorts," carrying the idea of the ship-as-hotel-at-sea to its logical extreme. His solution to the challenge of making Cunard ships over into that role, however, was to simply sell off four of the seven passenger ships in the fleet (the remaining seventy ships that Cunard owned were all cargo vessels), instead of converting or rebuilding them. The million-pound refit of the *Queen Elizabeth* was a half-hearted attempt at trying to make her over into Sir Basil's new vision, but it failed because it didn't go far enough. That there was merit in Smallpiece's concept would be proven by the success eventually enjoyed by the new ship that was even then being built in the John Brown yard, which would become the *Queen Elizabeth* 2. But there was always an element of hesitancy, of self-doubt, in Smallpiece's actions, as if he lacked sufficient belief in his own ideas to see them through with the determination, even ruthlessness, necessary to make them successful.

At the same time, Cunard became involved in a variety of undertakings that often had only marginal connections with ships or shipping. While acquiring large interests in the Atlantic Container Line and Associated Container Transportation, which gave Cunard a presence in the rapidly growing and highly profitable container-ship industry, made sound business sense, a venture into servicing North Sea oil rigs seemed a good bit more questionable. Of equally dubious wisdom was the decision to buy British travel companies, Lunn-Poly and Sunair Holidays. While the travel agencies offered an opportunity to make money for Cunard, they were in the rather surreal position of doing so by taking potential customers away from Cunard and booking them aboard ships and aircraft belonging to Cunard's competitors. Finally, Smallpiece decided to sell Cunard's 30% interest in BOAC-Cunard, claiming that, although the airline was making money, a 6% profit margin wasn't sufficient for him.

There can be little doubt that Smallpiece blundered in one of his first decisions as chairman, when he agreed to take the *Mauretania* out of service in 1965. Plans for a 75,000-ton replacement for the aging *Queen Mary*, known by the project name Q3, had first been considered by Sir John Brocklebank in 1961, but were rejected as being too costly. Two years later, another design was proposed, known as the Q4, which, though barely two-thirds the tonnage of the *Queen Mary*, still carried an estimated cost of £17,857,000 ($50,000,000). Yet the *Mauretania*, which had long been known as the *Queen Elizabeth*'s "first cousin", and had on occasion served as a substitute for one or the other of the *Queens* when it was necessary to take one of the larger ships out of service, was never considered for the role of the *Queen Mary*'s successor on the North Atlantic, despite having already proved herself to be eminently suitable for the role. Instead, Smallpiece approved the plans for the new ship, even though the financing arrangements would literally mortgage the company's future for the next decade. By contrast, even had it been necessary to completely rebuild the *Mauretania*'s interiors and appointments, the cost would have been only a fraction of that of the Q4. Critics who claimed that the *Mauretania* was too old and too worn out to remain in service had the lie put to their argument the next year, when the *Queen Elizabeth*, only a year newer than the *Mauretania*, underwent a £1,000,000 ($2,800,000) refit that was meant to extend the ship's life by at least ten years; the same could have been done for the *Mauretania*. Smallpiece had clearly "missed the bus;" the consequences would be unfortunate for Smallpiece—ultimately they would cost him his job—and disastrous for Cunard.

The *Elizabeth*'s refit was, admittedly, something of a fiasco. It was intended to bring the standard of her accommodations up to the levels expected, and even demanded by the typical ocean traveler of the mid-1960s. The single most important element of the refit was the addition of private bathroom and toilet facilities for every cabin, regardless of class, a feature the Italian liners had adopted almost a decade earlier, and one that the French had introduced on their immense new *France* when it entered service in 1962. It also came close to being the *Elizabeth*'s undoing. The plumbing being installed in the *Elizabeth* featured copper piping, still something of a novelty along the Clydebank and in the poorer neighborhoods of Glasgow in 1966. Consequently, a thriving black market in copper tubing sprang up while work was being done on the *Elizabeth*.

Pilfering fixtures and furnishings from ships under construction had long been a time-honored, if not exactly honorable, tradition in shipyards along the Clyde, and the John Brown works were no exception. What would happen was that a worker would spot a bulkhead where the piping was exposed, and when no one was looking he'd drive a nail into the tubing: if water spurted out, the line was pressurized and nothing more could be done. If there was no water, then a hacksaw would magically appear and the piping would be cut up into lengths that could be conveniently slid down the workman's trouser legs. At hornblow he would stroll out of the shipyard and into one of several nearby pubs where the proprietors would gladly buy the copper tubing, later reselling it to Glasgow area builders. Unfortunately, the pilfering led to an enormous number of leaks caused by the undetected nail holes in otherwise sound pipes, and when the *Elizabeth* was about to re-enter service and her entire plumbing system was pressurized, flooding occurred all over the ship, ruining thousands of pounds of carpeting and flooring, and causing a two-month delay in her return to service while repairs and replacements were made.

While perhaps the decision to modernize the *Queen Elizabeth* was justifiable, the failure to similarly refurbish the *Mauretania* would come back to haunt Cunard in a few years. But the worst decisions Smallpiece made were in the choices he made for upper management. Wearing his ignorance of ships and shipping like some perverse badge of pride, he chose to bring in men whose backgrounds, rather than making up for his own inexperience, were as alien to maritime industry as his own. Perhaps the most glaring case in point was Philip Shirley, who was named Cunard's chief financial officer in 1968: Shirley had previously worked for British Railways.

Still, it must be said that some of the more drastic changes Smallpiece introduced were not only beneficial but also long overdue. The company's bloated upper management structure was cut down to barely a fifth of its previous size, while the staff of general managers was reduced from thirty to just twelve; at the same time, stiff budgetary controls were implemented. In 1966, he transferred all of the company's offices from Liverpool to Southampton, an obvious move since the Channel port was now the focus of the line's business. Eventually, Cunard's famous old corporate headquarters in Liverpool, the red sandstone-and-granite pile known with varying degrees of affection within the company as "the Kremlin," both for its appearance and the secretive nature of executives who worked within its walls, would be sold for £2,500,000 ($7,000,000).

And at the same time, it's not fair to place the whole blame for Cunard's decline and fall on the shoulders of Smallpiece and his colleagues, for they were simply displaying the symptoms of a malaise that was creeping over the whole of Britain at the time. By the middle of the 1960s, Great Britain was undergoing an identity crisis. Shorn of power, having abandoned her empire, apparently at the mercy of the Common Market, Britain was seized by a paroxysm of self-doubt, as all of her old values and virtues were suddenly called into question by self-appointed opinion-makers and trend-setters. Anything that smacked of Empire, authority, tradition, anything that suggested the "greatness" of Great Britain had suddenly come to be regarded as clichéd, passé, and faintly ridiculous. Everything new, hip, and "mod," however trite and trivial, became the touchstone of the Britain of Harold Wilson and Edward Heath, two non-entities in the mold of Stanley Baldwin or Neville Chamberlain, who periodically alternated terms in No. 10 Downing Street during these declining years. If Sir Winston Churchill's signature gesture was flashing a two-fingered "V" for Victory, that of Wilson or Heath would have been the wetted finger held up to the wind, testing which way the breezes of popular opinion were blowing. OBE's could be awarded to four mop-top musicians from Liverpool in an absurd public-relations gambit to make Britain's government more appealing to the working classes, but somehow the commodores of the Cunard Line no longer rated a place on the Honours List.

This sense of self-doubt, along with an obsession with youth that went entirely against all corporate tradition, certainly played a role in the decisions made by Smallpiece. Where he went wrong—and he was not alone in this error as it was shared by many of Britain's so-called leaders in the 1960s—was in his understanding of what had happened to Great Britain, and in his case more specifically, what had fundamentally changed within the British passenger ship industry. The problem was not that the British Empire had become obsolete; instead, the reasons for its existence had diminished until it had simply become unnecessary.

This last reality became a crucial factor in the continued existence of the Cunard Line. Despite the claims by some commentators who should really know better, air power never truly supplanted sea power—there were, and still are, economic, social, political and military objectives that can only be obtained through sea power; indeed, in the closing decade of the 20th Century and the opening of the 21st, the need for sea power became more obvious and pressing than any time since the end of the Second World War. What *did* happen, however, was that air travel had become more *convenient* than sea travel, a factor that was decisive with an ever-increasing majority of travelers. When steamships were "the only way to cross," travelers had no choice, but by the mid-60s, the majority of transatlantic passengers, in particular businessmen for whom, in the age-old cliché, time meant money, and American holiday-makers who often had only two weeks for their European excursions, could no longer afford to spend a week crossing the Atlantic aboard an ocean liner. Just as critical was the speed which air travel imparted to communications, most vitally the mail. A letter that once would have taken a fortnight to reach its destination could now be sitting on the recipient's desk in as little as five days after it had been posted. The very reason for the Cunard Line's inception as the British and North American Royal Mail Steam Packet Company had been taken away. Sea power was still required, but the need was simply no longer as absolute. It was this reality that prompted Churchill's pronouncement of what he foresaw as the future of Great Britain: "You came into great things by an accident of sea power when you were an island. The world had confidence in you.... By an accident of air power, you will probably cease to exist." He could well have been speaking about the Cunard line.

Whatever hopes there might be for any future at all for Cunard, were resting on the keel that was laid in the John Brown shipyard on the Clyde on July 5, 1965. Referred to in the press by the project title "Q4," the new ship was assigned the yard number 736, and was known by that number to the builder and the company throughout her construction. The design of the new liner, which began in the summer of 1961 when the 75,000-ton Q3 project was canceled by Sir John Brocklebank while still on the drawing board, had taken more than three years to complete. The construction contract with John Brown and Sons, now styled John Brown Engineering, was finalized on December 30, 1964, and the same slipway that had been the cradle of the *Lusitania*, *Queen Mary* and *Queen Elizabeth* was readied for what would become one of the best-known and best-loved ships in Cunard's history.

The new ship would have less than three-quarters of the displacement of either of the *Queens* at just 66,000 tons, although her dimensions were only slightly smaller than the earlier ships: 963 feet in length, with a beam of 105 feet. She would be powered by six boilers providing steam for two sets of Parsons geared turbines, which would produce 160,000 horsepower, sufficient to drive the ship at 28½ knots. Her design called for a capacity of 1,820 passengers, divided into two classes, and from the outset she had been conceived as a sort of "composite" ship, spending six to nine months each year making transatlantic crossings, the remaining months being given over to tropical or around-the-world cruises. Consequently, from the beginning, the design of the Q4 featured amenities and appointments that weren't found on other Cunard ships, or else had been added as afterthoughts.

Among them were four swimming pools—two indoor, two outdoor—a casino, a twenty-four-hour fast-food grill, and more open deck space than had ever been featured on any previous transatlantic liner. One of the most distinctive features was the Sun Deck, a large open area just aft of the ship's single funnel. Open to the sky but enclosed on the sides by glass screens, the area was protected from the wind and sea spray, quiet and calm, ideal for sunbathing or simply spending a quiet afternoon reading in the fresh air, a feature not found on any other Cunard ship. In emergencies, it could even double as a helicopter landing pad.

Every feature of the ship was scrutinized and criticized, and that single funnel which towered over the Sun Deck was the most controversial feature of the new liner's design. Tall and spindly, with a massive air scoop at the base designed to help deflect exhaust gasses up and away from the decks, it looked more like a church spire than a ship's funnel, and seemed too small, too puny, completely out of proportion to the rest of the vessel. Even its colors struck a jarring note: gone was the traditional Cunard red-and-black livery, replaced with a pristine and characterless white. That peculiar funnel aside, the Q4 promised to be a handsome ship, with her carefully proportioned hull and superstructure carrying on the sleek, elegant look begun with the *Queen Elizabeth* and carried on by the second *Mauretania* and the *Caronia*.

Apparently there also remained some vestiges of tradition among the shipyard workers, for the same self-appointed generosity that had marked the *Queen Elizabeth*'s refit was also part of the Q4's construction. Shipyard workers liberally helped themselves to almost everything that wasn't nailed, bolted, or riveted in place aboard the new ship. Almost certainly the worst malefactor was the electrician who was caught red-handed stealing from the ship: when his home was searched by the Glasgow police, they found that he had managed to spirit an amazing array of furnishings off the ship. Among the items they seized as evidence were two chests of drawers, three bookcases, table settings for six, a radiator, five lampshades and thirty yards of carpeting. While such antics might seem amusing in retrospect, at the time their effect was critical, for they drove the cost of the *QE2* to astronomical heights.

This was a serious consideration, for at £22,142,000 ($62,000,000) the Q4 had already badly overrun all budget estimates, and was well on its way to becoming the most expensive liner ever built. The sooner the new ship entered service the sooner it could begin paying its way, erasing some of the huge deficit it had created in Cunard's corporate coffers. At the same time, Smallpiece decided that the day of the *Queens* was rapidly approaching its twilight.

The end, when it came, came suddenly. On May 8, 1967, when the *Queens* were in mid-ocean, the masters of both ships received a wireless message instructing them to open sealed envelopes which had been placed in their safes prior to sailing. Inside the envelopes were letters which revealed that Cunard's board of directors had made the decision, as each ship had been losing over £750,000 each year for the past three years, that both *Queens* would be retired and sold, most likely for scrap. The *Queen Mary* would be the first to go, ending her service that September; the *Queen Elizabeth* would finish hers the following autumn.

When the news was made public, millions of people on both sides of the Atlantic for whom the *Queens* represented not only the Cunard Line, but everything that was good and admirable about Great Britain herself, were at first stunned then shocked. In a statement of typical insensitivity, Smallpiece declared "we cannot allow our affection or our sense of history to divert us from the aim of making Cunard a thriving company, and no other decision will make commercial sense."

It wasn't affection or a sense of history that caused more than a few raised eyebrows in the shipping world, and within the Cunard offices in particular, at the announcement that the *Queen Elizabeth* was to be retired, it was frank astonishment. That the *Queen Mary* was beginning to show signs of age was seriously disputed by no one, but had the million pounds spent on refitting the *Queen Elizabeth* just a year earlier been, for all practical purposes, simply thrown away? What happened to the plans to keep the *Elizabeth* in service for another ten years? Like so many decisions made during Smallpiece's stewardship, while this one may have made the balance sheet more attractive at year's end, it made little sense in terms of long-range planning.

The *Queen Mary*'s fate was decided in the summer of 1967, and as events turned out, she would not be scrapped. Cunard had made it clear when it announced that the company would be accepting bids for her disposal that it would not permit her to be bought by another shipping line to be sailed as a competitor. Nor would they allow her to be purchased and employed in a way that would be degrading to the ship or her reputation. (Memories are long in the shipping world, and images still lingered of the vast but impotent *Great Eastern* tied up at a Liverpool pier, her sides festooned with advertisements; at the very least the *Mary* would be spared that indignity.) One of the more unusual proposals Cunard received came from the city of New York, which offered to buy her for £714,000 ($2,000,000), hoping to set her up as a floating high school in the old Brooklyn Navy Yard; fortunately, nothing came of this rather absurd idea. In the meantime, the usual collection of bids for scrap came from Japan, none of them attractive enough to Cunard to warrant acceptance.

Ultimately, though Japanese scrap metal merchants would offer £1,160,000 ($3,250,000) for the *Queen Mary*, it was the city of Long Beach, California, that submitted the winning bid: £1,230,000 ($3,450,000). Long Beach, which had just become the venue of a highly popular Grand Prix race that was run through the city streets *à la* Monaco, was quickly becoming a popular vacation destination on the American West Coast, and the city leadership had ambitious plans to convert the liner into a floating hotel and convention center. It isn't difficult to imagine the sighs of relief that went up among the ranks of Cunard employees when it was learned that the grand old ship wouldn't suffer the indignity of being sent to a breaker's yard. The only remaining question was whether or not the *Queen Elizabeth* would also be spared in a similar fashion.

Though they would no longer sail the oceans they once ruled, the *Queens* would not depart without a fanfare of their own, nor without a chance to offer each other one final salute. The time was just past midnight, September 25, 1967, the place was somewhere in the middle of the North Atlantic. The two great ocean liners, the *Queen Elizabeth* westbound for New York, the *Queen Mary* eastbound for Southampton, were about to pass one another. The *Elizabeth* had crossed the Atlantic with almost clockwork regularity for over twenty years, the *Mary* for more than thirty, and there had been scores of such meetings in that time. But this mid-ocean encounter of the two ships was different from any other: after twenty-one years of such meetings, this would be their last, ever.

Word of the encounter, as well as its significance, had been spread about both ships, and notices reminding the passengers were prominently posted. Yet, when the time came, only a few dozen hardy souls on either *Queen* were willing to brave the cold winds and late hour to watch the two sisters pay a final salute to each other. Anxious eyes on the bridges and upper decks of both ships watched as first one, then two masthead lights edged over the horizon, then suddenly what had been just a blur in the darkness began to take shape as a black and white ocean giant. At a word from each ship's captain, the upper decks of both the *Queen Mary* and *Queen Elizabeth* were illuminated, the red and black of their funnels glowing above their gleaming white superstructures. The ships were each racing at nearly 30 knots, closing with breathtaking speed. As they passed portside to portside, each captain—Captain John Treasure Jones on the *Mary*, Commodore Geoffrey Marr on the *Elizabeth*—stepped out onto the bridge wing to lift his hat in salute to the other. The great steam whistles bellowed out their own acknowledgment, but their stentorian accolade was as much a dirge as it was an honor....

Then as suddenly as it had come, the moment passed, and the ships sped away from each other into the darkness. The notes of their whistles faded into the night, and their deck lights were dimmed. Within half an hour they were almost out of sight of one another, and those few souls perceptive or romantic enough to understand the meaning of what they had just witnessed broke from their reveries and began to drift off to their cabins. Soon the masthead lights vanished over the horizon, leaving each ship alone on the ocean, bound for destinies that none of the men who built them could have imagined, let alone foreseen as inevitable.

So it was that just over a month later, on October 31, 1967, as tens of thousands of people watched from the shore and hundreds of small craft surrounded her, the *Queen Mary* steamed proudly out of Southampton for the last time, flying a paying-off pennant three hundred and ten feet long—ten feet for every year of service. It was as she was leaving Southampton that one last salute was paid to her in honor of her wartime career.

The aircraft carrier H.M.S. *Hermes*, one of the Royal Navy's most powerful warships, was entering the harbor as the *Queen* was departing. *Hermes'* skipper, Captain Terrence Lewin, always the gentleman, thought it fitting and proper to acknowledge the *Queen Mary*'s passing, not only for her greatness as a liner, but also as one of the Warrior Queens. *Hermes'* complement of Buccaneer bombers and Sea Vixen fighters took to the air to perform a fly-by for the old ship, while the aircraft carrier's crew manned the port side of the flight deck to give three rousing cheers to the departing *Queen*.

Though at this point the *Queen Mary* leaves the stage of Cunard history, the tale of her years that followed deserve at least a passing mention. In many ways for countless thousands of people, particularly those who were born after the Golden Age of transatlantic steamships had passed, she came to embody the Cunard Line, and all that it was and all it represented.

Once she was safely berthed at Long Beach, the next three years were spent in converting the *Queen Mary*'s interior to a hotel and restoring her exterior, a project that cost over £25,714,000 ($72,000,000), and required replacing all three of her funnels. (Two of the original funnels were so corroded that they collapsed as they were being removed; the third was laid on its side for a time, and visitors were allowed to drive their cars through it, reminiscent of a publicity stunt carried out back in 1906 with the funnels of the

A dramatic nighttime view of the Queen Mary, *preserved in graceful retirement in Long Beach, California. (Photo courtesy of Geri Jeffers.)*

Mauretania.) On May 10, 1971, she was opened to the public for the first time, but received mixed reviews: some guests were grateful that the ship had been saved from the breaker's yard, yet many were mortified by the commercialization, including the plethora of souvenir stands that lined her decks, which at times came close to violating the terms of sale regarding demeaning treatment of the ship.

Still, the *Queen Mary*'s twilight, while not entirely free from troubles and tribulations, was happier than that of nearly every one of her contemporaries—of them all, only two remain: the *France*, converted to a cruise ship by Norwegian Cruise Lines in 1979 and still sailing the Caribbean as the *Norway*; and the *United States*, retired in 1969, now lying forgotten, rusting and rotten, at a Philadelphia pier. Scrap yards have taken the rest.

While the city of Long Beach always retained ownership of the *Queen Mary*, the hotel operations and other on-board facilities passed into the hands of the Walt Disney Corporation in 1988. Disney apparently had plans to build a waterfront theme park centered around the giant liner, but without the benefit of its oversized singing, dancing mouse aboard, accompanied by the usual plethora of cartoon characters, the entertainment giant was unable to turn a profit, and sold the *Mary*'s operations back to the city of Long Beach at the end of 1992, at which time the liner was closed to the public.

However, in February 1993, the RMS Foundation, headed by Joseph Prevratil, negotiated a lease on the *Queen Mary*, and that same month the liner was reopened, this time as the Hotel *Queen Mary*. In June of the same year, fifty-five acres of property adjacent to the liner's berth were deeded by the city to be included in the newly-named *Queen Mary* Seaport. In the years that followed, slow but dedicated efforts have been underway to restore as much of the *Queen Mary*'s once-fading splendor as possible. There were critics who deplored the fact that her engineering spaces were mostly gutted, although she would never again have a need for her engines and boilers; knowledgeable observers found some of the "historical" tours of the ship either dismaying for their lack of accuracy or faintly ridiculous in content. But for tens of thousands of people who had never been aboard an ocean liner at sea, the *Queen Mary*'s staterooms and public rooms, now serving as a hotel and convention center, provided a glimpse of the vanished glories of the Golden Age of the transatlantic liner.

Just as the two *Queens* were offering each other their last salute, Cunard's newest ship was finally ready for launching. In an echo of that September day thirty three years earlier, when the beloved old *Mauretania* left New York on her last Atlantic crossing on the same day that the *Queen Mary* slid down the ways, so the new ship would be launched just two days after the *Queen Mary* said her final farewell to New York. It was probably the only gesture to tradition and history that Sir Basil ever allowed.

Not that he had a free hand in planning the details of the launch of the new liner. Sir Basil's publicity men wanted to create a media spectacle, going so far as to propose that the Beatles be commissioned to write a new song for the event, and debut it in a live performance at the launching. However appealing such an idea may have been to Cunard executives, it had no chance of coming to pass: John Rennie would have none of it; until she was turned over to Cunard, the new ship was his.

John Rennie was managing director of John Brown, Ltd., and the man most directly responsible for the actual construction of the new liner. He was also the last of the great Scottish shipbuilders, the end of a line that had begun when Robert Napier built Samuel Cunard's first four ships. Rennie was born in Clydebank, a quarter-mile from the John Brown shipyard, virtually growing up in the shadows of the *Queen Mary* and *Queen Elizabeth* as they were being built. At sixteen, he went to work at the yard as an apprentice boiler-maker, but a keen mind and a driving ambition allowed him to begin studies which led to becoming a naval architect. No one ever had a sharper sense of propriety and the traditions inherent in the ties between John Brown and Cunard, and their importance to the image that grew about a ship and the "tone" it would set throughout its career. Consequently, while he personally may have had no objections to John, Paul, George, and Ringo, there would be no "New Queen Goes to Sea with Diamonds" or whatever it was they had in mind for the launching. Instead, the pipe band of the Singer Sewing Machine Company was hired to play at the yard on launch day.

The morning of September 22, 1967, dawned bright and clear above Clydeside, the famously unpredictable Scottish weather proving cooperative for once. Her Majesty Queen Elizabeth II, accompanied by Prince Phillip, and her sister Princess Margaret, came down from Balmoral to the banks of the Clyde to preside over the launch of the new ship. She

The new Cunard flagship, Queen Elizabeth 2.

was greeted by a crowd of more than a hundred thousand people who had already gathered to watch a sight that might never again be seen in a Scottish shipyard. Using the same pair of golden scissors that her grandmother, Queen Mary, had used to launch the great ship that bore her name, and which her mother, Queen Elizabeth, had used to send the ship that carried hers on its way, Queen Elizabeth II cut the silk ribbon holding the bottle of champagne that broke across the new ship's bow and sent her sliding into the waiting waters of the Clyde.

As she did so, the Queen resolved the great mystery surrounding the name of the new ship. For more than four years, speculation had run rampant as to what Cunard would call their latest creation. Among the proposed names were the *Queen Victoria, William Shakespeare, Britannia, Great Britain,* and *Winston Churchill.* At one point, it was even suggested the new ship be called the *Queen Mary 2.* (Back in 1964 Sir John Brocklebank once half-jokingly commented that he was faced with such a variety of names that he was even considering the *Jackie Kennedy.*) Now, as the Queen sent the new liner down the ways, she announced that the ship was to be called the *Queen Elizabeth 2.* (It should be pointed out here that the name *Queen Elizabeth 2* is *not* a reference to the monarch herself: in maritime usage the arabic numeral 2 rather than the roman numeral II is a clear indication that this is the second Cunard ship to bear the name *Queen Elizabeth.*)

Inside the new ship, which almost immediately became known as simply the QE2, there was little, if anything, about her interior that recalled any of Cunard's earlier ships. Gone was any suggestion of the country-home-at-sea that had been a Cunard hallmark for three quarters of a century: there was nary a carved panel or expanse of wood molding in sight. Instead, stainless steel, aluminum, synthetic fabrics, and plastics dominated the decor. The Carnaby Street crowd howled with indignation when Lady Brocklebank, Sir John's wife, following a time-honored tradition among the wives of Cunard chairmen, appeared at the Cunard design offices one morning in 1964 with swatches of chintz fabric and leatherette in hand, intent on adding her own touches to the new ship's interior. To their general relief she was denied, prompting one of the more perceptive British columnists to astringently observe, "Those who have feared everything would come up roses, horse brasses, chintz and 'Tally-ho!' prints are, no doubt, sitting easier in their Barcelona chairs."

Instead, there would be discos, shopping arcades, and Las Vegas-style revues. The styles of the public and private rooms were a strange mix of Carnaby Street, Kings Row, and NASA, interior decor according to the Who and the Rolling Stones—and Project Apollo. The use of new, "space age" materials was accentuated by designs that were modern and "high tech," functional and decidedly minimalist. Some of the public areas—in particular the Queen's Room—were more than vaguely reminiscent of the sets of the film *2001: A Space Odyssey*. And yet, throughout the ship there was a faint but discernable air of self-consciousness, as if the *QE2* knew that she was a lady dressed up as a Picadilly tart.

The *QE2*'s interior decorators made extensive use of the bold and vivid colors that were the most popular of the time: red, orange, yellow, ochre and white. In those few places on board where wood could be found, rosewood, ash and cedar veneers were used. Wall panelings were covered in Swiss Pearl, velvet, or silk. In a radical but well-advised break from past standards of passenger accommodations, all of the passenger cabins were air conditioned, while each cabin included not only a telephone but a private toilet with either a bath or shower as well.

Passengers boarding the *QE2* would first enter the Midships Lobby, a large circular room that, depending on individual taste, could seem either dramatic or surreal. What would immediately catch every passenger's attention was the jet-black carpeting that was used throughout the public areas of the ship. In the center of the room was a large well, centered on a pillar that resembled nothing so much as a trumpet set on its mouthpiece, its flaring bell supporting a ceiling formed by a series of concentric circles. Around the perimeter of the well was a circular bank of green leather-covered bench seats, each topped with a chrome railing. To some passengers it would be oddly reminiscent of an American drive-in restaurant.

The motif of that peculiar trumpet-shaped pillar was repeated in the smaller columns that lined the Queen's Room, the largest public lounge on board the *QE2*. Flanked along its entire length by large floor-to-ceiling windows that looked directly out onto the ocean, the Queen's Room was awash with natural light in the daytime. At night, an interesting and pleasant mix of flourescent and incandescent lighting made the room a bright and comfortable place, if not particularly cozy or intimate. Unfortunately, the tables and chairs spread throughout the room appeared to be refugees from a science-fiction movie set, the chairs in particular, which resembled eggs sliced in half lengthwise, and by all reports were no more comfortable to sit in than they were to look at.

The two lounges that would prove to be the most popular areas of the ship were a study in contrast, the Midship Bar and the Theater Bar. The Midship Bar was dark and quiet, the dominant color being forest green, and the materials used were mohair, velvet, and deep pile carpet. Part of its popularity was due no doubt, to its imperturbable air of tranquility. In utter contrast was the Theater Bar, located on the starboard side of the Upper Deck, just aft of the Theater. A harsh, almost jarring red was used for the upholstery on the chairs, the fabric of the drapes, even the lacquer finish on the grand piano. An egg crate-like wall covering, made of fiberglass and colored in the same bright red, whose purpose was apparently purely decorative—at least no one could ever seem to figure out an actual use for it—was mounted on the wall behind the bar.

Of all the public rooms aboard the *Queen Elizabeth* 2 the least controversial and most mundane was the Coffee Shop. Its purpose was to provide around-the-clock service for passengers who wanted light meals and breakfast fare at unusual hours. There were none of the attempts to evoke any of the "Britain swings!" chic that pervaded the rest of the ship: it was nothing more or less than a typical American all-night diner. It struck a jarring note, not because it contrasted so greatly with the rest of the ship, but rather because it seemed so out of character aboard a luxury liner. Just what the traveling public's opinions of the ship's interiors would be, remained to be seen. And in fairness it should be said, that as ultra-modern as much of the interior of the *QE2* seemed to be, her designers managed to avoid the aesthetic excesses that plagued the French Line's five-year old superliner, the *France*, which "boasted" some of the most garish interiors, in cabins and public rooms alike, ever to be seen at sea.

While there was very little of the *Queen Elizabeth* 2's interior that suggested any ties to past Cunard traditions, the shipyard workers were doing their best to perpetuate a few time-honored Clydeside traditions of their own. The same plague of thefts that had visited the *Queen Elizabeth* on her final refit now descended on the *Queen Elizabeth* 2, and in the fourteen months it took to complete her fitting out, the new ship was plundered mercilessly. Almost everything moveable aboard the ship was at one time or another carted off, from radios, decorative wall panels, and carpets, to doorknobs, tableware, brass nameplates, and furniture. The level of theft rose to such levels that it made headlines in several British dailies. London's Daily Telegraph ran a story headlined "Piracy on the Clyde," remarking that entire truckloads of stolen furnishings were passing out the shipyard gates under cover of darkness. Eventually, though, enough progress was made so that in early November 1969, the *QE2* was finally declared finished and ready for her sea trials.

Lost in the glare of publicity surrounding the *Queen Mary*'s retirement and the launch of the *Queen Elizabeth* 2 was the announcement that the *Caronia* was also being taken out of service. Surpassed in luxury by the latest generation of cruise ships, her passenger lists gradually dwindled to nothingness, and in November of 1967 she was stricken from the Cunard registry and sold to a group of Greek investors. They hoped to emulate Long Beach and the *Queen Mary*, planning to turn her into a floating hotel moored off the Dalmatian coast. When those plans fell through, her new owners gave her a hasty facelift and returned her to cruising in the Caribbean as the *Caribia*. But on her second voyage she caught fire and was so badly damaged that she had to be towed back to New York. Her new owners had no money to pay for repairs, so she sat unused in New York harbor for the next five years, being shunted from one pier to another, falling further and further into the depths of desuetude and decay. At one point, the City of New York issued the forlorn liner a "parking ticket" for being moored illegally.

Finally, in December 1974, an auction was held aboard the *Caronia*, and everything that remained of value—and quite a bit that wasn't—was sold off before the ship was towed away by her new owners, a Taiwanese scrapping firm. While being towed across the Pacific, she was overtaken by a tropical storm and slipped her towline, running hard aground near the harbor entrance at Guam. The storm quickly broke the ship into three pieces, and as she presented a hazard to navigation, the wreck of the *Caronia* was quickly cut up and scrapped where it lay, a sad end to one of Cunard's most popular ships.

Tragically, the fate of the *Queen Elizabeth* would be no echo of that of the *Queen Mary*. The *Elizabeth* limped along her route between Southampton and New York for a year after the *Mary*'s retirement, the sole survivor of Cunard's once magnificent transatlantic fleet. On one round trip between New York and Southampton, she actually carried a total of two hundred passengers, eighty eastbound, one hundred twenty westbound, who were attended by a crew of eleven hundred, a situation readily apparent to all aboard as being more than faintly ridiculous. The end came for her in October 1968; on the last night of her final eastbound crossing, her passengers and crew gathered on the dance floor and sang "Auld Lang Syne"—there were more than a few tears. In a touching gesture, Queen Elizabeth, the Queen Mother came down from Glammis Castle in Scotland to where the liner was tied up at the Ocean Dock in Southampton, paying a last visit to the ship to which she had given her name and launched some thirty years before. Not wanting to embarrass the Queen Mother or the company, Cunard hurriedly assembled a work gang to scrub down the hull and upper works of the side of the ship facing the shore, so that the *Queen Elizabeth* could put on a good face for Queen Elizabeth. In December she bid farewell to Southampton for the last time. Her next port of call, and her intended final home, would be Port Everglades in the United States, near Fort Lauderdale on the east coast of Florida. When she finally arrived, Commodore Geoffrey Marr rang down "Finished with Engines" on the brass telegraphs for the last time, then opened a cablegram sent from Cunard's Southampton office, which read simply: "ACTS 27 VERSE 19." Consulting his New Testament, Marr found that the passage in question read, "And when it was day, they knew not the land: but they discovered a certain creek with a shore, into which they were minded, if it were possible, to thrust the ship."

A somewhat amorphous group of American speculators, trying to exploit a real estate boom in Florida in the late 1960s, had purchased the *Queen Elizabeth*, snatching her out of the hands of the scrappers, and planned to undertake a conversion of the liner into a floating hotel, shopping mall, museum, and convention center, an even more ambitious project than that planned for the *Queen Mary* in Long Beach. To promote the idea, they invited Commodore Marr to embark on an extensive speaking tour, hoping to attract investors and publicity; Marr cooperated, although he later said that the experience made him feel like a used car salesman.

The grandiose plans of the Florida real estate speculators were never to come about: the group quickly went broke, and for almost two years a succession of similar companies tried to make a going proposition out of the by now rapidly deteriorating liner. Great streaks of rust blemished the sides of the hull and upper works, while the harsh Florida sun quickly faded out the Cunard red of the funnels to an absurd shade of pink. Inside, with much of her interior decor removed, the *Elizabeth* echoed to the footsteps of the handful of visitors and caretakers who periodically came aboard.

Her agony seemed to come to an end in the late summer of 1970, when a Hong Kong businessman named C.Y. Tung bought the ship, announcing his intention to convert the *Queen Elizabeth* into a sort of seagoing academy for marine sciences and aspiring merchant marine cadets, to be called "Seawise University." Just what prompted Tung to such an undertaking has never been explained: more than one observer felt that he simply had more money than he could spend, and indulged in what was certainly the most conspicuous example of conspicuous consumption ever displayed. The thought was prompted by the sly pun in the new name of the ship—"Seawise" being a phonetic rendering of Tung's first and middle initials.

Whatever his motives, Tung brought aboard a Chinese crew, and with only part of the *Queen Elizabeth*'s power plant working, half-towed, half steamed the ship to Aruba, where repairs were made which allowed her to limp under her own power to Hong Kong, via Rio de Janeiro and Cape Town. Once there, extensive renovations began, with replicas of the Great Wall of Sages, the Moon Palace of the Emperor Tang, and the Imperial Peacock Lounge being installed. But something went very, very wrong, for on the morning of January 9, 1972, five fires simultaneously broke out at different locations throughout the ship, and within an hour the *Queen Elizabeth* (no one but Tung and his workers ever referred to her as the *Seawise University*) was ablaze from bow to stern. Fireboats crowded her side and began pumping hundreds of tons of water onto the fires; all they succeeded in doing was destroying the ship's stability. The fires continued to burn throughout the night and the following day, gutting the ship and causing the superstructure and upper hull to collapse and cave in on itself. The ship rolled over onto her starboard side, setting on the harbor bottom at an angle of 45 degrees, the fire eventually burning itself out.

A board of inquiry later ruled, not surprisingly, that arson was the probable cause of the *Queen Elizabeth*'s destruction, although no suspects were ever named and no arrests ever made. A scrap metal firm from Japan quickly bid on the wreckage and was awarded

Smoke billows from the superstructure of the Queen Elizabeth *as she burns in Hong Kong Harbor.*

the contract to dismantle the hulk. The task took more than two years, but by the summer of 1974, the last remains of the *Queen Elizabeth* had been hauled away. It was perhaps a significant indicator of the general disgust at what had been done to a once magnificent ship that the salvors never once referred to the *Queen Elizabeth* by name, but merely called her "the Hong Kong job."

In the meantime, a month before the *Queen Elizabeth* departed Southampton for the last time, the *QE2* was pulled out from her fitting-out berth at the John Brown shipyard, on November 19, 1968, and sent down the Clyde into the Western Approaches for her sea trials, under the command of Captain William "Bill" Warwick. It was one of Warwick's finest hours—command of one of the *Queens* was the ultimate dream for a British merchant captain, the pinnacle of a career, and he had already served as master of both the *Queen Mary* and the first *Queen Elizabeth*. It should have also been the ultimate vindication of Smallpiece's stewardship of the Cunard Line.

Instead, it was a fiasco. On her first set of runs along the measured mile at the mouth of the Firth of Clyde, the *QE2* performed magnificently. Under full power she made a top speed of 32.46 knots, an effort worthy of the first Queens, but disaster struck on a subsequent run. Barely had full speed been rung down to the engine room when the turbines began to emit a horrible cacophony of tortured metal. When they were stopped and the turbine casings opened up by the chief engineer, fractured and broken turbine blades poured out by the bucketful. Unsuspected and undetected flaws in the alloys used in forging the blades had created microscopic fractures in their structures, and when they were subjected to the stresses of high pressure and high speeds, the blades quickly disintegrated. Limping down the coast and into Southampton, the *QE2* spent six months tied up at the docks there, while engineers from John Brown Engineering sought a solution to the problem.

Just two months after the *QE2's* abbreviated sea trials, the *Carmania* ran aground in the Caribbean, and was forced to put into Newport News, Virginia, for repairs that took a month to complete. This left Cunard with just a single passenger ship in service in the first quarter of 1969, the *Franconia*. Suddenly Sir Basil Smallpiece's decision to prematurely retire the *Mauretania* began to look more and more like a mistake, and it was only the money that the cargo divisions generated that kept the company afloat. In early 1970 Cunard further consolidated its cargo operations when it combined Cunard Cargo Shipping Services Ltd., which had been formed out of the Atlantic Container Line and Associated Container Transportation, and with Cunard-Brocklebank, the Port Line, Moss Tankers and Offshore Marine. The new division continued to operate four container ships on the Atlantic run, but most of its tonnage operated between the Middle East, Australia, and the United States, which was one of the most profitable trade routes in the world at the time.

In May 1970, the day finally arrived for the *Queen Elizabeth 2* when Cunard declared that her engine woes had at last been cured. In apparent vindication of the vision of Sir John Brocklebank's decision taken in 1964 to go ahead and build the new liner, excitement had been building for months among the traveling public on both sides of the Atlantic. In anticipation of the new *Queen's* maiden voyage the demand for cabins aboard her was so great that Cunard announced that there would be five "first" passages: a two-day trial cruise from Southampton up to the Clyde and back; a four-day excursion out of Southampton; the maiden westbound crossing to New York; a two-week Caribbean cruise; and then the first eastbound crossing from New York to Southampton. This schedule prompted one reader of the London Guardian to write:

VIRGIN BERTH

Sir,—Can there be any more striking evidence of the influence of the new morality than the report that the new Cunard liner is to have five maiden voyages?

On May 2, the *QE2* left the Ocean Dock in Southampton bound for New York. Three days out she stopped at eight o'clock in the morning, and in a simple, quiet ceremony, the body of Ernest Sharp was committed to the deep. Sharp had been with Cunard for thirty-one years, serving as a steward on both of the first two *Queens*; it had been his fondest wish to serve aboard the third. Less than an hour after she stopped the *QE2* was once again on her way, arriving in New York five days after leaving Southampton, being greeted by the traditional New York welcome for a liner on her maiden voyage. Surrounded by a flotilla of fireboats throwing up curtains of spray, escorted by a dozen tugs up to Pier 92, the *Queen*

Elizabeth 2 was saluted by a United States Navy destroyer, the USS *Conway*, as she was eased into her berth for the first time.

Surprisingly, the critics loved the *Queen Elizabeth 2* as much as did the traveling public. Terrence Mullaly of the London Daily Telegraph, positively gushed, going so far as to declare that a crossing on the new liner would become a social fixture for everybody who had any ambitions to become anybody. The *Queen Elizabeth* 2 spent the summer of 1970 on the North Atlantic booked to capacity for almost every crossing. When she shifted to cruising the Caribbean in the autumn and winter, her popularity remained equally high. It appeared for a moment that the success of the *QE2* might become Cunard's salvation, but it was not to be: she was barely breaking even. Not even the profitable cargo operations could obliterate the red ink that was marring the company's books: the accumulated burden of debt had become overwhelming, and when the year ended with Cunard losing more than £2,000,000—almost $5,000,000—it was the eighth year out of the previous ten that the line had finished in the red.

Nothing in Sir Basil's bag of fiscal tricks was sufficient to overcome this sort of financial disaster, and in early 1971 Cunard's board of directors, fulfilling what had probably been Smallpiece's strategy all along since he assumed the Chairmanship, decided to put the company up for sale. The buyer was Trafalgar House PLC. Trafalgar House was founded in 1956 as a property development and building business, but in the following decade and a half, a series of acquisitions diversified the company away from its roots in real estate and construction, most notably moving it into the travel and leisure industries; it was this segment of its business that made Cunard attractive to Trafalgar. When the announcement was made, it created only a minor stir in the international business community. The prevalent attitude was that such a move had long been inevitable, and the only thing remarkable about the decision to sell the company was that it had been so long in coming.

So it was that on August, 1971, with very little fanfare or public notice, after one hundred-thirty-one years of business, the Cunard Line ceased to exist as an independent corporate entity.

CHAPTER SEVENTEEN

Limbo

So began the most enigmatic and disappointing passage in the whole history of the Cunard Line, a twenty-eight year-long odyssey that would see the company gradually lose its self-image, its identity, and its character, while nearly abandoning its heritage and coming within a hair's breadth of extinction. It would finally end when an American shipping magnate would chose to acquire the line for purely mercenary reasons, only to discover himself giving Cunard a rebirth and returning the line to its rightful place as the premier passenger ship company in the world.

When Trafalgar House absorbed Cunard, the new owners understood from the outset that they had inherited a problem child. Trafalgar's chairman, Nigel Broackes, candidly admitted that while the name Cunard was, in the public's perception, inseparably linked with ocean travel, and that the *QE2* was a major asset in attracting business, there was no disguising the fact that just this ship alone was losing nearly £50,000 every month. The challenge, as Broackes perceived it to be, was to find a way to turn that public awareness into fare-paying passengers.

The first step toward profitability was a reorganization of the company's front office that was as sweeping as anything that Sir Basil Smallpiece had attempted; certainly it was every bit as ruthless, and ultimately proved to be far more effective. Not surprisingly, Sir Basil was replaced as the chairman of Cunard, Victor Matthews taking his place. For six months Smallpiece clung, limpet-like, to a position on Trafalgar's board of directors, eventually resigning when he came to realize that he would play no meaningful part in developing or executing corporate policy. Even before Smallpiece's departure, Matthews fired or replaced sixteen top Cunard executives, all Smallpiece's men, cutting the Board of Directors down from twelve members to just five, and dismissing the top executives in several departments, including finance, personnel, and joint ventures, and combining several divisions. Like Smallpiece, Matthews had never worked in the shipping world prior to taking the helm at Cunard, but unlike his predecessor, he didn't perceive that as a sort of blessing in disguise. Rather he felt the need to make up for his own lack of knowledge of the industry, and believing that experience counted for more than paper credentials, he promoted four mid-level division managers who had spent their entire careers in the shipping business, to the top vacancies. Typical of them was Norman

Thompson, the head of Cunard's cargo division. At 51, Thompson had spent most of his life working on or around ships, beginning as an ordinary merchant seaman. Thompson's experience gave him the advantage of understanding how things were done in the shipping world, and allowed him to work more easily with his colleagues from other companies, men who had often found Smallpiece's underlings arrogant and abrasive. Few professions are as close-knit or tradition-bound as the shipping industry, and pompous "outsiders," such as the men who had worked for Smallpiece, rarely earned the respect, and usually only the most basic cooperation of men who grew up within sight and sound of a waterfront or shipyard.

All of the executive reshuffling, while certainly important to whatever future viability Cunard might have as a passenger ship company, was essentially invisible to the general public. A decision made by Trafalgar House just six months after the combine took over was, on the other hand, highly visible, and made headlines in business journals and daily newspapers across Europe and America. In a single stroke, Cunard's fleet of passenger ships was halved when it was announced on February 1, 1972, that the *Franconia* and *Carmania* were to be sold to a Japanese shipping line. It was a decision provoked by the refusal of the British seamen's union to allow Cunard to replace half the crews aboard the two ships with Asian crewmen, who could be employed at lower wages. (Such intransigence was typical of British labor unions in the 1960s and 1970s, with much the same results—essentially the seamen's union cut off its nose to spite its face, as the upshot of the whole affair was to leave the whole of both crews out of work.)

Selling the two ships—which were, admittedly, getting on in years—went far toward significantly cutting Cunard's operating expenses, the single largest short-term financial obstacle, but at the same time it created another problem. For much of the traveling public on both sides of the Atlantic the name "Cunard" was inseparably associated with passenger liners, yet with only two such ships remaining in the fleet, the company's opportunities to offer the service for which it was best known, were severely curtailed. It was a singularly unenviable situation: the demand for bookings aboard Cunard ships regularly exceeded the capacity of the two remaining vessels, yet was never quite great enough to justify constructing new ones. The entire burden of Cunard's passenger trade would have to be borne by the *QE2* and the *Cunard Adventurer*.

The question confronting Matthews and Trafalgar House was what form that passenger trade would take. While Smallpiece and his colleagues had clearly understood that the future of passenger ships lay in the cruise and excursion market, they never quite developed a coherent concept of the place which Cunard would take in that market. The result of that muddled vision was the *Cunard Adventurer*, a small vessel—484 feet long, 71 feet in beam, just 14,100 tons and accommodations for only 806 passengers—with a curiously symmetrical hull and superstructure that at times made it difficult to determine whether she was coming or going. She was built in Rotterdam for Overseas National Airways, a charter airline in which Cunard had acquired a 50% interest, which had plans to expand into the cruise industry. When the airline foundered in 1971, Cunard bought the unfinished ship outright; a sister already building, the *Cunard Ambassador*, would be added the following year.

The *Adventurer* was a queer sort of ship, which along with her sister, never quite found their place in the Cunard fleet. It was hoped to offer a level of passenger luxury aboard them that no other company in the cruise market could match, but their small size, which was intended to create an atmosphere of affluent intimacy, proved instead to be a handicap, as they felt cramped, rather than cozy, and they never quite caught on with the public, in particular with American travelers, who were—and still are—enthralled with big ships, and so were perennially attracted to the QE2 in ever growing numbers. In any case, the two ships' careers with Cunard were short. A fire aboard the *Adventurer* in 1974 left her so badly damaged that repairs were impractical and she was sold to a Danish shipyard that was eventually able to rebuild her as a sheep carrier. Two years later, the *Ambassador* was sold to the Norwegian Caribbean Line, which renamed her the *Sunward II*.

Two years after the *Adventurer* and *Ambassador* had been discarded, Cunard acquired two more orphans, this time with somewhat more success. The *Cunard Countess*, launched in 1976, and the *Cunard Princess* which followed a year later, had begun life as part of a projected octet of ships that were to be designed and built for MGM, the Hollywood movie studio, which was looking to diversify into the hotel and cruise businesses. The new pair of ships, as alike as two peas in a pod, were built in Denmark and fitted out in Italy in 1976 and 1977, and expanded the Cunard's modest presence in the Caribbean. With a length of 536 feet, a beam of 74 feet, and a tonnage of 17,500, they were appreciably larger than the *Cunard Adventurer* and *Cunard Ambassador*, but they carried fewer passengers at just 750 each. This actually worked to *Countess'* and *Princess'* advantage, as their larger size allowed them to create the sort of "floating country club" atmosphere that had been attempted on their predecessors.

In this sense, they were very much the later descendants of the *Caronia*. However, the comparison could only be carried so far, for they had their faults and limitations. It should have come as a surprise to no one that MGM had very little practical experience with ships, and that inexperience found ways to make itself manifest in the *Countess* and *Princess*. The same standards of construction and appointments that may have worked successfully on land rarely translated well to a ship at sea, and so it proved with the *Countess* and *Princess*. MGM had cut corners in the cost of their construction, using inexpensive materials and devoting little attention to soundproofing. As a result, both ships earned reputations for having paper-thin walls between cabins; the apparent lack of privacy was disconcerting to a large number of passengers, many of whom were put off from ever sailing aboard a Cunard ship again.

Sadly, what was happening to Cunard during these years was that the company was beginning to lose its identity, its sense of self. Sir Basil Smallpiece, for all of his errors, had been utterly correct in his perception that the future of any passenger ship company now lay in cruising rather than transportation, turning the ships themselves into a destination all their own. When Trafalgar House took over the line, Nigel Broackes and Victor Matthews had the good sense to continue pursuing Sir Basil's concept. The difficulty lay in determining how to do so. Certainly there was nothing wrong with the concept of having a large flagship—the *Queen Elizabeth 2*—to attract customers among the general public, and a number of smaller ships available to provide a more specialized service, or serve limited markets: that had been the formula for Cunard's success throughout the 20th Century. The difference now, and it was proving to be profound, was that rather than building new ships to its own specifications, Cunard was falling into the habit of picking up other companies' cast-offs. There is no question that it was a policy that was saving money for the line at a time when it had little capital for new construction, but the result was that the ships never really acquired a Cunard "personality." It was a situation that resembled the plight of the *Berengaria* after the Great War—she could never quite put her German origins behind her, and so always seemed a bit out of place in Cunard's fleet, a factor which ultimately played into her somewhat premature demise. Now, thirty years later, the only truly "British" ship in the Cunard fleet was the *QE2*; the others all had the look and feel of stopgaps.

To some degree, Chairman Matthews and his staff added to that impression. They never made any pretense of the fact that the *QE2* was something of a hybrid, half ocean liner, half cruise ship. In the words of a contemporary Cunard brochure, "*QE2* is not a modern version of the former Queens. She is a resort hotel that has the advantage of being able to follow the sun...." or as it is put in another part of the same advertisement, "*QE2* is not so much in competition with the air, which is transportation, as with land-based resort hotels, which are holiday and leisure centers." Perhaps no better proof of how far behind Cunard was leaving its transatlantic heritage was shown, when in 1971 the purser ceased to be the purser: he was now the "hotel manager."

The *QE2* herself had undergone an extensive makeover in November 1972, which had left some critics aghast. The addition of an entire deck of penthouse suites above the Boat Deck between the bridge and the funnel noticeably altered the ship's profile, although the change was not the desecration that some observers declared it to be. More immediately recognizable to her passengers—and of far more questionable taste—were the wholesale alterations made to the *Queen Elizabeth 2*'s interior. The most notable change was the disappearance of the Blue Room, which had been a quiet reading room on the port side of the Quarter Deck. In its place came a casino, complete with slot-machines, roulette wheels, and craps tables. Other changes, while not as drastic, were equally disconcerting: an arcade of shops replaced part of the grand ballroom, while a section of the First Class promenade deck was converted into a showroom for new cars; the *QE2* had become a sea-going automobile dealership. The new penthouse suites came under fire for their lack of discernable style: one designer, delivering a wit more cutting than any bitter critique, called them a

The Queen Elizabeth 2 *passing through the Panama Canal on one of her annual around-the-world cruises.*

collection from the Louis-the-Who? period.

Nineteen seventy-two had been a memorable year aboard the QE2 for other reasons as well. May saw the ship subjected to a bomb scare in mid-Atlantic: Cunard's New York office received an anonymous telephone call when the ship was in mid-Atlantic announcing that bombs already in place aboard her would be detonated if a ransom demand of $350,000 wasn't immediately and unquestioningly met. Cunard, as well as the British and American authorities, suspected a hoax but couldn't afford to take any chances, so a bomb disposal team, composed of a Royal Ordnance captain, a sergeant from 22 Regiment (SAS) and two men of the Royal Marine's elite Special Boat Service, was flown out to the *Queen Elizabeth 2* and parachuted into the water alongside the liner. Once they were aboard the demolition experts quickly swept the ship and found nothing. The threat had merely been an elaborate hoax. All the same, for a time the passengers were quite nervous, but Captain William Law, the QE2's master, was making regular announcements on the ship's Tannoy system, calming passengers' fears and gradually gaining everyone's confidence until the time came when it was realized that there was no danger to the *Queen Elizabeth* 2 or anyone aboard her.

Meanwhile, the American FBI had swung into action and discovered that the hoax had been inspired by a short story written for an undergraduate English class at Hunter College in New York. A few months later, the owner of a New York City shoe store would be convicted of perpetrating the hoax and making the threatening phone calls. He received a sentence of twenty years in prison for his efforts.

The next year saw one of the most bizarre and humiliating chapters in the *Queen*

Elizabeth 2's storied career. Chartered in April by Oscar Rudnick, a Jewish travel agent from Worcester, Massachusetts, she was expected to carry some fifteen hundred Jewish passengers to the Israeli port of Ashdod in celebration of the twenty-fifth anniversary of the establishment of the State of Israel. Announcement of the excursion brought the inevitable and immediate threats of violence from the lunatic fringe of the Arab world, and they were repeated with such frequency and vehemence that hundreds of would-be passengers were frightened away. Ultimately some five hundred sixty-six brave souls made the journey, when the QE2 sailed from New York into the Mediterranean.

The voyage, which coincided with Passover, reached its nadir as the ship was entering the Med. Manny Williams, an American entertainer and "comedian" brought aboard especially for this crossing, announced at one of his performances that the sixty-first anniversary of the sinking of the Titanic had just passed. He then reassured his audience that there would be no icebergs in the Mediterranean—"Goldbergs, yes; Steinbergs, yes; but no icebergs." The passengers didn't find it particularly amusing, either.

Two days later the QE2 docked at Ashod with a local youth band playing "When the Saints Go Marching In." It was insult added to injury, for the ship had made port on the Jewish Sabbath, offending many of her passengers and a sizeable portion of Israel's population. It would be difficult to judge who was more humiliated by the whole incident, Cunard or the State of Israel.

It was becoming clear to even the most casual observer that Cunard was beginning to lose its dignity. Gone were the days when formal dress at dinner was expected on every night of a crossing except the first and the last. Afternoon tea had degenerated from the days of quietly correct stewards in faultlessly starched white jackets pouring Earl Grey into china cups, into individual pots of hot water and tea bags, served with paper napkins; cruise directors no longer addressed the passengers as "Ladies and Gentlemen," but with a familiar, almost contemptuous, "Boys and Girls;" and Boat Drill, certainly the one shipboard activity that should never have been subject to mockery or derogation, had degenerated from a function attended by all passengers before leaving port to a pantomime performed at a single station and broadcast throughout the ship on closed-circuit television. Even the cuisine, for so many decades the feature that set an ocean voyage apart from anything ever experienced on land, was becoming bland, predictable, a sea-going imitation of the food offered at an American chain hotel. It was clear that Trafalgar House was missing the mark: while there was certainly no call for adherence to the stuffiness and excessive formality that had so dismayed John Rosellini in the early 60s, many travelers who had booked passage on one of the three Cunard ships had done so in the hope of experiencing a taste of the service, attitude, and attention to detail that had once characterized British ocean liners, envied and emulated throughout the shipping industry. Cunard and Trafalgar made no attempt to disguise their efforts to attract affluent Americans aboard the QE2, the *Princess*, and the *Countess*, but instead of bringing them aboard and presenting an introduction to the British concept of civilized living, they were offered a shipboard experience that, with each passing year became more and more like a stay in a Howard Johnson's. What they got was not even imitation, it was parody: egalitarianism had become the watchword of British society and industry, and it was proving to be Cunard's undoing. The result was inevitable: the line spent the rest of the 1970s slowly stagnating.

Most critically, what was passing beyond hope of recovery were the ties to the past that were provided by the Cunard crews, arguably even more important to the continuity of the Line than any ship in the fleet. In the middle years of the 1970s aboard the QE2, if you knew who to ask and when, it was still possible to get a Bloody Mary in the Chartroom Bar that was personally mixed by Ernie Breen, the chief bar steward. Breen had started with Cunard back on the old *Berengaria*, where he spent nine years before moving on to the *Queen Mary* and eventually the first *Queen Elizabeth*. Service on Cunard ships was something of a family tradition—he had an uncle who had been a crewman on the *Lucania*, the *Carmania*, and the *Lusitania*. He was Cunard through and through, and readily admitted it: "We talk American at times, we think American," he said when describing how the crew adapted to the changes in the business, "I'm not English, I'm Cunard."

Working for Cunard was a family tradition, too, for David Parkinson, a bedroom steward aboard the QE2, whose father had gone to sea aboard the *Umbria* before the turn of the century. The younger Parkinson's first ship was the *Aquitania*, which he had joined in 1934 at the age of sixteen, working for £1 16s a month. He recalled how, when he transferred to the *Queen Mary*, the ship had just started using a novel gold-plated table-service that tarnished horribly every time it was used, and was discarded after only a few crossings. Pride and nostalgia mingled as he remembered the bellboys—long vanished from Cunard decks—in their knife-edged black trousers and biscuit-colored jackets with their red chevrons and red pillbox hats. And he remembered, like so many who served aboard her, how the *Queen Mary* rolled in any kind of a seaway. But he also recollected how she would "glide" through a calm sea. Tom Davis, another QE2 barman, who had spent twenty years aboard the first *Queen Elizabeth*, was adamant in his belief that she rolled every bit as badly as the *Mary*.

These were the men who knew the days when the great Cunard liners had been in competition not with other ships, but with the great hotels and restaurants ashore—the Savoy, Claridge's, the Ritz-Carlton, the Waldorf-Astoria. To them, good service was a matter of not merely professionalism, but personal pride: they were the final incarnation of the breed of whom Theodore Dreiser had once written, "...as to manner: Heaven save the mark!"

One Cunard tradition that Trafalgar House perpetuated, although they did so unwittingly and unwisely, was a variation of a long-standing company policy, one that Sir Samuel Cunard had instituted as far back as 1850. Essentially conservative by nature, old Sir Samuel was suspicious of new technological innovations and new methods of doing business. He was quick to put this imprimatur on the company, and willingly, even cheerfully, allowed his competitors to introduce novelties to steamship travel on the North Atlantic, be they new methods of propulsion or added amenities for the passengers. In his opinion, it was wiser to allow others to be pioneers, to bear the burdens—and costs—of innovation. Should some new development prove successful, emulation would be neither difficult nor particularly expensive. On the other hand, should some novel idea prove a failure, it was best to let someone else bear the cost, be it moral or monetary. After all, there was nothing in the company motto "Speed, comfort, and safety" which required Cunard to be innovators. While such a corporate philosophy perhaps created an image of over-cautiousness in some circles, it also earned the company a reputation for soundness and utter reliability.

Unfortunately, Trafalgar House was bringing this same sort of conservative thinking into the last quarter of the 20th Century. Quick to follow any innovation introduced by a competitor that seemed to work successfully, but never ready to introduce any unique features of its own, or to establish its own identity, Cunard became the quintessential "me-too" cruise line. While such a business philosophy might work well for automobile manufacturers and fast-food restaurants, in the cruise industry it was a genuine handicap. The great appeal of cruising was, and remains, its novelty—there is no other travel experience like it. But within the industry, the differences between the offerings of the various cruise lines, be they in destinations, amenities, or distinctive ship-board experiences, were the lures which the cruise companies employed to draw their customers. Cunard gave up any opportunity of creating such distinctions by merely playing "follow-the-leader".

Happily, one tradition that still remained a constant was that of the captain's table. The origins of the custom were fairly humble, going back to the days of the packet steamer when the cabin class passengers would join the master of the ship at the table in the dining saloon at dinner time, where he would offer up the initial serving of each course. Toward the end of the 19th Century, when passenger ships were rapidly growing in size, captains had begun to pick and choose among the First Class passengers who would be invited to dine with them, and such invitations became marks of distinction, much coveted by the socially ambitious. By the 1930s, the custom had evolved its own traditions and rituals, and it became a matter of considerable import to determine just who merited an invitation. It became quite common for the captain, staff captain, chief officer, purser, and maitre d' to pore over the passenger lists to determine who among the sometimes hundreds of passengers might be worthy of the captain's attention, and were of sufficient social stature, prominence, or importance to the company to be welcome at his dinner table. It was not unknown for the assistant pursers, ship's surgeon, or chief engineer to become involved in the process. Some captains, like the formidably debonair Sir James Charles, would often draw up the list of those to be invited themselves; others, like "Bowler Bill" Turner, more at home on their bridge than when rubbing elbows with the rich and titled, would leave all such decisions to their pursers.

By the 1980s, when Cunard captains were expected to have manners as polished as their seamanship, the social cachet of an invitation to dine at the captain's table was still as attractive as ever. Ship's masters still had considerable discretion in determining who would be chosen, although the unwritten—and all the more binding for being so—law was that no one would be invited who might in any way prove an embarrassment to the ship or the company. Still, because the chance that such an invitation might be extended always existed, it served as a powerful inducement for potential passengers, who craved the opportunity to turn their less fortunate friends and neighbors back home all the appropriate shades of envious green when recounting how they had dined at the captain's table aboard the *QE2*.

Gradually, some sense of need to have ships in the fleet that were worthy companions to the *Queen Elizabeth 2* and the Cunard tradition began to percolate into the corporate consciousnesses within the offices of Cunard and Trafalgar House, and in early 1982 word was quietly circulated within the shipping world that the line was looking to add a pair of intermediate sized ships to its fleet. But events outside the cruise line industry intervened before any action could be taken. In the spring of 1982, the name Cunard suddenly became inseparably linked with a locale of which most of the world had never before heard, but would not soon forget: the Falkland Islands.

The Falklands are a collection of small, cold, isolated, somewhat desolate islands located in the South Atlantic some eight hundred miles off the coast of Argentina. Ownership of the islands, which once had great strategic value as a source of fresh water for sailing vessels and as a coaling station for naval forces in the first half-century of steam, had long been disputed between Great Britain and Argentina.

On March 27, 1982 the British Government began to receive intelligence indicating that an invasion of the Falkland Islands by Argentina was imminent. The military *junta* ruling in Buenos Aires, attempting to divert the Argentinean public's attention away from a rapidly deteriorating economy, chose this moment to reassert a long-dormant claim of Argentine sovereignty over the Falklands, or as the islands were known in Argentina, Las Malvinas. Under the guise of joint naval maneuvers with Uruguay, an Argentine invasion fleet consisting of two destroyers, two frigates, a landing ship, a troop transport and an escorting submarine set sail the next day, its actual destination the town of Port Stanley in the Falkland Islands. Twenty-four hours later, as a precautionary measure, Britain's Prime Minister, Margaret Thatcher, ordered two Royal Navy submarines, HMS *Spartan* and HMS *Splendid*, to take stations around the Falklands.

The actual invasion, Operation Azul, was delayed by bad weather for twenty-four hours, the Argentine forces landing at Port Stanley on April 1. All told, some 800 Argentine soldiers and marines were put ashore, reinforced later that day by a battalion of infantry just over a thousand strong, flown in by military transports after the airfield outside Port Stanley was secured. A small mixed force of Royal Marines, Royal Navy seamen, and local residents put up a fierce defense that cost the Argentine forces a significant number of casualties, but finally surrendered when the Governor, Rex Hunt, recognized that further resistance was pointless—Argentine strength was overwhelming.

Two days later, Prime Minister Thatcher formed a War Cabinet and announced the formation of the Falklands Task Force, which would be built around the aircraft carriers HMS *Invincible* and HMS *Hermes*. On April 5, the Task Force set sail from Portsmouth, gathering up additional ships on its way to the South Atlantic; by the time it reached Ascension Island, the Task Force numbered fourteen warships and a half-dozen support vessels. The Royal Navy was once more preparing to demonstrate to the world that Great Britain had not forgotten the meaning of *sea power*. Thatcher's government made it clear they meant business from the very beginning: one of the first steps taken was Britain's declaration of a 200 mile "exclusion zone" around the Falklands: any Argentine ship, man-o'-war or merchantman, found within the zone could be sunk without warning.

On April 20, the War Cabinet formally ordered the Task Force to retake the Falkland Islands, and five days later South Georgia, one of the outlying islands of the Falklands group, was recaptured by the Royal Marines. The swift action was a clear demonstration of Britain's determination to back her words with action; at the same time, it was of great strategic importance, as it secured the harbor at South Georgia as a base for amphibious operations against the rest of the islands.

The Task force sailed into the exclusion zone on the last day of April, and the next morning saw its first action as Mirage fighter-bombers of the Argentine Air Force attacked the Royal Navy ships. Warships of the Argentine Navy began moving into position to strike at the Task Force; unknown to them, the heavy cruiser *General Belgrano*, Argentina's most powerful ship and the centerpiece of the planned attack, was being shadowed by the British submarine HMS *Conqueror*. When *Belgrano* began a high-speed run toward South Georgia that would have carried her into the heart of the Task Force, she was torpedoed and sunk by *Conqueror*, even though the cruiser was technically outside of the exclusion zone; more than 500 Argentine officers and sailors lost their lives. There was no turning back now for either side, and no doubt left that Britain was in deadly earnest about her intention to retake the Falkland Islands. Argentina's revenge came two days later when the destroyer HMS *Sheffield* was sunk after being hit by an Argentinean Exocet missile.

As the confrontation in the South Atlantic escalated into a full-blown shooting war, the *QE2* was just a day out of Southampton on an eastbound crossing from Philadelphia when her master, Captain Alexander Hutcheson, received an urgent message from the company offices. Upon docking in Southampton, he was informed that the liner was being requisitioned for service with the Royal Navy as a troopship. The *QE2* was to join the ranks of the Warrior *Queens*.

The Ministry of Defense had already executed a Queen's Order in Council and appropriated two of the P&O Line's ships, the 45,000-ton *Canberra* and the 17,000-ton *Uganda*. The white-painted *Canberra* (soon to be affectionately dubbed "The Great White Whale" by British servicemen) was readied in just over three days to carry two thousand British troops down to the Falklands, while the *Uganda* was converted into a 1,000-bed floating hospital.

As soon as the *Queen Elizabeth 2* docked at Southampton on May 3rd, dockyard workers swarmed aboard and began clearing away many of the ship's furnishings, along with the bone china, crystal stemware, all of the table linens, most of the artwork, the weight equipment from the gymnasium, and all of the potted plants. At the same time, other work crews were installing military communications equipment, reinforcing deck plates where anti-aircraft guns would be mounted, and creating landing areas for helicopters. This latter task involved actually cutting away some sections of the aft superstructure on the Upper and Quarter decks and covering the swimming pools with prefabricated steel decking to provide space for the helipads. While all this was taking place, dozens of paint crews were applying a coat of the same "Light Sea Grey" to the *QE2's* hull that the *Queen Mary* and *Queen Elizabeth* had worn forty years earlier.

The Royal Navy's decision to take over the *QE2* was made public the day she arrived in Southampton, leaving some 1,700 would-be passengers who had planned on boarding her for a 13-day Mediterranean cruise, without a ship. There were surprisingly few complaints, however, as the urgency of the British navy's need was self-evident. It was almost as if the clock had been turned back forty years; a Ministry of Defense spokesman, unconsciously echoing the reasons that had compelled the British Government to call up the first two *Queens*, explained that the ship's size, speed and facilities made her "uniquely suited to carry a substantial number of troops, who must be kept fit and ready for operations should they be required." Clearly, the Royal Navy, although shrunk in size until it was a mere a shadow of its former power and glory, had not forgotten the potential of sea power. Equally clearly, it was a concept which the Argentinean generals and admirals never really grasped; they were about to be taught a very harsh lesson.

On May 12th, 5th Infantry Brigade, consisting of 2nd Battalion Scots Guards, 1st Battalion Welsh Guards and 1st Battalion 7th (Duke of Edinburgh's) Ghurka Rifles, embarked on the *QE2* at Southampton docks on May 11th. In addition to the three infantry battalion's headquarters of Major-General Moore (commander of the ground forces), a number of supporting units were embarked. The Guards were, of course, world-renowned for their reputation as tough, competent, highly professional soldiers, and deservedly so. The Ghurkas, on the other hand, were less well-known outside of military circles—something the Argentines would soon learn had little bearing on the Gurkhas' fighting abilities.

On the morning of the *QE2's* departure, a military band appeared at the Ocean Dock and began played a variety of patriotic tunes including "Rule Britannia," "Land of Hope and Glory" and "British Grenadiers." It was an emotion-filled moment as the ship began to ease away from her berth, a huge crowd forming on the dockside to bid the troops farewell. Among the thousands gathered were wives and families of many of the soldiers, brought down to Southampton by the Guards Division, and more than one of the men found himself with a lump in his throat, although later they would all swear that it was the sharp cold breeze off the Solent that had brought tears to their eyes.

What could have been a hopelessly maudlin scene was avoided when several young women who apparently had (or wanted!) husbands and sweethearts in the Scots and Welsh Guards decided to enliven the moment by stripping down to their underwear—or less— and waving their more intimate garments over their heads in farewell, much to the delight

The third Warrior Queen, seen from the deck of HMS Antelope, *the* Queen Elizabeth 2 *enters the South Atlantic on her way to the Falklands War.*

of the watching troops. (A few days later, one of these ladies, whose husband was a signaler in the 5th Brigade HQ & Signal Squadron, appeared topless as a "Page 3 Girl" in the tabloid *The Sun*, hundreds of copies of that issue later being flown out to the *QE2*. The soldier initially found it quite amusing, but the novelty began to fade when copies of the picture began appearing all around the ship. Only the British....)

Life on the ship was busy, and filled with as many idiosyncrasies as life aboard the *Queens* had been during the Second World War. In order to protect the decks and furnishings the troops were ordered to remove their boots and wear soft-soled shoes or trainers. Incongruities abounded: the Brigade headquarters, along with that of Major General Moore's staff, set up shop in the casino, various maps, charts, and reports spread out across blackjack and roulette tables and among the slot machines. The HQ section's Land Rovers were stowed on the Sun Deck, just behind the funnel around the perimeter of the helicopter landing pad. The Intelligence section found itself cleaning its weapons and testing its radios in the rather incongruous setting of the purple and pink decor of the hairdressing salon.

The *QE2* had been taken over by the Admiralty so hastily that there had been no opportunity to replace all of the civilian cuisine in the ship's pantries and cold storage lockers with the usual bland Ministry of Defense rations ordinary issued to the troops. True, the 17,000 bottles of champagne that normally graced the cellars of the *Queen Elizabeth 2* had been left behind in Southampton, along with a half-ton of caviar, but as far as the troops were concerned, the loss was more than adequately made up by the 100,000 bottles of beer brought aboard in their place. The three battalion's cooks made the most of this unique opportunity and for the next two weeks the men ate better than any British soldiers ever had aboard a troopship. It wasn't uncommon for a typical "salad lunch" to actually include cold duck, beef, chicken, turkey, and ham, plus a variety of salads and dressings. Even the weather seemed cooperative until the ship was approaching South Georgia: at one point, a pair of troopers were spotted sunbathing on one of the upper decks.

But when the *QE2* reached Ascension Island, a noticeable change in mood came over officers and other ranks alike. On May 19th the Task Force was officially placed on active service, and two days later when the landings at San Carlos were announced, it became clear to everyone aboard that they would soon be part of the fighting. Until then, the deployment had seemed more like an exercise than an actual military operation: from that moment on the war was real.

Mission-specific training began in earnest, and the first drill the troops began practicing was emergency evacuation. The Argentine Navy's submarines were considered a genuine threat to the *QE2*, and possibility of a fire breaking out if she were struck by torpedoes was very real. The greatest danger was toxic fumes released by many of the materials used in her construction as they burned, so the troops practiced crawling along the decks below the smoke layer—later, to simulate a loss of power and the resulting total darkness that would envelope the interior of the ship's subsequent darkness below deck, the men were blindfolded and had to find their way out by touch. As anyone who had sailed aboard the *QE2* in peacetime well knew, the ship was a maze of corridors and passageways, bewildering enough to someone walking upright, with their eyes open and the passageways fully lit, so it was hardly surprising for these drills to become highly unpopular among the troops. After the first half dozen or so, most of the men realized that, in truth, they had little chance of reaching the upper decks if the ship was torpedoed.

In the meantime, in the two weeks since the *QE2* sailed from Southampton, there had been numerous skirmishes and exchanges of fire between British and Argentine ground units and sporadic Argentine air attacks on the Royal Navy ships in the waters around the Falklands. Two British battalions, 45 Commando and 3 Paras, went ashore at San Carlos and set up a beachhead on May 21st. The Argentinean Air Force responded by launching its heaviest series of attacks yet, a furious assault on the fleet anchorage at San Carlos. HMS *Ardent* took multiple bomb strikes and sank, while HMS *Antrim* and HMS *Argonaut* were both hit by bombs which failed to explode (dud ordnance would plague the Argentine forces throughout the conflict, saving the Royal Navy from even more serious losses than it ultimately incurred), while HMS *Brilliant* and HMS *Broadsword* suffered slight damage. The cost for the Argentinean air force was equally heavy: at least thirteen aircraft were shot down and many more were badly damaged.

Two days later, HMS *Glasgow* and HMS *Brilliant* set up a missile trap off Port Stanley, and three Argentine attack planes were shot down by them. *Glasgow* was hit by a bomb which passed straight through the ship without exploding. That same day Argentinean ground gunners near Goose Green scored an "own goal" when they shot down an

Argentine Skyhawk. HMS *Broadsword* and HMS *Coventry* set up a similar missile trap May 25th and were promptly bombed by Skyhawks. In a scenario already too familiar to the Argentine air force, *Broadsword* was hit but the bomb failed to explode. *Coventry*, though, wasn't as lucky: hit by three bombs that exploded almost simultaneously, her back was broken and she capsized. At the same time the MV *Atlantic Conveyor*, acting as a floating supply depot for the British task force, suffered a fatal hit, and despite heroic efforts to save her, she sank three days later.

The courage and tenacity of the Argentine flyers earned the admiration of British land and naval forces alike—most of the pilots in the aircraft shot down were lost. Their determination also led the Royal Navy to take no chances with the *QE2*. As the ship passed Ascension island and moved deeper into the South Atlantic the threat of air attack became increasingly real, batteries of Browning .50 caliber heavy machine guns were set up on the upper decks and manned around the clock by troops from the infantry units. Accompanying the gun batteries were soldiers equipped with Blowpipe surface-to-air missiles, while even further protection was provided by an escorting destroyer, HMS *Antrim*.

When *Antrim* made her rendezvous with the *QE2* on May 27th, any remaining doubts about how real was the Falklands War, vanished. Easily visible from the *Queen Elizabeth 2*'s decks were the streaks and patches of rust along *Antrim*'s hull, testimony to the ferocity of the South Atlantic weather: equally visible were holes made by cannon fire from Argentine aircraft, as well as the hastily welded steel plates covering the hole in her deck where a dud bomb had punched through. *Antrim* escorted the *QE2* into the ice-filled approaches to South Georgia, and the liner's Chief Officer, R.W. Warwick, son of her first skipper, Captain Bill Warwick, watched a mist settle in over the ice field. He ordered the ship's radar switched on, and was startled to see over a hundred icebergs scattered across the screen, any one of which was large enough to sink the ship. It was a cautious approach into the harbor.

Once the three thousand troops of the 5th Brigade were either transferred to the *Canberra* or landed ashore, the *QE2* underwent yet another conversion, this time being turned into the world's largest hospital ship. Some six hundred and forty injured Royal Navy seamen taken off *Antelope*, *Coventry*, and *Ardent*, many of them seriously wounded, were brought aboard. Once they were safely bedded down, the *Queen Elizabeth* 2 left the waters of the Falkland Islands and returned to Great Britain.

In the meantime, relentless pressure from the men of 5th Brigade forced the Argentinean forces back on Port Stanley, the capital of the Falkland Islands and the ultimate objective. "Relentless pressure," while perhaps adequately descriptive from a purely military perspective, does little justice to the human experience of combat—or the cost in lives and suffering to both sides. The weather was cold, wet, and miserable, the terrain rugged and unyielding. If the Argentinean forces were determined to make a stand, it was going to be a bloody business, but both Her Majesty's Government and the British forces on and about the islands were determined to get this conflict over as quickly and decisively as possible.

From their beachhead near San Carlos, the British infantry advanced towards Port Stanley. On May 28, 2nd Battalion, the Parachute Regiment, outnumbered two to one and low on ammunition, took Darwin and Goose Green in the longest and hardest-fought battle of the war. Seventeen British soldiers and more than two hundred Argentineans were killed in this fight. Two weeks later, on June 12, the Parachute Regiment's 3rd Battalion attacked Mount Longdon, a commanding height overlooking Port Stanley. Before the assault was over, the fighting had become hand to hand, with bayonets and entrenching tools taking the place of rifles and grenades, as the Argentine troops had to be overcome position by position. British casualties were twenty-three dead, forty-seven wounded, with Argentinean losses more than twice those figures. That same day in another bloody battle, 2nd Battalion, the Scots Guards seized Mount Tumbledown. The ring around Port Stanley was closing fast, and two days later, on June 14, 1982, the Argentine garrison there, 9800 strong, surrendered. For all practical purposes, the war was over. By the "standards" of the Second World War, Korea, or Vietnam, it had been a "little war," the British dead numbering 236, the Argentineans 655. But it was a very expensive price to pay for a war that had been fought solely to prop up a tottering military regime in Argentina; if anything good came of it, it was that it hastened the fall of the *junta* of General Leopoldo Galtieri, and the restoration of democracy to Argentina.

By the time Port Stanley was taken, the *Queen Elizabeth 2* was already back in Southampton, arriving on June 11, where her welcome was a spectacle in itself. Tens of thousands of people lined the shores of the Solent and the docks and piers of the waterfront to watch the liner make her way into the port. Thousands of others took to a flotilla of small craft which formed a sort of escort for her as she steamed past the Isle of Wight. Waiting off Cowes was the Royal Yacht *Britannia*, where the Queen Mother, her famous smile beaming wider than ever, greeted the returning liner. It was almost a dress rehearsal for the tumultuous welcome that awaited the Falklands Task Force upon its return, at the end of July. On December 2nd, the Queen Mother came aboard the liner at the Ocean Dock in Southampton to unveil the Falklands War plaque, which commemorated the *QE2*'s service.

Shortly after the celebrations surrounding Britain's victory in the Falklands War and the hoopla of the safe return of the *Queen Elizabeth 2* had died down, Cunard acquired two new ships, the *Sagafjord* and *Vistafjord*, when it bought a controlling interest in their owner, Norwegian America Cruises. Originally a small cruise line called Norwegian America, it was sold in 1980 to Norway's Leif Hegh & Co., but after two and one half years of financial problems, Norwegian America Cruises was sold to Cunard, which promptly reorganized it as Cunard-Norwegian America Cruises. The two sisters, *Sagafjord* and *Vistafjord*, which also happened to be the sum total of Norwegian America's fleet, retained their original names and crews.

Handsome and elegant, they resembled the quartet of intermediates built in the 1950s, but in all respects they were thoroughly modern. Though nominally sister ships and very similar in appearance, they were far from duplicates of each other. The *Sagafjord* was the first to be built, constructed by the Société des Forges et Chantiers de la Mediterranée of Toulon, France, she was launched in 1965. Her length was 615 feet, beam 82 feet, with a displacement of 24,000 tons. Power was supplied by a pair of Sulzer diesels, driving twin screws that gave her a service speed of 20 knots; she could accommodate 789 passengers, served by a crew of 350. The *Vistafjord*'s dimensions and power plant were identical, as was her hull form, but she was built nearly ten years after her sister, at the Swan Hunter shipyard in Newcastle-on-Tyne, England, and new construction and safety regulations put in place after the *Sagafjord* had been built, meant that she had significant differences.

Most importantly, the *Vistafjord* was built entirely with inflammable materials; her entire superstructure was constructed of aluminum rather than steel, which allowed her designers to add an additional deck, as well as extend the superstructure fore and aft. Not only did this improve the newer ship's silhouette, it also allowed the *Vistafjord*'s passenger accommodation to be increased by almost one hundred fifty over her sister's capacity.

Inside, the changes to the *Vistafjord*'s superstructure placed the main dining room one deck higher than in the *Sagafjord*. On the older sister, this lower position restricted the size of the windows that could be used in the dining room, considerably diminishing the amount of natural light available, so by using a two-deck high design, a sense of brightness and feeling of spaciousness was obtained. In the *Vistafjord*'s dining room, one deck higher, both sides were lined with large picture windows, making the room seem brighter and larger, even though it was actually a much smaller space. Both ships though, were striking in their appearance, with sharply raked clipper bows, long, balanced superstructures, each sporting a single short, tapered funnel. Like the *Queen Elizabeth 2* they were specifically designed and built to serve as both ocean liners and cruise ships, and so their classic lines, like those of their larger cousin, were an elegant combination of transatlantic liner and floating resort.

Norwegian American Cruises wasn't the only acquisition made by Trafalgar House in the 1980s: another was the purchase in 1986 of John Brown Engineering, better known to most of the world by its previous name, John Brown & Sons, the shipyard that built the *Lusitania*, the *Aquitania*, and all three of the *Queens*. As the shipbuilding industry along the Clyde died its slow, bitter death, John Brown had gradually transformed itself into a leading process-engineering, offshore-drilling, and energy-production company; its particular specialty and expertise now lay in the construction, refitting and refurbishing of North Sea oil platforms.

That same year Cunard acquired two more ships and added another division, as it took over financially troubled Sea Goddess Cruises. With the addition of the *Sea Goddess I* and *Sea Goddess II*, the line's fleet now stood at seven ships, the largest it had been in more than two decades. Built in Helsinki, Finland at the Wärtsilä, the two *Goddesses* were very small ships, less than 4,200 tons, with cabins for just 116 passengers each. They were meant to be "the most luxurious passenger ships ever to sail," according to the advertising brochures, and with their casinos, gift shops, outdoor cafés, spas, health centers, and beauty salons, the claim wasn't unreasonable. Each ship even had its own sailboat and speedboat stowed aboard. Every cabin had a private dining room, as well as a private bar, library, television and video system, ship-to-shore telephone, and refrigerator—stocked, of course, with salmon and caviar. While Cunard-Sea Goddess Cruises was considered a separate division of the Cunard line, the ships both wore Cunard-red and black funnels, to ensure that no one would mistake who owned these elegant, yacht-like ships.

A momentous chapter of history was closed by the *Queen Elizabeth* 2, in October 1986, when she completed the last steam-powered crossing of the North Atlantic that would ever be made by a passenger ship. Due to begin a £100,000,000 ($162,000,000) refit in the Lloyd Werft shipyard in Bremerhaven in November, her worn-out boilers and troublesome turbines would be replaced by a diesel-electric power plant which would give her a top speed of over 32 knots. Although no one would rue the improvements in efficiency and reduced costs provided by the new engines, the passing of steam power on the North Atlantic was a watershed.

The Age of Steam had been one of the greatest, if not *the* greatest, period of human progress, change and development—social, political and technological. Human ingenuity had applied steam power to every form of machinery, save for aircraft, and there had even been attempts at steam-powered flight. Steam power had propelled more than ships and locomotives—it had literally driven the Industrial Revolution, which in turn spawned every subsequent social and technical sea-change which followed. Even more resonant

In 1986 the Queen Elizabeth 2 *was given a new funnel, new engines, and a remodeled upper superstructure, and enjoyed her most successful year to date.*

were the achievements that steam power had impelled, none more so than the great ocean liners. In every corner, every joint, every part, the level of craftsmanship they inspired had no parallels. From the keel plates to the double-bottom hulls, to the framing and shell-plating, the decking, the cast-steel frames for bows and sterns, through the superstructures, the boilers, reciprocating engines or turbines, to the sybaritic luxury of First Class staterooms, smoking rooms and dining saloons, or the stark simplicity of Third Class dormitories, steamships blended beauty and function as none of mankind's structures has ever done, coming closer to aesthetic and technical perfection than anything else in human history.

Ironically, the very success of steam had been its undoing, for it provided the power needed to develop the technologies which supplanted it. The factories that cast the steel for gigantic diesel engine-blocks and enormous electric generators and rotors had been powered by steam; steam shovels and steam tractors had dug the great excavations that became hydroelectric dams; steam power's success had ensured its obsolescence.

There was little doubt in the late 1980s that the Falklands War was Cunard's last hurrah, the line's final moment of glory before it resumed its slow downward slide into mediocrity. The late 1980s and early 1990s were the years when the cruise industry "grew up," as it were, assuming the general outlines and much of the substance of its present form. The cruise lines began developing their individual identities: Holland-America becoming the choice of traditionally-minded middle-aged travelers; Princess, capitalizing on the image created by the American television show "The Love Boat", establishing itself as the cruise line for young, affluent adults; Carnival, a newcomer to the industry, energetically appealing to young families and singles; Norwegian Cruise Lines (not to be confused with the defunct Norwegian American Line) carving out a niche for itself somewhat between Holland America and Princess. Yet Cunard persisted in its unspoken, unarticulated policy of being a "me-too" cruise line, content in trying to be all things to all travelers, and not being at all successful at it, but expecting what few echoes of its former glory and reputation that remained to continue to draw passengers to the line. The cold, hard, fact was that Cunard was now living in the past, as well as living off it. The balance of events in the 1980s and 1990s would simply put the seal on that truth.

In 1988, the Queen Mother once again came aboard, her third visit to the *QE2*, to commemorate the fiftieth anniversary of the launch of the first *Queen Elizabeth*. It seemed ironic that for all of her close association with the liner, the Queen Mother never sailed on her. Two years later Cunard celebrated its one hundred fiftieth anniversary, with the *QE2* going on a "'Round Britain" cruise. In a fit of nostalgia she put into Liverpool, where the Cunard Line had been founded, and sailed up the Clyde to the John Brown yard for the first time since her launch. Celebrating the tenth anniversary of Great Britain's victory in the Falklands War in 1992, the former Prime Minister, Lady Margaret Thatcher, boarded the *QE2* in Southampton for a three hour luncheon with several hundred veterans of the South Atlantic conflict.

Despite the spate of nostalgia and reminiscences, the *Queen Elizabeth* 2 hadn't seen the last of her moments of high drama. One incident came on September 11, 1995, when the *QE2* was crossing to New York with some twelve hundred passengers aboard: she was hit by an enormous rogue wave that was created by the seas being whipped up by Hurricane Luis. Suddenly rearing up ahead of the ship, it struck her bow-on with the crest at bridge level—more than ninety feet above the waterline. To her master, Captain Ronald Warwick, no stranger to the worst the Atlantic, North or South, had to offer, "it looked as if we were going straight into the White Cliffs of Dover. It was the biggest wave I have seen in 38 years at sea...." Fortunately, damage was minor, there were no serious injuries among passengers or crew, and the *QE2* arrived in New York only eight hours later than scheduled.

It was an incident that harked back to the similar encounters by other Cunard ships—the *Campania,* the *Lusitania,* and the *Queen Mary,* among them. Long dismissed as sailors' yarns, the truth is that such monster waves, known as "rogues"—seas that are capable of breaking a 600 foot-long ship in half and sending it to the bottom within seconds—have terrified seafarers for centuries and caused the disappearance of countless ships. It is believed that in the last quarter-century alone more than two hundred tankers, supertankers, and container ships have vanished without a trace after encountering rogue waves. The experience of the *Queen Elizabeth* 2 was a lesson that would not go unheeded.

Warwick had yet another opportunity to demonstrate the quality of his seamanship, this time in Milford Sound, a narrow fjord-like inlet of the Tasman Sea on the west coast of New Zealand's South Island. As the *QE2* was entering the Sound a powerful squall came up, and the wind was so strong that the ship wasn't able to reverse her course back into open water, but found herself being driven toward the rocks instead. Warwick would later recall that the power of the wind was so great that waterfalls along the cliffs of the fjord were actually being blown back upwards against the sides of the inlet. With the *Queen Elizabeth 2*'s bow less than twenty feet from the cliff face, he found a relatively calm and quiet patch of water, and judging time and distance to a nicety, he was able to coordinate screws, rudder, and bow thrusters to safely turn the ship around. The *QE2* made her way back to the open sea without further incident.

When the world-wide real estate market began to decline in late 1995, Trafalgar House found itself in trouble, and the following February, a Norwegian-based conglomerate, the Kvaerner Group, announced its intention to take over Trafalgar House. Formed in Oslo in 1853 as Kvaerner Brug, in little over a century Kvaerner had grown into a massive international operation of ten Norwegian-based companies employing over 32,000 workers, with business interests that ranged from shipbuilding, to commercial and industrial construction, to hydroelectric power generation. Kvaerner's interest in Trafalgar House centered on the British holding company's shipbuilding businesses, in particular the Scottish firm of John Brown Engineering, but the Norwegian giant had little desire to own a passenger ship line. However, Trafalgar House insisted on an all-or-nothing deal, saying that any take-over would have to include all the British holding company's businesses.

At a stockholders' meeting in March, 89% of Trafalgar House shareholders voted in favor of the take-over, and the next month Kvaerner paid $1,200,000,000 to acquire Trafalgar outright. The future of Cunard had suddenly become very uncertain: it was well known that Cunard's entire fleet was in desperate need of a refit, but even as Kvaerner bought Trafalgar, senior executives of the Norwegian company made it clear that they were unwilling to spend the money necessary to overhaul the ships; the question of either selling Cunard or dissolving the company and scrapping the ships began to be raised with some frequency at Kvaerner's board meetings. Speculation rapidly grew in the business community about who might want to take the company off Kvaerner's hands—the names most often mentioned were P&O and the new Disney Line.

The speculation wasn't idle, for on August 24, 1996, Kvaerner formally announced that it was looking to divest itself of Cunard. The situation then began to turn ugly, as barely a month later, Peter Ward, who had taken over as Cunard's chairman and chief executive only 15 months earlier, suddenly resigned. Ward, a former chairman of Rolls-Royce Motor Cars Ltd., had very little to say about Cunard that was complimentary, at one point telling *The New York Times* that when he became chairman in September, 1995, "Cunard was almost like a welfare state at sea."

Certainly there had been problems. In early 1996, the *Sagafjord* was chartered to Trans-Ocean Cruises for a period of six months, and renamed the *Gripsholm*. Departing from Fort Lauderdale, Florida on January 4, on an around-the-world cruise, she was a hundred miles off the Philippine island of Palawan on her way from Hong Kong to Malaysia, when a fire broke out in the generator room and spread throughout much of the ship. Although none of the four hundred seventy-six passengers were injured, the damage done by the blaze was severe enough to knock out her power plant, and she had to be towed back to port.

Although false reports about the extent of the damage grew in the telling—some sources still claim that the ship was "destroyed" by the fire—the *Sagafjord*'s hull and structural integrity were never compromised; her interior, however, was a shambles, and the cost of returning her to her previous appearance was simply more than Kvaerner was willing to spend. Instead, she was sold to Saga Holidays in late October 1996, for $17,000,000, and renamed the *Saga Rose*.

Fire also visited the *Vistafjord* on April 6, 1997, but the changes in her design and in the materials used in her construction caused the story to have a far different outcome than that of her sister. Halfway through a transatlantic crossing, a fire was discovered in a laundry room, and smoke began to spread; as a precaution, an abandon ship drill was started and the passengers quickly donned their life jackets and reported to the lifeboats. The fire spread slowly, allowing the crew to bring the blaze under control before the order to abandon ship was actually given, although one of the crewmen, a steward, died from smoke inhalation while fighting the fire. Unlike the *Sagafjord*, the *Vistafjord* remained in the Cunard fleet: although no one knew it at the time, an amazing future awaited her.

In early November 1997, events began moving rather quickly as rumors about Cunard began swirling throughout the business world: one report held that Prudential PLC, the

British financial services giant, had begun serious discussions with Kvaerner, with an eye on acquiring Cunard; Kvaerner was said to be asking $600,000,000 for the line. At the same time Captain Paris Katsoufis, Cunard's then-chairman, announced to the Norwegian Seaman's Union that Kvaerner was planning to hold onto Cunard, and might even expand the line. "The reason to keep the line," he explained, "is that there have not been any buyers interested in paying the price being asked."

A little more than a week later, Cunard made a stunning announcement: after a fierce bidding war and secretive negotiations with Dade and Broward counties in south Florida, Cunard was leasing a 36,000 square-foot office complex near Miami International Airport, abandoning the New York City offices the company had occupied since the mid-1800s. Tax incentives and lower operating costs, coupled with a $10,600,000 incentive package from Dade County, sealed the deal. New York City would continue to be the American terminus of Cunard's transatlantic service, but the move to Miami solidified the future of the line's focus on cruising.

While the move to Florida could only have been made with the parent corporation's approval, Kvaerner was still muddying the waters as far as its commitment to Cunard's future was concerned. Various sources within the company were saying that the Norwegian corporation wanted to sell Cunard so it could concentrate on shipbuilding, but the asking price was still too high. On March 14, Prudential PLC, believing that other corporations had submitted higher bids, withdrew its offer of $340,000,000 to buy Cunard from Kvaerner. It was at this point that Carnival Corporation abruptly stepped into the picture.

On April 3rd it was revealed that Carnival was buying a majority interest—68% of Cunard. The American conglomerate, based in Miami and sometimes described as a "behemoth", was the parent company for Carnival Cruise Lines, the largest cruise line in the world; its holdings included Holland America, Costa Cruises of Italy, and Windstar Cruises; it also had equity interests in the Seabourn ultra-luxury cruise line and owned 26% of Britain's Airtours. Carnival companies already boasted more than 48,000 berths, with ships on order that would add another 20,000 to that total. The deal cost Carnival $425,000,000 $375,000,000 of it in cash, and it was immediately announced that Cunard's fleet would be merged with Seabourn's luxury-cruise operations.

Suddenly, almost a century after Lord Inverclyde had deftly thwarted the "Yankee Pirate" J.P. Morgan and kept Cunard independent of his International Mercantile Marine cartel, the line had come into the possession of another ambitious American shipping magnate. The great question looming over Cunard's existence now was whether this new owner would choose to reclaim Cunard's distinctive place among the world's passenger ship lines, or if he would allow the company to fall into complete dilution and dissipation in the world of cookie-cutter, mass-produced cruises and cruise ships. His name was Mickey Arison.

CHAPTER EIGHTEEN

Resurrection

There is a charming tale told of how Micky Arison came to acquire Cunard, of how, as a five year-old boy, he came to America with his father aboard the *Mauretania*, and in so doing developed an affection for the ships with the distinctive red-and-black funnels, a fondness that, as he grew older, gradually evolved into a desire to someday own the line. Consequently, the story goes, when Kvaerner was ready to sell Cunard, Arison seized the opportunity to fulfill a life-long wish, and persuaded Carnival Corporation's board of directors to buy the company. There *is* an element of truth in the tale: Micky Arison *did* come to the United States with his father in 1954 aboard the *Mauretania*, but alas, beyond that, the story is so much latter-day mythmaking—Arison claims that all he can remember of the *Mauretania* are the lines that tied the ship to the dock. When Carnival bought Cunard from the Kvaerner conglomerate in 1999, it was for sound business reasons, not motives of sentiment.

Anyone who has met Micky Arison would find the truth much easier to believe than the legend. In person, Arison is a tall, barrel-chested man, now in his mid-fifties, his hair and beard straying toward iron grey, his grey eyes often narrowing in intelligent, even shrewd concentration. He carries about him an air of easy authority that, while it sometimes crosses over into arrogance, conveys a distinct sense that he is a man motivated by practicalities. It quickly becomes evident in any conversation that his mind is very much focused in the here and now, while his vision is directed toward the future, not the past, and he leaves little doubt that sentiment has no part to play in his decision making, save for those rare times when sentiment and good business practice coincide.

Indeed, critics have said that under Arison, Carnival Corporation has become the most ruthless competitor in the cruise industry, citing as proof Carnival's absorption of smaller, weaker lines such as Cunard, Holland-America, Seabourn, and Costa, although the case can be made that such practices have long been typical of the passenger shipping industry. Certainly in its heyday, Cunard never hesitated to acquire smaller competitors, the Anchor Line and the Brocklebank Line being just two examples. There is no doubt, though, that the Miami-based giant runs an efficient operation, noted throughout the business world for its tight financial discipline and rigorous cost-cutting. Arison takes a personal interest in absolutely everything that goes on within Carnival, and while his friends and admirers readily describe him as charming and fun, he leaves no doubt about who is in control of the company. While he clearly loves the shipping industry, his approach to it is utterly practical; he refers to ships as "products," calls cruise lines "brands," and characterizes countries as "markets."

Arison frankly admits that there was no nostalgia involved in the decision to acquire Cunard: "We were dealing with Kvaerner through their shipbuilding subsidiary in Finland, and they had offered us Cunard a couple of times...and we resisted the idea because Cunard seemed so disjointed, in such bad condition, with no 'brand focus.' It was a company with all those ships but no 'brand,' and it seemed like a pretty hopeless situation. But it appeared that Cunard was going to be sold, and we were concerned about what might happen if it became a competitor [to Carnival] with some financial clout.

"Atle Brynestad, who was our partner in Seabourn, had the thought that if we had the name Cunard we could use it to rebuild the line and create a 'brand,' so we decided to go ahead. We knew that the line was going to be sold, and if it got into someone else's hands, they would start building new ships and create a premium-type cruise line, a direct competitor to Holland-America and Crystal, and it wasn't in our interest to see that happen."

The existing relationship between Kvaerner and Carnival made the purchase of Cunard easier: Kvaerner had already built eight ships for the cruise giant, and orders were on the books for as many as six more. Senior executives, among them Antti Pankakoski, vice president of Kvaerner's shipbuilding division, and Captain Paris Katsoufis, the new chairman of Cunard, openly admitted that they preferred to see the American conglomerate become the line's new owner, as they felt that only Carnival had both the resources and the know-how to turn the debilitated company back to profitability, and restore the luster and prestige of the Cunard name. It quickly became clear that all that was required of Carnival was to match the best offer made by any other potential buyer. By mid-April an agreement had been reached, and Cunard was handed over.

Under the terms of the acquisition, Carnival Corporation became the majority shareholder in an investment group which controlled 68% of Cunard and 50% of the Seabourn Cruise Line. The balance of Seabourn shares was held by a Norwegian businessman, Atle Brynestad, who founded Seabourn in 1987. Brynestad, who with 17% of the new company was the single largest shareholder, was appointed chairman of the board. No sooner had the deal been closed than Carnival executives began planning the merger of Cunard with Seabourn, a move that would create the largest luxury cruise company in the world.

On May 18, Larry Pimentel, Seabourn's president since 1992, was named president and chief executive officer of the new Cunard Line Limited. It was an inspired choice. An amateur maritime historian, Pimentel was particularly conscious of Cunard's unique place in the chronicles of passenger shipping, and was determined to do it justice. Six weeks later, Pamela Conover was named as chief operating officer of Cunard. Born in Bangkok of British parents, Conover's business career began in banking, her first experience with the shipping world coming in the early 1990s when she was head of Citicorp's North American ship finance unit. Conover became the first woman to serve as the president of a major cruise line when she was hired to run Carnival's venture with the Epirotiki Line in 1994.

Giving substance to Carnival's claims of its commitment to Cunard's future, plans were finalized in mid-June for an $18,000,000 refit of the thirty-one year-old *Queen Elizabeth 2* at the Lloyd Werft shipyard in Bremerhaven, Germany. Scheduled from November 11 to December 12, 2000, the hotel accommodation of the ship was completely refurbished. Arison himself had been the moving force behind this decision. In an interview given in November 2002, he explained, "I had been aboard the *QE2* two or three times before Carnival got involved with Cunard, and always was extremely disappointed in the way the

Mickey Arison, Chairman and CEO of Carnival Corporation. (Photo courtesy of Carnival Corporation)

ship looked and the way she was maintained. I felt that if we owned her and she was going to carry the banner of Cunard she had to look good. I decided that when she came out of the refit she would look as good as she ever had." Everyone agreed that it was long overdue. In her first thirty years at sea the *QE2* had sailed four and one-half million nautical miles, more than the total distance traveled by the *Queen Mary* and *Queen Elizabeth* combined. During that time she carried over two million passengers—the exact number remains unknown—and the wear was beginning to show.

The *QE2* docked at the Lloyd Werft yard in Bremerhaven on November 11, and the work began immediately. Almost all of the "soft" furnishings—that is, the carpets, curtains, bedcovers, and upholstery—were replaced throughout the ship, while the corridors of the accommodation decks were given new paneling, a split-grain veneer that echoed the decor of the first two *Queens*. At the same time, many of the staterooms and cabins were reworked to make them more comfortable and add touches of former Cunard style. A bit more pedestrian, but of considerable importance to the passengers' comfort, the bathrooms in all the cabins were modernized. A quartet of new suites were added on One and Two Decks, all named after Cunard liners of the past, the *Aquitania, Mauretania, Carinthia,* and *Caledonia.*

The most dramatic changes though, were made in the public rooms, which were redesigned and redecorated by Tillberg Design, a Fort Lauderdale, Florida-based design house that previously had created the interiors of numerous ships in Carnival Corporation's various fleets. Tillberg employed styles that echoed the great Cunard and White Star liners of the past, in particular the *Queen Mary* and *Queen Elizabeth*, the *Lusitania* and *Mauretania*, and the "Pretty Sisters," *Carmania* and *Caronia*. Part of this was a conscious corporate decision in an attempt to re-establish ties to Cunard's past traditions, and part was simply the whim and whimsy of the designer studio.

Particular attention was paid to the Caronia Restaurant. Reworked to resemble the dining saloon of one of the crack transatlantic liners, it would greet passengers with expanses of dark mahogany-veneer paneling, carved and molded pilasters, and crystal chandeliers. The Queen's Room would once again become the social centerpiece of the ship, with a royal blue and gold color theme throughout, and a large parquet dance floor. The last remnants of the bizarre "space age" furniture were discarded; in its place were numerous overstuffed armchairs, sofas, and settees, the fabric of their upholstery adding Tudor Rose to the blue-and-gold decor theme. The bronze bust of Queen Elizabeth II was moved from an almost invisible niche in one wall to a position of prominence where it became the dominant fixture of the room. In what was perhaps the most charming touch of all, the ship was given a completely new set of teak deck chairs, modeled after a style that had first graced Cunard decks at the turn of the 20th Century.

At the same time, the *Vistafjord* was given a similar makeover, and with it came a name change. Most immediately noticeable was the coat of satin black that now graced her hull, with the traditional white stripe at the waterline separating the black paintwork from the

The Caronia, *the third ship to bear that legendary Cunard name, a worthy successor to the "Green Goddess."*

red boot-topping. Her new appearance echoed the handsome intermediate liners of the 1950s, and Carnival hoped that her completely new look, inside and out, would give *Vistafjord* the identity of a British ship, with a British character. At the same time, it was felt that changing her name to that of one of Cunard's most popular ships would even more clearly define her new status and position. On December 14, 1999, as she was tied up at Liverpool's ancient granite seawall, the *Vistafjord* was officially renamed the *Caronia* in a ceremony held in front of the old Cunard building before a crowd of thousands. Pamela Conover became the new godmother of the *Caronia*, and the British Deputy Prime Minister, John Prescott, announced that *Caronia* would be transferred to the British registry, and make her home port in Southampton. At midnight, to the accompaniment of a choir and orchestra, a massive mid-river firework display, the ringing of every church bell in Liverpool, and the shouts of a crowd cheering itself hoarse, the newest *Caronia* cast off and eased out into the Mersey, bound for her new home in Southampton.

While all this activity was going on aboard the QE2 and the *Caronia*, the *Sea Goddess I* and *Sea Goddess 2* were formally transferred to the Seabourn fleet, where they joined the *Seabourn Sun, Seabourn Pride, Seabourn Spirit,* and *Seabourn Legend*. As time passed, it would become clear that the idea of trying to combine the operations of Seabourn and Cunard was not a success: the styles of each company, as well as the clientele to which each line appealed, were simply too different. By the end of October 2000, Seabourn would cut all ties with Cunard and become an independent division of Carnival Corporation.

But the centerpiece of Carnival's plan for a revitalized Cunard had been revealed on June 8, 1999, when Cunard announced the *Queen Mary* 2 Project to the world. Its purpose was simple and clear-cut: to build what would be the largest and most luxurious "true ocean liner" ever constructed. According to Mickey Arison, the concept for the *Queen Mary* 2, or QM2 as the ship quickly became known, was the integral part of Carnival's acquisition of Cunard. "From the time we first considered purchasing Cunard, our plans always included building a new liner," he said in a November 2002 interview. "It would only make sense if we built a new ship for the line. To try to operate it the way the prior owners had, buying used ships and throwing them away, and being just a 'me-too' brand with thousand-passenger ships, just made no sense. We wanted to take advantage of the whole heritage of the *Queens* and the legacy of the *Queens*." So it was that the heart of the story of Cunard's resurrection would be the story of the *Queen Mary* 2.

The design brief was given to Stephen Payne, Cunard's chief naval architect, who was appointed as the project's executive director. It was expected that the design would be completed by the end of 2000, with construction beginning the following year, the liner entering service by the end of 2003. Immediately speculation began about who would build her: with the John Brown shipyard now only a memory, the leading contenders were Kvaerner of Norway, Fincantieri of Italy, Meyer Werft of Germany, Harland and Wolff of Northern Ireland, and Chantiers de l'Atlantique of France.

The original design called for a ship of 84,000 tons capable of carrying 2000 passengers. However, it wasn't long before the projected size of the new liner began to increase dramatically. The experience that Carnival had gained with 100,000-ton *Destiny* class cruise ships and the obvious popularity of Royal Caribbean's 137,000-ton *Voyager of the Seas* caused Carnival to rethink the design of the new ship.

The world-wide public reaction was astonishing. Final design specifications had yet to be determined, no one knew quite what the ship would look like, there were no working drawings or blueprints for her, nor had preliminary construction bids been sought—the line hadn't even decided on a name for her (although it was already pretty much an open secret that she would be called the *Queen Mary* 2), yet within a month of news of the project being made public, Cunard was already receiving inquiries from prospective passengers, asking where and how they could place deposits to secure passage on the new ship. "We've received 597 checks in the mail from people all anxious to have a place on the maiden voyage," Pimental told a reporter, "and we're not open for bookings yet. We're not even soliciting the sale of tickets. It's just amazing."

Cunard's director of public relations, Ernie Beyl, elaborated: "We expect this liner to be the most famous ship in the world, even before it starts sailing. Everywhere we go—here [Miami], London, Australia—we're asked questions about it. We like to think that we're bringing back the glory days of sea travel. We believe there's a major market for people who want to experience a liner crossing."

The effect of the *Queen Mary* 2 project on the people of Cunard was equally electric. When Captain Ronald Warwick spoke to the World Ship Society at New York on April 14, he declared that he was optimistic about Cunard's future for the first time in two decades. It was a far cry from the earlier observation that Warwick had made on more than one occasion that ocean liners would die with the *Queen Elizabeth* 2, and that when she retired it would be the end of that line. Young officers, engineers, and crew suddenly began to believe that they had a future with Cunard. Even in the corporate offices, people found a new vitality, as it became clear that business as usual, the old days of Cunard as the poor relation of the cruise industry, were over once and for all, and that the best of Cunard tradition would return.

Certainly Captain Warwick was in a position to know first-hand what effect the *Queen Mary* 2 would have on the company. He had gone to sea as a seventeen year-old apprentice on the cargo ships of the Port Line, sailing mainly between Britain and Australia and New Zealand. By 1961, at the age of twenty-one, he had his Second Mate's Certificate, and spent the next several years gaining experience on as many different types of ships as possible. It was a stint as Fourth Officer on the Royal Mail cruise liner RMS *Andes* that led him to choose to specialize in passenger shipping.

In 1968 he earned his Master's Ticket, and two years later he joined the Cunard Line as a junior officer aboard the *Carmania*, later moving to various officer berths on the *Cunard Adventurer*, the *Cunard Countess*, the *Cunard Princess*, and eventually the *QE2*. His first command was the *Cunard Princess* when she was sailing in Alaskan waters in 1986, and she always would remain a personal favorite. On the first world cruise of the *QE2* in 1975 he served as Navigator, later moving up to Chief Officer, the slot he occupied during the 1982 Falklands War.

Command of the *Queen Elizabeth 2* came to Captain Warwick in July 1990, and when it did it created a most unusual situation. His father, the late Commodore William E. Warwick CBE RD RNR, had served not only as the captain of the *Queen Mary* and the first *Queen Elizabeth*, but had also been the first master of the *Queen Elizabeth 2*, serving on her until his retirement in 1972, making him the only man who ever cap-

Captain R.W. Warwick, Commodore of the Cunard Line. (Photo courtesy of Carnival Corporation)

tained all three *Queens*. With his son now master of the *QE2*, it marked the first time in Cunard history that a father and son had served as captain of the same ship. The younger Warwick was the *QE2's* captain when the liner received Her Majesty Queen Elizabeth II and His Royal Highness the Duke of Edinburgh aboard for the 150th anniversary celebration of the Cunard Line, off Spithead in July 1990.

As soon as the *Queen Mary 2* project was announced, rumors began to circulate that Warwick would be named as her first captain, even though he would be past mandatory retirement age when the new liner entered service; it was believed an exemption to the retirement regulations would be made for him. Certainly it would be an opportunity that Cunard would be loathe to pass up, the son of the only man to command the first three *Queens* becoming the master of the last two. Certainly it seemed that having a Warwick on the bridge of one of the *Queens* had become something of a Cunard tradition.

All the same, Larry Pimentel's respect for Cunard tradition and British maritime history didn't extend to British maritime labor policies, and the day after Captain Warwick addressed the World Ship Society, Pimental was meeting with Britain's Deputy Prime Minister, John Prescott, to settle some thorny labor issues. Prescott, who at one time had worked for Cunard as a steward, was hoping to persuade Cunard to register the *QM2* under the British flag, but Pimentel was adamant that unless British shipping unions made significant concessions on pay and conditions, the new liner was unlikely to fly the red ensign. It would be several months before the issue was settled.

It was about this time that Raoul Fiebig, a German cruise industry writer with an international reputation and excellent connections within the industry, reported that Carnival

Corporation was seeking to renegotiate the price it had paid for Cunard when it purchased the line from Kvaerner. Carnival felt that Kvaerner had misrepresented both the condition of Cunard's ships and their earning potential, and was asking for close to $80,000,000 to be returned by the Norwegian industrial firm. With the need to undertake the *Queen Mary* 2 Project essential to ultimately making Cunard a going concern again, the added costs of refitting and refurbishing the *QE2* and the *Caronia*, as well as overhauling the entire business operation were becoming a burden to Carnival, one that it believed had been unfairly foisted on it by Kvaerner.

Meanwhile, the design for the new super-liner quickly began taking shape. In early June, some five hundred maritime enthusiasts boarded the *Queen Elizabeth* 2 in New York for a seven-day cruise that included stops at Bermuda, Nassau, and Newport News. On board was Stephen Payne, who gave an overview of the *Queen Mary* 2 project and presented the first look the public had at what form the ship would take. According to Payne, the new ship would have an overall length of 1,170 feet, a beam of 135, and a height from her keel to the top of her funnel of 237 feet; the projected displacement would be approximately 150,000 tons, with a total of fifteen decks. The *Queen Mary* 2 would accommodate over 2620 passengers and 1250 crew. At one point, he produced an artists' conception of the new liner's appearance, and the illustration created considerable consternation among the audience, for apparently they were expecting something quite different. One rather vocal passenger later described what he saw, making it clear after the voyage was over that he thought the new vessel would not be a proper ocean liner: "I got an impression of a sort of swollen *Queen Elizabeth* 2, with a *France*-ish rear superstructure and *Queen Mary* face, with a rather stunted funnel. [Payne] explained that the funnel could not be taller due to the need to clear New York's Verrazano Narrows Bridge and the already towering decks of the ship left no further height."

It's hard to conceive of what the audience expected, unless they were hoping for a reprise of one of the original *Queens*, as the final design was far from complete. According to Payne's presentation, there will be the same sort of "family resemblance" between the *Queen Mary* 2 and the *Queen Elizabeth* 2, much like that which existed between the first two *Queens*: the hull will be painted the satin black that graced Cunard hulls for more than a half-century, while a single massive funnel, similar in profile to that of the *QE2* and wearing the famous "Cunard Red" with two black bands, will be positioned just aft of amidships. The super-structure, painted the Ivory White that every Cunard ship has worn since the days of the first *Servia*, will be stepped well back from the clipper bow, and stepped aft as well, the classic liner profile. Diesel-electric power will drive four propulsion "pods" rather than the traditional shaft-mounted screws of previous liners, producing around 140,000 horsepower; the electrical output will be great enough to light a city with a population of 250,000. Unofficial reports initially maintained that the *Queen Mary* 2 was being designed for a top speed between 32 and 35 knots, but given her projected displacement and horsepower figures, such speeds seem highly unlikely, if not actually impossible.

The new liner's interiors, created by Tillberg Design, who had also done the reworking of the *QE2*, will attempt to re-create the high style and grace of the great Cunard and White Star ships. There will be grand staircases, elegant restaurants, a broad, covered promenade deck encircling the entire superstructure, a forward-facing observation lounge and a large Lido pool with a retractable dome for inclement weather. Two-thirds of the outside staterooms and suites will have private balconies, while the ship's public rooms will be on a scale of luxury not seen since the days of the *Aquitania*, or even the *Titanic* or *Olympic*.

Other features that Payne revealed included an onboard Maritime Museum highlighting the history of transatlantic liners; a Heritage Trail (a concept which originated on the *QE2*) displaying artifacts from Cunard's 160-year history (rumor has it that these may include the *Aquitania*'s bell and an engine telegraph from the first *Mauretania*, both of which are currently in the wardroom of the *QE2*); an extravagant spa and health center; a computer learning center; and even a pub with its own onboard microbrewery.

The whole design process for the new liner was a learning experience for Arison and most of the people at Carnival. "I remember seeing a PBS special about the *QE2* called 'The Last Liner,' which I was infuriated at—I thought we *were* building liners! What I didn't realize was that a 'liner' is something quite different from a cruise ship. We even nicknamed our *Fantasy* class 'super liners.' But when we got into what it means to be a liner, our technical guys put up slides of six or seven major events in the North Atlantic, like the *Michelangelo*'s bow being completely crushed by a giant wave, and they explained that you can't just build a cruise ship and send it across the Atlantic eighteen or twenty times a year—you have to build something different.

"What really drove me nuts was that you can't put a main lounge forward and a restaurant aft, like we've done before: if you look at all our new building, the main lounge is forward and the restaurant is aft. You start there and start building, it's like putting building blocks in between. But we basically had to start from scratch, taking whatever we learned from cruise ships and seeing where we could incorporate it, but mainly we started from scratch. It was a very difficult process, by far the longest we've ever gone through. Even the general arrangement plan took months and months! On our other designs that wasn't a difficult process, just lay it out a certain way for how you want people to move through the ship, but here everything was pushed toward the middle of the ship.... It was a very interesting process and took a very long time, but in the end we came up with a unique design. It's going to be an exciting ship."

One issue that arose quite early in the design process for the *Queen Mary* 2 was the positioning of the lifeboats. The International Convention for the Safety of Life at Sea, also known as SOLAS, mandates that lifeboats be nested in the hull forty-five feet above the waterline, that is, more or less in the middle of the ship. It's a provision that has its origins in the *Titanic* disaster, when hundreds of Third Class passengers were unable to reach the upper deck of the sinking liner where the lifeboats were stowed, until it was too late and all of the boats had been launched. Over the years the provisions for positioning the boats have been modified to reflect the changing nature of the passenger ship business, and with the overwhelming majority of passenger ships now engaged in cruising, SOLAS began to lose sight of some of the harsher realities of genuine ocean travel, one of which is the particularly vicious weather that the North Atlantic can unleash without warning at any time of the year. Cunard requested that SOLAS provide an exemption to the forty-five foot rule: on a transatlantic liner, lifeboats so positioned were actually in danger of being damaged or destroyed by heavy seas. It had happened to the *Queen Elizabeth* 2 in December 1998. At first SOLAS was unwilling to make such a concession, but when the U.S. Coast Guard endorsed Cunard's request, SOLAS relented; the *Queen Mary* 2 will have a proper Boat Deck somewhere between sixty-five and seventy-five feet above her waterline.

All the fuss about the *QM2* didn't mean that business maneuverings had come to a standstill. On October 20, 2000, Carnival Corporation exercised its option to purchase the outstanding 32% of Cunard Line Limited for $205,000,000. To Arison, purchasing the balance of the Cunard shares simply made good business sense. Despite fears in some circles that Carnival's acquisition of Cunard would lead to the line being "Americanized" and losing its British identity and character, exactly the opposite had happened. In many ways Cunard was more British under Carnival that it had been since the early 1960s, and the rise in bookings for the first ten months of 2000 were proof of the line's renewed popularity. The plans for the *QM2* also played a role. "Considering the strength of the Cunard brand and its plans to build the largest ocean liner in the world to complement the *Queen Elizabeth* 2, it simply makes sense for Carnival to own 100% of Cunard," Arison said. That same month Kvaerner reached a $50,000,000 settlement of Carnival's claim that in terms of performance and earnings capability, Cunard had been overvalued at the time of the sale.

It was about this time that an article in the British technical journal *The Engineer* revealed that the builder was finally selected from the five shipyards bidding to build the *QM2*. British yards were likely to be passed over; Germany's Meyer Weft or Italy's Fincantieri were considered to be the front runners. The British business community was furious, and Cunard, seeking to diffuse the impact of this report, said that regardless of who the builder might be, the liner's master and officers would be British, and assured the British government that she would home-ported at Southampton along with the *Queen Elizabeth* 2 and the *Caronia*, with all of the positive benefits that would bring to the British economy.

The controversy begun by that article was more than just a tempest in a teapot. Arison, who had visited the shipyard the same week the article in *The Engineer* appeared, and met with company officials and Ministers from the Northern Ireland Assembly, was quick to say that Harland and Wolff's chances of securing the contract to build the new liner were excellent. Arison had gone to Belfast as part of a series of visits to each of the five yards under consideration. The Belfast yard is owned by the Norwegian shipbuilding firm of Fred Olsen, and has faced declining numbers of orders for several years: when Carnival began looking for a builder for the new liner, Harland and Wolff had no pending orders on their books at all. Securing the *QM2* order would revitalize not only the yard but the entire region, so it was no small matter when it was reported that it had already been determined that the shipyard would receive short shrift when it came time to choose a builder. The controversy died down somewhat, though, when Larry Pimentel announced that the whole project was going to be delayed by a few months as changes in the design were worked out. The new target date was for the order to be placed in the early spring of 2000, with delivery set for the end of 2003.

Even though construction had yet to begin, the new liner was able to create still another controversy, this time on the other side of the world, when Carnival encountered problems in persuading the Sydney Ports Corporation in Australia to allow the new ship to berth in Sydney Harbour. To do so would require rebuilding the Sydney Cove Passenger Terminal, and the port authority wasn't convinced the return would be worth the investment. There were a number of factors working against Carnival and Cunard in the Australian market: a short cruising season, long and expensive air connections, regulations forbidding the operation of casinos and duty-free shops, and high fuel taxes. Most cruise lines don't regard Australia as a serious cruise market, even though one of the fastest growing segments in the industry is the Pacific Rim. Most observers within the business feel that the lack of interest on the part of the cruise industry in the Australian market has been due to the government's refusal to change the laws and regulations. After an initial abortive attempt at persuading Australian officials to make their regulations more friendly to the industry, and faced with an adamant refusal by the port of Sydney to modernize its facilities, Carnival let the matter drop, preferring to deal with it at a future date.

By the end of February 2000, the short list of prospective builders for the *QM2* was reduced to two: Chantiers de l'Atlantique of Saint-Nazaire, France, and Harland & Wolff. After meeting with Carnival executives in Miami, Harland and Wolff officials believed they had every chance of securing the order. At stake were the shipyard's 2,000 core jobs, plus thousands more that would be created in Northern Ireland and the rest of the United Kingdom. After reviewing what they had learned at Germany's Meyer Werft, Finland's Kvaerner Masa, and the Italian shipyard Fincantieri, Carnival's executives decided to eliminate those three shipyards, due to their lacking either the physical capacity or the technical skills necessary to undertake a project of the magnitude of the *QM2*. But Chantiers de l'Atlantique couldn't be so easily disposed of: the thorny question that remained to be settled was the size and nature of the government subsidy that would support the yard until the ship was finished. Both Carnival and Cunard were openly favoring the Belfast shipyard, but there was an enormous difference in the bids submitted by Harland & Wolff and Chantiers de l'Atlantique, rumored to be as much as $118,000,000. The fundamental problem was money—the new ship could eventually cost as much as $700,000,000, capital that Carnival simply did not have to put up front, and should there be any significant rise in labor costs, that figure could soar even higher. At the same time, Harland and Wolff was in no position to underwrite the cost of building the ship until it was complete and Carnival could be billed for payment. What both shipyard and cruise company were anticipating were loan and price guarantees from Her Majesty's Government, but the best that Prime Minister Tony Blair was willing to offer was an annual subsidy equal to 9% of the final cost of the ship, not enough to keep the yard operating, even with regular payments from Cunard and Carnival while the ship was being built.

Consequently, on March 9 Cunard revealed that the company would sign a letter of intent to build its super-liner at the one hundred-forty year-old Chantiers de L'Atlantique shipyard in Saint-Nazaire, France. Micky Arison made the announcement, declaring that "The signing of this letter of intent is a significant milestone in the birth of this unique vessel. Over the last months, our vision of the first true ocean liner to be built in a generation has evolved from a dream to a detailed plan on paper. We are satisfied that the shipyard which created the *Normandie*, the *France* and other legendary liners has the capability to make that dream a reality."

Owned by Alstom, a French consortium of transportation manufacturers, the Chantiers de L'Atlantique yard had a reputation for building ships of unusual size and style, including several coastal cruise ships. However, as Micky Arison had learned while the *QM2*'s design was being developed, a cruise ship and an ocean liner are very different vessels, from their basic layouts to the type and thickness of the steel that forms the shell plating for the hull. Still, Alstom executives were confident that their company could build what Cunard required. "We want to build this magnificent ship because of our history and because of our future," was how Chantiers de L'Atlantique Chairman Patrick Boissier put it. "We understand the character of the liner that Cunard wants, and we know how to build that kind of ship."

But despite Boissier's confidence, a letter of intent is not a contract, and confirmation of the order was delayed, although Cunard extended the duration of its letter of intent with the French shipbuilder. According to Cunard executives, the anticipated date for a contract confirmation was being postponed because of changes being worked into the final design. What was really happening was that Harland and Wolff was making one last, desperate play to secure the construction order.

The fight by the Belfast shipyard to secure the order for the *QM2* finally received some measure of substantial support from the British government. A quiet row had been brewing within the Government since Prime Minister Tony Blair's lukewarm offer of 9% subsidy—without guaranteed financing—back in March. The Northern Ireland minister, Adam Ingram, often an "invisible man" in the Blair Government—Blair had a tendency to otherwise ignore Northern Ireland when formulating Government policy—was suddenly able to impress on the Prime Minister the impact that the *QM2* contract would have on the economy of Great Britain as a whole, and Blair, leading as usual from the rear, immediately turned to follow his subordinates. The Department of Trade then disclosed that under the Home Shipbuilding Credit Guarantee Scheme, the Government could guarantee a loan of 80% of the cost of the *QM2*'s contract, a figure more than sufficient for the yard to be able to complete the project. Essentially what the guarantee meant was that the yard would have the cash to build, and to repay the money on completion and payment by the purchaser. It would assemble a funding package which would guarantee the financing necessary for the yard to compete, the announcement coming less than twenty-four hours after Harland and Wolff began issuing protective redundancy notices (layoff notices in American parlance) to 1,745 workers, nearly the yard's entire workforce. At a mass meeting of the workers they agreed to accept a request by management for a three-year agreement banning strikes—labor disputes that might severely disrupt the liner's construction was a major concern of Carnival—during the building of the ship, should the yard secure the order.

Sadly for Harland and Wolff, it was a classic case of too little, too late. The near-disdain with which the Blair government had treated Carnival early in the selection process, then the panicky measures taken in the eleventh hour led Carnival executives to quietly wonder how well thought-out the British proposals were, as well as how substantial they might be. When asked about making the final choice of the French shipyard over the British, it was clear from Arison's response that he would have preferred to build the *QM2* at Harland and Wolff. "We bent over backwards to give the people in Belfast a chance. We spent a lot of time at Harland and Wolff, and they have a lot of very good people who did a lot of good work. We really tried to give them an opportunity to secure the order, but in the end they just couldn't compete." Evident in the tone of his voice, if not in his words, was disappointment at not having the chance to build the new *Queen* in a British shipyard, as well as the implied insult of the Blair government in not taking Carnival seriously enough to become involved earlier in securing the order.

On November 2, 2000, Carnival Corporation confirmed the order for *Queen Mary* 2 with the Chantiers de l'Atlantique. Commenting on the *Queen Mary* 2's place in Cunard history at the signing ceremony, Larry Pimentel, the Cunard Chairman said, "Cunard has been carrying people between Europe and America and around the world for more than 160 years. For the last six decades, there has always been a Cunard *Queen* on the sea. *Queen Mary* 2 will be the heir to all that has gone before and she will be a showcase of the art of shipbuilding in its most refined and masterful form. *Queen Mary* 2 will carry the grace and elegance of a bygone era into the future."

Simultaneously with the announcement of Cunard's choice of the French shipyard as the builder of the *Queen Mary* 2, came the news that the new liner would be flagged under the Red Duster, the ensign of the British Merchant Marine. It was a tremendous boost for the British shipping industry, and was hugely welcomed by British Deputy Prime Minister John Prescott. Tough negotiations between Larry Pimental and Prescott over the terms and conditions of British maritime labor regulations finally came to fruition, and Prescott was happy to tell the press: "As a former Cunard employee, I am delighted that this prestigious ship will be flagged in the UK. This is yet a further sign that our new shipping policy and registration process are re-emphasizing the UK's prominence as a maritime center. Since I announced our new shipping policy for the UK less than 2 years ago, our shipping register

The Queen Mary 2 *under construction at the drydock of the Chantiers de l'Atlantique of Saint-Nazaire, France.*

has grown by almost one and a half million tons - including cruise ships, container ships and ferries - reversing decades of decline. Britain is regaining its merchant navy fleet."

Cunard revealed that it was planning to build a second luxury liner on December 14, projecting that the new ship would be in service by the summer of 2005. Rumors briefly swirled about the shipping world that the new vessel was to be a sister ship to the *Queen Mary* 2, but those were quickly dispelled. Mickey Arison went on record as saying, "We view the *Queen Mary* 2 for the time being, as one of a kind. The truth is that we don't envision a bunch of ships on the North Atlantic in the next three or four years—we view that as a unique, one-ship market. Otherwise we would be keeping the *QE2* on the trade with the *QM2*, but we don't believe there is a demand for more than one ship like the *Queen Mary* 2." Later that month Carnival signed a letter of intent with the Italian shipyard Fincantieri for the construction of the new ship. Early reports indicated that she would be around 82,000 tons displacement, with a capacity for 1,968 passengers, making her comparable to the slightly smaller *Queen Elizabeth* 2. The estimated cost of the new ship, which will be based in Southampton along with the *QE2*, is said to be $400,000,000. One of the design mandates for her is the capability to pass through the Panama Canal, something the *Queen Mary* 2 will be unable to do because of her immense size, allowing the new liner to be utilized on around-the-world cruises. Like the *QM2*, the new ship's propulsion system will feature diesel-electric motors and will employ the Azipod propulsion system for greater maneuverability.

At one point it was rumored in some circles that this latest ship would be known as the *Queen Victoria*, although there was no precedent for this name in the Cunard fleet, and many maritime enthusiasts were hoping to see her christened as the *Mauretania*. Rumors even swirled about that she might be called the *Queen Elizabeth* 3 though they were unrealistic because the new ship will be entering service in 2005, and Cunard currently plans for the *QE2* to be part of the fleet at least through 2010. Ultimately, in the late spring of 2003 it was quietly announced that the new ship would indeed be named the *Queen Victoria*.

Quite unexpectedly, on February 6, 2001, Larry Pimental, Cunard's president, resigned. In a prepared statement he told the press "It is with great difficulty that I have made the decision to step down from my current post. My years at Seabourn and Cunard have been extremely rewarding. However, from a personal perspective, this is the right decision for me and my family." Apparently, the strain of overseeing the *Queen Mary* 2 project while trying to run Cunard's day-to-day operations had become too much for him, and he began to believe his family's well-being was suffering as a consequence. Something of a workaholic, Pimentel had been in charge of Cunard since May 1998, and before that had spent six years as president and chief operating officer of Seabourn; if anyone had the right to claim they were burnt out from overwork, it was he. However, it seems that there were other reasons motivating his departure as well. Knowledgeable observers within the cruise industry hinted that disagreements between Pimental and Arison over marketing strategies and plans for Cunard's future made Pimental's decision to leave, inevitable.

In his place, Arison appointed Pamela Conover as Cunard's new president. It proved to be a fairly smooth transition, as Conover was already Cunard's chief operating officer. An earlier stint as vice president of strategic planning for Carnival Corporation meant that she already had a hand in developing corporate plans for the line, and implementing them would be less troublesome for her than apparently they had been for Pimental. To Pimental's credit, whatever disagreements he may have had with Arison had not created any major disruptions in Cunard's operations or plans, and the *Queen Mary* 2 project proceeded without interruption.

A major step forward in the design of the *Queen Mary* 2 was taken in late February when a scale model of the ship passed critical tank tests with flying colors. The Maritime Research Institute Netherlands (MARIN) built a 15-foot long, self- propelled model of the ship that perfectly duplicated the hull form and contours of the proposed design. The model was then placed in a large tank—almost a small lake—in which equipment was installed which could reproduce various sea conditions in scale with the model. This would allow the ship's designers to determine the efficiency and seaworthiness of the hull design, refine it, and eliminate any inherent problems even before the first keel plates were laid.

The tests were a triumph for the new hull and propulsion design. First came a series of maneuvering tests to determine the ship's handling characteristics. Next, a series of seakeeping tests were performed to examine the hull's performance in different sea conditions. The design performed flawlessly as it rode through a simulated 40-foot swell at a speed of 18 knots, with virtually no water being shipped over the bow. Even in simulated hurricane conditions, her raked bow split the waves cleanly and her wake trailed out straight astern, a sure sign that the design was stable and seaworthy. The success of the tests meant that no major revisions to the design were required; dimensions and specifications could now be finalized, and the process of assembling materials, cutting steel and fabricating structural components could begin.

Perhaps as a sign of the renewed vitality that has suffused Cunard, company traditions pop up in curious places and at curious times. So it was when Pam Conover expressed her satisfaction with the test results, and unconsciously gave expression to the old Cunard motto, "Speed, comfort, and safety." "It's always a big step to actually put a model in the water and see the design become real. Transatlantic service calls for speed, safety, reliability and comfort. We designed a hybrid vessel with classic lines above the water and very modern and innovative features below, and the design met or exceeded all our expectations."

The successful tank tests also allowed the Cunard designers to settle on a specific power plant for the liner. The propulsion system design for *Queen Mary* 2 is unique: she will be the first vessel to be propelled by four pod-mounted propellers called Azipods, that extend beneath the hull, rather than mount on long shafts at the extreme stern. The two forward pods are fixed and the two aft pods are steerable, an arrangement which allows the engineers to dispense with not only the bulky propeller shafts, but also the rudders and rudder machinery. The power plant arrangements underwent one significant change at this point, when it was decided to abandon diesel-electric propulsion in favor of a gas turbine-electric combination. The engines chosen to power the Azipods are GE Marine Engines' LM2500+ gas turbines, ironically, a design derived from passenger jet aircraft engines. A combined gas turbine-generator set, the LM2500+ engines offer the advantages of being compact, relatively quiet, virtually vibration-free, and extremely fuel efficient—they are as much an advance over steam-powered turbines as those turbines were over reciprocating engines.

Another system successfully tested in the model tank were the stabilizers. Rolls-Royce, who builds propulsion systems and stabilizers for the Royal Navy, was chosen to supply the Brown Brothers-designed stabilizers for the *Queen Mary* 2. There are four folding-fin stabilizers, two to a side, controlled by gyroscopes, which will be capable of reducing a 20º roll to less than a quarter of that distance. These are the same type of stabilizers that Cunard chose for retrofitting into the *Queen Mary* and *Queen Elizabeth* in the 1950s, eliminating both those ships' notorious rolling tendencies; they were installed on the *Queen Elizabeth* 2 when she was built.

While the technical details of the *QM2* were being settled, Cunard was also attending to the aesthetic details. A Dutch art house, the Enterprise & Art Consultancy of Amsterdam, was commissioned to provide original and reproduction artwork for the new liner—more than five thousand pieces in all. Internationally-known artists were commissioned by Cunard to create over three hundred original works especially for the *Queen Mary*

2. There will be the usual assortment of oil paintings, watercolors, and murals, as well as mosaics, bas reliefs, and free-standing sculptures of bronze and glass. The centerpiece of the *QM2*'s art collection will be a 1,200 square feet *trompe l'oeil* painted ceiling in the main dining room that will echo the famous transatlantic mural found in the original *Queen Mary*'s First Class Dining Room.

A well thought-out concept, careful planning, and thorough organization had brought the *QM2* to the brink of becoming a reality, as plans were made to begin cutting steel for the ship in January 2002. In the meantime, profiting for the first time in over a quarter century from a coherent vision of what the line was meant to be and how it was to be accomplished, Cunard had accomplished an astonishing turnaround in its first eighteen months under Carnival stewardship. At the end of 2000, Maritime World Online, one of the leading Internet websites covering the shipping and cruising industries, announced that Cunard had been voted the Best Cruise Line World-wide. The *QE2* was more popular than ever, with nearly every sailing booked to capacity, while the *Caronia* was living up to the heritage of her name, with cruises becoming some of the most sought-after passages in the industry. Cunard's resurrection, it appeared, was almost complete.

Then came that awful morning without reason....

On September 11, 2001, a score of Islamic fanatics hijacked four civilian airliners in the airspace over the United States, causing two of them to crash into the twin towers of the World Trade Center in New York City, which later crumbled to the ground as a result of their damage. A third aircraft plunged into the side of the Pentagon in Washington, D.C., while the fourth plane smashed itself into a field in western Pennsylvania after the passengers chose not to be the helpless pawns of madmen, but fought back, losing their lives but saving untold others who would have been the target of that aircraft. The world was stunned, shocked, outraged; the United States mourned, then gathered to itself a terrible resolve to bring retribution to the evil minds behind the atrocities.

For Cunard, the consequences of the attacks were felt both personally and in business operations. The Port Authority of New York had made its home in the North Tower of the World Trade Center, and it had been completely obliterated when it collapsed; sadly, several Port Authority employees were killed as the tower came down. They had been friends and colleagues of the Cunard personnel who staffed the line's New York facilities, and the company felt their loss keenly. The elimination of the Port Authority offices also meant that Cunard was forced to move the American operations of its transatlantic service, and in a hastily improvised, but remarkably successful operation, the western terminus was moved to Boston. It would be almost five months before the *QE2* and the *Caronia* were able to return to New York.

(In one of the spookiest coincidences ever, comparable to Morgan Robertson's novel *Futility*, published in 1898, which gave an eerie foreshadowing of the *Titanic* disaster fourteen years later, a chilling advertisement—prepared and printed months before the terrorist attacks—appeared in the Cunard brochure which presented the 2002 sailing schedules of the *Queen Elizabeth 2* and the *Caronia* that was released in the first week of September 2001. It depicted a stylishly dressed, attractive couple leaning against a ship's railing, looking out to sea. Behind them loom the twin towers of the World Trade Center. The caption of the advertisement read, "New York may have changed, the best way to get there hasn't...." The brochures were withdrawn and destroyed as soon as the photo and caption was brought to Cunard's attention.)

In the meantime, though, there was a backlash among travelers, as people around the world were fearful of where and how such terrorists might strike again. The number of airline passengers plummeted as people feared an attempt to repeat the September 11 hijackings, while for many, a cruise ship filled with carefree, happy passengers seemed to be too good a target for such twisted minds to let pass untouched. The cruise lines began to be flooded by cancellations of existing bookings, while new reservations virtually vanished. It was a crisis without precedent within the industry—every line was hit hard by the decline in bookings; losses for some became so great that their survival became doubtful. One of them was Renaissance Cruises, which had been living a more-or-less hand-to-mouth existence for several years. The rash of cancellations and the paucity of new bookings created a cash flow crisis for Renaissance, and with practically no reserves, the line simply folded up and vanished in the mists of bankruptcy less than two weeks after the September 11 disasters.

Though it wasn't readily apparent that the demise of Renaissance might threaten the *QM2*, within two weeks of the September 11 disasters, rumors began surfacing that the project faced cancellation. In part, these rumors were fueled by the effect the sudden collapse of Renaissance Cruises might have on the Chantiers de l'Atlantique yard, which currently had eight Renaissance ships either under construction or on order. It was feared that without payments from Renaissance for these ships, the yard would be unable to afford to pay its workers to continue on the *QM2*.

The failure of Renaissance Cruises threw into stark relief the terrible impact the terrorist attacks had on the cruise line industry, as well as some of its murkier financial practices. The shipbuilding business has always been something of an arcane art, and histories of shipyards are replete with tales of how directors, chairmen, and managers have cooked books, skimmed cash, and otherwise fleeced customers and stockholders. It was a matter of public record that Friedrich Krupp, the German steel manufacturer, made a profit of exactly 100% on each of the warships his Germaniawerft yard built for the Kaiser's navy. When Lord Pirrie, the chairman of Harland and Wolff, died in 1924, the yard had no idea exactly what it was worth or how much cash it had on hand, for Pirrie had been keeping several sets of books for decades. The relationship between Renaissance and Chantiers de l'Atlantique, while technically legal, certainly maintained the tradition. The way in which the Renaissance collapse affected the Chantiers de l'Atlantique yard offered a revealing insight into how the cruise industry worked.

Renaissance Cruises already operated several ships that had been built in various yards owned by Alstom, the French transportation conglomerate which owned the Chantiers de l'Atlantique. In order to pay off the loans used to build those ships, which were relatively short-term notes, Renaissance had mortgaged the ships and amortized them over their projected twenty-year life-spans. Alstom had retained an interest in these ships by holding the first mortgages on them, the mortgage payments being used to pay off loans that had financed the yard's operating costs during the ships' construction, as well as the company's other operations. (The situation was somewhat analogous to a prospective homeowner loaning the mortgage company the money it was going to lend him to buy a house.) Already financially shaky, the sudden rash of cancellations by would-be passengers now fearful of another wave of violence left Renaissance with no working capital, and little chance of finding new financing. The resulting failure of Renaissance left Alstom financially vulnerable, although at the time Alstom maintained that it was adequately insured against the risks. However, the issue was far from certain.

When Alstom's precarious position was made public, there was a flurry of rumors that Cunard, rather than risk having Chantiers de l'Atlantique suddenly close down with the *Queen Mary* 2 less than half finished, would pull the plug on the project before construction started. It was a legitimate fear: trading in Alstom shares had been suspended in Paris after the stock fell further than the stock market limit, when the news broke of the conglomerate's vulnerability following the Renaissance bankruptcy. The yard was said to have an "ultimate liability" of $1,400,000,000 in financing on those eight ships. In order to protect Alstom, a group of French banks hastily assembled a financing package which would cover 80% of the value of the ships, leading Alstom executives to declare that Alstom was "adequately covered" against any risks related to Renaissance, but the financial community wasn't so positive.

At this point Arison stepped in. Realizing that the slightest appearance of a loss of confidence by Carnival in Chantiers de l'Atlantique, and by implication, Alstom, would almost certainly doom the shipyard, and with it the *Queen Mary* 2, his office issued a statement which declared that with a fleet of forty-five ships in its six component cruise lines, Carnival had assets worth $1,200,000,000, plus another $1,600,000,000 in available credit, and could afford to see the *Queen Mary* 2 through to completion. In effect, Carnival was saying that it had the resources to prop up Chantiers de l'Atlantique long enough for them to finish the super-liner. While the announcement didn't exactly spur a fervid revival of confidence in Alstom or its subsidiary, it did halt the panic and allowed a certain equilibrium to prevail long enough for Alstom to reorganize its finances sufficiently to ride out the storm.

Work officially began on the *Queen Mary* 2 on January 16, 2002. With a projected 694 days to delivery, Pamela Conover pressed a button on a huge cutting machine at the Chantiers de l'Atlantique shipyard that began fabricating the first steel for the *QM2*. Much had changed in the technology of shipbuilding in the last half of the 20th Century so there would be no actual "launching" of the ship, with a bottle of champagne broken over her

An artist's impression of the Queen Mary 2.

bow and the huge hull sliding down a slipway into the waiting water. Consequently, the act of cutting the first steel plates took the place of a launching as the suitable venue for the requisite bunting-behung, speechifying Auspicious Occasion. Conover's remarks, like all of the other addresses made during the ceremony, were the usual predictable mixture of business-speak and corporate platitude: "I am absolutely delighted to officially initiate the construction of the successor to such great transatlantic liners as *Queen Mary, Queen Elizabeth* and *Queen Elizabeth* 2. This begins a new era in the history of Cunard." Patrick Boissier, chairman of the Chantiers de l'Atlantique, spoke in a similar vein and idiom: "Today is a great day which will be remembered for a very long time by all Chantiers de l'Atlantique employees and all our partners associated in this project. It marks the beginning of one of the most prestigious industrial projects of this century and we are proud that Cunard has selected our shipyard to be part of it."

Fortunately, businessmen and businesswomen are valued for their business acumen rather than their eloquence, and what made that January 16 a day to be long remembered was not what was said, but what was done. The symbolism of cutting the first plates for the *QM2* was tremendous, for it gave the first substance to what, up until now, had been nothing more than piles of drawings in an architect's office, reams of contract paper on lawyers' desks, and a fifteen-foot model in a Dutch testing tank. The *Queen Mary* 2 was about to become real, about to give the lie to the thought that the ocean liner was an anachronism, an exercise in nostalgia with no place in the modern world, about to revive the glory of Samuel Cunard's dream. Now she was steel; now she was real.

In February, Cunard, feeding the world's insatiable hunger for news about the new ship, released a preliminary schedule of the *Queen Mary* 2's sailings. Her maiden voyage would be from Southampton to Fort Lauderdale in early January 2004, followed by a series of Caribbean cruises until April. That month she would begin a regular schedule of six-night transatlantic sailings between Southampton and New York, taking the place of the *Queen Elizabeth* 2 on this route. The *QE2* would be shifting her operations to cruising in the Mediterranean and Scandinavian waters. On April 29, 2002 a thrill ran through the shipping world and the cruise industry alike when Cunard announced that an original seven foot-long, 1400 pound steam whistle from the first *Queen Mary* would be taken from the liner sitting at her permanent berth in Long Beach and mounted on the *Queen Mary 2*. Audible for a distance of over ten miles, the whistle is one of three installed on the Queen Mary when she was fitting out in 1936. Fittingly, the QE2 carried the whistle across the Atlantic to Southampton, where it was transferred to St. Nazaire by ferry. Already people were anticipating the day in April 2004 when the westbound *Queen Mary* 2 meets the eastbound *Queen Elizabeth* 2 in mid-Atlantic, and the stentorian sound of two *Queens* saluting one another, not heard for almost thirty-seven years, blasts out across the waves.

On July 4, 1840, the *Britannia*, Samuel Cunard's first ship, left Liverpool bound for Halifax and Boston. One hundred sixty-two years later, on what is celebrated as the birthday of the Cunard Line, the keel was laid for the *Britannia*'s newest successor on July 4, 2002. It wasn't quite the same sort of keel-laying ceremony that had been typical of all of Cunard's pervious ships. Instead of a series of plates being "laid" on a slipway floor and riveted or welded into the beginning of the new ship's keel, with a skeletal framework rising from that backbone to be gradually covered with shell plating and decking, the *QM2* is being constructed using modular technology. Her hull is divided into a series of ninety-four sections, or modules—the French call them "blocks,"—some of them weighing as much as six hundred tons. The modules are prefabricated, with bulkheads, decks, partitions, wiring, and plumbing all installed before the completed module is then hoisted by a crane into its place on the ship being assembled. So the first module, or section, of the *QM2* was lowered into place in the dry dock where she was to be built, serving as a surrogate keel for the occasion.

That's not to say that there was no acknowledgment of tradition when this was done: a gathering of shipyard workers and invited guests watched as two coins were solemnly placed inside the keel section. It was a custom dating back to the days of sail, when a coin would be placed at the foot of each mast as it was stepped. This time, symbolizing a British ship being built in a French yard, a new £5 Jubilee coin and a one hundred franc coin were placed inside keel section number 502 just before it was lowered into the dry dock.

Bookings for passage on the *Queen Mary 2* officially opened on August 1, and the next day reservations for the proposed January 12, 2004, maiden voyage were closed: the voyage had sold out. The itinerary for the voyage was finally confirmed: a 14-day cruise from Southampton to Fort Lauderdale, Florida, by way of Madeira, Tenerife and Las Palmas in the Canary Islands, Barbados and St. Thomas. In a masterly example of British understatement, a Cunard spokesman told the press that sales for the *Queen Mary* 2 had "exceeded all expectations." It's possible, despite his belief that "there won't be a bunch of passenger ships crossing the Atlantic in the next four or five years," Micky Arison has discovered a passion in the traveling public that few before suspected existed, a desire to experience life aboard not just a cruise ship but a true ocean liner, an opportunity to eschew the agony of being sealed inside a steel tube and shot across the ocean, compelled to endure for hours on end squalling babies, obnoxious teenagers, and rude tourists, along with bad food, bad movies, and bad seating. Certainly there will always be that hard core of travelers who cannot arrive at their destination soon enough, and the majority will continue to persuade themselves that it's preferable to fly, but certainly there are many thousands of people on both sides of the Atlantic for whom, as the Cunard Line advertised a half-century ago, "getting there is half the fun."

Carnival Corporation, and in particular Micky Arison, have a definite vision of the future for the Cunard Line. When the *Queen Mary* 2 goes into service in early 2004, she will, in essence, be bringing Cunard home. The company's primary operations are already shifting to Southampton—Pam Conover moved her office there two years ago—and Carnival expects that fully two-thirds of the line's future business will come from the United Kingdom. At the same time, the much beloved *Caronia*, undersized and beginning to show her age, will have finally reached the end of her career with Cunard, as it was announced in May 2003 that she would make her last voyage in the Line's livery in the summer of 2004: she would then be sold to Saga Cruises, where she would rejoin her sister, once the *Sagafjord*, now the *Saga Rose*, later that year, cruising the Baltic and Mediterranean Seas. By then, however, the *Queen Elizabeth* 2, the *Queen Mary* 2, and the *Queen Victoria*, still taking shape in Italy, will be more than sufficient to carry the name and traditions of Cunard well into the 21st Century. Far from becoming bland and Americanized, as so many had feared when Carnival bought Cunard, the line is becoming more and more British in tone and character, perhaps more than it has ever been in the past half-century.

The Cunard Line that exists today is a very different entity than what was created by Samuel Cunard more than 162 years ago, but then, it's a very different world. The company that Cunard had created, and the service it provided, had changed the world, propelling, in turn, British shipbuilding, steam engineering and steel-making to feats of construction and production that had never before been imagined. They in turn, were the driving forces behind the Victorian Era. At the same time, by example, Cunard showed the way for a score of steamship companies to turn the trickle of emigrants from Europe to America into a flood, changing the face and character of two continents. Yet the technologies that grew out of the industrial expansion which spawned the steamships ultimately made them obsolete. The need for the services which the Cunard Line had long provided ceased to exist, and so the company reinvented itself, ultimately successfully, so that when it could no longer fulfill a need, it satisfied a desire. It was a matter of practical business survival, and it would be hard to imagine old Sir Samuel disapproving, for he was above all else, a practical businessman. There can be no way of knowing for sure, yet it seems likely that Samuel Cunard, while perhaps looking with disdain on the stewardship of some of his latter-day successors, would be pleased by what has ultimately become of his British and North American Royal Mail Steam Packet Company. While perhaps wondering at the luxury and the apparent extravagance of these modern ships, he would approve of the fact that the service is still smart, the ships still neat and tidy, the seamanship still impeccable. While he might be more than mildly shocked at the idea of a woman as the chief executive officer of the line, he would no doubt find reassurance in hearing Pamela Conover's invocation of "Speed, Comfort, and Safety." And while he might be awed by the size of the *Queen Mary 2*, so large that the little *Britannia*, his first ship, would be lost inside her dining room, he would quickly appreciate that this new leviathan is the ultimate confirmation of everything he had striven to achieve. Once again, a Cunard ship will dominate the great northern ocean, putting the Cunard seal once and for all time over the age of North Atlantic passenger travel. It had been his age, the age of his ships, the age of his line. It had been the Age of Cunard.

EPILOGUE

The Dream and the Glory

It was just past 8:00 o'clock on the morning of May 18, 2002, in the port of Southampton. The *Queen Elizabeth 2* had drawn alongside the Ocean Dock two hours before, and as soon as the gangway was hauled into place, a team of the Crown's Customs officials set themselves up at the far end of it and began the ritual of debarkation for the *QE2*'s passengers. It was an old routine, well-rehearsed and well-honed, one that had been going on with minor variations for more than a hundred and fifty years. It was organized, low-key, and smoothly efficient. By 9:00 am the first passengers were making their way off the ship, some to waiting tour buses, others to taxis, still others into the arms of waiting family and friends. Outside the early morning gloom was giving way to a fitful sunshine, and as it did, an American author standing on the *Queen Elizabeth 2*'s Boat Deck suddenly found himself doing something he had once vowed never to do: he became part of the story he was writing.

The Southampton waterfront could finally be seen, as well as the length of the Ocean Dock, and for me it's a vista filled with mixed emotions. So much of Southampton has changed since the years when the great liners docked here, and yet so much is recognizable from a past that is hardly distant, when this city was one of the greatest seaports in the world. The debarkation terminal is abuzz with the rush and bustle of people leaving the ship for their holidays in Britain, or being whisked off to Heathrow or Gatwick to continue their travels by air. Southampton's city center is a pleasantly noisy urban center filled with trendy shops and fashions, the majority of the people making their way along the High Street are young and bright. But down by Ocean Dock, when the last of the departing passengers have gone, it seems for a few moments almost as if the place is haunted.

Stepping up to the *QE2*'s Sun Deck I gaze up and down the venerable Ocean Dock, now well over a century old, and the sights overwhelm my imagination and my emotions. Below me I can see rails still embedded in concrete running down the length of the dock; once they had borne the Boat Trains that come down from Waterloo Station in London, delivering the First and Second Class passengers to the boarding gangways of ships with names like *Caronia, Carinthia, Homeric, Majestic, Queen Mary, Aquitania*. There stand cranes and gantries, some dating back to the First World War, which had loaded and unloaded uncountable tons of cargo and luggage into and out of some of the most magnificent ships that ever sailed. Across the way is the Trafalgar Dry Dock and the Town Quay, the Empress Basin and the Prince of Wales Dock, empty moorings now, but somehow with still-lingering shadows cast by ships from a dozen different nations and twice that many steamships lines, but always, always dominated by the funnels bearing that curious, indescribable, but unmistakable shade of red....

I become suddenly conscious of a succession of memories, some my own, others recalled from photos and narratives that I had come across over the years, images that slowly unfold, like a motion picture being wound backwards. It was from this dock that the first *Queen Elizabeth* had sailed for the last time in 1968, on a voyage that would ultimately take her to oblivion, bringing the curtain thundering down on the greatest sea story of all time. The *Queen Mary* had pulled away from this same spot on October 31, 1967, saluted by HMS *Hermes* at the mouth of the Solent, as she departed for a graceful and beloved retirement. This same waterfront had said goodbye to the "Green Goddess," the elegant and much-loved *Caronia*; it had seen the grand old *Aquitania* doff her wartime grey and don the colors of peacetime as she resumed her majestic progressions across the Atlantic once the lowering clouds of the Second World War had lifted. In the King George V dry dock the *Queen Mary* and *Queen Elizabeth* had been returned to their civilian glory after their days as Warrior *Queens*.

War clouds had hovered over these docks for four years, while German bombers tried to destroy them and they sat empty of the great ocean liners. Somewhere beyond the rampart of buildings crowding the waterfront was the bombed-out remains of Holyrood Church, solemnly noble in its ruined grace, now Britain's memorial to the officers and men of her gallant merchant marine who gave their lives in two World Wars....

It was here that the *Mauretania*, her white hull streaked with rust, sailed slowly away to be broken up, a lone piper playing a lament for her passing. The *Olympic* and the *Homeric*, flying two house flags as they struggled to keep the ghost of the White Star Line alive in the last years of their own lives, had called Southampton their home port. Then came the image of the Southampton docks caught in the depths of the Great Depression, when ship after ship tied up and shut down her boilers, no passengers to carry, no freight to take aboard, nowhere to go and no reason to go there. And I thought of how close Cunard had come to dissolution in those years....

Then, as suddenly as it began, the progression of images stopped, and then reversed itself, now moving forward in time, and I was seeing a different succession of ships that had worn Cunard's colors, some Blue Ribband holders, others simply unforgettable, making a stately parade through my imagination. There were the first Cunarders, the *Britannia* and *Acadia*, giants in their day, yet ultimately so diminutive that they could have been placed inside the dining saloons of some of their descendants; the powerful *Persia* and the lovely *Scotia*, who brought the paddlewheel steamer to the pinnacle of perfection just at the moment when it became obsolete; the *Umbria* and *Etruria*, hardly pretty ships but fast and luxurious for their day; the *Campania* and *Lucania*, with their squat, dumpy superstructures and outsized funnels that belied their Blue Ribband speed; the *Caronia* and *Carmania*, the "Pretty Sisters," neither of which actually held the Blue Ribband, but which showed the way for the magnificent ships to come....

The *Lusitania*, big, bold, awkward-looking but awesomely powerful, that revolutionized shipbuilding at a stroke; there was her sister once again, the *Mauretania*, one of the most beloved ships of all time, whose demise caused grown men to weep; the *Aquitania*, stately and proud, the last of the majestic four-funneled liners; the *Berengaria*, the ugly German giant, an interloper who was never quite at home in her foreign clothes; once more there were the *Queens*, the most majestic passenger ships ever built, the ultimate embodiment of everything that Samuel Cunard had ever hoped to accomplish when he created the British and North American Royal Mail Steam Packet Company more than one hundred sixty years ago....

And there was the ship on whose decks I stood, the *Queen Elizabeth 2*, defying convention, defying all odds, a magnificent anachronism: the last passenger liner still making the transatlantic run, her services no longer truly needed but now more popular than ever. And just over the horizon, across the English Channel, an even more amazing ship was taking shape, the *Queen Mary 2*, which in eighteen months would set sail as the largest passenger liner that has ever been built, or likely ever will be. It will only be a matter of time, I realize, until once more the impossibly deep-voiced whistles of two *Queens* will bellow out their salutes to one another in passing on the North Atlantic....

What a story I had stepped into! From the brink of dissolution and oblivion, Cunard had been pulled back, rehabilitated, returned to its rightful place of honor as the oldest and greatest—and last—of the passenger lines on the transatlantic run.

And that was when it struck me, why the reverie was at once so glorious and yet seemed tinged so with melancholy: it had been all about speed, and yet, speed didn't matter much anymore. The voyage I had just made aboard the *Queen Elizabeth 2* had taken six days—six days from New York to Southampton, a crossing time that when I was a boy would have shamed the Cunard Line! The *Queens* had made their crossings in little more than four days, the *Lusitania* and *Mauretania* in five. A six-day crossing hadn't been known to a Cunard flagship for more than century—but now it was the standard, and no one seemed to mind. Even more startling, no one seemed to notice: it never occurred to anyone that when Samuel Cunard had formed the steamship line that would bear his name, he did so in order to satisfy a need for speed; the irregular, unpredictable departures and arrivals of sailing ships were no longer adequate to meet the needs and demands of the new Industrial Age of the 19th Century. It was Cunard's dream to change all that with his little flotilla of floating steam kettles, as they made what for his day were swift and regular passages across the Atlantic. It was a dream that became a reality. No sooner had he had proven it could be done, then the clamor began to be heard for faster crossing times: the next step, taken by Cunard and his competitors, was to begin to build ever swifter ships. As they did so, the dream turned to glory, as the span of each passage began to decline, from twelve days to eleven, eventually to nine, then to seven..five...four—until at last, with the appearance of Cunard's ultimate rival, the S. S. *United States*, the crossing of the Atlantic was reduced to barely more than three days.

And yet the clamor grew for still more speed, until it was answered by a method and medium that steamships could never hope to equal. When the advent of air travel had reduced the time to cross the Atlantic Ocean from days to hours, all of the efforts of a century of businessmen and financiers, architects and shipbuilders, engineers and stokers, skippers and quartermasters—the whole of the dream and the glory—were reduced to seeming insignificance. No longer were crossing times reduced by increments—the airplane had shortened them by orders of magnitude. If any proof were required that an era had well and truly passed, here it was: for the ships, speed didn't matter much anymore.

They had become anachronisms, and so did the companies that built and sailed them. One by one they vanished or were transformed into something far different than they had been: the United States Line, the C. G. T., the Italian Line, Hamburg-Amerika, Holland-America, Canadian Pacific, of them all only Cunard remained. And even so it was only a shell of its former self, once the mightiest steamship line in the world, it now boasted a fleet of a mere two ships. The company had become a mere division of a huge shipping combine, which ironically, possesses a fleet whose numbers rival those of Cunard's in the years when the line was at the height of its powers. But necessity became luxury; seapower gave way to airpower; the Atlantic, once an obstacle, is now only an inconvenience.

And so my reminiscences in Southampton came to an end that morning as the sun at last broke though the clouds, and what had been a cold, damp wind became a warm summer breeze. My reveries were over but they did not end with a pang of loss or a sigh of nostalgia, rather they closed with a faint echo of trumpets. If the dream was gone, the glory still remained: the Age of Cunard had been a story of ambition and vision; of shrewd businessmen seizing swiftly passing opportunities; of technological breakthroughs and triumphs; of glittering passenger lists filled with the most illustrious names of the day; of the largest, swiftest, most beautiful and glamorous ships in the world. And it still is: though Cunard's days of greatness have passed, its legacy flourishes. It had been magnificent, and continues to be so.

The Age of Cunard is far from over.

APPENDIX

The Cunard Fleet 1840-2002

(Dates indicate a ship's entire service career, not just years of service for Cunard; dimensions for length are between perpendiculars (pp); tonnage is Gross Registered Tonnage (GRT); ships that were solely cargo carriers are not listed.)

Britannia
1840—1880
Builder: Robert Duncan, Greenock (engines Robert Napier, Glasgow)
Gross Tonnage: 1,135
Dimensions: length 207 ft; beam 34 ft; (63.09 x 10.36 m)
Wood hull—Paddlewheels
Service speed: 9 knots
Passenger accommodation: 115 First Class

Acadia
1840—1858
Builder: John Wood, Port Glasgow (engines, Robert Napier, Glasgow)
Gross Tonnage: 1,154
Dimensions: length 207 ft; beam 34 ft; (63.09 x 10.36 m)
Wood hull—Paddlewheels
Service speed: 9 knots
Passenger accommodation: 115 First Class

Caledonia
1840—1851
Builder: R. Wood, Port Glasgow (engines Robert Napier, Glasgow)
Gross Tonnage: 1,138
Dimensions: length 207 ft; beam 34 ft; (63.09 x 10.36 m)
Wood hull—Paddlewheels
Passenger accommodation - 115 First class

Columbia
1841—1843
Builder: Robert Steele & Son, Greenock (engines Robert Napier, Glasgow)
Gross Tonnage: 1,175
Dimensions: length 207 ft; beam 34 ft; (63.09 x 10.36 m)
Wood hull—Paddlewheels
Service speed: 9 knots
Passenger accommodation: 115 First Class

Hibernia
1843—1868
Builder: Robert Steele & Son, Greenock (engines Robert Napier, Glasgow)
Gross Tonnage: 1,422
Dimensions: length 219 ft; beam 35 ft (66.74 x 10.67 m)
Wood hull—Paddlewheels
Service speed: 9 knots
Passenger accommodation: 120 First Class

Cambria
1845—1875
Builder: Robert Steele & Son, Greenock (engines Robert Napier, Glasgow)
Gross Tonnage: 1,423
Dimensions: length 219 ft; beam 35 ft (66.74 x 10.67 m)
Wood hull—Paddlewheels
Service speed: 9 knots
Passenger accommodation: 120 First Class

America
1848—1875
Builder: Robert Steele & Co., Greenock (engines Robert Napier, Glasgow)
Gross Tonnage: 1,826
Dimensions: length 241 ft; beam 38 ft (76.50 x 11.58 m)
Wood hull—Paddlewheels
Service speed: 10 knots
Passenger accommodation: 140 First Class

Niagara
1848—1875
Builder: Robert Steele & Co., Glasgow (engines Robert Napier, Glasgow)

Gross Tonnage: 1,824
Dimensions: length 241 ft; beam 38 ft
(76.50 x 11.58 m)
Wood hull—Paddlewheels
Service speed: 10 knots
Passenger accommodation: 140 First Class

Europa
1848—1867
Builder: John Wood, Port Glasgow (engines Robert Napier, Glasgow)
Gross Tonnage: 1,834
Dimensions: length 241 ft; beam 38 ft
(76.50 x 11.58 m)
Wood hull—Paddlewheels
Service speed: 10 knots
Passenger accommodation: 140 First Class

Canada
1848—1883
Builder: Robert Steele & Co., Greenock (engines Robert Napier, Glasgow)
Gross Tonnage: 1,831
Dimensions: length 241 ft; beam 38 ft
(76.50 x 11.58 m)
Wood hull—Paddlewheels
Service speed: 10 knots
Passenger accommodation: 140 First Class

Africa
1850—1868
Builder: Robert Steele & Co., Glasgow (engines Robert Napier, Glasgow)
Gross Tonnage: 2,226
Dimensions: length 265.5 ft; beam 40 ft
(81.07 x 12.19 m)
Wood hull—Paddlewheel
Service speed: 12 knots
Passenger accommodation: 130 First Class, 30 Second Class

Asia
1850—1876
Builder: Robert Steele & Co., Glasgow (engines Robert Napier, Glasgow)
Gross Tonnage: 2,226
Dimensions: length 265.5 ft; beam 40 ft
(81.07 x 12.19 m)
Wood hull—Paddlewheels
Service speed: 12 knots
Passenger accommodation: 130 First Class, 30 Second Class

Andes
1852—1859
Builder: William Deny & Bros., Dumbarton
Gross Tonnage: 1,440
Dimensions: length 235.5 ft; beam 33 ft
(72.10 x 10.12 m)
Iron hull—Single screw
Service speed: 9 knots
Passenger accommodation: 62 First Class, 122 Second Class

Alps
1853—1859
Builder: William Deny & Bros., Dumbarton
Gross Tonnage: 1,440
Dimensions: length 235.5 ft; beam 33 ft
(72.10 x 10.12 m)
Iron hull—Single screw
Service speed: 9 knots
Passenger accommodation: 62 First Class, 122 Second Class

Arabia
1853—1864
Builder: Robert Steele & Co., Glasgow (engines Robert Napier, Glasgow)
Gross Tonnage: 2,402
Dimensions: length 283.3 ft; beam 41 ft
(86.62 x 12.50 m)
Wood hull—Paddlewheels
Service speed: 12 knots
Passenger accommodation: 180 First Class

Emeu
1856—1880
Builder: Robert Napier & Sons, Glasgow
Gross Tonnage: 1,538
Dimensions: length 217.2 ft; beam 35.6 ft
(81.74 x 11.15 m)
Iron hull—Single screw
Service speed: 10 knots
Passenger accommodation: 80 First Class, 130 Second Class

Etna
1856—1896
Builder: Caird & Co., Greenock
Gross Tonnage: 2,215
Dimensions: length 305 ft; beam 37 ft
(92.96 x 11.46 m)
Iron hull—Single screw
Service speed: 10 knots

Jura
1857—1864
Builder: J. & G. Thomson, Glasgow
Gross Tonnage: 2,241
Dimensions: length 314 ft; beam 35.1 ft
(95.70 x 10.97 m)
Iron hull—Single screw
Service speed: 11 knots

Lebanon
1855—1859
Builder: J. & G. Thomson, Glasgow
Gross Tonnage: 1,373
Dimensions: length 242 ft; beam 30 ft
(76.80 x 9.14 m)
Iron hull—Single screw
Service speed: 10 knots

Persia
1856—1872
Builder: Robert Napier & Sons, Glasgow
Gross Tonnage: 3,300
Dimensions: length 404 ft; beam 45 ft
(114.60 x 13.71 m)
Iron hull—Paddlewheels
Service speed: 13.5 knots
Passenger accommodation: 200 First Class,
50 Second Class

Taurus
1853—1859
Builder: William Deny & Bros., Dumbarton
Gross Tonnage: 1,126
Dimensions: length 210 ft; beam 29.4 ft
(64.12 x 8.96 m)
Iron hull—Single screw
Service speed: 9 knots
Passenger accommodation: 40 First Class,
100 Second Class

Aleppo
1865—1909
Builder: J. & G. Thomson, Glasgow
Gross Tonnage: 2,057
Dimensions: length 292.5 ft; beam 37.2 ft
(89.15 x 11.64 m)
Iron hull—Single screw
Service speed: 11 knots
Passenger accommodation: 46 First Class,
593 Third Class

Australasian
(renamed Calabria in 1870)
1860—1898
Builder: J. & G. Thomson, Glasgow
Gross Tonnage: 2,902
Dimensions: length 331 ft; beam 42 ft
(101.09 x 12.83 m)
Iron hull—Single screw
Service speed: 12 knots
Passenger accommodation: 200 First Class,
60 Second Class

Balbec
1860—1884
Builder: William Deny & Bros., Dumbarton
Gross Tonnage: 774
Dimensions: length 209.2 ft; beam 30.2 ft
(63.76 x 9.23 m)
Iron hull—Single screw
Service speed: 9 knots
Passenger accommodation: 29 First Class,
157 Third Class

British Queen
1862—1899
Builder: William Deny & Bros., Dumbarton
(engines Caird & Co., Greenock)
Gross Tonnage: 772
Dimensions: length 196 ft; beam 29 ft
(59.43 x 8.84 m)
Iron hull—Single screw
Service speed: 9 knots
Passenger accommodation: 71 First Class,
166 Third Class

China
1862—1906
Builder: Robert Napier & Sons, Glasgow
Gross Tonnage: 2,638
Dimensions: length 319.5 ft; beam 40.4 ft
(99.42 x 12.31 m)
Iron hull—Single screw
Service speed: 12 knots
Passenger accommodation: 268 First Class,
771 Second Class

Cuba
1864—1887
Builder: Tod & McGregor, Glasgow
Gross Tonnage: 2,668
Dimensions: length 331 ft; beam 42.4 ft
(103.07 x 12.92 m)
Iron hull—Single screw

Service speed: 12 knots
Passenger accommodation: 300 First Class, 800 Third Class

Damascus
1860—1912
Builder: William Deny & Bros., Dumbarton
Gross Tonnage: 1,213
Dimensions: length 253 ft; beam 32 ft
(77.11 x 9.75 m)
Iron hull—Single screw
Service speed: 10 knots
Passenger accommodation: 40 First Class,(unknown) Third Class

Hecla
1863—1954
Builder: Robert Napier & Sons, Glasgow
Gross Tonnage: 1,785
Dimensions: length 276 ft; beam 36.3 ft
(84.12 x 11.09 m)
Iron hull—Single screw
Service speed: 10 knots
Passenger accommodation: 70 First Class, 800 Third Class

Java
1865—1895
Builder: J.& G. Thomson, Glasgow
Gross Tonnage: 2,696
Dimensions: length 335 ft; beam 42.8 ft
(102.74 x 13.07 m)
Iron hull—Single screw
Service speed: 12 knots
Passenger accommodation: 300 First class, 800 Third class

Kedar
1860—1897
Builder - William Deny & Bros., Dumbarton
Gross Tonnage: 1,783
Dimensions: length 275.8 ft; beam 35.5 ft
(84.05 x 11.03 m)
Iron hull—Single screw
Service speed: 10 knots
Passenger accommodation: 40 First Class, 494 Third Class

Malta
1866—1889
Builder: J.& G.Thomson, Glasgow
Gross Tonnage: 2,132
Dimensions: length 293 ft; beam 39 ft
(92.38 x 11.98 m)
Iron hull—Single screw
Service speed: 11 knots
Passenger accommodation: 40 First class, 535 Third class

Marathon
1861—1898
Builder: Robert Napier & Sons, Glasgow
Gross Tonnage: 1,784
Dimensions: length 276 ft; beam 37 ft
(84.12 x 11.15 m)
Iron hull—Single screw
Service speed: 10 knots
Passenger accommodation: 70 First Class, 850 Third Class

Melita
1860—1868
Builder: Alexander Deny, Dumbarton
(engines MacNab & Clark, Greenock)
Gross Tonnage: 1,254
Dimensions: length 231 ft; beam 28.9 ft
(71.01 x 8.84 m)
Iron hull—Single screw
Service speed: 9 knots
Passenger accommodation: First Class, 70, Third Class, 800

Nemesis
1869—1902
Builder: Tod & McGregor, Glasgow
Gross Tonnage: 2,717
Dimensions: length 352.5 ft; beam 41.5 ft
(107.46 x 12.65 m)
Iron hull—Single screw
Service speed: 11 knots
Passenger accommodation: Unknown

Olympus
1863—1891
Builder - J. & G. Thomson, Glasgow
Gross Tonnage: 1,794
Dimensions: length 276 ft; beam 36.4 ft
(84.12 x 11.15 m)
Iron hull—Single screw
Service speed: 10 knots
Passenger accommodation - 70 First Class, 900 Third Class

Palestine
1860—1896
Builder: Robert Steele & Co., Greenock
(engines Robert Napier, Glasgow)
Gross Tonnage: 1,800
Dimensions: length 276 ft; beam 36 ft
(84.12 x 11.15 m)
Iron hull—Single screw
Service speed: 10 knots
Passenger accommodation: 70 First Class,
900 Third Class

Palmyra
1866—1897
Builder: Caird & Co., Greenock
Gross Tonnage: 2,044
Dimensions: length 290.8 ft; beam 37 ft
(88.63 x 11.58 m)
Iron hull—Single screw
Service speed: 11 knots
Passenger accommodation - 46 First class,
650 Third class

Russia
1867—1902
Builder: J.& G. Thomson, Glasgow
Gross Tonnage: 2,960
Dimensions: length 361.8 ft; beam 43 ft
(109.11 x 13.10 m)
Iron hull—Single screw
Service speed: 13 knots
Passenger accommodation: 235 First class

Samaria (1)
1868—1882
Builder: J.& G. Thomson, Glasgow
Gross Tonnage: 2,574
Dimensions: length 330.5 ft; beam 39.4 ft
(97.71 x 12.04 m)
Iron hull—Single screw
Service speed: 12 knots
Passenger accommodation: 130 First class,
800 Third class

Scotia (1)
1862—1904
Builder: Robert Napier & Sons, Glasgow
Gross Tonnage: 3,871
Dimensions: length 379.4 ft; beam 47.8 ft
(115.63 x 14.56 m)
Iron hull—Paddlewheels
Service speed: 14 knots
Passenger accommodation: 573 First class

Siberia
1867—1882
Builder: J.& G. Thomson, Glasgow
Gross Tonnage: 2,498
Dimensions: length 320 ft; beam 39.2ft
(97.53 x 11.95m)
Iron hull—Single screw
Service speed: 12 knots
Passenger accommodation: 100 First class,
800 Third class

Sidon
1863—1885
Builder: William Deny & Bros., Dumbarton
Gross Tonnage: 1,872
Dimensions: length 275.8 ft; beam 57.5 ft
(83.99 x 11.03 m)
Iron hull—Single screw
Service speed: 10 knots
Passenger accommodation: 69 First Class,
550 Third Class

Tarifa
1865—1899
Builder: J. & G. Thomson, Glasgow
Gross Tonnage: 2,058
Dimensions: length 292.5 ft; beam 37.2 ft
(89.15 x 11.64 m)
Iron hull—Single screw
Service speed: 11 knots
Passenger accommodation: 50 First Class,
650 Third Class

Tripoli
1865—1872
Builder: J. & G. Thomson, Glasgow
Gross Tonnage: 2,057
Dimensions: length 292.5 ft; beam 37.2 ft
(89.15 x 11.64 m)
Iron hull—Single screw
Service speed: 11 knots
Passenger accommodation: 50 First Class,
650 Third Class

Abyssinia
1870—1891
Builder: J. & G. Thomson, Glasgow
Gross Tonnage: 3,376
Dimensions: length 362.5 ft; beam 42.2 ft
(110.78 x 12.86 m)
Iron hull—Single screw
Service speed: 13 knots
Passenger accommodation: 120 First class,
1,068 Third class

Algeria
1870—1903
Builder: J. & G. Thomson, Glasgow
Gross Tonnage: 3,428
Dimensions: length 360.5 ft; beam 41.2 ft
(110.08 x 12.53 m)
Iron hull—Single screw
Service speed: 13 knots
Passenger accommodation: 200 First class,
1,054 Third class

Atlas
1873—1896
Builder: J.& G. Thomson, Glasgow
Gross Tonnage: 2,393
Dimensions: length 328.5 ft; beam 35.8 ft
(100.27 x 11.12 m)
Iron hull—Single screw
Service speed: 11 knots
Passenger accommodation: 69 First class,
833 Third class

Batavia
1870—1891
Builder: William Deny & Bros, Dumbarton
Gross Tonnage: 2,553
Dimensions: length 327.4 ft; beam 39.3ft
(99.79m x 11.98 m)
Iron hull—Single screw
Service speed: 12 knots
Passenger accommodation: 150 First class
and 800 Third class

Bothnia
1874—1899
Builder: J. & G. Thomson, Glasgow
Gross Tonnage: 4,535
Dimensions: length 422.3 ft; beam 42.2ft
(128.71 m x 12.86m)
Iron hull—Single screw
Service speed: 13 knots
Passenger accommodation: 300 First class,
1,100 Third class

Gallia
1879—1900
Builder: J. & G. Thomson, Glasgow
Gross Tonnage - 4,809
Dimensions: length 430.1 ft; beam 44.6 ft
(131.09m x 13.59m)
Iron hull—Single screw
Service speed: 13 knots
Passenger accommodation: 300 First class;
1,200 Third class

Parthia (1)
1870—1955
Builder: William Deny & Bros., Dumbarton
Gross Tonnage: 3,167
Dimensions: length 360.5 ft; beam 40.4 ft
(109.87 x 12.31 m)
Iron hull—Single screw
Service speed: 12 knots
Passenger accommodation: 150 First class,
1,031 Third class

Saragossa
1874—1909
Builder: J. & G. Thomson, Glasgow
Gross Tonnage: 2,263
Dimensions: length 316.3 ft; beam 35.3 ft
(96.40 x 10.76 m)
Iron hull—Single screw
Service speed: 11 knots
Passenger accommodation: 74 First class,
548 Third class

Scythia (1)
1875—1899
Builder: J. & G. Thomson, Glasgow
Gross Tonnage: 4,557 tons
Dimensions: length 420.8 ft; beam 42.2ft
(128.25m x 12,86m)
Iron hull—Single screw
Service speed: 13 knots
Passenger accommodation: 300 First class;
1,100 Third class

Servia
1881—1902
Builder: J. & G. Thomson, Glasgow
Gross Tonnage: 7,392
Dimensions: length 515 ft; beam 52.1 ft
(156.96 x 15.88 m)
Steel hull—Single screw
Service speed: 16 knots
Passenger accommodation: 480 First class,
750 Second class

Catalonia
1881—1901
Builder: J.& G. Thomson
Gross Tonnage: 4,481
Dimensions: length 429.5 ft; beam 43 ft
(130.93 x 13.10 m)
Iron hull—Single screw
Service speed: 13 knots
Passenger accommodation: 200 First class,
1,500 Third class

Cephalonia
1882—1904
Builder: Laird Bros., Birkenhead
Gross Tonnage: 5,517
Dimensions: length 433.5 ft; beam 46.5 ft
(131.24 x 14.17 m)
Iron hull—Single screw
Service speed: 14 knots
Passenger accommodation: 200 First class,
1,500 Second class

Pavonia
1882—1900
Builder: J. & G. Thomson, Glasgow
Gross Tonnage: 5,588
Dimensions: 131.21 x 14.14m
Iron hull—Single screw
Service speed: 14 knots
Passenger accommodation: 200 First class,
1,500 Third class

Aurania (1)
1883—1905
Builder: J. & G. Thomson, Glasgow
Gross Tonnage: 7,269
Dimensions: length 470 ft; beam 57.2 ft
(143.25 x 17.43 m)
Steel hull—Single screw
Service speed: 16 knots
Passenger accommodation: 480 First class,
700 Third class

Oregon
1884—1886
Builder: John Elder & Co., Glasgow
Gross Tonnage: 7,324
Dimensions: 152.69 x 16.52m
Iron hull—Single screw
Service speed: 18 knots
Passenger accommodation: 340 First class,
92 Intermediate, 110 Third class and 1,000
Steerage

Umbria
1884—1910
Builder: John Elder & Co., Glasgow
Gross Tonnage: 7,718
Dimensions: 152.87 x 17.43m
Steel hull—Single screw
Service speed: 19 knots
Passenger accommodation: 550 First class,
800 Third class

Etruria
1885—1909
Builder: John Elder & Co., Glasgow
Gross Tonnage: 7,718
Dimensions: length 498.1 ft; beam 57.2 ft
(152.87 x 17.43 m)
Steel hull—Single screw
Service speed: 19 knots
Passenger accommodation: 550 First class,
160 Intermediate, 800 Third class

Campania
1893—1918
Builder: Fairfield Co. Ltd., Glasgow
Gross Tonnage: 12,950
Dimensions: length 601 ft; beam 63.2 ft
(183.17 x 19.87 m)
Steel hull—Twin screw
Service speed: 21 knots
Passenger accommodation: 600 First class,
400 Second class, 1,000 Third class

Lucania
1893—1909
Builder: Fairfield Co. Ltd., Glasgow
Gross Tonnage: 12,952
Dimensions: length 601 ft; beam 63.2 ft
(183.17 x 19.87 m)
Steel hull—Twin screw
Service speed - 21 knots
Passenger accommodation - 600 First class,
400 Second class, 1,000 Third class

Carinthia (1)
1895—1900
Builder: London & Glasgow Co., Glasgow
Gross Tonnage: 5,598
Dimensions: length 445.0 ft; beam 49.0 ft
(135.63 x 14.93m)
Steel hull—Twin screw
Engines: Six-cylinder triple-expansion
Service speed: 13 knots
Passenger accommodation: none

Sylvania (1)
1895—1910
Builder: London & Glasgow Co., Glasgow
Gross Tonnage: 5,598
Dimensions: length 445.0 ft; beam 49.0 ft
(135.63 x 14.93m)
Steel hull—Twin screw
Service speed: 13 knots
Passenger accommodation: none

Ultonia
1898—1917
Builder: Swan & Hunter, Wallsend-on-Tyne (engines by Sir C. Furness, Westgarth & Co. Ltd., Middlesbrough)
Gross Tonnage: 8,845
Dimensions: length 500.0 ft; beam 57.4 ft (152.39 x 17.49m)
Steel hull—Twin screw
Service speed: 13 knots
Passenger accommodation: none as designed, accommodation for 675 Third class passengers added during construction

Ivernia (1)
1900—1917
Builder: Swan & Hunter, Wallsend-on-Tyne (engines by Wallsend Slipway Co. Ltd.)
Gross Tonnage: 14,058
Dimensions: length 582 ft; beam 64.9ft (177.38 x 19.77m)
Steel hull—Twin screw
Service speed: 15 knots
Passenger accommodation: 164 First class, 200 Second class, 1,600 Third class

Saxonia (1)
1900—1925
Builder: - John Brown & Co. Ltd., Glasgow
Gross Tonnage: 14,281
Dimensions: length 580 ft; beam 64.2 ft (176.77 x 19.77m)
Steel hull—Twin screw
Service speed: 15 knots
Passenger accommodation: 164 First class, 200 Second class, 1,600 Third class

Carpathia
1903—1918
Builder: Swan & Hunter, Wallsend-on-Tyne (engines by Wallsend Slipway Co. Ltd.)
Gross Tonnage: 13,555
Dimensions: length 540 ft; beam 64.5 ft (164.58 x 19.65m)
Steel hull—Twin screw
Service speed: 14 knots
Passenger accommodation: (as built) 204 Second class, 1,500 Third class; (after 1905) 100 First class, 200 Second class, 2,250 Third class

Pannonia
1904—1922
Builder: John Brown & Co. Ltd., Glasgow
Gross Tonnage: 9,851 tons
Dimensions: length 486.5 ft; beam 59.3 ft (148.27 x 18.13m)
Steel hull—Twin screw
Service speed - 13 knots
Passenger accommodation - 90 First class, 70 Second class, 2,066 Third class

Slavonia
1904—1909
Builder: Sir J. Laing & Sons, Sunderland (engines by Wallsend Slipway Co. Ltd.)
Gross Tonnage: 10,606 tons
Dimensions: length 510 ft; beam 59.5 ft (155.44 x 18.13m)
Steel hull—Twin screw
Service speed: 13 knots
Passenger accommodation: 71 First class, 74 Second class, 1,954 Third class

Carmania (1)
1905—1932
Builder: John Brown & Co. Ltd., Glasgow
Gross Tonnage - 19,524 tons
Dimensions: length 650.4 ft; beam 72.7 ft (198.23 x 22m)
Steel hull—Triple screw
Service speed: 18 knots
Passenger accommodation: 300 First class, 350 Second class, 2,000 Third class

Caronia (1)
1905—1933
Builder: John Brown & Co. Ltd., Glasgow
Gross Tonnage: 19,687 tons
Dimensions: length 486.5 ft; beam 59.3 ft (198.11 x 22m)
Steel hull—Twin screw
Service speed: 18 knots
Passenger accommodation: (as built) 300 First class, 350 Second class, 2,000 Third class; (after 1926) 452 Cabin class, 365 Tourist class, 650 Third class

California
1907—1917
Builder: D.& W. Henderson Ltd, Glasgow
Gross Tonnage: 8,662 tons
Dimensions: length 470 ft; beam 58.3 ft (143.25 x 17.77m)
Steel hull—Twin screw
Service speed: 16 knots
Passenger accommodation: 232 First class, 248 Second class, 734 Third class

Folia
1907 - 1917
Builder: James Laing & Co, Sunderland
Gross Tonnage: 6,560 tons
Dimensions: length 430 ft; beam 53.7 ft
(131.06 x 16.06m)
Steel hull—Twin screw
Service speed: 14 knots
Passenger accommodation: 120 First class, 50 Second class, 1,500 Third class

Lusitania
1907—1915
Builder: John Brown & Co Ltd., Glasgow
Gross Tonnage: 31,550 tons
Dimensions: length 762.2 ft; beam 87.8 ft
(232.31 x 26.75m)
Steel hull Quadruple screw
Service speed: 25 knots
Passenger accommodation: 563 First class, 464 Second class, 1,138 Third class

Mauretania (1)
1907—1935
Builder: Swan, Hunter & Wigham Richardson, Wallsend-On-Tyne
Gross Tonnage: 31,938 tons
Dimensions: length 762.2 ft; beam 88.0 ft
(232.31 x 26.82m)
Steel hull—Quadruple screw
Service speed: 25 knots
Passenger accommodation: 563 First class, 464 Second class, 1,138 Third class

Albania (1)
1911—1930
Builder: C.S. Swan & Hunter, Wallsend-on-Tyne
Gross Tonnage: 7,640 tons
Dimensions: length 461.5 ft; beam 52.1 ft
(140.65m x 15.88m)
Steel hull—Twin screw
Service speed: 11 knots
Passenger accommodation: 50 Second Class; 800 Third Class

Alaunia (1)
1913—1916
Builder: Scotts Shipbuilding & Engineering Co., Ltd, Greenock
Gross Tonnage: 13,405 tons
Dimensions: length 520.3 ft; beam 64 ft
(158.58 x 19.50m)
Steel hull— Twin screw
Engines: Quadruple-expansion, eight
Service speed: 15 knots
Passenger accommodation: 520 Second class, 1,540 Third class

Andania (1)
1913—1918
Builder: Scott's Shipbuilding & Engineering Co., Ltd, Greenock
Gross Tonnage: 13,405 tons
Dimensions: length 520.3 ft; beam 64 ft
(158.58 x 19.50m)
Steel hull—Twin screw
Service speed: 15 knots
Passenger accommodation: 520 Second class, 1,540 Third class

Aquitania
1914—1950
Builder: John Brown & Co., Ltd, Glasgow
Gross Tonnage: 45,647 tons
Dimensions: length 868.7 ft; beam 97 ft
(264.76 x 29.56m)
Steel hull—Quadruple screw
Service speed: 23 knots
Passenger accommodation: 597 First class, 614 Second class, 2,052 Third class

Ascania (1)
1911—1918
Builder: Swann, Hunter & Wigham Richardson, Wallsend-on-Tyne
Gross Tonnage: 9,111
Dimensions: length 466.6 ft; beam 56.1 ft
(142.31m x 17.10m)
Steel hull—Twin screw
Service speed: 13 knots
Passenger accommodation: 200 Second Class; 1,500 Third Class

Aurania (2)
1916—1918
Builder: Swan, Hunter & Wigham Richardson, Wallsend-on-Tyne
Gross Tonnage: 13,936 tons
Dimensions: length 520.3 ft; beam 64 ft
(158.58 x 19.50m)
Steel hull—Twin screw
Service speed - 15 knots
Passenger accommodation: Unknown

Ausonia (1)
1911—1918
Builder: C. S. Swan & Hunter,
Wallsend-on-Tyne
Gross Tonnage: 7,907 tons
Dimensions: length 450.6 ft; beam 54.2 ft
(137.33m x 16.52m)
Steel hull—Twin screw
Service speed: 12 knots
Passenger accommodation: 90 Second Class;
1,000 Third Class
Cargo: 2,440 tons

Cameronia (1)
1915—1917
Builder: D & W Henderson Ltd, Glasgow
Gross Tonnage: 10,963 tons
Dimensions: length 515 ft; beam 62.3 ft
(156.96 x 18.99m)
Steel hull—Twin screw
Service speed: 16 knots
Passenger accommodation: 362 First class,
304 Second class, 802 Third class

Feltria
1916—1917
Builder: William Deny & Bros., Dumbarton
Gross Tonnage: 5,254 tons
Dimensions: length 420 ft; beam 48.2 ft
(128.01 x 14.69m)
Steel hull—Single screw
Service speed: 13 knots
Passenger accommodation: 400 Third class

Flavia
1917—1918
Builder: Palmers Co. Ltd, Jarrow-on-Tyne
Gross Tonnage: 9,285 tons
Dimensions: length 470 ft; beam 56.8 ft
(143.25 x 17.31 m)
Steel hull—Twin screw
Service speed: 13 knots
Passenger accommodation: 125 First class,
900 Third class

Franconia I
1911—1916
Builder: Swan, Hunter & Wigham
Richardson, Wallsend-on-Tyne
Tonnage: 18,150 tons gross; 11,247 tons net
Displacement: 25,000 tons
Dimensions: length 600.3 ft; beam 71.3 ft
(182.96 m x 21.73 m)
Steel hull—Twin screwed
Service speed: 17 knots
Passenger accommodation: 300 First Class,
350 Second Class and 2,200 Third Class

Olympic
(originally owned by White Star Line)
1911—1937
Builder: Harland & Wolff, Belfast
Gross Tonnage - 45,342
Dimensions: length 852.5 ft; beam 92.5 ft
(259.83 x 28.19m)
Steel hull—Triple screw
Service speed: 21 knots
Passenger accommodation: 735 First class,
674 Second class, 1,026 Third class

Laconia (1)
1912—1917
Builder: Swann, Hunter & Wigham
Richardson, Wallsend-on-Tyne
Gross Tonnage: 18,099
Dimensions: length 600.3 ft; beam 71.3 ft
(182.96m x 21.73m)
Steel hull—Twin screw
Service speed: 17 knots
Passenger accommodation: 300 First class;
350 Second Class; 2,200 Third Class

Orduna
1914—1921
Builder: Harland & Wolff, Belfast
Gross Tonnage: 15,499
Dimensions: length 550.3 ft; beam 67.3 ft
(167.72 x 20.51m)
Steel hull— Triple screw
Service speed: 15 knots
Passenger accommodation: Unknown

Berengaria (ex-Imperator)
1920—1946
Builder: A.G. Vulcan, Hamburg
Gross Tonnage: 52,226
Dimensions: 269.09 x 29.96m
Steel hull—Quadruple screw
Service speed: 22 knots
Passenger accommodation: 970 First class,
630 Second class, 515 Tourist class and 606
Third class

Majestic
(ex-*Bismarck*; war prize originally awarded to
White Star Line)

1921—1943
Builder: Blohm & Voss, Hamburg
Gross Tonnage: 56,551 tons
Dimensions: length 915.5 ft; beam 100.1 ft
(279.03 x 30.51m)
Steel hull—Quadruple screw
Service speed: 23 knots
Passenger accommodation: 700 First class,
545 Second class, 850 Third class

Albania (2)
1921—1941
Builder: Scott's Shipbuilding & Engineering
Co., Ltd, Greenock
Gross Tonnage: 12,768 tons
Dimensions: length 523.1 ft; beam 64 ft
(159.43 x 19.50m)
Steel hull—Single screw
Service speed: 13 knots
Passenger accommodation: 500 cabin class

Scythia (2)
1921—1958
Builder: Vickers Ltd., Barrow
Gross Tonnage: 19,730 tons
Dimensions: length 600.7 ft; beam 73.8 ft
(183.08 x 22.49m)
Steel hull—Twin screw
Service speed: 16 knots
Passenger accommodation: 350 First class,
350 Second class, 1,500 Third class

Ausonia (2)
1922—1965
Builder: Armstrong, Whitworth & Co. Ltd,
Walker-on-Tyne
Gross Tonnage: 13,912
Dimensions: length 520 ft; beam 65.3 ft
(158.48 x 19.90m)
Steel hull—Twin screw
Service speed: 15 knots
Passenger accommodation: 500 Cabin class,
1,200 Third class

Antonia
1922—1948
Builder: Vickers Ltd, Barrow
Gross Tonnage: 13,867
Dimensions: length 519.9 ft; beam 65.3 ft
(158.45 x 19.90m)
Steel hull—Twin screw
Service speed: 15 knots
Passenger accommodation: 500 Cabin class,
1,200 Third class

Andania (2)
1922—1940
Builder: Hawthorn, Leslie & Co. Ltd,
Hebburn-on Tyne
Gross Tonnage: 13,950 tons
Dimensions: length 520.2 ft; beam 65.3 ft
(158.55 x 19.90m)
Steel hull—Twin screw
Service speed: 16 knots
Passenger accommodation: 500 Cabin class,
1,200 Third class

Samaria (2)
1922—1956
Builder: Cammell Laird & C., Ltd,
Birkenhead
Gross Tonnage: 19,602
Dimensions: length 601.5 ft; beam 73.7 ft
(183.33 x 22.46m)
Steel hull—Twin screw
Service speed: 16 knots
Passenger accommodation: 350 First class,
350 Second class, 1,500 Third class

Laconia (2)
1922—1942
Builder: Swan, Hunter & Wigham
Richardson Ltd, Wallsend-on-Tyne
Gross Tonnage: 19,860 tons
Dimensions: length 601.3 ft; beam 73.7 ft
(183.27 x 22.46m)
Steel hull—Twin screw
Service speed: 16 knots
Passenger accommodation: 350 First class,
350 Second class, 1,500 Third class

Lancastria
(Originally entered service as the *Tyrrhenia*)
1922—1940
Builder: W. Beardmore & Co., Ltd., Glasgow
Gross Tonnage: 16,243
Dimensions: (168.48 x 21.45m)
Steel hull—Twin screw
Service speed: 15 knots
Passenger accommodation: 280 First Class,
364 Second Class, 1,200 Third Class

Aurania (3)
1924—1961
Builder: Swan, Hunter & Wigham
Richardson Ltd, Wallsend-on-Tyne
Gross Tonnage: 13,984
Dimensions: length 519.7 ft; beam 65.3 ft
(158.39 x 19.90m)

Steel hull—Twin screw
Service speed: 15 knots
Passenger accommodation: 500 Cabin class,
406 Tourist class, 500 Third class
1,200 Third class

Ascania (2)
1925—1956
Builder: Armstrong, Whitworth & Co., Ltd,
Walker-on-Tyne
Gross Tonnage: 14,013 tons
Dimensions: length 520 ft; beam 65.3 ft
(158.48 x 19.90m)
Steel hull—Twin screw
Service speed: 15 knots
Passenger accommodation: 500 Cabin class,
1,200 Third class

Carinthia (2)
1925—1940
Builder: Vickers Ltd, Barrow
Gross Tonnage: 20,277
Dimensions: length 600.7 ft; beam 73.8 ft
(183.08 x 22.49m)
Steel hull—Twin screw
Service speed: 16 knots
Passenger accommodation: 240 First class,
460 Second class, 950 Third class

Laurentic
(originally owned by White Star Line)
1927—1940
Builder: Harland & Wolff, Belfast
Gross Tonnage: 18,724
Dimensions: length 578.2 ft; beam 75.4 ft
(176.22 x 22.98m)
Steel hull—Triple screw
Service speed: 16 knots
Passenger accommodation: 594 Cabin class,
406 Tourist class, 500 Third class

Georgic
(originally owned by White Star Line)
1932—1956
Builder: Harland & Wolff, Belfast
Gross Tonnage: 27,759 tons
Dimensions: length 683.7 ft; beam 82.5 ft
(208.38 x 25.14m)
Steel hull—Twin screw
Service speed: 18 knots
Passenger accommodation: 479 Cabin class,
557 Tourist class and 506 Third class

Britannic
(originally owned by White Star Line)
1934—1960
Builder: Harland & Wolff, Belfast
Gross Tonnage: 26,943
Dimensions: length 683.7 ft; beam 82.5 ft
(208.38 x 25.14m)
Steel hull—Twin screw
Service speed: 18 knots
Passenger accommodation: 504 Cabin Class,
551 Tourist Class, 506 Third Class

Queen Mary
1936—1967
Builder: John Brown & Co., Ltd, Glasgow
Gross Tonnage: 80,774 tons
Dimensions: length 975.2 ft; beam 118.6 ft
(297.23 x 36.14m)
Steel hull—Quadruple screw
Service speed: 29 knots
Passenger accommodation: 776 Cabin class,
784 Tourist class, 579 Third class

Mauretania II
1939—1965
Builder: Cammell, Laird & Co., Ltd,
Birkenhead
Gross Tonnage: 35,738 tons
Dimensions: length 739.4; beam 89.4 ft
(225.36 x 27.24m)
Steel hull—Twin screw
Service speed: 23 knots
Passenger accommodation: 486 Cabin class,
390 Tourist class, 502 Third class

Queen Elizabeth (1)
1940—1972
Builder: John Brown & Co., Ltd, Glasgow
Gross Tonnage: 83,673
Dimensions: length 987.4 ft; beam 118.6 ft
(300.94 x 36.14m)
Steel hull—Quadruple screw
Service speed: 29 knots
Passenger accommodation: 823 First class,
662 Cabin class, 798 Tourist class

Parthia (2)
1948—1969
Builder: John Brown & Co., Ltd, Glasgow
Gross Tonnage: 13,345
Dimensions: length 531 ft; beam 70 ft
(161.5 x 21.25m)
Steel hull—Twin screw

Service speed: 18 knots
Passenger accommodation: 250 First class

Media
1947—1969
Builder: John Brown & Co., Ltd, Glasgow
Gross Tonnage: 13,345
Dimensions: length 531 ft; beam 70 ft
(161.5 x 21.25m)
Steel hull—Twin screw
Service speed: 18 knots
Passenger accommodation: 250 First class

Caronia (2)
1949—1974
Builder: John Brown & Co., Ltd, Glasgow
Gross Tonnage: 34,183
Dimensions: length 678.5 ft; beam 91.4 ft
(209.53 x 27.85m)
Steel hull—Twin screw
Service speed: 22 knots
Passenger accommodation: 581 First class, 351 Cabin class

Saxonia (2)
(renamed *Carinthia* (3) in 1963)
1954—1973
Builder: John Brown & Co., Ltd, Glasgow
Gross Tonnage: 21,637 tons
Dimensions: length 570 ft; beam 80.3 ft
(173.72 x 24.47m)
Steel hull—Twin screw
Service speed: 21 knots
Passenger accommodation: 110 First class, 833 Tourist class

Ivernia (2)
(renamed *Franconia* (2) in 1963)
1955—1973
Builder: John Brown & Co., Glasgow
Gross Tonnage: 21,947
Dimensions: length 570 ft; beam 80.3 ft
(173.72 x 24.47m)
Steel hull—Twin screw
Service speed: 21 knots
Passenger accommodation: 154 First class, 714 Tourist class

Carinthia (3)
1956—1988
Builder: John Brown & Co., Glasgow
Gross Tonnage: 21,947
Dimensions: length 570 ft; beam 80.3 ft
(173.72 x 24.47m)
Steel hull—Twin screw
Service speed: 21 knots
Passenger accommodation: 154 First class, 714 Tourist class

Sylvania (2)
1957—1968
Builder: John Brown & Co., Glasgow
Gross Tonnage: 21,989 tons
Dimensions: length 570 ft; beam 80.3 ft
(173.72 x 24.47m)
Steel hull—Twin screw
Service speed: 21 knots
Passenger accommodation: 154 First class, 714 Tourist class

Queen Elizabeth 2
1969—present
Builder: John Brown & Co., Glasgow
Gross Tonnage: 65,863 tons
Dimensions: length 963 ft; beam 105 ft
(296.3 x 32.30m)
Steel hull—Twin Screw
Service speed: 28.5 knots
Passenger accommodation: 564 First class, 1,441 Tourist Class

Cunard Adventurer
1971—1976
Builder: Rotterdam Dry Dock Company, Rotterdam
Gross Tonnage: 14,155 tons
Dimensions: length 484 ft; beam 71 ft
(148.92 x 21.84 m)
Steel hull—Twin screw
Service speed: 20.5 knots
Passenger accommodation: 806 First Class

Cunard Ambassador
1972—1974
Builder: Rotterdam Dry Dock Company, Rotterdam
Gross Tonnage: 14,155 tons
Dimensions: length 484 ft; beam 71 ft
(148.92 x 21.84 m)
Steel hull—Twin screw
Service speed: 20.5 knots
Passenger accommodation: 806 First Class

Cunard Countess
1976—1997
Builder: Burmeister & Wain Shipyards,

Copenhagen (completed by Industrie Navali
Mechaniche Affine Shipyard, La Spezia)
Gross tonnage: 17,495 tons
Dimensions: length 536 ft; beam 74 ft
(164.92 x 22.77 m)
Steel hull—Twin screw
Service speed: 20.5 knots
Passenger accommodation: 750 cruise
passengers

Cunard Princess
1977—1998
Builder: Burmeister & Wain Shipyards,
Copenhagen (completed by Industrie Navali
Mechaniche Affine Shipyard, La Spezia)
Gross tonnage: 17,495 tons
Dimensions: length 536 ft; beam 74 ft
(164.92 x 22.77 m)
Steel hull—Twin screw
Service speed: 20.5 knots
Passenger accommodation: 750 cruise
passengers

Sagafjord
1983-1997
Builder: Société des Forges de la
Mediterranee, France
Gross tonnage: 24,000 tons
Dimensions: length 615 ft; beam 82 ft
(188.10 x 25.23 m)
Steel hull—Twin screw
Service speed: 20 knots
Passenger accommodation: 789 cruise
passengers

Vistafjord
(renamed *Caronia* (3) in 1999)
1983—present
Builder: Swan Hunter Shipyards,
Newcastle-on-Tyne
Gross Tonnage: 24,492 tons
Dimensions: length 627 ft; width 82 ft
(192.92 x 25.23 m)
Steel hull—Twin screw
Service speed: 20 knots
Passenger accommodation: 688 cruise
passengers

Sea Goddess I
1984—1999
Builder: Wartsila Shipyards, Helsinki
Gross tonnage: 4,200 tons
Dimensions: length 344 ft; beam 58 ft
(105.84 x 17.84 m)
Steel hull—twin screw
Service speed: 18 knots
Passenger accommodation: 116 First class
passengers

Sea Goddess II
1985—1999
Builder: Wartsila Shipyards, Helsinki
Gross tonnage: 4,200 tons
Dimensions: length 344 ft; beam 58 ft
(105.84 x 17.84 m)
Steel hull—twin screw
Service speed: 18 knots
Passenger accommodation: 116 First class
passengers

AUTHOR'S NOTE

I suppose that I should have seen this book coming many, many years ago. My interest in the great liners of the North Atlantic first sprang up when I was around the age of ten, upon my discovering, more or less simultaneously, the stories of the *Titanic*, the *Lusitania*, and the *Queens*. More than thirty-five years have passed since then, and in those years my interest in the transatlantic liners grew—and its horizons expanded—as I came to understand that there was much more to the story of the North Atlantic passenger trade than just big ships. It gradually dawned on me that it was an industry which was one of the central, driving forces in the history of not just one, but two continents, Europe and America, and without it neither would have become what they are today. And no matter where I turned in that story, one name kept recurring time after time, more than any other—Cunard.

I have always striven in my writing to place the events I am describing in a larger context; sometimes social, sometimes political, sometimes military—and sometimes combining the three in varying degrees. The purpose is to provide my readers with an awareness that those events are not happening in a moral or temporal vacuum, but are influenced by what has come before, and will affect what comes after. This sense of context is essential to my own understanding of history as well as its presentation. Out of this concept, the idea came one day as I was writing my book, *Warrior Queens*, about the *Mary* and *Elizabeth* in wartime, that while I had succeeded in putting individual ships into the larger context of their times, what I should do is put *passenger liners* in the context of their whole day and age. It didn't take me long to realize that the unifying theme of that effort was the steamship company that had been the first, and ultimately the last regular transatlantic passenger line, the name that kept recurring every time I turned to the North Atlantic was—Cunard.

And so the idea for *The Age of Cunard* was born; it grew, matured, and ultimately became a finished work. As an author I find it difficult to imagine a project for which there has been such widespread enthusiasm among the people and institutions involved during its inception and creation, as there has for this book. Consequently, I would like to acknowledge the individuals and institutions who quite literally made *The Age of Cunard* possible.

From the outset, Diana Hunter and Peter Griffes at ProStar Publications were excitement personified. From the moment that the book was proposed through the very last stages of writing and preparation they have been consistent in offering encouragement while avoiding pressure—never once did they give deadlines pride of place ahead of quality, and it is my sincere hope that *The Age of Cunard* validates their dedication.

As always, the cooperation of staffs at the Public Records Office, the National Maritime

Museum, and the Imperial War Museum was exemplary, as was that of the Southampton City Heritage and the Southampton Maritime Museum. Their counterparts in Glasgow (The Museum of Transport) and Belfast (The Ulster Folk and Transport Museum) were equally helpful, if not more so. There seems to be a new sensibility developing within the British people, where they no longer look on their past accomplishments as something for which they should apologize or explain away; instead, the feeling is one of pride in their achievements, coupled with a willingness to share the credit where and when it is due. A similar attitude can be found throughout the Commonwealth, whether it be in Canada's capitol of Ottawa, in the cradle of the Maritimes at Halifax, or as far away as Sydney, Australia. Perhaps that attitude, so common in so many distant localities, came from a sense these individuals had that they were aiding in the creation of a "good" story, not one of squalor, exposé, or deconstruction, but rather a tale of accomplishment, achievement, a recounting of how the Cunard Line had a hand in building and shaping the character and destinies of nations and peoples. And perhaps it was a sense of pride in having had a part, however small or vicarious, in that story.

I've gone on record before as stating, and want to re-emphasize here, that good librarians and archivists are the people who make an historian's work possible: with their familiarity with the collections at their disposal, as well as their knowledge of the literature on a given subject, they can provide irreplaceable guidance for an author overwhelmed by the sheer volume of information available on his or her chosen subject. As some wit recently observed, the problem with the information age is the information; actually, it's the sheer volume of information that can be a problem, and without the librarians and their assistants, it would be insoluble. Consequently, I want to extend my thanks to the librarians, archivists, and pages at the Broward County Library System, Fort Lauderdale, Florida; the Orange County Library System, Orlando, Florida; the University of Michigan Library System, Ann Arbor, Michigan; the libraries of Florida State University, Tallahassee, Florida; and as always, the Library of Congress, Washington, D.C.

I would also like to extend my particular thanks to the Mariners' Museum of Newport News, Virginia; the Maritime Museum of the Atlantic, in Halifax, Nova Scotia; and the South Street Seaport Museum in New York City. What makes these museums so special is their close interest in, and understanding of, the transatlantic passenger trade, which offered very distinctive insights into the research I was undertaking. In particular, the connection between Halifax and Cunard made the role played by the Maritime Museum of the Atlantic especially valuable.

However essential the contributions of the formal institutions of research and learning to telling the story of the Cunard Line, without a doubt *The Age of Cunard* could not have been completed without the cooperation and encouragement of the people of Carnival Corporation and the Cunard Line, Ltd. Mickey Arison, the chairman of Carnival, went out of his way in the middle of grueling merger negotiations with P&O/Princess to make time available to sit down with an author whom he barely knew, in order to answer questions about Carnival's acquisition of Cunard, the relationship between the parent corporation and its subsidiary, and the vision he has for Cunard's future. At Cunard, Julie Davis, Director of Public Relations, and Maritza Perez, Director of Enrichment Services, never hesitated to do whatever they could to provide me with information, resources, or contacts. Also worthy of mention and thanks for their willingness to share their memories of Cunard's past or their hopes for the company's future are: Capt. Ronald W. Warwick, Commodore of the Cunard Line, whose candor about past mismanagement of Cunard was as entertaining as his tales of rough seas and high winds—and just as illuminating; Maureen Ryan, Cruise Hostess of the *Queen Elizabeth* 2, for her recollections of the last decade of the first two *Queens*; Andy Dinsdale and Colin Parker, Cruise Directors aboard the *QE2*, who provided remarkable insight into the workings of the modern passenger liner; Warren Smith, Cruise Host, who couples his enthusiasm for his current position with a well-founded knowledge of Cunard's history; and David Hamilton, Hotel Manager of the *QE2*. Whether reminiscing about the past glories of the line, recounting its present accomplishments, or musing about the promises that the future holds for Cunard, they were all quite open and ready, indeed anxious, to share with me their distinctive views and appreciations of Cunard. One characteristic common to all of these individuals, one that earned my undying respect, was their refusal, no matter what their position in Carnival or Cunard, to attempt to influence or interfere with the content of this book.

Also deserving of special mention are John Brown Engineering and Harland and Wolff. Sadly, the glory days of John Brown and Company, as well as the rest of those immense shipyards that once lined the banks of Scotland's River Clyde, are a fading memory; sadder still, even the firm's successor, John Brown Engineering, is no more: the last remnant of the once-great Scottish shipbuilder closed its doors for the last time on December 31, 2000. But I had the privilege, while researching *The Age of Cunard*, of being a guest at the yard before its demise. There was still immense pride among the staff, who exemplified Scottish hospitality and helpfulness, in the fact that their yard had given form to such magnificent ships as the *Lusitania*, the *Aquitania*, and the first three *Queens*. Their only rivals in courtesy were to be found in Belfast, Northern Ireland, at Harland and Wolff. Once the largest shipyard the world had ever seen, Harland and Wolff has shrunk to a fraction of its former size as the consequence of the eclipse of the British shipbuilding industry in the 1960s and 1970s. Even as this is being written, the future survival of the shipyard is in doubt, as there are no more orders on the books. Though there was no direct association between Cunard and the Belfast shipbuilder, the folks at Harland and Wolff were able to provide a wealth of background information, not only concerning the construction of great ocean liners, but also about the sort of men who built them.

A word of acknowledgement and thanks also, to people who aren't directly associated with Cunard, but who made material contributions to this book. This was the last work in which my father, Harold Butler, was able to directly provide technical advice, as well as recalling what it was like to sail the North Atlantic aboard a tanker in 1943: he passed away at the age of 75 while the manuscript was in its last stages of preparation—he's going to be missed. I was also able to avail myself of the memories of Lieutenant Commander Alan Young, RN (ret.), many of which were contemporary with those of my father, as he shared thoughts of his times in the Royal Navy during the Second World War. Chief Petty Officer Ivan Harris, RN (ret.), was a goldmine of information on the Royal Navy, and his recollection of the *Queen Mary*'s departure on her final voyage was priceless. CPO Harris, who served on HMS *Hermes* during the Falklands War, was also able to offer significant insights about that conflict.

My gratitude also goes out to Captain Tony Crompton, retired Master Mariner, and Ilya McVey, an officer in the British Merchant Marine. Over the last six years these two gentlemen offered many insights and real-life examples of the realities of life at sea and the challenges of seamanship. I'm fortunate in that they were willing to demonstrate how often the truth of experience differs from the fantasy of the ideals cherished by regulators and academics.

Three friends deserve to be singled out for their assistance. Once again Trish Eachus did yeoman work in research and proofreading. As her own career as an author is beginning to gain momentum, there will be little time in her future for repeating such efforts, and I will miss her assistance, but I'm also pleased to know that she is about to embark on great successes of her own. The critiques provided by Scott Bragg were invaluable, as was the ongoing encouragement, and the occasional much-needed "reality check"—everyone should have a friend like Scott. Kitty Bartholomew provided valuable input on layout, design, format, and presentation, as well as a certain impetus to complete the work. Her creativity is boundless and her energy is infectious; and she is the sort of person whose successes don't inspire envy, they create motivation. Someone who has a person like Kitty in their life is fortunate indeed. They all have my gratitude for their contributions which, while perhaps not always tangible or measurable, were nonetheless essential.

As ever, though, how those contributions were utilized was entirely of my own choosing. The final responsibility for the content of this book—good or bad—lies entirely with me.

I wouldn't have it any other way.

Daniel Allen Butler
February 12, 2003
Atlantic Beach, Florida, USA

BIBLIOGRAPHY

BOOKS:

Anderson, Roy. *White Star*. Prescott, Lancashire: T. Stephenson & Sons, Ltd., 1964

Armstrong, Warren. *Atlantic Bridge*. New York: John Day and Company, 1962.

_____. *The Collins Story*. New York: John Day and Company, 1956.

Bisset, Commodore Sir James. *Commodore; War, Peace and Big Ships*. London: Angus & Robertson, Ltd., 1961.

_____. *Ladies and Tramps*. Glasgow: Brown and Ferguson. 1955.

Bonsor, N. P. *North Atlantic Seaway*. Prescott, Lancashire: T. Stephenson & Sons, Ltd., 1955.

Braynard, Frank O., and William H. Miller. *Picture History of the Cunard Line 1840-1990*. New York: Dover Publications, 1991.

Brinnin, John Malcolm. *The Sway of the Grand Saloon*. New York: Delacorte Press, 1971.

Butler, Daniel Allen. *The Lusitania: The Life, Loss, and Legacy of an Ocean Legend*. Mechanicsburg: Stackpole, 1998.

_____. *"Unsinkable"—the Full Story of RMS Titanic*. Mechanicsburg: Stackpole, 2000.

_____. *Warrior Queens—RMS Queen Mary and Queen Elizabeth in World War Two*. Mechanicsburg: Stackpole, 2001.

Chidsey, Donald Barr. *The Day They Sank the Lusitania*. New York: Award Books, 1967.

Churchill, Winston S. *The World Crisis*, 6 volumes. New York: Charles Scribner's Sons, 1926-1931.

de Kerbrech, Richard, and David L. Williams. *Cunard-White Star Liners of the 1930's*. London: Conway Maritime Press, Ltd., 1988.

Dodman, Frank F. *Ships of the Cunard Line*. London: Adfard Coles, Ltd., 1955

Fletcher, R. A. *Traveling Palaces*. London: Sir Isaac Pitman and Sons, Ltd., 1913.

Gibbs, C. R. Vernon. *Passenger Liners of the Western Ocean*. London: Staples Press Ltd., 1952

Gilbert, Martin *The First World War, a Complete History*. New York: Henry Holt and Company, 1994.

Grattidge, Captain Harry. *Captain of the Queens*. London: Oldbourne Press, 1956.

Gray, Edwyn A. *The U-Boat War, 1914-1918*. London: Leo Cooper, 1994.

Harding, Stephen. *Gray Ghost: The RMS Queen Mary at War*. Missoula: Pictorial Histories Publishing, 1982.

Hayes, Sir Bertram. *Hull Down*. New York: E. P. Dutton & Co., 1925.

Haythornewaite, Philip J. *The World War One Sourcebook*. London: Arms and Armour Press, 1992.

Hoehling, A. A. and Mary. *The Last Voyage of the Lusitania.*
New York: Henry Holt and Company, 1956.

Hulderman, Bernhard. *Albert Ballin*, translated by W. J. Eggars. London: Cassell and Co., 1925.

Hutchings, David F. *Queen Elizabeth: From Victory to Valhalla*. Southampton: Kingfisher Productions, 1990.

_____. *Queen Elizabeth 2: A Ship for All Seasons*. Southampton: Kingfisher Productions, 1988.

_____. *Queen Mary: 50 Years of Splendour.* Southampton: Kingfisher Productions, 1986.

Jordan, Humphrey. *Mauretania.* London: Hodder and Stoughton, 1937.

Hyde, Francis E. *Cunard and the North Atlantic, 1840-1973.* London: The Macmillan Press, Ltd., 1975.

Johnson, Howard. *The Cunard Story.* London: Whittet Books, Ltd., 1987.

Kahn, David. *The Code Breakers.* New York: MacMillan and Company, 1967.

Keegan, John. *August 1914: Opening Moves.* New York: Ballantine, 1971.

Lewin, Ronald. *Ultra Goes to War.* London: Hutchinson, 1978.

Lightoller, Charles H. *The Titanic and Other Ships.* London: Ivor Nicholson and Watson, 1935.

Lobley, Douglas, ed. *The Cunarders 1840-1969.* London: Peter Barker Publishing, Ltd., 1969.

Lord, Walter. *A Night to Remember.* New York: Holt, Rinehart and Winston, 1955.

Lord. Walter. *The Good Years.* New York: Harper, 1960.

Lord, Walter. *The Miracle of Dunkirk.* New York: William Morrow, 1976.

Maddocks, Melvin. *The Great Liners.* In the series *The Seafarers.* New York: Time-Life, 1978.

Manchester, William. *The Arms of Krupp.* Boston: Little, Brown and Company, 1968.

Manchester, William. *The Last Lion, Winston Spencer Churchill: Visions of Glory, 1874-1932.* Boston: Little, Brown and Company, 1983.

Maxtone-Graham, John. *Cunard: One Hundred Fifty Glorious Years.* Newton Abbot, Devon: David & Charles, Ltd., 1989.

_____. *The Only Way to Cross.* New York: Macmillan, 1972.

Miller, William H. *British Ocean Liners: A Twilight Era, 1960-1985.* Wellingborough, Northamptonshire: Patrick Stephens, Ltd., 1986.

Miller, William H. and David F. Hutchings. *Transatlantic Liners at War: the Story of the Queens.* New York: David & Charles, 1985.

Newell, Gordon, *Ocean Liners of the 20th Century.* Seattle: Superior Publishing Co., 1963.

Oldham, Wilton J. *The Ismay Line.* Liverpool: The Journal of Commerce, 1961.

Padfield, Peter. *An Agony of Collisions.* London: Hodder & Stoughton, 1966.

Potter, Neil, and Jack Frost. *The Elizabeth.* London: George G. Harrap & Company, Ltd., 1965.

_____. *The Mary.* London: George G. Harrap & Company, Ltd., 1961.

Roskill, Captain S. W. *The War at Sea.* In the series *History of the Second World War,* Vols. I and II. London: HMSO, 1954 and 1956.

Rostron, Capt. Sir Arthur. *Home From the Sea.* London: Hodder and Stoughton, 1937.

Stevens, Leonard A. *The Elizabeth: Passage of a Queen.* New York: Alfred A. Knopf, 1968.

Taylor, David B. *Steam Conquers the Atlantic.* New York and London: Appleton-Century Company, 1939.

Thomas, David A. and Patrick Holmes. *Queen Mary and the Cruiser: the Curacoa Disaster.* Annapolis: Naval Institute Press, 1997.

Tuchman, Barbara. *The Guns of August.* New York: MacMillan and Company, 1962.

Tuchman, Barbara. *The Proud Tower.* New York: MacMillan and Company, 1962.

Van der Vat, Dan, with Christine Van der

Vat. *The Atlantic Campaign: World War II's Great Struggle at Sea*. New York: Harper & Row, 1988.

Villiers, Captain Alan. *Men, Ships, and the Sea*. New York: The National Geographic Society, 1973.

Winter, C. W. R. *Queen Mary: Her Early Years Recalled*. London: Hodder & Stoughton, 1986.

PERIODICALS:
Business Week
Colliers
Contemporary Review
Coronet
The Engineer
Engineering
Forbes
Harper's Weekly
Marine Review
National Geographic
Newsweek
Outlook
Saturday Review
Scientific American
Scribners Monthly
The Shipbuilder
Time
The Titanic Commutator
U. S. News and World Report
United States Naval Institute Proceedings
Washington Post Semi-Monthly Magazine

NEWSPAPERS:
Boston American
Boston Globe
Brooklyn Eagle
Chicago Tribune
Detroit News
Detroit Free Press
Edinburgh Review
Glasgow Herald
Illustrated London News
London Daily Mail
London Morning Post
London Times
New York American
New York Herald
New York Nation
New York Sun
New York Times
New York Tribune
New York World
Richmond Times-Dispatch
Washington Evening Star
Washington Post

MUSEUMS, ARCHIVES, AND COLLECTIONS

Australia
Australian War Memorial, Canberra.

Canada
Canadian War Museum, Ottawa, Ontario.
Maritime Museum of the Atlantic, Halifax, Nova Scotia.
Public Archives of Canada, Ottawa, Ontario.
Public Archives of Nova Scotia, Halifax, Nova Scotia

Republic of Ireland
Public Records Office of the County of Cork, Cobh.

United Kingdom
Cunard Archives, Liverpool and London.
Harland and Wolff Shipyards, Belfast, Northern Ireland.
Imperial War Museum, London.
John Brown Engineering, Ltd., Clydebank.
National Maritime Museum, Greenwich.
Naval Historical Branch, Ministry of Defence, London.
Public Records Office, London.
Southampton Maritime Museum (Wool House), Southampton.
Transport Museum, Glasgow, Scotland.
Ulster Folk and Transport Museum, Belfast, Northern Ireland.
University of Glasgow.
University of Liverpool.

United States
Library of Congress, Washington, D.C.
Mariner's Museum, Newport News, Virginia.
Port Authority of New York, New York, N.Y.
South Street Seaport Museum, New York, New York.
U. S. Army Military History Center, Washington, D.C.
U. S. Army Transportation Corps Museum, Ft. Eustis, VA.
U.S. Naval Historical Center, Washington, D.C.

INDEX

Ships belonging to major shipping lines are found with their parent companies; warships are listed with their respective navies. Other ships are listed alphabetically.

Photographs are listed in *italics*.

Admiralty, British...38, 39, 40, 51, 60-61, 78, 123-124, 143-144, 145, 203, 208, 218, 225, 230, 286, 287, 303
Alstom...420, 427
American International Navigation Company...100
Anchor Line...96, 197-198, 227, 233
   Ships
      Cameronia...227, 233
      Tuscania...227-228, 233
Ancona...221
Antiochia...299
ANZACS (Australia-New Zealand Army Corps)...225-226
Archduke Franz Ferdinand...200, 203
Archimedes...52
Argentina...395, 401
Argentine Air Force...396, 399
Argentine Army...395, 400-401
Argentine Navy...395, 396, 399
   General Belgrano...396
Arison, Mickey...407, 409-410, 411, *411*, 417, 418, 420, 421, 423, 430
Arnold-Foster, H. O. ...144
Astor, Vincent...239
Athenia...285, 294
Athinai...227
Atlantic Conveyor...400
Atlee, Clement...353
Auxiliary Cruisers (Armed Merchant Cruisers)...141-142, 208-209, 295

Bacall, Lauren...353
Baker, Bernard...139
Balfour, Arthur J. ...142-143
Ballin, Albert...133, 134-135, 136-137, 140-141, 173, 193, 261
Bankhead, Tallulah...239

Barr, Capt. James Clayton...199, 209
Bates, Col. Dennis...354
Bates, Sir Percy...340
Battle of the Atlantic...291, 295, 307, 329
Bayard, Sen. James Asheton...73
Belgian Prince...222
Ben Cruachan...214
Berenice...60
Betting pools...347-348
Beyl, Ernie...413
Bismarck, Otto von...131
Bisset, Cmdr. Sir James...181, 307, 315, 324, 339
Black Ball Line (The New York Packet Company)...21
"Black Gang"...164-165, *165*, 236-237
Blair, Prime Minister Tony...420, 421
Blyskawica (Free Polish destroyer)...319
BOAC-Cunard Airways...364
Boer War...174-175
Bogart, Humphrey...353
Boissier, Patrick...420
Booth, Alfred...210
Booth, George...210
"Booze Cruises"...262
Boston, city of...42-43, 44-45, 48, 64-65, 86
Boutwood, Capt. John W., RN...318, 319, 321
Bow, Clara...239
Boyer, Charles...353
Breen, Ernie...393
Bremen, city of...90, 129
Brinnin, John Malcolm...143, 247
Britannia (Royal Yacht)...401
British and North American Royal Mail Steam Packet Company (Cunard Line)...41, 60, 68, 111, 430, 435
British and North American Steam Navigation Company...31, 55, 57
   British Queen (ex-*Princess Victoria*)...31, 33, 51, 57
   President...51, 57
British Army...85, 86, 208,
   British Expeditionary Force (B.E.F.)
      In First World War...204-205
      In Second World War...297
      In Falklands War...395-399
   Regiments

Parachute Regiment...399, 401
Scots Guards...397, 401
Welsh Guards...397
7th Gurkha Rifles...397
22 Regiment (Special Air Service)...391
British European Airways (BEA)...362
British Overseas Airways Corporation (BOAC)...361, 362, 363, 367
Britten, Cmdr. Sir Edgar...271
Broackes, Nigel...387-388
Brocklebank, Sir John...361-362, 363, 367, 369, 372, 378
Brocklebank Line...350, 362
Brunel, Ismabard Kingdom...27-28, *27*, 29, 47, 51, 80, 96-98
Brynestad, Atle...410
Burns, George...38, 40-41, 101, 111

C. S. Swan & Hunter (shipbuilder)...151, 161, 223
Cammel Laird...278-279, 296
Captains...23-25, 116-118, 240-242, 394-395
Capper, Capt. R. ...224
Carnival Corporation...407, 409, 410, 415-416, 417, 418, 419, 430
Casanare...299-301
Cavell, Edith...222
Cerrachio, Sgt. Jerry...322
Chamberlain, Neville...260, 262, 281, 283
Chambers, James...103
Chantiers de l'Atlantique...413, 419, 420, 421, 426-427, 427-428
Chaplin, Charlie...239
Charles Wood (shipbuilder)...41
Charles, Cmdr. Sir James...239, 241-242
Churchill, Sir Winston...175, 203-204, 225, 285, 287, 306, 309, 310, 316, 328-329, 353, 371-372
Clarence...60
Coaling...120-121
Collins, Edward Knight...69, 72, *73*, 74, 75, 78-79, 81, 82, 83
Collins Line...73-74, 77, 79, 80, 82-83, 87, 93
  Ships
    Adriatic....74, 82-83
    Arctic....74, 79, 93
    Atlantic....74, 75-76, 82-83
    Baltic....74, 82-83
    Pacific....74, 76, 81-82, 93
Compagnie Generale Transatlantique (French Line)...96, 249, 253, 255, 259, 349, 358, 436
  Ships
    France (1)...249
    France (2)...358, 369
    Ile de France...249, 272
    Libert (ex-Europa)...349
    Normandie...249, 253, 255, 259, 269, 270, 271, 272, 279, 282, 349
Conover, Pamela...413, 423, 424, 427-428, 430
Cottam, Harold...179-180
Crimean War...85-87, 78, 80
Crown Prince Akihito of Japan...353
Cruiser Rules...214-215, 221
Cruising...249-251, 261-262, 364-365, 404
Cunard, Abraham...35-36
Cunard, Ann...47, 53
Cunard, Edward...44-45
Cunard, Margaret...35
Cunard, Sir Samuel...25, 33, 35-39, *37*, 43, 44, 45, 47, 48, 51-52, 53, 58, 64, 65-66, 78, 80, 81, 92, 96, 100, 101, 148, 377, 430-431
Cunard Cargo Shipping Services Ltd. ...384
Cunard Line...48, 51, 54, 66-68, 69, 76, 78, 85-86, 92, 93, 96, 109, 110, 111-112, 114, 125, 127, 129, 132, 142-143, 144-145, 147-148, 151-152, 155-156, 197-198, 200, 204, 208, 210, 221, 224, 225, 226, 233-234, 242-243, 245, 246, 253, 256-257, 260-261, 269, 270-271, 277, 287, 295, 299, 305, 339, 340-341, 345-347, 354-356, 358, 361, 362-363, 365, 370, 371-372, 385, 387-388, 392-393, 401, 402, 403, 406-407, 409-410, 418, 428-429, 430-431, 434, 435-436
  Attempted takeover by J. P. Morgan...141-145,
  Business policies of...65, 66, 68, 78, 80, 101, 111, 135, 147-148, 182-183, 246-247, 276, 361, 389-390, 392, 393-394, 404
  Effects of airlines on...357-358, 359, 361, 366-367, 371-372
  Founding of...40-41
  Funnel colors of...42, 416
  Merger with White Star Line...260, 262-263
  Safety record of...58, 100
  Sold to Carnival Corporation...407
  Sold to Kvaerner Group...405-406
  Sold to Trafalgar House...385
  Ships
    Abyssinia...110-111
    Acadia...35, 41, 46, 56, 58, 434
    Africa...76, 91
    Alaunia (1)...198, 223, 233

Alaunia (2)...245
Albania...198
Aleppo...95
Algeria...110-111
Alps...91, 92
America...68, 91
Andania (1)...198, 223, 233
Andania (2)...244, 296
Andes...91, 92, 93
Antonia...244
Aquitania...61, 114, 120, 183, 184, *184* 186-192,*197*, 236, 238, 240, 241-242, 262, 267, 274, 278, 287, 289, 331 332, 343-344, *344*, 344-345, 349, 356, 417, 434, 435
    Construction of...187-188
    Interiors of...186-191, *188*, *189*
    In Second World War...289, 302-303, 306-307, 309, 310-311
Arabia...77-78
Ascania (1)...233
Ascania (2)...245, 344, 354
Asia...76, 91
Aurania (1)...112
Aurania (2)...198, 223-224, 233
Aurania (3)...245, 301-302
Ausonia (1)...198, 224, 227-228
Ausonia (2)...244
Balbec...95
Batavia...198
Berengaria (ex-*Imperator*)...236, 238-239, 246-247, 262, 277-278, 390, 393, 435
Bothnia...119
Britannia...35, 41, 46, 47-48, 51, 53, 54-56, 58, 65, 429, 431, 434
Caledonia...35, 41, 46, 56
Cambria...61, 66-67, 68, 79,
Campania...127, 148, 230-231, 434
Canada...68, 76, 91
Carinthia (1)...244, 249, 250-251, 261, 295-296, 433
Carinthia (2)...355-356
Carmania (1)...159-160, 166, 199, 208-210, 244, 351, 393, 434
Carmania (2) (ex-Saxonia (2))...359, 384, 414
Caronia (1)...159-160, *160*, 166, *166*, 244, 433, 434
Caronia (2)...351-353, *352*, 359, 365, 380-381, 389, 434
*Caronia (3)*413, 425, 430
Carpathia...152-153, 155, 179-182, *182*, 183, 196, 229-230
Catalonia...112, 196
Cephalonia...112, 196
China...95
Columbia...35, 41, 46, 47, 56, 61,
Cunard Adventurer...388-389, 414
Cunard Ambassador...389
Cunard Countess...389, 392, 414
Cunard Princess...389, 392, 414
Damascus...95
Emperor of India (Kaisar-I-Hind—post-WW I charter)...234
Etruria...114, 119-123, 123-124, 126, 148, 434
Europa...68, 76, 91
Franconia (1)...226-227, 233
Franconia (2)...244, 249, 261, 344, 351, 354
Franconia (3) (ex-Ivernia (2))...359, 384
Hibernia...61, 68
Ivernia (1)...152, 155, 196, 226, 233
Ivernia (2)...355-356, 359
Kedar...95
Laconia (1)...227
Laconia (2)...243, 244, 249, 261, 294-295
Lancastria (ex-Tyrrhenia)...245-246, 261, 297-299, *298*
Lucania...127, 129, 156, 393, 434
Lusitania...61, 145, 156, 159, 161-162, 164, 169-170, *170*, 175, 176, 183, 187, *192*, 193, *217*, 221, 233, 240, 256, 302, 393, 405, 435
    Design and construction of...156-157, 160
    Destruction of...216-220, 221
    Interiors of...166-169
    Speed records of...170
Mauretania (1)...120, 145, 156, 159, 164, 170-173, *172*, 175, 176, 183, 187, 193, *205*, 223, 237, 240, 251-252, *252*, 261, 267, 275-276, 417, 435
    Construction of...161, 162
    Interiors of...166-169, *167*, *168*
    Popularity of...171-173, 237-238
    Retirement of...276
    Speed records of...171, 249, 252
Mauretania (2)...278-279, *279*, 287, 289, 303, 304, 306-307, 309, 331-332, 341, *350*, 351, 354, 365, 369, 370
Media...350-351, 365

Niagara...68, 91
Olympus...95
Oregon (ex-Guion Line)...113-114
Palestine...95
Pannonia...197
Parthia (1)...110-111
Parthia (2)...350-351, *350*, 365
Pavonia...112, 196
Persia...80, 81, 92-93, 434
Princess Julianna (post-WW I charter)...234
Queen Elizabeth...61, 274, 278, 279, 280, 281, 282, 283, 287-289, 325, 335-336, *336*, 345, *345*, 346, 349, 353, *354*, 357, 364, *364*, 366, 367, 368, 369-370, 373, 377, 381-383, 434
   Conversion to troopship...321-324
   Design and construction of...279-280, 281-282, 283, 286
   Destruction of...381-383, *383*
   Escapes to United States...288-289, *290*
   Interiors...282
   Launching of...281
   Maiden voyage...340-341
   Refitted as troopship...311-312
   Retirement of...373-375,
   Returned to Cunard service...338-339
   Wartime service of...303, 304-305, 306-307, 309, 312-314, 315, 325, 327, 328-329, 396
Queen Elizabeth 2...61, 368, 378-380, *378*, 385, 390, *391*, 391-392, 404-405, 414, 415, 423, 425, 428-429, 430, 433, 435
   As Project Q4...372-373
   Design and construction of...372-373, 378-379
   Interiors...378-380
   Launching of...377-378
   Maiden voyage...384-385
   Refits...390-391, 403, 411-412
   Sea trials...383-384
   Service as troopship...396-399, *398*, 400, 401
   Struck by rogue wave...404-405
Queen Mary...61, *266*, *268*, 272-273, 274, 275, 278, 280, 282, 285, 287, 325, 334-335, *335*, 336, 337, 344, 345, 349, *350*, 353, 357, *362*, 365, 366, 368, 368, 377, 429, 433, 434
   As Hull 534...253-254, 256, 260, 262-263, *263*, 289, 365
   Collision with HMS *Curacoa*...
   Construction of...253-254, 256, 260, 262-263, *263*, *264*, 266-267
   Conversion to troopship...321-324
   Interiors of...269-270, *270*, *273*, 274
   Launching of...264-266, *264*
   Maiden voyage of...270-272
   Naming of...263-264
   Popularity of...272, *273*, 274
   Refitted as troopship...311-312
   Retirement of...373-377, *376*
   Restored to Cunard service...335, 341-342
   Speed records of...271, 272, 342
   Struck by rogue wave...316-317, 405
   Wartime service of...303-304, 306-307, 309, 312-314, *313*, *314*, 315, 325, 327-328, 329, 396
Queen Mary 2...413-414, 416-418, 421-422, 423, 424-425, 427-430, 430, 435
Queen Victoria...422-423, 430
Russia...95-96
Sagafjord...401-402, 406
Samaria (2)...243-244, *244*, 302, 354,
Saxonia (1)...152, 155, 196
Saxonia (2)...355-356, 359
Scotia...93-94, 434
Scythia (1)...119
Scythia (2)...242-243, 244, 245, 306, 344, 354
Sea Goddess 1...402-403, 413
Sea Goddess 2...402-403, 413
Servia...112
Slavonia...197, 198-199
Sylvania...355-356, *356*,
Transylvania...227-228
Ultonia...197
Umbria...114, 123-124, 126, 434
Unicorn...44-45, 48
Vistafjord...401-402, 406, 412-413
Cunard-Eagle Airways...363-364
Cunliffe-Owen, Sir Hugo...341

D-Day (Allied invasion of Europe)...309, 325, 327, 328
Dardanelkles Campaign...224-226
Davis, Arthur...186
Davis, Tom...393

De Roebeck, Adm. John...225
Dean, First Officer H. ...179-180
Dempsey, Jack...239
Deny, William II...91
Dickens, Charles...54, 55-56
Dietrich, Marlene..353
Doenitz, Gr-Adm. Karl...212, 293, 295
Douglass, Frederick...66-68
Dover Castle...227
Dramatic Line....73
Dreiser, Theodore...192
Driver...23
Duke of Windsor (ex-King Edward VIII)...277, 357

Eagle Airways...363
Eisenhower, Gen. Dwight D. ...333
Ellerman, John R. ...139
Emergency Quota Act ("Three Percent Act")...246
Ericsson, John...44
Ewing, Capt. J. ...61

Falaba...215-216
Falkland Islands...63, 395-396
Fairbanks, Douglas, Sr. ...239
Fairfield Shipbuilding and Engineering...113
Feibig, Raoul...415-416
Fincantieri (shipbuilder)...413, 418, 419, 423
Ford, Henry...353
Frederick Leyland and Company (Leyland Line)...139

Gallipoli...224-226
Gamblers...193, 239-240
Garbo, Greta...353
German Army...204-204, 208, 222
German Navy...174, 175, 203-204, 211-212, 213, 293-294, *294*, 295
    Ships
        DKMS *Admiral* Hipper...293
        DKMS *Bismarck*...293
        DKMS *Deutschland*...286
        DKMS *Gneisenau*...286
        DKMS *Graf Spee*...286
        DKMS *Prinz Eugen*...293
        DKMS *Scharnhorst*...286
        SMS *Eber*...209
        SMS *Magdeburg*...*213*
    U-boats (WW I)

U-9...211
U-17...211
U-20...*215*, 217-218, 221, 240
U-21...211
U-24...221
U-28...216
U-33...227
U-38...221
U-44...222
U-46...223
U-47...226
U-55...222
U-63...228
U-86...222
U-103...276
UB-47...227
UB-67...223
UB-77...229
    U-Boats (WW II)
        U-30...285, 294
        U-46...296
        U-99...299-301
        U-129...307
        U-156...294-295
        U-161...307
Gibbs, William...356, 357
Glitra...211
Grant, Capt. Noel, RN...209
Grattidge, Capt. Henry...297-298,
Great Britain...71-72, 133, 173-174, 370-371, 395
Great Depression...254-256,
Great Western Railway...26, 27, 29, 51, 62
Great Western Steamship Company...51, 63, 64
    Ships
        Great Britain...27, 62-64, 68, 80, 90, 96
        Great Eastern...27, 96-98,
        Great Western...27, 29-30, *29*, 31-32, 33, 43-44, 47, 51, 64, 96
Griscom, Clement...139
Guion, Stephen...100
Guion Line...96, 100-101, 109, 112-113, 132, 148
    Ships
        Alaska...109, 113
        Arizona...109, 113
        Chicago...100
        Colorado...101
        Dakota...101
        Idaho...101
        Montana...101

Oregon...112-113

Hadrian's Wall...153
Halifax, city of...25, 33, 35, 36, 42, 44, 108, 341, 354
Hall, Samuel...26
Hamburg-Amerika...96, 108, 129, 131, 132, 132, 134, 135, 138, 140-141, 148, 186, 193, 233, 256, 259, 436
    Ships
        Amerika...235
        Bismarck...194, 196, 235
        Cap Trafalgar...209-210
        Deutschland...134, 135, 141
        Fürst Bismarck...132
        George Washington...235
        Imperator...194-196, 199-200, 235
        Kaiserin Augusta Victoria...132, 173, 262
        Vaterland...194, 196, 235
Hamburg-Amerikanische Packetfahrt Aktien Gesselschaft...129
Hamilton, Gen. Ian...225
Hardy, Oliver...239
Harrison, Rex...353
Harland, Edward J. ...104
Harland & Wolff (shipbuilder)...104, 105, 106-107, 137, 140, 176, 253, 306, 413, 418, 419, 420-421, 426
Hartenstein, *Kapt-Lt.* Werner...294-295
Helensburgh...60
Hemingway, Ernest...353
Hepburn, Katherine...353
Hermann...66
Hesperian...221
Hickson, Robert...104
Hitler, Adolf...280-281, 283, 316
Hoover, President Herbert...255
Hunt, Governor Rex...395
Hughes, Chief Steward Henry...181
Hutcheson, Capt. Alexander...396
Huxley, Aldous...353

Illingworth, Capt. Cyril Gordon...315-316, 318-319, 320, 321, 341
Immigrants...22, 91, 100, 153-155, 246
Imrie, William...104
Inman, William..89-90, 139
Inman and International...139
Inman Line...90, 91, 94, 95, 96, 100, 109, 132, 139, 148
    City of Baltimore...91

City of Berlin...107, 108, 109
City of Boston...100, 107
City of Brussels...94, 100
City of Clyde...90, 91
City of Glasgow...23, 90, 100
City of Manchester...90, 91
City of New York...100, 124, 127
City of Paris...124, 127
City of Philadelphia...90, 91, 100
City of Rome...129
City of Washington...91, 100, 107
Interiors, ships'...130, 131, 136, 166-169, 186-191, 194-195, 269-270, *270*, *273*, 274, 282, 378-380
International Mercantile Marine (IMM)...139, 140-141, 142, 143, 198, 253
International Navigation Company...139
Inverclyde, 1st Lord (George (John) Burns II)...101, 111, 265
Inverclyde, 2nd Lord (John Burns)... 142-143, 144, 145, 160-161
Ismay, Bruce...110, 140, 176
Ismay, Thomas...103-104, 105, *105*, 110, 127, 137, 140, 176
Ismay, Imrie and Company...104
Italian Line...253, 256, 349, 365, 436
    Ships
        Conte di Savoy...253, 272
        Leonardo da Vinci...368
        Michaelangelo...368
        Raffaello...368
        Rex...253, 272

J & G Thomson (shipbuilder)...61, 95
James Monroe...21-22
Jardin, David...124
Jones, Capt. John Treasure...375
John Brown & Company, Ltd. (also John Brown & Sons, John Brown Engineering)...95, 151, 159, 160, 253-254, 256, 263, 265, 280, 282-283, 368, 377-378, 402, 404, 413
John Elder & Co. (shipbuilder)...114
John Wood (shipbuilder)...41
Jordan, Humphrey...133, 171
Judkins, Capt. C.H.E. ...81

Kaiser Friedrich...132
Kaiser (King) Wilhelm I...130
Kaiser Wilhelm II...137-138, 141, 175, 220, 222, 259

Katsoufis, Capt. Paris...407
Kilroy's Patent Stoking Indicator...164
King George V...263-264, 264-265,
King George VI...281, 339
King Peter of Yugoslavia...353
Kirkwood, David...259
Kitchener, Field Marshal Lord...210
Kretchmer, Kapt-Lt. Otto...300-301
Kryslant, Lord...253
Kvaernar Group...405-406, 409, 410, 413, 416, 418, 419

"*Laconia* Order"...295
Lansing, Asst. Sec. of State Robert...221
Laurel, Stan...239
Law, Capt. William...391
Lemp, Lt. Julius...285, 294
Lewin, Capt. Terrence...375
Leviathan (ex-*Vaterland*)...235, 248-249
Liman von Sanders, Gen. Otto...225
Liverpool, city of...21, 22, 45-46, 91, 367, 404, 413
Llandovery Castle (hospital ship)...222
Lloyd George, David...239
Lloyd Werft (shipbuilder)...411
Lohmann, Johann...130, 132
Long Beach, city of...375, 377, 381
Luce, Capt. James...79
Luftwaffe (German Air Force)...287, 288, 291, 292-293, *292*, 297-298, 305, 306, 327

MacDougal, Capt. John...26
MacLaren, Sir Charles...161
Maclean, Capt. Peter...228
MacNeil, Capt. James...252
Mahan, Capt. Alfred Thayer...208, 289-291
Marr, Cmdr. Geoffrey Marr...375
Marshall, Gen. George C. ...309, 310
Masefield, John...266
Mathews, Victor...388, 390
Maxtone-Graham, John...345
McIver, Charles...67
McIver, David...40-41, 111
Melville, James...38
Mewés, Charles...173, 186
Meyer Werft (shipbuilder)...413, 413, 419
Mills, Edward...65, 68
Molotov, Commissar Vyacheslav...340
Moore, Maj.-Gen. ...397
Morgan, J. Pierpont...138-142, 143, 144

Murdoch, William...118

Nantucket Lightship...276
Napier, Robert...31, 38-40, 41, 45, 49, 52, 58-61, *59*, 68, 377
National Line...96
New York, city of...21, 22, 30, 32, 42-43, 64, 65, 66, 263-264, 279,285, 289
New York and Liverpool United States Mail Steamship Company (Collins Line)....73
New York Packet Company (Black Ball Line)...21
Norddeutscher-Lloyd AG...109, 129, 130, 131, 132, 138, 140-141, 148, 233, 249, 255, 259, 349
   Ships
      Bremen (1)...200
      Bremen (2)...249, 251, 272, 349
      Europa...249, 251, 272, 349
      Fulda...114
      Grosser Kurfurst...199, 235
      Havel...132
      Kaiser Wilhelm II...132, 135, 141, 156, 162, 169,251
      Kaiser Wilhelm der Grosse...132-133, *133*, 141, 208
      Kronprinz Wilhelm...135, 141, 235, 251
      Kronprinzessin Cecile...141, 235
      Main...200
      Prinzess Irene...198
      Saale...200
      Spree...132
Norwegian America Cruises...401, 402

Ocean Queen...23
Ocean Steam Navigation Company...65, 66, 68
Oceanic Steam Navigation Company (White Star Line)...104,
Oronsay...297, 299

Packet boats...21, 24-25
   conditions aboard...23-24
   described...22-23
Paganini, Nicolo...47
Parkinson, David...393
Parry, William Edward...38
Patroclus...300-301
Patzig, Oblt. Helmut...222
Pavlova, Anna...239

Payne, Stephen...413, 416
Peninsula & Orient Line (P&O)...396
    Canberra...396, 400
    Uganda...396
Peskett, Leonard...155, 156, 161, 165, 183
Pickford, Mary...239
Pilkington, John...103
Pimental, Larry...410, 415, 419, 423
Pirrie, Lord William...140, 426
Pohl, V-Adm. Hugo von...204, 208
Poppe, Johannes...130, 131, 137, 173
Port Stanley...63, 395, 400, 401
Prescott, John...413, 415, 421-422
Prevatil, Joseph...376
Prince Philip, Duke of Edinburgh...377, 415
Princess Margaret...339, 377
Prinzip, Gavrillo...200

Queen Elizabeth (wife of King George VI,
    the Queen Mother)...281, 378, 401, 404
Queen Elizabeth II...339, 377-378, 415
Queen Mary (wife of King George V)...264,
    265, 269, 378
Queen Victoria...100
Queenstown (Cobh), city of...90, 91, 148,
    197, 219

Reciprocating engines...132-133, 157-
    158, *157,*
Renaissance Cruises...426-427
Rennie, John....377
Ritz, Caesar...137
Ritz-Carlton...137
RMS Foundation...376-377
Robert Duncan (shipbuilder)...41
Robert Steele & Sons (shipbuilder)...41, 77
Robert F. Stockton...44
Roberts, Capt. Richard...32
Rogue waves...57-58, 148, 404-405
Roosevelt, President Franklin D. ...173, 276,
Rosselli, John...365-366, 392
Rostron, Cmdr. Arthur...179-182, 240
Royal Air Force...326, 327
Royal Mail Group...253
Royal Marines...391, 395, 396
    45 Commando...399
    Special Boat Service (SBS)...391
Royal Navy...38, 86, 87, 137, 144, 145, 159,
    174, 175, 203-204, 211-212, 212-213,
    230, 283, 286, 287, 295, 314-315, 349,
    395-396

Ships
    HMS *Aboukir*...211
    HMS *Achates*...301
    HMS *Antrim*...399, 400
    HMS *Ardent*...399, 400
    HMS *Argonaut*...399
    HMS *Antelope*...399
    HMS *Bramham*...319, 321
    HMS *Brilliant*...399
    HMS *Bristol*...400
    HMS *Broadsword*...399, 400
    HMS *Bulldog*...319
    HMS *Conqueror*...396
    HMS *Coventry*...400
    HMS *Cowdray*...319, 321
    HMS *Cressy*...211
    HMS *Curacoa*...317, 318-319, 319-321
    HMS *Dreadnought*...142, 159
    HMS *Duke of York*...283
    HMS *Glasgow*...399
    HMS *Havelock*...299
    HMS *Hermes*...375, 395, 434
    HMS *Highflyer*...208
    HMS *Highlander*...299
    HMS *Hogue*...211
    HMS *Invincible* (Battlecruiser)...142
    HMS *Invincible* (VSTOL carrier)...395
    HMS *Irresistible*...225
    HMS *Pathfinder*...211
    HMS *Queen Elizabeth*...225, 236
    HMS *Rifleman*...226, 227
    HMS *Saladin*...319, 321
    HMS *Sheffield*...396
    HMS *Skate*...319, 321
    HMS *Snowdrop*...230
    HMS *Spartan*...395
    HMS *Splendid*...395
Royal William...25-26, 37, 39, 51
Royden, Lord...263-264
Rudnick, Oscar...392
Runciman, Sir Walter...210

Sagu Rose (ex-*Sagafjord*)...430
Sailing Day...119-123
Samuels, Capt. Samuel...23
Savannah...25
Schichau Werft (shipbuilder)...132
Schneider, Kapt-Lt. Rudolf...221
Schwabe, Gustavus...104-105
Schwieger, Kapt.-Lt. Walther...217-218,
    218, 221
Scotts Shipbuilding & Engineering...198

Seabourn Cruise Lines...407, 410, 413
Selborne, Lord...143
Sharp, Ernest...384
Shipboard life...54-56, 346-349
Shirley, Philip...370
Sirius...31-32, 33, 51
Slattery, Sir Matthew...363
Smallpiece, Sir Basil...361, 367-368, 369, 370, 377, 385, 387, 388
Smith, Sir Francis Pettit...62
Smith, Junius...30-31, 51, 57
SOLAS...417-418
Southampton, city of...242, 267, 276, 285, 288, 302, 335, 336, 338, 339, 341, 345, 367, 384, 396, 397, 422, 433-434
Spedding, Purser Charles...240
Stayner, J. N. ...40
Stewards and stewardesses...191-193,
Stokers...164-165, *165*, 236-237
Sultan of Jahore...239

Thatcher, Lady Margaret...395-396, 404
Thresher, Leon C. ...216
Thomas Cook, Ltd. ...114-116
Thomas Ward (breaker's yard)...344
Thompson, Norman...387-388
Thorneycroft, Peter...363
Tillberg Design Group...411-412, 417
Tirpitz, Adm. Alfred...175, 204, 209
Tracy, Spencer...353
Trafalagar House PLC...385, 387-388, 392, 393, 394, 395, 401, 402, 405-406
Tuchman, Barbara...131
Tung, C. Y. ...382
Turbines...158-159, *159*, 162, 163
  on *Caronia*...159-160
  on *Lusitania* and *Mauretania*...162-163, 237, 276
  on *Queen Elizabeth 2*...383-384, 403
  on *Queen Mary*...267
Turner, Lana...353
Turner, Capt. William...217, *217*, 220, 240-241
Twain, Mark...136, 147, 151

United States...356-357, 358, 435
USS *Conway*...385

Vesta...78
Vishinski, Commissar Andrei...340

Volstead Act (Prohibition)...248
Volturno...199
Vulkan Werft (shipbuilder)...132, 133

Wallace, Edgar...239
Ward, Peter...406
Warwick, Capt. Ronald...400, 406, 414-415, *415*
Warwick, Capt. William...383, 400, 415
Washington...65-66, 73,
Watkinson, Capt. James...21, 22
Watson, William...161
Watt, Capt. J. B. ...169
Weddigen, Kapt-Lt. Otto...211
White Star Line...94, 103, 104, 108-109, 110, 132, 140, 148, 176, 233, 253, 255, 260, 359, 365
  Ships
    Adriatic (1)...94, 106, 107, 108
    Adriatic (2)...277
    Afric...233
    Albertic...277
    Arabic...221, 233
    Atlantic...105, 106
    Baltic (1)...105, 106, 107
    Baltic (2)...277
    Britannic (1)...108, 109, 124
    Britannic (2) ex-*Gigantic*...176, 233
    Britannic (3)...253, 277, 358-359
    Calgaric...277
    Cedric...277
    Celtic...106, 108
    Cymric...233
    Delphic...233
    Doric...277
    Georgic (1)...233
    Georgic (2)...253, 277, 305-306, 358
    Germanic...108, 109, 124
    Homeric...253, 277, 433, 434
    Laurentic (1)...233
    Laurentic (2)...299-301
    Majestic (1)...110, 125-126
    Majestic (2) (ex-*Bismarck*)...235, 277, 433
    Oceanic (1)...105, 106, 107, 111
    Oceanic (3)...253, 255, 365
    Olympic...176, 183, 184, 187, 261, 269, 276-277, 417, 434
    Republic (1)...105, 106
    Teutonic...110, 124, 125-127, 137
    Titanic...176-177, 179-180, 181, 182, 183, 184, 185-186, 187, 233, 269, 417

White Star Line of Australian Packets... 103-104
White Star Line of Boston Packets...103
   Ellen...103
   Red Jacket...103
   Royal Standard...103
   White Star...103
William Deny & Son (shipbuilder)...92
William Patterson (shipbuilder)...31
Wilson, Henry Threlfall...103
Wilson, President Woodrow...221
Winthrop, Mrs. Thomas...244
Wintour, D. F. ...210
Wirth, Kapt. Julius...209
Wolff, Gustav...104
Wood and Napier (shipbuilder)...60
Woodruff, Capt. Henry, RN...46, 53, 54-55, 56

Zimmermann, Robert...129